The Gendered 'I' in Ancient Literature

Philologus

Zeitschrift für antike Literatur und ihre Rezeption /
A Journal for Ancient Literature and its Reception

Supplemente /
Supplementary Volumes

Herausgegeben von / Edited by
Sabine Föllinger, Sotera Fornaro, Tobias Reinhardt,
Christoph Schubert, Jan R. Stenger

Volume 18

The Gendered 'I' in Ancient Literature

Modelling Gender in First-Person Discourse

Edited by
Lisa Cordes and Therese Fuhrer

DE GRUYTER

ISBN 978-3-11-153674-3
e-ISBN (PDF) 978-3-11-079525-7
e-ISBN (EPUB) 978-3-11-079530-1
ISSN 2199-0255

Library of Congress Control Number: 2022938345

Bibliographic information published by the Deutsche Nationalbibliothek
The Deutsche Nationalbibliothek lists this publication in the Deutsche Nationalbibliografie; detailed bibliographic data are available on the internet at http://dnb.dnb.de.

© 2024 Walter de Gruyter GmbH, Berlin/Boston Typesetting: Integra Software Services Pvt.

This volume is text- and page-identical with the hardback published in 2022.

www.degruyter.com

Contents

Lisa Cordes, Therese Fuhrer
Introduction: Gender-Specific Elements in First-Person Statements in Classical Literature —— 1

I The Rhetorics of a Gendered 'I'

Judith P. Hallett
The Gender and Third-Person Parameter in the Shaping of First-Person Discourse in Roman Literature —— 11

Florence Klein
Construire un « je » genré dans les traductions de Catulle (*c.* 51 et 66) : Érotique de l'appropriation littéraire et féminisation rétrospective des modèles grecs —— 25

Lisa Cordes
***Virgo, virago*, Vestal – Gender and Fiction in Seneca the Elder's *Controversia* 1.2** —— 43

II Gendering a Non-Human 'I'

Markus Hafner
***Pythia poetrix*? Oracular Polyphony between Poetic Collaboration and Delphic Politics** —— 71

Luca Basso
Costruire un 'io' divino: Ovidio e le dee —— 93

Helge Baumann
In Memory of Reading Matrons and Eloquent Dogs: Female Voices and Role Constructions in Martial's Epigrams 10.63 and 11.69 —— 105

III The Gendered 'I' in Choral Lyric and Tragedy

Emily Hauser
Making Men: Gender and the Poet in Pindar —— 129

Valentina Moro
A Theatre of Vulnerability: Lamentation as a Gendered Self-Narration in Sophocles' *Antigone* —— 151

Therese Fuhrer
A Female View of the Tragic Action: On the Function of Collective First-Person Statements in the Women's Choruses in the (ps.-)Senecan Tragedies *Troades* **and** *Hercules Oetaeus* —— 179

IV The Gender Parameter in Erotic First-Person Discourse

Giulia Sissa
Elle sait. Elle dit. Elle rit. L'éloge paradoxal d'éros par Diotime de Mantinée —— 203

Christoph Mayr
Gender und Rollen in Horaz *carm.* **1,13** —— 243

Jacqueline Fabre-Serris
Enquête sur l'identité du « je » féminin de l'élégie 3.11 du *Corpus Tibullianum* **: méthodes et conjectures** —— 257

V The Gender Parameter in Ovid's First-Person Discourse

Alison Sharrock
Living to Tell the Tale: Male and Female First-Person Narrators of Metamorphosis —— 285

Federica Bessone
***Autofiction* al femminile. Arte di raccontare ed effetti di genere in Ovidio** —— 307

Alison Keith
Gender and Genre in First-Person Discourse: Three Case Studies in Ovid's *Metamorphoses* —— 329

VI The Gendered 'I' in the Poetry of Late Antiquity

Henriette Harich-Schwarzbauer
In den Wind gesprochen – Die Ich-Reden der Ceres in Claudians *De raptu Proserpinae* —— 357

Ann-Kathrin Stähle
Medea *virago* in Dracontius' *Romulea* —— 375

Notes on Contributors —— 391

General Index —— 395

Index locorum —— 403

Lisa Cordes, Therese Fuhrer

Introduction: Gender-Specific Elements in First-Person Statements in Classical Literature

In his *progymnasmata*, the earliest surviving treatise on ancient rhetorical school exercises, dating probably from the first century CE, the orator Aelius Theon points to the fundamentally different natures of the speech of men and women. When discussing the exercise of *prosopopoeia*, 'speech in character', he instructs his readers that "different ways of speaking would be fitting by nature for a woman and for a man . . ." (διὰ φύσιν γυναικὶ καὶ ἀνδρὶ ἕτεροι λόγοι ἁρμόττοιεν ἄν . . .).[1] In addition to other aspects such as age, social status, origin, and emotional state, students of rhetoric are taught to consider the aspect of gender when assigning appropriate words to the character that they are introducing as a speaker.

Aelius' instructions are of relevance for the present volume, as research has long established that ancient texts are informed by the formal training of their male and – in the case of Sappho and Sulpicia[2] – female authors, and of the ancient audience. We can expect that since at least the fifth century BCE, authors received rhetorical training, which continued into Late Antiquity and was further formalised.[3] In ancient rhetoric classes, speaking in roles was practised in order to learn how to convincingly represent, as an orator, the position of a defendant or plaintiff in court, or a cause from a certain perspective in political institutions or in public.[4] Yet, the technique of role modelling and construction of character was relevant to the composition of literary texts as well, whether in drama,[5] lyric poetry,[6] epic,[7] the novel,[8] historiography, or in philosophical dialogues.[9] As poets, rhetors, lawyers, and politicians were all former students of rhetoric, there was naturally an exchange of knowledge and skills between

---

1 Aelius Theon, *Progymnasmata* 116.2 (Sprengel), transl. Kennedy (2003) 48 with an introduction to the work.
2 See the contributions by Florence Klein, Judith Hallett, and Jacqueline Fabre-Serris.
3 On the "intellectual habits instilled by rhetorical training" in Greek and Roman culture, see Connolly (2009), quotation on p. 136. On the role of rhetoric in the educational system and literary production of late antiquity, see Sandnes (2009), esp. 16–39.
4 See the contribution by Lisa Cordes.
5 On first-person speeches in tragedy, see the contributions by Valentina Moro and Therese Fuhrer; on comic examples, see the remarks by Judith Hallett (p. 12f.), and Lisa Cordes (p. 60f.).
6 See the contributions by Emily Hauser, Florence Klein, Christoph Mayr, and Ann-Kathrin Stähle.
7 See the contributions by Alison Sharrock, Federica Bessone, Alison Keith, and Henriette Harich-Schwarzbauer.
8 See the contribution by Lisa Cordes.
9 See the contribution by Giulia Sissa.

rhetoric and literary production. The technique of moulding an 'I' is considered to have been common knowledge in the Greek and Roman cultural elites.[10] This 'I' does not have to be a human being: with the technique of *prosopopoeia*, gods and goddesses or other supernatural voices, animals, and even objects can be modelled as *personae* speaking in human language.[11]

Based on these considerations of the widespread rhetorical training in 'speech in character', the present volume starts from the premise that every first-person statement that we find in the ancient texts is in some way rhetorically modelled and aesthetically shaped. The nature of the shaping depends on the role that the speaker has to play in a certain speech context, in accordance with intra-literary logic, genre conventions, etc. Moreover, it is informed by the compartmentalised notion of ancient character. As can be seen from Aelius' remarks, rhetorical theory defines a number of parameters that are deemed relevant for the representation of a person and need to be displayed in their manner of speaking. As Koen De Temmerman points out with a view to the ancient rhetorical training and the literary practice influenced by it, in antiquity, "the complex notion of what constitutes a human being is broken down into a series of discrete pockets of information about a person that can be discussed and analysed separately."[12] Just as with other parameters, the speaker's gender has to be modelled according to the rhetorical situation – speaking in the terminology of modern social sciences: the behaviour setting or the script – in order for the role to be rhetorically successful. As authors and audiences alike were taught about the persuasive effects of language, we can assume that the ancient texts employ gender-relevant motifs and use gender-specific elements in a controlled and recognisable way to virtuously model types, roles, and perspectives with regard to a certain persuasive or literary goal.[13]

The contributions in this volume analyse the use and modelling of such gender-specific elements in first-person speech. Focusing on different types of text, in Greek and Latin, poetry and prose, from the Archaic Age to Late Antiquity, they ask: What gender-specific elements are attributed to the speaker? How is the gender parameter used in statements about a specific subject, about other characters and their speeches and actions, and about the speaker's emotions and those of others? How are gender-specific elements combined when the empirical author is male but the voice shaped by him is to be considered as female? With what further parameters is the role of the

---

10 On the specific problems with gendered 'I's that arise in translations and transformation from Greek to Latin texts, see the contribution by Florence Klein.
11 For non-human speech, see the contributions by Florence Klein, Markus Hafner, Luca Basso, Helge Baumann, and Alison Sharrock. On the use of the terms *ethopoeia*, and *prosopopoeia* in this context, see Cordes (in this volume) p. 44 n. 4.
12 De Temmerman (2019) 107.
13 Cf. Fuhrer/Zinsli (2003b) and see the contributions by Christoph Mayr and Lisa Cordes in this volume.

first-person speaker endowed? How do these parameters relate to the parameter of gender, and what function does gender have in the overall composition of a first-person discourse? Finally, how are gender roles or gender-specific role models – also role stereotypes – staged and discussed in first-person speech, and how do the texts work with role expectations concerning gender that are given by frame, context, and setting?

By concentrating on first-person speech, we ask specifically how the gender parameter is moulded in the process of talking about oneself, and what possibilities arise from the subjectivisation of perspective. Prime examples of such subjectivisation are the specifically Roman form of subjective love elegy, and the "undelivered speeches of indignant women" in Ovid's *Heroides*.[14] In the latter, poetological reflections and subjective experiences in the realm of erotics, as well as other gender-specific experiences regarding social status, (loss of) prestige, (loss of) authority, and emotionality, are expressed in the first-person statements and played through in changing combinations. In the process, the 'I' can explore boundaries and test risks, without the statements formulated from the speaker's perspective claiming objective validity. The ancient authors are familiar with these possibilities regarding the literary staging of subjective experience and experiment with them continuously.

The volume analyses the use and modelling of the gender parameter in different types of first-person speech, be it that the speaker is (represented as) the author of a work, be it that they feature as characters in the work, narrating their own story or that of others, from a homo- or a heterodiegetic position. With that, the volume does not only promise new insights into the rhetorical strategies and literary techniques used to construct a gendered 'I' in ancient literature,[15] but it also addresses questions concerning the form and function of first-person discourse in classical literature. It thus concerns intersecting fields of research that have increasingly come into focus in recent years, such as authorship studies,[16] studies concerning the ancient notion(s) of the literary *persona* and their various manifestations,[17] and studies concerning a historical narratology that discuss the understanding of concepts like the narrator or the character in ancient literary theory and practice.[18]

---

14 The quotation refers to the German (untranslatable) title of Christine Brückner, *Wenn du geredet hättest, Desdemona. Ungehaltene Reden ungehaltener Frauen* (Hamburg 1983), who puts fictional speeches into the mouths of famous women, as, e.g., Sappho, Katharina von Bora, Effi Briest, Eva Hitler (née Braun), Christiane von Goethe (née Vulpius), Gudrun Ensslin. See Schubert (1985) 85–96.
15 Some earlier treatments of the topic can be found in Fuhrer/Zinsli (2003a) and Formisano/Fuhrer (2005).
16 Cf., e.g., Marmodoro/Hill (2013), Guzmán/Martínez (2018).
17 Cf. most recently McCarthy (2019) and Bitto/Gauly (2021) with an overview on the long-running, controversial debate.
18 Cf. the contributions in von Contzen/Tilg (2019), Feddern (2021), as well as Whitmarsh (2013) and Grethlein (2021).

By bringing together studies that analyse first-person speech in a wide range of texts while focusing on one single parameter, the volume offers perspectives – on aspects such as the modelling of a gendered 'I', or the depicted relation between the inner-literary speakers and the author – that can be compared and related to each other. Since the individual papers are summarised at the beginning of each chapter, in the following we point to some recurring aspects and overlaps between them, which invite complementary readings.

Most contributions examine first-person speech uttered by an individual human being. Judith Hallett adds a perspective by concentrating on individual human speakers who refer to themselves using a third-person singular verb form. Emily Hauser, Therese Fuhrer, and Valentina Moro examine gender-specific elements in collective speech. There are several chapters about non-human speakers, as well. The contributions of Luca Basso, Federica Bessone, Markus Hafner, Alison Sharrock, Henriette Harich-Schwarzbauer, and Ann-Kathrin Stähle concentrate on divine speakers or on speakers that are depicted as being connected to the superhuman. Helge Baumann and Alison Sharrock examine animal speakers and human speakers who are transformed into animals. Florence Klein shows that a speaking object, the lock of Berenice, can be subject to a gendered literary modelling. The (non-)human or divine status of the speakers does not necessarily influence the way the parameter gender is employed – Luca Basso and Helge Baumann demonstrate that a divine and an animal 'I' may be gendered in an anthropocentric way, according to contemporary discursive norms and role patterns. Yet, as Alison Sharrock shows, by looking at first-person narrative of metamorphosis in Ovid's *Metamorphoses*, a speaker's gender can influence the process of their involuntary transformation.

As the papers show, the speaking 'I' is often designed as clearly male or female, but it can have an ambiguous gender status, as well. This ambiguity is created when the speakers cross gender boundaries in their behaviour or self-presentation. A female speaker may take on a stereotypically male role (Cordes, Stähle), while a male speaker may explicitly appropriate behaviour with female connotations (Mayr). In other cases, the speakers appear as 'hybrids' in which different voices, e.g., of male god and female priestess (Hafner), of muse and (male) bard (Hauser), or of male declaimer and female litigant (Cordes), merge. In cases where the speaking 'I' appears as a hybrid, and in texts with female auctorial speakers, the discussion of the speaker's gender is linked to questions of authorship and agency. This is shown by Markus Hafner with regard to the Delphian Pythia, and by Jacqueline Fabre-Serris regarding the poet Sulpicia. In both cases, the gender of the speaking 'I' has influenced the discussions about authorship from antiquity well into modern times. As is shown by Florence Klein with regard to Catullus' translation of Sappho's fr. 31, and by Emily Hauser with regard to Pindar's depiction of the Graces in *Olympian* 14, the authors may playfully address the issues of gender and agency when they transform the female author or singer into the object of a narrative, turning the person singing into the person 'being sung of'.

In the case of female character speech, the relationship between the female speaker and the male author comes into focus. Luca Basso shows how Ovid (in his auctorial *persona*) interacts with female characters in the *Fasti* on the same diegetic level. Federica Bessone argues that in the *Metamorphoses* Ovid can be seen as engaging with the female characters in a 'narrative complicity'. Helge Baumann argues that the 'self'-presentations of the hunting dog Lydia and the anonymous matron in Martial's *Epigrams* 11.69 and 10.63 ultimately serve the fashioning of the male author and his patron Dexter. Lisa Cordes shows how female *sermocinatio* in Seneca the Elder's *Controversia* 1.2 is used to demonstrate the quick-wittedness of the male declaimers. Applying modern feminist theory, Alison Sharrock asks how gendered first-person narrators can gain access to the Symbolic, the world order controlled by men, which includes the author, and what role the (modern) reader plays in granting this access. Similarly, Federica Bessone analyses whether and how the 'narrative complicity' between the primary narrator and the female voices in Ovid's *Metamorphoses* can be reconciled with the palpable irony in the accounts of his mythical characters.

Another recurring topic among the contributions is how ancient gender norms and role patterns influence the modelling of the 'I' and how the first-person speech may endorse or question them. By analysing the gendering terms for 'poet' in Pindar's poetry, Emily Hauser shows how the author builds a masculinising image of himself and his community. Therese Fuhrer shows how the women's choruses in the (ps.-)Senecan tragedies *Troades* and *Hercules Oetaeus* provide an additional perspective on the action of each play, based on the gender and low social status of their members, and which questions the male-connoted values of the tragic heroes and heroines. Luca Basso analyses how the self-presentation of female deities in the *Fasti* offers an alternative perspective on the concept of Roman civilisation. With a view to the Minyads' Tales in the *Metamorphoses*, Alison Keith addresses the close connection between narrators and their narratives. She argues that the Ovidian account is shaped by, and lends credence to, the popular notion of a stereotypically female interest in romance and elegiac poetry. The high proportion of erotic themes in the texts studied in this volume corresponds to this.

A close connection between the gender of the speaker and the style and content of what is said is also shown in the contribution by Giulia Sissa. She is able to gain fundamentally new aspects from the text of Plato's *Symposium*. According to her, the pederastic relationship between male teachers and pupils, which Diotima presents as Socrates' ideal of imparting knowledge, is readable with ironic distance through the female voice: the homoerotic and specifically male Eros is not only a cipher for the ascent of desire and thus for a mystical energy, but corresponds to the actual practice of the Athenians. It takes a woman, however, who is interested in and experienced with real reproduction and childbirth to evoke this deeply ironic understanding. The gender of the speaker thus gains philosophical relevance.

Conventions of genre influence the way the gendered first-person speech is shaped, as well. The speakers may know these conventions and fashion themselves and their narratives accordingly, as is shown by Helge Baumann regarding Martial's *Epigrams* 10.63 and 11.69, and by Federica Bessone regarding Arethusa's account in Ovid's *Metamorphoses*. Conventions of the epistolary genre and historiography seem to influence the use of the third-person verb forms analysed in the contribution of Judith Hallett. The declaimers in Seneca the Elder's *Controversia* 1.2 use the female first-person speech and their reaction to it as a means to reflect the declamation's fictional genre (Cordes). Besides conventions of genre, the literary tradition and intra-textual connections have an effect on the shaping of the gendered 'I'. Dracontius deviates from his literary predecessors in depicting his Medea as a priestess and *virago* (Stähle), as does Claudian by giving his Ceres an extraordinary number of I-speeches compared to Ovidian pretexts on the rape of Proserpina in the *Metamorphoses* and *Fasti* (Harich-Schwarzbauer). The gendered self-depiction of the speaker in Horace *Carmen* 1.13 plays with the expectations of an audience that 'knows' the speaking *persona* from its intra-textual reading experience (Mayr).

Moreover, the use of the gender parameter in shaping the first-person speech can have a metapoetic or poetological dimension. Florence Klein interprets the inversion of gender in Catullus' translations from a metapoetic perspective as an erotic relationship, in which the male translator figures as the conqueror of the translated authoress. Alison Sharrock argues that the flight of Cornix in the second book of the *Metamorphoses* could be interpreted poetologically, and that such a reading would give the female narrator access to the Symbolic that the text seems to grant to a greater extent to the male narrator Hippolytus.

Finally, several contributions that focus on female speakers ask about the relation between self-presentation and self-assertion in moments of weakness. Therese Fuhrer argues that the essential competence of the women's choruses in the (ps.-) Senecan tragedies is their ability to assist in the lamentations of others, while there is no room for any reference to their own situation. Henriette Harich-Schwarzbauer shows how the increasing amount of self-affirmation observable in Ceres' speeches in Claudian's *De raptu Proserpinae* paradoxically corresponds to her *loss* of authority. Similarly, Valentina Moro, following modern feminist theory, interprets vulnerability as an idea that enhances a demand for self-determination. In this perspective, Antigone's lamentation, which is accompanied by a constant search for belonging, can be seen as staging her own vulnerability.

Coming from different national traditions of classical philology (which is reflected in the multilingualism of the volume), the contributions offer a wide range of perspectives and methods trying to seek answers to the question of how a gendered 'I' is designed in texts by Greek and Latin authors in different literary genres. Our interest is not primarily in the study of gendered speech and gendered language, as interpreted in linguistics,[19] and most contributions do not place the modern theories of gender studies or feminist theories at the centre of their textual analysis. Exceptions are Alison Sharrock (see above), and Valentina Moro who analyses gendered vocal performance in Sophocles' tragic language and refers to the Lévinasian research tradition on embodiment, (female) dependence and vulnerability. Overall, the studies represent different approaches to the subject matter, from tried and tested historical-critical methods to approaches informed by modern literary theory. By analysing gendered first-person speeches and narratives, they aim to shed light on how ancient notions of gender influenced literary depictions, discussions about authorship and agency, and questions of self-presentation and self-assertion.

The volume collects papers given at the tenth meeting of the 'European network on Gender Studies in Antiquity' (EuGeStA) at LMU Munich on 7–9 November 2019, and additional papers that were commissioned afterwards in order to further broaden the scope of the publication. The volume thus also documents the discussions that took place during the conference and in the ensuing exchange between the contributors. We take here the opportunity to thank all invited speakers, chairpersons, and participants for a stimulating conference, which raised many fascinating ideas and generated lively discussions. We are also extremely grateful to the authors who were not present at the conference and who enrich the volume with their contributions.

All contributions have undergone a rigorous interactive and collaborative peer-review process and have benefited greatly from the feedback provided by the anonymous peer reviewers. The arduous task of compiling the indices was undertaken by our graduate students Anna Demeter, Sophia Jellema, Tobias Gräbert, and Johannes Ostermeier who also carefully proofread the texts. Clare O'Neill did the linguistic editing of the articles written in English by non-native speakers. We sincerely thank the editors of Philologus Supplements for including the volume in the series.

---

[19] On the question of "gender differences in speech" and "male speech" cf. Dutsch (2008), esp. 1–12; Clackson (2015) 124–37.

Bibliography

Bitto/Gauly (2021): Gregor Bitto and Bardo Maria Gauly (eds.), *Auf der Suche nach Autofiktion in der antiken Literatur*, Berlin/Boston.
Clackson (2015): James Clackson, *Language and Society in the Greek and Roman Worlds*, Cambridge.
Connolly (2009): Joy Connolly, "The politics of rhetorical education", in: Erik Gunderson (ed.), *The Cambridge Companion to Ancient Rhetoric*, Cambridge, 126–141.
von Contzen/Tilg (2019): Eva von Contzen and Stefan Tilg (eds.), *Handbuch Historische Narratologie*, Berlin.
De Temmerman (2019): Koen De Temmerman, "Figur – Antike / Character – Antiquity", in: von Contzen/Tilg (2019), 105–115.
Dutsch (2008): Dorota M. Dutsch, *Feminine Discourse in Roman Comedy: On Echoes and Voices*, Oxford.
Feddern (2021): Stefan Feddern, *Elemente der antiken Erzähltheorie*, Berlin/Boston.
Formisano/Fuhrer (2005): Marco Formisano and Therese Fuhrer (eds.), *Gender-Inszenierungen in der antiken Literatur*, Trier.
Fuhrer/Zinsli (2003a): Therese Fuhrer and Samuel Zinsli (eds.), *Gender Studies in den Altertumswissenschaften: Rollenkonstrukte in antiken Texten*, Trier.
Fuhrer/Zinsli (2003b): Therese Fuhrer and Samuel Zinsli, "Einleitung", in: Fuhrer/Zinsli (2003a), 7–13.
Grethlein (2021): Jonas Grethlein, "Author and Characters: Ancient, Narratological, and Cognitive Views on a Tricky Relationship", *CPh* 116, 208–230.
Guzmán/Martínez (2018): Antonio Guzmán and Javier Martínez (eds.), *Animo Decipiendi? Rethinking fakes and authorship in Classical, Late Antique, & Early Christian Works*, Groningen.
Kennedy (2003): George A. Kennedy (ed.), *Progymnasmata. Greek Textbooks of Prose Composition and Rhetoric, Translated with Introduction and Notes*, Atlanta.
Marmodoro/Hill (2013): Anna Marmodoro and Jonathan Hill (eds.), *The Author's Voice in Classical and Late Antiquity*, Oxford.
McCarthy (2019): Kathleen McCarthy, *I, the Poet. First-person Form in Horace, Catullus, and Propertius*, Ithaca/London.
Sandnes (2009): Karl O. Sandnes, *The Challenge of Homer: School, Pagan Poets and Early Christianity*, London.
Schubert (1985): Werner Schubert, "'Quid dolet haec?' – Zur Sappho-Gestalt in Ovids 'Heroiden' und in Christine Brückners 'Ungehaltenen Reden ungehaltener Frauen'", *A&A* 31, 76–96.
Whitmarsh (2013): Tim Whitmarsh, "An I for an I: reading fictional autobiography", in: Marmodoro/Hill (2013), 233–247 (originally 2009 in: *CentoPagine* 3, 56–66).

I The Rhetorics of a Gendered 'I'

Judith P. Hallett

The Gender and Third-Person Parameter in the Shaping of First-Person Discourse in Roman Literature

Abstract: My paper examines several Latin texts by or placed in the mouths of women – beginning with the letter ascribed to the brothel slave Phoenicium in Plautus' *Pseudolus*, and including "Sulpicia" 8, 10 and 12, and passages from Vergil's *Aeneid* – in which what is apparently the first speaker employs third person singular verb forms to refer to herself. In exploring and elucidating this puzzling usage, I will be looking at Julius Caesar's use of the third person when describing his own military experiences, and Catullus' use of the third person when representing himself in such poems as 8, 11, 56, 58 and 79. I will be accounting for this usage by considering several possible explanations, none of which excludes the other: the metrical advantages of third person singular verb forms over first person forms; the influence of the epistolary convention whereby the letter writer begins words of greeting with the third person formula *salutem dicit*; and the affinities between these 'women's words' and those of Greek and Roman historians.

Keywords: illeism, illaism, women speakers/authors, Plautus, Vergil, Sulpicia

"A new trial of an ancient rhetorical trick finds it can make you wiser." So reads the headline of an article by science journalist David Robson in the *British Psychological Society's Research Digest* for May 2019. Robson continues, and seeks to add prestige and authority to his words, by invoking classical antiquity, asserting,

> We credit Socrates with the insight that 'the unexamined life is not worth living' and that to 'know thyself' is the path to true wisdom. But is there a right and a wrong way to go about such self-reflection? Simple rumination – the process of churning your concerns around in your head – isn't the answer . . . Research has shown that people who are prone to rumination also often suffer from impaired decision-making under pressure, and are at a substantially increased risk of depression. Instead, the scientific research suggests that you should adopt an ancient rhetorical method favored by the likes of Julius Caesar and known as 'illeism' – or speaking about yourself in the third person (the term was coined in 1809 by the poet Samuel Taylor Coleridge from the Latin *ille* meaning 'he, that') . . . A bulk of research has already shown that this kind of third-person thinking can temporarily improve decision making.

. . . and, according to Canadian psychologist Igor Grossman, it "can also bring long-term benefits to thinking and emotional regulation." Grossman's latest experiment evidently establishes that, after keeping a diary in the third person for four weeks about how they dealt with day-to-day conflicts, those "using illeism improved in their intellectual humility, perspective-taking and capacity to find a compromise", not to mention "greater emotional regulation and stability." Citing such well-known examples as Elmo on the children's program *Sesame Street*, Jimmy in the TV sitcom *Seinfeld*, and Donald Trump, Robson does acknowledge that illeism is often thought to be infantile, and the sign of a narcissistic personality. "Clearly", he ruminates, "politicians might use ille-ism for purely rhetorical purposes." But, "when applied to genuine reflection, it appears to be a powerful tool for wiser reasoning."[1]

My paper explores a phenomenon that I will call "illaism", from *illa*, the feminine singular form of the masculine singular Latin adjective/pronoun *ille*. It examines several Latin texts by, or placed in the mouths of, women, in which what is apparently the first person speaker employs third person singular verbs to refer to herself.[2] These texts include passages that I have earlier scrutinized in other published studies: the letter ascribed to the brothel slave Phoenicium in a second century BCE Roman comedy, Plautus' *Pseudolus*; words uttered by Dido, Queen of Carthage, in Book 4 of an epic poem from the Augustan era, Vergil's *Aeneid*; and poems 8, 10 and 12 of the eleven elegies connected with a female poet named Sulpicia, in Book 3 of poems connected with another Augustan poet, the elegist Tibullus. They also include the opening elegiac couplets of several poems in another Augustan-era collection, Ovid, *Heroides* 1, 4, 13 and 14.[3] In elucidating this puzzling usage, I have benefited from Kurt Raaflaub's analysis of the illeistic writings by *Ille ipse*, Julius Caesar, who famously favored the third person when describing his own military experiences.[4] I have similarly profited from Marilyn Skinner's research about Catullus' use of the third person when representing himself as poet-speaker in such poems as 8, 11, 56, 58 and 79.[5]

To account for these third person singular verbs in first-person discourse, I will ponder several possible explanations, none excluding the others. First, the influence of the Latin epistolary convention whereby letter writers begin words of greeting

---

[1] Quotations by Robson (2019) and Grossman *et al.* (2021). I recognize that a sarcastic tone permeates my summary of Robson's discussion, owing to my skepticism about Grossman's findings, and their application to the use of the third person in Latin literary texts written, or scripted, as spoken by women. A subsequent effort on my part to write my own autobiography in the third person has not substantially diminished that skepticism. Indeed, my adoption of a third-person narrative style did nothing to minimize the powerful emotional anguish I felt when recalling and retelling painful episodes both from my past and in the present, such as abusive treatment by an alcoholic stepfather and public, gratuitously anti-Semitic attacks on me by a colleague I had thought a friend.

[2] For the use of the first person in three Roman poets who at times represent female figures as speaking – Catullus, Horace and Propertius –, see McCarthy (2019). For women's voices in the poetry of Catullus and Horace, see Hallett (2002a) and (2006). For Catullus' own use of the third person in his first person poetry, see Skinner (2015) and the discussion below.

[3] Hallett (2002a), (2002b), (2006), (2011) and (2021).

[4] Raaflaub (2022, in print).

[5] Skinner (2015), esp. 251; there she seeks to explicate poem 31 (*Paene insularum, Sirmio, insularumque . . .*) and in that context cites poem 56.

with the formula *salutem dicit* (or, in instances I discuss, *salutem mittit* and *salutem expetit*), employing a third person singular verb before switching to the first person singular.[6] Second, the metrical advantages of third person singular verb forms over first person singular verb forms in Latin comic, epic and elegiac verse. Third, various affinities between the words of women who use, or are represented as using, third person singular verbs when referring to themselves and similar, illeistic, modes of writing by several men: Julius Caesar, the earlier Greek historians Thucydides and Xenophon, and the poet Catullus. Despite the suggestion by Robson and Grossman that I would do well to consider whether the women depicted as expressing themselves with illaisms in these Latin texts display heightened intellectual humility, enhanced perspective-taking or superior capacity for finding a compromise, I will not pursue those questions. But were I to judge the illaistic texts by these standards, I would be tempted to conclude that the illaistic women reveal few if any indications of self-effacing, externally focused, and accommodating thinking. In fact, all appear determined to have their own way, dismissive of objections raised by others, and prone to confrontation, issuing *ultimata* rather than proposing solutions that entail mutual adjustments by the parties concerned.

One reason this phenomenon of illaism intrigues me is that scholars have long fixated on the third person singular verbs describing Sulpicia in elegies 8, 10 and 12. Each elegy is immediately followed by another elegy (and in the case of elegy 12, six elegies) in which the poet-speaker uses verbs in the first person singular when referring to herself. Such scholars regard these third-person singular verbs as evidence that Sulpicia could not have written these three poems herself, even if they believe that she wrote elegies 13 through 18. Indeed, scholars conventionally view the sequence of elegies 8 through 12 as the work of an anonymous male "friend" or "garland poet", since these elegies are longer and ostensibly more learned than the sequence of elegies 13 through 18.[7] Hence I would ask if self-descriptions with third-person singular verbs, in discursive environments where we would expect, and often encounter, first person singular verbs, can only be illeisms. Can women similarly adopt, or be realistically portrayed as adopting, this rhetorical ploy?

Let us first look at the two third person singular verb forms opening the letter supposedly penned by the Athenian brothel slave Phoenicium to her freeborn young lover Calidorus in Plautus' *Pseudolus*, because Plautus' comedy is earliest chronologically. And, as I contend elsewhere, because this representation of a woman's words in 191 BCE may have influenced later decisions by a female poet such as Sulpicia, or male poets who represent the speech of such female characters as Dido, Penelope and Phaedra, to use verbs in the third person singular rather

---

[6] For Latin epistolary *formulae*, see Lanham (1975).
[7] See, for example, the studies of Tränkle (1990) 255–98; Skoie (2002); Fulkerson (2017), esp. 237 and 268–70; and Hallett (2002a) and (2021).

than the first.[8] Phoenicium launches her letter with the phrases *salutem mittit*, and *salutem expetit*, "sends good wishes . . . seeks good wishes", in line 43, both of them featuring a third person singular verb. She thereby utilizes a variant form of *salutem dicit*, a well-known introductory expression from the realm of Latin epistolary language. To be sure, Plautus does not portray Phoenicium herself as employing the more common phrase *salutem dicit*. Yet he attests to its existence in the Latin parlance of his own time by assigning the phrase to male letter-writing characters in his *Bacchides* and *Curculio*.[9]

It merits our notice that four of the twenty-one fictitious letters in Ovid's elegiac *Heroides* – written approximately 200 years after Plautus' comedy, and purporting to represent the written words of various Greek mythic female figures to their male lovers – also begin with statements referring to their authors with the third person singular verb form *mittit*, only to switch to first person verbs thereafter. In the very first elegiac couplet of the very first of the *Heroides*, lines 1f., Ovid gives Penelope's opening words to Ulysses as "Your Penelope, Ulysses, sends (*mittit*) these words to you, slow to return: it does not matter that you write me nothing in return, come yourself." In *Heroides* 4, addressed by Phaedra to Hippolytus, Ovid similarly has Phaedra use *mittit* as well as the third person singular verb form *est* in referring to herself, stating in its opening couplet, lines 1f., "The Cretan girl sends (*mittit*) to the man of Amazonian parentage good wishes, which, unless you will have given them, she herself is (*est*) going to be lacking." The opening couplet of *Heroides* 13, to Protesilaus from Laodamia, employs *mittit* as well as *optat* in lines 1f.: "Laodamia of Haemonia sends (*mittit*), to her Haemonian husband, good wishes and affectionately desires (*optat*) for these wishes to travel where they are sent." So, too, *mittit* appears in the opening couplet of 14, lines 1f., from Hypermestra to Lynceus: "Hypermestra sends (*mittit*) [*salutem* is presumably to be understood] to the one brother surviving from so many, the rest of the crowd lies dead owing to the crime of their new brides."[10]

It warrants attention, however, that in the first two lines of *Heroides* 18 Ovid represents its putative male author, Leander, as also using the third person singular verb *mittit* to his female lover Hero. Leander begins: "The man from Abydos sends (*mittit*)

---

8 See Hallett (2011) and (2021). All translations from the Latin are my own.
9 So *Bacchides* 734 (Mnesilochus): *Mnesilochus salutem dicit suo patri* ("Mnesilochus wishes his father good health") and *Curculio* 429–31 (Lyco): *Miles Lyconi in Epidauro hospiti / suo Therapontigonus Platagidorus plurimam / salutem dicit* ("The soldier Therapontigonus Platagidorus sends many greetings to his guest-friend Lyco in Epidaurus"). On Phoenicium's letter, see also the discussion of Jenkins (2005).
10 Strikingly, with *tibi, rescribas* and *veni* at *Heroides* 1.11f., and *dederis* in 4.2, Ovid has both Penelope and Phaedra use second person singular forms for their male addressees while referring to themselves in the third person; with e.g. *scires, ames* and *simules* at *Pseudolus* 72f., Plautus has Phoenicium eventually do the same in addressing Calidorus.

to you, girl of Sestos, good wishes of the sort he would prefer to bear personally, if the wave of the sea should fall."[11] The use of third person singular verbs at the start of poetic epistolary texts otherwise written in the first person singular does not, therefore, appear to be a stylistic peculiarity that Ovid, at least, restricts to female correspondence, such as "love letters" of the kind attributed to Plautus' Phoenicium and his own mythic heroines. It is also possible that illaisms at the start of a text which soon switches to describing its female speaker with first person singular verbs, especially a text voicing strong erotic feelings, may seek to imitate actual "love letters" by women: through providing both key descriptive context and formal distance from the more emotionally charged statements expressed by first person singular verbs.

It merits attention, too, that the remainder of Phoenicium's emotionally charged letter to Calidorus in the *Pseudolus* barely employs first person singular verbs. Indeed, other than various first person singular pronouns and adjectives, the only indications that she is writing about her own actions and her own feelings do not show up until the end of the letter, with her assertion at lines 72f.: "I have taken care (*curavi*) that you may know all of these matters I have known of (*scivi*): now I will try to determine (*experiar*) what you do by way of loving and what you do by way of pretending." Significantly, both *curavi* and *scivi*, perfect tense forms which end with vowels, are immediately followed by words beginning with vowels, *ut* and *omnia* respectively, requiring elision for the Latin meter – in this case iambic senarii – to work. Similar metrical challenges confronted the authors of poetic texts such as the *Aeneid* (in dactylic hexameter), the Sulpicia poems and Ovid's *Heroides* (both in elegiac couplets). The first person singular verb forms available to them include active indicative verb forms in the present tense that end in "o"; future and future perfect active indicative forms that also end in "o", perfect indicative forms ending in "i"; and other active forms such as the imperfect and pluperfect indicative, and the present subjunctive, ending in "am". These final syllables need to be elided, or, even worse, left in gaping hiatus, if followed by a word beginning with a vowel. The invariable "t's" that conclude all Latin active verb forms in the third person singular did not present these same metrical challenges.

I would maintain, too, that metrical contingencies may play a role in two passages from Book 4 of Vergil's *Aeneid* noteworthy for their anomalous third person singular verb forms. Both of these passages depict Dido and Aeneas as speaking to one another face-to-face, rather than as in separate locales and dependent upon epistolary communication. In the first passage, lines 307f., Vergil portrays Dido as using a third person singular present active indicative verb form to refer to herself and her actions when addressing Aeneas. In the second, lines 369f., Vergil depicts

---

[11] With the personal pronoun *tibi* in line 1, Ovid's Leander uses a second person singular form for his addressee, much as his Penelope and Phaedra do.

Dido as employing several perfect active indicative third person singular verb forms to describe her second person addressee Aeneas, also apparently in his presence.

The first passage is a rhetorical question that Dido poses to Aeneas, after accusing him of concealing his planned departure from her shores: "Does not our love (*amor*), nor the right hand given at one time in marriage (*data dextera quondam*), nor Dido about to die in a cruel death hold (*tenet*) you, you (repeated *te*) here?" To be sure, there are three nouns – *amor* and *dextera* as well as Dido's name – that govern the verb *tenet* here. But the third person plural present indicative form *tenent* would have fit the meter as well. What is more, Dido's name and its modifiers come last, and are closer to the verb than the other two nouns; Vergil clearly forges a special connection between *Dido* and *tenet*. Why, then, does he have Dido use the third person singular present active indicative verb form *tenet* and not the first person singular present active indicative verb form *teneo*? Metrically speaking, because the final two syllables of *teneo* would not create the spondee (nor the caesura) furnished by the final syllable of the third person *tenet*. Yet there is a literary advantage to the third person singular *tenet* as well. The combination of *tenet* and Dido's name impart an impersonal, distancing tone to a highly emotional demand, particularly because the interrogative mood implies an external audience in addition to Aeneas himself from whom Dido seeks validation.

Dido's use of the third person for Aeneas when she addresses him in lines 369 and 370 similarly occurs in a series of rhetorical questions: "He did not lament (*ingemuit*) at our weeping, did he? He did not move (*flexit*) his gaze, did he? He did not, emotionally overcome, shed (*dedit*) tears or take pity (*miseratus est*) on his lover, did he?" Here, of course, one would expect Vergil to have Dido use second person singular active indicative forms of the perfect tense. But *ingemuisti*, *flexisti*, and *dedisti* would not fit the meter even if *miseratus es* would. And here again, the interrogative mood affords the impression of an external audience, this time an audience that may or may not include Aeneas himself, and an audience invited to judge him and agree with her.[12]

Both Alison Keith and I have argued that Sulpicia evokes Vergil's Dido in such elegies as 9 and 13 through her use of such literarily charged words as *fama* and *indago*.[13] Sulpicia may be doing the same with her use of third person singular verbs. It is also possible to argue, as I have, that the use of third person singular verb forms in 8, 10 and 12 of the Sulpicia elegies recalls the words that Plautus uses in Phoenicium's letter to Calidorus.[14] For one might read 8, introducing Sulpicia to her audience, as a letter of sorts to its physically distant second person addressees, first the god Mars, and later the Pierian Muses; 10 as a letter of sorts to both the

---

12 See the discussion of these passages in Hallett (2021) 188f.
13 See Keith (1997) and Hallett (2002a), (2002b) and (2021); see also the discussion of Fulkerson (2017) 240 and 273–9.
14 Hallett (2021) 191.

physically distant god Apollo and her currently absent lover Cerinthus; and 12 as a letter of sorts to the distant goddess Juno.

But metrical considerations may also help to explain why we find third person singular verb forms referring to Sulpicia in these elegies. In the case of her poetry, however, it is because in certain circumstances these forms allow for elision and at others they allow for the avoidance of elision. In elegy 8, for example, the elided *est* of the first line, *Sulpicia est tibi culta tuis, Mars magne, kalendis* ("Great god Mars, Sulpicia is arrayed for you on the Kalends, the first day of March") could not be replaced by *sum* if the first four syllables are to comprise a dactyl and long syllable. On the other hand, *sumam*, whose final syllable would need to be elided, could not take the metrical place of *sumet* in the penultimate line, 23, *hoc sollemne sacrum multos haec sumet in annos* ("let her welcome this traditional holy rite for many years"). In elegy 10 *sum* could not replace *est* in line 16, *tu modo semper ama: salva puella tibi est* ("only you love always: your girl is safe") and in line 17 *at nunc tota tua est* ("but now she is yours entirely") without elision and metrical irregularity. For the same reasons, *cogito* could not replace *cogitat* in line 18 (17f.: *te solum candida secum / cogitat, et frustra credula turba sedet*, "the luminous girl thinks to herself of you alone, and a trusting throng sits at her side in vain").

Furthermore, in elegy 12, line 3, *tota tibi est hodie* ("she is all yours today"), *sum* could not substitute for *est*. Nor could *starem* substitute for *staret* in line 4, *staret ut ante tuos conspicienda focos* ("in order that she might stand before your hearth to be gazed upon"); nor *uror* for *uritur* in line 17, *uritur ut celeres urunt altaria flammae* ("she is set on fire as rapid flames set the altars on fire"). It merits attention that elegy 12 actually contains, in line 8, *sed iuveni quaeso mutua vincla para* ("but prepare for the young man, I beseech you, chains that bind him in the same way"), a first person singular present active indicative verb form *quaeso* as well as these and other third person singular verb forms to describe Sulpicia. Its use indicates that its author could well have chosen to utilize other first person singular verb forms for apparent self-description, but chose not to. In addition, even in the poems where Sulpicia as poet-speaker refers to herself with first person singular verbs, she does not do so all that often, and in those instances these forms often conclude a hexameter or pentameter line, or allow for elision, or (as passives or deponents) end in the letter "r."[15] Incorporating third-person as well as first-person singular verb forms poses its challenges for Latin poets, even those who resort to elision far more frequently than Ovid does.

---

15 For first person singular forms that conclude a hexameter or pentameter line, see e.g., 11.8 *rogo* and 14.7 *relinquo*; for those that allow for elision, see, e.g., 8.1 *Sulpicia est* and 16.1 *ne cedam ignoto*; for those which, as passives or deponents, end in the letter "r", see, e.g., 9.16 *arguar*, 11.5 *uror* (2x), 11.12 *precor* and as well as 13.10 *ferar*. For the interpretation of first-person statements in the Sulpicia-elegies in a more general sense, cf. the chapter by Jacqueline Fabre-Serris in this volume.

In a forthcoming essay, Kurt Raaflaub has insightfully tackled Julius Caesar's embrace of illeism, observing that Caesar followed in the footsteps of such earlier Greek writers as Thucydides and Xenophon. Recalling "third-person narrative was well-known long before Caesar", Raaflaub remarks that "Thucydides applies it when mentioning his own writing and actions, aligning himself with all the other actors in his *History*"; he also notes that "Thucydides, like Caesar, only rarely uses the authorial 'I' for a personal comment." As for Xenophon, Raaflaub maintains "Xenophon too uses it when describing his own leadership role, placing himself on the same level as all the other generals." Indeed, he continues, "Xenophon goes even farther in separating author and actor by attributing the *Anabasis* to another author, most probably a fictitious person."[16]

Raaflaub contends "[this narrative technique] separates Caesar the author/narrator from Caesar the actor, and encourages the reader to see the actor's achievement from the outside, not the inside. . . . It is a way to depersonalize and objectify the narrative, to allow evaluation of the actions it describes, and to lift it above the level of personal memoir (one of the functions of a *commentarius*) toward that of history, reflecting 'an attempt to provide a definitive account in the manner of an historian'."[17] What is more, these third-person forms signal that the expressed utterances are intended to be read by others in addition to specific addressees, and locate the narrator as a member of the reading audience as well as a performer in the scenario of the text.

The feelings and experiences that Sulpicia, an actual female poet, shares with her audience, may not deserve the label of *commentarius* or even personal memoir, capable of elevation to the level of history; the same holds true for feelings and

---

16 Raaflaub (2022, in print).
17 Raaflaub's comments merit quotation in full: "Caesar generally writes: 'Caesar did,' not 'I did.' This strikes modern readers such as T.P. Wiseman as odd, even as 'unnecessarily mannered.' Governors' letters to the Senate were written in the first person; Caesar's choice of the third person is thus deliberate. It separates Caesar the author/narrator from Caesar the actor and encourages the reader to see the actor's achievement from the outside, not the inside. [As John Marincola has noted], it is a way to depersonalize and objectify the narrative, to allow evaluation of the actions it describes, and to lift it above the level of personal memoir (one of the functions of a *commentarius*) toward that of history, reflecting 'an attempt to provide a definitive account in the manner of an historian.' Moreover, it was typical of Roman writers to refer to their army as 'our men' and to include themselves by emphasizing 'we' and 'us.' By using 'us' and 'our' for the Romans but 'he' for Caesar, the narrator [as Luca Grillo argues] locates himself within his audience, conveying a sense that he is 'one of us' reporting someone else's deeds." – Third-person narrative was well-known long before Caesar. Thucydides applies it when mentioning his own writing and actions, aligning himself with all the other actors in his *History* – and he, like Caesar, only rarely uses the authorial 'I' for a personal comment. Xenophon too chooses it when describing his own leadership role, placing himself on the same level as all the other generals. Raaflaub goes even farther in separating author and actor by attributing the *Anabasis* to "another (most probably fictitious) author." See also Pelling (2013), a discussion of Xenophon which actually uses the term "illeism."

experiences voiced by such fictional female literary characters as Plautus' Phoenicium, Vergil's Dido, and Ovid's mythic heroines. Nevertheless, the use of third person verb forms, illaisms, in expressing these feelings and experiences reminds their audiences that these women are to be read by many others as well as by named addressees, that these female characters wish to be viewed from the outside as well as the inside, and evaluated accordingly, and that they seek to be defined as belonging to as well as performing for their audiences.

Marilyn Skinner, perhaps the most prominent among Catullan scholars who has interpreted Catullus as a public performer of his verse, is concerned with his poetry itself as vehicle for performance.[18] She has recently suggested that the name "Catullus" itself is not a hereditary but an individual *cognomen*, perhaps a nickname, which could "shed light upon the poet's references to himself in the third person."[19] Skinner focuses on the hendecasyllabic poem 56, in which the poet-speaker does not refer to himself with third person singular verbs, merely the first person singular perfect active verb forms *deprendi* and *cecidi*:

> *deprendi modo pupulum puellae*   5
> *trusantem: hunc ego, si placet Dionae,*
> *pro telo rigida mea cecidi.*

> I just now caught the little boy of my darling girl jerking off, and I knocked him off, so help me Venus' mother, weaponizing my stiff dick.

Catullus does however, refer to himself here as "Catullus" (much as Vergil has Dido refer to herself as "Dido" and Sulpicia elegy 8 refers to her as "Sulpicia"). Poem 79, in elegiac couplets, does not portray the poet-speaker as the subject of any verb.

> *Lesbius est pulcer. quid ni? quem Lesbia malit*
>   *quam te cum tota gente, Catulle, tua.*
> *sed tamen hic pulcer vendat cum gente Catullum,*
>   *si tria natorum suavia reppererit.*

> Lesbius is beautiful. Why not? He's the kind of man Lesbia prefers over you, with your kin, Catullus. But nevertheless this beautiful man would sell Catullus and his kin, if he shall have found three [passionate kisses of male offspring?].

It does, however, depict him as addressing himself by the vocative form of his name, *Catulle*, and then as employing his name in the accusative case to make an uncharitable claim about the poem's male subject "Lesbius" (presumably the tribune Publius Clodius Pulcher, actual brother of Clodia Metelli, whom Catullus celebrates by the metrically equivalent, literarily charged pseudonym Lesbia).[20]

---

18 See, for example, Skinner (1993).
19 Skinner (2015).
20 For Clodius, see Skinner (2011).

In the hendecasyllabic poem 58, Catullus uses the third person singular perfect active indicative form *amavit* to describe his own emotions *and* refers to himself as "Catullus", evoking his description of his *puella* in line 5 of poem 8, to be discussed below.

> *Caeli, Lesbia nostra, Lesbia illa.*
> *illa Lesbia, quam Catullus unam*
> *plus quam se atque suos amavit omnes,*
> *nunc in quadriviis et angiportis*
> *glubit magnanimi Remi nepotes.* 5

> Caelius, our Lesbia, that Lesbia, that Lesbia whom Catullus loved alone, more than himself and all near and dear, now in crossroads and alleyways performs handjobs on the descendants of great spirited Remus.

While 56 does not mention Lesbia by name, nor represent her in a critical light, both 79 and 58 do, permitting the inference that the use of the poet-speaker's *cognomen*, and in one instance of a third person verb form, functions as a distancing mechanism which facilitates and seeks judgment from readers as well as the addressees of a poem.

But Catullus' poems 11 and 8 deserve closer scrutiny. In 11 he mentions the illeistic Julius Caesar by name as well as his own *cognomen*, and provides details of Caesar's conquests as well as of a lengthy journey that his addressees Furius and Aurelius are prepared to undertake with Catullus himself.

> *Furi et Aureli comites Catulli,* 1
> *sive in extremos penetrabit Indos,*
> . . .
> *sive trans altas gradietur Alpes,*
> *Caesaris visens monimenta magni,* 10
> *Gallicum Rhenum horribile aequor ulti-*
>   *mosque Britannos,*
> . . .
> *pauca nuntiate meae puellae* 15
>   *non bona dicta.*
> *cum suis vivat valeatque moechis,*
> *quos simul complexa tenet trecentos,*
> *nullum amans vere, sed identidem omnium*
>   *ilia rumpens;* 20
> *nec meum respectet, ut ante, amorem,*
> *qui illius culpa cecidit velut prati*
> *ultimi flos, praetereunte postquam*
>   *tactus aratro est.*

> Furius and Aurelius, companions of Catullus, whether he will penetrate into most remote India . . . or whether he will stride across the lofty Alps, gazing at the achievements of great Caesar, and Gallic Rhine and the bristling sea and the most distant Britons . . . convey a few

words, not good words, to the woman I loved. Let her live and thrive with her illicit lovers, three hundred of whom she has embraced at the same time, loving no man truly, but repeatedly smashing the groins of all. And may she not look back, as she did before, at my love, which by her fault has fallen like a flower at the meadow's rim, after it has been touched by a plow passing by.

Readers struck by the emotional power packed into poem 11, written in the Sapphic meter and including an unmistakable allusion to Sappho's marriage hymns, often fail to notice that Catullus shares his searing personal pain without ever using a first person verb, or mentioning Lesbia by name. Or that Catullus here writes in an unusually ambitious vein. The geographical scope and temporal sweep of this poem, achieved in part by allusions to both Sappho's lyrics and other Catullan verses (such as the opening line of poem 5 – *vivamus, mea Lesbia, atque amemus* – evoked by *cum suis vivat valeatque moechis*) liken it to a personal memoir if not a *commentarius*; the third person verbs thus elevate Catullus' words to a mode of historical writing, insisting that the audience assess the actions described.

Like 11, poem 8 does not mention Lesbia by name, merely, in the fashion of 8, referring to her as his *puella*.

> *miser Catulle, desinas ineptire,*
> *et quod vides perisse perditum ducas.*
> . . .
> *nunc iam illa non vult: tu quoque impotens noli,*
> *nec quae fugit sectare, nec miser vive,*   10
> *sed obstinata mente perfer, obdura.*
> *vale puella, iam Catullus obdurat,*
> *nec te requiret nec rogabit invitam.*
> . . .
> *at tu, Catulle, destinatus obdura.*   19

> Wretched Catullus, stop playing the fool, and consider what you see to have been lost destroyed. . . . Now she is unwilling: be unwilling yourself, as it is out of your control. Don't pursue one who flees, don't live in a wretched state. But endure with resolved mind, be tough. Farewell, woman once loved, now Catullus is tough. Nor will he seek you nor will he ask you against your will. . . . But you, Catullus, be tough, resolved.

While it does mention Catullus by his *cognomen* in its first line, poem 8 does so in the vocative case, and – for the poem's first ten lines – addresses him with second person singular indicative, subjunctive and imperative verb forms. Yet in lines 12 and 13 he suddenly addresses his *puella*, and, perhaps in an effort to persuade himself (as Christopher Pelling has suggested), switches to third person singular verbs – *obdurat, requiret,* and *rogabit* – when describing his hardened resistance to her appeal:

separating author/narrator from actor, demanding the reader witness and judge his achievement from the outside by joining the reader.[21]

Catullus' use of these illeisms in both 8 and 11 set a memorable performative example for future poets eager to share and engage their audiences with their emotions and experiences, an example that in my estimation Sulpicia followed successfully with her illaisms. I trust I have established that illaism was a mode of expression potentially available to female as well as male speakers in Latin poetry, and that the illaistic portions of the Sulpicia elegies argue for, and not against, her authorship.

In his 1948 historical novel about Julius Caesar, *The Ides of March*, Thornton Wilder represents Catullus' lyrics about Lesbia as "verses of unbounded obscenity ... scribbled over the walls and pavements of all the baths and urinals in Rome" (p. 11). He thereby prefigures the claim of Simon and Garfunkel seventeen years later (1965) that "the words of the prophets are written on subway walls and tenement halls", whispering in "the sound of silence". Perhaps illeisms, and illaisms, by elevating personal feeling to a more distanced, relatable and readily evaluative mode of communication, have helped protect the words of, and ascribed to, women poets and poetic topics, from the oblivion that silence may create.

Bibliography

Bellandi (2007): Franco Bellandi, *Lepos e pathos: studi su Catullo*, Bologna.

Fulkerson (2017): Laurel Fulkerson, *A Literary Commentary on the Elegies of the Appendix Tibulliana*, Oxford.

Grossman *et al.* (2021): Igor Grossman, Anna Dorfman, Harrison Oakes, Kathleen D. Vohs, Henri Carlo Santos and Abigail Schoeler, "Training for Wisdom: The Distanced-Self-Reflection Diary Method", Psychol. Sci. 32:3, 381–394.

Hallett (2002a): Judith P. Hallett, "The eleven elegies of the Augustan elegist Sulpicia", in: Laurie J. Churchill, Phyllis R. Brown and Jane E. Jeffrey (eds.), *Women Writing Latin from Roman Antiquity to Early Modern Europe, vol. 1: Women Writing Latin in Roman Antiquity, Late Antiquity, and the Early Christian Era*, London, 45–65.

Hallett (2002b): Judith P. Hallett, "Women's Voices and Catullus' Poetry", *CW* 95.4, 421–424.

Hallett (2006): Judith P. Hallett, "Catullus and Horace on Roman Women Poets", special thematic issue "Catullus in Contemporary Perspective", *Antichthon* 40, 65–88.

Hallett (2011): Judith P. Hallett, "Ballio's Brothel, Phoenicium's Letter, and the Literary Education of Greco-Roman Prostitutes: The Evidence of Plautus' *Pseudolus*", in: Allison Glazebrook and Madeleine M. Henry (eds.), *Greek Prostitutes in the Ancient Mediterranean 800 BCE–200 CE*, Wisconsin, 172–196.

---

21 Pelling, personal communication, October 24, 2019. Cf. Florence Klein's chapter in this volume on Catullus' use of *ille* at the beginning of 51, referring to a 'rival', then switching, in the fourth stanza, to the vocative *Catulle* and second-person statements, referring to the poet's "I", as well as Bellandi (2007); Möller (2008).

Hallett (2021): Judith P. Hallett, "Latin Literary Lenses on Phoenician Female Speech", in: Jacqueline Fabre-Serris, Alison Keith and Florence Klein (eds.), *Identity, Ethnicity and Gender in Antiquity*, Berlin, 175–193.

Jenkins (2005): Thomas Jenkins, "At Play with Writing: Letters and Readers in Plautus", *TAPA* 135, 359–392.

Keith (1997): Alison Keith, "*Tandem Venit Amor*: A Roman Woman Speaks of Love", in: Judith P. Hallett and Marilyn B. Skinner (eds.), *Roman Sexualities*, Princeton, 295–310.

Lanham (1975); Carol Lanham, *Salutatio Formulas in Latin Letters to 1200: Syntax, Style and Theory*, Hildesheim.

McCarthy (2019): Kathleen McCarthy, *I, the Poet: First-Person Form in Horace, Catullus and Propertius*, Ithaca, NY/London.

Möller (2008): Melanie Möller, "Subjekt riskiert (sich) – Catull, *carmen* 8", in: Alexander Arweiler and Melanie Möller (eds.), *Vom Selbst-Verständnis in Antike und Neuzeit / Notions of the Self in Antiquity and Beyond*, Berlin/New York, 3–20.

Pelling (2013): Christopher Pelling, "Xenophon's and Caesar's third-person narratives – or are they?", in: Anna Marmodoro and Jonathan Hill (eds.), *The Author's Voice in Classical and Late Antiquity*, Oxford, 39–73.

Raaflaub (2022, in print): Kurt A. Raaflaub, "Tradition, Innovation, and Authority: Caesar's Historical Ambitions", in: K. Scarlett Kingsley, Giustina Monti and Timothy Rood (eds.), *The Authoritative Historian: Tradition and Innovation in Ancient Historiography. Essays in Honor of John Marincola*, Cambridge.

Robson (2019): David Robson, "Why speaking to yourself in the third person makes you wiser", *British Psychological Society's Research Digest*, May 24: https://digest.bps.org.uk/2019/05/24/a-new-trial-of-an-ancient-rhetorical-trick-finds-it-can-make-you-wiser (03/05/2022).

Skinner (1993): Marilyn B. Skinner, "Catullus in Performance", *CJ* 89, 61–68.

Skinner (2011): Marylin B. Skinner, *Clodia Metelli: The Tribune's Sister*, Oxford.

Skinner (2015): Marilyn B. Skinner, "A Review of Scholarship on Catullus, 1985–2015", *Lustrum* 57, 91–361.

Skoie (2002): Mathilde Skoie, *Reading Sulpicia: Commentaries 1475–1990*, Oxford.

Tränkle (1990): Hermann Tränkle, *Appendix Tibulliana*, herausgegeben und kommentiert von H.T., Berlin/New York.

Florence Klein
Construire un « je » genré dans les traductions de Catulle (*c.* 51 et 66) : Érotique de l'appropriation littéraire et féminisation rétrospective des modèles grecs

Abstract: This paper investigates the gendered dimension of the translation process, as thematized within the texts themselves, and thus considers how the translator shapes the first-person's gender when translating a poem. In order to make this investigation, it analyses and compares the two translations by Catullus of a Greek model, namely Sappho in *c.* 51, and Callimachus in *c.* 66, as they present us with opposed gendered paths: in the former poem, a female 'I' in the Greek text becomes male while transposed in the Latin text; while in the latter one, a male 'I' becomes female. This inversion is explained by a common metapoetic scenario that figures the act of translation as an erotic relationship, with the male translator as the lover and conqueror of the feminized translated author. The second part of the article explores how this way of representing the translation as a strongly gendered process does retroactively affect the translated texts themselves.

Keywords: Callimachus, Sappho, gender in translation, transgendered voice, gender ambivalence, metapoetics of translation

Pour étudier le rôle joué par le paramètre du genre dans l'élaboration d'une voix poétique à la première personne, la poésie de Catulle semble nous offrir un terrain d'observation incontournable, tant elle nous donne à lire des oscillations, des tensions et des métamorphoses entre la voix masculine et la voix féminine d'un même « je », que ce soit celui d'un personnage mythologique[1] ou celui de la *persona* du poète amoureux de Lesbie.[2] Dans cet article, je considérerai les jeux de transforma-

---

[1] On pense par exemple à l'Attis du *c.* 63, dont le monologue à la première personne épouse la transformation, par sa castration, d'homme en femme. Sur ce poème, voir *e.g.* Skinner (1993).
[2] Le « je » qui dit sa passion au fil du recueil se donne alternativement comme une voix féminine, ou féminisée, et comme une voix masculine, et il est remarquable qu'un poète par ailleurs tout à fait soucieux d'affirmer avec force sa virilité (qu'on songe au *c.* 16) puisse se féminiser comme il le fait, notamment dans son expression de la plainte personnelle (considérons par exemple l'usage de la figure de Laodamie dans le *c.* 68, introduite par le biais de la mention de Troie et qui sert à la fois de comparant explicite à Lesbie pour leur commune beauté (v. 131 s.), et de comparant implicite au « je » catulléen, pour la semblable intensité avec laquelle ils vivent chacun l'amour et la perte). Par ailleurs, sur l'oscillation de la voix du poète, entre masculine et féminine, dans les *c.* 8, 72 et 76, on se reportera aux analyses de Greene (1995), qui réinterprète en termes de genre la fragmentation de la voix locutrice dans ces textes qui disent la douleur extrême et l'impossibilité de se défaire de

tions entre voix féminine et masculine dans la poésie de Catulle à un autre niveau, celui de la relation métapoétique qui lie l'auteur latin à ses modèles grecs, archaïque ou hellénistique, lorsqu'il les 'traduit' et les transfère à Rome :[3] pourquoi et comment le traducteur modifie-t-il (y compris rétroactivement) le genre de la voix locutrice des poèmes qu'il importe dans son propre recueil ? Par quels moyens et avec quels enjeux s'élabore ainsi l'image d'une relation éminemment genrée entre le modèle grec et son émule latin ? A quel point peut-on considérer en outre que la construction d'une telle relation, qui féminise les modèles traduits, a pu rétrospectivement affecter ces derniers, et la perception que nous en avons ?

Pour répondre à ces questions, nous relirons, en regard l'un de l'autre, les poèmes 51 et 66 du *liber Catulli*, qui traduisent respectivement le fragment 31 de Sappho et la *Boucle de Bérénice* qui clôt le quatrième livre des *Aitia* de Callimaque. Ces deux textes sont chacun écrits à la première personne, donnant la parole, pour le premier, à l'amante éperdue de passion face à la femme qu'elle aime, et, pour le second, à un arrangement de cheveux de la reine Bérénice, voué aux dieux pour le retour de l'époux absent, coupé et finalement transformé en constellation. Or dans les deux cas, la traduction catulléenne entraîne un changement de genre du « je », puisqu'elle modifie le triangle homo-érotique en relation hétéro-érotique dans le *c.* 51, et attribue les plaintes du βόστρυχος callimachéen à une *coma* dans le *c.* 66. Ces deux traductions sont par ailleurs considérées comme étonnamment proches du texte grec qu'elles transposent en latin (au point que pour le *c.* 66, on se sert de la traduction latine pour reconstituer le texte de Callimaque, et que pour le *c.* 51, la quatrième strophe a pu être considérée comme apocryphe parce qu'elle rompait brutalement avec l'apparente proximité du texte de Sappho). Dans le contexte de cette 'fidélité' d'ensemble, ces modifications de genre de la première personne ne sont pas anecdotiques. Si on les considère alors comme signifiantes, comment expliquer qu'elles semblent résulter d'itinéraires inversés – du féminin au masculin dans le premier cas, du masculin (au moins au sens grammatical du terme) au féminin dans le second ? Parce que le changement de genre semble en apparence symétriquement opposé dans les deux traductions, il est d'autant plus important de les considérer ensemble,[4] pour observer la façon dont poète latin

---

l'amour pour Lesbie : la voix féminine, ou féminisée, serait celle qui subit la passion amoureuse destructrice, et qui appelle 'à la rescousse' son alter ego masculin pour la sauver des effets débilitants de l'amour.

3 J'emploie le verbe « traduire » en sachant bien que la réalité antique diffère de notre conception moderne de la traduction. Sur cette question théorique et sur la pratique catulléenne de la traduction comprise au sens large comme appropriation, voir Young (2015).

4 Comme le note Thorsen (2019), les études sur chacune des deux traductions de Catulle ont la plupart du temps été menées en parallèle l'une de l'autre, et non de manière croisée (82, « it appears curious and striking that there are still few works of scholarship that compares Catullus' Sappho-translation with his Callimachus-translation as two sides of the same phenomenon, namely Catullus' translational technique, and, by extension, Catullus' translational technique as emblema-

construit l'identité genrée de la première personne, non seulement dans son propre texte mais également dans celui du modèle qu'il s'approprie : nous verrons ainsi comment le poète manipule le genre de la voix locutrice – dans l'image qu'il contribue à forger du texte grec 'traduit' tout autant que dans la traduction latine –, et quels sont les enjeux de telles interventions qui (re-)modèlent le genre du « je » dans ces textes passés du grec au latin.

Ajoutons enfin que le cas particulier des traductions est intéressant à deux niveaux : tout d'abord parce que l'analyse des variations et des écarts volontaires avec le modèle traduit, transposé ou imité, nous permet d'analyser plus précisément les modalités de présentation genrée de la première personne, mais aussi, et surtout, parce que dans ces deux textes, l'opération de traduction, de transfert d'un texte d'une culture à l'autre, est lui-même intimement lié à l'enjeu de ces changements de genres. La manipulation rétrospective du genre du « je » dans ces poèmes écrits à la première personne permet à Catulle de suggérer, à un niveau métapoétique, une représentation genrée du rapport du 'traducteur' latin à ses modèles grecs. Dans un premier temps, nous reviendrons sur les deux itinéraires inversés – du féminin au masculin dans le *c.* 51 ; du masculin au féminin dans le *c.* 66 – comme deux moyens convergents et complémentaires de figurer l'opération de traduction comme une relation genrée. Puis, dans un second temps, nous examinerons la manière dont les traductions de Catulle n'ont pas seulement modifié le genre de leurs modèles dans les vers latins qui en sont issus, mais ont pu contribuer à infléchir la lecture que l'on a faite de ces textes grecs eux-mêmes, avec en quelque sorte une 'féminisation rétroactive' de ces derniers dans la tradition littéraire.

1 Figurer l'opération de traduction comme une relation genrée : deux itinéraires métapoétiques complémentaires

Commençons par le fragment 31 de Sappho et sa traduction dans le *carmen* 51, en rappelant ce qui est bien connu, et d'abord les quatre premières strophes du poème d'amour composé par la poétesse grecque :

---

tic of his poetic project »). On peut néanmoins mentionner les paragraphes intitulés « Catullus' Literary Amours » et « Catullus' Transgendered Voice » d'Höschele (2009) 146–151 qui suggèrent un lien stimulant entre les deux textes, et les analyses, certes successives mais convergentes, de Young (2015) qui consacre le dernier et l'avant-dernier chapitres de son livre respectivement à chacune des deux traductions. Les analyses qui suivent s'inscrivent dans la lignée de ces deux contributions.

φαίνεταί μοι **κῆνος ἴσος** θέοισιν
ἔμμεν' **ὤνηρ, ὄττις ἐνάντιός** τοι
ἰσδάνει καὶ πλάσιον ἆδυ **φωνείσας** ὐπακούει

καὶ **γελαίσας** ἰμέροεν, τό μ' ἦ μὰν
καρδίαν ἐν στήθεσιν ἐπτόαισεν,
ὠς γὰρ ἔς σ' ἴδω βρόχε' ὤς με φώναι-
   σ' οὐδ' ἒν ἔτ' εἴκει,

ἀλλὰ κὰμ μὲν γλῶσσα †ἔαγε λέπτον δ'
αὔτικα χρῶι πῦρ ὐπαδεδρόμηκεν,
ὀππάτεσσι δ' οὐδ' ἒν ὄρημμ', ἐπιρρόμ-
   βεισι δ' ἄκουαι,

κὰδ' ἴδρως ψῦχρος κέεται, τρόμος δὲ
παῖσαν ἄγρει, **χλωροτέρα** δὲ ποίας
ἔμμι, τεθνάκην δ' ὀλίγω 'πιδεύης
   φαίνομ' **ἔμ' αὔται**.⁵

Le poème met en relation trois personnages : le « je » semble tout d'abord s'intéresser à un homme, désigné à la troisième personne et comparé aux dieux (κῆνος ... ὤνηρ – ἴσος θέοισιν), non pour ses qualités propres mais pour la sérénité avec laquelle ce dernier peut contempler une jeune femme (désignée à la deuxième personne) dont la douce voix et le rire désirable bouleversent profondément le « je ». L'homme évoqué au début est alors immédiatement oublié, et la suite du poème se concentre sur les effets dévastateurs de la vue de l'aimée sur le « je » qui détaille les symptômes cliniques de sa passion. Du point de vue du genre, si la troisième personne est d'emblée présentée au masculin dans les deux premiers vers, et si la féminité du « tu » apparaît par le biais des participes φωνείσας et γελαίσας dès les vers 3–5, le « je » est finalement donné comme féminin aux vers 14 et 16 (χλωροτέρα, ἔμ' αὔται).

Comme le notent les commentateurs, la virtuosité de la traduction de Catulle a consisté à changer radicalement le scénario, tout en semblant au premier abord n'avoir modifié qu'à la marge le texte traduit (dans ses trois premières strophes du moins), pour décrire une situation profondément différente, centrée sur l'expression du désir érotique masculin et la mise en avant de la rivalité entre hommes dans un espace public lui aussi exclusivement masculin. De fait, si l'on considère les sept premiers vers (*c.* 51,1–7),

---

[5] Fr. 31,1–16 Voigt, « Un rival des dieux, tel me semble l'homme / Que je vois assis devant toi, de face, / lui qui peut t'entendre, si proche – douce, / lorsque tu parles / saisissante, lorsque tu ris – ce rire / qui, en moi, a bouleversé mon âme. / Car à peine je t'aperçois, je reste / toute muette ; / Et ma langue est comme brisée ; se glisse, / Sous ma peau, soudain, une fine flamme ; / Et mes yeux, aveugles, se vident ; mes o-/reilles bourdonnent ; / La sueur ruisselle sur tous mes membres ; / Un frisson me prend ; plus livide encore / Qu'herbe jaunissante, je crois sentir la / mort qui s'approche » (trad. Brunet 1991).

> *ille* mi par esse deo uidetur,
> *ille*, si fas est, superare diuos,
> *qui* sedens aduersus identidem te
>   spectat et audit
>
> dulce ridentem, **misero** quod omnis
> eripit sensus **mihi** : nam simul te,
> **Lesbia**, aspexi . . .[6]

on retrouve immédiatement le « il » au masculin pour le rival jalousé (*ille, ille . . . qui*), mais c'est également au masculin qu'est qualifié le « je », au vers 5 (avec l'adjectif *misero*, apposé au pronom *mihi*). C'est donc un homme désormais qui rivalise avec un autre pour l'amour d'une femme. On note cependant que la féminité du « tu » n'apparaît pas grammaticalement par le même canal que le grec : le participe qui dit le doux rire du « tu » contemplé et écouté par le « il » (*te / spectat et audit / dulce ridentem*) ne porte pas de marque morphologique du féminin comme c'était le cas en grec ; par contre, il est désigné comme féminin par l'insertion d'un nom au vocatif au vers 7, *Lesbia*.

Cette interpellation de la femme aimée par son prénom, qui ne figurait pas dans le texte grec, s'avère ici particulièrement retorse : si Lesbia est bien le surnom de la femme aimée dans la fiction du *libellus*, il désigne aussi la Lesbienne / la poétesse de Lesbos, Sappho donc (et cette lecture est en outre favorisée par la présence d'un autre nom de poète, celui de Catulle lui-même – au vocatif, *Catulle* – dans la dernière strophe[7]). Le contexte particulier qui est celui de la traduction d'un poème de Sappho, précisément, donne nécessairement à ce terme une connotation métapoétique, en créant l'impression que l'auteur latin interpelle directement, de l'intérieur du texte qu'il lui reprend, l'auteure grecque qu'il est en train de traduire. Parce que de cette manière Sappho prend en quelque sorte la place de la femme adorée, contemplée par les hommes du poème, la traduction de son poème amoureux par un auteur masculin se double, au niveau métapoétique, d'une déclaration d'amour du poète latin à celle qui l'inspire et qu'il traduit ; mais cette déclaration d'amour a la violence d'une conquête impérialiste autant qu'érotique.[8] Catulle fait sienne (la poésie de) Sappho, dans un geste d'appropriation culturelle, qui est aussi, littéralement, une forme d'expropriation. En plaçant Sappho dans la situation de la femme aimée, de

---

6 « Celui-là me semble être l'égal d'un dieu, il me semble, si c'est possible, surpasser les dieux celui qui, assis en face de toi, peut souvent te contempler et entendre ce doux rire, qui me ravit, malheureux que je suis, l'usage de tous mes sens ; car à peine t'ai-je aperçue, Lesbia . . . » (trad. Lafaye 1998 légèrement modifiée, car je n'ai pas souhaité reprendre la traduction de *misero . . . mihi* par « qui ravit *à ma pauvre âme* l'usage de tous mes sense » – une métonymie qui, en quelque sorte, féminiserait la voix locutrice sur le modèle du *c.* 65, voir *infra* p. 33).
7 *C.* 51,13, *otium, Catulle, tibi molestum est*. Au sujet de l'adresse à soi-même de la part du « je » voir la contribution de Judith Hallett dans ce volume.
8 Voir Young (2015) 166–181.

l'objet de la parole érotique, Catulle la dépossède également de son statut d'auteur : Sappho n'est plus le sujet de son propre texte, elle n'est que la femme sur laquelle on écrit – ou 'que l'on écrit', comme la future *scripta puella* des élégiaques[9] –, elle passe du statut d'auteur écrivant au statut d'objet écrit.[10] Il est alors d'autant plus significatif que ce soit l'insertion de ce nom *Lesbia* au vocatif qui permette de désigner le « tu » comme féminin, contrairement au texte grec qui indiquait cela par la morphologie du participe présent aux vers 3–5 : cette insertion qui transforme « Sappho » (l'auteure) en « Lesbie » (l'objet d'amour) est justement, du fait de la disparition de la marque du genre grammatical sur le participe présent, le moment précis où l'on désigne cet autre – exproprié de son texte, privé de sa parole, donc – comme féminin. Ainsi Catulle souligne la nature éminemment genrée du scénario par lequel l'homme prive la femme de son statut de sujet de la parole et du désir, en faisant d'elle l'objet muet de son amour et de son poème.

Ainsi, dans une forme de dramatisation érotique de l'émulation littéraire, nous sommes invités à lire le *c.* 51 également à un niveau métapoétique, dans lequel le traducteur décrit sa relation à son propre modèle littéraire par les mots mêmes qu'il traduit. Catulle dit à la fois son amour pour la poétesse Sappho (/ Lesbie), et la violence de l'appropriation par laquelle il la spolie de sa parole en la réduisant à une position d'objet. Le changement de genre du « je » dans la traduction de Catulle, tel qu'il s'accompagne de la conversion de Sappho, de sujet du désir et de la parole poétique, en objet de ce désir et de cette parole désormais masculine, permet de mettre en scène, sur le plan métapoétique, une vision genrée de la relation qui unit le poète romain et son modèle grec, où le masculin prend le rôle de sujet désirant qui dit l'autre et le réduit au silence, où le désir de possession érotique permet de suggérer l'appropriation littéraire.

Qu'en est-il dans le *c.* 66 ? Dans l'élégie de Callimaque (fr. 110 Pf.), le « je » qui parle et dit son désarroi d'avoir été arraché de la tête de sa maîtresse après que celle-ci l'a voué aux dieux pour le retour de son mari, avant d'être transporté au ciel, sur les genoux d'Aphrodite, puis transformé en constellation, est – grammaticalement du moins – un « je » masculin. Dès son apparition dans le texte, comme complément d'objet direct du verbe de vision dont le sujet est l'astronome Conon, il

---

9 Sur la *scripta puella*, Wyke (1987). On peut par ailleurs également s'interroger, avec Alison Sharrock, sur ce qu'a de troublant la propension, antique comme moderne, à qualifier Sappho de « dixième muse » : « It is only a small step from calling a woman poet 'a Muse' to constructing her as 'poetry' rather than 'poet', as the 'blank page' who 'is a poem' rather than being someone who writes a poem' » (Sharrock 2002, 209 s. ; la fin de la citation fait référence à Gubar 1982). Pour les femmes qui sont 'chantées' et sont l'objet plutôt que le sujet du chant dans la poésie grecque ancienne, voir aussi la contribution d'Emily Hauser (section 3) dans ce volume.
10 Greene (1999) ; Young (2015).

est désigné comme un βόστρυχος ;[11] plus loin, aux vers 47 s., le βόστρυχος s'assimile au groupe (masculin) des πλόκαμοι.[12] Et lorsqu'il décrit son catastérisme, il se désigne là encore au masculin, comme Βερενίκειος καλὸς ἐγὼ πλόκαμος, « moi, le bel arrangement de cheveux de Bérénice ».[13]

Le genre de la voix locutrice ne fait pas consensus dans la critique.[14] Si grammaticalement, on l'a vu, le « je » qui parle est masculin, les lecteurs du poème ont pu l'identifier à une figure féminine, un des arguments mis en avant étant, en dépit du genre grammatical, le fait que le πλόκαμος a des expériences et un comportement traditionnellement féminin, comme la plainte, l'arrachement forcé aux siens etc. Mais en ce cas, l'argument n'est-il pas, dans une certaine mesure, circulaire ? On juge le « je » féminin parce qu'il/elle agit (ou plutôt subit) comme on juge que le fait une femme. Quoi qu'il en soit, en admettant, à raison certainement, que ces comportements sont traditionnellement féminins, il faut au minimum considérer l'ambivalence et la tension qui résultent des noms de genre masculin pour désigner le locuteur du poème – et qui sont certainement comme le reflet inversé de l'ambivalence de genre qui caractérise la présentation de la reine Bérénice elle-même, affublée de qualité supposément masculines.[15] Notons encore que dans les discussions sur le genre de la voix locutrice dans le poème callimachéen, une des situations jugées typiquement féminines se trouve au vers 50, quand le πλόκαμος évoque ses sœurs, les boucles (κόμαι) qui le pleurent après qu'il a été coupé :

ἄρτι [ν]**εότμητόν με** κόμαι ποθέενσκον ἀδε[λφαί[16]

On a alors pu identifier la situation du « je » à celle de la future jeune épouse qui doit quitter ses proches – ses sœurs ou un cercle de jeunes filles non mariées – pour être donnée à un époux. Parce que l'adjectif νεότμητος est épicène, on a pu voir dans le με une forme féminine, par assimilation aux κόμαι ἀδελφαί, aux « boucles sœurs » du même vers. Mais d'autres chercheurs ont également interprété le vers en

---

11 Fr. 110,1 ; 7 s., πάντα τὸν ἐν γραμμαῖσιν ἰδὼν ὅρον ᾗ τε φέρονται / . . . / †η με Κόνων ἔβλεψεν ἐν ἠέρι τὸν βερενίκης / βόστρυχον ὅν κείνη πᾶσιν ἔθηκε θεοῖς, « Voyant tout le ciel dans les signes tracés et où se meuvent . . . Conon me vit dans l'air, moi, le vrillon de cheveux de Bérénice, qu'elle consacra pour tous les dieux » (trad. Durbec 2006 modifiée, pour tenter de traduire le βόστρυχος par un nom masculin en français).
12 Ibid. 47 s., τί πλόκαμοι ῥέξωμεν, ὅτ' οὔρεα τοῖα σιδή[ρῳ / εἴκουσιν ;, « Que ferons-nous, cheveux tressés, quand de telles montagnes cèdent au fer ? » (trad. Durbec 2006 modifiée, pour la même raison avec πλόκαμοι).
13 Ibid. 61 (trad. Durbec 2006 modifiée, pour la même raison).
14 Pour une voix locutrice masculine : Koenen (1993) ; pour une voix locutrice féminine : Puelma (1982) ; Gutzwiller (1992) ; pour une voix locutrice au genre ambivalent : Barchiesi (1997) ; Vox (2000).
15 Voir *e.g.* Prioux (2011) 210 s.
16 « Les boucles, mes sœurs, me pleuraient, moi que l'on venait de couper » (trad. Durbec 2006 modifiée – sa traduction par « Les cheveux, mes frères, me pleuraient, moi qui venais d'être coupée » inversant, étonnamment, les genres des noms / pronoms).

conservant le genre masculin de la première personne, si l'on songe qu'un homme peut-être pleuré par sa sœur lors de son départ – en l'occurrence à la guerre, c'est-à-dire la situation précise de Ptolémée pleuré par sa « sœur »/épouse (ou du moins celle qui était présentée comme telle par l'idéologie Lagide, dans la lignée du couple « Philadelphe »). Comme le rappelle en outre Évelyne Prioux, cette identification du πλόκαμος à Ptolémée, contraint de quitter Bérénice qui pleure son départ, fait sens par la logique de substitution de l'ex-voto, la reine ayant offert son arrangement de cheveux en échange du retour de son mari.[17]

En traduisant le poème de Callimaque, Catulle a évincé toute ambiguïté et fait de la boucle de cheveux de la reine une locutrice résolument féminine. Tout d'abord, grammaticalement, le βόστρυχος / πλόκαμος devient une *coma*[18] ou une *caesaries*, qui entraîne l'accord au féminin comme on peut le voir dès le tout début du poème,

†ἣ **με** Κόνων ἔβλεψεν ἐν ἠέρι **τὸν** βερενίκης
 βόστρυχον ὅν κείνη πᾶσιν ἔθηκε θεοῖς[19]

*idem **me** ille Conon caelesti in lumine uidit*
 *e Bereniceo uertice **caesariem***
*fulgentem clare, **quam** multis illa dearum*
 leuia protendens bracchia pollicita est[20]

ou plus loin, lorsqu'est évoqué le catastérisme par lequel la boucle prend place à côté de la couronne d'Ariane dans le ciel,

ὄφρα δὲ] μὴ νύμφης Μινωίδος ο[
 : . .]ος ἀνθρώποις μοῦνον ἐπι.[
φάεσ]ιν ἐν πολέεσσιν ἀρίθμιος ἀλλ[ὰ γένωμαι
 καὶ **Βερ**]**ενίκειος καλὸς ἐγὼ πλόκαμ[ος**,
ὕδασι] **λουόμενόν με** παρ' ἀθα[νάτους ἀνιόντα
 Κύπρι]ς ἐν ἀρχαίοις ἄστρον [ἔθηκε νέον[21]

---

17 Prioux (2011).
18 *C.* 66,93 : *sidera corruerint ; utinam **coma** regia fiam !*.
19 Callimaque, fr. 110,7 s., « Conon me vit dans l'air, moi, le vrillon de cheveux de Bérénice, qu'elle consacra pour tous les dieux » (trad. Durbec 2006 modifiée).
20 Catulle, *c.* 66,7–10 : « celui-là même, Conon, dans la lumière céleste, m'a vue, boucle détachée du front de Bérénice, jeter des feux éclatants, après que cette reine m'eut promise à plusieurs déesses en tendant vers elles ses bras lisses » (trad. Lafaye 1998). – On peut noter qu'au vers 47, c'est le terme *crines* qui est employé (*quid facient crines, cum ferro talia cedant ?*) : le masculin est certes ainsi représenté, mais cantonné à une forme de généralité.
21 Callimaque, fr. 110,59–64, « Pour éviter que la jeune épouse, la fille de Minos, . . . pour les hommes seulement, mais [que je sois] moi, le bel arrangement de cheveux de Bérénice. Moi, baigné des flots, auprès des immortels . . . Cypris me plaça entre les anciens astres, moi le nouvel astre » (trad. Durbec 2006 légèrement modifiée).

> *hic dii uario ne solum in lumine caeli*
>   *ex Ariadneis aurea temporibus*
> *fixa corona foret, sed nos quoque fulgeremus*
>   *deuotae flaui uerticis exuuiae,*
> ***uuidulam*** *a fletu cedentem ad templa deum* ***me***
>   *sidus in antiquis diua nouum posuit.*[22]

En outre, en soutien de ce changement de genre grammatical, la féminisation de la voix locutrice est renforcée par plusieurs jeux intratextuels qui associent la *coma* à des figures féminines ou féminisées – à commencer par celle du poète lui-même dans le texte qui précède et accompagne la traduction du poème de Callimaque : le *c.* 65, billet par lequel le poète justifie auprès de son ami Ortalus son incapacité à lui envoyer une production entière personnelle, tant la douleur de la mort de son frère le prive d'inspiration poétique. L'auteur qui parle à la première personne y construit l'impression d'une voix locutrice féminine, alors même que le « je » est bien donné comme masculin (1–4) :

> *etsi* ***me*** *assiduo* ***confectum*** *cura dolore*
>   *seuocat a doctis, Ortale, uirginibus,*
> *nec potis est dulcis Musarum expromere fetus*
>   ***mens animi*** *(tantis fluctuat* ***ipsa*** *malis . . .*[23]

Alors que l'accord de *confectum* apposé au pronom *me* dans le premier vers désigne d'emblée le locuteur comme un homme, le reste du poème brouille cette première information en féminisant la voix locutrice par divers procédés : par exemple, la métaphore de l'enfantement – en l'occurrence de la stérilité – (poétique), *nec potis . . . expromere fetus*, associée à la métonymie par laquelle le « je » est remplacée par sa *mens animi*, un nom féminin, qui de fait sera repris dans la parenthèse qui suit par le pronom *ispa*. On peut aussi mentionner, toujours dans ces quatre premiers vers, le rôle de l'intratextualité, la formule *tantis fluctuat ipsa malis*, à propos de la *mens* du « je » (supposément masculin) convoquant comme modèle, par le parallélisme des deux fins de vers soutenu par d'autres échos verbaux, la figure d'Ariane représentée dans le poème précédent comme « ballotée sur une immense mer de soucis » *magnis curarum* ***fluctuat*** *undis* (*c.* 64,62). Le *c.* 65 qui prépare la lecture du *c.* 66 nous présente déjà, en acte, une transformation de la voix masculine en voix féminine – sur laquelle nous reviendrons plus tard.

---

[22] Catulle, *c.* 66,59–64, « Alors elle décida qu'on ne verrait plus seulement, fixée au milieu des flambeaux épars dans le ciel divin, la couronne d'or détachée du front d'Ariane, mais que j'y brillerais aussi, dépouille sacrée d'une tête blonde ; et quand j'arrivai, toute baignée de larmes, au séjour des dieux, la déesse fit de moi un astre nouveau, qui prit place parmi les anciens » (trad. Lafaye 1998).
[23] « Même si le chagrin cruel qui m'accable sans relâche me tient éloigné des doctes vierges, Ortalus, même si mon âme ne peut plus donner naissance aux douces productions des Muses (elle est agitée par de si grands maux . . .) » (trad. Lafaye 1998 modifiée).

De plus, ce premier effet de suggestion se double d'échos intratextuels dans le *c.* 66 associant la boucle locutrice avec plusieurs figures féminines qui encadrent le poème dans le *libellus* catulléen : d'une part, les jeunes femmes passionnément amoureuses que sont l'Ariane du *c.* 64 – déjà, comme on l'a vu, rappelée à l'esprit du lecteur par le début du *c.* 65 – et la Laodamie du *c.* 68 ; d'autre part, les vierges ravies à leurs familles par leur futur époux des épithalames que sont les *c.* 61 et 62.[24] J'ai analysé ailleurs ces jeux d'échos qui associent la *coma* à des figures de jeunes femmes amoureuses et/ou enlevées contre leur gré par leur amant, et ainsi contribuent, au-delà de la seule transformation grammaticale, à renforcer la féminité de la boucle.[25] En outre, le contexte de ces poèmes ainsi mis en réseau par le jeu de l'intratextualité renforce l'idée de rapt amoureux, qui s'actualise dans la complainte de la *coma* décrétant que c'est contre son gré, *inuita*, qu'elle a quitté la tête de sa maîtresse (*c.* 66,39 s.) :

> *inuita, o regina, tuo de uertice cessi,*
>   *inuita ; adiuro teque tuumque caput.*[26]

Ainsi accordé au féminin, l'expérience de l'arrachement forcé loin des siens se charge indubitablement d'une connotation érotique ;[27] dès lors aussi, l'image des boucles sœurs qui pleurent (v. 51 s.) – quelle que soit la situation qu'elle évoquait chez Callimaque – corrobore encore l'idée du rapt amoureux qui traverse le texte de Catulle (ce qui, réciproquement, accentue encore la nature féminine de la locutrice enlevée malgré elle à ses proches).

Or cette image du rapt peut, comme l'a montré Regina Höschele, se doubler d'une valeur métapoétique, la boucle arrachée et déplacée étant alors l'image de la *Boucle*, le poème callimachéen, lui-même arraché de son contexte d'origine (le dernier livre des *Aitia*, composé dans le contexte de l'Alexandrie ptolémaïque au IIIe s. avant J.-C.) pour prendre place dans un contexte nouveau, un recueil de poèmes composés en latin au Ier s. avant J.-C.[28] Le transfert de la *coma*, de la tête de la reine lagide jusqu'au ciel où elle a rejoint la couronne d'Ariane,[29] figure aussi l'opération de traduction elle-

---

24 Voir, pour un développement de ces éléments, Klein (2020) 529–533 ; Klein (2022).
25 Klein (2022).
26 « C'est bien malgré moi, ô reine, que j'ai quitté ton front, oui, malgré moi ; j'en fais serment par toi, par ta tête » (trad. Lafaye 1998).
27 L'adjectif *inuita* fait entendre le terme grec ἀέκουσα volontiers associé à l'évocation des rapts de vierge, et notamment à leur modèle archétypal : le rapt de Perséphone dans *l'Hymne homérique à Déméter*, où la jeune fille est dite à plusieurs reprises enlevée « contre son gré » (*cf.* notamment *H. Cer.* 19 s., ἁρπάξας δ' **ἀέκουσαν** ἐπὶ χρυσέοισιν ὄχοισιν / ἦγ' ὀλοφυρομένην . . ., « il l'enleva et, malgré sa résistance, l'entraîna tout en pleurs sur son char d'or . . . »).
28 Höschele (2009) 145 s.
29 *C.* 66,59-62, *hic dii uario ne solum in lumine caeli / ex Ariadneis aurea temporibus / fixa corona foret, sed nos quoque fulgeremus / deuotae flaui uerticis exuuiae* (voir *supra* p. 33 n. 22 pour la traduction).

même qui transpose la *Coma Berenices* callimachéenne – « astre nouveau » de la constellation des poèmes de Catulle – dans le *liber* latin où sa place à côté d'Ariane prend un véritable sens métapoétique puisque, de fait le groupe de *c.* 65 et 66 (la traduction de Callimaque précédée de son billet d'accompagnement) y suit immédiatement le *c.* 64 qui nous fait entendre les plaintes d'Ariane.[30] C'est ainsi que, comme le fr. 31 de Sappho, le poème de Callimaque acquiert rétrospectivement, en tant que texte traduit, arraché à sa culture d'origine dont il déplorerait d'avoir été séparé contre son gré, une dimension métapoétique qu'il n'avait évidemment pas à l'origine et par laquelle, dans les mots mêmes du poème, se dirait l'expérience de la traduction du grec au latin. On observe alors que, dans ce cas-ci, le scénario métapoétique implique une voix locutrice féminine, en jouant sur l'image du rapt érotique, l'enlèvement de la future épouse par un amant entreprenant. Tout se passe donc comme si la nette féminisation du « je » était inséparable de la construction, en parallèle de la traduction du texte, d'un sens métapoétique évoquant cet acte même de traduction en des termes genrés, en l'occurrence comme un rapt amoureux : le texte grec, féminisé par son traducteur, est assimilé à une jeune fille enlevée malgré elle – à ce qu'elle en dit, du moins[31] – à son milieu d'origine par son soupirant / conquérant romain.

Ainsi, dans les deux poèmes qu'il traduit du grec, Catulle semble aboutir au même résultat – l'assimilation du texte traduit du grec à une femme désirée et, d'une certaine manière, possédée par son amant romain dans un scénario métapoétique fortement genré – par des procédés inversés : la transformation de la première personne du féminin au masculin dans le *c.* 51, du masculin (au moins grammatical) au féminin dans le *c.* 66. Cette inversion est logique, puisque dans le poème de Callimaque, le « je » était l'objet du rapt, tandis qu'il était le sujet du désir dans le fragment de Sappho : en réécrivant le premier au féminin et le second au féminin, Catulle peut raconter la même 'histoire métapoétique', assimilant la poésie grecque à une femme passionnément aimée, enlevée, mais aussi bousculée voire violentée par son traducteur latin dans une

---

30 Voir Höschele (2009) 140 s., qui suggère que le passage callimachéen correspondant a pu inspirer à la fois le *c.* 64 (pour Ariane), et le *c.* 66 (pour la boucle elle-même).

31 Höschele (2009) 145 s. – suivie par Young (2015) 147 – suggère, de manière tout à fait stimulante, que la résistance de la boucle à quitter la tête de sa maîtresse figurerait une forme de réticence, évidemment projetée par Catulle, du poème grec à être transposé en latin (« Could it not be that, within its new textual surroundings, Berenice's tress, so to speak, voices the anxiety of the text, as it is taken away from its author? »). Pour ma part, dans le sillage de cette suggestion, je défends l'idée que Catulle, tout en faisant dire cette réticence à la boucle (/ *Boucle*), nous donne à douter de sa sincérité, à la fois par les jeux d'échos intratextuels avec des vierges consentant à leur enlèvement et par le décodage qu'offre la boucle elle-même sur les larmes feintes des jeunes épousées (*c.* 66,11–20), ce qui lui permettrait alors, sur le plan métapoétique, de proposer – avec la mauvaise foi de ceux qui considèrent qu'une victime de violence y a de quelque manière consenti ? – une représentation de l'appropriation poétique à laquelle il soumet ses modèles hellénistiques comme un rapt qui doit peut-être moins à la force et à la contrainte qu'il n'y paraît d'abord (Klein, 2022).

conception érotique en même temps qu'impérialiste de l'appropriation des modèles grecs à Rome.

Ainsi les deux poèmes catulléens, aux itinéraires apparemment opposés en ce qui concerne le genre de la voix locutrice, convergent en un même scénario métapoétique et genré. On peut cependant aller plus loin, au-delà de cette première impression de procédés en miroir. Car dans les deux cas, en réalité, le résultat est bien que Catulle a contribué à féminiser rétrospectivement son modèle grec. C'est assez net pour la *Boucle de Bérénice* callimachéenne : difficile de considérer que l'intermédiaire de la traduction latine par laquelle on a souvent accès au texte incomplet de Callimaque n'a joué aucun rôle dans notre perception d'une voix locutrice féminine en dépit du genre grammatical du βόστρυχος / πλόκαμος qui y prend la parole. Mais je voudrais aussi suggérer qu'il en va de même à propos du fr. 31 de Sappho, avant d'observer comment cette féminisation rétrospective des deux modèles grecs se nourrit d'effets d'échos et de croisements qui, par le jeu des traductions catulléennes, les rapprochent l'un de l'autre.

2 La féminisation rétrospective des modèles grecs

S'il paraît légitime de se demander dans quelle mesure la traduction au féminin de Catulle (*caesaries, coma*) a influencé rétrospectivement notre interprétation du genre de la voix locutrice dans le texte de Callimaque, on songe moins à se poser la question pour le poème de Sappho, déjà considéré en lui-même comme l'expression du désir au féminin. J'adopterai désormais une perspective légèrement différente, en rappelant qu'à y regarder de près le « je » n'y est pas immédiatement donné comme grammaticalement féminin, et en suggérant dès lors que c'est la réécriture de Catulle qui, par contraste, a pu contribuer à accentuer la dimension genrée de la voix locutrice dans son modèle même.

Comme je l'ai souligné plus haut en effet, les éléments grammaticaux permettant d'identifier une voix locutrice féminine dans le texte grec n'apparaissent que dans la quatrième strophe du fragment (contre la première strophe pour les indications de genre des troisième et deuxième personnes). Avant l'apparition des formes χλωροτέρα et αὖται caractérisant la première personne comme féminine, respectivement aux vers 14 et 16 du poème – c'est-à-dire à la toute fin du fragment tel que nous le possédons –, l'essentiel du poème ne permet pas d'attribuer de genre à la voix qui dit son désir et sa passion amoureuse. Autrement dit, si le but de Catulle avait uniquement été de se réapproprier le poème de Sappho pour lui faire dire une histoire différente, la sienne, et de transformer, avec le minimum de changements possible, le triangle homoérotique en triangle hétéroérotique, il aurait pu le faire de manière plus frappante encore, en profitant de l'ambiguïté de son modèle quant au genre de la voix locutrice dans la majeure partie du fragment. Mais, comme on l'a vu dans la première partie de cet article, son but était moins de profiter de la relative indétermination de son modèle sur le genre du « je » pour adapter les mots de la poétesse à un contenu érotique nouveau que de mettre en avant une vision fortement genrée de la relation unissant le poète romain et son modèle grec – cette vision genrée impliquant la masculinisation du premier, comme sujet du désir et de la parole, et la féminisation du second, comme leur objet, réduit au silence par le jeu de l'appropriation culturelle.

Ajoutons ici que ce qui permet que la voix du « je » dans le poème de Sappho ne soit que très tardivement donnée comme féminine est lié à ce que l'on a appelé le caractère « objectif » de la description de son désir souffrant. Comme le note le Pseudo-Longin, le « je » est dispersé en éléments distincts vus comme de l'extérieur :

> οὐ θαυμάζεις, ὡς ὑπὸ ταὐτὸ τὴν ψυχήν, τὸ σῶμα, τὰς ἀκοάς, τὴν γλῶσσαν, τὰς ὄψεις, τὴν χρόαν, πάνθ ὡς ἀλλότρια διοιχόμενα ἐπιζητεῖ, καὶ καθ ὑπεναντιώσεις ἅμα ψύχεται κάεται, ἀλογιστεῖ φρονεῖ (ἢ γὰρ φοβεῖται ἢ παρ' ὀλίγον τέθνηκεν) ἵνα μὴ ἕν τι περὶ αὐτὴν πάθος φαίνηται, παθῶν δὲ σύνοδος ;

> N'admires-tu pas comment d'un seul coup, Sapho va chercher l'âme, le corps, l'ouïe, la langue, les yeux, le teint, tout comme autant de choses qui lui sont étrangères et qui se séparent d'elle, comment sous l'alternance de sentiments contraires, en même temps elle est transie de froid et elle brûle, elle s'égare et elle est sensée (car elle est soit terrifiée soit presque morte), si bien que ce n'est pas une seule passion qui se manifeste en elle, mais un concours de passions ?[32]

De fait, c'est l'éclatement de la première personne en parties distinctes (son âme, ses organes, ses sens . . .) qui fait que le « je » n'est qualifié, et ainsi identifié comme féminin par l'effet des accords grammaticaux, qu'à la toute fin du poème. Or, en lieu et place de ce procédé (qui débute au vers 5 chez Sappho, τό μ' ἦ μὰν / καρδίαν ἐν στήθεσιν ἐπτόαισεν), Catulle introduit (au vers 5 également) l'adjectif *misero* qu'il appose au pronom *mihi*,[33] marquant ainsi sa première personne comme masculine précisément à l'endroit où le texte de Sappho aurait pu lui permettre, s'il l'avait voulu, de se modeler sur son indistinction de genre en évitant, comme cette dernière, de qualifier directement le « je » au masculin ou au féminin. Au-delà des aspects dépendants de la langue même (comme la non distinction genrée du participe présent en latin, par opposition au grec), certaines modifications stylistiques apparaissent comme plus signifiantes encore, parce qu'elles ne sont pas déterminées par le changement linguistique. Si Catulle avait voulu se mouler le plus possible dans le texte de Sappho, il aurait pu conserver les effets de l'éclatement métonymique du « je » qui prolongeait l'indétermination du genre de la voix locutrice ; il les a au contraire neutralisés, précisément pour pouvoir mieux identifier son propre « je » comme masculin.

Par cette présence du pronom *mihi* immédiatement donné comme masculin par l'accord de l'adjectif apposé *misero*, le texte latin nous donne en même temps, de

---

32 Pseudo-Longin, *Du Sublime* X 3 (texte et trad. Lebègue 1939).
33 C. 51,5 s., *misero . . . omnis / eripit sensus mihi*. Voir *supra* p. 29.

manière indissociable, le sens d'un moi, d'une première personne rassemblée, et sa caractérisation au masculin, par opposition à la dislocation du « je » chez Sappho, dont Ellen Greene a noté à quel point elle apparaissait comme une caractéristique féminine.[34] Mais il faut souligner, il me semble, que cette nature supposément féminine du « je » disloqué, éclaté est fortement accentuée, sinon rétrospectivement créée, par le contraste que crée Catulle avec son modèle lorsqu'il choisit, en rupture avec ce dernier, d'associer directement au masculin la préservation de l'intégrité du « je ». Autrement dit, l'association du féminin à la désintégration du moi serait une construction favorisée par la traduction / transformation contrastive opérée par Catulle : c'est parce qu'il s'en distingue en insistant sur la masculinité d'un « je » qui a, malgré les affres de la passion, conservé le sens d'une intégrité personnelle, que Catulle désigne rétrospectivement le « je » éclaté de Sappho comme féminin, et contribue donc à établir comme caractéristique de la voix féminine cette dislocation dans une multiplicité éparse, étrangère à elle-même.

Or, il apparaît que par cette dislocation pointée comme féminine, le texte grec se voit doté d'une dimension métapoétique supplémentaire, et complémentaire de celle que nous avons déjà relevée. Lorsque le « je » se dit réduit au silence et formule sa propre désintégration, c'est comme si le poème, au féminin, racontait sa privation de parole suite à l'appropriation par la traduction latine. Comme le commente le Pseudo-Longin, Sappho cherche ce qui devrait constituer son « je » « comme autant de choses qui lui sont étrangères et qui se séparent d'elle ». Richard Hunter souligne combien la formule évoque l'acte même de traduction : « if πάνθ ὡς ἀλλότρια διοιχόμενα ἐπιζητεῖ could be said of anyone, it could be said of Catullus, for 'translation' is precisely the finding of the οἰκεῖον, 'what is one's own', in the ἀλλότριον, 'what belongs to someone else' » ;[35] ou, pourrait-on nuancer, si le traducteur fait en effet sien « ce qui appartient à autrui », la formule de Pseudo-Longin pourrait bien plutôt être reprise pour désigner plus précisément ce que la traduction de Catulle *fait à Sappho*, qu'elle dépossède de ses mots propres pour les lui rendre étrangers à elle-même, comme les parties éclatées de son être dans lesquelles la poétesse ne reconnaît pas le sens d'un « je ». Là encore, donc, la dimension métapoétique peut s'appliquer de manière rétrospective au modèle grec traduit, qui dirait, en même temps que les symptômes cliniques de la passion amoureuse, sa propre dépossession par sa traduction latine, l'expropriation de la poétesse qui n'est plus sujet d'une parole que s'est appropriée son traducteur.

Dès lors, si l'on considère que ce qui caractérise le poème de Sappho est moins, en réalité, la nature féminine de sa voix locutrice que son éclatement,[36] que c'est la traduction de Catulle qui, associant par contraste le sens d'un « je » unifié et la nature

---

34 Greene (1999).
35 Hunter (2019) 53.
36 Voir Prins (1996).

masculine de ce dernier, a rétrospectivement désigné comme féminine cette « étrangèreté à soi » qui ressort du fr. 31 et que, donc, la voix féminine, qui n'apparaissait pas immédiatement comme telle dans le poème grec, le devient, à la lumière de sa traduction contrastive, quand (et parce qu')elle est arrachée à elle-même, alors on peut admirer la manière dont le texte de Catulle projette sur son modèle ce scénario métapoétique qui fait de la dispersion de la parole la caractéristique d'une poésie féminisée : la traduction est représentée comme une forme d'appropriation virile, agressive tout autant que mue par l'amour, de la voix locutrice féminine qui accomplirait ainsi, par la dislocation de son « je », sa supposée nature d'« étrangère à son propre texte ».

Observons maintenant comment cette féminisation rétrospective de la poésie de Sappho a pu également permettre à Catulle de renforcer encore la féminisation de son autre modèle grec, Callimaque, dans le couple de poèmes 65 et 66.

J'ai déjà suggéré plus haut que la féminisation de la voix locutrice dans le *c.* 66, principalement réalisée par le changement de genre grammatical des noms de la boucle s'appuyait, en outre, sur un premier brouillage de la masculinité du « je » dans le *c.* 65 qui précède et introduit directement la traduction du poème callimachéen (voir p. 33) : observons maintenant ce que ce brouillage, cette première forme de féminisation de la voix locutrice, doit à la présence de Sappho, et d'une Sappho 'féminisée' par Catulle lui-même. De fait, on a vu le rôle joué, dans ce glissement de genre, par la métonymie du début du *c.* 65, où la première personne s'identifie dès les premiers vers à sa *mens animi* impuissante à écrire et ballotée dans une tempête de souffrances : cette substitution est un des moyens de féminiser la voix locutrice (masculine, puisqu'il s'agit de celle du poète lui-même) dans ce texte, engageant un processus de féminisation du « je » qui prépare au changement de genre du πλόκαμος en *coma* dans le *c.* 66. Or il apparaît intéressant de mettre en regard ce procédé avec la traduction contrastive du fr. 31 de Sappho dans le *c.* 51, qui, mettant l'accent sur la masculinité d'un « moi » unifié (*mihi*) par contraste avec la dispersion métonymique du « je » de la poétesse en diverses parties de son être, avait contribué, comme on vient de le suggérer, à désigner comme typiquement féminin cet éclatement de la première personne. Pour le formuler autrement, tout se passe comme si, après avoir « féminisé » rétrospectivement le modèle de Sappho, Catulle s'en servait pour brouiller le genre de la voix locutrice du *c.* 65 et, ainsi, préparer la féminisation de la boucle / *Boucle* callimachéenne.[37]

---

37 Cette hypothèse peut être confortée par la présence d'une autre évocation de Sappho en lien avec un brouillage du genre du « je » dans le *c.* 65, qui s'achève sur l'étrange comparaison entre la relation du poète à son correspondant Ortalus, d'une part, et celle d'un couple d'amoureux, d'autre part. Une des lectures possibles de cette comparaison consiste à assimiler le poète, qui se défend d'avoir laissé échapper de sa mémoire les paroles de son ami, à la jeune vierge qui, oublieuse, a laissé rouler par mégarde la pomme qu'un jeune homme lui avait envoyée en présent d'amour (v. 15–24), ce qui contribue à féminiser la voix locutrice du *c.* 65. Or, comme l'a relevé Acosta-Hughes (2010), l'image

Mais revenons pour finir à cette dernière. Dans les débats critiques sur le genre de la voix locutrice dans le poème de Callimaque, un argument en faveur d'une voix féminine, ou du moins ambivalente, a été apporté par Onofrio Vox, qui postule une allusion à un passage de Sappho au vers 39 du poème callimachéen, que nous n'avons pas conservé. Vox se fonde sur la traduction de Catulle, dans les vers dont j'ai par ailleurs plus haut souligné l'importance pour la féminisation de la voix locutrice par l'assimilation à la jeune fille enlevée *inuita* « malgré elle » aux siens dans le cadre d'un rapt érotique ou d'un mariage (*c*. 66,39 s., voir texte cité p. 34). Si le vers 39 manque dans le texte grec, le fait que l'on ait au vers 40 l'équivalent exact de la fin du serment tel qu'on le trouve en latin (σήν τε κάρην ὤμοσα σόν τε βίον cf. *adiuro teque tuumque caput*) peut laisser penser que le texte de Callimaque comportait bien, à cet endroit, une protestation de réticence comparable à celle que l'on peut lire chez Catulle, *inuita, o regina, tuo de uertica cessi*. Mais, si on l'admet, à quel genre s'accordait-elle ? Pour certains, on doit supposer une forme au masculin. Comme le rappelle Alessandro Barchiesi à une époque où on reconstruisait volontiers le modèle grec en se servant du texte de Catulle, « Barber e Lenchantin avevano azzardato un esametro aperto da ἄκων 'contravoglia' » ;[38] et, en dépit de ses réserves sur ces pratiques de reconstitution, Barchiesi lui-même imagine plutôt une forme masculine pour formuler la réticence du πλόκαμος à son catastérisme.[39] Vox, quant à lui, propose de prendre en compte la présence d'une forme féminine dans un vers de Sappho (fr. 94,5 Voigt) : Ψάπφ', ἦ μάν σ' **ἀέκοισ'** ἀπυλιμπάνω, « Sappho c'est malgré moi que je te quitte », placé par la poétesse dans la bouche d'une tendre aimée forcée de la quitter et enjointe à se rappeler tous les moments passés ensemble, dans une intimité toute féminine que peut rappeler la situation de la boucle attachée à sa maîtresse. Il est néanmoins difficile de savoir si Callimaque convoquait effectivement l'intertexte de ce vers de Sappho, et, le cas échéant, comment cette référence éventuelle fonctionnait, quels effets de sens elle créait, et si notamment cela faisait vaciller le genre de la boucle (il aurait été étonnant qu'il reprenne littéralement la forme ἀέκοισα au féminin en tout cas, dans la mesure où le terme serait *a priori* apposé à un sujet grammaticalement masculin). Bref, il semble difficile de se prononcer sur les effets de cette citation de Sappho, s'il y en avait bien une.

---

de la pomme associée aux jeunes fiancés évoquait sans doute le modèle d'un épithalame de Sappho (en plus de celui, bien identifié, du récit callimachéen de Cydippe et Acontius) : fr. 105A Voigt, « Telle la pomme sucrée qui rougit tout au bout de la branche / La plus haute de l'arbre, oubliée par les cueilleurs de pommes – / Non ce n'est pas un oubli, le fruit est resté hors d'atteinte » (trad. Brunet 1991), les motifs conjoints de la pomme, du rougissement, de l'oubli ainsi que le contexte érotique étant commun à ce texte et à celui de Catulle. On observe donc, encore, la présence de Sappho dans les passages du *c*. 65 où le « je » se trouve virtuellement féminisé, comme une préparation à la féminisation de la boucle dans le poème suivant.

38 Barchiesi (1997) 214.
39 *Ibid*. 215 : « non escluderei che Callimaco già avesse qualcosa come *inuitus* più che *inuita* ».

Par contre, on peut penser que dans le poème de Catulle, par un effet d'allusion-fenêtre, lorsque la *coma* est désormais tout à fait féminine, le 'retour' éventuel à une forme féminine, *inuita*, le strict équivalent donc du ἀέκοισα de Sappho, permettrait d'activer le souvenir de cette dernière, et donc de doter, plus encore, la boucle d'une voix féminine, celle de la poétesse grecque que l'auteur avait traduite dans le *c.* 51, en contribuant, comme on l'a vu, à la construire comme essentiellement féminine par cette traduction même.

D'ailleurs, comme indice du souvenir par Catulle de ce fr. 94, on peut se demander si l'insertion du vocatif *Lesbia* – désignant comme objet de l'amour non seulement Lesbie, mais Sappho elle-même – dans la deuxième strophe du *c.* 51, qui ne figurait pas dans le fr. 31, ne pourrait pas lui aussi se fonder sur le souvenir de ce même vers, avec les deux interpellations de la femme aimée également en début de vers (cf. *nam simul te / **Lesbia** aspexi, nihil est super mi . . .* ~ **Ψάπφ'**, ἦ μάν σ' ἀέκοισ' ἀπυλιμπάνω) qui, suivant le scénario métapoétique mis en place par Catulle, désigneraient en réalité la même personne : la poétesse Sappho. En ce cas, on aurait un jeu de croisement supplémentaire entre les *c.* 51 et 66, puisque les deux traductions catulléennes feraient allusion conjointement au même fragment de la poétesse grecque. On mesure alors l'importance de considérer de concert les deux poèmes de Catulle qui, non seulement esquissent, par des moyens complémentaires, un scénario métapoétique convergent, assimilant la littérature grecque à une femme passionnément aimée en même temps qu'enlevée par un époux-conquérant et dépossédée d'elle-même, mais aussi, d'une certaine manière, confortent par des phénomènes d'échos et d'influences réciproques l'établissement de cette relation genrée du poète romain aux modèles qu'il traduit.

Bibliographie

Éditions et traductions

Callimaque, *Fragments poétiques*, textes traduits et commentés par Yannick Durbec, Paris 2006.
Callimachus, *Aetia*, 2 vols., ed. Annette Harder, Oxford/New York 2012.
Catulle, *Poésies*, texte établi et traduit par Georges Lafaye, revu par Simone Viarre et Jean-Pierre Néraudau, Paris 1998.
Longin, *Du sublime*, éd. et trad. par Henri Lebègue, Paris 1939.
Sappho, *Poèmes et fragments*, texte établi et traduit par Philippe Brunet, Lausanne 1991.

Articles et ouvrages de critique

Acosta-Hughes (2010): Benjamin Acosta-Hughes, *Arion's lyre: Archaic Lyric into Hellenistic Poetry*, Princeton.
Barchiesi (1997): Alessandro Barchiesi, "Otto punti su una mappa dei naufragi", *MD* 39, 209–226.
Clark (2008): Christina A. Clark, "The Poetics of Manhood? Nonverbal Behavior in Catullus 51", *CP* 103, 257–281.
Greene (1995): Ellen Greene, "The Catullan Ego: Fragmentation and the Erotic Self", *AJP* 116, 77–93.
Greene (1999): Ellen Greene, "Re-figuring the feminine voice: Catullus translating Sappho", *Arethusa* 32, 1–18.
Gubar (1982): Susan Gubar, "The Blank Page and Female Creativity", in: Elizabeth Abel (dir.), *Writing and Sexual Difference*, Brighton, 73–93.
Gutzwiller (1992): Kathryn Gutzwiller, "Callimachus' *Lock of Berenice*: Fantasy, Romance, and Propaganda", *AJP* 113, 359–385.
Höschele (2009): Regina Höschele, "Catullus' Callimachean *Hair*-itage and the erotics of Translation", *RFIC* 137, 118–152.
Hunter (2019): Richard Hunter, "Notes on the Ancient Reception of Sappho . . . ", in: Thea S. Thorsen et Stephen Harrison (dir.), *Roman Receptions of Sappho*, Oxford, 45–60.
Klein (2020): Florence Klein, "Métamorphoses intertextuelles et intersexuelles d'une voix 'trans-genre' : la *Boucle de Bérénice* relue par Catulle, Virgile et Ovide", in: Christophe Cusset, Pierre Belenfant et Claire-Emmanuelle Nardone (dir.), *Féminités hellénistiques: voix, genre, représentations*, Leuven et al., 527–549.
Klein (2022): "Objets arrachés / femmes enlevées : le rapt des vierges et les images du transfert culturel dans les poèmes 64, 65 et 66 de Catulle", in: Henriette Harich-Schwarzbauer et Cédric Scheidegger-Lämmle (dir.), *Women and Objects in Antiquity*, Trier, 149–170.
Koenen (1993): Ludwig Koenen, "The Ptolemaic King as a Religious Figure", in: Anthony Bulloch, Erich S. Gruen, A. A. Long et Andrew Stewart (dir.), *Images and ideologies: self-definition in the Hellenistic world*, Berkeley, 25–115.
Prins (1996): Yopie Prins, "Sappho's Alterlife in Translation", in: Ellen Green (dir.), *Re-Reading Sappho: Reception and Transmission*, Berkeley.
Prioux (2011): Évelyne Prioux, "Callimachus' Queens", in: Benjamin Acosta-Hughes, Luigi Lehnus et Suzan Stephens (dir.), *Brill's Companion to Callimachus*, Leiden/Boston, 201–224.
Puelma (1982): Mario Puelma, "Die *Aitien* des Kallimachos als Vorbild der römischen Amores-Elegie", *MH* 39, 221–246; 285–304.
Sharrock (2002): Alison Sharrock, "An A-musing Tale: Gender, Genre, and Ovid's Battles with Inspiration in the *Metamorphoses*", in: Efrossini Spentzou et Don Fowler (dir.), *Cultivating the Muse. Struggles for Power and Inspiration in Classical Literature*, Oxford, 207–227.
Skinner (1993): Marilyn B. Skinner, "*Ego mulier*: The Construction of Male Sexuality in Catullus", *Helios* 20, 107–130.
Thorsen (2019): Thea S. Thorsen, "As Important as Callimachus? An Essay on Sappho in Catullus and Beyond", in: Thea S. Thorsen et Stephen Harrison (dir.), *Roman Receptions of Sappho*, Oxford, 77–94.
Vox (2000): Onofrio Vox, "Sul genere grammaticale della Chioma di Berenice", *MD* 44, 175–181.
Wyke (1987): Maria Wyke, "Written Women: Propertius' *scripta puella*", *JRS* 77, 47–61.
Young (2015): Elizabeth Marie Young, *Translation as Muse. Poetic Translation in Catullus' Rome*, Chicago/London.

Lisa Cordes

Virgo, *virago*, Vestal – Gender and Fiction in Seneca the Elder's *Controversia* 1.2

Abstract: This paper analyses the use of female *sermocinatio* in Seneca the Elder's *Controversia* 1.2. The gender status of the 'prostitute-priestess', who is at the centre of the *Controversia*, is ambiguous, as she is depicted at times as a weak *virgo*, at times a manly *virago*, who may, or may not, be suitable for priesthood. The paper shows how this ambiguity is employed in the first-person speech that the declaimers put into the woman's mouth. Focusing on their rhetorical, literary, and aesthetic dimensions, the paper analyses these *sermocinationes*, and the alleged 'interactions' that they initiate between the woman and the advocates, first with regard to the excerpts from the declaimers' individual speeches, second with regard to the *Controversia* as it is compiled by Seneca. With a view to this declamatory 'womanufacture', the paper demonstrates the importance of a holistic approach to Seneca's 'collages'. Moreover, by looking at parallels in Roman comedy and the ancient novel, it shows how the *Controversia* combines the construction of gender with a self-conscious discussion of the declamation's fictional genre.

Keywords: declamation, *sermocinatio*, oral/written communication, fictionality, *virago*, womanufacture

1 Introduction: Female *sermocinatio* in declamation

In the *Controversiae* of his "declamatory anthology", Seneca the Elder collects excerpts from fictitious juridical speeches of famous orators of his time.[1] In the fictitious

---

[1] The term "anthology" is used by Fairweather (1981). Seneca's work, entitled *Oratorum et rhetorum sententiae divisiones colores* in the manuscript tradition, consists of a collection of excerpts from declamations by various orators who were active between the 30s of the first century BCE and 40 CE (on the dates, see Feddern 2013, 60). The excerpts are taken from two types of declamatory speeches: from fictitious juridical speeches (*controversiae*) and from fictitious deliberative speeches (*suasoriae*). To differentiate between the original declamations, and the compilations that Seneca assembled from the excerpts of these declamations, I capitalise the term *Controversia* when I refer

---

Acknowledgments: I thank the participants in the discussion in Munich, especially Alison Sharrock, Judith Hallett, and Jaqueline Fabre-Serris, as well as Nicola Hömke, for their valuable feedback. Clare O'Neill corrected my English. This paper was written during a lockdown due to the Coronavirus pandemic. I am grateful to the university libraries of Humboldt-Universität Berlin and Ludwig-Maximilians-Universität München for their helpful online services. My warmest thanks go to my mother, Maria Cordes, for her invaluable help in this situation.

https://doi.org/10.1515/9783110795257-004

lawsuits underlying these speeches, women play different roles. They may be victims and plaintiffs, defendants, or the cause of a dispute between men. In accordance with Roman custom, they usually do not plead their own cases. Instead, they are represented by their advocates, i.e., by the role-playing male declaimers. As Danielle van Mal-Maeder emphasises, the declamatory 'I' is essentially male.[2] However, in most *Controversiae* involving female characters we find what Martin Bloomer called "snippets of speech":[3] short fragments of what the women are imagined to have said during their fictitious trials.

Unlike the more extensive discourses spoken by female characters in the pseudo-Quintilian *Major Declamations* and unlike the long *ethopoeiae* (or, in Latin, *sermocinationes*) of mythical characters practised in rhetorical education,[4] the fragments of female speech in Seneca's *Controversiae* have not attracted much scholarly attention.[5] The reason is probably that, formally speaking, they are simple rhetorical figures, short *sermocinationes*. According to ancient theory, such *sermocinationes* are fictions of speech that are placed into the mouth of a person in order to characterise

---

to the latter. Seneca's anthology contains 10 books of *Controversiae* with excerpts from speeches on a total of 74 different topics, and one book of *Suasoriae* with excerpts from speeches on a total of seven topics. According to the tripartite division in the title of the anthology, the excerpts are usually arranged into three categories: *sententiae* (short, pointed catchphrases), *divisiones* (schematic depictions of a speech's proposed structure), and *colores* (additional 'colourings' or interpretations that the declaimer gives to facts and characters mentioned in the topic). On the structure of Seneca's work and the meaning of the terms *sententia*, *divisio*, and *color* see the introductions of Berti (2007) 17–28 and Feddern (2013) 36–59. For the literary quality of the *sententiae* and *colores* collected by Seneca, see below n. 8.

2 On the representation of women in Roman declamation see van Mal-Maeder (2003), (2007) 95–107. She gives an overview of declamatory settings in which women may play a role and emphasises their novel-like depictions. Pointing to the fact that the women usually do not plead their own cases but are represented by their male advocates, she characterises the declamatory universe as "un monde essentiellement masculin" (2007, 95).

3 Bloomer (1997) 68. Van Mal-Maeder (2007) 42, 99 uses the term "discours cités" when referring to the quoted speech of men and women who belong to the fictional declamatory universe.

4 For an overview on the inconsistent use of the terms *sermocinatio*, *ethopoeia*, and *prosopopoeia* (used by Quintilian in this context) in ancient rhetoric, see Hömke (2009) 244f. with further literature. Kraus (2007) 455f. distinguishes between three meanings of *ethopoeia/sermocinatio* in ancient rhetoric: the display of a speaker's good character, a type of schoolroom exercise (the long *ethopoeia/sermocinatio* mentioned here), and a rhetorical figure of a fiction of speech (the short *ethopoeia/sermocinatio* on which this paper will concentrate).

5 For female discourse in the ps.-Quintilian *Decl. mai.* see van Mal-Maeder (2003), (2007) 101–7, Hömke (2009) 250–55. For *ethopoeiae* of female mythical characters, see Kraus (2007) 457–9 with further literature. Due to their thematic orientation, there is almost no female speech in the *Suasoriae*. However, in *Suas.* 1.13 about Alexander the Great one declaimer is said to have used a *sermocinatio* of Alexander's mother.

him or her.[6] They are a common rhetorical device, hence their presence in the *Controversiae* may not seem particularly intriguing. In this paper, however, I will show that they are worth a closer look.

The present volume is based on the premise that every first-person statement in a speech situation in literature is somehow shaped, i.e. formed, in literary and aesthetic terms. When it comes to *sermocinatio*, this is true in a very explicit sense. The snippets of female speech in Seneca's work are most obviously shaped: they are invented, styled, and performed by the role-playing male declaimers. Moreover, due to their brevity, they often do not stand by themselves, but they are combined with the advocate's 'reaction' to the opponent's fictitious speech. The rhetorical effect is thus based not on the *sermocinatio* itself, but on the fake interaction it initiates. In principle, this applies to *sermocinationes* of both men and women, but, as will be shown, the gender difference of the persons 'speaking' in these interactions has specific effects.

In the following, I will concentrate on *Controversia* 1.2 which is about the 'prostitute-priestess', a young woman who aspires priesthood after having escaped the brothel (see below for the details). On the one hand, I will address the rhetorical side of female *sermocinatio* in this text. Focusing on the parameter gender, I will analyse its persuasive potential in the context of the fictitious juridical setting, and its potential for a positive self-representation of both the declaimer and the advocate whom he is impersonating.[7] It is not surprising that *sermocinationes* play a significant role in Seneca's collection of memorable *sententiae* and *colores*.[8] As the declaimers are responsible for inventing the women's words as well as for their own responses to these words, the snippets of speech provide a perfect base for their seemingly quick-witted replies.

On the other hand, I will look at the literary and aesthetic aspects of these *sermocinationes*. In recent years, scholarship has emphasised the literary dimension of declamation in general and Seneca's work in particular, with regard to both the

---

6 Cf. Lausberg §§ 820–25, Quint. *Inst.* 9.2.29–32.

7 Van Mal-Maeder (2007) 41f. distinguishes between three levels in the declamatory communicative situation: on the first, a real declaimer speaks in front of a real audience ("monde extratextuel, réalité"). On the second, the real declaimer plays the role of a fictitious advocate (plaintiff, defendant) before a fictitious jury ("monde intratextuel, univers fictionnel"). On the third, the fictitious advocate 'cites' the words of his fictitious opponents ("monde cité, discours cités"). If I say that a *sermocinatio* provides a good base to prove ingenuity, this holds for both the declaimer (who demonstrates this ingenuity to his audience) and the advocate (who aims at winning his fictitious case with it). As Seneca collects the excerpts under the names of real declaimers, in the following, I will speak of *the declaimer's* ingenuity. With that, I refer to the declaimer as he is impersonating an advocate in the fictitious case. The structure of *Contr.* 1.2 contributes to the impression that each declaimer impersonates his 'own' advocate. See below, p. 58–60

8 On the assessment of the literary and aesthetic quality of the *sententiae* see Connolly (2009) 338f., Faure-Ribreau (2016) 216–18. On the literary potential of the *colores* see Zinsmaier (2009) 259–63, Feddern (2013) 44–59.

anthology as a whole and the speeches excerpted in it. Emanuele Berti emphasised that Latin declamation evolved from being a school exercise into a form of epideictic spectacle, aiming at *ostentatio* and *voluptas audientium*.[9] Joy Connolly analyses the declaimers' "sententious art", stating that Seneca's assortment of sophisticated *sententiae* and *colores* is written for well-educated, adult Roman men, among whom declamation became popular at the end of the first century BCE.[10] Accordingly, over recent years, scholars have pointed out the proximity of declamation to poetry and the novel,[11] the genre's dramatic and performative elements,[12] and the intertextual quality of the *Controversiae*.[13] As regards the anthology as a whole, scholarship has emphasised that it is not "a fragmentary collection of isolated argumentations or sententiae, but . . . an elaborate and skilfully arranged art work in its own right".[14]

Remarkably, this increased interest in the literary dimension of declamation has not had a great influence on the analysis of female representation in Seneca's work. Traditionally, scholarship has addressed gender issues in declamation from a socio-cultural perspective. Focusing on the didactic scope of declamation, Martin Bloomer argued that it represented "the right to speak in gendered terms" and taught the schoolboy when and on what a woman could speak.[15] Similarly, Manfred Kraus showed how female impersonation trained the orators to express emotions that they wouldn't be allowed to display in their own *persona*.[16] Danielle van Mal-Maeder combined an analysis of declamation as a literary genre with socio-cultural questions when she asked whether the eccentricity of the genre's novel-like fictions fostered an innovative discourse on gender relations. She concludes that, far from experimenting with unorthodox gender roles, female speech in declamation confirms existing social norms, as it depicts the speakers without exception as stereotypically 'good' or 'bad' women.[17] Building on these observations, I will examine the snippets of female speech in *Contr.* 1.2 with a focus on their rhetoric, literary, and aesthetic dimensions.

---

9 Berti (2015) 20f., Stramaglia (2016) stress that no clear-cut distinction can be made between *Schau-* and *Schuldeklamation*. On *ethopoieia* between school exercise and literary form, see Heusch (2005). Seneca alludes to the educational background of declamation in *Contr.* 1 *praef.* 4: *fiat quod vultis: mittatur senex in scholas*.
10 Connolly (2009) 332–4. La Bua (2010) 195f. and van Mal-Maeder (2020) argue that the literary character of the work corresponds to its didactic goals.
11 See van Mal-Maeder (2007) 65–93, Berti (2015) for the relation to poetry; van Mal-Maeder (2007) 115–45 for the relation to the novel.
12 See Pianezzola (2003), Hömke (2009) on the declaimers' multi-layered roleplay; Nocchi (2015) and Hömke (2017) on the influence of comedy and tragedy; Huelsenbeck (2015) on the declaimers' interactions in the original performative context.
13 See e.g. Stoffel (2017) on *Contr.* 6.8.
14 Stoffel (2017) 164 n. 10, following Gunderson (2003).
15 Bloomer (1997) 68.
16 Kraus (2007) 465f. For socio-cultural analyses of gender and declamation see also Richlin (1997) and Connolly (1998).
17 Van Mal-Maeder (2003), (2007) 95–107.

The connection between gender issues and the fictional setting is important, here as well. As I will show, the *Controversia* closely combines the construction of gender with a self-conscious discussion of the declamation's fictional genre.

I will consider the rhetoric and aesthetic effects of the *sermocinationes*, and the alleged 'interactions' they initiate between the prostitute-priestess and the advocates on two levels: first, with regard to the excerpts from the speeches of the individual declaimers; second, with regard to the *Controversia* as a whole, i.e. with regard to the 'collage' compiled by Seneca from these excerpts. With this twofold focus I will add to the voices of those who stress that Seneca's *Controversiae* should be read as deliberately arranged literary units. Moreover, I will show how the two levels of engagement with the topic – the excerpts from orally presented speeches on the one hand, and their arrangement in the written collection of Seneca, on the other – interact.[18]

2 *Virago* and aspiring Vestal: The ambiguous gender status of the 'prostitute-priestess'

Let us start by recapitulating the *thema*, the proposed subject of *Controversia* 1.2, and the law underlying the case.[19] They read as follows:

> sacerdos casta e castis, pura e puris sit.

> quaedam virgo a piratis capta venit; empta a lenone et prostituta est. venientes ad se exorabat stipem. militem, qui ad se venerat, cum exorare non posset, colluctantem et vim inferentem occidit. accusata et absoluta remissa ad suos est; petit sacerdotium.

> A priestess must be chaste and of chaste <parents>, pure and of pure <parents>.

> A virgin was captured by pirates and sold; she was bought by a pimp and made a prostitute. When men came to her, she asked for alms. When she failed to move a soldier who came to her, he struggled with her and tried to use force; she killed him. She was accused, acquitted, and sent back to her family. She seeks priesthood.[20]

With this subject, the *Controversia* is particularly interesting in the present context. Although the captured girl is referred to as *virgo* and thus explicitly marked as female, her gender status is not unambiguous. First, according to the case's description, the girl was able to defend herself against and even kill the armed soldier who

---

18 On the combination of verbal and textual communication, see Henderson (2018) 179f., Santini (2006) 613–16 (with focus on the *praefationes*), La Bua (2010).
19 On the structure of the *Controversiae*, and the *thema* see Berti (2007) 25f. Longer treatments of *Contr.* 1.2 include Helms (1990), Pailler (2004), Langlands (2006) 253–64, Berti (2007) 95–9, Mastrorosa (2016) 296–302. Unlike in other *Contr.*, the law cited here resembles an actual pontifical rule regarding the selection of Vestal Virgins, cf. Bonner (1949) 104.
20 Text: Håkanson (1989), translation: Winterbottom (1974), modified.

tried to rape her.²¹ This makes her appear as a *virago*, a female with virile character who is physically and psychologically capable of crossing the limits of her nature to kill a man.²² The peculiarity of the narrative becomes clear if we compare the girl's behaviour with that of young women in Roman comedy who find themselves in similar situations. As Stelios Panayotakis points out, freeborn girls in Plautine comedy who are captured and held by pimps do usually not take action themselves to escape the brothel. Instead, they rely on the help of their male lovers or are rescued by the means of a scheming slave.²³ The actions of the girl in the *Controversia* deviate from this rather passive attitude. As we will see, they are comparable to the behaviour of captured women in the ancient novel.

Second, the girl in the *Controversia* wants to become a priestess. Although no specification is given, the declaimers (and modern scholars²⁴) interpret the *sacerdotium* mentioned in the *thema* as referring to the cult of Vesta. With her request to become a Vestal Virgin, the girl aspires to a position that is marked by a gender ambiguity as well. As Mary Beard showed, the Vestal priestesses did not only take on the apparently contradictory roles of virgin and *matrona*, but did also convey a male aspect. They were accompanied by a lictor, a right specifically associated with men, and they seem to have been the only women who were seen as capable of giving evidence and who had testamentary powers.²⁵ The Temple of Vesta was the only female space in the otherwise male-connoted forum.²⁶ According to Beard, the ambiguity of the Vestals' gender status was crucial for their sacredness.²⁷

The very setting of the *Controversia* thus focuses on the negotiation of gender issues, not only by discussing the norms of *castitas* and *puritas* in the extreme case of a virgin prostitute, but also by juxtaposing *virago* and Vesta, two female figures that are at opposite poles of the evaluative spectrum concerning the transgression of gender boundaries. As we will see, the declaimers work with the ambiguous gender status of the girl when they make her speak, and use it to their advantage.

---

21 This is one possible interpretation. The question of whether she was able to defend herself against his advances prior to killing him plays an important role in the *Controversia*.
22 Seneca does not use the term, but the type of the *virago*, as it is described here, is found elsewhere in declamation, see Pingoud/Rolle (2016) 148, 151f. In the following sections, I use the term in the sense of this type description. The term is also applied to goddesses (Minerva, Diana), and to heroic women (Polyxena, Cassandra), see *OLD* s.v. *uirago*. Negative examples, who are not always called *viragines*, however, include Medea, cf. Stähle in this volume, and Clytaemnestra.
23 Panayotakis (2002) 106.
24 See Pailler (2004).
25 Beard (1980) 12–19. She points out that similar ambiguities can be observed in the Pythia (*ibid.* 22). On the ambiguous gender of priestesses see again Stähle (cf. above n. 22). On Pythia's voice see Hafner in this volume.
26 Richlin (1997) 92.
27 Beard (1980) 19–22.

3 Arguing against the girl – excerpts from individual declamations

The first part of the *Controversia* contains excerpts from speeches in which the declaimers plead against the *puella*.[28] They contend that, after all that she has experienced, she is not eligible for priesthood. The declaimers make the girl argue her case in numerous *sermocinationes*, only to counter her arguments with witty replies. As Rebecca Langlands observes, in most of the *sermocinationes* it is assumed that the girl's defence is that, despite her misfortune, she was able to preserve her virginity.[29] In the snippets of speech in which she maintains this, she is made to emphasise either the 'male' or the 'female' aspect of her ambiguous gender status. In the first case, she foregrounds the *virago*-part of her story, stressing that she was able to kill the soldier when he tried to harm her. In the second case, she doesn't mention the struggle with the soldier. Taking on a pleading rather than a defiant role, she concentrates on the *virgo*-part of her story and emphatically denies that she has had any sexual relations.

When the *puella* draws on the *virago*-part of her story, the declaimers respond to this by downplaying or completely ignoring her argument. They do not use the downside of the male-connoted image of the heroic *virago* to argue against the girl, by depicting her, e.g., as a cruel and relentless murderess.[30] On the contrary, they emphatically foreground the female aspect of her gender status. They describe her as a weak girl who, after all, was not able to protect herself from being defiled. With this, they undo, as it were, the transgression of gender boundaries that is implied in the image of the *virago*. An example is found in the excerpted speech of Porcius Latro (1.2.1,4–7[31]):

---

28 As the *virgo* mentioned in the *thema* has no name, and the question of whether she is a virgin is disputed, I will refer to her as *puella* (as some declaimers do) or, in English, as 'girl' or 'young woman'.
29 In only a few *sermocinationes* the girl defends herself against the allegation that she is ineligible for priesthood because she killed a man, cf. Langlands (2006) 255.
30 The only *sententia* that uses the downside of the *virago*-image to criticize the girl is attributed to Blandus, cf. 1.2.4,24f.: *non videbatur iste virginis vultus, ista constantia et ne armatum quidem timens audacia*. The declaimer foregrounds strong and male-connoted traits of the girl's character (*constantia*, *audacia*, fearlessness) to argue that she is unfit for priesthood. In comparison, the belittling effect of the other reactions becomes obvious. Another point of reference that shows how the girl's depiction could have looked like is *Contr.* 7.8 about a raped girl who may choose to marry her rapist or have him executed. The girl chose to marry but now wants to change her vote. The declaimers depict her as indulging in her position of power and express their fear and aversion (cf. 7.8.2,12–15: *quid est, puella? ecquid te horum lacrimae movent? 'non', inquit, 'ille ad magistratum veniat'. non dissimulo: metuo te, puella, si nusquam rogari vis, nisi ubi occidere potes*).
31 The citation of Seneca follows the edition of Håkanson (1989). The numbers after the comma indicate the lines in the edition.

> *o egregium pudicitiae patrocinium: 'militem occidi'; at hercule lenonem non occidisti. Deducta es in lupanar, accepisti locum, pretium constitutum est, titulus inscriptus est: hactenus in te inquiri potest; cetera nescio.*
>
> O, what a marvelous defence of chastity: "I killed the soldier." But, in the name of Hercules, you didn't kill your pimp. You were led to the brothel, you took your place, the price was fixed, the name tag was written: this much can be enquired about you; about the rest, I don't know anything.

The advocate impersonated by Latro does not dwell for long on the girl's statement that she has killed the soldier. He briefly ironises it and then goes on to demonstrate that it doesn't actually matter. In an asyndetic sequence of short phrases he directly addresses the *puella*, painting a vivid picture of her miserable situation in the brothel. In his description, he turns the courageous and successfully self-defending *virago* as whom she presents herself in the *sermocinatio*, into a weak *virgo*, who, although she might have defeated the soldier, was not able to defend herself altogether against being humiliated, defiled and, as he implies, raped.

A comparable interaction is staged by Argentarius (1.2.6,10). He makes her say, "I killed an armed man" (*armatum occidi*), a comment that is primarily aimed at defending her murder as self-defence. When he replies, "What about the ones who were unarmed?" (*quid inermes?*), he demonstrates a lack of interest for this *virago*-part of her story. Instead, he draws the attention to the *virgo*-part. The punch line of his *sententia* is based on the fact that, contrary to what she seems to think, he is not interested in whether the killing was self-defence or cold-blooded murder. What matters is whether she preserved her virginity; which, in this case, she is implied to have lost by wilfully engaging with the suitors who were unarmed. While she depicts herself as someone who, in a situation of extreme danger, was able to cross the limits of her nature and defend her virginity, the declaimer's words crush this aura of extraordinariness. In his reply, he does not address a strong and potentially frightening *virago*, but a deplorable young girl who, in her misfortune, became just an ordinary prostitute.

A third declaimer who turns the discussion about self-defence into one about virginity is Cornelius Hispanus (1.2.2,15f.). His *sententia*, too, starts from the *virago*-part of the story. He accuses the girl of murdering the soldier and asks what she has to say to that (*occidisti hominem; quid respondes?*, "You killed a man. What is your reply?"). When she defends herself by pleading self-defence (*vim adferebat mihi*, "He was attacking me"), his reply is short. In a surprising twist, he says: *etiam, puto* ("Yes, I thought so"). The punch-line of his reply is based on the ambiguity of *vim adferre*, which can be taken to mean 'to attack someone' as well as 'to rape someone'.[32] He uses this ambiguity to wittily turn the attention to the *virgo*-part of the story. Deliberately misunderstanding the girl, he takes her statement as a confession

---

32 *OLD* s.v. *uis* 2a ("force used to obtain sexual gratification").

that she was raped.[33] His reply is followed by silence – she is not able to talk if he doesn't compose another *sermocinatio* for her – and thus creates the impression that its astute brevity left her defeated and lost for words. Once more, the declaimer turns the frightening murderess who she appears to be at the beginning of the dispute (*occidisti hominem*), into a girl who has been overpowered and humiliated by a man. The way the *puella* is treated in court seems to mirror the way she was allegedly treated in the brothel. We will return to this observation and to the persuasive potential of such a depiction below.

In the case of *sermocinationes* in which the *puella* focusses on the *virgo*-part of her story, there is no need to 'undo' a crossing of gender boundaries with an opposing narrative. Instead, the declaimers build on the image of the pleading virgin as whom the girl presents herself. The basic effect is the same, though: with their reactions, the declaimers humiliate the girl and turn her words against her. The first *sermocinatio* of this kind is taken from the speech of Porcius Latro. He makes the girl emphatically declare that nobody took her virginity (*'nemo' inquit 'mihi virginitatem eripuit'*). To this, he replies (1.2.1,9f.):

> *sed omnes quasi erepturi venerunt, sed omnes quasi eripuissent recesserunt.*
>
> But everybody came intending to take it away, everybody went as though they had succeeded.

Latro's answer is comparable to his reaction cited above. He forms an astute stichomythia by readopting the verb the girl used in a kind of inter-personal polyptoton (*eripuit* – *erepturi, eripuissent*; cf. also: *nemo* – *omnes, omnes*), and counters her assertion of virginity by painting a humiliating picture of her situation in the brothel. He thus implies that her testimony doesn't matter. Regardless of whether she was able to preserve her virginity or not, she was defiled by the men who came to visit her.[34]

Another strategy the declaimers choose is to counter the girl's words by evoking negative female stereotypes. Iunius Gallio depicts her as wheedling. He makes her claim that she moved all suitors to spare her by beseeching them, and then goes on to argue that this very behaviour demonstrates that she was a prostitute (1.2.12,17–19):

---

33 The ambiguity is also used by Iunius Gallio in *Contr.* 1.2.12,21–3: *cum dico: 'vim passa es', 'occidi' inquit; cum dico: 'hominem occidisti', 'inferebat' inquit 'vim mihi': sacerdos nostra stuprum homicidio, homicidium stupro defendit.*
34 Langlands (2006) 255–60 shows how the declaimers work with the question of "whether or not *pudicitia* is identical to virginity", to argue that there are "things other than penetrative sex that pose a threat to it". She shows how the declaimers describe the girl in a sordid light and make it difficult for the audience to envisage her as a virgin priestess. The *sermocinationes* and the declaimers' 'reactions' to them have a similar effect. The notion that the girl has been defiled in the brothel, independently of whether or not she was raped, is discussed by Panayotakis (2002) 106–9.

> '*omnes*' inquit '*exorabam*': *si quis dubitabat, an meretrix esset, audiat, quam blanda sit.*
>
> "I begged them all off", she says. – If anyone doubted whether she was a whore, let him hear how wheedling she is.

The declaimer turns the words that he himself placed into the girl's mouth against her. With his reply, he leaves her defeated and, we may assume, discouraged from her aspiration to priesthood.[35]

Still other declaimers react to the girl's pleas in a seemingly sympathetic manner at first, but then take a pointed turn to argue against her. An example is given by Blandus, who makes the *puella* speak more than the usual two- and three-word phrases. In the *sermocinatio*, she not only claims to be a virgin, but she emphatically argues for her case by presenting witnesses who support her claim (1.2.4,21–3):

> '*virgo sum*', inquit '*interroga, si dubitas, archipiratam, interroga gladiatorem, an rogatus virginitati pepercerit.*' *non refello, dum scias clausa esse testibus tuis templa.*
>
> "I am a virgin", she says, "if you doubt it, ask the chief pirate, ask the gladiator, whether, when begged to do so, they spared my virginity." I don't refute you – so long as you realise that your witnesses are banned from entering temples.

The declaimer initially seems to agree with the girl, saying that he does not challenge her claim of virginity. Then, in a pointed twist, he implies that her argument is irrelevant. Condescendingly, he reminds her that the witnesses she names are at the lowest end of the social spectrum and are thus not suitable to argue for someone who is aspiring to priesthood. The interaction implies that, even though the declaimer is generally benevolent towards the girl, he cannot change the fact that her past excludes her from becoming a Vestal virgin.

A similar twist can be found in a *sententia* attributed to Publius Vinicus. In his *sermocinatio* the girl's argument does not concern the individual facts of her past, but the question of culpability. Referring to the workings of fate, she rejects responsibility for what happened, and demands pity (1.2.3,10–11):

> '*fortuna*' inquit '*haec me coegit pati; misereri debent omnes mei.*' *et ego misereor tui, puella, sed non facimus miserandas sacerdotes.*
>
> "Fortune", she says, "compelled me to suffer this. All must pity me." – And I pity you, girl, but we don't make priestesses of women who need pity [or: we don't make deplorable priestesses].

This declaimer, too, demonstrates a patronising sympathy at first and then coldly rejects the girl's request to become a priestess. In a witty 'stichomythia' he takes on her demand for compassion, again creating an interpersonal polyptoton (*miserere – misereor, miserandas*). He plays with the different notions of *miseranda*, which can

---

[35] Cf. also 1.2.2,21f. where Marullus implies that she is lying.

be taken to mean 'to deserve sympathy', but also 'to be deplorable'. His rejection and damning verdict leave the girl defeated and lost for words; they crush her hopes to become a priestess once and for all.

The passages show how the declaimers use the girl's *sermocinationes* not only to prove their ingenuity but also to give their arguments an almost irresistible persuasiveness. The words that the declaimers place into the girl's mouth are modelled in a way so as to form the ideal basis for their epigrammatic punch lines and astute replies.[36] This makes their counter-arguments extremely powerful. Since the declaimers are responsible for formulating the words to which they then react, their retorts are perfect hits, suited to nullifying the girl's arguments.[37] As a result, the declaimers' reactions have a strong performative power. The men do not only *argue* that the girl has been disgraced and is thus ineligible for priesthood. By leaving her defeated and humiliated with their sharp responses, they *make* her the very person they need her to be in order to win the argument: a degraded young girl who is not (any longer) suitable to attain a priesthood. By interacting with her in the manner described – and by being successful and convincing in crushing her arguments – the declaimers make her lack of eligibility a fact. As will be shown below, this impression is reinforced if the *Controversia* is read as a whole.

The use of female *sermocinatio* presented here could be called 'declamatory womanufacture' or 'womanufacture *al negativo*', to borrow a term coined by Alison Sharrock.[38] Referring to the myth of Pygmalion, she uses it to describe how the elegiac *poeta/amator* creates his *puella* and falls in love with her, i.e. with his own poetic creation. The 'womanufacture' in the *Controversiae* has a comparable effect. By inventing a *sermocinatio*, the declaimer, too, creates a woman, and (emotionally) reacts to his creation. He does not fall in love with the *puella* he created, but feels contempt for her or is indignant over her behaviour. Yet, as one function of the *sermocinatio* is the demonstration of his wit and ingenuity, one could say that the declaimer who is responsible for inventing both the woman's words and the advocate's reaction to these words, and who is self-consciously playing with the possibilities created by his use of *sermocinatio*, is actually indulging in – or, as it were, falling in love with – his literary creation.

---

36 Faure-Ribreau (2016) 216f. defines the *sententia* as a concise 'punch-line' formula that must be considered regarding its effect on the listener, an effect intended by the declaimers seeking applause.
37 This description of the rhetorical power is also true for *sermocinationes* given to male opponents. Yet, the interactions initiated by 'male' *sermocinationes* in the collection are usually not as degrading as the ones discussed here. One reason is that the topics of *Controversiae* involving only male characters are rarely as potentially shameful as the issues of rape and virginity.
38 Sharrock (1991).

4 Arguing for the girl – excerpts from individual declamations

Before we analyse the effect of a linear reading of *Contr.* 1.2, it is worthwhile to take a look at excerpts from individual speeches in which the declaimers argue in favour of the girl. The favourable part of the *Controversia* is shorter than the accusing part. In it, the girl speaks only twice. In the first *sermocinatio*, Albucius imagines what she is supposed to have said during her confrontation with the soldier. Like the declaimers cited above, he draws on the ambiguous gender status of the self-defending *virago*. He uses it to imply that this very ambiguity makes the girl suitable to become a priestess. In bright colours he pictures the moment when the soldier attacked the *puella*. He endows the situation with an aura of the miraculous by suggesting that the soldier was sent by the gods themselves in order "to save the chastity of the future priestess, not to violate it" (1.2.18,14–16: *ipsis credo dis illum impellentibus, ut futurae sacerdotis non violaret castitatem <sed> vindicaret*[39]). He thus paves the way for a lofty speech in which the girl addresses her attacker (1.2.18,16–20):

> *praedixit illi, abstineret a sacro corpore manum: 'non est, quod audeas laedere pudicitiam, quam homines servant, dii expectant.' ridenti et in perniciem ruenti suam 'en' inquit 'arma, quae nescis te ferre pro pudicitia', et raptum gladium in pectus stupratoris mersit.*

> She announced that he should keep his hands off her holy body: "You must not dare to harm chastity that men preserve and gods await." When he laughed and came rushing to his doom, she said, "Look, your weapon – you do not realise that you carry it in the cause of chastity."[40] And seizing the sword she drove it into her attacker's breast.

The male aspect of the *virago*-image is linked here to the ambiguous gender status of the future priestess. The girl confronts the soldier determinedly and without fear, and, in the role of the manly heroic virgin, kills her attacker. On the other hand, she addresses the soldier in a lofty and imperative style. She does not use first-person speech, but a distancing third-person phrasing (*non est, homines servant, dii expectant*). She thus assumes the role of a priestess who speaks with divine authority. The fact that the soldier laughs at her, and is immediately punished for his hubris, supports the impression that the woman speaking here is called to higher things. Accordingly,

---

[39] *Vindicaret* is an emendation of Håkanson (1989), which replaces the earlier emendation *ostenderet*. It emphasises the miracle to which the declaimer draws the attention. The earlier Teubner edition by Kiessling (1872/1967) reads *videret*.

[40] Langlands (2006) 262 n. 43 suggests an appealing alternative translation of the phrase ("Behold the weapons that you do not know how to wield on behalf of *pudicitia*"). She reads the girl's words "as a reference to the traditional idea that soldiers should be fighting to protect *pudicitia* . . . and not plundering it."

the declaimer does not retort her words, but comments on them, suggesting once more that the *puella* has been helped by the gods (1.2.18,22–4):

> nemo credebat occisum virum a femina, iuvenem a puella, armatum ab inermi; maior res videbatur, quam ut posset credi sine deorum immortalium adiutorio gesta.

> No-one could believe a man had been killed by a woman, a youth by a girl, one armed by one unarmed. It was too great a feat for it to be supposed to have taken place without the aid of the immortal gods.

The crossing of gender boundaries on the part of the heroic *virago* is emphasised through the juxtapositions of *vir – femina* and *iuvenis – puella*. Yet, the norm-threatening potential of this image is mitigated and discursively controlled. In the speeches against the girl the declaimers 'neutralised' this potential in a humiliating manner, transforming the alleged *virago* into a weak and defeated *virgo*. In the present case, the potential is contained in a way that supports the girl's aspiration to priesthood: the declaimer attributes her crossing of gender boundaries to the gods. With the suggestion of divine intervention, he also responds to the potential objection that the *virago*-part of the story lacks credibility. We will come back to that.

The second *sermocinatio* used in favour of the girl is not set in the brothel, but at a later point of events, probably during a questioning after the supposed murder. The declaimer Triarius makes the girl describe the confrontation with the soldier. Remarkably, despite the focus on the *virago*-part of the story, she presents herself markedly as female (1.2.21,21f.):

> 'altior' inquit 'humana visa est circa me species eminere et puellares lacertos supra virile robur attollere.'

> She said, "a form taller than human seemed to loom around me, raising my girlish arms above a man's strength".

It is not a manful *virago* who speaks about the murder here, but a girl who struggles to explain how she was able to commit such an act. The crossing of gender boundaries (cf. *puellares lacertos – virile robur*) is depicted as temporary and attributed to a higher entity. Accordingly, the declaimer makes the girl assert that she is not responsible for the killing at all: "The girl said she had not done it, she said he had not fallen by her hand" (1.2.21,20f.: *negabat se puella fecisse, negabat illum suis cecidisse manibus*).

If we compare this *sermocinatio* to the one discussed above and to the *sermocinationes* in the first part of the *Controversia*, it becomes obvious that the image of the *virago* is highly ambivalent. Its evaluation depends on the situation in which the girl is depicted as acting as a *virago*. In speeches against the girl, the declaimers let her speak as a defiant *virago* long after the fight in the brothel, making her confidently refer to the murder during court proceedings. In the favourable *pars altera*, on the other hand, the girl acts and speaks like a *virago* only in the life-threatening situation in the brothel. Here, the image is associated with the notion that a divine favour has been bestowed on her. When a favourable *sermocinatio* is put into her mouth at a later moment of events, the girl acts and speaks like a *virgo* again. This implies that she did not act autonomously when she appeared as a *virago* during her fight with the soldier, but was but a tool in the hands of the gods – she is not the subject, but the object of the action described in the *sermocinatio*, which in turn is attributed to a superhuman being: *visa est species puellares lacertos attollere*.

Triarius' speech does not end here. He continues by suggesting that it was the experience in the brothel that made the *puella* want to become a priestess (1.2.21,22–5):

> *quicumque estis, dii immortales, qui pudicitiam ex illo infami loco cum miraculo voluistis emergere, non ingratae puellae opem tulistis: vobis pudicitiam dedicat, quibus debet.*

> Whoever you are, immortal gods, who wished chastity to emerge miraculously untouched from that ill-famed spot, the girl you helped is not ungrateful. She owes you her chastity – and she vows it to you.

The editions differ on the question of whether these words are still part of the girl's *sermocinatio* or whether they should be read as a comment of the declaimer. While Håkanson and Schönberger/Schönberger attribute the sentences to the declaimer, Winterbottom imagines them to be spoken by the girl.[41] The passage is written in the third person, so an attribution to the declaimer is certainly the *lectio facilior*. Yet, we saw how the girl uses an august third-person phrasing when the declaimer wants to emphasise her sacerdotal role. One can therefore well imagine that the girl is still speaking. In this case, her words would reflect the transformation from *virgo* to *virago* in the first part of the *sermocinatio* (*puellares lacertos – supra virile robur attollere*) and from *virago* to (aspiring) Vestal in the second part of the *sermocinatio* (*supra virile robur attollere – vobis pudicitiam dedicat, quibus debet*).

5 Reading the *Controversia* as a whole

The effects described so far are reinforced if we perceive the *Controversia* in the form in which it was compiled by Seneca. Originally, the speeches excerpted in Seneca's collection were performed by the declaimers in front of an audience. During his performance, a declaimer could additionally emphasise the parameter gender. When uttering the girl's *sermocinationes*, he could imitate a female voice. We can imagine, for example, how Iunius Gallio sexualises the 'wheedling' *sermocinatio* quoted above (1.2.12,17f.: *omnes exorabam*) by pronouncing it in a seductive way, and thus supports his argument that the girl's behaviour proves her indecent

---

[41] Håkanson (1989) 25, Schönberger/Schönberger (2004) 41, Winterbottom (1974) vol. I, 84f.

past. Blandus' *sermocinatio* about the witnesses whom the girl adduces (1.2.4,21f.: *Virgo sum . . . interroga . . . archipiratam, interroga gladiatorem . . .*) can be imagined to be said in a desperate and urging voice. This would intensify the effect of the declaimer's seemingly sympathetic reply, which turns out to be a cold refusal. In any case, the imitation of a female voice during the performance of the *sermocinationes* in the first part of the *Controversia* would highlight the contrast between the girl and the declaimers and thus emphasise the latter's dominance. It would probably also have a comic effect, first because it is based on a crossing of gender boundaries on the part of the declaimer,[42] second because it creates a kind of complicity between the declaimer and his audience. Both the declaimer and the audience, know how the device of *sermocinatio* works. Together they can enjoy the declaimer's "sententious art"[43] and the way it exposes the girl whose momentary position of argumentative strength is – as they know, while she doesn't – doomed to be destroyed by the declaimer's reply.[44]

If we perceive the excerpted speeches in the form of Seneca's written collection, on the other hand, the *sermocinationes*, and the reactions to them have another effect. Jonathan E. Mannering has recently described Seneca's compilation from a perspective of the aesthetics of reception:

> For Seneca has vetted the full, original declamations in favour of the more refined and sparkling epigrams. These fly thick and fast in unrelenting, asyndetic transitions from one declaimer to the next throughout the anthology, challenging the reader to keep up with the seemingly endless permutations and rhetorical refinements of the same themes, but also leaving us open to surprise and thrill. . . . By virtue of the anti-narratological volatility of Seneca's text the declamatory competitions attain uncanny resonance as the imaginary space of an arena . . . is constructed. Faced with authorial blow-by-blow recap the reader assumes the role of a spectator to a cavalcade of speakers jousting for their audience's attention and respect.[45]

Mannering refers here to the textualization of the first level of the declamatory communication situation,[46] i.e. to the historical orators whom Seneca, the self-proclaimed *munerarius*, makes compete in the textual 'arena' of his written collection.[47] As I will show in the following, the imagery is also fitting regarding the second level of

---

[42] Stoffel (2017) 166 emphasises the humour and irony of such a cross-gender performance with regard to *Contr.* 6.8.
[43] For the term, see Connolly (2009).
[44] Langlands (2006) 264 links the idea of entertainment to the ethical discussion that can be observed in the text: "Declaimers have their gruesome fun with *pudicitia*, but in doing so trace out actual grey areas in Roman ethics."
[45] Mannering (2020) 222.
[46] See above, n. 7.
[47] Seneca compares himself to a *munerarius* (4 *praef.* 1,1) and refers to a *pompa* in the circus (1 *praef.* 24,2). Fairweather (1981) 29 describes the collection's design as inspired by the "arrangement of a gladiatorial show". On the effect of a holistic reading, see also Connolly (2009) 339 who

communication, i.e. the textual 'arena' of the fictitious trial, in which the different advocates plead their case and "blow-by-blow" refute their opponent.

It is important to note that the ontological difference between the role-playing declaimer and the girl whom he 'creates' and causes to speak in the *sermocinatio*, is obvious to the audience in an oral performance, but is not as apparent in the written collection. For a *reader* of Seneca's work, both the declaimers and the girl are textual entities that interact with each other on the textual stage created by Seneca.[48] Moreover, if the reader reads the *Controversia* as a whole, they get the impression that it is always the same girl who speaks on this stage, but always a different advocate who reacts to her. This is due to the basic structure of *Contr.* 1.2.

The *Controversiae* of Seneca's corpus can be divided into two groups. The majority concerns 'civil cases', mostly between men, i.e. cases in which two male individuals – often a father and a son – argue against each other.[49] In this setting, the declaimers usually impersonate the opponents, playing the role, say, first of the father, and then of the son. They also use *sermocinationes* to make their respective opponent speak, and react to his words. As the opponents are clearly identified, the personnel in these interactions seems to remain the same throughout Seneca's *Controversia*. A reader who reads this type of *Controversia* and perceives the collected excerpts in a linear reading, gets the impression that they watch the same characters arguing over and over again, discussing different aspects of their dispute.

Contr. 1.2, on the other hand, belongs to a second, smaller group of *Controversiae* which can be classified as 'public'.[50] In these, an individual person argues against a counterparty representing a public interest. When the declaimers speak on behalf of this counterparty, they impersonate an advocate who is not further identified in the *thema*. The text gives no reason to believe that in this setting all declaimers impersonate the same advocate. Rather, the structure of the collection in which Seneca names one declaimer after another and cites highlights from their individual speeches, suggests that each declaimer is creating 'his own' fictional advocate.[51] In this case, a linear reading of the *Controversia* and of the *sermocinationes*

---

stresses that Seneca's presentation creates "a cascade of dramatic effects". On polyphony of voices in the *Controversiae*, see Berti (2007) 28, van Mal-Maeder (2020).

48 I thank Alison Sharrock for this observation.

49 Of the 74 *Controversiae* in Seneca's corpus, 52 concern 'civil cases'. In 10 of them there is a female litigant (2.2, 2.5, 2.7, 3.7, 4.6, 5.3, 6.4, 6.6, 7.4, 7.8). Van Mal-Maeder (2007) 41–64 distinguishes between three "modes d'énonciation" in declamation, that differ with regard to the declaimer's personal involvement. He can play the role of the applicant or respondent in a case, the role of an advocate representing a client, the role of an advocate pleading in a public charge.

50 There are 22 *Controversiae* of this type in Seneca's corpus. Three of them concern women as defendants, always (aspiring) Vestal priestesses (1.2, 1.3, 6.8).

51 One reason is that there is no institution of public prosecution in Roman Republican law, cf. Manthe (2019) 85. Thus, the declaimers do not impersonate the same 'state attorney'.

and reactions collected therein gives the impression that one individual is arguing against several opposing advocates.[52]

With regard to the accusing part of *Contr.* 1.2, this means that the girl seems to defend herself against 14 different advocates. In a linear reading we get the impression that the *puella* is defeated by one man after the other. As seen above, the defeats are often accompanied with a humiliating depiction of the girl. If perceived as a whole, the *Controversia* thus reinforces the arguments of the single declaimers and the way they depict the *puella* in their individual speeches: it is not credible that the woman whom we encounter in the first part of Seneca's *Controversia*, who is overpowered by several men and repeatedly degraded in a sexualised manner, was able to defend herself against even more men, with even baser intentions, in the brothel, and preserve her virginity. Moreover, a woman like this, who is treated without respect by everybody she 'meets' on the textual stage, seems – in fact, is – not eligible to aspire to the highest priesthood.

And there is yet another way in which the overall *Controversia* reinforces the critical judgement of the single declaimers. Although the girl is portrayed as helpless and weak on the level of the individual *sermocinationes*, and although this portrayal is reinforced at the level of the written collection, she appears as someone who speaks a lot on her own behalf. If we consider the *Controversia* as a whole, the *sermocinationes*, which were originally created and performed in different declamatory speeches, add up to the image of a woman who rises to speak time and again in the

---

[52] A comprehensive study that analyses the use of *sermocinatio* in different types of *Controversiae* is a *desideratum*. In it one would have to differentiate not only between 'civil' and 'public' cases, but also between cases with and without a female litigant. It goes beyond the scope of this paper to address this in detail. I want to raise two points that concern the question of whether the impression described here with regard to *Contr.* 1.2, of reading a dispute of 'one-against-many', can be found in *Controversiae* with male litigants, too. As said, *Controversiae* concerning 'civil cases' between two male litigants do not create this effect, but give the impression of a 'one-against-one'-situation. As women are usually represented by an advocate, one could imagine that the situation is different in 'civil' *Controversiae* involving one female party, as, in this case, several advocates could be seen as arguing against one man. Interestingly though, advocates representing a woman rarely make the opposing male litigant speak. Of the 10 'civil cases' involving women, eight contain *sermocinationes*; of these, five contain *sermocinationes* mostly or only of the female party (2.2, 2.5, 6.6, 7.4, 7.8), two contain *sermocinationes* of men who are not the opposing litigant in the case (2.7, 4.6). In only one case (5.3) an advocate makes the male opponent speak in a *sermocinatio* and reacts to it in a manner that is comparable to *Contr.* 1.2. As regards 'public cases', there are some *Controversiae* involving male litigants, which create the impression that one man is opposed to several advocates (e.g. 4.4, 7.2, 9.4, 10.4, 10.5). In these we find 'interactions' between the litigant and the advocates that are comparable to *Contr.* 1.2, insofar as the advocates' reactions to the litigant's *sermocinationes* are witty retorts that ridicule the opponent and create a gap in hierarchy between the defendant and the accusing advocate. The retorts are not as degrading, though, as in the case of *Contr.* 1.2. It is interesting that several of the 'public' *Controversiae* with a male litigant contain *sermocinationes* not of the accused man, but of a woman (e.g. 1.5, 8.1, 9.2, 9.6).

public situation of a court hearing, and thus behaves in a way that is not befitting to a decent woman.⁵³ In this perspective, the *puella* depicted in the *Controversia* might be helpless, but she is also bold, and therefore, indeed, not a suitable candidate for the College of the Vestals.

This reading is supported if we consider the second, favourable part of the *Controversia*. Although it is shorter than the first part, it is striking that the *puella* is made to speak much less here. Moreover, the girl's *sermocinationes* are not set in the situation in court. Instead, the *puella* is imagined to have spoken only in and shortly after the life-threatening situation in the brothel, where she supposedly could not help but to speak in the face of the extraordinary events. In court, she recedes into the background and is silent. Her minimised appearance on the textual stage supports the claim in the individual speeches that she is chaste, modest, and thus worthy of a priesthood.

6 Literary parallels – constructing gender, discussing fiction

The story underlying the *Controversia* – a freeborn girl, captured by pirates and made a prostitute, is able to escape her misfortune – has parallels in Roman comedy and in the ancient novel. In the last section of this paper, I will discuss them in order to situate the observations made so far in a literary context. I want to show that the way the parameter gender is discussed in the *sermocinationes* and in the declaimers' reactions to them has a meta-literary dimension that concerns the fictitious nature of the *Controversia*. Scholarship has long recognised the parallels between declamation, comedy, and the novel, also referring to *Contr.* 1.2.⁵⁴ Building on these observations I will focus on the spectrum of possibilities that the texts attribute to a woman who finds herself in the situation described.

As previously discussed, freeborn women made prostitutes in comedy often rely on the help of male characters to escape their misfortune.⁵⁵ This is reflected in the way they speak. Taking on stereotypically female roles, they appear frightened and desperate for help. If they take on a more active role, they are depicted as sweet-

---

53 See Kraus (2007) 456, van Mal-Maeder (2007) 98. If we consider the temporary difference between the speeches excerpted in the collection (Feddern 2013, 60), the criteria according to which Seneca compiles the excerpts come into focus. This paper argues that these are i.a. literary and aesthetic.
54 Cf. Panayotakis (2002) 106–9, van Mal-Maeder (2007) 115–45, with further literature. Hömke (2017) 213–18 points out the structural and conceptual relation between the *Decl. mai.* and Plautine Comedy.
55 Panayotakis (2002) 106.

talking their male lovers into rescuing them. An example of the first scenario can be found in Plautus' *Rudens*. Having temporarily escaped their pimp and fled to a temple of Venus, the young women Palaestra and Ampelisca are rediscovered by their tormentor. In this situation, Palaestra begs Trachalio, the slave of her young lover, to protect her (683: *nisi quid re praesidium apparas, Trachalio, acta haec res est*, "unless you bring us some protection in action, Trachalio, we're done for"), while Ampelisca laments her fate. For a moment, she gathers courage, declaring that she is determined to die if the pimp harms her. But she shrinks back from the deed, confessing that, due to her "female mind" (685: *muliebris animus*), she is too frightened to kill herself.[56]

Planesium in Plautus' *Curculio* is another free-born girl who is made a prostitute. Her description is comparable to that of Seneca's *puella* in several regards. When her lover Phaedromus describes her as *pudica* (57), his slave reacts in a way that resembles the sardonic remarks of the declaimers in *Contr.* 1.2: "I'd believe it – if any pimp had chastity" (58: *credam, pudor si quoiquam lenoni siet*). Planesium behaves in the second of the ways mentioned above. She tells Phaedromus that she loves him, she kisses him, and gives him affectionate names. When he declares his love to her (211), she asks him to prove it to her by ransoming her: "If you love me, buy me and don't ask for me, but make sure you win the highest bid" (213f.: *si amas, eme, ne rogites, facito ut pretio pervincas tuo*).

In the ancient novel, in contrast, we find women who themselves act to preserve their chastity and escape their misfortune. In Xenophon of Ephesus' novel *Anthia and Habrocomes*, which might date to the mid-first century CE,[57] the heroine Anthia stabs a man who tries to rape her (4.5.4f.), and is able to preserve her chastity in a brothel by faking an epileptic seizure (5.7.4). There are several parallels to *Contr.* 1.2 in the account of Anthia's misfortunes, e.g. when the narrator describes Anthia's situation in the brothel where she is dressed up, presented, and marvelled at by "an instreaming crowd of men".[58] What is important in the present context is

---

56 Plaut. *Rud.* 684–6: *certumst moriri quam hunc pati <saevire> lenonem in me. / sed muliebri animo sum tamen: miserae <quom venit> in mentem / mihi mortis, metus membra occupat. edepol diem hunc acerbum!* ("I'm resolved to die rather than let this pimp treat me cruelly. But still, I have a woman's mind; poor me, when death comes to my mind, fear grips my limbs. Goodness, this day is bitter!"). Text and translations from Plautus: De Melo (2011), (2012).
57 Henderson (2009) 209f. assumes that Xenophon predates Chariton of Aphrodisias, who can be dated to the time between the second half of the first century BCE and 150 CE, and rather earlier than later within this frame, as his novel was probably known in Neronian Rome. Holzberg (2006) 69f. dates Xenophon to the second half of the first century CE.
58 Xen. *Eph.* 5.7.1–3 ὁ δὲ πορνοβοσκὸς ὁ τὴν Ἀνθίαν ὠνησάμενος χρόνου διελθόντος ἠνάγκασεν αὐτὴν οἰκήματος προεστάναι. καὶ δὴ κοσμήσας καλῇ μὲν ἐσθῆτι, πολλῷ δὲ χρυσῷ ἦγεν ὡς προστησομένην τέγους . . . ὡς δὲ ἦλθε καὶ προέστη πλῆθος ἐπέρρει τῶν τεθαυμακότων τὸ κάλλος, οἱ δὲ πολλοὶ ἦσαν ἕτοιμοι ἀργύριον κατατίθεσθαι τῆς ἐπιθυμίας ("In due course the pimp who had bought Anthia made her display herself in front of the whorehouse. He dressed her up in a beautiful costume and lots of gold and took her to her spot outside a stall. . . . When she got there and

that Anthia explicitly points to her active role after having dreamt that her husband Habrocomes had cheated on her. Contrasting herself with him, she emphasises that she was able to cross the limits of her nature to preserve her conjugal fidelity (5.8.7):

> ἐγὼ μὲν καὶ πόνους ὑπομένω πάντας καὶ ποικίλων πειρῶμαι δυστυχὴς συμφορῶν καὶ τέχνας σωφροσύνης ὑπὲρ γυναῖκας εὑρίσκω.
>
> I put up with every kind of struggle, I am beset in my misfortune by manifold predicaments, and I find resources of virtue beyond a woman's means.

In contrast to Plautus' Ampelisca, Anthia does not foreground her female status, but the fact that she has overcome its limitations. Accordingly, she is determined to end her life (5.8.7f.). Besides lovesickness, it is the prospect of preserving her chastity that brings her to this decision (5.8.8: ἐμοὶ δὲ ἀποθανεῖν καλῶς ἔχει σωφρονούσῃ). The idea that suicide is the only honourable option for a woman in her situation has a parallel in *Contr.* 1.2, where a declaimer says to the *puella*: "You were led off to a place where you could do nothing more upright than to die" (1.2.3,8f.: *eo deducta es, ubi tu aliud nihil honestius facere potuisti quam mori*).

In the second century novel *Leucippe and Clitophon* by Achilles Tatius, the heroine is able to preserve her virginity, as well. In this case she resists her master Thersander, to whom she came as a slave after having been kidnapped.[59] Danielle van Mal-Maeder has demonstrated the declamatory quality of the main characters' speeches and has shown parallels to Seneca's *Contr.* 2.5 and 1.2.[60] Important for us is the way Leucippe confronts Thersander when he threatens to use force on her. She opposes him without fear, confidently affirming that she is a virgin and not afraid of torture (6.22.1–3). With pathos she proclaims that, although she might be "defenceless, alone and a woman" (6.22.4: γυμνή, καὶ μόνη, καὶ γυνή), she will not surrender to his violence. The impression of an authoritative attitude is reinforced by the fact that Leucippe uses a *fictus interlocutor* to praise her virginity, thus seeming to speak about herself in the third person (6.22.2f.):

---

took her position out front, a crowd of men streamed over, marvelling at her beauty and many of them ready to lay out money for what they wanted", transl. Henderson 2009), cf. *Contr.* 1.2.1,5f.; 1.2.7,17–19 (*stetisti cum meretricibus, stetisti sic ornata, ut populo placere posses, ea veste quam leno dederat*); 1.2.8,30 (*omnis sordida iniuriosaque turba huc influit*); 1.2.10,25f. (*convenit omnis libidinosorum turba et concurrit ad meretricem novam*).

59 On the dating cf. Whitmarsh/Morales (2001) xiv–xv.

60 Van Mal-Maeder (2007) 136–45. She shows how Thersander's questioning of Leucippe's alleged virginity resembles the objections of several declaimers in *Contr.* 1.2, cf. Ach. Tat. 6.21.3 (παρθένος; εἶπεν ὁ Θέρσανδρος· ὢ τόλμης καὶ γέλωτος· παρθένος τοσούτοις συννυκτερεύσασα πειραταῖς. εὐνοῦχοί σοι γεγόνασιν οἱ λῃσταί; φιλοσόφων ἦν τὸ πειρατήριον; οὐδεὶς ἐν αὐτοῖς εἶχεν ὀφθαλμούς; – "Virgin indeed!" cried Thersander. "The ridiculous impudence of the baggage! You a virgin, who passed night after night among a gang of pirates! I suppose your pirates were eunuchs? Or was the pirates' lair a Sunday-school? Or perhaps none of them had eyes?", transl. Gaselee 1984) with, e.g. *Contr.* 1.2.8.

καί τις ἐρεῖ, κἂν νῦν μαινόμενος φονεύσῃς· 'Λευκίππη παρθένος μετὰ βουκόλους, παρθένος καὶ μετὰ Χαιρέαν, παρθένος καὶ μετὰ Σωσθένην.' ἀλλὰ μέτρια ταῦτα· τὸ δὲ μεῖζον ἐγκώμιον, 'καὶ μετὰ Θέρσανδρον παρθένος, τὸν καὶ λῃστῶν ἀσελγέστερον. ἂν ὑβρίσαι μὴ δυνηθῇ, καὶ φονεύει.'

> If you kill me now in your mad passion, people will say; 'This is Leucippe, who remained a virgin after falling among buccaneers, who remained a virgin after her abduction by Chaereas, who remained a virgin after passing through the hands of Sosthenes!' This would be but little; I shall have a still greater meed of praise: 'She remained a virgin even after her encounter with Thersander, who is more lecherous than any robber; if he cannot gratify his lust, he kills its object!'

With her explicit and multiple self-description as παρθένος, on the one hand, and the fearless and respect-demanding attitude of a manly heroine, on the other, Leucippe resembles the heroic *virgo-virago* that is depicted in Seneca's *Contr.* 1.2. Her sublime appearance makes Thersander let go of her.

Finally, let us look at late-antique narrative *Historia Apollonii Regis Tyri*.[61] Again, there are parallels between the description of the misfortunes of the heroine Tarsia, who is kidnapped by pirates and sold into a brothel, and the experiences of the *puella* as they are told in *Contr.* 1.2. Stelios Panayotakis has pointed them out, focusing on the relationship between space and the individual.[62] If we concentrate on the action the heroine takes in order to save her virginity, we are reminded of the '*virgo*-part' of the *Controversia*.[63] In the brothel Tarsia falls on her knees before her suitors and begs for pity. She convinces the men to spare her and give her money so that she can buy her freedom. Through pleas and tears (35: *preces et lacrimae*) as well as eloquence (36: *facundia*), Tarsia succeeds in preserving her virginity (34–6). With this depiction, the narrator almost seems to elaborate the theme of *Contr.* 1.2, in which it is said that the girl asked for alms from the men who came to her (*venientes ad se exorabat stipem*). The *virago*-part, on the other hand, has no place in the *Historia*.[64]

Given the numerous parallels between declamation and the ancient novel, it has been assumed that the latter developed from the former. Danielle van Mal-Maeder has argued that the parallels rather indicate a common socio-cultural background.[65] The observations made in this chapter support this. The passages from the novels quoted here cover the whole spectrum of actions that the declaimers

---

[61] The earliest surviving version of the tale probably dates to the late fifth or early sixth century CE and derives from a narrative that was originally composed in the third century CE, cf. Panayotakis (2002) 98.
[62] Panayotakis (2002) 107–9.
[63] The focus on the innocent *virgo* is visible in the fact that Tarsia's virginity is mentioned 15 times in §§ 34–6.
[64] The Vestal-part of the *thema* can be recognised in parallels between the *Historia* and tales of Christian martyrs where the idea of virginity being saved by divine intervention reoccurs, cf. Panayotakis (2002) 109–12.
[65] Van Mal-Maeder (2007) 116–18.

consider for the *puella* in *Contr.* 1.2, as well: tears, pleas, flattery, courageous eloquence, authoritative demeanour, deceit, murder – each of these types of action is attributed to the girl at some point in the *Controversia*, whether in relation to her behaviour in the brothel, in court, or both. With their arguments and their sharp and damning replies, however, the declaimers reject this spectrum of actions. In their depiction, the version of events that the girl presents in the *sermocinationes* is portrayed as what it was to become in later literary history: as the plot of an unrealistic *fabula*.

In a passage from Cestius Pius' narration, which can be read as a winking discussion of declamation's fictitious nature,[66] the declaimer makes this explicit. He doubts the credibility of the girl's story (1.2.8):

> non est credibile temperasse a libidine piratas omni crudelitate efferatos, quibus omne fas nefasque lusus est . . . a stupris removere potuisti quibus inter tot tanto maiora scelera virginem stuprare innocentia est? sed lupanar excepit: omnis sordida iniuriosaque turba huc influit, nec quisquam eo, ut †iudicet†, venit. at omnes favere fabulis tuis, at omnibus persuasum est? nemo in tanta euntium redeuntiumque turba inventus est, qui fortunae tuae vellet inludere?

> It is incredible that pirates abstained from lust, men brutalised by every sort of cruel deed, for whom right and wrong are a jest. . . . you could turn men aside from their desires, for whom, amid so many greater crimes, the rape of a virgin is an act of innocence? But the brothel took you in. To this place flows a crowd of all filthy and dangerous men: no-one comes there to play the judge. Yet everyone sympathised with your tales? Everyone believed them? No-one was to be found in such a throng of comers and goers who wanted to make a joke of your ill-fortune?

The objection voiced here at the level of the individual declamation is enacted at the level of the *Controversia* as a whole. A linear reading of Seneca's compilation gives the impression that a young girl has indeed no chance of succeeding with any line of action when she is confronted by 14 hostile men. If she presents herself as a *virago* – killing the attacker, courageously standing up for herself, eloquently arguing her case – she is cut down to size by the men who can easily overpower her (1.2.1, 1.2.4, 1.2.6, 1.2.11). If she uses deceit, it is seen through (1.2.2). If she uses flattery, she is despised (1.2.11). If she takes on the role of the supplicatory *virgo*, she does not succeed in restoring her honour (1.2.3). Thus, with their counter-narratives and sharp replies, the declaimers do not only reverse the transgression of gender boundaries that is implied in the *thema* of the *Controversia*, they also restore 'realism' to the state of affairs. The girl's narrative, it is implied, is, in fact, a *fabula*. In the 'real world', stories like the one underlying the *Controversia* do not create brave *viragines*, respectable virgins or, much less, a priestess. A girl who is kidnapped

---

[66] In this case, the differentiation between the real declaimer and the fictitious advocate is particularly interesting. While the latter searches for the truth in the fictious case, the former, tongue-in-cheek, plays with the accusation of implausibility, which the genre was subjected to (on this see Hömke 2017, 209 with further literature).

and forced into prostitution has no chance to prevail. She cannot expect a happy ending – nor the restoration of her social status and a reunion with her husband or lover, as in comedy or in the novel; nor, as is argued in *Contr.* 1.2, a priesthood. In this perspective it is no coincidence that the second part of the *Controversia*, where the declaimers use the very incredibility of the story to argue that the girl should become a priestess, is much shorter.[67]

7 Conclusion

The way in which the gender parameter is used and implemented in the girl's *sermocinationes* in *Contr.* 1.2, and in the declaimers' reactions to them, has a strong meta-literary component. It is linked to a discussion about the fictivity and plausibility of the declamatory genre. The *Controversia*, then, does not only determine what is socially acceptable, as scholarship has argued, providing a normative discussion of gender. It also determines what is 'realistic', providing a descriptive discussion of gender. By staging the 'interactions' between the girl and the role-playing declaimers – who, with the power given to them *qua* gender and the undeniable force of reality, are able to demonstrate their argumentative ability – the *Controversia* discusses what possibilities are available to a woman in her gender-specific contingency. It does so both on the level of the individual declamations and on the level of the *Controversia* as a whole. The analysis of the gender parameter and its presentation on the textual 'stage' of *Contr.* 1.2 thus shows from a new perspective the aesthetic and literary quality of the work, as well as the high degree of self-reflection about questions of genre that the *Controversiae* of the elder Seneca exhibit.

Bibliography

Texts and translations

Achilles Tatius with an English transl. by Stephen Gaselee, Cambridge, MA/London 1984 (orig. 1917).
Achilles Tatius, *Leucippe and Clitophon*, transl. with notes by Tim Whitmarsh, introduction by Helen Morales, Oxford 2001.
Historia Apollonii regis Tyri, ed. Gareth Schmeling, Leipzig 1988.
Longus, *Daphnis and Chloe*, Xenophon of Ephesus, *Anthia and Habrocomes*, ed. and transl. by Jeffery Henderson, Cambridge, MA/London 2009.

---

67 Seneca points out that it is easier to argue against the girl than for her, cf. *Contr.* 1.2.21,26f.

Plautus, *Casina, The Casket Comedy, Curculio, Epidicus, The two Menaechmuses*, ed. and transl. by Wolfgang De Melo, Cambridge, MA/London 2011.
Plautus, *The little Carthaginian, Pseudolus, The Rope*, ed. and transl. by Wolfgang De Melo, Cambridge, MA/London 2012.
Annaei Senecae *Oratorum et rhetorum sententiae divisiones colores*, rec. Adolphus Kiessling, Leipzig 1967 (orig. 1872).
L. Annaeus Seneca Maior, *Oratorum et rhetorum sententiae, divisiones, colores*, rec. Lennart Håkanson, Leipzig 1989.
Seneca The Elder, *Declamations*, 2 vols., transl. Michael Winterbottom, Cambridge, MA 1974.
Lucius Annaeus Seneca der Ältere, *Sentenzen, Einteilungen, Färbungen von Rednern und Redelehrern*, Übersetzung und Anmerkungen von Otto und Eva Schönberger, Würzburg 2004.

Books and articles

Beard (1980): Mary Beard, "The Sexual Status of Vestal Virgins", *JRS* 70, 12–27.
Berti (2007): Emanuele Berti, *Scholasticorum Studia. Seneca il Vecchio e la cultura retorica e letteraria della prima età imperiale*, Pisa.
Berti (2015): Emanuele Berti, "Declamazione e poesia", in: Mario Lentano (ed.), *La declamazione latina. Prospettive a confronto sulla retorica di scuola a Roma antica*, Napoli, 19–57.
Bloomer (1997): W. Martin Bloomer, "Schooling in Persona: Imagination and Subordination in Roman Education", *CA* 16, 57–78.
Bonner (1949): Stanley F. Bonner, *Roman Declamation in the Late Republic and the Early Empire*, Liverpool.
Connolly (1998): Joy Connolly, "Mastering Corruption. Constructions of Identity in Roman Oratory", in: Sandra R. Joshel and Sheila Murnaghan (eds.), *Women and Slaves in Greco-Roman Culture. Differential Equations*, London/New York, 130–151.
Connolly (2009): Joy Connolly, "The Strange Art of the Sententious Declaimer", in: Philip Hardie (ed.), *Paradox and the Marvellous in Augustan Literature and Culture*, Oxford, 330–379.
Fairweather (1981): Janet Fairweather, *Seneca the Elder*, Cambridge.
Faure-Ribreau (2016): Marion Faure-Ribreau, "Présence et fonctions de la *sententia* dans la Déclamation Latine", in: Rémy Poignault and Catherine Schneider (eds.), *Fabrique de la Déclamation antique (Controverses et suasoires)*, Lyon, 211–226.
Feddern (2013): Stefan Feddern, *Die Suasorien des älteren Seneca: Einleitung, Text und Kommentar*, Berlin/Boston.
Gunderson (2003): Erik Gunderson, *Declamation, Paternity, and Roman Identity. Authority and the Rhetorical Self*, Cambridge.
Helms (1990): Lorraine Helms, "The Saint in the Brothel: Or, Eloquence Rewarded", *Shakespeare Quarterly* 41, 319–332.
Henderson (2018): John Henderson, "Tales of the Unexpurgated (Cert PG). Seneca's Audionasties (*Controversiae* 2.5, 10.4)", in: Monica R. Gale and J. H. D. Scourfield (eds.), *Texts and Violence in the Roman World*, Cambridge, 179–214.
Heusch (2005): Christine Heusch, "Die Ethopoiie in der griechischen und lateinischen Antike: von der rhetorischen Progymnasma-Theorie zur Literarischen Form", in: Eugenio Amato and Jacques Schamp (eds.), ἨΘΟΠΟΙΙΑ. *La représentation de caractères entre fiction scolaire et réalité vivante à l'époque impériale et tardive*, Salerno, 11–33.
Hömke (2009): Nicola Hömke, "The Declaimer's One-man Show. Playing with Roles and Rules in the Pseudo-Quinitilian *Declamationes maiores*", in: *Rhetorica* 27, 240–255.

Hömke (2017): Nicola Hömke, "Mit Gift und Dirnen römische Werte bewahren? Die pseudoquintilianischen *Declamationes maiores* 14 und 15 zwischen Kontinuität und Wandel", in: Armin Eich, Stefan Freund, Meike Rühle and Christoph Schubert (eds.), *Das dritte Jahrhundert. Kontinuitäten, Brüche, Übergänge*, Stuttgart, 203–220.

Holzberg (2006): Niklas Holzberg, *Der antike Roman. Eine Einführung*, Darmstadt.

Huelsenbeck (2015): Bart Huelsenbeck, "Shared Speech in the Collection of the Elder Seneca (*Contr.* 10.4): Towards a Study of Common Literary Passages as Community Interaction", in: Eugenio Amato, Francesco Citti and Bart Huelsenbeck (eds.), *Law and Ethics in Greek and Roman Declamation*, Berlin/Boston, 35–62.

Kraus (2007): Manfred Kraus, "Rehearsing the Other Sex: Impersonation of Women in Ancient Classroom Ethopoeia", in: José Antonio Fernández Delgado *et al.* (eds.), *Escuela y Literatura en Grecia Antigua. Actas del Simposio Internacional, Universidad de Salamanca, 17–19 Noviembre de 2004*, Cassino, 455–468.

La Bua (2010): Giuseppe La Bua, "*Aiebat se in animo scribere* (Sen. *Contr.* 1 *praef.* 18): Writing in Roman Declamations", in: Lucia Calboli Montefusco (ed.), *Papers on Rhetoric X*, Roma, 183–199.

Langlands (2006): Rebecca Langlands, *Sexual Morality in Ancient Rome*, Cambridge.

van Mal-Maeder (2003): Danielle van Mal-Maeder, "L'autre voix. Représentations de femmes dans les déclamations latines", in: Therese Fuhrer and Samuel Zinsli (eds.), *Gender Studies in den Altertumswissenschaften. Rollenkonstrukte in antiken Texten* (Iphis 2), Trier, 93–105.

van Mal-Maeder (2007): Danielle van Mal-Maeder, *La fiction des déclamations*, Leiden.

van Mal-Maeder (2020): Danielle van Mal-Maeder, "Controversial Games. Didactical Voices and the Construction of Discourse in Seneca's *Controversiae* and *Suasoriae*", in: Martin T. Dinter, Charles Guérin and Marcos Martinho (eds.), *Reading Roman Declamation: Seneca the Elder*, Oxford, 318–331.

Mannering (2020): Jonathan E. Mannering, "Objection! Contesting Taste and Space in Seneca's Declamatory Arena", in: Martin T. Dinter, Charles Guérin and Marcos Martinho (eds.), *Reading Roman Declamation: Seneca the Elder*, Oxford, 221–239.

Manthe (2019): Ulrich Manthe, *Geschichte des römischen Rechts*, 6. durchgesehene und aktualisierte Aufl., München.

Mastrorosa (2016): Ida Gilda Mastrorosa, "Istituzioni religiose e pratica declamatoria in età augustea e tiberiana. Il culto di Vesta in Seneca il Vecchio", in: Rémy Poignault and Catherine Schneider (eds.), *Fabrique de la Déclamation antique (Controverses et suasoires)*, Lyon, 293–307.

Nocchi (2015): Francesca Romana Nocchi, "Declamazione e teatro", in: Mario Lentano (ed.), *La declamazione latina. Prospettive a confronto sulla retorica di scuola a Roma antica*, Napoli, 175–209.

Pailler (2004): Jean-Marie Pailler, "La prêtresse prostituée ou les trois vœux de la Vestale", in: *Histoire, espaces et marges de l'Antiquité. Hommages à Monique Clavel-Lévêque*, Vol. 3, Besançon, 88–101.

Panayotakis (2002): Stelios Panayotakis, "The Temple and the Brothel. Mothers and Daughters in *Apollonius of Tyre*", in: Michael Paschalis and Stavros Frangoulidis (eds.), *Space in the Ancient Novel*, Barkhuis, 98–117.

Pianezzola (2003): Emilio Pianezzola, "Declamatori a teatro. Per una messa in scena delle *Controversiae* di Seneca il Vecchio", in: Isabella Gualandri and Giancarlo Mazzoli (eds.), *Gli Annei. Una famiglia nella storia e nella cultura di Roma imperiale* (Atti del Convegno internazionale di Milano-Pavia 1–6 maggio 2000), Como, 91–98.

Pingoud/Rolle (2016): Julien Pingoud and Alessandra Rolle, "*Noverca et mater crudelis*. La perversion féminine dans les *Grandes Déclamations* à travers l'intertextualité", in: Martin

T. Dinter, Charles Guérin and Marcos Martinho (eds.), *Reading Roman Declamation: The Declamations Ascribed to Quintilian*, Berlin/Boston, 147–166.

Richlin (1997): Amy Richlin, "Gender and Rhetoric: Producing Manhood in the Schools", in: William J. Dominik (ed.), *Roman Eloquence. Rhetoric in Society and Literature*, London/New York, 90–110.

Santini (2006): Carlo Santini, "Oralità e scrittura in Seneca il Vecchio: Sulla vestale che scrive versi", in: Carlo Santini, Loriano Zurli and Luca Cardinali (eds.), *Concentus ex dissonis. Scritti in onore di Aldo Setaioli*, Vol. II, Napoli, 613–633.

Sharrock (1991): Alison Sharrock, "Womanufacture", *JRS* 81, 36–49.

Stoffel (2017): Christian Stoffel, "The Inter- and Intratextuality of Seneca the Elder's Controversia 6.8: The Vestal Virgin Writer and her Challenging *persona*", *Philologus* 161, 162–177.

Stramaglia (2016): Antonio Stramaglia, "The Hidden Teacher. 'Metarhetoric' in Ps.-Quintilian's *Major Declamations*", in: Martin T. Dinter, Charles Guérin and Marcos Martinho (eds.), *Reading Roman Declamation: The Declamations Ascribed to Quintilian*, Berlin/Boston, 25–48.

Zinsmaier (2009): Thomas Zinsmaier, "Zwischen Erzählung und Argumentation. *Colores* in den pseudoquintilianischen *Declamationes maiores*", *Rhetorica* 27, 256–273.

II **Gendering a Non-Human 'I'**

Markus Hafner
Pythia poetrix? Oracular Polyphony between Poetic Collaboration and Delphic Politics

To Emily, Julia, and Rose

Abstract: This contribution takes its starting point from two opposite traditions found in Imperial texts, which both concern the role of the Pythia at Delphi. Whereas the first tradition underscores her poetic creativity, the second considers that priests or bards supplied the verse oracles to the Pythia and thus denies her agency. According to the latter, influential view, she was a dependent mouthpiece of the Delphic institution with hardly any poetic ability. Given that earlier texts exhibit an emergence of the Pythia's onymity and authorship, it is surprising that later authors and scholars, ancient and modern, silenced this prominent female voice. I will argue that her ἔπεα neither wholly conformed to the status of oral poetry, nor were they considered sacred texts. However, the shaping of a multi-layered and polyphonic oracular 'I' in Late Archaic and Classical Greek Literature, which appears as a gender-hybrid (i.e., male oracular god vs. female priestess) and ontologically hybrid (i.e., human vs. divine agent) collaboration, results in a co-creative authorial voice. This indistinct 'acting in unison', which transcends gender-specific and status-specific elements of the speaking figures' voices, is firmly rooted in Early Greek poetry.

Keywords: verse oracle, Apollo, attribution, oracular 'I', hybridity, collaborative authorship

---

Acknowledgments: I have had the great opportunity to present earlier versions of this paper at the University of North Carolina (Chapel Hill), the University of Kentucky (Lexington), the Goethe University Frankfurt (all 2019) and the University of Graz (2020). Special thanks to Jackie Murray (University of Kentucky, Lexington) and David Kaufman (Transylvania University, Lexington, KY), who kindly invited me to contribute to the *Bluegrass Lectures*. Moreover, to Emily Baragwanath (Chapel Hill, NC), Veronika Lütkenhaus, Thomas Paulsen (Frankfurt) and Anna-Katharina Rieger (IGS "Resonant Self-World Relations in Ancient and Modern Socio-Religious Practices", Erfurt and Graz), who offered me platforms to present my paper and to receive helpful questions or comments. Lastly, I wish to thank Lisa Cordes and Therese Fuhrer for accepting my contribution for their volume.

https://doi.org/10.1515/9783110795257-005

1 Two opposite traditions in Imperial Greek Literature

The ambivalent image of the Delphic Pythia and the contradictory qualities that have been attributed to this mysterious figure[1] – ever since antiquity – can be especially well observed if one takes a glimpse at her appearances in Imperial Greek Literature. According to some authors, the Pythia played a foundational role in the development of Greek poetry and wisdom. In the second century CE, Pausanias (10.5.7) reports that a woman called Phemonoe ("who perceives [is sensible of] oracular utterances") became the first prophetess (πρόμαντις)[2] of Apollo. What is more, according to Pausanias, the arch-Pythia Phemonoe became the – as it were – πρώτη εὕρετις (*prima inventrix*) of hexameter verse. Moreover, the first century CE historian Diodorus (4.66.6) mentions that a certain Daphne (her name, "laurel", credits her with Apollonian sovereignty), daughter of the seer Tiresias, became a proto-poetess and the teacheress of Homer.[3] Like her father she was well versed in the art of soothsaying (μαντικὴ τέχνη), which she even improved in comparison with him. She also produced many written oracles on her own (χρησμοὺς ἔγραψε παντοδαπούς), and some say that Homer appropriated her poetry and embellished his own works with it (παρ' ἧς φασι καὶ τὸν ποιητὴν Ὅμηρον πολλὰ τῶν ἐπῶν σφετερισάμενον κοσμῆσαι τὴν ἰδίαν ποίησιν).[4] Finally, the second century CE biographer Diogenes Laertius in the *Life of Pythagoras* (D.L. 8.1–50) informs us that according to the Peripatetic philosopher Aristoxenus of Tarentum (fourth century BCE), Pythagoras had taken most of his ethical doctrines from a Pythia called Themistocleia ("known for her judgments"), an arch-philosopher (D.L. 8.8). Phemonoe, Daphne, and Themistocleia were probably fictitious figures. However, all the Imperial texts mentioned above are dedicated to the prophetess' poetic autonomy, considering her a primordial source of creativity.

---

[1] On the Pythia and her prophesies in general, cf. Fauth (1963), Schnurr-Redfort (2006); on Greek female seers, Flower (2008) 211–39, Hagedorn (2013); on prophetesses in the Hebrew Bible, Fischer (2002). On Greek divination, Burkert (2005), Rosenberger (2013); on ancient prophesy in general, Nissinen (2017). On the Delphic oracle, Parke (1939), Amandry (1950), Lloyd-Jones (1976) and, more recently, Bowden (2005) and Kindt (2016). Parke/Wormell (1956) and Fontenrose (1978) offer collections and classifications of Ancient Greek oracles. On the archeological and geological explorations in Delphi, cf. Hall (2014) 17–34.
[2] Herodotus, e.g., uses πρόμαντις as the title of the Delphic Pythia (Hdt. 6.66, 7.111). Further names are μάντις (A. *Eu.* 29) or προφῆτις (E. *Ion* 42).
[3] Diodorus (16.26.6) describes the generic Pythia as a woman of around fifty years (before the raping of one Pythia, she had been an unmarried virgin), which accords with Aeschylus (*Eu.* 38). Cf. Amandry (1950) 115–18.
[4] Other sources mention further Homeric 'borrowings' from female poets, such as from Helen, daughter of the legendary Musaeus. This episode from Ptolemy Chennus' (early second century CE) *Novel History* (Καινὴ ἱστορία) is summarized by Photius (*Bibl.* 190, 149b22–5). What is more, in 190, 151a37–b5 the Egyptian priestess Phantasia appears as the authoress of an early *Iliad* and *Odyssey*.

Other authors chose a different approach, by quoting widespread allegations (φασι), according to which the Pythia was an untrained and unpoetic figure to whom male priests or bards supplied the actual verse oracles. Hence, the first/second century CE philosopher Plutarch in his dialogue *De Pythiae oraculis*, which treats the problem that the Pythia does not deliver oracles in verse anymore, but only in prose, has the speaker Theon deliver an apologetic monologue in favour of the new Delphic custom.[5] Against those who maintain that the oracle has become useless,[6] Theon contrasts the former ambiguity of the oracle with a new simplicity and directness in the present age. For him, divine inspiration is independent from poetic expression. In *De Pyth. or.* 25.407B, Theon – in order to denigrate earlier poetic practices at Delphi – quotes a rumour, portraying the Pythia as a mouthpiece in need of "certain (male) assistants in poetry" (ποιητικοί τινες ἄνδρες), who converted her inarticulate 'stammering' into an artificial form as a means of conveying an oracle.[7]

The geographer Strabo (first century BCE/first century CE) quotes another authorless rumour, saying that poets in the service of Delphi's institution impose a metric form on Pythia's prose utterances (Str. 9.3.5). Although this a more moderate view, it still highlights the Pythia's dependence from versifiers. A last passage, again from Plutarch, who served as a priest of Apollo at Delphi himself, mentions that divine forces exert strong influence on the Pythia. According to a statement from *De defectu oraculorum*, uttered by Plutarch's brother Lamprias, who held an office at the Oracle of Trophonius in Lebadeia (*Def. or.* 38.431C–D), daimonic pneuma and other divine influences take control of the Pythia's divinatory capability (50.437D).

Thus, Imperial writers considered the Pythia an autonomous and creative agent on the one hand, or a passive mouthpiece of the Delphic institution and/or divine forces on the other. Surprisingly, the second view became much more influential in

---

5 On Theon's speech (403A9–409D7) in this essay, cf. Schröder (1990) 10–24. On Plutarch's writings that deal with oracles, divination, and divine inspiration, such as *De genio* (on the *daimonion* of Socrates) and *De defectu oraculorum* (on the question, why many oracles and religious sites for prophesy were in decay), cf. Schröder (2010). Moreover, Plutarch's dialogue *De E apud Delphos* displays a handful of philosophical speeches (as interlocutors appear, amongst others, Theon, Plutarch's brother Lamprias, and 'Plutarch' himself), which offer profound, yet ultimately aporetic, enquiries into the enigmatic signs of Delphi's divine 'arch-philosopher' Apollo (Thum, 2013).
6 An exemplary skeptical view on prophesy is uttered in Cic. *Div.* 1.38 (Cicero's brother Quintus: *minus oraculorum veritas excellit*) and, more fiercely, 2.117 (Marcus Cicero: *non modo nostra aetate, sed iam diu tam otiosa iacent, ut nihil possit esse contemptius?*). On further testimonies, cf. Bendlin (2006) 181f. n. 68, who generally deals with the Imperial discussion on the problems of traditional religion and authority.
7 πολλῶν δ' ἦν ἀκούειν ὅτι ποιητικοί τινες ἄνδρες ἐκδεχόμενοι τὰς φωνὰς καὶ ὑπολαμβάνοντες ἐπικάθηνται περὶ τὸ χρηστήριον, ἔπη καὶ μέτρα καὶ ῥυθμοὺς οἷον ἀγγεῖα τοῖς χρησμοῖς ἐκ τοῦ προστυχόντος περιπλέκοντες (ed. Schröder, 1990) ("[T]here was the oft-repeated tale that certain men with a gift of poetry were wont to sit about close by the shrine waiting to catch the words [of the Pythia] spoken, and then weaving about them a fabric of extempore hexameters or other verses as 'containers,' so to speak for the oracles", transl. Babbitt, 1936).

modern scholarship (see section 2). This is especially surprising since, although both Strabo and Plutarch explicitly refer to rumours concerning the Delphic Pythia, such statements were taken for granted in later times.

In the following section, I shall examine the ways in which later commentators, ancient and modern, silenced this prominent female voice and show which particular 'obstacles' prevented the Pythia from being considered an autonomous agent in the cultural history of her reception (2).[8] This is especially remarkable, given that earlier texts, such as Herodotus' *Histories*, exhibit an emergence of the Pythia's authorial onymity and agency (3).[9] Next, I will argue that her ἔπεα neither wholly conformed to the status of oral poetry, nor were they considered sacred texts (4). However, the shaping of a multi-layered and unresolvable polyphony of oracular 'I's (5) that I shall compare to other forms of hybrid – human-divine and male-female – collaboration (6) in Late Archaic literature results in a co-creative authorial voice, which as an indistinct 'acting in unison' is firmly rooted in Early Greek poetic production.

2 'Obstacles' to Pythian autonomy, or The silencing of female voice

A passage from Herodotus, who lived during the heyday of the Delphic oracle (fifth century BCE), displays the first verse oracle in direct discourse in the *Histories* (Hdt. 1.47).[10] When the Lydian king, Croesus son of Alyattes, who plotted to challenge

---

8 Cf. Hauser (2016) 136f.: "women's voices were largely silenced in the ancient world, both literally and figuratively in their survival in the textual record. [. . .] The layered, fragmentary, mediated tradition in which we receive female-authored texts [. . .] requires that we problematise the extent to which we can, or should, attempt to recover an 'authentic' female voice in the works of ancient Greek women authors. This, in turn, becomes the source of the second difficulty that arises in the study of female authorship: the tension between gender and self-expression that arises when women speak/perform/write, challenging cultural expectations about women's silence in public, inevitably becomes an integral feature of the few surviving female-authored texts that cannot be ignored." See also Alison Sharrock's reflections on the Symbolic, i.e. the world order controlled by men, as discussed in feminist theory, in this present volume.
9 In Herodotus, the priestess often speaks directly and without intermediary to her inquirers or comments on Apollo's decisions, cf. e.g. Amandry (1950) 120f.; Maurizio (1995) 71f. Her autonomy is acknowledged as early as Pi. *P*. 4.60 (αὐτομάτῳ κελάδῳ, "through the spontaneous cry [sc. of the Delphic Bee]", transl. Race, 1997). A *schol.* ad loc. explains that the inspired Pythia answered before she was asked the question (ἤτοι αὐτοκελεύστῳ· οὐ γὰρ κατὰ ἐπίταγμα τῶν χρησμῳδουμένων ἡ προφῆτις τοὺς χρησμοὺς ἐκφέρει, ἀλλ' ἐπιπνοίᾳ).
10 The first oracle in Hdt. 1.13, which is given to Croesus' Lydian ancestor Gyges, is presented in indirect discourse. On the significance of the Delphic shrine for the *Histories* and on Herodotus' description of the mantic session, cf. Fairbanks (1906), Compton (1994), Kindt (2006). On the role of religion in Herodotus, see Mikalson (2003).

the Persian kingdom, tries to consult and test a series of oracular shrines, the Delphic oracle gives a hexametric response to the Lydian messengers that have arrived from Sardis. The oracle begins as follows (1.47.3):

ἡ Πυθίη ἐν ἑξαμέτρῳ τόνῳ λέγει τάδε·
οἶδα δ' ἐγὼ ψάμμου τ' ἀριθμὸν καὶ μέτρα θαλάσσης,
καὶ κωφοῦ συνίημι καὶ οὐ φωνεῦντος ἀκούω.
(ed. Wilson, 2015)

the priestess – the Pythia – began to speak as follows, chanting in perfect hexameters:
I can count an infinitude of grains of sand and I have the measuring of the sea,
I understand the talk of the dumb, and I can hear what the voiceless say.
(transl. Holland, 2013)

The verses reveal the self-asserted authority of its speaker, who lists several *adynata* to prove her or his own omniscience (pretending to have knowledge of the number of the grains of sand etc.), emphatically using the first-person pronoun ἐγώ (cf. οἶδα δ' ἐγώ). However, the identity of the oracular 'I' remains quite unclear – are we dealing with the god Apollo, the shrine itself, or the Pythia? Whereas the miraculous and supernatural *adynata* point to the omniscient god,[11] scholarship tends to attribute the verses to the oracle, thus equaling its rank to the Lydian king Croesus.[12] However, the narrative frame surrounding the oracle makes an authorial attribution to the Pythia plausible, who spoke to the Lydians in hexameter verses (ἡ Πυθίη ἐν ἑξαμέτρῳ τόνῳ λέγει τάδε). Thus, for the first time in the *Histories*, we come across oracular polyphony, in which the ambiguously speaking 'I' can be attributed to one of the three instances 'god' (as higher omniscient being), 'oracle' (as impersonal political entity) and 'Pythia' (as marked by the narrative frame). Surprisingly, scholarship resolved this ambiguous polyphony of the oracular first-person voice mostly in favour of the realm of oracular politics. Such an 'institutional' reading considers Delphi as a place of great authority in dealing with political rulers.[13] Accordingly, it

---

11 In Pi. *P.* 9.46–9, the wise centaur Chiron addresses Apollo, praising the god for knowing, amongst other things, "how many leaves the earth puts forth in spring, and how many grains of sand in the sea and rivers are beaten by the waves and blasts of wind, and what will happen and whence" (transl. Race, 1997). (ὅσσα τε χθὼν ἠρινὰ φύλλ' ἀναπέμπει, χὠπόσαι | ἐν θαλάσσᾳ καὶ ποταμοῖς ψάμαθοι | κύμασιν ῥιπαῖς τ' ἀνέμων κλονέονται, | χὠ τι μέλλει, χὠπόθεν | ἔσσεται, εὖ καθορᾷς, ed. Snell/Maehler, 2008).
12 Cf., e.g., Chamberlain (2001) 24, who attributes the verses to the Delphic oracle, which replies to Croesus' envoys. He thus parallels the Delphic institution with the historian Herodotus himself: "'I know (*oida d'egô*) the number of the sands and the measure of the seas'– that is, if you like, 'I am the consummate *histor*, I know the ultimate superlatives,' so don't try to out interpret me (1.47.3). [. . .] The figure of authority, the one who knows and who signals, asserts this authority by marking his discourse with the first person pronoun."
13 Although Fontenrose (1978) doubted the authenticity of the colonization oracles, Maurizio (2001) connects the rise of Delphi in Archaic Times with the movements of colonization and

stresses the (male) sphere of international relations and diplomacy, thus allowing the Pythia to fade into irrelevance.[14] However, once Croesus and the Lydian empire have fallen, the Pythia offers the now remorseful Croesus Apollo's true will (Hdt. 1.93).

Apart from these difficulties surrounding the polyphonic oracular 'I' (see more in section 5), further obstacles have been brought to bear against Pythian agency. Modern scholarship has adduced, amongst other things, that male poets and versifiers assisted the Pythia in composing (verse) oracles.[15] This assumption, however, does not rest on solid ground, because, first, both Plutarch (*De Pyth. or.* 25.407B) and Strabo (9.3.5) only refer to rumours (φασι)[16] concerning 'literary assistants' of the Pythia. Secondly, in earlier texts, e.g. in Herodotus, male ministers or interpreters (προφῆται) do not play a major role at the Delphic oracle (cf. Hdt. 8.37). However, the following lines became an often-quoted classic of modern scholarship:

> the Pythoness ascended into the tripod, and, filled with the divine afflatus which at least the later ages believed to ascend in vapour from a fissure in the ground, burst forth into wild utterance, which was probably some kind of articulate speech, and which the [. . .] 'holy ones,' who with the prophet sat around the tripod, knew well how to interpret [. . .]. What was essential to Delphic divination, then, was the frenzy of the Pythoness and **the sounds which she uttered in this state which were interpreted by the 'holy ones' and the 'prophet' according to some conventional code of their own.**[17]

As a reference for his description of the Pythia's practices, the scholar points to a passage from Plutarch's *De defectu oraculorum* (49.437A7–10). However, in Plutarch the speaker Lamprias only generally remarks on the recruitments of "priests and

---

tyranny – cf. Forrest (1957). During times of critical change, Delphi became an important institution for the Greek city-states to consult. The Pythias, according to Maurizio (2001) 42, thus responded to the needs of oikists and tyrants and mirrored linguistically the uncertainties of their respective ventures. Kindt (2006) 36f., however, considers that the Pythia's opaque and enigmatic speech reflected the alterity of divine speech vs. human utterances. Cf. Kindt (2017).

14 This is mirrored, at first sight, in the following narrative. Once the Delphic shrine has won Croesus' approval, he sends rich gifts to Delphi (1.50f.). When the oracle advises Croesus that an expedition against Persia will destroy a great empire, he overjoys and sends two gold staters to each Delphian (1.54.1). In return, the city grants to Croesus and the Lydians outstanding rewards and privileges (1.54.2). Among these are προμαντηίη (i.e., the right of first consulting the oracle), ἀτελείη (i.e., freedom from all charges, waiving of payment for consultation), προεδρίη (i.e., the chief seats at festivals) and ἐξεῖναι τῷ βουλομένῳ [. . .] γίνεσθαι Δελφὸν ἐς τὸν αἰεὶ χρόνον (i.e., perpetual right of honorary Delphian citizenship to members of an entire foreign community). Asheri et al. (2007) ad loc. mention that "Herodotus echoes the official formula used in decrees of this kind".
15 Cf. McLeod (1961) on oral bards in Delphi; Burkert (1985) 116 ("the utterances of the Pythia are then fixed by the priests in the normal Greek literary form, the Homeric hexameter."); Bowden (2005) 22–4, 33–9; *contra* Dodds (1951) 212, 218f.
16 Ustinova (2009) 126 points out, too, that the phrase "they say" in Strabo means that there is no eyewitness account.
17 Farnell (1907) 189 (my emphasis). Cited also in Fontenrose (1978) 196.

holy men" performing sacrifices and perceiving the presence of the god at the Delphic shrine.[18] Thus, a connection between the Pythia, who goes unmentioned in this passage, and her alleged male interpreters lacks any clear evidence in ancient sources. A footnote by the same scholar at the bottom of the page is self-revealing: "This theory of the relations between the Ὅσιοι and the Πυθία rests on no direct authority, but on general probabilities and a combination of evidence."[19]

Another assumption resolves the oracular polyphony in favour of 'divine motivation' and considers the god Apollo as the speaking 'I' of the οἶδα δ' ἐγὼ in Hdt. 1.47.3. According to this view, the Pythia acted as a passive and mediumistic mouthpiece of the god. This view, however, became prominent in ancient texts of relatively late date, which often rely on particular generic conventions and aesthetic principles. Thus, the most drastic text that depicts the surrender of consciousness of the ecstatic Pythia to Apollo is Lucan's Imperial epic on the Civil War (*Pharsalia*, first century CE).[20] During the violent questioning of the Pythia Phemonoe by Appius Claudius Pulcher,[21] the possessed Pythia appears in a state of furious frenzy (5.190–93).[22]

The popular image of a furious Pythia as a passive figure who is exposed to the violent seizure and grip of divine principles of inspiration, which emerges from Imperial texts (e.g. Plu. *Def. or.* 50.437D) and which might owe a lot to the Pythia's representations in Greek tragedy,[23] further developed in Late Antiquity. Particularly

---

[18] On this passage, cf. Amandry (1950) 118–25, Maurizio (1995) 83f.
[19] Cf. Farnell (1907) 189. He goes on saying that "It is not really contradicted by such common phrases as ἡ Πυθία χρᾷ (equivalent to ἔχρησεν ὁ θεός) in Herodotus and others, nor by stories of the Pythoness being bribed [. . .]: for [. . .] it would be the cue of the Ὅσιοι to maintain officially that the utterances came directly and spontaneously through the Pythoness from the god. If the latter had really free hand and could say what she liked and could accept bribes, she would scarcely have been the commonplace character that Plato and Plutarch were familiar with [. . .], and we must then reject the stories about the enthusiasm and frenzy, or regard her as a deliberate impostor." On the view that priests interpreted, or composed, oracles, cf. Amandry (1950) 168, Parke/Wormell (1956) 38. Fabre-Serris, in this volume, shows how modern scholars discussed female authorship and agency with regard to Elegy 3.11 in the *Corpus Tibullianum*.
[20] The description, which is vividly rendered by the epic primary narrator, is probably based on the encounter of Aeneas and the ecstatic Cumaean Sibyl in Verg. *Aen.* 6.45–54, 77–80, 99–101. Cf. Amandry (1950) 19–24; Fontenrose (1978) 210; Casali (2011) 101–4. *Contra* Ustinova (2009) 140f.
[21] Appius Claudius held a censorship in 50 BCE and administrated the territory of Greece on behalf of Pompey.
[22] Wild frenzy, loud groaning, inarticulate cries with panting breath, and dismal wailing are the consequences of the Pythia's prophetic inspiration, cf. 5.96–8a. The domination of the god, with its sexual connotation (cf. 5.166f. *artus* [. . .] *inrupit*), only slowly recedes to seize power over the priestess, cf. 5.210b–211. This image of the *Pythia furens* in Imperial Latin Literature is also palpable in fable no. 8 of the Phaedrus appendix.
[23] One might think of the portrayal of the Trojan Cassandra (e.g. A. *Ag.* 1150, 1207, 1216, E. *Tr.* 408f.), cf. Ustinova (2009) 125–7, Hagedorn (2013) 106–14.

Christian writers used the image of a Pythia who is penetrated by the god to discredit pagane religious practices and beliefs.²⁴

However, an earlier, 'classical' passage – certainly well known to the Platonist Plutarch – deals with the enthusiastic and 'maniac' Pythia who is not yet an irrational being lacking divinatory capability. In the Platonic *Phaedrus*, Socrates even mentions the countless benefits that humankind has received through prophetic madness (*Phdr.* 244a5–b5):

> εἰ μὲν γὰρ ἦν ἁπλοῦν τὸ μανίαν κακὸν εἶναι, καλῶς ἂν ἐλέγετο· νῦν δὲ τὰ μέγιστα τῶν ἀγαθῶν ἡμῖν γίγνεται διὰ μανίας, θείᾳ μέντοι δόσει διδομένης. ἥ τε γὰρ δὴ ἐν Δελφοῖς προφῆτις αἵ τ' ἐν Δωδώνῃ ἱέρειαι μανεῖσαι μὲν πολλὰ δὴ καὶ καλὰ ἰδίᾳ τε καὶ δημοσίᾳ τὴν Ἑλλάδα ἠργάσαντο, σωφρονοῦσαι δὲ βραχέα ἢ οὐδέν· καὶ ἐὰν δὴ λέγωμεν Σίβυλλάν τε καὶ ἄλλους, ὅσοι μαντικῇ χρώμενοι ἐνθέῳ πολλὰ δὴ πολλοῖς προλέγοντες εἰς τὸ μέλλον ὤρθωσαν, μηκύνοιμεν ἂν δῆλα παντὶ λέγοντες. (ed. Burnet, 1901)

> For if it were a simple fact that insanity is an evil, the saying would be true; but in reality the greatest blessings come to us through madness, when it is sent as a gift of the gods. For the prophetess at Delphi and the priestesses at Dodona when they have been mad have conferred many splendid benefits upon Greece both in private and in public affairs, but few or none when they have been in their right minds; and if we should speak of the Sybil and all the others who by prophetic inspiration have foretold many things to many persons and thereby made them fortunate afterwards, anyone can see that we should speak a long time. (transl. Fowler, 1925)

Notwithstanding the beneficial role, which Plato's representative Socrates attributed to the Pythia's μανία, modern scholarship, starting from the seminal monograph "Psyche" by Erwin Rohde – a friend of the young Nietzsche –, has tended to underscore the 'maniac' dimension of the Pythia's mantic μανία.²⁵ What is more, scholars have not shied away from uttering biologistic statements about the Pythias, who qua their female sex are attributed a certain disposition or an aptitude to certain influences.²⁶ Thus, Michael Flower has pointedly summarized the difficulties surrounding arbitrary a priori assumptions concerning the Pythia's authorial status:

---

24 Cf. Orig. *Cels.* 7.3f., Joh. Chrys. *in 1 Cor. hom.* 29.12.1, and the discussion in Amandry (1950) 196–230. An important starting point for church fathers and scholarly commentators was a passage from the third century Neoplatonist author Iamblichus (*Myst.* 3.11), who claimed that the Pythia was giving herself up entirely to the divine spirit and to the god (ὅλη γίγνεται τοῦ θεοῦ).
25 Rohde (1898) 60f.: "Was sie dann ‚mit rasendem Munde' verkündigt, das spricht aus der Gott; wo sie ‚ich' sagt, da redet Apollo von sich und dem was ihn betrifft. Was in ihr lebt, denkt und redet, so lange sie rast, das ist der Gott selbst". On the 'penetrated' Pythia, cf. Parke (1939) 39, Dodds (1951) 70, Parke/Wormell (1956) I, 12f., 33–8. On the metaphor of daemonic possession as a male strategy for controlling women in Classical Athens, cf. Padel (1983) 14: "Erotic penetration becomes one of the main images for any possessing deity in relation to the human soul."
26 Cf., e.g., Bonnechere (2007) 154: "There was no need for the seer to have an advanced education: the Pythia at Delphi just had to have, like children used as mediums in magic, a pure soul, one that was not too much bogged down in the passions [. . .]. If prophets were numerous, prophetesses were also respected, perhaps particularly for tangible factors, such as an emotional condition better adapted to the psychic demands of possession."

> The classic problem is whether the Pythia herself delivered intelligible oracles or whether she spoke unintelligibly, and her words were put into order either by attendant male priests or by professional versifiers [. . .]. [T]his is an ideologically charged set of problems, since basic issues of gender roles and of the nature of religious authority are at stake.[27]

3 The emergence of Pythian onymity and agency in Herodotus

In Herodotus, for the first time in Greek Literature, a Pythia bears a personal name and thus emerges from anonymity. In Hdt. 6.66, we hear about the manipulation and bribery of a Pythia by the name Perialla (another manuscript tradition offers the version Periallos) and the subsequent political scandal. When the royal legitimacy of the new Spartan king Demaratus is questioned, his rival Cleomenes starts an intrigue and corrupts a powerful Delphian. The latter bribes the Pythia in favour of Cleomenes. Once the scandal becomes known, Perialla is ousted from her honorary position. This episode about this questionable Pythia called Περίαλλα (a speaking name?)[28] shows that the rise of authorship follows the need to attribute[29] responsibility and liability to a named agent.[30] Surprisingly, further archaic authors,

---

27 Flower (2008) 215f. Fontenrose (1978) 196 ('rational' and 'prosaic' Pythia) offers another moderate view.
28 Cf. LSJ s.v. περίαλλος, ον (adj.), "before all others: Adv. περίαλλα before all, h.Pan. 46, Pi.P.11.5, Ar.Th.1070". Thus, Greek ears did certainly perceive the 'uniqueness' or 'peculiarity' resounding with her personal name.
29 Hartmut Leppin rightly points out to me that the attribution (*Zuweisung*) of authorship to the Pythia is based on the general possibility of imputing (*Zurechnung*) to her responsibility and agency. For only if the Pythia, the mediator of Apollo, appears to be sound of mind (*zurechnungsfähig*), can authorship be attributed to her. Remarkably, the relevant texts from Greek antiquity distribute agency during the collaborative act of prophetic communication between the Pythia and the divine instance (see below in this article): the Pythia appears as a more or less discernible agent within this communication. Thus, oracular authorship can be considered as a product of cultural networks and their acts of authorization, which run counter to concepts of autonomous agency, original creativity and intellectual ownership (cf. Berensmeyer *et al.*, 2012, 8). On authorship as a social performance within a complex field of agency, see Biggs/Travlou (2010) 29. On the distribution of agency among human and non-human actors, see Latour (2005).
30 Foucault (1969) connected the notion of authorship with attribution and liability. His *fonction-auteur* localizes literary works in a modern universe, which is governed by juridical forces and legalistic principles, such as copyright. Qua their names, authors become 'owners' of their work and must therefore fear expropriation in case of plagiarism. Some decades later, the typology of author-functions (*authemes*), or phases of authorial activity, in Love (2002) differentiates Foucault's notion of the *fonction-auteur*. On the poetical and institutional agency associated with the author's name already in Greek Literature, see Calame (2004) 37: "Le nom d'auteur en Grèce est donc susceptible à la fois de conférer à un genre et à une tradition poétiques une certaine «agency» poétique et

and most prominently Homer, are named for the first time in texts which criticize their works as inappropriate.[31]

The second Pythia who is granted onymity by Herodotus, is Aristonike (again a speaking name?), who foretells the Athenians how to "win in the best (possible) way" the Battle of Salamis (Hdt. 7.140–42). Her second oracle, famously mentioning the 'wooden walls' (i.e. the Athenian ships), leads to the victorious strategy against the Persian forces (480 BCE). However, a previous oracle (Hdt. 7.140) had predicted disaster and ruin for Athens at the hands of the Persians. Contrary to later sources, Herodotus names the Delphic priestess Aristonike as the author of the oracle ("the priestess, whose name was Aristonike [τῇ οὔνομα ἦν Ἀριστονίκη], uttered the following prophecy").[32] When the Athenians returned to the shrine as suppliants and asked Lord Apollo for a more favourable answer, Aristonike gave the second 'wooden wall oracle' (Hdt. 7.141). Surprisingly, later sources referring to this oracle obliterate Aristonike's role during the Persian invasion and attribute the oracle to divine authority only.[33] The Severan writer Claudius Aelianus (second/third centuries CE), e.g., compiles both Delphic oracles into one sentence and refers generally to οἱ χρησμοί, "the oracles" (Ael. *NA* 12.32),[34] invoking both Aristotle (fr. 399 Rose) and Philochorus (FGrHist 328 F 116) as his sources. In other words, a compilation of both oracles circulated as early as the fourth and third centuries BCE. Herodotus is therefore the only author to highlight the Pythia's agency during the Persian Wars, which he underlined by giving her a personal name. Thus, 'Aristonike' – literally a *vaticinatio ex eventu* – foreshadows the Athenian victory from Herodotus' later point of view.[35] Even if the

---

institutionelle; il est aussi susceptible de fixer l'acte de composition du poème dans sa relative autonomie par rapport à son execution."

31 Homer: Xenoph. 21 B 11, 12, 14–16, 23–6 DK, Heraclit. 22 A 22 DK, B 42, 56. Cf. the earliest mentions of Archilochus in Heraclit. 22 B 42 DK and in Pindar *P.* 2.52–6, both in polemical contexts.

32 Divergent attributions of the oracle refer to Apollo (Clem.Al. *Strom.* 5.14), the anonymous god (Suid. α 2371), or the seer Bakis (Tz. *H.* 9.812).

33 Attributions point to Apollo (Luc. *JTr.* 20; Clem.Al. *Strom.* 5.14), the anonymous god (e.g. Suid. α 2371) or the oracle (Eust. *Il.* 8.97 p. 701). Prose paraphrases attribute the oracle to Apollo (Max.Tyr. 13.1; Arg. 1 A. *Pers.*) or are anonymous (Ael. *NA* 12.32). Further testimonies refer to Apollo (Lyc. 1416–20) or the oracle (Paus. 1.18.2).

34 μετοικιζομένων γὰρ τῶν Ἀθηναίων εἰς τὰς ναῦς, ἡνίκα τοῦ χρόνου ὁ Πέρσης τὸν μέγαν πόλεμον ἐπὶ τὴν Ἑλλάδα ἐξῆψε, καὶ ἔλεγον οἱ χρησμοὶ λῷον εἶναι τοῖς Ἀθηναίοις τὴν μὲν πατρίδα ἀπολιπεῖν, ἐπιβῆναι δὲ τῶν τριήρων (ed. García Valdés *et al.*, 2009) ("The Athenians moved into the ships when the Persian kindled the Great War against Hellas, and the oracles said that it was better for the Athenians to leave their country and embark on the triremes").

35 Cf. Dewald (1981) 113: "the Pythia [is] the most important woman in the *Histories*; she [. . .] advises kings, tyrants, aristocrats, and commoners, both Greek and barbarian. She predicts the outcome of war and directs the foundation of colonies [. . .]. The Pythia represents the intersection of politics and morality for those who consult her. [. . .] As the representative of one of the few Greek institutions open to all Greek cities alike she works for the benefit of the society as a whole rather than in the narrow self-interest of an individual *polis*."

Pythia Perialla appears as a questionable figure, the *Histories* clearly throw into relief the emergence of both prophetesses' authorship.[36]

4 The ἔπεα of the Pythia – oral poetry or sacred texts?

Plutarch's *De Pythiae oraculis* offers a discussion on the value of the Pythia's utterances (cf. *De Pyth. or.* 7.397C). Theon, the self-asserted defender of Apollo, responds to those who maintain that the oracles have become useless that in cases in which oracles lack standards of clarity or comprehensibility it is not the god's fault.[37] In fact, his female mouthpiece is to blame.[38]

It is an ironical twist in this Plutarch passage that the Pythia's responsibility and liability for her verses are only asserted *ex negativo*. Following this logic, whenever an Apollonian oracle seems faulty, authorship is attributed to the Pythia. Thus, Theon concedes that many Pythias of the past – contrary to contemporary prophetesses – possessed a thorough poetic inclination.[39] And indeed, Herodotus, e.g., has the Pythias often present the oracles not only in an elaborate hexametric shape, but also in the speaking verses of the iambic trimeter.[40]

The poetic constitution of oracles, especially the formal similarities between oracular verses and Early Greek Poetry, has led scholars to draw divergent conclusions about Pythian poetry in the context of Archaic Song Culture. According to one view, archaic communities transmitted the highly regarded knowledge implied in oracular

---

[36] Neither bribery (cf. Hdt. 5.63, 6.66 and 75), obscurity (1.66.3, 1.75.2, 5.91.2), nor false (8.141, 9.95), falsely applied (9.43) or forged (7.6.3) oracles limit Herodotus' belief in oracular infallibility (1.91, 8.20, 8.77, 8.96.2).
[37] The attempt to defend the oracles' legitimacy becomes relevant once we take into consideration accusations from contemporary sources, charging the oracular prophesies for their malicious ambiguity and fraud. Cf. P.Berol. 11517 and further passages, especially in Lucian, in Jones (1986) 4f. with n. 57.
[38] οὐ γάρ ἐστι <τοῦ> θεοῦ ἡ γῆρυς οὐδ' ὁ φθόγγος οὐδ' ἡ λέξις οὐδὲ τὸ μέτρον ἀλλὰ τῆς γυναικός· ἐκεῖνος δὲ μόνας τὰς φαντασίας παρίστησι καὶ φῶς ἐν τῇ ψυχῇ ποιεῖ πρὸς τὸ μέλλον· ὁ γὰρ ἐνθουσιασμὸς τοιοῦτόν ἐστι (ed. Schröder, 1990) ("As a matter of fact, the voice is not that of a god, nor the utterance of it, nor the diction, nor the metre, but all these are the woman's; he puts into her mind only the visions, and creates a light in her soul in regard to the future; for inspiration is precisely this", transl. Babbitt, 1936).
[39] Earlier times, Theon states, produced "personal temperaments and nature which had an easy fluency and a bent towards composing poetry" (*De Pyth. or.* 23.405E εὔρουν τι καὶ φορὸν [. . .] πρὸς ποίησιν).
[40] Hexametric: 1.47.2, 5.92β, 6.86γ; trimetric: 1.174. Cf. Parke (1981). Ca. one third of the 581 oracles collected in Parke/Wormell (1956) are hexametric, whereas two third of them are supposedly prose paraphrases of a later date.

verses orally and brought them to bear in ever-new applications. Such procedures might, e.g., explain the linguistic mutability of prophesies[41] and the presence of epic formula in many oracles.[42] Hence, alternative versions of an oracular text would rely on different performances. During re-compositions and re-orderings, the exact words of the Pythia were, so to say, lost in authorless, or collective, transmission.[43] This approach, which is oriented towards studies on oral poetry and performance, considers oracles as shaped diachronically by the *vox populi*. However, it underestimates the role of writing in the course of transmission. After all, already Herodotus reports on collections of written oracles.[44]

According to another view, Greek conservatism perceived oracles as sacred texts of a different ontological status in comparison with Archaic Poetry. Whereas performative agents such as the professional rhapsodes modified poems during subsequent re-performances, oracles in this view contained the god's unchangeable words. Thus, oracles were held sacrilegious and were preserved *verbatim*.[45] This logic of an oracular *Urtext* that contained the god's unchangeable utterances bases itself on a passage from the elegiac poet Theognis (sixth century BCE, vv. 805–10):

> τόρνου καὶ στάθμης καὶ γνώμονος ἄνδρα θεωρόν | εὐθύτερον χρὴ <ἔ>μεν Κύρνε φυλασσόμενον, | ὦιτινί κεν Πυθῶνι θεοῦ χρήσασ' ἱέρεια | ὀμφὴν σημήνηι πίονος ἐξ ἀδύτου· | οὔτέ τι γὰρ προσθεὶς οὐδέν κ' ἔτι φάρμακον εὕροις, | οὐδ' ἀφελὼν πρὸς θεῶν ἀμπλακίην προφύγοις.
>
> (ed. West, 1998)
>
> It is necessary for the man who is a *theoros* [i.e. a sacred ambassador], Cyrnus, to be straighter than a carpenter's compass, rule, and square, that man to whom the priestess of the god at Pytho [i.e. Delphi] in her response reveals the god's voice from the rich *adyton* [inner room].[46]

---

41 Cf., e.g., Thuc. 2.54.2f., where the Athenians are shown in disagreement about the exact wording of the oracle and whether it had predicted a pestilence (λοιμός) or a famine (λιμός).
42 McLeod (1961) considered that the oracles were, as a rule, carried out by male bards, who drew on traditional material from Homer and other poets. Cf. Hall (2014) 30.
43 Cf. Maurizio (1997). Maurizio (2001) problematizes the conflict of female authorship and subsequent male transmission. She is pessimistic about the historicity of the Pythia's oracles, cf. 39 n. 8: "Oracular texts reflect an oral tradition in which the effect of male transmission is problematic if not impossible to evaluate. No oracles, because of their oral transmission and reformulation in writing, represent the exact words of any one Pythia".
44 On writing down oracles after their oral delivery, cf. Hdt. 1.48 (the Lydian messengers take notes of the Pythia's words: συγγραψάμενοι οἴχοντο ἀπιόντες ἐς τὰς Σάρδις ["the Lydians wrote it down and returned home to Sardis", transl. Holland, 2013]. Cf. 7.142. On the oracular compilations produced by the Greek chresmologue Onomacritus, whose *floruit* was under the Pisistratids in Athens, Hdt. 7.6.3 (at the same time, Onomacritus interpolated and forged written oracles). Hdt. 8.96.2 and 9.43.2 mention compilations of oracles given by the legendary poet Musaeus. Overall, Herodotus' mention of archives of authoritative oracles reveals their significance for the Greek poleis, cf. Nissinen (2017) 137–43. Ar. *Av.* 961–90 attributes the chresmologue and his βιβλίον of oracular verses a pivotal role for the foundation of the comic city.
45 This is the view in Flower (2008) 219.
46 On the ἄδυτον as the consultation place in the temple of Apollo, see Pi. *O.* 7.32 and Hdt. 7.141.2.

For neither adding anything would you still find a remedy, nor subtracting anything would you avoid giving offence in the eyes of the gods.

(transl. and explanatory notes Flower, 2008, 219)

The verses seem to postulate the steady preservation of oracles, since they contain the vox dei, i.e. the ipsissima verba of both Pythia and the Delphic god. It is doubtful, however, whether these verses are suited to prove an oracular orthodoxy. The warning directed at the young addressee Cyrnus, neither to add words to an oracle, nor to take away anything from it, rather corresponds with Theognis' general anxiety concerning the written transmission of the elegies, which we encounter throughout the corpus. Verses 805–10, like the σφρηγίς verses (Thgn. 19–23), which are also addressed to Cyrnus, rather self-consciously anticipate the unreliability of written verses, which can be stolen or altered by anyone (Thgn. 20f. οὔποτε κλεπτόμενα | οὐδέ τις ἀλλάξει) during future re-performances. Hence, the mention of the acknowledged Delphic oracle emphasizes the wish that the elegies should not be varied. At the same time, it clearly anticipates future re-composition.

An intermediate position between both 'oralist-performative' and 'unitarian' viewpoints – which seem to mirror the controversies surrounding Homeric epic – admits that oracles might well have been re-told orally, but that scripture also played a role in preserving and archiving oracles for particular communities. It is plausible that when writing techniques spread widely during the sixth century BCE, and grew popular in the book culture (late fifth and fourth centuries BCE), the tradition of orally transmitted verse oracles became replaced by new textual archives. According to Plutarch, the fourth century BCE historiographer Theopompus of Chios noticed that there existed only a small number of verse oracles any more (Fr5GrHist 115 F 336 = De Pyth. or. 19.403E–F).[47] This testimony shows that the decay of verse oracles happened synchronically with the transition from song culture to the book age in (Late) Classical Time. That is, the corpus of verse oracles did face similar medial conditions as did non-oracular Greek poetry. What is more, the multi-layered polyphony of the oracular 'I', in which terms such as collaboration, co-agency and mutual co-authorship describe the Pythia's role within the context of oracular performances,[48] reveals further convergences between oracular and non-oracular poetry in Archaic and Classical texts. Hence, whereas the next section deals with the Pythia's co-creative authorial voice in Herodotus, Aeschylus and the 'Homeric' Hymn to Hermes, the final section (6) roots this hybrid – in terms of gender and ontology – collaboration in Early Greek poetic production.

---

47 In his fourth century BCE speech Against Meidias (51f.), Demosthenes quotes an oracle in both prose and verse, which points to the contemporary coexistence of the two media.
48 Cf. Lewis (2014) 146 on the role of social relations within the institutional context at Delphi. Kindt (2016) and (2017) considers Delphi and its oracular shrine a paradigmatic place of religious communication. For her Herodotus' stories thus illustrate problems surrounding human-divine communication.

5 The oracular voice: a polyphonic 'I'

As section 2 has shown, the oracles delivered by Herodotus, be they in direct or indirect discourse, reveal a multi-layered oracular voice which is hardly attributable to a single speaking instance – the god Apollo, the shrine itself, or the Pythia (cf. Hdt. 1.47.3). There are only few exceptions. Accordingly, Apollo, the divine owner of the shrine, seems to speak in Hdt. 1.65, as the possessive pronoun indicates ("Ηκεις, ὦ Λυκόοργε, **ἐμὸν** ποτὶ πίονα νηὸν ["You have come, Lycurgus, to **my** rich temple"]). Moreover, 1.66 (Ἐγὼ δέ τοι οὔτι μεγαίρω ["But not all will I grudge you"]) points to Apollo's grudge,[49] the *ira dei*, and 4.157.2 and 7.141.3 have masculine participles.[50] Other passages, however, center on the Delphic shrine itself (τὸ χρηστήριον) as a neutral, quasi-impersonal agent, to which oracular commands are attributed. This is the case in Hdt. 1.13 (first mention of the oracle's agency in Herodotus), 5.79f. (on the intention of the oracle: τὸ θέλει λέγειν ἡμῖν τὸ μαντήιον) and 6.19.1f. (the shrine advises the Argives). Sometimes, however, we detect the soothsaying Pythia behind the verses, e.g., when there is a difference of the speaking voice from the male god in the third person, as in Hdt. 4.155 (Βάττ', ἐπὶ φωνὴν ἦλθες· **ἄναξ δέ σε Φοῖβος Ἀπόλλων** | ἐς Λιβύην πέμπει μηλοτρόφον οἰκιστῆρα ["Battus, though for a voice you have come, our lord, Phoebus Apollo, | Sends you to Libya – there, amid its sheep, to found a colony"]) and 4.163 (**διδοῖ ὑμῖν Λοξίης** βασιλεύειν Κυρήνης ["Loxias [. . .] permits [. . .] to sit upon the throne of Cyrene"]).[51] Another, yet weaker, criterion is information offered in the narrative frame of an oracle, such as "The Pythia gave them this response: [. . .] That, they say, was the response from the Pythia" (e.g. 1.174, 3.57f., 7.148). Finally, we read about speculations on authorial intentions, when "The Pythia ordered/meant" (1.167.3f.), or when she instructed or urged someone to follow her advice, e.g. to found a city (4.150f.).

However, any differentiation and attribution of oracular voices remains quite speculative. Instead of *one* oracular 'I', we encounter an unresolvable polyphony, or plural oracular 'I's. Thus, the principally gender-hybrid (male god vs. female priestess) and ontologically hybrid (human vs. divine agent) shaping of the oracular 'I' in Herodotus appears as a polyphonic authorial collaboration.[52] In the collaborative act, the role of the gender parameter in the oracular first person discourse grows rather indistinct and the specific peculiarities of the speaking figures' voices are blurred. As to the functions of the authorial voices included, we can hardly differentiate between the voice of the declarative author of an oracle, i.e. the god Apollo as a validator who confers divine dignity on oracles and makes sure they are

---

49 As, e.g., in Hom. *Il.* 23.865b.
50 Cf. also Hdt. 1.69.2, 4.155.3f. and 157.2, 5.80.1.
51 Yet, except from Hdt. 6.66 (Perialla) and 7.140–42 (Aristonike), we never learn the Pythia's proper name.
52 On authorial collaboration and different types of author functions, see Love (2002).

taken seriously,⁵³ and the voice of the executive-performative agent, i.e. the Pythia, who delivers the oracle in the *hic et nunc* of the mantic performance.⁵⁴ Rather, the clients at Delphi listen to both Apollo's divine voice and the Pythia's human voice, which sound in unison. Whoever cuts out one single voice of this polyphony runs the risk of muting the other one.

The co-creative role of Herodotus' Pythias in the course of her mantic sessions finds parallels in two other texts from Late Archaic and Early Classical Ages. The first is Aeschylus' final play from the extant trilogy *Oresteia* (458 BCE), the *Eumenides*, in which an anonymous Pythia delivers the prologue. At the beginning, the Delphic priestess appears in front of Apollo's temple, where Orestes has sought asylum from his pursuit by the relentless Erinyes. First, she sets out her genealogy (*Eu.* 1–8), starting from the goddesses Themis and Phoebe, the first Delphic prophetesses and drawing it down to herself. Her subsequent analogy parallels the relation of Apollo with Zeus on the one hand (*Eu.* 19 Διὸς προφήτης δ' ἐστὶ Λοξίας πατρός ["Loxias is thus the spokesman of his father Zeus"])⁵⁵ and of herself with her master Apollo on the other hand (*Eu.* 33 μαντεύομαι γὰρ ὡς ἂν ἡγῆται θεός ["for I prophesy as the god guides me"]).⁵⁶ By this, the Pythia places herself in a prophetic genealogy of divine authorization. Moreover, she sets her own role in analogy to the Delphic god and thus appears as the human collaborator of soothsaying Apollo.

The second text, yet of earlier date than the *Oresteia*, gets us closer to the Pythia's mantic co-authorship. In the 'Homeric' *Hymn to Hermes* (sixth century BCE), Apollo boasts his prophetic supremacy (vv. 533–63) in a speech to his brother, the trickster god Hermes.⁵⁷ In v. 556, he goes on mentioning his "teachers in the mantic arts" (μάντεις [. . .] διδάσκαλοι), three winged maiden figures who live at an isolated place near Mount Parnassus (i.e. Delphi). In vv. 558–63, Apollo characterizes the three mysterious sisters as follows:

---

53 Love (2002) 44f. Love presents a typology of four author-functions (*authemes*), or phases of authorial activity, which he denotes as declarative, precursory, executive, and revisionary functions of authorship. Love is here elaborating Michel Foucault's notion of the *fonction-auteur*, the classificatory function of the author's name: Foucault (1969). For recent studies in the field of literary authorship, cf. Berensmeyer *et al.* (2019).
54 On the executive author function of "the deviser, orderer, wordsmith, reformulator", cf. Love (2002) 43.
55 Cf. Flower (2008) 86.
56 See also Eur. *Ion* 321, 1322, Pl. *Phdr.* 244b.
57 Remarkably, the Pythia is absent from the *Hymn to Apollo*, often dated to the early sixth century BCE. Fontenrose (1978) 204, 215 thus suggests that she did not serve as the original mouthpiece for Apollo.

ἐντεῦθεν δἤπειτα ποτώμεναι ἄλλοτε ἄλλη | κηρία βόσκονται καί τε κραίνουσιν ἕκαστα. | αἱ δ᾽ ὅτε μὲν
θυίωσιν ἐδηδυῖαι μέλι χλωρὸν | προφρονέως ἐθέλουσιν ἀληθείην ἀγορεύειν· | ἢν δ᾽ ἀπονοσφισθῶσι
θεῶν ἡδεῖαν ἐδωδὴν | ψεύδονται δἤπειτα δι᾽ ἀλλήλων δονέουσαι.   (ed. Vergados, 2013)

> From their home they fly now here, now there, | feeding on honey-comb and bringing all
> things to pass. | And when they are inspired through eating yellow honey, | they are willing to
> speak truth; | but if they be deprived of the gods' sweet food, | then they speak falsely, as they
> swarm in and out together.   (transl. Athanassakis, 2004)

Two aspects of Apollo's speech about his prophetic teacheresses are remarkable. The first is their use of prophetic honey, which throughout antiquity was regarded not only as a symbol of sweetness, but also as a divine nourishment and source of inspiration,[58] through which poetry achieved the quality of truth.[59] Thus, the winged beings conform to a poetic image of honeybees, symbolizing the creative potential of soothsaying. Secondly, the prophetic ambiguity of the maidens "to speak truth", but also to "speak falsely", when deprived of divine honey, comes close to the warnings of the Muses in the proem of Hesiod's *Theogony* (vv. 27f.). Prior to Hesiod's poetic inspiration on Mount Helicon, they confess to know how to tell many lies that sound like the truth, but also how to sing about true things, when they are willing. Such license of poetic ambiguity characterizes Apollo's winged prophetesses in the *Hymn to Hermes*, too. Both Bee Maidens and Muses act on behalf of the same deity, Apollo, the Μουσηγέτης and Delphic Πύθιος respectively. That is, the poetry offered by the Muses and the mantic technique practiced by the Pythias appear as commensurable. Thus, the *Homeric Hymn* offers a perspective on the archaic conception of 'mantic poetry', in which the dimensions of poetry and soothsaying have merged.

This commensurability of ποιητικὴ and μαντικὴ τέχνη survives well into Plato's times. In the *Phaedrus*, which, among other things, deals with divine inspiration and the state of μανία ("madness"), Socrates offers a typology of different μανίαι, i.e. forms of divine possession (265a9–b5). He links every type of μανία to a single god as a source of legitimacy for madness.[60] While Socrates assigns prophetic

---

[58] On inspiration in ancient poetry, cf. Tigerstedt (1970), Murray (1981), Thraede (1998), Spentzou/Fowler (2002).

[59] On bees and honey as ancient means for poetical or divinatory inspiration, cf. Waszink (1974) 9–11, Nünlist (1998) 300–306; on the Pythia as "Delphic bee", Pi. *P.* 4.60. On the 'Bee oracle', Scheinberg (1979) 22–4; Vergados (2013) 17–22, ad loc. On the so-called Μέλισσαι ("Bee maidens"), who served as priestesses of the Ephesian Artemis, von Fritz (1931) 526 and Scherrer (2007) 325, who also mentions the supposed connection of the Latin word *apis* ("bee") with the Hittite name of Ephesos, Apaša.

[60] Socrates makes four divisions of the divine madness, thus ascribing prophecy to Apollo, the mystic madness to Dionysus, the poetic to the Muses, and the madness of love to Aphrodite and Eros.

madness to mantic inspiration (μαντικὴ ἐπίπνοια)⁶¹ caused by the god Apollo, he connects poetic madness with the inspirational gift of the Muses. This parallelism of both types of divinely motivated madness reveals that still Plato (or his spokesperson Socrates) considered divination and poetry as two adjacent phenomena and cultural techniques (τέχναι).⁶²

6 Closing remarks on Pythian authorship and hybrid collaboration

From the literary portrayals of the Pythia and the oracular god in Herodotus and in Aeschylus' *Eumenides*, and of the Muse-like Bee Maidens in the *Hymn to Hermes*, we can conclude that their mutual relationship appears as a hybrid collaboration. The underlying hybridity is twofold, in terms of the ontological status – between human and divine being⁶³ – and of the gender parameter involved – between female prophetess and male deity. During the inspirational process, i.e. in the *hic et nunc* of the oracular performance, the hybrid voices of Pythia and Apollo merge and become indistinguishable. Such 'acting in unison' forms the characteristic ambiguity of oracular polyphony.⁶⁴

However, the oracular practice of hybrid collaboration and co-creative authorship forms no exception in the realm of Early Greek poetic production. Another, yet most prominent example is the collaboration between inspired singer and Muse in Archaic poetry. Accordingly, the bard Phemius in the *Odyssey* calls himself a poetic autodidact who is also inspired by the goddess (*Od.* 22.347–348a αὐτοδίδακτος δ' εἰμί, θεὸς δέ μοι ἐν φρεσὶν οἴμας | παντοίας ἐνέφυσεν). This 'dual motivation',⁶⁵

---

61 Similarly, the first century CE author of *On the Sublime* – [Longin.] (13.2) – considers that the Pythia acquired divine inspiration through an extraneous spirit, causing her to pronounce oracles through exhalation (ἐπίπνοια).
62 Pl. *Ap.* 21a reveals the exceptional significance of Delphi for Socrates. The Pythia gave an oracle to Socrates' friend Chairephon, saying that no man is wiser than Socrates, which was the beginning of lifelong attempts to falsify this hypothesis. In the same speech (*Ap.* 22c), Socrates compares poets to those who pronounce oracles, who are all ἐνθουσιάζοντες ("filled with the god"). Cf. Pl. *Ion* 533e–534a, *Men.* 99d. See also Maurizio (1995) 77.
63 Only the Bee Maidens of the *Hymn*, who consume the "gods' sweet food" (v. 562), appear as quasi-divine beings.
64 However, the Pythia can explain or interpret a particular oracle in retrospect (cf. Hdt. 1.93), thereby gaining a certain degree of autonomy and religious authority at her service for the Delphic Apollo. Thus, she mediates and communicates divine knowledge and lends it a human dimension by making it accessible to her clients at Delphi.
65 On this concept of poetic production, cf. Lesky (1961), Murray (1981), Schlesier (2004) and (2006).

which oscillates between the poles of human technique and the divine gift of inspiration, is a widespread phenomenon, which has found various expressions throughout Archaic Greek poetry, inside[66] and outside Homeric epic.[67] The relation of Pythia and Apollo, however, appears as gender-inverted in comparison with the relation of bard and Muse. In both gender-hybrid (and ontologically hybrid) connections, agency and responsibility are divided between divine instance and human performer.[68] The omniscient divine agents (Apollo, the Muses) impart information to, and complement the spatio-temporally limited knowledge of, the deficient human agents (seers or singers). The latter communicate this knowledge to their audiences and recall remote places and times, making them 'present' during the poetic/mantic performance.[69] Such conveyance of divine knowledge legitimates the high prestige of both bard and prophetess. Whereas the blindness of the singer Demodocus is the somatic symptom of aoidic impartiality – unable of autopsy, he conveys the knowledge of the Muses as a substitute (*Od.* 8.63f.) – that discerns the singer from his audience, the Pythia's mantic knowledge does not stem from her own experience either. To conclude, in terms of successful hybrid collaboration, on which their knowledge bases, the Pythia and the archaic singer become commensurable agents in the context of Early Greek poetry.

Someone might argue that poetic, or literary, entertainment – τέρψις is a principal effect of Homeric song according to epic itself (*Od.* 8.367f.)[70] – is alien to the concept of Delphic truth. Yet, most of our fragmentary knowledge of the Pythia rests on literary depictions that follow generic conventions and narrative agendas, which also aim to create aesthetic pleasure. The enigmatic oracular god himself, however, shall give the ultimate response. In the *Hymn to Hermes*, Apollo advises

---

66 The successful collaboration between epic singer and the Muses is also a theme in the proem of the Iliadic Catalogue of Ships (*Il.* 2.484–93). The mnemo-technical achievement of the resulting catalogue itself proves this success. However, the embedded episode of the Thracian singer Thamyris deals with the critical change from poetic synergy to antagonism between human agent and deity in the same catalogue (*Il.* 2.594–600). After Thamyris boasted his superiority to the Muses, they took away from him the art of singing (ἀοιδή) in revenge. On the relation between the (male) bard and the female Muses and Graces in Pindar see Hauser in this volume, esp. p. 134–136.
67 Hes. *Th.* 31b–32, Archil. fr. 1 W. juxtapose external forces of inspiration and internal first-person voices, too.
68 On the role of gender and female contribution to prophetic communication, implying both divine and human agency, in the Ancient Near East and Ancient Greece, cf. Nissinen (2013) and (2017) 297–325.
69 Cf. the poet's praise of the Muses' omniscience in *Il.* 2.485 (ὑμεῖς γὰρ θεαί ἐστε, πάρεστέ τε, ἴστέ τε πάντα). Similarly, the amazed Odysseus in *Od.* 8.491 praises Demodocus' artful ability to guide his listeners to places and landscapes, which the blind singer himself has never seen himself (ὥς τέ που ἢ αὐτὸς παρεών).
70 ταῦτ' ἄρ ἀοιδὸς ἄειδε περικλυτός· αὐτὰρ Ὀδυσσεὺς | τέρπετ' ἐνὶ φρεσὶν ᾗσιν ἀκούων ἠδὲ καὶ ἄλλοι (ed. van Thiel, 1991) ("That was the poet's song. Odysseus | was happy listening; so were they all", transl. Wilson, 2017).

Hermes to consult the prophetesses on Mount Parnassus – i.e. the Delphic Pythias – and to delight on their answer (564b–565a): "Inquire of them exactly for the truth | and delight your heart" (σὺ δ' ἀτρεκέως ἐρεείνων | σὴν αὐτοῦ φρένα τέρπε).

Bibliography

Texts and translations

Claudius Aelianus. *De natura animalium*. Ediderunt Manuela García Valdés *et al.*, Berlin/New York 2009.
Herodoti *Historiae*. *Tomus prior libros I–IV continens*. Recognovit breviuqe adnotatione critica instruxit Nigel G. Wilson, Oxford 2015.
Herodotus, *The Histories*. Translated by Tom Holland. With an Introduction and Notes by Paul Cartledge, London 2013.
Homeri *Odyssea*. Recognovit Helmut van Thiel, Hildesheim *et al.* 1991.
Homer, *The Odyssey*. Translated by Emily Wilson, New York 2017.
The Homeric Hymn to Hermes. Introduction, Text and Commentary by Athanassios Vergados, Berlin/Boston 2013.
The Homeric Hymns. Translation, Introduction, and Notes by Apostolos N. Athanassakis, Baltimore ²2004.
Iambi et elegi Graeci ante Alexandrum cantati. Edidit Martin L. West. Volumen 1. Archilochus, Hipponax, Theognidea, Oxford ²1998.
Lucan, *The Civil War. Books I–IX*. English translation by James D. Duff, Cambridge, MA 1928.
Pindari *carmina cum fragmentis*. Pars I. Epinicia post Brunonem Snell. Edidit Hervicus Maehler. Editio stereotypa editionis octavae (MCMLXXXVII), Berlin/New York 2008.
Pindar, *Olympian Odes. Pythian Odes*. Edited and translated by William B. Race, Cambridge, MA/London 1997.
Plato in Twelve Volumes, Vol. 9. English translation by Harold N. Fowler, Cambridge, MA 1925.
Platonis *Opera. Tomus II tetralogias III–IV continens*. Recognovit breviuqe adnotatione critica instruxit Ioannes Burnet, Oxford 1901.
Plutarch's *Moralia* in Sixteen Volumes, *Vol.* 5. English Translation by Frank C. Babbitt, Cambridge, MA 1936.
Plutarchs Schrift *De Pythiae Oraculis*. Text, Einleitung und Kommentar von Stephan Schröder, Stuttgart 1990.

Books and articles

Amandry (1950): Pierre Amandry, *La mantique Apollinienne à Delphes. Essai sur le fonctionnement de l'oracle*, Paris.
Asheri et al. (2007): David Asheri, Alan Lloyd and Aldo Corcella (eds.), *A Commentary on Herodotus: Books I–IV. Edited by Oswyn Murray and Alfonso Moreno*, Oxford.
Bendlin (2006): Andreas Bendlin, "Vom Nutzen und Nachteil der Mantik: Orakel im Medium von Handlung und Literatur in der Zeit der Zweiten Sophistik", in: Dorothee Elm von der Osten,

Jörg Rüpke and Katharina Waldner (eds.), *Texte als Medium und Reflexion von Religion im römischen Reich*, Stuttgart, 159–207.

Berensmeyer et al. (2012): Ingo Berensmeyer, Geert Buelens and Marysa Demoor, "Authorship As Cultural Performance: New Perspectives in Authorship Studies", *ZAA* 60/1, 5–29.

Berensmeyer et al. (2019): Ingo Berensmeyer, Geert Buelens and Marysa Demoor (eds.), *The Cambridge Handbook of Literary Authorship*, Cambridge.

Biggs/Travlou (2015): Simon Biggs, Penny Travlou, "Distributed Authorship and Creative Communities", in: Scott Rettberg, Patricia Tomaszek and Sandy Baldwin (eds.), *Electronic Literature Communities*, Morgantown, WV, 29–44.

Bonnechere (2007): Pierre Bonnechere, "Divination", in: Daniel Ogden (ed.), *A Companion to Greek Religion*, Chichester, 145–159.

Bowden (2005): Hugh Bowden, *Classical Athens and the Delphic Oracle: Divination and Democracy*, Cambridge.

Burkert (1985): Walter Burkert, *Greek Religion*, transl. John Raffan, Cambridge, MA (German Stuttgart 1977).

Burkert (2005): Walter Burkert, "Signs, commands, and knowledge: Ancient divination between enigma and epiphany", in: Sarah I. Johnston and Peter T. Struck (eds.), *Mantikê: Studies in Ancient Divination*, Leiden, 29–49.

Calame (2004): Claude Calame, "Identités d'auteur à l'exemple de la Grèce classique: signatures, énontiations, citation", in: Claude Calame and Roger Chartier (eds.), *Identités d'auteur dans l'Antiquité et la tradition européenne*, Grenoble, 11–39.

Casali (2011): Sergio Casali, "The *Bellum Civile* as an Anti-*Aeneid*", in: Paolo Asso (ed.), *Brill's Companion to Lucan*, Leiden, 81–109.

Chamberlain (2001): David Chamberlain, ""We the Others": Interpretive Community and Plural Voice in Herodotus", *ClAnt* 20/1, 5–34.

Compton (1994): Todd Compton, "The Herodotean Mantic Session at Delphi", *RhM* 137, 217–223.

Dewald (1981): Carolyn Dewald, "Women and culture in Herodotus' *Histories*", *Women's Studies* 8, 93–127.

Dodds (1951): Eric R. Dodds, *The Greeks and the Irrational*, Berkeley.

Fairbanks (1906): Arthur Fairbanks, "Herodotus and the Oracle at Delphi", *CJ* 1/2, 37–48.

Farnell (1907): Lewis R. Farnell, *The Cults of the Greek States*, vol. 4, Oxford.

Fauth (1963): Wolfgang Fauth, "Pythia", in: *RE* 24/1, coll. 515–547.

Fischer (2002): Irmtraud Fischer, *Gotteskünderinnen. Zu einer geschlechtsfairen Deutung des Phänomens der Prophetie und der Prophetinnen in der Hebräischen Bibel*, Stuttgart.

Flower (2008): Michael A. Flower, *The Seer in Ancient Greece*, Berkeley et al.

Fontenrose (1978): Joseph E. Fontenrose, *The Delphic Oracle. Its Responses and Operations with a Catalogue of Responses*, Berkeley.

Forrest (1957): William G. F. Forrest, "Colonisation and the Rise of Delphi", *Historia* 6, 160–175.

Foucault (1969): Michel Foucault, "Qu'est-ce qu'un auteur?", *Bulletin de la Société française de philosophie* 63, 75–104.

Hagedorn (2013): Anselm C. Hagedorn, "The Role of Female Seer/Prophet in Ancient Greece", in: Jonathan Stökl and Corrine Carvalho (eds.), *Prophets Male and Female. Gender and Prophesy in the Hebrew Bible, the Eastern Mediterranean, and the Ancient Near East*, Atlanta, 101–125.

Hall (2014): Jonathan M. Hall, *Artifact and Artifice. Classical Archeology and the Ancient Historian*, Chicago/London.

Hauser (2016): Emily Hauser, "In Her Own Words: The Semantics of Female Authorship in Ancient Greece, From Sappho to Nossis", *Ramus* 45/2, 133–164.

Jones (1986): Christopher P. Jones, *Culture and Society in Lucian*, Cambridge, MA/London.

Kindt (2006): Julia Kindt, "Delphic Oracle stories and the beginning of historiography: Herodotus' Croesus logos", *ClassPhil* 101, 34–51.
Kindt (2016): Julia Kindt, *Revisiting Delphi. Religion and Storytelling in Ancient Greece*, Cambridge.
Kindt (2017): Julia Kindt, The Inspired Voice. Enigmatic Oracular Communication, in: Richard J. A. Talbert and Fred S. Naiden (eds.), *Mercury's Wings: Exploring Modes of Communication in the Ancient World*, Oxford, 211–228.
Latour (2005): Bruno Latour, *Reassembling the Social: An Introduction to Actor-Network-Theory*, Oxford.
Lesky (1961): Albin Lesky, *Göttliche und menschliche Motivation im homerischen Epos*, Heidelberg.
Lewis (2014): Rosemary Lewis, *The Role of the Pythia at Delphi: ancient and modern perspectives*, Pretoria 2014 (dissertation: http://uir.unisa.ac.za/handle/10500/18723, 03/05/2022).
Lloyd-Jones (1976): Hugh Lloyd-Jones, "The Delphic Oracle", *Greece and Rome* 23, 60–73.
Love (2002): Harold Love, *Attributing Authorship. An Introduction*, Cambridge.
Maurizio (1995): Lisa Maurizio, "Anthropology and Spirit Possession: A Reconsideration of the Pythia's Role at Delphi", *JHS* 115, 69–86.
Maurizio (1997): Lisa Maurizio, "Delphic oracles as oral performances: authenticity and historical evidence", *ClAnt* 16/2, 308–334.
Maurizio (2001): Lisa Maurizio, "The voice at the center of the world: the Pythias' ambiguity and authority", in: André Lardinois and Laura McClure (eds.), *Making Silence Speak: Women's Voices in Greek Literature and Society*, Princeton, 38–54.
McLeod (1961): Wallace E. McLeod, "Oral bards at Delphi", *TAPhA* 92, 317–325.
Mikalson (2003): Jon D. Mikalson, *Herodotus and Religion in the Persian Wars*, Chapel Hill, NC.
Murray (1981): Penelope Murray, "Poetic Inspiration in Early Greece", *JHS* 101, 87–100.
Nissinen (2013): Martti Nissinen, "Gender and Prophetic Agency in the Ancient Near East and in Greece", in: Jonathan Stökl and Corrine Carvalho (eds.), *Prophets Male and Female. Gender and Prophesy in the Hebrew Bible, the Eastern Mediterranean, and the Ancient Near East*, Atlanta, 27–58.
Nissinen (2017): Martti Nissinen, *Ancient Prophesy. Near Eastern, Biblical, and Greek Perspectives*, Oxford.
Nünlist (1998): René Nünlist, *Poetologische Bildersprache In der frühgriechischen Dichtung*, Stuttgart/Leipzig.
Padel (1983): Ruth Padel, "Women: Model for Possession by Greek Daemons", in: Averil Cameron and Amélie Kuhrt (eds.), *Images of Women in Antiquity*, Detroit, 3–19.
Parke (1939): Herbert W. Parke, *A History of the Delphic Oracle*, Oxford.
Parke (1981): Herbert W. Parke, "Apollo and the Muses, or Prophecy in Greek Verse", *Hermathena* 130/31, 99–112.
Parke/Wormell (1956): Herbert W. Parke and Donald E. W. Wormell (eds.), *The Delphic Oracle. Vol. I: The History. Vol. II: The Oracular Responses*, Oxford.
Rohde (1898): Erwin Rohde, *Psyche. Seelencult und Unsterblichkeitsglaube der Griechen*, vol. 2, Freiburg et al.
Rosenberger (2013): Veit Rosenberger, *Divination in the Ancient World: Religious Options and the Individual*, Stuttgart.
Scheinberg (1979): Susan Scheinberg, "The Bee Maidens of the *Homeric Hymn to Hermes*", *HSPh* 83, 1–28.
Scherrer (2007): Peter Scherrer, "Von Apaša nach Hagios Theologos – Die Siedlungsgeschichte des Raumes Ephesos von prähistorischer bis in byzantinische Zeit unter dem Aspekt der maritimen und fluvialen Bedingungen", *Jahreshefte ÖAI* 76, 321–351.
Schlesier (2004): Renate Schlesier, "Künstlerische Kreation und religiöse Erfahrung – Verwendungsgeschichtliche Anmerkungen zum Begriff der Inspiration", in: Gert Mattenklott

(ed.), *Ästhetische Erfahrung im Zeichen der Entgrenzung der Künste. Epistemische, ästhetische und religiöse Formen von Erfahrung im Vergleich*, Hamburg, 177–194.

Schlesier (2006): Renate Schlesier, "Platons Erfindung des wahnsinnigen Dichters. Ekstasis und Enthusiasmos als poetisch-religiöse Erfahrung", *Zeitschrift für Ästhetik und Allgemeine Kunstwissenschaft* 51, 45–60.

Schnurr-Redfort (2006): Christine Schnurr-Redfort, "Weissagung und Macht: Die Pythia", in: Thomas Spät and Beate Wagner-Hasel (eds.), *Frauenwelten in der Antike. Geschlechterordnung und weibliche Lebenspraxis*, Stuttgart/Weimar (revised and reprinted version of Darmstadt 2000), 132–146.

Schröder (2010): Stephan Schröder, "Plutarch on Oracles and Divine Inspiration", in: Heinz-Günther Nesselrath (ed.), *On the Daimonion of Socrates*, Tübingen, 145–168.

Spentzou/Fowler (2002): Efrossini Spentzou and Don Fowler (eds.), *Cultivating the Muse – Struggles for Power and Inspiration in Classical Literature*, Oxford.

Thraede (1998): Klaus Thraede, "Inspiration", in: *RAC* 18, coll. 331–334.

Thum (2013): Tobias Thum, *Plutarchs Dialog De E apud Delphos. Eine Studie*, Tübingen.

Tigerstedt (1970): Eugène N. Tigerstedt, "*Furor Poeticus*: Poetic Inspiration in Greek Literature before Democritus and Plato", *Journal of the History of Ideas* 31, 163–178.

Ustinova (2009): Yulia Ustinova, *Caves and the Ancient Greek Mind: Descending Underground in the Search for Ultimate Truth*, Oxford.

von Fritz (1931): Kurt von Fritz, "Melissa", in: *RE* XV/1, coll. 524–528.

Waszink (1974): Jan H. Waszink, *Biene und Honig als Symbol des Dichters und der Dichtung in der griechisch-römischen Antike*, Opladen.

Luca Basso
Costruire un 'io' divino: Ovidio e le dee

Abstract: The paper examines Ovid's conversations with some of the most important goddesses in the *Fasti* (Juno, Venus, and Flora), and underlines the features that define their feminine qualities as a strategy of self-representation, investigating how the definition of an 'I' shaped according to a gender parameter, even at the level of non-human characters, interacts with male cultural codes and values. The focus on divinities, i.e., on characters imbued with cultural significance and highly conscious of their own civilizing role, allows us to better understand the Ovidian model of construction of a complex Roman identity, based on the interaction of manifold forces, including the relationship between masculine and feminine.

Keywords: *Fasti*, Roman identity, Juno, Venus, Flora, divine informants

1 Introduzione

In una recente monografia dedicata ai *Fasti*, Angeline Chiu ha illustrato le strategie impiegate da Ovidio per costruire un'idea di romanità più complessa e dinamica rispetto al modello virile rappresentato dalla tradizione virgiliana e liviana, e patrocinato dalle politiche culturali del principato augusteo.[1] La studiosa, con un'analisi di tipo contrastivo, discute diversi episodi ovidiani facendoli interagire con le versioni parallele presenti nell'*Eneide* o nella narrazione liviana, e dimostra come il poeta dei *Fasti* tenda a valorizzare elementi trascurati (o messi in secondo piano) dai suoi modelli, tra i quali spiccano in modo particolare le figure femminili. Personaggi femminili di varia natura, umani e divini, nobili e popolari, prima assenti o secondari, si impongono come protagonisti forti nella narrazione dei *Fasti*, introducendo un punto di vista alternativo su importanti vicende della tradizione. La sfida di Ovidio è a un paradigma di identità romana che rischia di essere parziale: per inserire voci alternative, il poeta sfrutta l'elemento 'altro' per eccellenza, la donna, in modo da arricchire le prospettive del lettore su una realtà culturale e sociale più complessa di quanto possa suggerire una visione troppo rigida della tradizione.

Prendendo le mosse da questa stimolante lettura della Chiu, vorrei qui soffermarmi su una categoria ristretta di personaggi femminili, cioè le dee. La mia attenzione va, in particolare, a quelle che entrano in relazione diretta con il poeta, comparendo davanti

---

[1] Chiu (2016). Il lavoro della Chiu si inserisce in una feconda corrente di studi, che esplorano la tendenza dei *Fasti* a valorizzare elementi culturali sacrificati da una tradizione letteraria ormai consolidata (virgiliana *in primis*): cfr. per es. Fantham (1992); Brugnoli/Stok (1992); Fantham (2002); Murgatroyd (2005).

a lui come interlocutrici, e che contribuiscono a costruire in prima persona la propria immagine divina.[2] Attraverso una valutazione degli elementi che definiscono la qualità femminile di questi personaggi, cercherò di valutare come la definizione di un 'io' costruito secondo il parametro del genere interagisca con codici e valori di stampo maschile. È interessante portare questo tipo di lettura al livello dei soggetti non umani, perché le divinità sono personaggi particolarmente densi di significato a livello culturale, e peraltro, nei *Fasti*, sono anche discretamente consapevoli della propria valenza civilizzatrice e identitaria. Valutare l'apporto dell'elemento femminile nell'autorappresentazione divina è perciò un buon modo per mettere alla prova quel paradigma ovidiano di costruzione della romanità fondato su una interazione di forze molteplici.

2 Giunone

Ab Iunone principium. La regina degli dei compare in diversi punti del poema sul calendario, e oltre ad essere menzionata come destinataria di culti, entra in scena anche come personaggio.[3] All'inizio del sesto libro dei *Fasti*, in una disputa erudita relativa all'etimologia del nome di giugno, Giunone interviene per prima a rivendicare il dominio su tale nome (6,21–64): *Iunius* deriverebbe da *Iuno*, come omaggio rivolto dai Romani alla loro regina. Giunone entra in scena in modo solenne, per non dire minaccioso. Il suo ingresso è anticipato da un riferimento al giudizio di Paride (15sq.: [*deas uidi*] *nec quas Priamides in aquosae uallibus Idae / contulit: ex illis sed tamen una fuit*, "[scorsi le dee] né quelle che il Priamide giudicò nelle valli dell'Ida ricco di acque: ma una di esse vi era"),[4] richiamo assai poco opportuno nell'introdurre la dea che meno di tutte aveva mandato giù la scelta del Troiano. L'analogia infelice di Ovidio, nell'abile costruzione di un contesto, ha l'effetto di porre fin da subito il poeta in una posizione delicata, diciamo pure potenzialmente pericolosa, che fa risaltare per contrasto l'imponenza di Giunone. Quando la dea entra in scena, il poeta la riconosce subito, per averla vista più volte raffigurata sul Campidoglio (17sq.), e subito rabbrividisce di paura (19). È Giunone stessa, nell'esordio del discorso, a rassicurare il poeta, sostenendo che il diritto di vedere una divinità gli è attribuito in virtù della sua funzione di *Romani conditor anni* (21–24). Da subito, dunque, il rapporto tra poeta e interlocutrice è improntato a una notevole distanza, e Giunone stessa fa emergere, con la propria condiscendenza, l'orgoglio del proprio rango.

---

[2] Sulla presenza e il ruolo degli dei come informanti nel poema vd. per es. Rutledge (1980); Miller (1983); Murgatroyd (2005); Graf (2016).
[3] Studi piuttosto circostanziati sulla figura di Giunone nei *Fasti* sono Lieberg (1969); Kötzle (1991) 89–176; più recentemente Poletti (2017).
[4] Il testo italiano dei *Fasti* è quello di Canali (1998), eccetto che per i passi dei colloqui con Venere e Flora, per i quali adotto una mia traduzione. Per le *Metamorfosi* la traduzione è di Chiarini in Rosati (2009).

La tesi centrale del discorso (26: *Iunius a nostro nomine nomen habet*, "il nome di giugno deriva dal mio nome") è argomentata da Giunone sulla base della propria rilevanza nel contesto della civiltà romana (rilevanza che da sola dovrebbe squalificare qualsiasi tesi concorrenziale). Fondamentale, dunque, è il ritratto che Giunone costruisce di sé all'interno del discorso per rendere evidente questa sua centralità culturale; e tale immagine appare orientata prima di tutto dalla sua identità femminile. La dea, infatti, definisce la sua posizione nel panorama religioso in relazione alle figure maschili della propria famiglia. Per prima cosa ricorda di essere sposa e sorella di Giove (27sq.: *est aliquid nupsisse Ioui, Iouis esse sororem: / fratre magis dubito glorier anne uiro*, "conta qualcosa essere la sposa di Giove, e di Giove sorella: non so se gloriarmi maggiormente del fratello o dello sposo"), saldando l'elemento del matrimonio alla componente del *genus* (Giove è suo fratello), quest'ultima poi ampliata dalla menzione del padre (29sq.: *si genus aspicitur, Saturnum prima parentem / feci*, "se si guarda alla stirpe, io per prima chiamai padre Saturno"); da qui torna ancora al matrimonio (33: *si torus in pretio est, dicor matrona Tonantis*, "se il talamo è in pregio, mi spetta il titolo di consorte del Tonante").[5] La dignità di Giunone è dunque definita preliminarmente in base a due rapporti familiari presentati in parallelo (29, 33: *si genus aspicitur – si torus in pretio est*). Si noterà facilmente l'esito lievemente paradossale dell'uso di *matrona* nell'espressione *matrona Tonantis* (Littlewood parla di "humorously incongruous juxtaposition"),[6] ma l'umorismo sotteso a una tale qualifica serve proprio a denunciare l'operazione con cui Ovidio trasferisce un modello di costruzione dell'identità femminile entro le soglie del pantheon romano. Come qualsiasi donna romana, Giunone è, prima di tutto, figlia e moglie di qualcuno.

Ma un secondo esito paradossale è ravvisabile all'interno del tema matrimoniale e nell'orgoglio di Giunone per la propria condizione matronale. Subito dopo aver proclamato la sua relazione con Giove, la dea cita a sostegno della sua tesi il caso di Maia, che avrebbe dato il nome al mese precedente (*Maius*): se questo onore fu concesso a una concubina, perché non dovrebbe toccare alla moglie del sommo dio? (35sq.: *an potuit Maio paelex dare nomina mensi, / hic honor in nobis inuidiosus erit?*, "Ma come! Una concubina poté dare il suo nome al mese di maggio, e invece tale onore sarà negato a me?"). Il ragionamento *a fortiori* sarebbe perfettamente logico, se il soggetto maschile coinvolto non fosse in entrambi i casi Giove (con cui Maia si era unita dando alla luce Mercurio). Certo, Ovidio non rinuncia a farci sorridere della *nonchalance* di Giunone, che poco più avanti tornerà a ribadire la concordia matrimoniale che a Roma la unisce al suo sposo (52: *hic colar, hic teneam cum Ioue templa*

---

5 Un motivo, quello della *soror-coniunx* di Giove, che Ovidio riprende anche nelle *Metamorfosi* dall'epica virgiliana, cfr. Verg. *Aen.* 1,46sq., Ov. *Met.* 3,265sq. con la nota ad loc. di Barchiesi/Rosati (2007).
6 Littlewood (2006) ad loc.

meo, "qui io sia venerata e occupi il tempio insieme con il mio Giove").[7] Ma in realtà nel cortocircuito che si crea tra la volontà di ostentare la propria relazione matrimoniale e quella di stabilire la propria superiorità sull'amante del marito, leggiamo la complessità di un personaggio che, nelle esigenze dell'autorappresentazione, deve affrontare aspetti contrastanti del proprio ruolo femminile: Giunone è matrona, ma, come molte matrone, deve anche fare i conti con un marito infedele.

Il quadro delle relazioni familiari di Giunone è completato infine dalla sua linea di discendenza, che comprende personaggi tra i più rappresentativi della tradizione virile di Roma, Marte e Romolo. È stato Marte, infatti, a stabilire l'influenza della madre sulla città del nipote (53sq.: *ipse mihi Mauors 'commendo moenia' dixit / 'haec tibi: tu pollens urbe nepotis eris'*, "Marte stesso mi disse: 'ti affido queste mura; tu sarai potente nella città di tuo nipote'"; un riferimento a Romolo è poi ancora al v. 64: *nostri Roma nepotis erat*). Nell'accorta costruzione del suo discorso, dunque, Giunone sfrutta un paradigma tradizionale di rappresentazione femminile, allineandosi al ruolo di figlia, sposa e madre che ci si aspetta da una donna di alto livello. L'interazione con le componenti maschili centrali del pantheon romano rientra tra le strategie di argomentazione della brillante retorica di Giunone, che sa quale effetto possa produrre l'esibizione di una dignità matronale, perfettamente integrata nella mentalità sociale di Roma.

3 Venere

Su tutt'altro linguaggio punta Venere, la grande patrona del mese di aprile, che da lei (o meglio, dal suo nome greco), secondo Ovidio, prende il nome. Il quarto libro si apre in modo brillante, con uno scambio di battute tra il poeta e la dea, e anche questa volta il contesto narrativo rivela molto del tipo di relazione che si instaura tra gli interlocutori.[8] Non c'è nulla della gravità che caratterizza l'entrata in scena di Giunone. Ovidio invoca Venere chiedendo la sua protezione (4,1: *'alma faue', dixi 'geminorum mater Amorum'*, "'Vieni propizia, alma Venere', dissi, 'madre dei due Amori'"), e prima della risposta fornisce un dettaglio narrativo (2: *ad uatem uoltus rettulit illa suos*, "lei rivolse lo sguardo al poeta"). Tutta la grazia di Venere è racchiusa nel piccolo gesto di condiscendenza: non si tratta, come per Giunone, della degnazione di una sovrana, ma della cortese attenzione di una donna che sa di essere oggetto di desiderio. Il brevissimo dialogo che segue ha le movenze di un *flirt*: Venere risponde facendo l'offesa (3: *'quid tibi' ait 'mecum? certe maiora canebas'*, "'che hai da fare con me? Non volevi cantare argo-

---

[7] L'unità dei due coniugi era evocata dalla menzione del tempio condiviso già al v. 34: *iunctaque Tarpeio sunt mea templa Ioui*, "e il mio tempio è congiunto con quello di Giove Tarpeo".

[8] Sul ruolo di Venere, e in particolare sul proemio al quarto libro, vd. Barchiesi (1994) 45sq.; Pasco-Pranger (2006); Fucecchi (2010).

menti più impegnati?'"), e poi passa all'ironia pungente (4: *num uetus in molli pectore uolnus habes?*, "porti forse ancora nel cuore l'antica ferita?"). Il poeta, da parte sua, si limita a una risposta piena di sottinteso, che tradisce la confidenza tra i due, fondata su una consuetudine passata (5: *'scis dea', respondi, 'de uolnere'*, "tu sai tutto, o dea, della mia ferita"). Tra Ovidio e Venere si instaura una vera relazione, fondata su una componente fisica: la dea guarda il poeta, ride alla sua battuta (5sq.), e infine, per confermare la sua investitura, lo tocca con un ramo di mirto (15sq.). Il rapporto tra i due si configura come una naturale attrazione tra i sessi. L' 'io' femminile di Venere interagisce strettamente con quello di Ovidio (emerge bene dalla dialettica *tibi-mecum* nella risposta piccata della dea: *quid tibi, ait, mecum?*), sfruttando un paradigma di civetteria funzionale all'affermazione dell'identità del personaggio. Fin dal proemio la grazia di Venere è costruita come una caratteristica femminile tale da attrarre un uomo, prima ancora che un poeta.

Questa accentuata femminilità si trova a interagire con codici e valori ad essa estranei. Prima di tutto il lettore è invitato a instaurare un confronto ideale con la figura divina che inaugura il libro precedente, cioè Marte. Marzo e aprile, infatti, costituiscono una coppia tematica e i due libri si aprono, rispettivamente, con Marte e Venere, i progenitori divini di Roma.[9] Se paragonata alla brillante apparizione di Venere all'inizio del quarto libro, la figura di Marte, nel terzo, è caratterizzata da un evidente imbarazzo: fin dalle prime parole Ovidio commenta l'incompatibilità teorica del dio con il contesto del poema religioso (3,1-4) e l'invito a presentarsi *depositis clipeo et hasta* suggerisce la difficoltà di adattare questa figura tradizionale ai codici e ai linguaggi dell'opera presente.[10] Dopo una lunga sezione relativa alle origini di Roma, Marte interviene in prima persona a parlare, ed egli stesso ammette di ritrovarsi in un ruolo che non è il suo (173sq.: *nunc primum studiis pacis, deus utilis armis / aduocor, et gressus in noua castra fero*, "ora per la prima volta, io, nume fatto per la guerra, sono chiamato a impegni di pace ed entro in un nuovo campo"). L'autopresentazione di Marte, com'è comprensibile, mette in primo piano elementi che si possono facilmente ricondurre al mondo virile e guerresco: *armis* (messo in risalto dall'*enjambement*), *gressus* (termine che rimanda alle marce militari, da cui il nome di *Gradiuus*), *castra*. Tale modello è esibito appunto per rendere più scoperto il problema della sua adattabilità al poema, e ad intensificare il paradosso di un Marte elegiaco concorre anche la domanda di Ovidio, che chiede come mai il suo mese si apra, alle Calende, con una delle feste più 'femminili', i *Matronalia*, celebrata solo dalle donne. L' 'io' di Marte, che non sa rinunciare a un paradigma fortemente maschile di rappresentazione (si noti che l'invito a togliersi le armi il dio lo accoglie solo a metà,

---

9 Sulla struttura 'a coppie tematiche' del calendario ovidiano vd. Braun (1981); Hübner (1999); Pasco-Pranger (2006).
10 La figura di Marte nei *Fasti* è stata approfonditamente indagata da Merli (2000), soprattutto per la sua presenza problematica, in quanto dio della guerra, in un poema elegiaco che tratta di argomenti pacifici; importanti osservazioni sul ruolo 'metapoetico' di Marte anche in Hinds (1992).

171sq.), non instaura con il poeta un rapporto armonico, dà l'impressione di rimanere 'fuori posto' nel poema, tanto che, dopo aver tentato qualche spiegazione alla domanda sui *Matronalia*, il dio sparisce improvvisamente, lasciando il poeta nella necessità di trovare un'altra fonte di informazioni (259sq.).

La contrapposizione con Venere è perciò ricca di significato. La dea si trova perfettamente a suo agio nel poema, e sembra che la sua 'adattabilità' sia in qualche modo mediata a livello narrativo dalla costruzione di una (attraente) identità femminile. Anche Venere (come Marte, ma in modo rovesciato) si trova a interagire con codici diversi dal suo. Il suo dialogo con il poeta, infatti, è seguito da una lunga sezione sulla gloriosa storia di Roma, a partire dai re di Alba Longa, passando per Romolo e Remo e arrivando, ovviamente, alla casata dei Giulii, di cui lei è patrona. Si tratta di una storia essenzialmente maschile, aderente alla tradizione eroica e virile di Roma, ma l'immagine di Venere non è danneggiata dalla competizione con questo filone culturale. La dea risulta perfettamente integrata in un discorso ampio sulla romanità, e anzi la sua figura finisce per conciliare in modo programmatico le diverse anime del poema.

4 Flora

Su un terreno simile, ma in forma più complessa, si muove anche Flora, uno dei personaggi più generosi di dettagli autobiografici nei *Fasti*. La dea è invocata a maggio, in coincidenza con la parte finale dei *Floralia*, e già l'invocazione mette a fuoco la complessità del personaggio: *mater ades florum, ludis celebranda iocosis*, "vieni, madre dei fiori, cui spettano giochi spensierati" (5,183). Flora è *mater*, ma allo stesso tempo anche destinataria del *iocus*, termine che in Ovidio si riferisce generalmente all'*eros* non inquadrato in un contesto coniugale.[11] Fin da subito, dunque, l'identità femminile di Flora, nel suo complesso, è soggetta a una sorta di diffrazione: da un lato abbiamo la *mater*, la matrona, dall'altro la donna degli *ioci*, del mimo e, in generale, dell'amore libertino.[12]

Quando Flora prende la parola, Ovidio rileva un solo dettaglio della sua immagine esteriore: il profumo che esce dalle sue labbra (194: *dum loquitur, uernas efflat ab ore rosas*, "mentre parla, la sua bocca effonde profumo di rose"). Il dettaglio non è solo motivato da una basilare associazione tra la divinità e il suo ambito di perti-

---

[11] Cfr. per es. nei *Fasti* la storia di Fauno e Onfale, *fabula plena ioci* (2,304), con la nota di Robinson (2011) ad loc. per maggiore documentazione.

[12] Credo che la solennità sottesa all'appellativo *mater* non sia sminuita dalla combinazione con il genitivo *florum*, che pure serve a limitare, com'è comprensibile, l'area di influenza della dea. Il nesso richiama l'analogo *frugum mater*, usato per Cerere e Tellus in *Fasti* 1,671 (per Cerere anche in *Met.* 6,118). Si noti, peraltro, che Flora è chiamata *mater* anche da Cicerone (*Verr.* 2,5,36) e Lucrezio (5,739), e da ciò si può forse supporre il richiamo a una consuetudine rituale.

nenza, ma dice anche qualcosa sul rapporto tra la dea e il poeta, dato che il profumo è elemento di seduzione, spesso applicato a un oggetto di desiderio.[13] Da questo capiamo che il rapporto tra i due (almeno nella testa del narratore) non è privo di una componente emozionale e, di nuovo, il fatto che l'intervistatore sia un uomo e l'intervistata una donna appare rilevante.

Flora esprime fin da subito la sua 'doppia identità', aprendo il suo discorso con un esibito accostamento di due distinti livelli cronologici: *Chloris eram quae Flora uocor*, "ero Clori, io che ora mi chiamo Flora" (195). Prima di essere Flora, Clori era una ninfa come tante, senza una particolare funzione nella vita (la troviamo a passeggiare spensierata in una qualsiasi giornata primaverile), ovviamente bellissima. La sua bellezza le attira le attenzioni di Zefiro, che inizia a inseguirla, con conseguenze prevedibili. Il passaggio è caratterizzato da un'azione rapidissima e da uno stile leggero (199–202):

> *quae fuerit mihi forma, graue est narrare modestae;*
>   *sed generum matri repperit illa deum.*
> *uer erat, errabam; Zephyrus conspexit, abibam;*
>   *insequitur, fugio: fortior ille fuit.*

> Quale fosse la mia bellezza, son troppo modesta per dirlo,
>   ma procurò a mia madre un genero divino.
> Era primavera, andavo a spasso; Zefiro mi vide, scappavo;
>   mi insegue, scappo ancora: fu più forte lui.

Nella vivace autorappresentazione della dea emerge il primato, tutto ovidiano, della *forma*. Il malcelato compiacimento di Flora per la propria avvenenza serve a introdurre tematicamente la 'personalità' della dea e dei suoi riti, caratterizzati da una spiccata esteriorità. Allo stesso tempo, per un personaggio alla costante ricerca dell'autopromozione, il motivo della bellezza costituisce la base ideale su cui costruire uno sviluppo narrativo di grande prestigio (l'unione con un dio). Dato che quella di Flora è l'unica storia di violenza nei *Fasti* a essere narrata dalla vittima stessa, sorge spontaneo il confronto con il racconto di un'altra famosa vittima 'omodiegetica', Aretusa, nel quinto libro delle *Metamorfosi*, che appare però antitetica rispetto a Flora. Per Aretusa, infatti, la bellezza è motivo di reale imbarazzo (*Met.* 5,580–584):

> *sed quamuis formae numquam mihi fama petita est,*
> *quamuis fortis eram, formosae nomen habebam.*
> *nec mea me facies nimium laudata iuuabat,*
> *quaque aliae gaudere solent, ego rustica dote*
> *corporis erubui, crimenque placere putaui.*

---

[13] Cfr. per es. il ritratto di Onfale, che attira le attenzioni di Fauno in *Fasti* 2,309, *ibat odoratis umeros perfusa capillis*, con Robinson (2011) ad loc. per ulteriori esempi.

> Sebbene, pur essendo prestante, non avessi mai
> cercato la fama di bella, avevo fama di bella.
> Un aspetto tanto lodato non mi appagava: le altre
> sono solite goderne, io di queste doti fisiche arrossivo
> inurbana com'ero, e piacere mi pareva un delitto.

Va ricordato che il racconto di Aretusa si inserisce in una raffinata architettura di discorsi riportati da dee ad altre dee, e tutto il resoconto appare sottoposto a pressioni esterne che ne influenzano l'andamento.[14] L'insistita 'sconfessione' della propria avvenenza è ingegnosamente avanzata quasi a discolpa di fronte a un pubblico che, a tutti i livelli intra-diegetici, ha in antipatia il tema della violenza erotica. Flora, invece, da narratrice perfettamente autonoma (e autoreferenziale), ha interesse a impostare il racconto di violenza in vista di uno scioglimento ben diverso. Condivide senz'altro con Aretusa un certo imbarazzo per la propria bellezza, ma il suo è assai poco credibile, e anzi non si può escludere che la sua grossolana reticenza (199: *quae fuerit mihi forma graue est narrare modestae*) contenga una risposta arguta a certe pretese di modestia di alcune 'colleghe' del mito. Ma quella che per Aretusa è la conseguenza gravosa della propria bellezza (l'attenzione non richiesta di un dio) per Flora è invece il vero motivo di orgoglio, dal momento che la violenza di Zefiro è addotta, di fatto, proprio come prova di tale bellezza. Dal punto di vista di Flora, dunque, la violenza in sé è concepita come un fatto secondario, un corollario inevitabile della sua identità di 'femmina del mito'. Che la sua attenzione sia altrove lo dimostra anche il fatto che la vicenda erotica sia inquadrata vistosamente in un contesto 'di famiglia', in modo abbastanza singolare per la versione di una vittima: la bellezza di Flora fa acquisire alla madre di lei un genero divino (200); Zefiro, con la sua intraprendenza, rende omaggio a una tradizione di famiglia (203sq.); ma soprattutto Zefiro rimedia al suo atto prepotente prendendo Flora come moglie (205sq.: *uim tamen emendat dando mihi nomina nuptae, / inque meo non est ulla querella toro*, "però compensa la violenza dandomi il nome di sposa, e nel mio letto non ho mai avuto di che lamentarmi"). Il matrimonio non è lo scioglimento più consueto in questo genere di vicende, ma qui, al contrario, assorbe tutta l'attenzione, perché è il vero interesse di Flora.[15] Nella sua autobiografia, dunque, Flora costruisce la propria identità femminile seguendo piste diverse: il motivo mitologico di inseguimento e violenza, che riguarda tante donne del mito, è un tassello necessario, ma su questo si innesta uno

---

[14] Le parole di Aretusa sono contenute nel canto di Calliope di fronte alle ninfe, e questo a sua volta è riferito da una Musa anonima a Minerva. Il fatto che il resoconto di Aretusa non termini, a dispetto della tradizione, con la vittoria del rapitore è stato messo in relazione con la sensibilità dell'uditorio coinvolto. Su questi aspetti vd. il commento di Rosati (2009) ad loc., Bessone (2020) e ora Bessone in questo volume.

[15] Infatti, se si considera *a posteriori* la narrazione della violenza, la sintesi estrema con cui Flora racconta il fatto dà adito a dubbi legittimi sulla sua resistenza (si confronti ancora, per converso, la tenacia di Aretusa in *Met.* 5,601–620).

sviluppo che porta in un'altra direzione, verso il raggiungimento di una dignità matronale coerente con la mentalità sociale di Roma. Flora dunque da ninfa qualsiasi diventa una donna regolarmente sposata, e in virtù di questa condizione acquisisce uno spazio stabile e chiuso (un *hortus*) e una potestà divina sui fiori, che le è conferita direttamente dal marito (209–212). Seppure su un altro livello, dunque, l'autodefinizione di Flora come donna non è distante da quella di Giunone, perché anche lei sfrutta a proprio vantaggio dei paradigmi di rappresentazione femminile, passando anche attraverso la relazione con (e dipendenza da) importanti ruoli maschili.

Più avanti, rispondendo alle domande circa l'istituzione dei *Ludi Florales* (277–330), Flora si rivela assai interessata alla ricerca di un avanzamento sociale. In un precedente articolo ho ripercorso le modalità e il significato di questa 'carriera' di Flora, che culmina nell'istituzione, da parte del Senato, di giochi annuali, come riparazione alla precedente trascuratezza degli uomini.[16] Qui mi limito a osservare come anche Flora, dopo aver presentato una precisa immagine di sé come donna (donna del mito greco, donna romana), sappia muoversi in un contesto che si potrebbe supporre poco congeniale al suo sesso, cioè la storia socio-economica di Roma, parlando con scioltezza di condanne penali, interventi urbanistici, disastri agricoli (da lei causati) e ostentando, infine, il proprio trionfo, comprovato dall'omaggio del ceto senatorio. Ora, questa positiva interazione di Flora con una prospettiva storico-politica assume tanto più valore quanto più si accentua, a livello ideale, la nozione di una divinità convenzionalmente legata ai piaceri, ai banchetti, agli *ioci*, cioè ad argomenti anti-virili per eccellenza. È proprio lo spiccato carattere femmineo di Flora e del suo culto a rendere produttiva l'integrazione con diverse anime della civiltà romana. E proprio su questi aspetti, infatti, torna Ovidio dopo la lunga narrazione storica, mettendosi a ripercorrere le componenti più note dell'atmosfera rilassata dei *Floralia*.

L'ultima sezione del passo su Flora è incentrata su aspetti puntuali riguardanti il culto cittadino, ma più che i dettagli eruditi, ci interessa qui il contesto narrativo.[17] Come già per Venere, la dialettica tra Ovidio e Flora è influenzata dal fascino personale della dea. Quello che dovrebbe essere un neutrale scambio erudito è ancora, prima di tutto, un dialogo tra un uomo e una donna. Un esempio: Ovidio chiede perché durante i *Floralia* si usino vesti variopinte. L'ovvietà della risposta fa sospettare qualche secondo fine da parte di Ovidio, e il sospetto si rivela fondato. L'abbigliamento variopinto dei *Floralia* viene contrapposto alle vesti bianche usate ai *Cerialia* (355–361):

> *cur tamen, ut dantur uestes Cerialibus albae,*
>   *sic haec est cultu uersicolore decens?*
> *an quia maturis albescit messis aristis,*
>   *et color et species floribus omnis inest?*

---

16 Basso (2019).
17 Per tutti i dettagli eruditi è ora fondamentale Fabbri (2019).

> *adnuit, et motis flores cecidere capillis*
> *accidere in mensas ut rosa missa solet.*
>
> Ma perché, se nelle feste di Cerere si usano vesti bianche,
>   lei invece è incantevole nella varietà dei suoi colori?
> Magari perché le spighe mature imbiancano la messe,
>   mentre nei fiori vi è ogni splendore di forme e colori?
> Fece segno di sì, e dalle chiome scrollate caddero fiori,
>   come cade la rosa sparsa sulla mensa.

Bisogna ammettere che la contrapposizione è costruita ingegnosamente per tornare ad esclusivo vantaggio di Flora: nella parte che la riguarda, infatti, emergono parole solo apparentemente neutrali, come *decens* (356) e *species* (358), mentre a Cerere tocca l'associazione con l'area semantica di *albus, albescere* (355–357), un'indicazione cromatica assai poco entusiasmante.[18] Come se non bastasse, Ovidio si risponde da solo, con malcelata retorica (*an quia* ... ?, "forse perché ... ?"), avanzando una risposta che è, appunto, ovvia. Flora, da parte sua, si limita ad annuire a una spiegazione che in realtà serviva solo a compiacere la sua vanità femminile, senza tralasciare il dettaglio (sempre gradito) della superiorità su un'ipotetica rivale. Nel congedo, poi, ritorna ad anello il tema del profumo, perché la dea lascia dietro di sé una fragranza grazie alla quale, dice Ovidio, *posses scire fuisse deam*, "avresti capito che c'era stata una dea" (376); il profumo non è la traccia di una divinità in generale, ma di una divinità femminile, e anche particolarmente seducente.[19] E ancora, il poeta chiede un contatto fisico (378: *sparge, precor, donis pectora nostra tuis*, "ti prego, cospargi il mio cuore con i tuoi doni"), che possiamo paragonare al gesto di toccare le tempie con il mirto, compiuto da Venere. Al di là del significato metapoetico e programmatico che questi due gesti assumono (su cui molto è stato scritto),[20] i due dettagli, in senso letterale, rientrano nella costruzione di un rapporto che comprende una forte componente emotiva, e nel quale, perciò, l'identità sessuale dei due parlanti è un elemento non secondario.

---

18 Meno frequente di *flauus*, *albus* va riferito alla piena maturazione delle messi, quando queste iniziano a sbiadire sotto il sole estivo (cfr. anche l'uso di *canere, Am.* 3,10,39, *Met.* 1,110). Ma *albus* sembra indicare una sfumatura più vicina al *pallor* che al *candor*, e accresce perciò la vitalità dei colori di Flora; su questa terminologia vd. André (1949) 25–42.
19 L'esempio più celebre è senz'altro il profumo di Venere nell'*Eneide*, che tradisce la sua identità divina camuffata (1,402–405); cfr. anche il profumo di Artemide in Eur. *Hipp.* 1391sq.
20 Oltre a Chiu (2016) 171sq., vd. anche Miller (1983); Barchiesi (1994) 123; Pasco-Pranger (2006) 171; Tola (2009).

5 Conclusione

Come si diceva all'inizio, è stato ormai messo bene in evidenza che la figura femminile nei *Fasti* è spesso cruciale per ampliare le prospettive sul concetto di civiltà romana. Ovidio mette davanti al lettore figure femminili importanti per mostrare un lato dell' 'essere romani' messo in ombra da una tradizione fatta di codici e valori virili, primi fra tutti quelli della guerra e della politica. Come ho cercato di mostrare in queste pagine, l'analisi di alcune divinità-chiave del poema porta alla consapevolezza che anche la (auto)rappresentazione divina è influenzata da un'importante componente di genere. Questo fa sì che anche le divinità femminili, proprio in quanto femmine, interagiscano con valori tipici della società maschile, con scopi e esiti differenti. La dignità matronale di Giunone ha un significato diverso (e potremmo dire più lineare) rispetto alla femminilità 'elegiaca' di Venere, integrata in un discorso genealogico e celebrativo, e anche rispetto al complesso delle identità femminili di Flora, che da classica vittima del mito passa a essere (più o meno) classica e 'realizzata' matrona dello Stato. Qualunque sia il senso dei casi specifici, è un fatto assai rilevante che questa tendenza all'apertura verso elementi culturali 'altri' agisca anche al livello diegetico del narratore principale, intendendo con questo il maestro-ricercatore Ovidio (Ovidio *agens*, per così dire). Giunone, Venere, Flora, infatti, nella loro funzione di informanti o divinità patrone, non sono prodotti di storie narrate né da altri personaggi né dal narratore-ricercatore, ma si costruiscono da sé, entrando in dialogo diretto, in prima persona, con quest'ultimo, e ponendosi perciò sul suo stesso livello diegetico (diversamente, per esempio, da una Carmenta, da un'Anna Perenna e così via). E proprio in virtù della relazione diretta e paritaria con l' 'io' narrante, la loro figura è in grado di influenzare in modo più forte e vistoso l'orientamento culturale del poema. Per le esigenze di Ovidio (l'Ovidio *auctor*, questa volta) non c'è strategia migliore che guadagnare anche il mondo divino alla causa di una civiltà composita e inclusiva.

Bibliografia

Testi e traduzioni

P. Ovidii Nasonis *Fastorum libri sex*, rec. E. H. Alton, D. E. Wornell, E. Courtney, Leipzig 1978.

Ovidio, *Metamorfosi. Vol. II (libri III–IV)*, a cura di Alessandro Barchiesi e Gianpiero Rosati, trad. di Ludovica Koch, Milano 2007.

Publio Ovidio Nasone, *I Fasti*, Introduzione e traduzione di Luca Canali, note di Marco Fucecchi, Milano 1998.

Ovidio, *Metamorfosi. Vol. III (libri V–VI)*, a cura di Gianpiero Rosati, trad. di Gioacchino Chiarini, Milano 2009.

Libri e articoli

André (1949): Jacques André, *Étude sur les termes de couleur dans la langue latine*, Paris.
Barchiesi (1994): Alessandro Barchiesi, *Il poeta e il principe. Ovidio e il discorso augusteo*, Bari.
Basso (2019): Luca Basso, "Storia di una dea alla ricerca del tempo. Flora e i *Ludi Florales* nel calendario ovidiano (fast. V 183–378)", *Maia* 71.3, 683–698.
Bessone (2020): Federica Bessone, "L'illusione del lettore. Aretusa e i suoi racconti in Ovidio, *Metamorfosi* 5", *Dictynna* 17.
Braun (1981): Ludwig Braun, "Kompositionskunst in Ovids *Fasti*", *ANRW* 2.31.4, 2344–2383.
Brugnoli/Stok (1992): Giorgio Brugnoli e Fabio Stok (edd.), *Ovidius παρῳδήσας*, Pisa.
Chiu (2016): Angeline Chiu, *Ovid's Women of the Year. Narratives of Roman Identity in the Fasti*, Ann Arbor.
Fabbri (2019): Lorenzo Fabbri, *Mater florum. Flora e il suo culto a Roma*, Firenze.
Fantham (1992): Elaine Fantham, "The role of Evander in Ovid's *Fasti*", *Arethusa* 25, 155–171.
Fantham (2002): Elaine Fantham, "Ovid's *Fasti*: Politics, History, and Religion", in: Barbara Weiden Boyd (ed.), *Brill's Companion to Ovid*, Leiden/Boston, 197–233.
Fucecchi (2010): Marco Fucecchi, "Tra ospitalità e integrazione. Cibele (e Venere) nel libro IV", in: Giuseppe La Bua (ed.), *Vates operose dierum. Studi sui Fasti di Ovidio*, Pisa, 65–92.
Graf (2016): Fritz Graf, "The Gods in Ovid's *Fasti*", in: James J. Clauss, Martine Cuypers e Ahuvia Kahane (edd.), *The Gods of Greek Hexameter Poetry. From the Archaic Age to Late Antiquity and Beyond*, Stuttgart, 353–366.
Hinds (1992): Stephen Hinds, "Arma in Ovid's *Fasti*", *Arethusa* 25.1, 81–153.
Hübner (1999): Wolfgang Hübner, "Zur Paarweisen Anordnung der Monate in Ovids Fasten", in: Werner Schubert (ed.), *Ovid. Werk und Wirkung. Festgabe für Michael von Albrecht zum 65. Geburtstag*, Frankfurt, M., 539–557.
Kötzle (1991): Martina Kötzle, *Weibliche Gottheiten in Ovids «Fasten»*, Frankfurt, M.
Lieberg (1969): Godo Lieberg, "Iuno bei Ovid. Ein Beitrag zu Fasten VI, 1–100", *Latomus* 28, 923–947.
Littlewood (2006): R. J. Littlewood (ed.), *A Commentary on Ovid's Fasti. Book VI*, Oxford.
Merli (2000): Elena Merli, *Arma canant alii. Materia epica e narrazione elegiaca nei fasti di Ovidio*, Firenze.
Miller (1983): John F. Miller, "Ovid's Divine Interlocutors in the Fasti", in: Carl Deroux (ed.), *Studies in Latin Literature and Roman History III*, Bruxelles, 156–192.
Murgatroyd (2005): Paul Murgatroyd, *Mythical and Legendary Narrative in Ovid's Fasti*, Leiden/Boston.
Pasco-Pranger (2006): Molly Pasco-Pranger, *Founding the Year. Ovid's Fasti and the Poetics of the Roman Calendar*, Leiden/Boston.
Poletti (2017): Beatrice Poletti, "Juno in the Proemium of Ovid's Fasti 6. Considerations on the Reconciliatory Role of the Goddess", *Acta Antiqua Academiae Scientiarum Hungaricae* 57, 189–206.
Robinson (2011): Matthew Robinson (ed.), *A Commentary on Ovid's Fasti Book 2*. Ed. with Intr. and Comm., Oxford/New York.
Rutledge (1980): Eleanor S. Rutledge, "Ovid's Informants in the Fasti", in: Carl Deroux (ed.), *Studies in Latin Literature and Roman History II*, Bruxelles, 322–331.
Tola (2009): Eleonora Tola, "La celebracion de Flora en los Fastos de Ovidio (V, 183–378). Mito de origen y poética metamorfica", *Euphrosyne* 37, 317–325.

Helge Baumann
In Memory of Reading Matrons and Eloquent Dogs: Female Voices and Role Constructions in Martial's Epigrams 10.63 and 11.69

Abstract: This case study deals with the epitaphs Mart. 10.63 and 11.69, the two only instances of female first person speakers/narrators within the *Epigrammaton libri*. As the paper seeks to demonstrate, Martial in the role constructions of the anonymous matron in 10.63 and the hunting dog Lydia in 11.69 intensively draws upon expectations of genre and gender and establishes strong intertextual ties to other poems in the *Books of Epigrams* and, in the case of 11.69, to Greco-Roman epic. While the honourable matron of 10.63 fashions herself as an avid reader of Martial's epigrams, Lydia presents herself as a canine *virago* of epic stature. Even though they each portray a self-confident female protagonist, both poems at the same time serve the fashioning of male participants in the literary communication, namely Martial in 10.63 and his patron Dexter in 11.69.

Keywords: Intertextuality, epic, literary patronage, non-human, anthropomorphism, metapoetics

Martial's epigrams abound with first-person statements of the multifaceted and at times utterly elusive Martial-*persona*.[1] The impression that as readers we seem to be in steady contact with this epigrammatic *persona* extends even to many of those epigrams that do not contain a grammatical first-person at all: poems that immediately address a second person and/or refer to a third person are generally also to be understood as voiced by the Martial-*persona*. Accordingly, one might think that the first-person voice of this *persona* rules supreme in Martial's *œuvre*, but there are exceptions to the rule, i.e. epigrams in which the first-person voice is held by an unambiguously different figure or thing. A total of 66 such epigrams can be found in

---

[1] If not signified as "Martial-*persona*", by the sole name "Martial" I refer to the empirical author. On the Martial-*persona* cf. especially Lorenz (2002) 4–42. Becker (2008) 284f., setting out from early Greek epigram and communication theories of modern literary theory, emphasises the deictic function of first-person statements related to the Martial-*persona* that enables an immediate and effortless situational framing typical of Greco-Roman and especially Martialian epigram. Interestingly, Becker's statement that a first-person speaker does not have to introduce himself holds true for many utterings of the Martial *persona*, but not for the two surprisingly different speakers discussed in this paper.

Acknowledgement: I would like to thank Calum Maciver, the participants of the EuGeStA Conference in Munich and the Mittelrheinische Symposion 2020 in Marburg for their welcome feedback on this paper.

https://doi.org/10.1515/9783110795257-007

the gift-inscriptions of the *Xenia* and *Apophoreta* (Mart. 13 and 14; 18,9%)² and a mere 15 in the *Epigrammaton libri* (Mart. 1–12; 1,3%).³ In this tableau, that, as far as I can see, has not yet received attention as distinct group, two aspects are striking: firstly, with the exception of only two poems⁴ the subset exclusively consists of epigrams that are – or at least pretend to be – inscriptions of objects, predominately of gifts and tombs.⁵ Secondly, in the *Epigrammaton libri* only two of those poems – both of them epitaphs – are voiced by a female ego: an anonymous matron in Mart. 10.63 and a hunting dog in Mart. 11.69.⁶ It is this exceptional female duo that will be at the core of this paper. As I seek to demonstrate by means of a close reading, Martial carefully shapes both deceased speakers through role-constructions that are intensively concerned with expectations, appropriations, and deviations of gender and genre. While the matron assumes decidedly epigrammatic role patterns and reflects on the interrelations of a chaste life, pleasure, and reading, the hunting dog Lydia by way of a strong anthropomorphism is shaped through references to mythical exempla and epic intertexts. The fact that the matron and the dog speak on their own behalf surprisingly lets their own sepulchral self-fashioning enable a parallel self-fashioning of the male participants in the immediate literary communication, namely Martial in epigram 10.63 and Lydia's Master as well as Martial in epigram 11.69. Both poems, in other words, develop a gendered double vision that negotiates both female and male patterns of literary representation.

---

2 Mart. 13: edible items; 16 out of 127 poems; 12,6%; Mart. 13.22, 25, 26, 33, 35, 49, 50, 59, 71, 72, 76, 82, 83, 87, 94, 103). Mart. 14: non-edible items; 39 out of 223 poems; 22,4%; Mart. 14.3, 9, 15, 29, 37, 39, 41, 43, 44, 46, 47, 52, 56, 58, 61, 62, 63, 64, 73, 76, 80, 88, 90, 94, 95, 99, 101, 103, 104, 107, 119, 120, 121, 122, 123, 133, 135, 136, 138, 139, 145, 148, 149, 151, 152, 154, 156, 178, 202, 213.
3 In the following list an asterisk (*) marks epigrams without pronouns or verbs in the first-person. – Still living speaker: Mart.1.5 (emperor Domitian); 10.7* (Thybris addressing Rhenus). – Inscribed material objects speaking: Mart. 2.59 (building, the *Mica Aurea*); Mart. 9.28 (portrait); 10.1 (the book itself). – Epitaphs with speaking tombs: Mart. 1.116; 6.28*; 6.52*; 10.61; 11.13*; 11.91*. – Epitaphs with speaking deceased: Mart. 7.96; 10.53; 10.63; 11.69. – Totals: 15 out of 1.170 poems; 1,3 %; no matches in Mart. *spect.*
4 Mart. 1.5; 10.7.
5 This bias is certainly best explained as a reflex of generic history: The early Greek, i.e. inscriptional, epigram relied on an immediate, often deictically marked co-presence of objects, voices of the deceased, texts, and passers-by and readily has any of them speak in the first person. On this aspect of communication in early Greek – especially sepulchral – epigram cf. Meyer (2005) 25–88; Tueller (2008) 12–56 and (2010); Schmitz (2010); Vestrheim (2010); Christian (2015) 28–60. On the probable roots of the gift inscription of Mart. 13 and 14 in dedicatory epigrams (and literary catalogues) cf. Leary (1996) 22 and (more confident) (2001) 14f.
6 There are other female animals speaking in the first person in the *Xenia*, but other than the poem on Lydia they do not consider questions of the speaker's gender.

1 "My reading was wanton, but my life was virtuous." – Mart. 10.63 and the confessions of a dead matron of rank

Marmora parva quidem sed non cessura, viator,
  Mausoli saxis pyramidumque legis.
bis mea Romano spectata est vita Tarento
  et nihil extremos perdidit ante rogos:
quinque dedit pueros, totidem mihi Iuno puellas,   5
  cluserunt omnes lumina nostra manus.
contigit et thalami mihi gloria rara fuitque
  una pudicitiae mentula nota meae.

The marble you are reading, traveller, is small indeed, but will not yield to the stones of Mausolus and the pyramids. My life was twice approved at Roman Tarentos [i.e. at the *ludi saeculares*] and lost nothing down to my dying day. Juno gave me five boys and as many girls; their hands all closed my eyes. Rare glory of wedlock was my lot, and my chastity knew but one cock.[7]

More than any other epitaph in the *Epigrammaton libri*[8] epigram 10.63 evokes and explodes stereotyped expectations of genre and gendered role patterns. The ending of this – as it eventually turns out – mock-epitaph is a prime example of an "explosive"[9] *aprosdoketon*-point that takes the reader by surprise. This is even though the continuous rhetoric of hyperbole increasingly casts doubts upon the authenticity of the matron, who exceeds all role expectations for Roman married women and thus, as Watson/Watson put it, simply seems too good to be true.[10] Epigrammatic exaggeration – a device that Martial uses in non-satirical (sepulchral) contexts, too[11] – is wittily intertwined here with a very close observation of generic conventions. Leaving aside that the matron oddly and suspiciously does not give her name and even uses strong language, epigram 10.63 conforms to the generic repertoire to the same

---

7 Citations and translations of Martial follow Shackleton Bailey (1993).
8 The other epitaphs in the *Epigrammaton libri* are: 1.116; 6.28, 52; 7.96; 10.53; 10.61; 11.13; 11.69 (Lydia, the hunting dog); 11.91. Henriksén (2006) 357 n. 25 further lists epigrams connected with actual deaths without taking the form of tomb inscriptions (1.114; 5.34; 6.18; I would also add 10.26) and epigrams shaped as epitaphs without being primarily concerned with actual deaths as they either are encomia for addressees different from the defunct (6.76; 7.40; 10.71) or satirical and fictitious (10.63; 10.67). On life, death, and consolation in Martial cf. also Heilmann (1998); Lorenz (2009).
9 Shackleton Bailey (1993) vol. II, 382.
10 Cf. Watson/Watson (2003) 350f.
11 Cf. e.g. the panegyric Mart. 8.11 with Schöffel (2002) 167f., 173, and – as regards *epitaphia* – 7.96.5 with Galán Vioque (2002) 508 ad loc. See also below on Mart. 11.69.

degree as Martial's non-satirical epitaphs do.¹² Accordingly, the following features are in keeping with the inscriptional and literary tradition:¹³
a) The matron speaks in the first-person voice (third-person voiced epitaphs are also found, though).¹⁴
b) She deictically refers to her tomb – not without comparing the small tombstone in stark antithetical hyperbole with the pyramids and the Mausoleum at Halicarnassus, the two sepulchral monuments amongst the Seven Wonders of the World (ll. 1f.).
c) She addresses by means of apostrophe a passer-by (*viator . . . legis*; ll. 1f.).
d) She both indicates her social status and . . .
e) . . . hints at the length of her life by boldly claiming to have twice been chosen and granted the honour of taking part in the ritual programme of the secular games, which date to 47 and 88 CE (ll. 3f.).
f) She tells us about her role as mother – note the suspiciously symmetric and hyperbolic number of five girls and boys who all survived her (ll. 5f).
g) She outlines her marital status, disclosing that she was *univira*, married to one husband only (ll. 7f.).

While Martial does not suggest the gender of the deceased in the first half of the poem, he fashions the anonymous voice as perfect *matrona* in the second half. Within four distiches we witness a highly condensed epigrammatic role construction of the ideal matron of rank.¹⁵ In sum, until she uses strong language the matron appears not so much as an individual but an stereotyped paradigm of motherhood, fidelity, piety, and virtuous chastity, i.e. *pudicitia*, which is a – if not *the* – traditional key value for Roman married women.¹⁶ All the more provoking is the end of the epigram: the presentation of female chastity culminates in the last line with Martial

---

12 Henriksen (2006) 358–62 categorises characteristics typical of Martial's sepulchral epitaphs referring to Tolman (1910) and Lattimore (1942). On types and main topics of ancient sepulchral stone inscriptions cf. also Peek (1960), and, specifically interested in gendered role constructions in Roman epigraphic culture, Keegan (2014). On the concept of the generic repertoire cf. Harrison (2007) 10f., 21–33.
13 Cf. Watson/Watson (2003) 350–52 and Scherf (2004) 236 for parallels between 10.63 and literary and/or inscriptional epitaphs.
14 In Martial's epitaphs (both serious and satirical) four have the deceased speak as first person (7.96; 10.53; 10.63; 11.69) and ten refer to the same in the third person (1.116; 6.28; 6.52; 6.76; 7.40; 10.61; 10.67; 10.71; 11.13; 11.91).
15 Watson/Watson (2003) 350, call this "the complete embodiment of the matronal ideal".
16 Treggiari (1991) 231 notes that – despite the importance of sexual fidelity in the conception of Roman marriage (cf. ibid. 232–8) – in the *CIL* only very few epitaphs in Rome attribute *uxores* explicitly with adjectives like *castissima* or *fidissima* (23 and 24 instances in 3.728 Epitaphs) but significantly more often with much broader concepts like *bene merens* (1.305), *sanctissima* (208), and *optima* (156), that inter alia can be related to *pudicitia* as well.

putting *pudicitia* (not that by any chance a reader otherwise would have missed the concept) verbatim in the text – only to let it collide spectacularly with a penile intruder, the *mentula*. Masterly arranged around the pentameter juncture this stark juxtaposition of the chaste and the obscene, of the female and the male is one of the most striking examples of register shifting in Martial's epigrams that I am aware of. The sudden intrusion of the common word *mentula* is particularly spectacular because it is framed by an otherwise over-elevated linguistic register and above all pronounced by the matron herself: publicly using the basic obscenity *mentula* is a taboo for high standing women (and men alike, for that matter).[17] This unexpected linguistic blast massively contradicts gendered and generic expectations and thus urges us to reconsider the preceding epitaph and role construction. The obscenity reveals the poem immediately to be a mock-epitaph – a kind of epigram that Martial presents us only once more five poems later in a companion-piece on old Plutia who is still lustful in her tomb (*hoc tandem sita prurit in sepulchro / calvo Plutia cum Melanthione*; 10.67.6f.).

Interestingly though, our anonymous matron is not revealed as an impostor that has never been chaste at all or as sexually deviant or excessive like the *vetula* Plutia. Therefore, the setting differs significantly from Martial's manifold witticisms and criticisms by which he often aggressively discredits female and male targets of epigrammatic satire. On the contrary, I agree with Adams who classifies the use of *mentula* in 10.63 as "neutral", i.e. non-abusive[18] since it, in fact, also stands as a hilarious *pars pro toto* for her one and only husband. Incompatible as it conventionally may be, the matron's lexical breach of etiquette does not cross out the preceding fashioning as a perfect upper-class lady (cf. *nihil . . . perdidit*; l. 4) but rather, expands it: this unusual matron both speaks a frank Martialian idiom and lived a chaste life. One aspect of this stark point of the epigram certainly is to remind overly prude opponents in the *Epigrammaton libri* (we will encounter one of those in a minute) that living in a happy marriage and giving birth to children even for the chastest and most faithful *matronae* might involve sex and hence the *mentula*.[19] With this stance Martial takes up a motto that he articulates only a small number of poems before in reflecting upon the ideal of the *vita beata*, part of which is "a marriage bed not austere and yet modest" (*non tristis torus et tamen pudicus*; 10.47).

---

17 Cf. Watson/Watson (2003) 353 referring to Mart. 10.68 (cf. ibid. 226 for further reference) and Adams (1982) 217. On *mentula* as basic obscenity and the etymologic uncertainties associated with it, cf. ibid. 9–12. As regards men of rank avoiding the word *mentula* cf. Cic. *Fam.* 9.22.3 hinting at it as *mentam pusillam*, which would yield *mentula* when expressed by way of diminutive. On the other hand, Martial claims Numa used the word *mentula* (Mart. 1.15.10) and cites verse of Augustus implementing it (Mart. 11.20., with Kay, 1985, 110 giving further references).
18 Cf. Adams (1982) 12.
19 On the *mentula* as source of life cf. 11.15.7–9: *illam, / ex qua nascimur, omnium parentem, / quam sanctus Numa mentulam vovabat*.

Patricia Watson concludes under the heading of this very verse that Martial in a number of poems . . .

> acknowledges the reality that the traditional concept of the desiccated asexual *matrona* is obsolete and needs to be redefined. He does this by breaking down the boundaries between the *meretrix* and the *matrona* in the area of sexuality, making his ideal *matrona* familiar with *artes meretriciae*. . . . Martial adher[es] to a view which was no doubt approved by his upper-class readers: that a *casta matrona* who was sexually aware might make an attractive wife.[20]

Using sexualised strong language might be appropriate for conjugal dirty talk[21] but, as stated by Watson, was "confined in theory to the meretrix".[22] The role construction of the anonymous matron in 10.63 can be seen, then, as part of the discourse of the sexually aware matron as analysed by Watson. But where or from whom does our matron adopt the word *mentula*? While we can assume that basic obscenities have been generally part of the known vocabulary but muted through social norms, *mentula* in the context of literature and all the more so within the *Epigrammaton libri* has a specific Martialian ring to it: though we find the word *mentula* famously in Catullus and the *Carmina Priapea*, Martial with 49 instances is the author who uses it by far the most.[23]

Setting out from this lexicographic scenario, I want to argue that the matron by usage of *mentula* demonstrates that she is a reader and connoisseur of minor poetry and above all of the *Epigrammaton libri*.[24] To clarify this new aspect of the point further, I want to cite epigram 1.35, in which we find the very first instance of *mentula* in the collection[25] and in which this characteristic obscenity – similarly as in the *Carmina Priapea*[26] – appears as a programmatic key word evocative not just of the obscene quality of the epigrammatic book but the book per se:

---

20 Watson (2005) 86 concluding her careful analysis of 1.34, 35; 3.68, 69; 4.14; 9.40; 10.35, 38, 47; 11.104.
21 Adams (1982) 7f., 217.
22 Watson (2005) 81.
23 In comparison, we find 8 matches in Catullus and 25 in the *Priapea*. *Mentula* is not used in books 4, 5, 8. Books 5 and 8, advertised in 5.2, 8.pr, and 8.1 as being decorous, are significantly less obscene in vocabulary than the rest but they by no means eschew erotic or sexual topics (cf. Lorenz 2002, 21f.; Schöffel 2002, 19f.).
24 In fact, one grows so accustomed to having the Martial-*persona* voicing this characteristic obscenity that one might even wonder if it really is only the matron drastically shifting her sociolinguistic register or if we witness something like a "voice-switch", an illegitimate breach of the speaker continuity with the Martial-*persona* taking over the first-person voice with a chuckle. As will be shown below, the Martial-*persona* indeed is visible behind the matron, but she nevertheless uses the obscenity in her own first-person and female voice.
25 Only one instance in Martial's œuvre dates earlier, 14.74.2.
26 On sexual metapoetics in Catullus, Martial, and the *Carmina Priapea* cf. Hallett (1996). On Priapic motifs in Martial cf. O'Connor (1998).

Versus scribere me parum severos
nec quos praelegat in schola magister,
Corneli, quereris: sed hi libelli,
tamquam coniugibus suis mariti,
non possunt sine mentula placere. 5
quid si me iubeas thalassionem
verbis dicere non thalassionis?
quis Floralia vestit et stolatum
permittit meretricibus pudorem?
lex haec carminibus data est iocosis, 10
ne possint, nisi pruriant, iuvare.
quare deposita severitate
parcas lusibus et iocis rogamus,
nec castrare velis meos libellos.
gallo turpius est nihil Priapo. 15

Cornelius, you grumble that I write risqué verses, not the sort a schoolmaster would dictate in class. But these little books are like husbands with their wives – they can't please without a cock. You might as well tell me to sing a wedding song without using wedding song words. Does anybody put clothes on Flora's festival or allow whores the modesty of the matron's robe? There's a law laid down for merry verses: they can't be good for anything unless they itch. So please put prudery aside and spare my jests and jollities; and don't try to emasculate my little books. There's nothing uglier than a neutered Priapus.

Following the preface of Book 1 that reflects upon the importance of obscenity for his poetry Martial here programmatically comments on the collection's very first instance of strong language in the preceding epigram 1.34.[27] In doing so, he metaphorically depicts his first book of epigrams as having a penis with substantial phallic potential if we consider the closing reference to Priapus. Excessive prudery and chastity (*severitas* and *pudor*; ll. 1; 9; 12) threaten the playful and jocose character of his poetry (cf. *lusibus et iocis*; l. 13). This trifling and – as Martial puts it in line 11 – itchy quality relies not only but yet significantly on the inclusion of obscenity. Martial casts the thread of this disposition in the strong metaphor of a literary *Kastrationsangst*, of his book being castrated.[28] In this image of the text as male body the *mentula* stands for the essence of Martial's playful poetry and can therefore been understood as a cipher or emblem for his epigrams.[29] With its imagery of

---

[27] Mart. 1.34 deals with the *meretrix* Lesbia and uses *futuere* for "having sex" (l. 10). Mart. 1.35 is a prime exemplar of Martial's use of literary apology on which cf. Sullivan (1991) 56–77 and especially Banta (1998) who concludes his comprehensive study with Mart. 1.35 (pp. 230–35).
[28] On actual, metaphorical, and metapoetical castration in Martial, cf. Hallett (1996); Obermayer (1998) 195–7; 273f.; Wells (2019) 97–130.
[29] On the metaphor of the epigrammatic text as (predominantly male) body cf. Williams (2002); Wells (2019). On the *mentula* as symbol for Martial's poetry cf. especially O'Connor (1998) 188: "The *mentula Priapi* recurs as a symbol of the piquancy of epigram as a genre . . . Without it, epigram ceases to be itself."; cf. also Williams (2002); Wells (2019), especially 119, 134.

body and body parts, epigram 1.35 is also interesting for the interpretation of our mock-epitaph in so far as it establishes a figurative nexus of poetry, sex, pleasure and marriage in ll. 3–5.[30] In this passage Martial conflates pleasurable conjugal sex and pleasurable reading: the text takes on the role of the husbands (*hi libelli; mariti*) and the reader – both female and male – the passive role of the wives (*coniugibus*) pleased by the male partners/texts and their *mentula*/risqué wittiness (*non possunt sine mentula placere*).[31] This metaphorical correspondence of sex and literature seems surprisingly modern in at least three ways: firstly because it lets both sex and literature appear ideally as matters of pleasure (< *plaisir* < *placere*); secondly because the metaphor takes into account female conjugal pleasure whereas Martial otherwise focusses on the pleasure wives give or should give their husbands;[32] thirdly because the idea of literature as pleasure and also specifically erotic pleasure – in 11.16.5–8 Martial claims that his piquant epigrams arouse female and male readers alike[33] – fits all too well in the scope of postmodern literary theory.[34]

Set against this backdrop, the collision of *pudicitia* and *mentula* within the, at first heavily stereotyped, role construction of an honourable deceased matron takes up an explicit metapoetic discourse about the relation between decency, obscenity, and pleasure established by Martial at the very beginning of the collection. The excessive amount of *severitas* and *pudicitia* that we find in our poem up until the last penthemimeres is not compatible with Martial's idea of poetry and thus countered with a bold gesture of epigrammatic appropriation. By no means does he leave the first-person voice to a representative of old-fashioned moralisers but rather shapes the anonymous matron in the role of the perfect *epigrammatic* matron – and this is a woman who, independent from her social status in life, on her tomb pointedly confesses with her own voice to have been both a positively lustful wife and reader. Taken *pars pro toto* for the husband, *mentula* points to pleasure in conjugal sexuality; taken as citation and emblem of Martial's playful poetry, it points to pleasure in reading the *Epigrammaton libri*. In the end, pleasure in reading corresponds to pleasure in sex as it does in 1.35. That epigram 10.63 is a poem about reading is already hinted at in the first distich where the passer-by is addressed as reader (*marmora . . ., viator, . . . legis*) and the matron's last resting place is hence explicitly presented as readable

---

30 Cf. on this nexus in Mart. 1.35 especially Hallett (1996) 323–7.
31 As Hallett (1996) 327 points out to separate him from the "Catullan and Priapean complexity" in this metaphoric field, "Martial credits his verses with and dissociates himself from sexual pleasure-giving . . .".
32 Cf. Watson (2005) especially p. 80, giving only Mart. 10.35.3f. on the poetess Sulpicia as another instance of the focus of female marital pleasure. See below on this motif in Mart. 10.63.
33 The text runs as follows: *o quotiens rigida pulsabis pallia vena, / sis gravior Curio Fabricioque licet! / tu quoque nequitias nostri lususque libelli / uda, puella, leges, sis Patavina licet.*
34 On pleasure and reading in modern literary theory cf. Barthes (1973) and the comprehensive study Anz (1998), dealing with aspects of the erotic and pornographic on pp. 205–28.

tomb.³⁵ But the idea of identifying the matron as reader relies much more on having her speak in the first person: her acquaintance with Martial's epigrams and poetics of *mentula* would have been conveyed significantly less immediate if we were told by an author/speaker what her words and readings would be like. Instead, as textual first-person reader/speaker she performs on her own means through the single use of *mentula* the adoption of a characteristically epigrammatic linguistic register and mindset.³⁶

As it turns out, by envisioning his readership, the shaping of the deceased matron serves the assertion and reflection of epigrammatic reach and hence a crucial aspect of Martial's authorial self-fashioning.³⁷ The claim that his poems are and will be read everywhere and by everybody independent from gender, age and social status is a key feature of Martial's self-advertising as poet known in the whole world, *toto notus in orbe*, as he boldly puts it at the very outset of the *Epigrammaton libri* in 1.1.2.³⁸ Explicitly included in this self-confident scope are Roman matrons, whom the author in 3.68 and 3.86 conceptualises and addresses as readers especially of his licentious poems.³⁹ 3.68 gives a trigger warning for prude ladies that turns out to be an overt strategy of attracting and affirming the readerly attention of matrons by way of announcing and including obscene language and topics. By the end of the epigram the Martial-*persona* is convinced that he has caught the matron's undivided attention: *si bene te novi, . . . totum* (sc. *libellum*) *nunc studiosa legis* (3.68.11f.). He reaffirms this point in a witty case of textual performativity in the companion piece 3.86 that follows after a series of obscene epigrams: *tu tamen, ecce, legis* (3.86.2). The matron of 10.63 obviously is a reader who did not put book 3 aside but conformed to Martial's concept of the ideal matron as articulated in the two trigger warning epigrams.⁴⁰ But in the fiction of our epitaph the imagination of an all-encompassing epigrammatic range not only transgresses borders of gender but also of life and death since the matron – and this is made possible only by giving her the first-person voice – recites

---

35 Cf. similarly Mart. 7.96.6: *da lacrimas tumulo, qui legis ista, meo*.
36 In the performance or recitation of the poem the textual reader/speaker relies on extratextual reader/speakers. The matron owes her voice to both the author and his readers. Cf. Häusle (1979) 100–104 and Tueller (2008) 150–54 regarding Greek archaic and Hellenistic epigram.
37 Martial 10.63 thus reflects the same function that Watson (2005) 78 assumes for other epigrams that deal with the sexuality of the Roman matron: "In books 3 and 11 . . . the poet exploits the sexuality of the married woman to his own advantage, appealing to an assumed fascination on the part of female readers . . ., in order to expand his readership." Cf. also Banta (1998) 235 on Martial's apologetic epigrams regarding obscenity: "The *apologia* . . . for Martial plays a role prior to that of the obscenity itself. Verbal obscenity allows for apology and enhances generic dialectic, rather than the other way around. Martial's *apologia* for obscenity aims at an extension of the range and readership and scope of appropriateness (and hence authority) of his epigrams . . .".
38 Cf. additionally Mart. 5.13; 7.88; 9.84; 10.9; 11.3.
39 For a discussion of both epigrams cf. e.g. Banta (1998) 212–17; Watson (2005) 78f. Cf. also Mart. 5.2.1; 11.16 (another trigger warning); 10.64 with Adams (1982) 217.
40 Are we in the end even to identify her with the anonymous matron in 3.68 and 3.86?

and keeps reciting one of Martial's epigrams even after having met her death. While Plutia in 10.67 is discredited as being a lecherous dead *vetula*, the matron is granted the privilege of indulging in her *Leselust* in eternity.

The single obscenity *"mentula"* marks her as a creation of Martial but cannot strike out the hyperbolically outlined accomplishments of her imagined life that leads to the birth of ten children and the ambition to be remembered for the time to come in high esteem. The matron articulates this claim for eternal memory boldly in the opening distich in which she – despite its antithetically small size – lets her tomb compete with the pyramids and the Mausoleum at Halicarnassus in their property as enduring sepulchral and memorial monuments (*marmora parva quidem sed non cessura . . . Mausoli saxis pyramidumque*).[41] This monumentalising gesture seems drastically hyperbolic as voiced by the matron but is highly reminiscent of authors especially of minor poetry laying claim to eternal memory for their work, often by way of a text as monument-allegory or by asserting that their texts will even outlast such physical monuments.[42] Martial is very fond of the latter variety and uses it amongst others in two preceding poems in Book 10.[43] Since our literary matron is asserting eternal remembrance for her small textual tomb she necessarily does so for Martial's poetry, too, and hence acts as spokeswoman for her author who otherwise makes such claims through the first-person voice of the author *persona*. In the end, the ambitious, frank matron with her ten children corresponds puzzlingly well to the ambitious, frank author Martial with his – at this point in the chronology of the *œuvre* – ten Books.[44] This similarity between the matron and Martial may luckily be undermined by the *dissimile* that Martial did not meet his death after his tenth book but produced two more books including 11.69, our next text due for close reading; but the remarkable resemblance extends to the vexed question of how the poetry one writes or reads intersects with

---

[41] Cf. the similar pattern in Stat. *Silv.* 2.3.62f. (*haec tibi **parva quidem** genitali luce paramus / dona, sed ingenti forsan **victura** sub aevo*) with van Dam (1984) 328. Watson/Watson (2003) 351 take a somewhat different stance and refer to the topos of the small tomb as opposed to the grandeur of the inhabitant, but both topoi can well be understood as having been combined here.

[42] Cf. van Dam (1984) 328 giving further references on the topos. On monumental architecture as allegory for literary works cf. prominently Pind. *O.* 6.1–5 and Hor. *carm.* 3.30.1 (*Exegi monumentum*) with further references in Nisbet/Rudd (2004) 365–8. On inscriptions claiming that physical monuments warrant eternal afterlife cf. Häusle (1980).

[43] Van Dam (1984) 328 lists amongst others Mart. 7.84.5–8 (a textual portrait [*parva dona*; cf. Stat. *Silv.* 2.3.62f. cited above n. 41] will outlive the paintings of Apelles); 8.3.5–8 (Martial's poetry will outlast the sepulchral monuments of Mesalla and Licinius [*Licini marmora*]); 10.2.9–12 (the monumental tombs of Mesalla [*marmora Messallae*] and Crispus will perish but Martial's books are the only monuments that do not know how to die [*solaque non norunt haec monumenta mori*]); 10.26.5–7 (Varus had no proper burial as he drowned but Martial's everlasting poem gives him a name that will live forth [*sed datur aeterno victurum carmine nomen*]).

[44] As we have seen above, in comparison to the matron's five girls and five boys, all of Martial's books must be regarded as male. As to a much stronger similarity of writing and giving birth to children cf. Hallett (1996) 330–33 on Catull. 50.

one's very life. Epigram 1.4.8 gives us an answer that fits both the deceased matron and the author: *lasciva est nobis pagina, vita proba* – "my page is wanton, but my life is virtuous".[45]

2 "I was called Lydia" – A canine case of gender and role construction in Mart. 11.69

Amphitheatrales inter nutrita magistros
  venatrix, silvis aspera, blanda domi,
Lydia dicebar, domino fidissima Dextro,
  qui non Erigones mallet habere canem,
nec qui Dictaea Cephalum de gente secutus   5
  luciferae pariter venit ad astra deae.
non me longa dies nec inutilis abstulit aetas,
  qualia Dulichio fata fuere cani:
fulmineo spumantis apri sum dente perempta,
  quantus erat, Calydon, aut, Erymanthe, tuus.   10
nec queror infernas quamvis cito rapta sub umbras.
  non potui fato nobiliore mori.

Reared among the trainers of the Amphitheatre, a huntress, fierce in the woods, gentle in the house, I was called Lydia, most faithful to my master Dexter, who would not have preferred Erigone's dog (i.e. Maira) or him of Dicte's breed (i.e. Lailaps) that followed Cephalus and came with him to the stars of the light-bringing goddess. It was not length of days nor useless age that carried me off, as was the fate of the Dulichian dog. I was slain by the lightning tusk of a foaming boar, as huge as him of Calydon or him of Erymanthus. Nor do I complain, though snatched untimely to the nether shades. I could not die by a nobler fate.

With epigram 11.69 Martial pays tribute to the epigraphic and literary tradition of epitaphs for animals.[46] Not only do we find a cluster of literary epitaphs for animals in Book 7 of the *Greek Anthology* – there also is epigraphic evidence of tombs and inscriptions for deceased dogs and other animals in the Greco-Roman world, documenting the potentially very close and affectionate relationship between humans and animals.[47] Measured against these social and literary practices, our poem

---

45 Cf. similarly Mart. 11.15.13: *mores non habet hic meos libellus*. Hallett (1996) 327 refers to Catull. 16.5f. as prototype for both passages in Martial.
46 For an extended analysis of Mart. 11.69 in conjunction with its companion piece 7.27 that is centred around role constructions through epic intertextuality cf. Baumann (2019) 162–220, esp. 195–219.
47 Cf. *AG* 7.189–216. On animal epicedia including Mart. 11.69 cf. still Herrlinger (1930); mainly on Latin poems for deceased animals, Fögen (2018); Mindt (2020) specifically on speaking dead animals. For the epigraphic evidence cf. Herrlinger (1930) 39–53; Keller (1909) 130–34, including *exempla* for faithful dogs and sumptuous funerals for dogs in ancient historiography; Kay (1985) 215. Cf.

could have well been put on a stone slab but, as will be discussed later – without reducing its qualities as consolation for the dog's master – it implies that it should be best kept in the *Epigrammaton libri*.[48] As regards generic conventions, in the way of a strong anthropomorphism that is typical of animal epitaphs Lydia's funerary epigram takes up many common features of epitaphs for humans that we have also noticed above in Mart. 10.63: Lydia speaks in the first-person voice,[49] she gives – other than the *matrona* of Mart. 10.63 – her name, tells us about her life, death, profession, and character, and even roughly indicates her age: she died young (cf. *cito rapta*,[50] l. 11). As will be discussed in detail, this generic rooting in the tradition of epitaphs for humans enables Martial to steadily intertwine human and animal frames of reference, especially mythical canine and human *exempla*, which is a crucial aspect of Lydia's intensely gendered role construction. Another important frame of reference to consider is the system of literary patronage, because we can infer from the companion piece Mart. 7.27 that the dog's master Dexter is apparently friends with and patron of the *poeta cliens* Martial.[51] In both poems Dexter appears as indulging in the pastime of hunting which not only in the Greco-Roman world but also in

---

also Frings (1998) 93–6 on the epitaph of the dog Margarita. On interactions between animals and humans in Greco-Roman antiquity cf. Fögen/Thomas (2017). For the construction of gender regarding (humans turned into) animals see also Sharrock in this volume.

48 As with all epitaphs – or any epigram, for that matter – that have been transmitted only in literary corpora and are not as obviously fictitious as Mart. 10.63 and 67, we will not be able to tell finally if 11.69 was composed for a "real" occasion or was even intended to be carved in stone. As to 11.69 as suited to be used as consolation and, potentially, even inscription cf. Herrlinger (1930) 103–5; Fögen (2018) 144 and 152, rejecting a general stance against the at times "bittersweet" literary animal epicedia as being ironic or parodistic. *Pace* Henriksén (2006) 358 and 365 with note 57 who considers both Lydia and her master Dexter fictional figures, taking exception to the missing deictic indication of the burial plot, the close literary link between Mart. 7.27 and 11.69, and the hyperbolic and thus supposedly parodistic usage of mythological comparisons. Stat. *silv.* 2.4 on the dead parrot of Atedius Melior, though, is an exemplar for massive mythological hyperbole in a poem that generally is not considered as satire or parody.

49 As a comparison, out of the 28 animal epigrams *AG* 7.189–216 seven are in the first-person voice (*AG* 7.191, 197, 198, 200, 207, 215, 216). Except for *AG* 7.200 Mindt (2020) analyses these poems and, amongst others, also inscriptional examples (cf. the useful overview on p. 210f.). On speaking animals in ancient literature in general cf. the substantial edited volume Schmalzgruber (2020).

50 Martial uses the expression *cito rapta* also in 1.116.3, the epitaph on Antulla, where it is the only indication of age, too; cf. also humorously transferred in 3.2.3 on his book imagined to be ruthlessly recycled as paper lid or bag.

51 Martial suggests Dexter as *amicus/patronus* in calling him *meus Dexter* in 7.27.3; cf. ThLL 8.0.916.46–83 *OLD* s.v. 2.b for this connotation of the possessive pronoun. As regards Dexter, cf. briefly Kay (1985) 217 and Galán Vioque (2002) 198, both referring to PIR^2, D 60. Shackleton Bailey (1990) 500 categorises Dexter as *poetae amicus* and does not mark him as fictitious name or figure in his *index nominum*. On the significant name of Dexter, who is a dexterous hunter cf. Giegengack (1969) 87; Galán Vioque (2002) 198. – On Flavian literary patronage cf. Nauta (2002); Zeiner (2005); Rühl (2006) and (2015).

other ancient cultures is conceptualised as a mainly aristocratic and male activity.[52] As will be discussed later, Lydia's first-person account is a highly efficient means to fashion not only Lydia but also her master Dexter as abounding in virtue and education.

Lydia plausibly opens her biographical account with her early childhood and concludes it with the circumstances of her sudden death fighting an enormous wild boar. Her life begins in the context of the amphitheatre (note the heavy, 6 syllables long *incipit "amphitheatrales"*).[53] There she obviously was brought up as hunting dog for spectacular public hunting shows, so called *venationes*, carried out by professional hunters, the so called *bestiarii*.[54] With verse two, though, Lydia leaves the amphitheatre for forests and a home, two spheres that she opposes by means of a chiastic antithesis (*silvis aspera, blanda domi*). It is here already, that we can see her having been adopted by Dexter and having accompanied him not only when out hunting but at home as well. In the domestic context Lydia characterises herself as *blanda*, as "tame" in the non-human meaning of the word that – in the strong anthropomorphic impetus of the poem – also evokes human associations. Eloquent as she thanks to Martial's epigrammatic intervention posthumously is, she states not only to have been a faithful dog that knew how to behave at home but also to have been emotionally close to Dexter. Beyond that, in speaking in the first-person voice, she also performs human characteristics of being *blanda* as she speaks in a very flattering and winning manner about her master.[55] In the further development of Lydia's self-fashioning, the domestic sphere does not seem to be of great importance anymore – but we shall return to that point later. First though, it is much more important for her account that she as a *venatrix* is outdoors in the forests, where she is *aspera*, "fierce", and thus the very opposite of *blanda*.[56] While it is not at all surprising to learn that a professionally trained dog – or even any other untrained predator, for that matter – is fierce when hunting for prey, I would like to argue that there is more to the use of this adjective when we, again, consider the specific human and female connotations of it: in erotic literature the adjective applies to *puellae* or *dominae* who are erotically reluctant and pitiless, otherwise it is especially used for resolute *viragines*, e.g. Camilla who is famously termed *aspera virgo* on the outset of her aristeia in *Aeneid* 11.664.[57]

---

[52] On hunting as leisure pursuit of the ancient upper classes cf. Anderson (1985), on Roman hunting cf. the substantial study Aymard (1951), esp. 297–329 dealing with the boar-hunt.
[53] This adjective is used in Latin Poetry here for the first time (cf. Kay, 1985, 216, referring to *ThLL* 1.1983.77f.).
[54] On the term *bestiarius* as opposed to *venator* cf. Coleman (2000) 251 n. 169.
[55] Cf. *ThLL* 2.0.2036.40–2037.84. Cf. below on the lapdog Issa in Mart. 1.109.
[56] For *asper* in use for animals cf. *ThLL* 2.0.814.24–45.
[57] Cf. *ThLL* 2.0.813.79–814.14 with the heading "*de feminis, maxime de puellis amorem spernentibus et de viraginibus*". For literary uses of the concept of *virago* see also Cordes and Stähle in this volume.

That Martial indeed models Lydia as a canine version of a mythical *virago* or heroine becomes obvious when we consider that there are a mere six instances of *venatrix* in the literary tradition before Martial, five of them in epics, namely the *Aeneid* (3 x), the *Metamorphoses,* and the *Thebaid.* As it turns out, the word is only used for divine or mythical figures, i.e. Venus, Arge, Atalante, Callisto, Camilla, and Ida.[58] Hence, by calling herself *venatrix*, Lydia inscribes herself in antiquity's most exclusive – i.e. female, mythical, and very epic – hunting club and becomes its only animal member. As regards Camilla, I want to argue that Lydia resembles her in even one more aspect: not only are both called *aspera* and *venatrix*, but also have both been raised by men. While the loss of Camilla's mother is not specifically addressed, Diana in *Aen.* 11.539–73 explains how her father Metabus saved little Camilla from approaching enemies by throwing her, bound to a spear, over a river and later raised her by putting her, in the stricter sense of *nutrire* as 'suckle',[59] to animal udders (ll. 571f.).[60] The aetiological impetus of this narrative is clear: it is through the upbringing by her father, through male agency, that Camilla exceptionally adopts male gendered role patterns and is not only ready to hunt from her earliest childhood on but also to fight and die in epic combat as a young woman.[61] Though in the *Liber spectaculorum* we also find a female *bestiaria*,[62] Lydia's upbringing in l. 1 is unmistakably marked as being also dominated by human male agency since she does not mention her mother who in the original sense of the verb *nutrire* would have suckled her with mother's milk but male dog breeders or trainers (cf. *amphitheatrales inter nutrita*

---

58 Venus (Verg. *Aen.* 1.319); the nymphs Callisto (Ov. *Met.* 2.492) and Arge (Hyg. *fab.* 205.1.1); Camilla (Verg. *Aen.* 11.780); Atalante (Stat. *Theb.* 9.616); Ida (Verg. *Aen.* 9.178); Val. Fl. 3.335 uses it attributively. Diana, the hunting godess par excellence, is called *venatrix* only from Iuv. 13.80 onward.
59 Cf. *OLD* s.v. 1 and the etymology s.v. *nutrix*.
60 Cf. Verg. *Aen.* 11.570–72 (*hic natam in dumis interque horrentia lustra / armentalis equae mammis et **lacte ferino / nutribat teneris immulgens ubera labris***.). This very motif – Horsfall (2003) 332 ad loc. calls it "the paradox of the mothering father" – also appears in Hyg. *fab.* 193.1 on Harpalyce (HARPAL<Y>CVS. *Harpal<y>cus rex Amymneorum Thrax cum haberet filiam Harpal<y>cen, amissa matre eius **uaccarum equarumque eam uberibus nutriuit** et crescentem armis exercuit . . .*). In Verg. *Aen.* 1.314–20 Venus is said to look like a Spartan girl or Harpalyce because the goddess appears disguised as *venatrix*.
61 On Camilla's transgression of gender norms, cf. Keith (2000) 27–31; Sharrock (2015) 159–68, with 161f. addressing the aetiological dimension of Camilla's rescue and upbringing. – After having taken her first steps, Camilla has been equipped – and obviously trained – as huntress by Metabus (cf. *Aen.* 11.573–80) and pursuing the spoils of the priest Chloreus in her aristeia she is famously termed *venatrix* shortly before she got killed by Arruns: *hunc [sc. Chloreum] uirgo, siue ut templis praefigeret arma / Troia, captiuo siue ut se ferret in auro / **uenatrix**, unum ex omni certamine pugnae / caeca sequebatur . . .* (Verg. *Aen.* 11.778–81). Calling her a huntress for precious spoils gloomily echoes Camilla killing the hunter Ornytus, whom she ridicules by asking if he thought the battle would be just another hunt (*siluis te, Tyrrhene, feras agitare putasti? Aen.* 11.686).
62 Cf. *spect.* 7, 8 (6, 6b) with Coleman (2006) 70–75 for further references on women in the arena.

magistros).⁶³ The opening distich, subtly enriched with motifs and vocabulary pointing to mythic and especially epic *viragines*, lets completely normal aspects of a professionally trained hunting dog's biography – to be a fierce huntress and reared by male human trainers – appear in a significantly different light: Martial makes Lydia's animal life and death a question of human gender difference and thus lets her seem as exceptional as the exemplary mythic huntresses he associates her with.⁶⁴ Additionally, through epic overtones he anticipates Lydia's mortal combat with the boar later in the poem, that also draws on epic models. Originally trained to entertain the crowds in the amphitheatre, Lydia envisions her spectacular dead for a different but probably even greater audience: Martial's readership.

In the midsection of the poem Lydia in the esteem of her master surpasses some of the most paradigmatic dogs of ancient mythology (*nec mallet habere*, l. 4). But what qualities do the other dogs stand for? Maira – usually considered the dog of Icarius but called the dog of his daughter Erigone by Martial – is a paradigm of canine loyalty: on behalf of Dionysus, Icarius let the shepherds of Attica for the first time ever taste wine. Getting inebriated, they thought Icarius has poisoned them and subsequently killed him. Erigone was led to her dead father by Maira and griefstricken hanged herself with the dog following her into death.⁶⁵ Cephalus' dog Lailaps on the other hand, can be considered the fastest dog in Greco-Roman mythology, since he was fated never to let a prey escape and was appropriately named "Hurricane". He was stalemated only in the hunt for the Teumessian fox, that in turn was destined to never be caught.⁶⁶ Both situations – i.e. the sorrowful end of Maira, as well as the endless chase of Lailaps – lead to divine intervention, as both dogs, in acknowledgement of their virtues, were by way of *katasterismoi* put on the night sky as stars for everyone to see and to remember forever (cf. *venit ad astra*; regarding Lailaps in l. 6).⁶⁷ Since their mistress or master also went to heaven (Icarius and Erigone

---

63 As regards the education of hunting dogs by their owners themselves or by professional *magistri canum*, cf. Aymard (1951) 242–4.

64 Roughgarden (2004) argues in her disputed study, that the concept of gender in certain contexts indeed applies to animals defining it as "the appearance, behavior, and life history of a sexed body" (p. 27).

65 On Maira cf. Schultz (1890–1894) 111f.; Heeg (1914) 973–5; Pochmarski (1986); Kay (1985) 217 referring, inter alia, to Hyg. *astr.* 2.4.2–5, *fab.* 130, Apollod. 3.14.7, and Eratosthenes' fragmentary epyllion *Erigone*.

66 Cf. Bömer (1976) 383f. and Fontenrose (1981) 101, n. 23 with further references. Hephaistos created Lailaps of bronze, originally for Zeus. The dog came into Cephalus' possession via his wife Procris, who in turn received it from King Minos or Diana in Crete. In skilfully intertwining mythological and huntsman's knowledge, Martial may hint us with the attribute *Dictaeu . . . de gente* (l. 5) both at Lailaps' former masters from Crete and the breed he resembled, as hunters in Greco-Roman antiquity held dogs from Crete in high esteem (cf. Kay 1985, 217, *inter alia* referring to Aymard 1951, 246–51).

67 As regards Lailaps, the mythological tradition varies between two strands, the *katasterismos* of the dog or his petrification. The former is presented by Eratosth. 1.33.1–10 (ed. Olivieri) and Hyg.

as stars and Cephalus as lover of the goddess Eos[68]) the dogs stay together with or close to them in heaven for all time. Despite this loyalty of cosmic scale, Lydia by way of superlative claims to be the most loyal of all: she is *fidissima* (l. 3).

Outdone by Lydia is also Odysseus' dog Argos who – after twenty years of separation and despite the fact that his master with the help of Athena is disguised as an old beggar – is the only non-divine figure on Ithaka that immediately recognises the returned hero, only to die immediately afterwards.[69] This famous and touching scene in *Odyssey* Book 17 makes Argos a prime exemplar for canine *fides* but beyond that, the once excellent hunting dog[70] is exemplary in another sense as well: he strikingly resembles the state of the *oikos* he belongs to, its inhabitants and the master himself. In Homeric scholarship this pattern of resemblance between dog, *oikos*, and master has long been noticed and is often called the "watchdog motif".[71] This motif appears several times in the *Odyssey*,[72] but pitiful Argos dying neglected and louse-ridden in front of Odysseus' palace is arguably the most famous instance of it. It is exactly this scenario that Lydia evokes in ll. 7f. in pointing out the high age and uselessness of Argos (cf. *inutilis aetas . . . longa dies*). The dying dog not only resembles Odysseus disguised as old beggar but particularly the moral and economical decline of the palace since the freeloading suitors seized control of it. In evoking Argos and hence the watchdog motif of *Odyssey* 17, Martial gives us the blueprint for a reading of epigram 11.69 in this very vein, which results in a literary double vision, a duplicated role construction for both Lydia and her master: the fierce huntress Lydia represents the eager hunter Dexter and his *domus*. As Lydia in a hyperbolic image typical of Martial attacked a boar larger than the Calydonian or the Erymanthian (cf. l. 10), Dexter flatteringly appears as greater a hunter than Meleager and Hercules have been. As I argued elsewhere, the short description of the fight with the boar in l. 9 (*fulmineo spumantis apri sum dente perempta*) contributes to this heroising and epicising of Lydia and Dexter because it resonates with associations to epic intertexts.[73] Within

---

astr. 2.35 (where the dog at first is petrified, though) the latter by Ov. *Met.* 7.759–93. As to the question into which stars they have been transformed, the ancient tradition varies as well: under discussion are the constellations Canis Major and Canis Minor, as well as their brightest star each, i.e. Sirius and Procyon (cf. Eratosth. 1.33.1–10 [ed. Olivieri]; Hyg. *astr.* 2.4.4, 2.35, *fab.* 130.5).

68 As to Cephalus and Eos cf. Kay (1985) 217 referring to Eur. *Hipp.* 455f. and Apollod. 1.9.4.
69 Cf. Hom. *Od.* 17.291–327. For the adjective *Dulichius* referring to Odysseus cf. *OLD* s.v.
70 Cf. Hom. *Od.* 17.313–17.
71 Cf. de Jong (2001) 177 with further references; Rose (1979); Beck (1991); Scodel (2005).
72 Cf. Hom. *Od.* 10.212–19 (men turned into lions and wolves by Kirke and behaving like tame dogs in front of her house), 14.29–36, 16.4f. and 16.162f. (the watchdogs of Eumaios).
73 Generally, in Homer and Ovid epic hunting scenes, especially the killing of the game, follow in many aspects epic combat scenes (cf. de Jong 2001, 256f. and 478; Tsitsiou-Chelidoni 2003, 195f.) As regards Mart. 11.69.9, *fulmineus* in epic contexts is used for deadly weapons, for hands wielding such weapons, and for heroes in combat (cf. *ThLL* 6.1.1532.7–10 referring to Vergil, Lucan, Valerius Flaccus, Silius Italicus, and Statius). Furthermore, the combination of *fulmineus dens* and *spumans*

the context of literary patronage this is an important aspect of the poem: it serves not only as consolation of the master who lost his favourite dog but also as encomium of Dexter, who is displayed by Lydia or Martial, respectively, as a hunter abounding in heroic *virtus* of epic scale.[74]

The interpretation of Mart. 11.69 in the vein of the watchdog motif can be deepened further, if we consider not only the heroising and epicising content of the poem but also its representation through Lydia as first-person speaker. While we find first-person voiced animals not only in Aristophanes, Aesop, Phaedrus, the aforementioned animal epicedia, as well as in Martial's *Xenia* and *Apophoreta*, Lydia is the only articulate animal in the *Epigrammaton libri*.[75] How much she stands out through her command of language becomes apparent in epigram 1.109 on the lapdog beauty Issa that is presented and gendered completely different from Lydia (Mart. 1.109.1–7, 14–16):

> *Issa est passere nequior Catulli,*
> *Issa est purior osculo columbae,*
> *Issa est blandior omnibus puellis,*
> *Issa est carior Indicis lapillis,*
> *Issa est deliciae catella Publi.*   5
> *hanc tu, si queritur, loqui putabis;*
> *sentit tristitiamque gaudiumque.*
> . . .
> *castae tantus inest pudor catellae,*

---

aper is highly reminiscent of the introduction of the Calydonian boar in Ov. *Met.* 8.287–9 (*fervida cum rauco latos stridore per armos / **spuma** fluit, **dentes** aequantur **dentibus** Indis; / **fulmen** ab ore venit, frondes adflatibus ardent*) and might also refer to Hom. *Il.* 9.539, the prototypical description on the Calydonian boar (ὦρσεν ἔπι χλούνην σῦν ἄγριον ἀργιόδοντα . . .). For detailed discussion cf. Baumann (2019) 206–10.

74 The boar hunt was as a matter of fact nothing for the faint hearted: In the northern Mediterranean territories, boars were by far the most prestigious and dangerous game that hunters could aim for (cf. Aymard, 1951, 328). The boar hunt required not only close combat (cf. Dexter's kill in the companion piece Mart. 7.27.1–3: *aper . . . quem meus intravit splendenti cuspide Dexter*) but also – as Xen. *kyn.* 10.1 and 3 reports – hunting dogs of the best possible quality. The death of Adonis (cf. e.g. Ov. *met.* 10.710–16), Odysseus' famous scar (Hom. *Od.* 19.449–51), and the deadly wounded heroes in the Calydonian hunt (cf. e.g. Ov. *met.* 8.362–4, 399–402) demonstrate how risky a pastime the boar hunt was.

75 Cf. Arist. *Av.*, *Ran.*; Mart. 13.59 (dormouse), 71 (flamingo), 72 (pheasant), 76 (woodcock), 82 (oyster), 83 (prawns), 87 (murexes), 94 (does), all of them intended to be eaten; 14.73 (parrot), 76 (magpie), 202 (monkey). Interesting in this context is the cluster of Mart. 14.73–6 on parrot, crow, nightingale, and magpie, as they reflect upon the ability of these birds to speak. A key difference between the monodistichs of Mart. 13 and 14 and 11.69 is the depth of figure development: While the gift inscriptions are in principle supposed to match any bird that is trained to repeat specific words and belongs to the species indicated by the lemma, Lydia – in conjunction with a complex role construction – is displayed as an individual with a distinctive biography and particular character traits.

> *ignorat Venerem; nec invenimus*   15
> *dignum tam tenera virum puella.*

> Issa is naughtier than Catullus' sparrow, Issa is purer than a dove's kiss, Issa is more winning than any girl, Issa is more precious than Indian pearls, Issa is a lapdog, Publius' darling. If she whines, you will think she's talking; she feels both his sadness and his joy. . .
> Such is the inborn modesty of this chaste little dog, she knows nothing of love; nor can we find any husband worthy of so tender a maid.

Even though Lydia (at least at home) and Issa have in common to be charming (*blanda*, l. 3) and to be emotionally attached to their masters, Issa's role construction as lovely and chaste girl (cf. *casta catella* and *tenera puella*; ll. 14, 16) is the outright antithesis to the canine *virago* Lydia and her assumption of human male-gendered role patterns. Despite the opening animal comparisons referring to Catullus' sparrow and a dove's kiss (ll. 1f.) Martial on the outset of the poem is wittily leading the reader to believe Issa was human and is giving away her canine identity in l. 5 only.[76] Even though one might think she could speak (*loqui putabis*; l. 6), Issa's most eloquent articulation is to whine and thus utterly non-human. Quite differently, Lydia in the fiction of the epitaph is easily one of the most eloquent and most well-educated dogs in ancient literature.[77] She speaks in polished verses and navigates authoritatively through the literary canon. If we consider this implication, the reference to the watchdog motif makes the house of Dexter appear as a place of educated literary contemplation. Through first person voiced Lydia the indirect role construction for Dexter thus gains a decisive completion: he not just seems to be a reckless killer of dangerous beasts like prominent *bestiarii* featured elsewhere in Martial's work, but rather a well-educated man, familiar with the social codes of Roman nobility. He is, thanks to the eloquent Lydia, to be imagined as spending his *otium* with pursuits appropriate for a distinguished *patronus* – like hunting, reading, and promoting writers like Martial.

In such a reading of the epitaph Lydia's closing words *non potui fato nobiliore mori* can be understood in different ways: they display her *asperitas* as *virago* or canine heroine, willing to fight till the bitter end. But this noble end can also be read as Lydia claiming for herself the human social status of a *nobilis* or at least to belong to the household of *nobilis*. This kind of assertion would be typical of human epitaphs as we have seen above regarding the distinguished anonymous matron of Mart. 10.63. But above that, Lydia's last words can also be read as a metapoetic commentary on Martial's refined and skilful poetry that literarily ennobles

---

[76] Lydia only in l. 4. explicitly tells us that she is a dog. But even before it is clear that it can hardly be a human female being, that is raised and trained in the Amphitheatre which she then leaves for her new master's house and forests.

[77] For talking dogs in sepulchral epigrams cf. the synopsis in Mindt (2020) 210f. and especially pp. 225–8 on the, as Mindt puts it, "*docta catella*" Margarita. For other literary speaking dogs cf. e.g. Aesop. 41, 52, 92, 127, 134, 223; Phaedr. 1.19, 23, 25, 3.7, 15, 5.10.

Lydia's life and death in letting her and Dexter intertextually interact with but the best dogs, huntresses and hunters and hence appear as hunters of mythic and epic scale. What could after having passed away be more noble than having such an epitaph composed for oneself by the unchallenged master of the Roman epigram? As we have seen above in the discussion of Mart. 10.63, the poet repeatedly claims for his work to withstand the ravages of time even better than the most famous and endurable sepulchral monuments. Quite similarly, in Mart. 11.69 even being set amongst the stars on heaven like Maira and Lailaps does not seem to be as constant let alone noble as to be included in Martial's *Epigrammaton libri*.

Martial shapes the first-person speakers of the epigrams 10.63 and 11.69 by way of intensely gendered role constructions as women (or anthropomorphised female animal, respectively) who, on the one hand, take up existing role models and concepts, but, on the other hand, diverge drastically from traditional social norms for women and associated role expectations: the otherwise impeccable matron brakes a taboo in using strong language and reflecting upon sexual and readerly pleasure; Lydia's hunting prowess might be absolutely expected for a professionally trained dog but in anthropomorphic translation her biography appears exceptional because it is likened to human *viragines* who extraordinarily adopt male role patterns. Different as the role constructions of the two female speakers may be, they are surprisingly similar in that they are implicitly intertwined with role constructions for male participants of the literary communication. Both female egos literally speak *pro domo*: the matron of epigram 10.63 reflects upon Martial's elsewhere phallocentrically defined poetics that especially aim at readerly pleasure and range; Lydia, however, by means of the watchdog motif speaks not least for her master but also points out the merits of Martial's poetry. In the end, like so many other figures in Martial's epigrammatic microcosm, the two only female first-person voices in the *Epigrammaton libri* cannot escape the gravitation of their literary creator Martial. His ego looms large even when it in rare cases gives way to such self-confident speakers such as the matron and Lydia.

Bibliography

Texts and translations

Griechische Grabgedichte, griech. und dt., ed. Werner Peek, Berlin 1960.
M. Valerii Martialis *Epigrammata* post W. Heraeus ed. David R. M. Shackleton Bailey, Stuttgart 1990.
Martial, *Epigrams*, lat./engl., ed. Shackleton Bailey, 3 vols., Cambridge, MA 1993.

Books and articles

Adams (1982): James N. Adams, *The Latin Sexual Vocabulary*, London.
Anderson (1985): J. K. Anderson, *Hunting in the Ancient World*, Berkeley.
Anz (1998): Thomas Anz, *Literatur und Lust: Glück und Unglück beim Lesen*, München.
Aymard (1951): J. M. Aymard, *Essai sur les chasses romaines des origines à la fin du siècle des Antonins (Cynegetica)*, Paris.
Banta (1998): David Samuel Banta, *Literary Apology and Literary Genre in Martial*, Diss. Duke University, Durham, N.C.
Barthes (1973): Roland Barthes, *Le plaisir du texte*, Paris.
Baumann (2019): Helge Baumann, *Das Epos im Blick: Intertextualität und Rollenkonstruktionen in Martials Epigrammen und Statius' Silvae*, Berlin/Boston.
Beck (1991): William Beck, "Dogs, Dwellings, and Masters: Ensemble and Symbol in the Odyssey", *Hermes* 119, 158–167.
Becker (2008): Maria Becker, "'Ich will nicht die Frau meiner Frau sein': zur Funktion von Ich-Aussagen bei Martial", *Philologus* 152, 282–293.
Bömer (1976): Franz Bömer, *P. Ovidius Naso. Metamorphosen. Kommentar. Buch VI–VII*, Heidelberg.
Christian (2015): Timo Christian, *Gebildete Steine: zur Rezeption literarischer Techniken in den Versinschriften seit dem Hellenismus*, Göttingen.
Coleman (2000): Kathleen M. Coleman, "Entertaining Rome", in: Jon C. N. Coulston and Hazel Dodge (eds.), *Ancient Rome: The Archaeology of the Eternal City*, Oxford, 210–258, ill. carte.
Coleman (2006): Kathleen M. Coleman, *M. Valerii Martialis Liber spectaculorum*, Oxford/New York.
Dam (1984): Harm-Jan van Dam, *P. Papinius Statius, Silvae Book II: A Commentary*, Leiden.
de Jong (2001): Irene J. F. de Jong, *A Narratological Commentary on the Odyssey*, Cambridge/New York.
Fögen (2018): Thorsten Fögen, "Zum Sterben und Tod von Tieren in lateinischen Trauergedichten", *A&A* 64, 130–155.
Fögen/Thomas (2017): Thorsten Fögen and Edmund Thomas, *Interactions between Animals and Humans in Graeco-Roman Antiquity*, Berlin/Boston.
Fontenrose (1981): Joseph Eddy Fontenrose, *Orion: The Myth of the Hunter and the Huntress*, Berkeley.
Frings (1998): Irene Frings, "Mantua me genuit: Vergils Grabepigramm auf Stein und Pergament", *ZPE* 123, 89–100.
Galán Vioque (2002): Guillermo Galán Vioque, *Martial, Book VII: A Commentary*, translated by J. J. Zoltowski, Leiden/Boston.
Giegengack (1969): J. M. Giegengack, *Significant Names in Martial*, Diss. Yale University, New Haven, CT.
Hallett (1996): Judith P. Hallett, "Nec castrare velis meos libellos: Sexual and Poetic lusus in Catullus, Martial and the Carmina Priapea", in: Claudia Klodt (ed.), *Satura lanx: Festschrift für Werner A. Krenkel zum 70. Geburtstag*, Hildesheim, 321–344.
Harrison (2007): Stephen J. Harrison, *Generic Enrichment in Vergil and Horace*, Oxford/New York.
Häusle (1979): Helmut Häusle, *Einfache und frühe Formen des griechischen Epigramms*, Innsbruck.
Häusle (1980): Helmut Häusle, *Das Denkmal als Garant des Nachruhms. Beiträge zur Geschichte und Thematik eines Motivs in lateinischen Inschriften*, München.
Heeg (1914): Joseph Heeg, "Ikarios", *RE* IX.1, 973–977.
Heilmann (1998): Willibald Heilmann, "Epigramme Martials über Leben und Tod", in: Farouk Grewing (ed.), *Toto notus in orbe: Perspektiven der Martial-Interpretation*, Stuttgart, 205–219.

Henriksén (2006): Christer Henriksén, "Martial's Modes of Mourning: Sepulchral Epitaphs in the 'Epigrams'", in: Ruurd Robijn Nauta, Harm-Jan Van Dam and Johannes Jacobus Louis Smolenaars (eds.), *Flavian Poetry*, Leiden, 349–367.

Herrlinger (1930): Gerhard Herrlinger, *Totenklage um Tiere in der antiken Dichtung, mit einem Anhang byzantinischer, mittellateinischer und neuhochdeutscher Tierepikedien*, Stuttgart.

Horsfall (2003): Nicholas Horsfall, *Virgil, Aeneid 11: A Commentary*, Leiden/Boston.

Kay (1985): N. M. Kay, *Martial Book XI: A Commentary*, London.

Keegan (2014): Peter Keegan, *Roles for Men and Women in Roman Epigraphic Culture and Beyond: Gender, Social Identity and Cultural Practice in Private Latin Inscriptions and the Literary Record*, Oxford.

Keith (2000): Alison Keith, *Engendering Rome: Women in Latin Epic*, Cambridge/New York.

Keller (1909): Otto Keller, *Die antike Tierwelt. Erster Band: Säugetiere*, Leipzig.

Lattimore (1942): R. Lattimore, *Themes in Greek and Latin Epitaphs*, Urbana.

Leary (1996): T. J. Leary, *Martial Book XIV: The Apophoreta. Text with Introduction and Commentary*, London.

Leary (2001): T. J. Leary, *Martial Book XIII: The Xenia. Text with Introduction and Commentary*, London.

Lorenz (2002): Sven Lorenz, *Erotik und Panegyrik: Martials epigrammatische Kaiser*, Tübingen.

Lorenz (2009): Sven Lorenz, "Der 'ernste' Martial: Tod und Trauer in den Epigrammen", *Gymnasium* 116, 359–380.

Meyer (2005): Doris Meyer, *Inszeniertes Lesevergnügen: das inschriftliche Epigramm und seine Rezeption bei Kallimachos*, Stuttgart.

Mindt (2020): Nina Mindt, "Rede toter Tiere. Tierrede in antiken Epigrammen und im *Culex*", in: Hedwig Schmalzgruber (ed.), *Speaking Animals in Ancient Literature*, Heidelberg, 207–251.

Nauta (2002): Ruurd R. Nauta, *Poetry for Patrons: Literary Communication in the Age of Domitian*, Leiden/Boston.

Nisbet/Rudd (2004): R. G. M. Nisbet and Niall Rudd, *A Commentary on Horace: Odes, Book III*, Oxford/New York.

Obermayer (1998): Hans Peter Obermayer, *Martial und der Diskurs über männliche "Homosexualität" in der Literatur der frühen Kaiserzeit*, Tübingen.

O'Connor (1998): Eugene Michael O'Connor, "Martial the moral jester: priapic motifs and the restoration of order in the epigrams", in: Farouk Grewing (ed.), *Toto notus in orbe: Perspektiven der Martial-Interpretation*, Stuttgart, 187–204.

Pochmarski (1986): Erwin Pochmarski, "Erigone I", *LIMC* III.1, 823f.

Rose (1979): G. P. Rose, "Odysseus' Barking Heart", *TAPA* 109, 215–230.

Roughgarden (2004): Joan Roughgarden, *Evolution's Rainbow: Diversity, Gender, and Sexuality in Nature and People*, Berkeley.

Rühl (2006): Meike Rühl, *Literatur gewordener Augenblick: die Silven des Statius im Kontext literarischer und sozialer Bedingungen von Dichtung*, Berlin.

Rühl (2015): Meike Rühl, "Creating the Distinguished Addressee. Literary Patronage in the Works of Statius", in: William J. Dominik, Carole Elizabeth Newlands and Kyle G. Gervais (eds.), *Brill's Companion to Statius*, Leiden, 91–105.

Scherf (2004): Johannes Scherf, "Epigramm 63: Epitaph für eine keusche Ehefrau", in: Gregor Damschen and Andreas Heil (eds.), *Marcus Valerius Martialis, Epigrammaton liber decimus, Das zehnte Epigrammbuch. Text, Übersetzung, Interpretationen. Mit einer Einleitung, Martial-Bibliographie und einem rezeptionsgeschichtlichen Anhang*, Frankfurt am Main, 236f.

Schmalzgruber (2020): Hedwig Schmalzgruber, *Speaking Animals in Ancient Literature*, Heidelberg.

Schmitz (2010): Thomas A. Schmitz, "Speaker and Addressee in Early Greek Epigram and Lyric", in: Manuel Baumbach, Andrej Petrović and Ivana Petrović (eds.), *Archaic and Classical Greek Epigram*, Cambridge/New York, 25–41.

Schöffel (2002): Christian Schöffel, *Martial, Buch 8: Einleitung, Text, Übersetzung, Kommentar*, Stuttgart.

Scodel (2005): Ruth Scodel, "Odysseus' Dog and the Productive Household", *Hermes* 133, 401–408.

Sharrock (2015): Alison R. Sharrock, "Warrior Women in Roman Epic", in: Jacqueline Fabre-Serris and Alison M. Keith (eds.), *Women and War in Antiquity*, Baltimore, MD, 157–178.

Sullivan (1991): J. P. Sullivan, *Martial, the Unexpected Classic: a Literary and Historical Study*, Cambridge/New York.

Tolman (1910): Judson A. Tolman, *A Study of the Sepulchral Inscriptions in Buecheler's "Carmina Epigraphica Latina"*, Chicago.

Treggiari (1991): Susan Treggiari, *Roman Marriage: Iusti Coniuges from the Time of Cicero to the Time of Ulpian*, Oxford/New York.

Tsitsiou-Chelidoni (2003): Chrysanthe Tsitsiou-Chelidoni, *Ovid, Metamorphosen, Buch VIII: narrative Technik und literarischer Kontext*, Bern/Frankfurt am Main.

Tueller (2008): Michael A. Tueller, *Look who's Talking: Innovations in Voice and Identity in Hellenistic Epigram*, Leuven/Dudley, MA.

Tueller (2010): Michael A. Tueller, "The Passer-by in Archaic and Classical Epigram", in: Manuel Baumbach, Andrej Petrović and Ivana Petrović (eds.), *Archaic and Classical Greek Epigram*, Cambridge/New York, 42–60.

Vestrheim (2010): Gjert Vestrheim, "Voice in Sepulchral Epigrams: Some Remarks on the Use of First and Second Person in Sepulchral Epigrams, and a Comparison with Lyric Poetry", in: Manuel Baumbach, Andrej Petrović and Ivana Petrović (eds.), *Archaic and Classical Greek Epigram*, Cambridge/New York, 61–78.

Watson/Watson (2003): Lindsay Watson and Patricia Watson, *Martial. Select Epigrams*, Cambridge Greek and Latin Classics, Cambridge/New York.

Watson (2005): Patricia Watson, "Non Tristis Torus et Tamen Pudicus: The Sexuality of the Matrona in Martial", *Mnemosyne* 58, 62–87.

Wells (2019): Jessica Rose Wells, *Gender, Text, and the Body in Martial's Epigrams*, Diss. University of Illinois.

Williams (2002): Craig A. Williams, "Sit nequior omnibus libellis: Text, Poet, and Reader in the Epigrams of Martial", *Philologus* 146, 150–171.

Zeiner (2005): Noelle K. Zeiner, *Nothing Ordinary here: Statius as Creator of Distinction in the Silvae*, New York.

III **The Gendered 'I' in Choral Lyric and Tragedy**

Emily Hauser
Making Men: Gender and the Poet in Pindar

Abstract: The identity of Pindar's "I" has long proven difficult to interpret. This chapter moves the focus away from the ἐγώ and the poet/chorus debate, onto the gendered terms which are used to construct the persona of the poet and his milieu. A close reading of the gendering of terms for "poet" in Pindar shows how a masculinizing image of the poet and his community is built up, from the mechanisms of inspiration between (female) goddess and (male) prophet-poet, to the valorizing "man-making" function of Pindar's songs. By using gender as a lens for the discussion of first-person statements, the aim is to shift the conversation from simplified dichotomies around the identity of the "I" in Pindar to the poetics of the discourse of masculinity which pervades Pindar's poetry and which crosses between poet, chorus, audience, and the subjects of song.

Keywords: choral 'I', choral community, poetics, authorship, subjects of song

1 The problem of Pindar's ἐγώ

Pindar is particularly well-known for the first-person statements which appear throughout his victory odes.[1] Take, for example, the opening of *Olympian* 2, line 2: "what god, what hero, what man shall we sing of?" (τίνα θεόν, τίν' ἥρωα, τίνα δ' ἄνδρα κελαδήσομεν;). This first-person verb ("we shall sing") clearly draws on the tradition of first-person statements by archaic bards (ἀοιδοί): compare "sing to me, Muse, of a man" (ἄνδρα μοι ἔννεπε, μοῦσα, Hom. *Od.* 1.1) at the opening of the *Odyssey*. Pindar's first-person κελαδήσομεν in *Ol.* 2.2 aligns with Homer's μοι (*Od.* 1.1); even the topic – ἄνδρα – is the same. But in Pindar's second *Olympian*, Homer's singular pronoun ("sing to me") is transformed into a plural first-person verb ("we shall sing"). This gestures to a transition from Homer's lone bard (ἀοιδός) to the communal performance context of the victory ode, which saw a soloist performing with, or in response to, a wider chorus.[2] These first-person statements thus serve both to connect Pindar to the poetic tradition which looked back to Homer, and, at

---

[1] There has been much controversy around the use of the first person in Pindar (see further below, n. 3). The debate flourished in the late 1980s and early 1990s in particular: see Anzai (1994), Bremer (1990), Burnett (1989), D'Alessio (1994), Gentili (1990), Goldhill (1991) 142–66, Lefkowitz (1963), (1991) and (1995), Morgan (1993), Pfeijffer (1999a). Pindar is quoted from the edition by Snell/Maehler (1980) throughout; translations are my own.

[2] For a helpful overview of the available evidence for and bibliography on the performance context of Pindar's odes, see Carey (2007); see also Carey (1989) and (1991), Heath (1988), Heath/Lefkowitz (1991).

the same time, subtly to translate Pindar's poetry into the performance context of epinician.

Much of the scholarship around Pindar's first-person statements has focused on the extent to which we can take these first-person statements as referring to Pindar, or to the chorus with whom the soloist may have performed his odes.³ The problem is compounded by the fact that we know very little for sure about the performance context of the victory odes: although the scholia tell us that the odes were performed by a chorus, we find a combination of different types of first-person statements in Pindar's poetry. Some seem to gesture to a communal performance, or at the very least other performers – as with the first-person plural κελαδήσομεν in *Ol.* 2.2, or the "celebration-band" (κῶμος) of young men at *Nem.* 3.5.⁴ Others appear to emphasize the voice and authority of the poet, as at *Nem.* 9.54: "I pray to sing of this excellence" (εὔχομαι ταύταν ἀρετὰν κελαδῆσαι), or *Ol.* 1.17f., "take the Dorian lyre down from its hook" (Δωρίαν ἀπὸ φόρμιγγα πασσάλου / λάμβαν'). An additional issue is whether we can see any of these first-person statements as expressions of biographical fact, and – if not – how we might interpret the function of the intrusion of the authorial (or choral) "I" from a literary-critical perspective.⁵

As often, the answer is likely more complex than a simple straight reading would suggest: it is not a case of *either* a solo poet *or* a communal chorus. The most helpful analyses of Pindar in recent years have suggested that we can instead see the poet's voice shifting between his own and that of the chorus in ways that tie in the solo voice with that of the civic community, and performing a wide-ranging authorial persona which projects the poet's (as well as the victor's) achievements into the future through the anticipation of solo reperformances.⁶ In particular, the move towards reading Pindar's first-person statements as complex and shifting constructions of a poetic persona engaging in different "communicative strategies" (following Giambattista D'Alessio)

---

3 For the choral hypothesis, see Carey (1989) and (1991), Stehle (1997) ch. 3. For the solo hypothesis, see Lefkowitz (1988) 3f. and (1991) ch. 9, Heath (1988), Heath/Lefkowitz (1991). For an argument for an oscillation between poet and chorus, see Currie (2013).
4 μελιγαρύων τέκτονες / κώμων νεανίαι, "young men, craftsmen of honey-voiced celebrations" (*Nem.* 3.4f.). On the κῶμος, see Agócs (2012), Eckerman (2010), Heath (1988), Morgan (1993).
5 Bowra (1964) represents the old school where Pindar's first-person statements were seen as instances of biographical fact; these are now typically understood to be motivated by genre, following Bundy (1962), and fictional/mimetic (Lefkowitz 1963; Lefkowitz 1980; Miller 1993).
6 Morgan (1993) 2 puts it particularly well: "a more complicated dynamic wherein the poet's voice is imposed upon a chorus of multiple voices that in turn draws the κῶμος into its orbit." Compare D'Alessio (1994) esp. 117 on "the image of the *persona loquens*" as "an authoritative voice speaking to and/or on behalf of a community to which he may or may not belong". See further Currie (2013), Goldhill (1991) 144f., Parmentier/Felson (2016); and, for an exploration of the different elements of the poet's persona, Gentili (1990) and Lidov (1993) 76. On the importance of reperformance for interpreting the opaque references to performance context, see Currie (2004), Hubbard (2004), Morgan (1993) 12, Morrison (2007) 42–5, Nagy (1989) 62, Phillips (2017).

has been particularly useful.⁷ I intend here to pick up on this emphasis on persona, but transfer the focus onto a different aspect of the first-person statements in Pindar's odes in ways that refract back onto questions of male authorship and male community – by looking specifically at the *terminology* used for the persona of the poet, and the strategies these words use to reflect or create norms around gender and authorship.⁸ The intention here is not to disassociate the poet from the chorus, or to argue for the poet's sole performance of the odes in the first instance, but rather to investigate what using the lens of gender on the nouns used to claim poetic identity might tell us about the constructed norms of epinician authorship in relation to gender. In a sense, then, we are investigating the (male) poet's strategy of self-creation in tandem with the (male) communal context of the odes' performance, as well as anticipating their reperformance by and for men as markers of the poet's subsequent fame. These statements, I suggest, then, work together with the original and subsequent performance contexts to build and shore up the persona of the male poet and his connection with his male-normative choral community, as well as the masculine subjects of his song.⁹ By using gender as a lens for the discussion of these first-person statements of poetic identity, we can thus avoid simplified dichotomies between poet and chorus, and instead focus on the generalizing discourse of masculinity which pervades the odes and which crosses between poet, chorus, audience, and the subjects of song.

2 Words for (male) poets: From ἀοιδός to ποιητής

The most common noun to describe the male poet in the archaic period was ἀοιδός, "bard" – a term used by both Homer and Hesiod, as well as in the Homeric Hymns.¹⁰ Moving into the fifth century BCE, new terms came to displace the old: in particular, a family of words for "making" poetry (ποιεῖν), pre-eminent among them the term

---

7 D'Alessio (1994) 117: "the image of the *persona loquens* is the result of a complex construction whose understanding involves the comprehension of the particular communicative strategy chosen each time by the poet."
8 For a survey of gender and performance in Pindar (with a focus on performance rather than authorship, and an emphasis on the choral nature of the odes), see Stehle (1997) ch. 3. I will be focusing on poetic authorship here, although it is worth noting that Pindar mentions prose-writers (λόγιοι) twice, at *Nem* 6.45 and *Pyth* 1.94. On the "professional" statements made by Pindar, see Lefkowitz (1963) 178f. and Morgan (1993).
9 I use "subject" here and throughout to mean "subject-matter", rather than in the grammatical sense ("subject" vs. "object").
10 See the passage in *Odyssey* 17, in which Eumaeus lists the male bard (ἀοιδός, 385) amongst a list of "skilled craftsmen" (δημιοεργοί, 383). See also *Il.* 24.720, *Od.* 3.267, 3.270, 4.17, 8.87 etc., and Hes. *Theog.* 95, 99, *Op.* 26. On the epic bard, see Ford (1994) 90–130; on the semantics of the term ἄοιδος, see Maslov (2009). On terms for female poets, see Hauser (2016), and for a fuller discussion of the relationship between authorship terms and gender, Hauser (2023).

ποιητής ("poet, maker"). Andrew Ford provides an excellent overview of the changes which took place, and their significance for mapping shifts in attitudes to poetry, arguing that their derivation from the verb ποιεῖν suggests a move towards a more artisanal, craft-focused vision of poetry.[11] With the shift in the fifth and fourth centuries away from orality towards "a sense of songs as texts to be studied rather than performed",[12] the overwhelming preponderance of ποιητής and its cognates demonstrates, according to Ford, "an increasing awareness of the lasting powers of texts [which] supported the conception of song as a stable work rather than a performance."[13] This technical, formal visualization of poetry-making came from a reconceptualization of writing (and the function and dissemination of texts) as a technical skill and lasting artefact, like craftsmanship – mostly among writers who wanted to emphasize their technical expertise –, deriving from critics who were writing in the tradition of Ionian *historia*. This, in turn, enabled the increasing professionalization of literature and the continuation of a semantics for authorship rooted in -ποιός ("-maker") suffixes into the Hellenistic period.[14]

Where ἀοιδός continued to be used, it now had an archaizing flavor, referring back to the original discourse of male poetry initiated by Homer and Hesiod. Pindar demonstrates this at the opening of *Nemean* 2, where he refers to the Homeridae, the group of poets who claimed to be both literal (genealogical) and poetic descendants of Homer: Ὁμηρίδαι / ῥαπτῶν ἐπέων . . . ἀοιδοί ("the Homeridae, singers [ἀοιδοί] of stitched verses", *Nem.* 2.1f.).[15] The term ἀοιδοί here refers to a very specific genre and tradition: the poetic lineage that goes back to Homer, suggesting that ἀοιδός has already acquired a specialized sense of "male epic bard", most often with reference to Homer and those who claimed literal or poetic descent from him. The masculinity of this tradition is underlined by the use of Ὁμηρίδαι, a male patronymic – literally "sons of Homer" – figuring the lineage of ἀοιδοί descending from Homer as a male father-to-son relationship.

---

[11] Ford (2002) ch. 6; see also Braun (1938), Graziosi (2002) 41–7, Svenbro (1984) 155–79.
[12] Ford (2002) 154.
[13] Ford (2002) 157.
[14] Ford (2002) 134, 294.
[15] See below p. 144. Pindar is giving an etymology of the term "rhapsode" (ῥαψῳδός) here: see Nagy (1989) 7, Pfeijffer (1999b) ad loc.

3 "Sung of" women, "singing" men: The male poet as singing prophet

The term ἀοιδός only occurs twice elsewhere in Pindar's victory odes, in *Pythian* 1.[16] In another ode, *Nemean* 3, however, we find an adjective – ἀοίδιμος ("sung of") – which is connected to ἀοιδός both through its etymology (both derive from the verb ἀείδειν) and its literary history. Towards the end of the ode, the poet moves into the first person to dedicate the song to his patron, Aristocleides of Aegina: χαῖρε, φίλος· ἐγὼ τόδε τοι / πέμπω . . . / πόμ' ἀοίδιμον ("cheers, my friend: I send you this drink of song", *Nem* 3.76–9). The phrase "drink of song" clearly anticipates the context of a toast raised to the dedicatee (χαῖρε),[17] with the offering of the wine and the gift of the song conflated into the phrase "song-drink".[18] At the same time, the adjective ἀοίδιμος has a special literary resonance: it appears first in Greek literature in a markedly metapoetic, and gender-significant, passage in Homer's *Iliad*. In book 6, during Hector's visit to the women of Troy, Helen – a female character whose mimetic speech and metapoetic weaving often associates her problematically with the figure of the poet[19] – appears to look through the mechanism of her own creation in poetry: ὡς καὶ ὀπίσσω / ἀνθρώποισι πελώμεθ' ἀοίδιμοι ἐσσομένοισι ("that in future we will be subjects of song for generations to come", *Il*. 6.357f.).[20] Where Helen uses ἀοίδιμος to mean "subject of song", however, here at *Nem*. 3.79 it is clearly not that the "drink" (πόμα) is the *subject-matter* of the song with which Pindar is presenting his patron, but rather that the drink itself, through metonymy, has come to *represent* song: a "song-drink". The passive force of Helen's ἀοίδιμος, "sung of", here becomes more active: "of song, singing". The change in the gender of the speaker, and their relation to song – Helen as sung of female character, Pindar as male singer – almost seems to occasion a change in the agency and meaning of the word.

But there is even more going on here. The strange collocation of "song-drink", with the characteristically dense metaphor of the poet toasting his patron through the offering of a song that is compared to wine, draws attention to the phrase as a metonym for song. Apart from the thematic connection of the dedication of the song to toasting with wine, there is another, more linguistic, punning level to Pindar's choice of this phrase – in the similarity between the nouns πόμα, "drink", and

---

[16] *Pyth* 1.3 πείθονται δ' ἀοιδοὶ σάμασιν, *Pyth* 1.94 οἷον ἀποιχομένων ἀνδρῶν δίαιταν μανύει / καὶ λογίοις καὶ ἀοιδοῖς. See also *Pae*. 21 (= fr. 70, 249b (70)) where ἀοιδός is used adjectivally of the reed: τὸν ἀοιδότατον . . . κάλαμον.
[17] See Instone (1996) ad. *Nem*. 2.76, Pfeijffer (1999b) 397f. with n. 380.
[18] Agócs (2012) 203, Neer/Kurke (2019) 121, Pfeijffer (1999b) 398f. On the question of the performance of *Nem*. 3, see Eckerman (2014), and also Instone (1996) 168f.
[19] Blondell (2010), Roisman (2006), Worman (2001).
[20] Blondell (2010) 20.

ποίημα, "poem".²¹ The attribution of the adjective ἀοίδιμος to the πόμα hints that Pindar is making a playful pun on the new vocabulary for "making" poetry here, linking the "singing πόμα" to the new word for poetry as a made object, a ποίημα. It is as if the addition of the adjective creates a false etymology or gloss for ποίημα, from a conflation of the sound of πόμα and the literary pedigree of ἀοίδιμος to gesture to the new word, ποίημα, to which Pindar's song-offering is compared. And this new type of ἀοίδιμος song is translated from Helen's awareness of her passivity as a female poetic character into a new, and markedly male, context of a toast shared between men – from male agentic poet to male (φίλος) patron.

The gendered aspect to ἀοίδιμος here is underlined by contrast with another instance of the term, this time in *Olympian* 14, again in a gendered context.²² The ode, celebrating Asopichus of Orchomenus, opens with an address to the Graces: ὦ λιπαρᾶς ἀοίδιμοι βασίλειαι / Χάριτες Ἐρχομενοῦ ("Graces, shining sung-of queens of Orchomenus", lines 3f.). The Graces are called on to favor Pindar's prayer; in particular Thalia, who is addressed as ἐρασίμολπε ("lover of song", 16). The Graces had already been described together with the Muses in Hesiod (*Theog.* 64), the *Homeric Hymn to Apollo* (3.189–95) and Sappho (frr. 103, 128), and were depicted singing together with the Muses at the wedding of Cadmus by Theognis (15); as we will see, we also find them connected to the Muses elsewhere in Pindar's poetry, at the opening of *Paean* 6.²³ Thalia's identification with song, and the connection between Graces and Muses, suggests that we are meant to read ἀοίδιμος in the opening invocation to the Graces as not only "sung of" (i.e. subjects of song) but also "singing" (i.e. they are singers as well as "queens").²⁴ The Graces are renowned in song, but also connected to song, Pindar seems to suggest, making them ideal patrons for the opening of his ode –

---

21 Especially with the short form πόμα, as opposed to the Attic πῶμα; see Pfeijffer (1999b) ad loc.
22 The other two instances of ἀοίδιμος in Pindar also show an interaction with gender and the same fluidity and tension between the active and passive senses of the term. *Pyth.* 8.59 describes Delphi as the ὀμφαλὸν . . . ἀοίδιμον ("singing/sung of navel"): on the one hand this is a description of Delphi's fame in song, on the other it must recall the voice of the (female) Pythia who prophesied in poetry; see further Markus Hafner's chapter in this volume on the Pythia's "I". The other example of ἀοίδιμος occurs at fr. 76, in praise of Athens, where the (female) city Ἀθᾶναι is described as λιπαραὶ καὶ ἰοστέφανοι καὶ ἀοίδιμοι ("shining and violet-crowned and sung-of/singing", line 1), again both a reference to Athens' "sung-of" fame, and to the well-known poets who made it "sing". For the different uses of ἀοίδιμος in Pindar, see Pfeijffer (1999b) 548.
23 See also *Hom. Hymn* 27.15. On the connection between Graces and Muses, see Lefkowitz (1963) 244 n. 54, Verdenius (1987) 104f.
24 Contra Verdenius (1987) ad loc., who acknowledges the active meaning of ἀοίδιμος at *Nem.* 3.79 and *Pae.* 6.6, but argues for a purely passive meaning "much sung of" here. It is important to note that I am not suggesting (as Bowra 1935, ad loc., Radt 1958, 107f.) that ἀοίδιμοι βασίλειαι should be taken as "queens of song" (with ἀοίδιμοι dependent on βασίλειαι), but rather that ἀοίδιμοι should be taken as an attribute of the Graces ("full of songs, singing"). See Florence Klein's chapter in this volume on how Catullus transforms Sappho from being an authoress to being 'sung of' and the object of song in his translation of fr. 31 in *c.* 51.

fitting replacements and counterparts for the Muses, the ultimate female inspirers of song.[25] But their active role only goes so far before the passive force of ἀοίδιμος in connection to female voices reinstates itself. After all, it is patently *not* the Graces who are singing here, but the male voice which is describing the Graces in song.[26] This is made explicit by the male speaking voice a few lines below, who claims that he has arrived ἀείδων ("singing", 18) this very ode. The masculinity of this act is ring-fenced by the masculine participle ἀείδων, contrasting with the feminine ἰδοῖσα ("having looked", 16) of one of the Graces two lines above. While the Graces may indeed be connected to singing, therefore, the re-appropriation of the verb ἀείδειν to the male voice means that the sense in which Helen had used ἀοίδιμος – "renowned in song, sung of" – rears its head again, to subvert the apparent praise of the Graces. The term ἀοίδιμος, with its connection to the activity of the male who "sings" (ἀείδων) about those who are "sung-of" (ἀοίδιμος), serves as a reminder that it is a male poet and his associates in song who have the real power as singers here – and it is these female figures who are ultimately shaped by them. This seems to show a very different dynamic to the use of ἀοίδιμος in *Nem.* 3, where the sense of the word was twisted to create a new vocabulary for Pindar's poetry in the context of active exchange between men.[27] Here, appearing to praise the Graces while simultaneously reminding that it is the male poet who constructs them in song, Pindar hints at the same unease with women's voices as in the portrayal of Helen in Homeric epic. As with Helen, it is the latent passive force of ἀοίδιμος, in connection with the performance by the ἀοιδός/poet of his song, which serves to put Helen (in Homer) and the Graces (here in *Ol.* 14) in their place – reminding them, and us, that it is the male poet who has sole control in poetry over the depiction of women and their voices.

This active re-assignment of ἀοίδιμος from female figures who – even though they are "singers" – are "sung of" in the male voice (the Graces in *Ol.* 14), to the male poet as "singing" (as in *Nem.* 3), is demonstrated again in *Paean* 6. This paean, performed at the Theoxenia at Delphi, opens with a similar request from the Graces – this time allied with Aphrodite – to welcome the poet and chorus to the Delphic festival (*Pae.* 6.1–6):

Πρὸς Ὀλυμπίου Διός σε, χρυσέα
   κλυτόμαντι Πυθοῖ,
λίσσομαι Χαρίτεσ-
   σίν τε καὶ σὺν Ἀφροδίτᾳ,

---

25 On the Muses in Pindar, see Kuhn-Treichel (2020), Maslov (2016), and see further more generally Spentzou/Fowler (2002).
26 For similar readings of the Muses as a figure for women's disempowerment through the transferral of inspiration to the male bard, see Gubar (1981) and Klindienst (2002). On Pindar's depiction of women, see Kyriakou (1994).
27 On the ideology of aristocratic exchange in Pindar, see Kurke (1991) ch. 4.

ἐν ζαθέῳ με δέξαι χρόνῳ
ἀοίδιμον Πιερίδων προφάταν·

By Olympian Zeus, I beg you, golden
Delphi famous for seers,
along with the Graces
and Aphrodite,
to welcome me – the singing prophet
of the Muses – at this sacred time

This passage has been a contentious one for arguments around the choral/solo hypothesis. Do we take the first person singular με who is asking to be welcomed here (5) – the ἀοίδιμος προφάτας (6) – to refer to Pindar alone, or as a self-reference by the chorus?[28] Mary Lefkowitz suggests that the invocation to the Graces here – given their close connection with the Muses and song – "seems to be a certain indication that these lines are addressed to [Pindar] himself".[29] Stefan Radt also takes Pindar as the speaker, though he reads this from the context given in the paean's opening lines (where the speaker claims to have come to Delphi to replace its chorus, lines 7–10).[30] And although some scholars still hold to a choral reading of the ἐγώ of *Pae.* 6.1–6,[31] Staffan Fogelmark has shown that the chorus is never referred to as προφάτας in Pindar and Bacchylides, while Giambattista D'Alessio argues convincingly that all the descriptors here – connection to the Muses and poetic production – point to the construction of the persona of a poet.[32] (This is not to say that the chorus' voice does not appear elsewhere in the paean, for example in the first person plural at line 128 εὐνάξομεν:[33] as I have said above (p. 131), part of the complexity of Pindar's use of the first-person is precisely the fluidity and slippage between the persona of the poet and the voice of the chorus, between self and community, the present of performance and the future of reperformance.)

---

28 For a summary of the debate, see Kurke (2005) 86–9.
29 Lefkowitz (1963) 244 n. 54; this note was excised from the version of the article printed in her 1991 book. This initial footnote acknowledging the voice of the poet in *Pae.* 6 is rather ironic, as Kurke (2005) 87 notes, given that Lefkowitz's major argument in her 1963 article is for a distinction between the voice of the poet in the epinician odes and that of the chorus in the paeans.
30 Radt (1958) 105–8.
31 Burnett (1998), Hoekstra (1962) 9–13, Stehle (1997) 139–47 and 139 n. 62 for further bibliography.
32 Fogelmark (1972) 119 n. 16, D'Alessio (1994) 125. See also Kurke (2005) 89. Stehle (1997) 140 gives the counterargument that "the Muses inspire not just poets but singers as well" (with examples given at her n. 66); but she cites Alcman fr. 3, where again we have to make the argument that this is the voice of the chorus invoking the Muses and not the poet; Eur. *Tro.* 511–14 is clearly a parody of the opening of Homer's *Iliad*, and therefore a parody of the *bardic* invocation of the Muses, not the chorus invoking them on their own account; the same can be said of the choral invocations at Ar. *Ach.* 665 and *Lys.* 1297, which are also clearly parodic of the epic bard.
33 As also Hoekstra (1962) 11.

This reading of the opening of *Pae.* 6 as a figuration of the persona of the poet is only underlined by the use of the adjective ἀοίδιμος, which, as we have seen, claims an etymological link with ἀοιδός, which indicates the bard-figure.³⁴ The phrase ἀοίδιμος Πιερίδων προφάτας here should therefore be interpreted as tying in with Pindar's self-presentation as poet in a line of bards who could claim inspiration by the Muses, stretching back to Homer (as we saw in the description of the Homeridae as ἀοιδοί at *Nem.* 2.2). Where, in *Olympian* 14, the Graces were invoked as ἀοίδιμοι only to be corralled into the male singers' voice, here the transfer and balance of power seems to be clear: the Graces (and Aphrodite) are being asked for inspiration, and it is their inspiration that will both enable Pindar to sing as a poet (ἀοίδιμος as "singing"), and to be renowned (ἀοίδιμος as "sung of"), through the vessel of his poetry.³⁵

This relationship between female goddess-inspirer and male poet is underlined by the noun which accompanies the poetically resonant ἀοίδιμος: "prophet" or "spokesman" (προφάτας). We have seen that Pindar uses the term ἀοιδός elsewhere for the general tradition of male poets in *Nem.* 2 and *Pyth.* 1, but he never makes use of the noun to construct the persona of the speaking poet himself. The use of πόμ' ἀοίδιμον at *Nem.* 3.79 suggests an awareness of the new vocabulary for poetry, ποίημα/ποιητής – which, however, Pindar also avoids, just like ἀοιδός, in figurations of his own poetic persona (the noun ποιητής appears nowhere in Pindar's poetry, in spite of its increasing popularity). At *Pae.* 6.6, instead, he chooses a periphrastic construction and an unusual noun for his self-construction as a poet.³⁶ As with the πόμ' ἀοίδιμον in *Nem.* 3, the adjective ἀοίδιμος is appended to a term – προφάτας, "prophet", "announcer" – that might not immediately be connected with poetry,³⁷ specifically to designate its status as a metapoetic term.³⁸ ἀοίδιμος serves to link the poet speaker to the tradition of male ἀοιδοί, while also enabling him to construct a new vocabulary of poetic authorship for himself by modifying and manipulating a different noun.

So what can Pindar's use of the noun προφάτας tell us about the male poetics being forecasted here? What "particular communicative strategy" does it play in terms of poetics and gender?³⁹ In the first instance, the poet as prophet is a trope of early Greek poetry, connecting to the poet's divine inspiration by the Muse.⁴⁰ But

---

34 On ἀοίδιμος here as active "singing", not passive "sung of", see Radt (1958) 105–8; D'Alessio (1994) 125 sees it as having both meanings.
35 D'Alessio (1994) 125 also identifies both these meanings to ἀοίδιμος here.
36 See, for example, Maslov (2015) 201: "This is not a case of appropriation of religious authority, but an improvised metapoetic term that marks the professionalization of poetic discourse."
37 Cf. e.g. *Nem.* 9.50 on a crater of wine as the κώμου προφάταν ("announcer of the celebration").
38 Though note the comparable use of the term "prophet of the Muses" in Bacchylides: Μουσᾶν γε ἰοβλεφάρων θεῖος προφ[άτ]ας, Bacchyl. 9.3.
39 D'Alessio (1994) 117.
40 Nagy (1989) 23–9, who suggests that the term μάντις ("prophet") "could once have been [an] appropriate designation for an undifferentiated poet/prophet" (p. 23); see also Radt (1958) 108.

the προφάτας actually had a very specific role, particularly in relation to the oracle at Delphi where Pindar is positioning himself: we must remember that the paean opens with an invocation not only to the Graces and Aphrodite, but to Delphi itself, "famous for seers" (κλυτόμαντι, 2). This adjective, κλυτόμαντις, contains within it two elements: the adjective κλυτός ("famed"), and the noun μάντις, "seer". This noun, used to describe oracles and seers, was also applied to the most famous oracle of them all, the female Pythia at Delphi, who was inspired by the god Apollo to utter divinely-inspired prophecies.[41] If we were not already primed to think of the Pythia through the adjective κλυτόμαντις, the fact that Pindar calls Delphi by the name Πυθώ – from which the Pythia derived her title – surely acts as a stimulus to make the connection between Delphi and the female oracle. In relation to the divine oracle at Delphi (the μάντις or "seer"), the προφάτας (literally "speaker-for", i.e. "interpreter") was the middle man who interpreted the gods' words, as relayed by the oracle, into poetry. He was, in other words, as Gregory Nagy succinctly puts it, a "recomposer of the inspired message in poetic form".[42]

What Pindar does here is to transfer the role of the προφάτας from the interpreter of the Delphic oracle to the poet as the προφάτας of the Muses. The comparison is set up not only in terms of the similarity of the roles they carry out (mortal interpreter into poetry of a divine message), but also in the alignment of their gender roles. The male προφάτας (indicated for us by the masculine noun) interprets the female oracle (the μάντις of κλυτόμαντις); similarly, the male poet-προφάτας channels the inspiration of the female Muses, the "goddesses of Pieria" (Πιερίδες), to produce his poetry. So when Pindar claims to be the "singing prophet of the Muses", what he is actually doing is comparing the relationship between the (female) god-inspired μάντις at Delphi and her (male) prophet-interpreter προφάτας, to that between the (female) goddess-Muses and the (male) poet.

We see this happening explicitly elsewhere in Pindar's poetry at fr. 150, where the Muse is told to "be a μάντις, Muse, and I will be a προφάτας": μαντεύεο, Μοῖσα, προφατεύσω δ' ἐγώ. Again, there has been debate over the identity of the ἐγώ, and whether it belongs to the poet or the chorus.[43] To me, however, it seems that the opposition drawn here between the male speaking voice and the female Muse is of more significance than that between the (male) poet or the (male) chorus, who are in fact both united in the discourse of their masculinity (even if not in their roles in performance).[44] The point of the line is surely the contrast between the roles of female

---

41 E.g. Aesch. *Eum.* 29. On the figure of the seer, see Bremmer (1996), Griffith (2009) 475–82, and for a survey of the μάντις in Pindar, Maslov (2015) 188–201. Again, see also Hafner in this volume (cf. above n. 22).
42 Nagy (1989) 26; see also Fontenrose (1978) 215–19.
43 See, for example, Nagy (1989) 27 for the poet, Maslov (2015) 197 for the chorus.
44 On the chorus of the victory odes as male, see Carey (2007) 207; for examples, see *Pyth* 5.22 κῶμον ἀνέρων, *Nem.* 3.4f. μελιγαρύων τέκτονες / κώμων νεανίαι; cf. also *Pyth.* 10.6 on the

Muse, on the one hand, as mantic inspirer, and male speaker on the other (whether poet or chorus) as poetic interpreter. Both the opposition and interrelationship between μάντις and προφάτας, female Muse and male poetic voice, are made explicit – and again, the vocabulary of προφάτας is used to delineate the male poetic voice.[45]

By calling himself an ἀοίδιμος Πιερίδων προφάτας at *Pae.* 6.6, then, Pindar is rewriting the relationship between Muse-poet into the μάντις-προφάτας interaction to lay claim to a very specific gendered relationship, between female goddesses of inspiration and the male interpreter who claims the woman's inspired voice and words as his own, and uses them as a vehicle for creating his poetry. This reading of *Pae.* 6 also clarifies the use of ἀοίδιμοι for the Graces in *Ol.* 14, because *Pae.* 6 opens with a proliferation of female divine figures who might inspire the poet and provide him with the substance for his poetry, including, once again, the Graces. The Graces' connection to song in *Ol.* 14 can thus be seen as twofold, in that a) they provide the subject for the male singer through his opening invocation to the female goddesses for inspiration; and b) their powers of song are invoked in order to be exploited and re-interpreted into poetry by the male poet-prophet, to enable him to sing poetry and thus to be renowned through his song. In other words, it is by reading the poetry through the lens of this gendered relationship that we can see that it is the appropriation of female powers of song (the Graces as ἀοίδιμοι in *Ol.* 14) and divine inspiration (the Muses' mantic properties in *Pae.* 6 and fr. 150) which enable the male poet to become ἀοιδός-like, and to channel women's association with song to interpret into his poetry: to be an ἀοίδιμος Πιερίδων προφάτας.

4 Making men: The male poet as craftsman

Pindar's self-construction as a poet-prophet who assimilates the female voice is not the only gendered construct he adduces to shape the persona of the poet. Another metaphor which threads through Pindar's poetry (and has often been commented on) is that of craftsmanship – the "poet-as-craftsman".[46] Both Homer and Hesiod group the ἀοιδός together with other "artisans" (δημιοεργοί): Homer lists the seer (μάντις), doctor (ἰητήρ), carpenter (τέκτων) and bard (ἀοιδός) among a group of

---

ἐπικωμίαν ἀνδρῶν κλυτὰν ὄπα. Snell/Maehler (1980) ascribe this fragment to the lost sections of *Isthm.* 9, which if correct would indicate an epinician chorus.

45 Cf. fr. 94a.5f. μάντις ὡς τελέσσω / ἱεραπόλος ("that I, a prophet priest, may fulfil"), where μάντις and ἱεραπόλος ("priest") are placed in apposition. This has previously been read as a *partheneion* (Burnett 1998, 495 n. 5), but this is unlikely as the masculine participle at line 11 (φιλέων) identifies the speaker as male; it may be another instance of the male first-person voice appropriating the mantic properties of the *partheneion* chorus. See Klinck (2001) 276, Kurke (2005) 88 n. 24.

46 E.g. Fearn (2017), Ford (2002) ch. 5, Segal (1998) ch. 8, Shapiro (1994) 72–98, Steiner (1986) 41–52.

δημιοεργοί at *Od.* 17.383–5, and Hesiod juxtaposes the ἀοιδός with the carpenter (τέκτων) and the potter (κεραμεύς) at *Op.* 25f.⁴⁷ With Pindar and his contemporary Bacchylides, however, we find a proliferation of craft metaphors for the poet. Ford has shown how these craft metaphors both amplify specific aspects of song – its monumentalization of glory, its ability to endure – and yet, at the same time, emphasize that sung poetry is more than a made artefact.⁴⁸ Here, I am interested not only in metaphors of craft for poetry but, more specifically, their application to name the poet, and how that interacts with the gendering of poetic authorship.

In their ability to fashion and piece together words, the poet and the chorus-members are compared directly to "craftsmen" (τέκτονες) twice in Pindar's odes: first at *Nem.* 3.4f., where the young men of the chorus are called μελιγαρύων τέκτονες / κώμων νεανίαι ("craftsmen of the honey-sounding celebrations"),⁴⁹ and again at *Pyth.* 3.113, where the poets of tales of men like Nestor and Sarpedon are called ἐπέων ... τέκτονες σοφοί ("wise craftsmen of words").⁵⁰ τέκτονες appeared in Homer – as we saw above, in close conjunction with ἀοιδοί in *Od.* 17 – but never for the figure of the poet.⁵¹ In *Pythian* 3, however, Pindar speaks of the "wise craftsmen" (τέκτονες) of "words" (ἐπέων) about Nestor and Sarpedon – a not-so-veiled reference to Homer, whose *Iliad* tells of both heroes and whose epics had already come to be referred to as ἔπεα by the fifth century BCE.⁵² Both these instances of terms of craftsmanship for singers at *Nem.* 3 and *Pyth.* 3 contain implicit or explicit gendered undertones: the νεανίαι ("young men") of the chorus at *Nem.* 3.5 specifically designates these τέκτονες as male; while the τέκτονες referred to in *Pyth.* 3 are valorized for the stories they tell of men like Nestor and Sarpedon, linking into Homer's subject as the κλέα ἀνδρῶν ("glorious deeds of men").⁵³ This may be drawing directly on a Homeric paradigm for connecting τέκτονες and men: a quarter of all occurrences of τέκτων in Homer give it in apposition to ἀνήρ (τέκτονες ἄνδρες, "craftsmen-men").⁵⁴ In Homer, then, the craftsman is doubly underlined as a man through the gender of the word and its frequent juxtaposition with ἀνήρ; and he is associated with the ἀοιδός through the list of δημιοεργοί in *Od.* 17. Pindar takes the final step, drawing on the craft metaphor for song, to make the association between

---

47 See Nagy (1989) 19, (1990) 56.
48 Ford (2002) ch. 4; cf. Fearn (2017) 19–23, 34.
49 See Instone (1996) ad loc., Neer/Kurke (2019) 113f., Pfeijffer (1999b) ad loc.
50 Other examples of τέκτων in Pindar (not referring to the poet/chorus) occur at *Pyth.* 3.6, *Pyth.* 5.36, *Nem.* 5.49.
51 Svenbro (1984) 156–79. There are twelve instances of τέκτων in Homer, all of carpenters: *Il.* 4.110, 5.59, 6.315, 13.390, 15.411, 16.483, 23.712; *Od.* 9.126, 17.340, 17.384, 19.56, 21.43.
52 Ford (1981) 137–52, Martin (1989) 13. For an example of ἔπος as epic in Pindar, see *Isthm.* 6.67 on the Ἡσιόδου ... ἔπος ("word/epic of Hesiod"); Nagy (1999) 238.
53 Nagy (1990) 196f.
54 Hom. *Il.* 6.315, 16.483, *Od.* 9.126.

the male τέκτων-singer, the male chorus (*Nem*. 3), and their male subjects (Nestor and Sarpedon, *Pyth*. 3).

There is another interesting instance of the craft metaphor for the poet-persona interacting with gender – but here it is in the negative, a definition by what he is not. *Nemean* 5, composed for Pytheas of Aegina, opens with a famously blunt statement of self-definition (*Nem*. 5.1f.):

Οὐκ ἀνδριαντοποιός εἰμ', ὥστ' ἐλινύσοντα ἐργά-
   ζεσθαι ἀγάλματ' ἐπ' αὐτᾶς βαθμίδος
ἑσταότ'·

I am not a statue-maker who fashions statues
that stand still on the same
bases

The poet then goes on to describe what his song does, flying on the ships and boats from Aegina to spread Pytheas' fame.[55] Charles Segal identifies a tension here "between song (poetry) on the one hand and monumentalization in statuary". Other critics – including Andrew Ford – follow his lead to read this passage as contrasting (and criticizing) statuary as static, against the ability of song to travel and spread fame.[56] Yet – as David Fearn has recently pointed out – the opposition is not so clear-cut as this.[57] The statues fashioned by the sculptor are called ἀγάλματα (*Nem*. 5.1), from ἄγαλμα, a noun whose meaning stretched from "glory, honor" to "delight, ornament", "gift", and thus "statue" dedicated to a god.[58] The epinician ode as an ἄγαλμα is a central aspect of the depiction of song as craft:[59] *Nem*. 8, for example, has Pindar specifically define the gift of his poetry as a Νεμεαῖον ἄγαλμα, and we see the same metaphor being applied in Bacchylides.[60]

In this sense, we can read Pindar's claim not to be an ἀνδριαντοποιός here in multiple ways: as an outright rejection of the role of artisan (as Segal, Ford and others); an implicit foregrounding of the role of statuary as a representation of song (as Deborah Steiner); a "wry, hyperbolical statement" that serves provocatively to

---

55 ἀλλ' ἐπὶ πάσας ὁλκάδος ἔν τ' ἀκάτῳ, γλυκεῖ' ἀοιδά, / στεῖχ' ἀπ' Αἰγίνας διαγγέλλοισ' (*Nem*. 5.2f.). On the proem to *Nem*. 5, see Fearn (2017) 17–28, Ford (2002) 119–23, Pavlou (2010), Pfeijffer (1999b) 62f. and 99–108, Segal (1974), Steiner (1993).
56 Segal (1986) 156, see also Segal (1974); Ford (2002) 119f., who sees it as following a Simonidean emphasis on the power of song over craft. See also Smith (2007) 92 on Pindar's "clearly hostile" attitude to statuary, Svenbro (1984) 187–212.
57 Fearn (2017) 17–28 (though note that Fearn does not read this, as I do, as an act of displacement, but rather suggests simply that there is more nuance to Pindar's critique of statuary than is usually assumed); see also Steiner (1993), (2001) 251–65.
58 On ἀγάλματα in Pindar, see Kurke (1991) 163–94, Steiner (1993) 161–7.
59 Ford (2002) 115–19, though Ford suggests a different usage of ἄγαλμα here: "such passages present songs as signs of rank and mutuality rather than as products of craft" (p. 117).
60 Bacchyl. 5.3–6, 10.11.

draw attention to issues around object value and memorialization (as Fearn);⁶¹ or, I would suggest, as a displacement and replacement of the one-dimensional artisan who can only produce static objects, with a new kind of craftsman whose songs are supple and mobile. This reading deals with the problem that Pindar does not provide any nominal term following the negative statement, "I am not a statue-maker", to describe the activity of the poet, to create a contrast with the vivid craft term which opens the ode: it is, instead, the *song*, ἀοιδά (and not the singer, ἀοιδός) which becomes the subject of the next line.⁶² By my reading, the contrast is not between the ἀνδριαντοποιός and the ἀοιδά, but the kind of ἀνδριαντοποιός who produces static ἀγάλματα – a statue-maker – and a craftsman like Pindar, who produces the mobile ἄγαλμα of song. The statement "I am not a statue-maker" is therefore not rejecting the category of artisan outright – it is superceding the kind of ἀνδριαντοποιός who fashions static ἀγάλματα, with a new sort of ἀνδριαντοποιός: Pindar.

This interpretation of the ἀνδριαντοποιός of *Nem.* 5 as a displacement and replacement of the statue-maker with a new kind of ἀνδριαντοποιός is shored up by the etymology of the term. It is made up of two parts: a nominal stem from ἀνδριάς ("statue, image of a man"), itself derived from ἀνήρ ("man"),⁶³ and the suffix -ποιός, meaning "maker" and cognate with ποιητής ("maker, poet"). This is the only time in the entirety of Pindar's corpus where he uses the suffix -ποιός to create a noun, which, as we have seen, was becoming increasingly popular in the fifth century BCE as conceptions of poetic "making" led to a new family of terms around ποιεῖν (ἐποποιός, τραγῳδοποιός and so on).⁶⁴ I have already suggested that Pindar's use of πόμ' ἀοίδιμον in *Nem.* 3 demonstrates an awareness of the new vocabulary for poetry as ποίημα (see above, pp. 133f). Here, I think, he goes further, building on the new fashion for forming craftsmen's names from -ποιός to come up with a new term that subtly elucidates both what he does not do – fashioning static statues – and what he does: crafting poetic images of men which are mobile enough to spread their glory abroad. He might not be a statue-maker in the literal sense, but with ἀνδριαντοποιός suggesting "man-fashioning" and -ποιός associated with poetic making, he is, surely, a "poet-fashioner of men".

This connects to many other passages in Pindar's odes where he describes his task as one of building up men's status and manhood through his poetry. We have seen how the poet, chorus and subject of poetry are tied into the same metaphorical

---

61 Fearn (2017) 19.
62 γλυκεῖ' ἀοιδά, / στεῖχ' ("go, sweet song", *Nem.* 5.2f.).
63 Note that ἀνδριάς normally means "statue of a man"; Pfeijffer (1999b) ad loc. notes that it is only occasionally (and much later) used of statues of women (Ath. 10.425f.). Fearn (2017) 24–7 demonstrates that we should understand the types of statue referenced here as more than simply athletic statues.
64 The only other instance of -ποιός in Pindar occurs to form an adjective at *Nem.* 8.33, κακοποιὸν ὄνειδος ("ill-doing disgrace").

language and simultaneously delineated as male through the image of the male τέκτων. Gregory Nagy has argued for close links between the hero of Homeric epic and the athlete of epinician, both of whom undergo trials and are reintegrated into the male community through the medium of poetry.⁶⁵ In both the κλέα ἀνδρῶν of epic and the recitation of the past and present achievements of men in victory odes, "there is a presupposition of an unbroken succession extending from the men of the past to the men of the present, both those men who are the subjects of the glory and those men who perpetuate the glory through song."⁶⁶

Pindar's continuation of Homer's theme of κλέα ἀνδρῶν is highlighted throughout the odes – perhaps most clearly at the opening of *Isthmian* 8, a celebration of Kleandros of Aegina, which opens with the resonant Kleandros' name, itself a combination of κλέα and ἀνδρῶν ("he who has the glories of men").⁶⁷ The glory of men is a theme which often recurs: *Olympian* 2, for example, opens with a request as to the poem's subject with three masculine nouns, one of which is ἀνήρ itself: τίνα θεόν, τίν' ἥρωα, τίνα δ' ἄνδρα κελαδήσομεν; ("what [male] god, what [male] hero, what man shall we celebrate?", *Ol.* 2.2). Meanwhile, *Olympian* 1 contains the noun ἀνήρ six times in the space of just over a hundred lines (and this is by no means unusual). Men (ἄνδρες) are defined again and again as the subject of Pindar's poetry: *Ol.* 6, *Ol.* 9, *Pyth.* 1, *Pyth.* 5, *Nem.* 1, *Nem.* 2, *Isthm.* 1 and *Isthm.* 4 all announce their subject as "that/this man",⁶⁸ *Ol.* 7 honors a "mighty man" (πελώριον ἄνδρα, line 15), *Pyth.* 4 a "beloved man" (ἀνδρὶ φίλῳ, line 1), *Pyth.* 9 a "blessed man" (ὄλβιον ἄνδρα, line 4) and so on. It is up to "writers and singers" (καὶ λογίοις καὶ ἀοιδοῖς), the poet tells us in *Pyth.* 1, to tell the tales "of men gone by" (ἀποιχομένων ἀνδρῶν, lines 93f.), and in *Pyth.* 10 it is only a prize-winning "man" (ἀνήρ) who is "told of in song" (ὑμνητὸς, line 22); meanwhile, *Nem.* 7 tells us that the poet will "bring genuine κλέος to a man who is dear to him" (φίλον ἐς ἄνδρ' ἄγων κλέος / ἐτήτυμον, lines 62f.), and *Isthm.* 2 announces the poet's job as bringing the Muses' honors "to the homes of famous men" (εὐδόξων ἐς ἀνδρῶν, line 34). Men are also the poet's audience and arbiters of fame and glory: excellence is honored "among men" (παρ' ἀνδράσιν, *Ol.* 6.10), and is won "as a man among men" (ἐν ἀνδράσιν ἀνήρ, *Nem.* 3.72), celebrated among the "men's" festival (κῶμον ἀνέρων, *Pyth.* 5.22), dancing (ἀνδρῶν χορεύσιος, *Pae.* 6.8) and symposium (ἀνδρῶν . . . συμποσίου, *Isthm.* 6.1). Often these different categories of men – the man as the subject of poetry, the reveler, and audience – are blurred to create a male-normative society of male poets, male victors and male audience. Thus, when Pindar claims to be "weaving a many-colored song for warrior men" (ἀνδράσιν αἰχματαῖσι

---

65 Nagy (1990) 136–45; see also Currie (2005).
66 Nagy (1990) 201.
67 Nagy (1990) 204–6.
68 κεῖνος ἀνήρ, *Ol.* 6.7; ἀνδρὸς / τόνδ' ἀνέρα, *Ol.* 9.13, 110; ἄνδρα . . . κεῖνον, *Pyth.* 1.42; ἄνδρα κεῖνον, *Pyth.* 5.107; κείνου . . . ἀνδρός, *Nem.* 1.9; ὅδ' ἀνήρ, *Nem.* 2.3; τοῦδ' ἀνδρός, *Isthm.* 1.34; ὅδ' ἀνήρ, *Isthm.* 4.70. On κεῖνος in Pindar, see Bonifazi (2004).

πλέκων / ποικίλον ὕμνον, *Ol.* 6.86f.), the dative "for men" (ἀνδράσιν) works loosely to encompass *all* men – both patrons, subjects, and audience of his song.[69]

Many of these statements stating the subject of the odes as "a man" come at the poems' openings: for example, *Pyth.* 4 composed for a "beloved man" which has ἀνδρὶ in line 1; or *Nem.* 6, which opens with the "race of men" (ἐν ἀνδρῶν . . . γένος, line 1). As I observed at the beginning of this chapter, opening with the subject of "a man" unavoidably recalls the beginning of Homer's *Odyssey*, with its first word ἄνδρα (*Od.* 1.1). *Nemean* 2 opens, as we have seen (see above, p. 132), with a reflection on the usual practice of the Homeridae ("singers of stitched verses", ῥαπτῶν ἐπέων . . . ἀοιδοί, *Nem.* 2.2) to begin with a prelude to Zeus (προοιμίου, line 3). By way of comparison, the ode continues, "this man" (ὅδ' ἀνήρ, line 3) has won a hymn in his honor for his victory in the Nemean Games.[70] The epic proemion to Zeus sung by the ἀοιδοί and the epinician's opening with the man (ἀνήρ) are balanced opposite each other in the same line,[71] thus explicitly linking the praise of the ἀνήρ in Pindar's epinician to the proemia of epic, and to the male ἀοιδός. If we compare this to the opening of *Nemean* 5, then, with its ἀνήρ-cognate in ἀνδριαντοποιός, we can see that ἀνδριαντοποιός in that context thus similarly draws on not only the masculinity of epinician's subject, but also a poetic tradition of opening with the praise of men.

The prevalence of words for men (ἄνδρες) in Pindar's poetry, and the connection of ἀνήρ to conventions of poetic openings stretching back to the *Odyssey*, thus suggests that there is a more complex subtext to the negative in the opening lines of *Nemean* 5. It argues for a reading of Pindar's relationship to the ἀνδριαντοποιός as one of competition and replacement with his own poetic vision of "man-image-making", rather than outright rejection. The performance of men's praise through the medium of victory odes, stressed through the continual deployment of ἀνήρ, means that the performative context of the statement "I am not a man-image-maker" counters its own meaning, and instead asks us to define what *kind* of man-image-maker Pindar is. This is underlined by the occurrence of ἀνήρ and its derivatives several more times during the ode: first at line 9, where the celebrant's native Aegina is praised as "having good men" (εὔανδρον) – a reflection on the young man who is being celebrated, as well as the function of the ode in drawing out the gendered praise of his (female) home (ματρόπολιν, line 8) as a nurse of "good men". Two heroic examples of these kinds of men are given, Peleus and Telamon – not mentioned by name, but denoted as "brave men" (ἄνδρας ἀλκίμους, line 15). Again, as with the *recusatio* of the opening statement, Pindar makes as if to shrink from telling their

---

[69] Compare *Ol* 7.7f. on Pindar sending his poetry ἀεθλοφόροις / ἀνδράσιν ("to victorious men").

[70] Note that it is not simply the victor's achievement which is being compared to the poetic practice of the Homeridae, as Instone (1996) 145 suggests (although of course this is the main force of the comparison): it is also a self-reflexive commentary on the ode itself, whose proemion begins with the praise of the victor.

[71] ῥαπτῶν ἐπέων τὰ πόλλ' ἀοιδοί / ἄρχονται, Διὸς ἐκ προοιμίου, καὶ ὅδ' ἀνήρ . . . (*Nem.* 2.2f.).

tale.⁷² Yet Peleus' and Telamon's designation as "heroes" (ἥρωας, line 7), "warriors" (αἰχματὰς, line 7) and "brave men" (ἄνδρας ἀλκίμους, line 15) constructs a discourse of praise of masculinity which runs against the poet's self-avowed silence.

The final link between masculinity, man-making and the poet comes towards the end of the ode (lines 48f.), in the praise of Pytheas' trainer Menander – a name which literally means "man-strength" (formed of μένος, "strength, courage", and ἀνήρ).⁷³ Pytheas' homeland Aegina is εὔανδρος, and has produced two mythical warrior-ἄνδρες, Peleus and Telamon; Pytheas' trainer, "Man-strength", acts as the final connection that ensures that Aegina's legendary manliness will be continued in the present-day victor, and which cements the praise of masculinity as a theme which runs through the ode. But there is more to it than this. Menander is termed, not a trainer, but a "craftsman of athletes" (τέκτον' ἀθληταῖσιν, line 49) – echoing the metaphor of craftsmanship with which the ode started, and linking in to the discourse of poet-as-τέκτων which we have seen elsewhere in Pindar's poetry. If Menander has crafted the man Pytheas' victory in the games through his sculpting of his athletic body, then the τέκτων-metaphor forms the last link in the chain to draw the parallel to Pindar as ἀνδριαντοποιός, as "man-maker" – for Pindar, in the end, is the one who has crafted his fame as a man through song (ἀείδειν, line 50).

5 Conclusion

Focusing on the construction of the poetic persona in Pindar through authorship terms and its interaction with gender provides one way into the difficult territory of interpreting the first-person statements in Pindar's poetry. Reading these terms as concerted constructions of the persona of the male poet and his chorus within a normative masculine community, celebrating and building up the male subjects of his song, enables us to see them as a series of attempts to draw the audience into a poetic world which centred around the construction of men. As in the case of the earlier poets, this masculine poetic construction often takes place at the site of contested gender relations – as in *Olympian* 14, for example, where the application of ἀοίδιμος to the Graces is countered by its use in *Paean* 6 to indicate the poet's appropriation of the female voice. Rather than drawing on old terms for poetic authorship, like ἀοιδός, or the new family of words around ποιητής and -ποιός, Pindar generates new metaphors for the persona of the poet which root it deeply in a gendered context. The προφάτας of *Paean* 6 demonstrates the channeling of the female

---

72 αἰδέομαι μέγα εἰπεῖν ἐν δίκᾳ τε μὴ κεκινδυνευμένον ("I hesitate to tell of a great deed, unjustly done", line 14).
73 On the apparently negative treatment of Menander here, see Pfeijffer (1999b) 81–4; he does not note the etymology of the name.

voice as the man ventriloquizes the inspired woman's words and turns them into his own poetry. Meanwhile, the ἀνδριαντοποιός of *Nemean* 5 sets Pindar up as a new kind of "man-image-maker", programmatically setting up poetry over other kinds of masculinizing to make the poet the pre-eminent maker of men.

The poetic persona which emerges is vibrantly new, generating a novel vocabulary to describe his identity as a poet that departs from traditional terms. Yet, despite the newness of the words, the gender paradigms and constructs which both frame the persona of the poet and generate his poetry mean that we are still in a very familiar world. Women who attempt to lay claim to their voices, just like Helen in the *Iliad*, are subverted from singers to the subject-matter of song, and are relegated to the backdrop of men's tales. Male poets draw on divine women's inspiration, like Homer's and Hesiod's Muses, to generate their own poetry. And finally, men come together in the context of poetic creation, performance and celebration, to generate images of men in the male voice, together as men, for an audience of men and male future generations. The dichotomy of solo poet and communal chorus is not, then, after all, the most nuanced way of reading the first-person statements of the odes; another dichotomy – that of gender – can be seen as a different, and no less important, structuring principle to Pindar's poems. In the end, it is deeply ironic that it is the one term which Pindar says he is not which best describes the poetic persona which runs through his poetry. This poet is, truly, a maker of men.

Bibliography

Texts and translations

Pindari *Carmina*, ed. C. M. Bowra, Oxford 1935.
Pindar, *Selected Odes: Olympian One, Pythian Nine, Nemeans Two & Three, Isthmian One*, ed. Stephen Instone, Liverpool 1996.
Pindari *Carmina Cum Fragmentis*, ed. Bruno Snell and Herwig Maehler, t. 1 and 2, Leipzig 1980.

Books and articles

Agócs (2012): Peter Agócs, "Performance and Genre: Reading Pindar's κῶμοι", in: Peter Agócs, Christopher Carey and Richard Rawles (eds.), *Reading the Victory Ode*, Cambridge, 191–223.
Anzai (1994): Makoto Anzai, "First-Person Forms in Pindar: A Re-Examination", *BICS* 39, 141–150.
Blondell (2010): Ruby Blondell, "'Bitch That I Am': Self-Blame and Self-Assertion in the *Iliad*", *TAPhA* 140 (1), 1–32.
Bonifazi (2004): Anna Bonifazi, "ΚΕΙΝΟΣ in Pindar: Between Grammar and Poetic Intention", *CP* 99, 283–299.
Bowra (1964): Cecil M. Bowra, *Pindar*, Oxford.

Braun (1938): Alfonsina Braun, "I verbi del fare nel greco", *SIFC* 15, 242–296.
Bremer (1990): Jan M. Bremer, "Pindar's Paradoxical Ἐγώ and a Recent Controversy About the Performance of His Epinicia", in: Simon Slings (ed.), *The Poet's 'I' in Archaic Greek Lyric*, Amsterdam, 41–58.
Bremmer (1996): Jan N. Bremmer, "The Status and Symbolic Capital of the Seer", in: Robin Hägg (ed.), *The Role of Religion in the Early Greek Polis*, Stockholm, 97–109.
Bundy (1962): Elroy Bundy, *Studia Pindarica*, Berkeley/Los Angeles.
Burnett (1989): Anne Pippin Burnett, "Performing Pindar's Odes", *CP* 84, 283–293.
Burnett (1998): Anne Pippin Burnett, "Spontaneity, Savaging, and Praise in Pindar's Sixth Paean", *AJP* 119, 493–520.
Carey (1989): Christopher Carey, "The performance of the victory ode", *AJP* 110, 545–565.
Carey (1991): Christopher Carey, "The victory ode in performance", *CP* 86, 192–200.
Carey (2007): Christopher Carey, "Pindar, place, and performance", in: Simon Hornblower and Catherine Morgan (eds.), *Pindar's Poetry, Patrons, and Festivals*, Oxford, 199–210.
Currie (2004): Bruno Currie, "Reperformance scenarios for Pindar's odes", in: Christopher J. Mackie (ed.), *Oral Performance and Its Context*, Leiden, 49–69.
Currie (2005): Bruno Currie, *Pindar and the Cult of Heroes*, Oxford.
Currie (2013): Bruno Currie, "The Pindaric First Person in Flux", *ClAnt* 32, 243–282.
D'Alessio (1994): Giambattista B. D'Alessio, "First-person problems in Pindar", *BICS* 41, 117–139.
Eckerman (2010): Chris Eckerman, "The Κῶμος of Pindar and Bacchylides and the Semantics of Celebration", *CQ* 60, 302–312.
Eckerman (2014): Chris Eckerman, "On the Performance of Pindar's *Nemean* 3", *Mnemosyne* 67, 289–292.
Fearn (2017): David Fearn, *Pindar's Eyes: Visual and Material Culture in Epinician Poetry*, Oxford.
Fogelmark (1972): Staffan Fogelmark, *Studies in Pindar with Particular Reference to Paean VI and Nemean VII*, Lund.
Fontenrose (1978): Joseph Fontenrose, *The Delphic Oracle: Its Responses and Operations with a Catalogue of Responses*, Berkeley.
Ford (1981): Andrew Ford, *A Study of Early Greek Terms for Poetry: 'Aoide', 'Epos' and 'Poiesis'*, Ph.D. Diss., Yale University.
Ford (1994): Andrew Ford, *Homer: The Poetry of the Past*, Ithaca.
Ford (2002): Andrew Ford, *The Origins of Criticism: Literary Culture and Poetic Theory in Classical Greece*, Princeton.
Gentili (1990): Bruno Gentili, "L' 'io' nella poesia lirica greca", in: *A.I.O.N. Sez. Filologico-Letteraria* 12, 20–22.
Goldhill (1991): Simon Goldhill, *The Poet's Voice: Essays on Poetics and Greek Literature*, Cambridge.
Graziosi (2002): Barbara Graziosi, *Inventing Homer: The Early Reception of Epic*, Cambridge.
Griffith (2009): Mark Griffith, "Apollo, Teiresias, and the Politics of Tragic Prophecy", in: Lukia Athanassaki, Richard P. Martin and John F. Miller (eds.), *Apolline Politics and Poetics*, Athens, 473–500.
Gubar (1981): Susan Gubar, "'The Blank Page' and the Issues of Female Creativity", *Critical Inquiry* 8, 243–263.
Hauser (2016): Emily Hauser, "In Her Own Words: The Semantics of Female Authorship in Ancient Greece, From Sappho to Nossis", *Ramus* 45, 133–164.
Hauser (2023): Emily Hauser, *How Women Became Poets: A Gender History of Greek Literature*. Princeton.
Heath (1988): Malcolm Heath, "Receiving the *komos*: the context and performance of epinician", *AJP* 109, 180–195.

Heath/Lefkowitz (1991): Malcolm Heath and Mary Lefkowitz, "Epinician performance", *CP* 85, 173–191.
Hoekstra (1962): A. Hoekstra, "The Absence of the Aeginetans: On the Interpretation of Pindar's Sixth Paean", *Mnemosyne* 15, 1–14.
Hubbard (2004): Thomas K. Hubbard, "The dissemination of epinician lyric: Pan-Hellenism, reperformance, written texts", in: Christopher J. Mackie (ed.), *Oral Performance and Its Context*, Leiden, 71–93.
Klinck (2001): Anne Klinck, "Male Poets and Maiden Voices: Gender and Genre in Pindar and Alcman", *Hermes* 129, 276–279.
Klindienst (2002): Patricia Klindienst, "The Voice of the Shuttle Is Ours", in: Laura McClure (ed.), *Sexuality and Gender in the Ancient World*, Oxford, 259–286.
Kuhn-Treichel (2020): Thomas Kuhn-Treichel, "Pindar's Poetic 'I' and the Muses: Metaphorical Role Characterization in Different Genres", *CJ* 116, 152–171.
Kurke (1991): Leslie Kurke, *The Traffic in Praise: Pindar and the Poetics of Social Economy*, Ithaca.
Kurke (2005): Leslie Kurke, "Choral Lyric as 'Ritualization': Poetic Sacrifice and Poetic *Ego* in Pindar's Sixth Paian", *ClAnt* 24, 81–130.
Kyriakou (1994): Poulheria Kyriakou, "Images of Women in Pindar", *MD* 32, 31–54.
Lefkowitz (1963): Mary Lefkowitz, "ΤΩ ΚΑΙ ΕΓΩ: The first person in Pindar", *HSCPh* 67, 177–253.
Lefkowitz (1980): Mary Lefkowitz, "Autobiographical Fiction in Pindar", *HSCPh* 84, 29–49.
Lefkowitz (1988): Mary Lefkowitz, "Who sang Pindar's victory odes?", *AJP* 109, 1–11.
Lefkowitz (1991): Mary Lefkowitz, *First-person Fictions: Pindar's Poetic "I"*, Oxford.
Lefkowitz (1995): Mary Lefkowitz, "The first person in Pindar reconsidered – again", *BICS* 40, 139–150.
Lidov (1993): Joel Lidov, "What Am I? What Am I Not?: Three Recent Pindars", *CJ* 89, 69–79.
Martin (1989): Richard P. Martin, *The Language of Heroes: Speech and Performance in the Iliad*, Ithaca.
Maslov (2009): Boris Maslov, "The Semantics of Ἀοιδός and Related Compounds: Towards a Historical Poetics of Solo Performance in Archaic Greece", *ClAnt* 28, 1–38.
Maslov (2015): Boris Maslov, *Pindar and the Emergence of Literature*, Cambridge.
Maslov (2016): Boris Maslov, "The Children of Mnemosyne: A Contrastive Metapoetics of Pindar and Bacchylides", *Philologia Classica* 11, 223–243.
Miller (1993): Andrew Miller, "Pindaric Mimesis: The Associative Mode", *CJ* 89, 21–53.
Morgan (1993): Kathryn Morgan, "Pindar the Professional and the Rhetoric of the ΚΩΜΟΣ", *CPh* 88, 1–15.
Morrison (2007): Andrew Morrison, *The Narrator in Archaic Greek and Hellenistic Poetry*, Cambridge.
Nagy (1989): Gregory Nagy, "Early Greek Views of Poets and Poetry", in: George A. Kennedy (ed.), *The Cambridge History of Literary Criticism: Volume 1, Classical Criticism*, Cambridge, 1–77.
Nagy (1990): Gregory Nagy, *Pindar's Homer: The Lyric Possession of an Epic Past*, Baltimore.
Nagy (1999): Gregory Nagy, *The Best of the Achaeans: Concepts of the Hero in Archaic Greek Poetry*, 2nd ed., Baltimore.
Neer/Kurke (2019): Richard Neer and Leslie Kurke, *Pindar, Song, and Space: Towards a Lyric Archaeology*, Baltimore.
Parmentier/Felson (2016): Richard Parmentier and Nancy Felson, "The 'Savvy Interpreter': Performance and Interpretation in Pindar's Victory Odes", in: Richard Parmentier (ed.), *Signs and Society: Further Studies in Semiotic Anthropology*, Bloomington, 208–238.
Pavlou (2010): Maria Pavlou, "Pindar *Nemean* 5: Real and Poetic Statues", *Phoenix* 64, 1–17.
Pfeijffer (1999a): Ilja Leonard Pfeijffer, *First Person Futures in Pindar*, Stuttgart.

Pfeijffer (1999b): Ilja Leonard Pfeijffer, *Three Aeginetan Odes of Pindar: A Commentary on Nemean V, Nemean III, and Pythian VIII*, Leiden.

Phillips (2017): Tom Phillips, "Pindar's Voices: Music, Ethics and Reperformance", *JHS* 137, 142–162.

Radt (1958): Stefan Radt, *Pindars Zweiter und Sechster Paian*, Amsterdam

Roisman (2006): Hanna Roisman, "Helen in the *Iliad*: 'Causa Belli' and Victim of War: From Silent Weaver to Public Speaker", *AJP* 127, 1–36.

Segal (1974): Charles Segal, "Arrest and Movement: Pindar's Fifth Nemean", *Hermes* 102, 397–411.

Segal (1986): Charles Segal, *Pindar's Mythmaking: The Fourth Pythian Ode*, Princeton.

Segal (1998): Charles Segal, *Aglaia: The Poetry of Alcman, Sappho, Pindar, Bacchylides, and Corinna*, London.

Shapiro (1994): H. Alan Shapiro, *Myth Into Art: Poet and Painter in Classical Greece*, London.

Smith (2007): R. R. R. Smith, "Pindar, Athletes, and the Early Greek Statue Habit", in: Simon Hornblower and Catherine Morgan (eds.), *Pindar's Poetry, Patrons, and Festivals: From Archaic Greece to the Roman Empire*, Oxford, 83–139.

Spentzou/Fowler (2002): Efi Spentzou and Don Fowler (eds.), *Cultivating the Muse: Struggles for Power and Inspiration in Classical Literature*, Oxford.

Stehle (1997): Eva Stehle, *Performance and Gender in Ancient Greece: Nondramatic Poetry in its Setting*, Princeton.

Steiner (1986): Deborah Steiner, *The Crown of Song: Metaphor in Pindar*, London.

Steiner (1993): Deborah Steiner, "Pindar's 'Oggetti Parlanti'", *HSCPh* 95, 159–180.

Steiner (2001): Deborah Steiner, *Images in Mind: Statues in Archaic and Classical Greek Literature and Thought*, Princeton.

Svenbro (1984): Jesper Svenbro, *La parola e il marmo: Alle origini della poetica greca*, Torino.

Verdenius (1987): Willem Jacob Verdenius, *Commentaries on Pindar: Volume 1, Olympian Odes 3, 7, 12, 14*, Leiden.

Worman (2001): Nancy Worman, "This Voice Which Is Not One: Helen's Verbal Guises in Homeric Epic", in: André Lardinois and Laura McClure (eds.), *Making Silence Speak: Women's Voices in Greek Literature and Society*, Princeton, 19–37.

Valentina Moro
A Theatre of Vulnerability: Lamentation as a Gendered Self-Narration in Sophocles' *Antigone*

Abstract: This chapter offers a new reading of Antigone's lamentation (lines 806–928) as a specifically gendered vocal performance in Sophocles' tragic language. Lamentation is a ritual linguistic structure traditionally attributed to female voices. It has therefore become a relevant topic for studies on women and gender in ancient Greek society and literature. This chapter analyses lexical elements, linguistic formulas, and narrative descriptions in the agonistic exchange between Antigone and the Chorus of Theban elders. My reading focuses on the gender parameter in Antigone's speech, in which she interprets her life as a constant and ongoing movement searching for a place where she fully belongs. Firstly, she compares herself to Kore/Persephone, daughter of Demeter, imagining her own ideal marriage to Hades. Secondly, she refers to the myth of Niobe, daughter of Tantalus and mother of many sons and daughters, who was punished by the gods after boasting of her fertility. Ultimately, she remarks that she is Jocasta's and Oedipus' offspring, which makes her both Polyneices' and Eteocles' sister. She continuously evokes and reaffirms these ties, considering them to be more important than the link with Haemon that would make her a wife and a mother. I argue that Antigone uses the performance of mourning in order to stage her own vulnerability and that the Chorus provides active engagement in her self-narration. The conceptual framework that informs this chapter is the "vulnerability paradigm" in feminist theory, which interprets vulnerability in positive terms, as an idea that enhances a demand for self-determination rather than a request for recognition.

Keywords: performance of mourning, Persephone, Niobe, marriage, sisterhood, motherhood, *metoikia*, vulnerability paradigm

1 Tragic lamentation as a gendered vocal performance

Lamentation, a ritual linguistic structure, recurs frequently in tragic language and has captured the attention of several scholars in different disciplines. In particular, it has become a relevant topic for studies on women and gender in ancient Greek society and literature, because ritual laments were performed almost exclusively by women.¹ This chapter interprets Antigone's lamentation in Sophocles' *Antigone* (lines 806–928) as a specifically gendered vocal performance in Sophocles' tragic language, by analysing the way in which Oedipus' daughter uses it to narrate her own story.

Lyric expressions of grief performed by tragic characters reveal how much the form of Attic drama owes to ancient Greek mourning practices and to lamentation as a poetic genre, namely the mourning song.² As Naomi Weiss highlights, the conceptualization of lament as a genre included both individual wailing (γόος) and collective songs performed by professional singers (θρῆνος).³ This performance was a social ritual and had political significance in archaic Greece: in all *poleis*, funeral ceremonies were public occasions at which the powerful families could display their wealth. The lamentations were performed not only by kin but also by professional mourners. In the late sixth and early fifth centuries BCE, many cities passed funerary legislations aimed at restricting and regulating all aspects of the ceremonies that were considered excessive. Examples of such restrictions included the number of gifts that could be buried with the corpse; the number of people (especially women) participating in the ritual, now limited to next of kin; and above all, lamentations – with all the connected ritual gestures, like the tearing of clothes.⁴ In the same period, the lamentation was adapted for use in literary genres and became a characteristic moment both in epic poetry and in Attic tragedy. In tragic drama, it appears as a recognizable ritual performance, called κομμός, with reference to the gesture of hitting one's own chest as a sign of mourning (from κόπτω, "to hit"). It is an antiphonal dialogue between an individual mourner and a collective voice (the Chorus). Although in Attic drama there are several examples of male characters who lament and express grief, often for the loss of a loved one or for their own tragic destiny, lamentations are nonetheless considered a female prerogative. In Sophocles' works, this is particularly remarkable in the play *Women of Trachis*, where Heracles, in excruciating pain after realising that he has been poisoned, laments his own feminization: "But now in my misery I have been found a woman (θῆλυς), instead of the man I used to be" (*Tr.* 1075, transl. Jebb). Therefore, a gender parameter characterizes the lamentations throughout Attic drama.

Taking into account lexical elements, linguistic structures and formulas, and narrative descriptions, similarities can be traced in two examples of lamentation performed by Sophocles' characters Antigone and Electra, respectively, in the eponymous plays. The sections of the two plays to which I refer are 806–928 in *Antigone* and 86–327 in *Electra*, which are equivalent neither in length nor in terms of their internal structures. They also refer to very different parts of each play. While Electra's

---

1 See for instance Loraux (1990); McClure (1999); Foley (2001).
2 See Murnaghan (2009) 322.
3 Weiss (2017) 246.
4 Foley (2001) 22f.

lamentation and interaction with the Chorus happen at the beginning of the play, Antigone laments only when she realizes she is going to die soon and will not have another chance to speak to her fellow citizens. Another difference is that, while in *Antigone* the Chorus members are Theban male citizens, in *Electra* the Chorus is female. Nonetheless, the two scenes have several relevant aspects in common. In both dramas there is one mourner (the female protagonist) who engages in an agonistic exchange with the Chorus; each lament reveals that the female mourner wants to be heard and that there is a dialogue, since neither Chorus solely consoles the mourner. Instead, both interactions have an agonistic connotation and, in both cases, the Chorus' questions and remarks allow the female protagonist to add some details to her narration.

Some of the features of these narrations have a specific gender association, such as the reference to institutional roles and ritual practices. For instance, both Antigone and Electra bewail that they will never marry or have children, which is a recurrent formula in tragic laments performed by female voices (i.e. *Ant.* 814, 867, 876, 917; *El.* 164f., 188). They compare themselves to female mythological characters; in particular, they both mention Niobe, a goddess who, according to the myth, was punished for her ὕβρις by Apollo and Artemis, who killed her offspring, and afterwards was turned into a weeping stone (*Ant.* 823–33; *El.* 150–52). They call into question their own kinship relationships and even gender norms by refusing to obey those who are in charge of their respective city and family. Significantly, both evoke the signs of desperation on their own bodies and describe their condition of social exclusion from a community which is both their family and the State, by comparing this status to foreignness. Indeed, while Antigone calls herself a μέτοικος (*Ant.* 852, 868) – a lexical choice that I will discuss in detail in the following pages –, Agamemnon's daughter describes herself as "a despised foreigner who serves in the house" (ἔποικος ἀναξία οἰκονομῶ, *El.* 189f.).[5] In both cases Sophocles chooses a recognisable linguistic structure such as lamentation as a tragic moment in which his female protagonists can speak and denounce not only the absence of mourning for the death of their male relatives (Antigone's brother and Electra's father, respectively), but also the lack of empathy and support on their fellow citizen's part for their own tragic fate.[6]

My reading adopts the fruitful comparison between the two performances of mourning as its point of departure and focuses on Antigone's lamentation by examining specific lexical and semantic elements. The fact that Antigone insists on her attachment to Polyneices, often interpreted as a repetition of the incestuous relationship by

---

[5] In the play, the term ἔποικος does not refer to a specific juridical condition; generically speaking, it identifies someone who comes from outside a household or another kind of community and moves in. See Finglass (2007) 158.

[6] For a further comparison between the two lamentations, a recent commentary on Electra's is Nooter (2011). On gendered language in *Electra* see Lewis (2015).

scholars and commentators,⁷ rather reveals a political attitude. What emerges from this reading is that Antigone claims the right to choose how to narrate the story of her family and how to identify herself. In particular, I focus on a selection of female characters referred to by Antigone in her lamentation. I will argue that the way in which she narrates their stories and describes their bodies and desires allows her to indirectly add details to her self-narration from the perspective of gender.

Moreover, this chapter invites readers to linger on the role that the Chorus plays in relation to the female protagonist's self-narration. I will read this section as an agonistic exchange based on the alternation and combination of two voices – Antigone's and the collective voice of the Chorus members. The agonistic construction of the lamentation is due to the individual mourner framing her own self-narration by interacting with the Chorus members and responding to their statements, questions, and provocations. The Chorus sings *together* with the mourner, but is not necessarily *aligned* with her claims. This is particularly relevant in as much as the function of most tragic Choruses in Attic drama is to mirror a larger community, namely the real audiences at the theatre, framing and building their experience into the play.⁸

The aim of this chapter is to demonstrate that, through her lamentation, Antigone delivers a first-person discourse and "stages" her own vulnerability as a theatrical performance, thus establishing a communication with the Thebans but also with the audience of the play.⁹ I call her lamentation a "theatre of vulnerability", using the notion of vulnerability to designate a connotation of human life in its bodily, gendered dimension. In modern Western philosophical thought, the notion has been used as an ethical response to the mainstream interpretation of violence.¹⁰ It is beyond the scope of this chapter to delve into the considerable amount of literature concerning the topic of vulnerability and its critical readings. Therefore, I summarize here some of the arguments which explain my use of the notion as a conceptual framework in order to contribute an original reading of Sophocles' play. Emmanuel Lévinas first argued that vulnerability is an ontological aspect of each human life, ambivalently linked both to

---

7 See the recent Mills (2018).
8 Murnaghan (2009) 327. – My reading of Antigone's exchange with the Chorus of Theban citizens is enriched by the reference to Therese Fuhrer's chapter in this volume, which focuses on women's choruses in two (ps.-)Senecan tragedies. Those readers who are interested in lamentations as antiphonal exchanges between a female character and the Chorus might find the comparison between Fuhrer's reading of this lyric performance and mine helpful. While Fuhrer remarks on the specificity of first-person statements pronounced by a collective female voice, I will show that the relationship between Antigone and a Chorus composed of her elderly and male fellow citizens is gendered and agonistically constructed.
9 Honig (2013) 135: "Staging dissensus by working with the materials provided by the city of consensus, Antigone conspires with language to work the interval between lamentation and *logos*, singularity and equality, between the infinite *aiai* of tragedy and the finite *aei* of the city."
10 Guaraldo (2018).

violence and to the ethical choice not to commit violence.[11] In feminist theories, the topic of vulnerability has been addressed through the lens of a *relational* model in the study of politics. It entails the critique of the sovereign subject paradigm that has characterized Western political thought from Hobbes and the social contract tradition onwards.[12] In particular, Martha Fineman, Judith Butler, Adriana Cavarero, and Sara Ahmed have addressed the Lévinasian topic by reflecting upon embodiment. They have remarked upon the constitutive exposure of each human body to the possibility of being hurt (*vulnus* is the Latin word for "wound" from which vulnerability stems).[13] They have claimed that each subject is vulnerable precisely because she is in relation to other subjects and depends upon infrastructures.[14] In particular, Adriana Cavarero has envisioned a "postural ethics", insisting on the image of inclination, symbolized by the maternal figure, as a model to think about human relationality in terms of vulnerability and dependence.[15] Therefore, the "vulnerability paradigm" can be considered as an ethical response to the philosophical interpretation of violence as an inevitable human drive.[16] Among the different critiques regarding the use of vulnerability as a paradigm, both in philosophical and in political and juridical literature, some of them concern its understanding as an ontological concept (namely vulnerability as a shared human condition) and others its use as a political and legal identification of specific groups or individuals as "vulnerable subjects".[17] In relation to the idea of vulnerability as an ontological concept, Judith Butler has remarked on the fact that each individual has different resources with which to cope with her precarity. Hence, the feminist thinker has differentiated between two notions: on the one hand, she considers *precariousness* a shared bodily condition that characterizes human life inasmuch as it is relational and dependent; on the other hand, she uses the term *precarity* to stress that each human life has different social, cultural, ethnic, racial, economic, and gender conditions.[18] As for the "particularistic" account of vulnerability as characterising specific groups and/or identities, it would be too complex listing and explaining here critiques within legal studies and it would require an expert in the field. One of the most prominent arguments in the fields of philosophy and political

---

11 Lévinas (1996).
12 See Pateman (1988) and Pulcini (2009b).
13 Maragno (2018).
14 Butler (2004).
15 Cavarero (2016).
16 See Guaraldo (2012).
17 Giolo (2018) 253f. differentiates between the two approaches to vulnerability, the "universal" one (in the fields of political philosophy and philosophy of law) and the "particularistic" one (in the fields of political science and legal studies). Nevertheless, she remarks that both of them strictly link the notion of vulnerability to the perspective of the subject, although this nexus does not correspond to the one originally introduced by liberal thinkers. On the use of the notion of the "vulnerable subject" in legal studies see Fineman and Grear (2013).
18 See Butler (2009) and Birmingham (2018).

science is the idea that such an account insists only on the *negative* aspect of vulnerability. The claim is that this categorization reproduces and even fosters the isolation and marginality of groups and individuals identified as in need of *protection*.[19]

Nevertheless, I agree with the approach taken by many feminist theorists which allows us to think about the *generative* character of vulnerability, being a site of resistance that produces new political subjects not by isolating them, but rather by making their voices heard in the public space.[20] Moreover, it can be thought of as an epistemic resource for rethinking and questioning social and political relations, as well as the role of institutions from a historical perspective.[21] Therefore, I have chosen this conceptual framework to analyse Antigone's lamentation because it interprets vulnerability in positive terms, as an idea that enhances a demand for self-determination rather than a request for recognition.

2 Antigone's exceptionality

"Look at me" (ὁρᾶτ' ἔμ', 806) Antigone utters when she appears on stage for the last time, after the Chorus has anticipated her arrival by saying "I see Antigone making her way to the chamber where all are laid to rest, now her bridal chamber" (804f.).[22] Creon, the king of Thebes, had issued a decree forbidding the burial of Polyneices, who was considered guilty of treason (21–36). Antigone, Polyneices' sister and Creon's niece, tried to bury the corpse anyway, thus violating the king's edict, but she was caught red-handed and Creon condemned her to be buried alive. At this point in the play, Antigone knows that she is going to die and she decides to address her fellow citizens (ὦ γᾶς πατρίας πολῖται: citizens of my fatherland, 806), asking them to turn to her and watch the pitiful sight of her body. She is looking for an audience while lamenting and she directly addresses her fellow citizens.

Her final appearance on stage happens in a section of the play (806–943) that can be divided into three parts. It starts (a) with a lyric-epirrhematic amoebaean[23] between an actor and the Chorus (806–82): Antigone pronounces a κομμός that Mark Griffith describes as a "quasi-ritual lament",[24] and the Chorus responds to her lyrics, firstly chanting in recitative anapaests (817–22; 833–8), and afterwards in

---

19 See Casadei (2018).
20 See for instance Ferrarese (2017).
21 See for instance Gilson (2014) and Pulcini (2009a).
22 Unless otherwise indicated, for the translation of Sophocles' *Antigone* I refer to Jebb (1966).
23 The genre of the amoebaean belongs to the archaic pastoral poetry in Greece. Originally, it was a singing contest in a pastoral setting. The lyric-epirrhematic characterization entails that its structure alternates lyrics and spoken parts. In Attic drama, it is mostly used to stress highly conflictual or pathetic situations, as in the case taken into account by this paragraph.
24 Griffith (1999) 13.

lyric metres (two short stanzas: 853–6; 872–5). The section continues (b) with a dialogue between Creon (883–90) and Antigone (891–928), whose ῥῆσις is long and articulate. The third part of the section is (c) a short anapaestic dialogue between the Chorus, Creon, and Antigone (929–43). In this crucial section of the play, the choral voice of the elderly Thebans engages with her agonistically and apparently keeps contradicting Antigone – which is typical of the structure of the amoebaean. Mark Griffith remarks that, from a stylistic perspective, there is a musical climax in this passage.[25] It is produced by the alternation of Antigone's and the Chorus' voices, in the intertwinement of speeches and lyrics.

Antigone recursively mentions images linked to death and mourning in her lamentation, which, for this reason, has been interpreted as her singing a dirge. Two aspects probably produced disorientation in the ancient audience. On the one hand, the dirge she is singing is, in fact, dedicated to herself.[26] On the other hand, while a κομμός (which is structured as a dialogue between a single and a collective voice) usually involves a group of people expressing grief and support to a single mourner, in this scene the Chorus keeps alternating sympathy with blame, although never in open contrast with Antigone.[27] A recurrent element in the lines pronounced by the Chorus is the idea that Antigone's action, so bold and fearless, is on the edge between heroism and ὕβρις. When they call her αὐτόνομος (821), the Chorus evokes her transgression, but at the same time remarks that she has taken full responsibility for it. The term literally means "someone guided by her own laws"; it can also designate a person who independently decides which rules to follow. Both Richard Jebb and Mark Griffith remark that the term also means, more generally, "voluntarily"; they argue that it is not clear whether, in using it, the Chorus aims to blame Antigone or not. The term is remarkable not only because it is extremely rare, but also because it expresses how Antigone's destiny is entirely different from anyone else's. She embodies an *exception*, since Creon condemns her to be buried "still alive, unlike any mortal before" (ζῶσα μόνη δὴ θνητῶν, 821f.).

While telling Antigone that she has been acting by following only her own rules, the elderly citizens of Thebes remark on the exceptionality of her act. Antigone's existence has always been considered unique, because of both her family and her refusal to compromise on Creon's political arguments. As Thebans, the Chorus members are certainly aware that part of their fellow citizens are unhappy with Creon's authoritative methods, covertly cry for Antigone and even support her claims, as Haemon tries to explain to his father at 690–99:

τὸ γὰρ σὸν ὄμμα δεινὸν, ἀνδρὶ δημότῃ
λόγοις τοιούτοις, οἷς σὺ μὴ τέρψει κλύων:

---

[25] Griffith (1999) 260.
[26] As remarked by Rehm (1994) 64; Goldhill (2012) 110; Honig (2013) 109.
[27] See Griffith (1999) 267f. and Goldhill (2012) 110.

> ἐμοὶ δ' ἀκούειν ἔσθ' ὑπὸ σκότου τάδε,
> τὴν παῖδα ταύτην οἶ', ὀδύρεται πόλις,
> πασῶν γυναικῶν ὡς ἀναξιωτάτη
> κάκιστ' ἀπ' ἔργων εὐκλεεστάτων φθίνει.
> ἥτις τὸν αὑτῆς αὐτάδελφον ἐν φοναῖς
> πεπτῶτ' ἄθαπτον μήθ' ὑπ' ὠμηστῶν κυνῶν
> εἴασ' ὀλέσθαι μήθ' ὑπ' οἰωνῶν τινος.
> οὐχ ἥδε χρυσῆς ἀξία τιμῆς λαχεῖν;

For dread of your glance forbids the ordinary citizen to speak such words as would offend your ear. But I can hear these murmurs in the dark, how the city moans for this girl, saying: 'No woman ever merited death less – none ever died so shamefully for deeds so glorious as hers, who, when her own brother had fallen in bloody battle, would not leave him unburied to be devoured by savage dogs, or by any bird. Does she not deserve to receive golden honor?'[28]

A close reading of the text allows us to raise questions concerning the Chorus members' sympathy for the protagonist and their real intentions, given the fact that Antigone is openly countering the king. There is no certain response to these questions; nonetheless we see that, when Antigone pronounces her last words in this section of the play, her claim already resounds among her fellow citizens and, although she dies lamenting her solitude, her message has already reached many people.

3 An all-female genealogy in Antigone's self-narration

Antigone structures her self-narration by rooting it in her own mythological imagery. Indeed, in the first *strophe* of the amoebaean she pronounces, she compares herself to Kore, Zeus' and Demeter's daughter (806–16), a mythical female figure whom Hades, god of the Underworld, carried off in his chariot.[29] According to the best-known versions of the myth, after her daughter's abduction, Demeter makes every possible effort to see Kore again. Deprived of her daughter, Demeter no longer gives birth and her desperation renders the soil unproductive and fruitless. An infertile earth is a threat to the preservation of all forms of life and therefore Demeter eventually reaches an agreement with Hades: Kore will spend part of her life in the guise of

---

28 The analysis of the speech with which Haemon bravely addresses his father is beyond the scope of this essay. Nevertheless, my opinion is that most of the political readings of *Antigone* have failed to remark on how relevant this father-son agonistic exchange is for understanding the play. It reveals that, among the Theban citizens, there is indeed not just sympathy for the pitiful sight of Antigone approaching her death chamber. Rather, some of them understand her denouncement and support her cause.
29 Hes. *Theog.* 912–14. For Ceres' lament in Claudian's Late Antique epic *De raptu Proserpinae* see Harich-Schwarzbauer in this volume.

Persephone, queen of the Underworld, and the other part of it on earth, where she lives with her mother, the goddess of agriculture. In much the same cyclical way as the earth changes, Demeter's body is alternately fertile (when her daughter is with her) and infertile.

By means of the comparison with Kore/Persephone, Antigone represents herself as a bride, leaving her family's residence to start a new life in her husband's home. She even describes this event as a wedding, as if she herself had to repeat Kore's fate by becoming Hades' new wife. In ancient Greek sources, the term κόρη indicates the status of a woman before getting married, but was not necessarily linked to a moral judgement of purity.[30] In classical Athens (and in many other Greek *poleis* whose customs and traditions we have evidence for), marriage was not an institution established by documentations; rather, it was a matter of material and cultural practices.[31] By behaving and being socially recognized as a married person, one could present his or her children as legitimate. The betrothal (ἐγγύησις) entailed several legal and economic features and was marked by ritual practices. It required a legal transaction and, mostly, the exchange (ἔκδοσις) of a property in the form of a dowry (προίξ) from the woman's father (or any other man who was legally responsible for her) to the spouse, who also became the woman's new legal tutor (κύριος). Therefore, marriage legally established a homosocial connection (between the woman's former and current tutor) and, most importantly, a connection between two οἶκοι (households). The ritualized passage from the paternal household to the new one (which corresponded to a processional ceremony: γάμος) was symbolically linked to the transformation undergone by the female body.[32] In ancient Greek literature, a rich semantic imagery interpreted the female body as an uncultivated field, which had the passive function of spontaneously generating. From the fifth century BCE onwards, the parallel between the cycle of generation and death in nature and female reproductive capabilities was connected to the idea of a woman's normative role within a household. Therefore, marriage was represented as having a civilizing function, since it made a woman ready to fit into a new house and start a new family. Nevertheless, as Violaine Sebillotte Cuchet has pointed out, women's sexual desire was not considered dangerous in itself, and neither was sexuality framed as more natural or ethical when aimed at procreation, as has frequently been assumed by critical interpretations.[33] As several judiciary orations evidence, the legal and customary control over seduction had

---

30 Sissa (1987) addresses the topic of virginity in ancient Greece by focusing on how the female body has been thought about and represented. Sissa takes several ritual aspects that characterize the interpretation of virginity in different geographic and cultural contexts, as narrated in historical, literary, and medical sources.
31 On the legal and social aspects connected to marriage in ancient Greece, see: Sebillotte Cuchet (2017); Lyons (2012); Cantarella (2005); Ormand (1999); Todd (1993) 214.
32 King (2002).
33 Sebillotte Cuchet (2017) 6.

only one aim: that of preserving the integrity of a family's fortune. If a woman lied about the identity of her child's father, the household's inheritance could be appropriated by an illegitimate heir.

More broadly, in the literary representation of women and marriage, two remarkable features were associated. On the one hand, there is a clear co-implication between the "marriage transaction" with the idea of women's mobility (within and outside the household, and within the *polis*) and their right to live in a specific place as a proper member. On the other hand, there is an opposition between the stability of the agricultural world, with its recursive and cyclic connotation, and the wild and unstable world of the animals, dominated by means of hunting – imagery strictly connected to sexual desire. Indeed, in ancient Greek literary sources, the image of taming or hunting wild animals was also metaphorically associated with the erotic sphere.[34] At the same time, Kirk Ormand remarks, both in vase painting and in poetry the ritual aspects related to the wedding have often been portrayed as an abduction scene, in which a hyper-masculine man carries a frightened bride away.[35]

The ritual and symbolical imagery linked to marriage in ancient Greece is particularly relevant in Antigone's case. The way in which she insists on the ideas of marriage (as something she has been deprived of) and mobility by comparing herself to Kore/Persephone visually evokes rituals of passage, recreation, and fertility, but all of this can even seem grotesque when one considers her imminent death. Antigone makes the ambiguity of the association between marriage and death explicit. Indeed, Oedipus' daughter describes her own journey towards the Acheron river, a prefiguration of death, not as a choice but, instead, as an abduction. She mentions both ritual customs and practices connected to nuptial celebrations and her own funeral. In these lines, the presence of terms meaning "bridal hymns and songs" (ὑμεναίων . . . ἐπινύμφειός . . . νυμφεύσω) alternating with terms designating "processional chants" (the figura etymologica: ὕμνος ὕμνησεν) necessarily captures the audience's attention (806–16):

> ὁρᾶτ' ἔμ', ὦ γᾶς πατρίας πολῖται,
> τὰν νεάταν ὁδὸν
> στείχουσαν, νέατον δὲ φέγ-
> γος λεύσσουσαν ἀελίου,
> κοὔποτ' αὖθις. ἀλλά μ' ὁ παγ-
> κοίτας Ἅιδας ζῶσαν ἄγει
> τὰν Ἀχέροντος
> ἀκτάν, οὔθ' **ὑμεναίων**

---

34 See Sourvinou-Inwood (1987) 138 and Ormand (1999) 91.
35 On the abduction scenes in Attic vase paintings see Sutton (1997/8) 28–32. On this point see Ormand (1999) 29.

ἔγκληρον, οὔτ' **ἐπινύμ-**
φειός πώ μέ τις **ὕμνος ὕ-**
μνησεν, ἀλλ' Ἀχέροντι **νυμφεύσω**

> No, Hades who lays all to rest leads me living to Acheron's shore, though I have not had my due portion of the chant that brings the bride, nor has any hymn been mine for the crowning of marriage. Instead the lord of Acheron will be my groom.

In the first portion of the lamentation, Antigone represents herself as a bride within the framework of a mythological self-narration, replacing Kore/Persephone in the role of Hades' wife. At the same time, she refers to marriage as something that she has been denied. Mark Griffith remarks that the "marriage to Hades" motif is widespread in Greek literature, arguing that, for a woman, there were many similarities between nuptial rituals and funeral ceremonies.[36] Two remarkable juxtapositions of terms, Ἅιδας ζῶσαν (811) and Ἀχέροντι νυμφεύσω (815), respectively, express that death is intertwined with life, just as, according to Antigone's self-narration, it is always present in marriage. Indeed, as death recursively appears in Antigone's speech, so does life (ζῶσαν, 811) and the same topics are echoed by the Chorus (life: ζῶσα, 821; ζῶσαν, 838; and death: φθινάσιν, 819; Ἅιδην καταβήσει, 822; φθιμένη, 836; θανοῦσαν, 838). Taking this idea further, one might argue that each marriage entails a loss since, once a virgin gets married, she has to move away from her parental household. This is also the representation of an ideal departure from the body she used to inhabit, which is now *becoming* something new – the body of a woman who is expected to get pregnant. However, the focus of my commentary is not the association between a woman's experience of marriage and death in the literary sources, which has been abundantly discussed.[37] Rather, it is relevant to stress these aspects within the framework of this chapter, as they characterize the way in which Antigone narrates her journey towards death as a bodily experience in the dirge she is performing for herself. The procession towards her tomb appears to be an unaccomplished and impossible wedding.

Antigone's attempt to compare herself with Kore/Persephone is unsuccessful for several reasons. Antigone describes herself as being *on the move* at the beginning of the lamentation (τὰν νεάταν ὁδὸν στείχουσαν: "see me setting out on my last journey", 807f.)[38] and her fellow citizens echo this as well (ἐς τόδ' ἀπέρχει κεῦθος νεκύων: "you depart to that deep place of the dead", 818). Nonetheless, figuratively speaking, she is not moving as a bride is supposed to move, namely towards her

---

[36] In particular, Griffith (1999) 267 refers to "torches, veils, the escorted journey to a new and unfamiliar 'home', fear and lamentation at loss of loved ones, delivery into the hands of the new 'owner'".

[37] See Ormand (1999) 25–8 on this aspect.

[38] Insofar as this expression is positioned between two lines, within the lyric-epirrhematic amoebaean, these lines were probably pronounced with a relentless pace.

spouse (Haemon, in this case) and their nuptial household. Instead, in this symbolical prefiguration, she is moving *backwards* towards her paternal family, with whom she is going to live for the eternity.[39] Moreover, Kore is not responsible for her own living conditions, which have been decided by the male god who has become her husband. Conversely, the members of the Chorus stress that Antigone has made her own choices: the word αὐτόνομος fully expresses the idea that she is responsible for violating the king's edict since the moment in which she established her own agenda. By prioritising Polyneices' burial, Antigone has expressed her will *not* to move towards a new household which, within the symbolical framework of an ideal marriage, represents the entire *polis*.

As a response to the Chorus' words, in the first *antistrophē* of her lamentation, Antigone compares herself to another goddess, Niobe. According to the mythological narration, Niobe was responsible for having boasted about her numerous children, thus offending Leto, Apollo's and Artemis' mother.[40] As a consequence, Niobe's children were killed and, since she could not stop crying, she was turned into a stone. Antigone does not narrate this part of the story; instead, she describes the metamorphosis of Niobe's body, her feelings and perception, dramatically focusing on her suffering as a mourning mother. Niobe's body has been deprived of its fertility and of the beneficial effects of touching her children; the only physical perceptions she has are the coldness of the stone that has taken control over her body and her tears. Niobe is fated to consume herself under the snow and the rain (826–33):

> τὰν κισσὸς ὡς ἀτενὴς
> **πετραία βλάστα** δάμασεν,
> καί νιν ὄμβροι τακομέναν,
> ὡς φάτις ἀνδρῶν,
> χιών τ' οὐδαμὰ λείπει, τέγ-
> γει δ' ὑπ' ὀφρύσι παγκλαύτοις
> δειράδας: ᾇ με δαί-
> μων ὁμοιοτάταν κατευνάζει.

> Like clinging ivy, the sprouting stone subdued her. And the rains, as men tell, do not leave her melting form, nor does the snow, but beneath her weeping lids she dampens her collar.

As Davide Susanetti remarks, the juxtaposition between the terms πετραία and βλάστα, right at the beginning of line 827, is an oxymoron, which combines the immobility and infertility of a stone with the idea of offspring, something new that is

---

39 Ormand (1999) 18 argues that both Antigone and Electra do not get married precisely because they remain devoted to their respective families of origin: "Particularly when the focus of the tragedy is on unmarried women, the daughter's devotion to the father has the potential to interrupt the marriage transaction."
40 See e.g. Hom. *Il.* 24.602–17 and Ov. *Met.* 6.146–312. On Antigone's self-comparison to Niobe, see Honig (2013) 140f.

generated.[41] This is a highly evocative example of how Antigone dwells on the detailed physical descriptions, indirectly involving her own body in the comparison with the mythological figures. The inanimate stone serves as an eternal cage for Niobe's body, thus prefiguring the tomb in which Antigone is going to be buried alive. Just as Niobe's very body becomes the deadly element that makes generation impossible for her, Antigone's graveyard is the stony jail that will prevent her from becoming a mother. While describing Niobe's condition through a floral metaphor – she is becoming cold, unable to sprout and bloom – Antigone is in fact alluding to her own body.

However, she also insists on marriage and motherhood, both things denied to her. Earlier in the play, while Creon's guard described to the king the moment in which he captured Antigone, he compares her to a bird that "looks at the nest/bed bereft of hatchlings" and insists on "the bedding empty" (424f.),[42] with a double metaphorical association. Indeed, the bird symbolizes both marriage and motherhood, since the terms that designate the empty nest in the bird metaphor (occupying a highlighted position as the first and last words in the line: εὐνῆς . . . λέχος, 425) commonly refer to the nuptial bed.[43] Both Kore's and Niobe's stories concern a transition and a bodily transformation linked to marriage and motherhood. First and foremost, both of these references include remarkable gendered features concerning the female body. On the one hand, Kore's life is a mythical representation of the earth's cyclic power of recreation; her abduction is the prefiguration of marriage, the most meaningful transformation of a woman's status, life, *and* body. On the other hand, before undergoing a physical metamorphosis into stone, Niobe represents a very fertile mother in the first place.

Aware that she is pronouncing her last words in front of her fellow citizens, Antigone combines images of life and death in order to denounce Creon's abusive decisions. She probably aims to gain the Chorus' sympathy when she evokes her own female desire and laments that it is impossible for her to accomplish it since she is going to die. She insists on the fact that her body has been deprived of its female attributes, after sacrificing all the inclinations and aspirations a woman was supposed to long for. Therefore, the construction of a "personal mythology" allows Antigone to frame her self-narration by using the reference to her own body and lamenting her *vulnerability*. As explained at the beginning of the essay, I use this notion in order to draw attention to the bodily, gendered dimension in Antigone's self-narration. This conceptual framework is particularly helpful because vulnerability appears as the way in which Antigone chooses to represent herself in front of the *polis*. Her self-portrait reveals that she wants to actively communicate with her fellow citizens and visual descriptions are a prominent aspect in her narration.

---

41 Susanetti (2012) 321.
42 Translation by Ormand (1999) 90f.
43 Ibid.

My critical hypothesis is that this is not just a rhetorical strategy, but rather a way to narrate her personal bodily experiences in terms of relationships and desires. Indeed, instead of picturing herself as a victim, Antigone insists on the imagery of fertility. As Bonnie Honig argues, her "alliance with hypermaternity" reveals tragic irony.[44] Antigone embodies an "excess" that can be interpreted in two opposite ways: as both an augmented and a diminished female power of fertility. On the one hand, she knows that the exceptionality of her destiny makes her someone who cannot fully belong to the city and fit into its political community. For this reason she compares herself to two goddesses, and the Theban citizens, member of the Chorus, acknowledge that she dies "in glory and with praise" (κλεινὴ καὶ ἔπαινον ἔχουσ', 817) like an epic hero.[45] On the other hand, in the moments before her death, Antigone feels her fully human and, most importantly, female desires much more strongly: not only does she lament the things she has been deprived of (becoming a wife and a mother), holding Creon accountable for this, but she suffers for the loved ones she has lost and cannot properly mourn. Antigone's desire is aimed not at meeting social expectations, but rather at being free to create her own relationships of φιλία (love).

With a striking metaphorical association, Antigone establishes a connection between the idea of inhabiting a place (a house) and that of inhabiting a body, thus implying that she feels like an outsider within the *polis*. She describes herself as homeless: "I have no home among men or with the shades, no home with the living or with the dead" (851f.). This evidently emerges in the choice she makes of mythological references. Kore/Persephone spends her entire life moving from the Earth to the Underworld and then back to her mother's home, and although she is considered both a queen among the dead and a beloved daughter among the living, still she does not fully belong to either place. Moreover, Niobe is both a "foreigner" in Phrygia – as Antigone remarks by calling her ξέναν (824) – her father's land where she spends her lifetime after being turned into a stone, and a foreigner in the body she is forced to inhabit. Indeed, the stone symbolically represents Niobe's embodiment of her own sorrow, with which she will live for the rest of her life. Antigone also describes herself in a condition of displacement and foreignness, of exteriority and marginality, by using the term μέτοικος (852; 868), as I will explain later. Significantly, in *Electra*, when the female protagonist refers to Niobe, she associates the goddess' stony body precisely with a tomb, nonetheless remarking that the goddess keeps crying and that therefore life still flows in her body: "Ah, all-suffering

---

44 Honig (2013) 263. On Niobe's hypermaternity see also Cavarero (forthcoming).
45 Both terms κλεινή (from κλέος) and ἔπαινον mean fame and praise in public opinion and express the idea of a collective celebration. The term κλέος and its variants recur in Homer's poetics, e.g. *Il.* 4.197, 5.3, 7.91, 8.192; *Od.* 8.74, 9.20. Both terms frequently appear in contexts in which they are linked to an all-male aristocratic register and attributed to heroes celebrated for military success, who deserve to be remembered.

Niobe, you I count divine, since you weep forever in your rocky tomb (τάφῳ πετραίῳ)!" (*El.* 150–52, transl. Jebb).

Although the Chorus too remarks that Antigone's destiny is exceptional, both because of what she has done and the way in which she dies, it does not accept the comparison between her and the two mythological figures she mentions, since she is not an immortal goddess. The members of the Chorus argue that, on the contrary, she is one of *them*, namely a human being, fated to die: "Yet she was a goddess, as you know, and the offspring of gods", they say, speaking of Niobe, "while we are mortals and mortal-born" (834f.). They remark that they share her condition of finitude, since they use the pronoun ἡμεῖς ("we", 835) including Antigone and themselves in the same group of θνητογενεῖς ("mortal-born", 835). The compound word is directly opposed to θεογεννής ("god-born", 834), the term used by the Chorus to describe Niobe, and the terms' correspondence with one another clearly emerges as they are in the same emphatic position at the end of their respective lines. This is an attempt at consolation, and the Chorus members, therefore, prove to be something more than mere detached commentators. Moreover, they are reminding Antigone that she is a citizen of Thebes, something that has a clear political implication. Since she has chosen to disobey the king, they stress that she has in fact refused another symbolical marriage – that with the *polis* itself. Therefore, they will share with her the consequences of her choice: a seed of civil war, the misfortune of Oedipus' offspring, will continue to exist in the community.

The fact that the members of the Chorus are male citizens marks a significant difference when compared to other Sophoclean tragedies, such as *Electra* and *Women of Trachis*, where the Choruses are composed of women, as previously mentioned in this chapter. The most evident aspect is that, when Antigone tries to gain the Chorus' sympathy by evoking her own vulnerability, she knows she is describing an entirely different condition from the ones that any male citizen could experience. Conversely, when the two other Sophoclean female protagonists lament their unfair destiny and their respective losses (while Electra mourns the death of her father and brother, Deianeira laments her husbands' infidelity), they can rely on the fact that they are talking to other women who can share similar experiences and feelings. In *Electra*, the Chorus of female citizens blames Agamemnon's daughter's lament for being excessive and dangerous, but nevertheless they express solidarity with her by immediately saying that her father has been "betrayed" by the "corrupt hand" of Electra's "false mother" (*El.* 124–6; transl. Jebb). They engage with the girl by comparing themselves to "a true-hearted mother" (*El.* 234; transl. Jebb), thus constructing an affective *liaison* with her based on the parameters of age and, above all, gender. With regard to Heracles' wife, the protagonist of *Women of Trachis* explicitly asks the female Chorus to "cry together with her"[46] (*Tr.* 535). The

---

[46] My own translation.

term συγκατοικτιουμένη arguably evokes a lamentation as a collective and all-female performance aimed at loudly expressing grief.

Given the age, the sex, and the social position ("wealthy citizens", 843) of the members of the Chorus, Antigone could never ask them to cry with her. Nonetheless, the way in which they engage in the antiphonal exchange with her reveals an attempt to console her and even a way to express solidarity. They do it from their own social position – as elderly men – by calling her "daughter" (855). The members of the Chorus are elderly and male, and belong to distinguished families in Thebes. Therefore, they do not lament with Antigone. Nevertheless, they *engage with her* in her lamentation and even try to console her.[47] Indeed, by using the pronoun "we" (835), as previously explained, they remind Antigone that she belongs to the community of the "mortal-born" (835). Remarkably, when they use a first-person utterance, they include Antigone in their "choral we", not just as a mortal human being, but, most importantly, as a fellow citizen.

The way in which the Chorus reframes the whole story of Antigone's family either interrupts or intersects and enriches her self-narration by remarking that she belongs to a city which has already suffered a lot because of its internal discords and fights. In both cases, they remind Antigone that her actions and her self-narration are heard and remembered within the city: "Still it is a great thing for a woman who has died to have it said of her that she shared the lot of the godlike in her life, and afterwards, in death" (836–8). Antigone reacts to these words by accusing the Chorus of "mocking" (οἴμοι γελῶμαι, 839) and "insulting" (ὑβρίζεις, 840) her. At this point in the agonistic exchange, the disagreement between Antigone and the Chorus seems to have reached a climax. Nevertheless, every time the Theban citizens interrupt and contradict Antigone, they also give her the chance to add several details of her self-narration.

Antigone makes an open critique of Creon's authoritative discourse visible and understandable. She declares that, although Creon claims the goal of his edict is to preserve the internal cohesion between the Theban citizens by publicly punishing Polyneices for being a traitor, it is instead a way to attack Antigone's family, whose position is already compromised within the political community. By marking a distinction between Eteocles' and Polyneices' corpses, Creon has violated a ritual prescription which establishes that every citizen has the right to be buried with a proper funeral ritual. Although the king claims that his edict is equivalent to a law,

---

47 In her chapter in this volume, Therese Fuhrer has proposed to study the first-person utterances pronounced by the two (ps.-)Senecan Choruses in the respective Latin dramas as a way to understand the gendered connotation of the Chorus' identity. In her conclusions, Fuhrer argues that the specificity of the "choral we" in the dramas on which she focuses in her reading is determined by the social status of the members of the Chorus precisely because they are women. Their fate is subordinated to that of the members of the ruling family: they have to share their suffering and, inasmuch as they are professional mourners, their task is to lament for their city.

and therefore that the Theban citizens must obey it without any exceptions, it in fact *produces* an exception within the city.⁴⁸ As a response, Antigone deconstructs the temporality of Creon's narration of her family's story, framed by the opposition between friends and enemies of Thebes. She does so by installing her own story into a mythological past of her choosing.

When Antigone eventually mentions her dead kin, she represents herself as the last heir of the house of Labdacus, claiming that she belongs with them and that she is ready to dwell alongside them in the realm of the dead.⁴⁹ She responds to the citizens of Thebes with the following words, right after they have mentioned her father (πατρῷον δ' ἐκτίνεις τιν' ἆθλον, 856; 858-71):

> ἔψαυσας ἀλγεινοτάτας ἐμοὶ μερίμ-
> νας, πατρὸς τριπόλιστον οἶκτον
> τοῦ τε πρόπαντος
> ἁμετέρου πότμου
> κλεινοῖς Λαβδακίδαισιν.
> ἰὼ ματρῷαι λέκτρων ἆται κοι-
> μήματά τ' αὐτογέννητ'
> ἐμῷ πατρὶ δυσμόρου ματρός,
> οἵων ἐγώ ποθ' ἁ ταλαίφρων ἔφυν:
> πρὸς οὓς ἀραῖος ἄγαμος ἅδ'
> ἐγὼ μέτοικος ἔρχομαι.
> ἰὼ δυσπότμων
> κασίγνητε γάμων κυρήσας,
> θανὼν ἔτ' οὖσαν κατήναρές με.

You have touched on my most bitter thought and moved my ever-renewed pity for my father and for the entire doom ordained for us, the famed house of Labdacus. Oh, the horrors of our mother's bed! Oh, the slumbers of the wretched mother at the side of her own son, my own father! What manner of parents gave me my miserable being! It is to them that I go like this, accursed and unwed, to share their home. Ah, my brother, the marriage you made was doomed, and by dying you killed me still alive!

---

48 Creon's prohibition is a κήρυγμα (an edict), as Antigone remarks in line 8, which is radically different from the ἄγραπτα νόμιμα (the "unwritten laws" given to human beings by the gods) that she mentions in lines 454f. As Susanetti (2012) 158 argues, from a procedural perspective a κήρυγμα required a public announcement to be made by the herald and it concerned the entire population. Although at 447 Creon himself defines his ban as a κήρυγμα, right afterwards he calls it νόμος (law), at 449. Harris (2006) 41-80 discusses the topic of Antigone's disobedience precisely on the basis of the distinction between κήρυγμα and νόμος. He remarks that, although Creon uses both terms, he does so in different contexts and with different aims within his speech. By using the term νόμος, his goal is to state the coercive power of his ban.
49 Murnaghan (2009) 325f. compares Antigone's acceptance of her inability to survive to Ismene's "instinct for survival", which is also the fear of being the only survivor of her family once her sister is gone: "What is the point of life for me, if I'm deprived of you?" (548).

Antigone refers here to the events that Sophocles narrates in *Oedipus Tyrannus*, as she explicitly evokes the incestuous relationship between her parents, which initiated a μίασμα (contamination) that hit the city hard in the form of permanent internal conflict, the outcome of which was the civil war between Oedipus' sons. When Antigone mentions her natal household – the "house of Labdacus" – she indeed refers to the intergenerational transmission of guilt and punishment, something that moves her "constantly repeated compassion" (τριπόλιστον οἶκτον) for her father (πατρὸς) and for the entire family (τού τε πρόπαντος ἁμετέρου πότμου κλεινοῖς Λαβδακίδαισιν). The word τριπόλιστον literally means "thrice turned-over" and metaphorically refers to the action of the plough, which loosens or turns the soil before seed sowing. Therefore, Antigone expresses the intensity of her lament (οἶκτον) for her father's destiny by using a term (τριπόλιστον) that evokes once again the agricultural metaphor according to which the female body (and desire) is something that becomes "domestic" and productive after marriage.[50] In Antigone's description of sorrow, she indirectly evokes her mother's body. Indeed, she mentions her mother twice (862 and 865), in both cases in relation to the incest (κοιμήματά τ' αὐτογέννητ'),[51] by bringing up Jocasta's bed (λέκτρων).

Just as she did when she was describing herself in the role of Kore/Persephone comparing her own destiny to Niobe's, Antigone evokes a bodily representation of her mother too – lying down with Oedipus. In this way, Jocasta becomes part of her daughter's personal "genealogy" of female characters. The striking thing is that the three women mentioned by Antigone have experienced desire and fertility with their bodies. Even Kore, although forced to live in the land of the dead, was able to experience a wedding, something which Antigone was not, and each time Kore cyclically joins her mother Demeter on the Earth, her body experiences the fertility of life again. As for Niobe, although her body has been turned to stone, it used to be extremely fertile, since she has had a full experience of motherhood. Nevertheless, Antigone is willing to build a link between herself and the two mythological figures in her narration, by bringing their bodies and their transformations into an imaginary scene she herself produces. She also does it when she talks about her mother and the incestuous relationship between her parents, even describing in clear terms all the sorrow that this tragic episode has caused her family. Nonetheless, such a relationship was also produced by Jocasta's fully human, and particularly female, desire, and therefore when Antigone evokes her mother, she portrays Jocasta's body while involved in the conjugal act that initiated their family. Antigone does not refuse any part of her family's story, rather lamenting that none of them expected their misfortune, and all of them have shared or still share that sorrow. It is

---

50 Griffith (1999) 272; Susanetti (2012) 327.
51 The formula αὐτογέννητα κοιμήματα μητρός, which means "a mother's intercourse with her own child", has only been found in this play, so it might be Sophocles' innovative solution to express incest.

also for this reason that she refuses to betray Polyneices and abandon his corpse: not only was he her brother, they also have in common the fact that they are tragic heroes with a tragic destiny.

4 The constant movement of Antigone the metic

As can be seen from the critical commentary presented in this chapter, Antigone narrates a story to her fellow citizens that begins with a mythological entanglement. When she compares herself to two female mythological characters in her lamentation, she dwells, in particular, on a physical description of female bodies that experience things which she has been deprived of. By comparing these experiences to the events she is undergoing, she involves her own body in the narration and the performance of mourning. In so doing, Antigone reinterprets her act of disobedience in the opposite way: while she has attempted to bury her brother in secret, now that she has avowed it, she decides to make her own death a spectacular performance of lamentation. In order to realise such a performance, she retraces and narrates its larger dramatic context, namely the disturbing events that happened to her family in connection with Oedipus' "contamination". Her aim is to assert that Creon's edict is the outcome of his political choice to make her family appear to be dangerous outsiders in relation to the *polis*. When she takes responsibility for her act of disobedience, Antigone herself remarks that it is exceptional and therefore dangerous for the stability of the city, but she laments that she had no other choice, since the king has produced a political exception by forbidding Polyneices' funeral rituals.

The Chorus members criticize Antigone's argument at 834–8, remarking upon a radical opposition between her and the goddesses who are not fated to die. As I have argued, this critique can be read as a way in which the citizens of Thebes express support for Antigone and remind her that, no matter how radical the opposition is between her and the king after the violation of the edict, she is still part of a community and her words and acts will be received. She declares that she looks for "witnesses" (ξυμμάρτυρας, 846) of her death, especially because she cannot be "mourned by her loved ones" (οἵα φίλων ἄκλαυτος, 846), who are all dead. She is going to die unwept and without any funeral rituals, just like Polyneices, and she wants to make clear that in both cases Creon's arbitrary decision is to blame. In this case, she herself calls it a "law" (νόμοις, 847), but she seems to be mocking the king by intentionally twisting his linguistic strategies: a law's coercive power is supposed to target the entire population, not just specific families or individuals. Mark Griffith writes that in this passage Antigone, disappointed with her male fellow citizens (the Chorus), invokes the "spring of Dirce" and the "holy ground of Thebes" (844f.) as her witnesses. Nevertheless, she is in fact addressing the whole community and delivering a political message.

Among the people who are listening is also Ismene, Antigone's surviving sister, who has just declared that she is willing to die with her sister: "I performed the deed – as long as she concurs – and I share and carry the burden of guilt" (536f.).[52] Antigone has denied any involvement on Ismene's part (538f.), and Creon has spared the latter's life. Ismene is, therefore, still alive, and she might recognize herself as part of the all-female group whose stories Antigone has retraced and narrated by connecting Jocasta's and her own life to two mythological figures of desiring women.

Antigone compares her journey towards death once again to a wedding ceremony at 891–4, by mentioning Kore/Persephone: "Tomb, bridal-chamber, deep-dug eternal prison where I go to find my own, whom in the greatest numbers destruction has seized and Persephone has welcomed among the dead!". She again uses words that describe her body in movement: πορεύομαι ("go"/ "walk" / "march", 892), in the quoted sentence; but also κάτειμι ("descend", 896) and ἐλθοῦσα (participle in the aorist tense from ἔρχομαι: "come" / "go", 897), both in a highlighted position as the first words of each line. This time she says that this journey will take her to her dead parents and brother, stressing that she has chosen to go and live with them. She declares that her suffering is mitigated by the idea that she will be welcomed by her family in the Underworld because of the funeral rites she performed for them (897–903). The final destination of her journey, the place where she will eventually arrive, is a place for Antigone to live, but not a proper home: "I have no home among men or with the shades, no home with the living or with the dead" (851f.). She uses a term, μέτοικος (in an emphatic position as the first word at 852), that she will repeat at 868.[53]

The term is significant in the Athenian legal vocabulary, as it designated the juridically recognized condition of a foreigner who was allowed to reside and work in Athens for a specific period.[54] This legal status was established in Athens over a period of time ranging from the 470s or maybe later to 450 BCE – when Pericles promulgated his citizenship law, which identified as legitimate citizens those whose parents were both γνήσιοι (born citizens). It aimed to institutionally identify a category of people as immigrants who were probably registered (although we do not know if there was a specific register) and had to pay a tax (μετοίκιον). Metic men were often merchants who traded within the territory of the *polis* or people who escaped from political persecution. Metic women could either settle in the city with their family or on their own, if they happened to be a widow, a freed slave, or simply unmarried but

---

[52] Ismene insists with these words: "But now with this sea of troubles around you, I am not ashamed to sail in a sea of suffering at your side" (540f.). I have commented extensively on the sororal relationship between Antigone and Ismene, and particularly on the nautical imagery at 540f. in Moro (2021).

[53] The term also appears at 890, when Creon remarks that Antigone is forbidden to reside among the living anymore, and therefore forces her to descend into her tomb.

[54] The term appears in Hdt. 4.151; Thuc. 2.13; Aesch. *Th.* 548 and *Supp.* 994 as defining a juridically recognized mode of hospitality within a *polis*. See Kasimis (2018) and Lape (2010).

without a male relative. Their independent status was recognized by law.[55] All metics had an Athenian sponsor who spoke for them in legal contexts. As a juridical status, μετοικία granted legal protection, but identified a group of people by a negation, since they had the right to live and work in the *polis* but were excluded from landownership and citizenship rights, e.g. participating in the political assemblies and serving as jurors.

In his later play *Oedipus at Colonus*, Sophocles portrays Antigone and her father, both still alive, as stateless migrants after being exiled from Thebes, forced to ask for shelter and hospitality in Colonus. Therefore, the choice of the term μέτοικος is particularly significant in *Antigone*, as the protagonist is located in her city and no mention is made by Sophocles of her previously migrating with her father outside Thebes. Antigone describes herself in motion while travelling from Thebes to the land of the dead, in the condition of not being resident in either places, since in both cases she does not properly belong. Indeed, she laments that she cannot be a μέτοικος ("among the mortals", 851) anymore, but she cannot properly be "among the dead" (851) either, insofar as she is still alive. Rather, she says that she *is going* "to reside as a guest" among her dead relatives: at 858, Sophocles links the condition of μετοικία to a verb expressing movement, by pairing the terms μέτοικος and ἔρχομαι. The status of μετοικία is less a condition that Antigone embodies than the way in which she describes herself – and a role she plays: μετοικία is a symbolical interpretation of her condition after being excluded from her community and condemned to death.[56] It is a narration and a performance in which she includes herself in her own all-female "genealogy" by both comparing and distinguishing the bodily experiences and desires of the woman she is in relation to those of the characters she describes. In this way, Antigone *becomes* a μέτοικος, describing this condition in her self-narration and shaping it through gendered elements.

This is particularly relevant for the scope of this essay: Antigone adopts a gender-based framework when she interprets her living conditions as a constant and ongoing movement in search for a place where she fully belongs. The gender parameter emerges in this self-narration when she compares her movement towards becoming a μέτοικος, which is in fact her last journey, to a bridal procession: firstly, she identifies her tomb with a nuptial chamber (ὦ τύμβος, ὦ νυμφεῖον, 891); afterwards, she stresses that she is embarking on this journey without being married (ἄγαμος, 867). The movement that Antigone describes is not temporary, as a migration would be; rather it characterizes her entire life insofar as she is Oedipus' offspring and therefore the political community can never assimilate her as they would any other citizen. Despite what the Chorus says, she has never been and will never become one of *them*.

---

[55] On metic women and the political relevance of legislating upon mixed marriage between citizens and metics, see Futo Kennedy (2014).
[56] Griffith (1999) 272 remarks on Antigone's "in-between status", but he does not interpret it as a movement.

Antigone interprets her own life as being constantly in transition from one condition to another: first she was a daughter and a sister, but, after losing her parents and brothers, she has never become a wife and a mother; and she is not even a citizen anymore, since she refused to accept Creon's legal restrictions which required her to sever her bonds with her family so as to remain loyal to the city. She knows she cannot live in the city anymore, and this is the only thing on which Creon agrees with her, even using the same vocabulary, when he says: "She will find herself deprived of her right to live (μετοικίας) here above"[57] (890). Nevertheless, the reading presented in this chapter suggests that Antigone's membership in the city has never been equal to anyone else's. The condition of μετοικία seems to describe her entire life fairly well. She says that her tomb will be "the house in which she is going to stay (buried) forever" (κατασκαφὴς οἴκησις ἀείφρουρος, 891f.):[58] paradoxically, this is the only time that she can imagine living somewhere "forever" (ἀείφρουρος).

Henao Castro has compared Antigone's status to that of contemporary refugees, undocumented immigrants, and non-citizens, remarking that her claim to be a foreign resident is performative in denouncing the ontological condition of the impossibility of being recognized as a member of a political community. According to this reading, Sophocles' protagonist is staging an act of "counter-politics" against the "secured juridical-political position of the citizen".[59] In Antigone's lamentation the condition of μετοικία indeed concerns, one's right to inhabit a place and to identify oneself as a member of a particular community. However, Antigone is not a ξένη (stranger), as she describes Niobe at 824, and she does not seek to gain recognition, if recognition is accorded on the king's conditions. Her reason for feeling displaced is that she has been forbidden to honor the memory of her dead parents and brother and is compelled to leave the latter's disgraced corpse unburied. She uses the term μέτοικος metaphorically, on the one hand to denounce the excessive violence of the king's decision to bury her alive, which is the expression of his ὕβρις, and on the other hand to claim that she is not a member of the Theban community either, as she refuses the king's authority and the city's legislation.[60] For her, the μετοικία symbolizes the temporary nature of her life in the city, but also – and most importantly – the fact that she has chosen to interrupt her bond with the city when the king has required her to betray her bond to her family. She has refused to submit to the king's restrictions, as a way to fight not only for Polyneices' memory but also for her own identity, which is not just that of a Theban citizen but that of a member of the house of Labdacus, too. Her lamentation is, therefore, a self-narration.

---

57 My translation.
58 My translation.
59 Henao Castro (2013) 311.
60 In his translation, at 852 Susanetti (2012) significantly glosses the term μέτοικος as "someone (Antigone) who has *no home, no city* in which to live" (my italics).

5 Conclusions

The regulations that made coexistence possible for the citizens of a *polis* and organized everyone's public life were produced by each individual city's laws. It was not possible for a citizen to be "disconnected" from the *polis*, because in that case he or she would become an outlaw and lose their citizenship rights; nor could a metic live within the *polis* without fully submitting to its legislation. The legislation normalized the foreigners' "exteriority" by granting them the permission to live in its territory under specific conditions, something that was denied to criminals and traitors. In the case of Sophocles' Thebes, the king has promulgated his edict demanding that the Thebans respect it as a law. He blames Antigone's disobedience as a dangerous attack not just on him, but on the city itself, and for this reason he sentences her to death. However, Antigone adopts a strategical way to address her fellow citizens, in order to explain the reasons for her disobedience, and to be heard by them. She retraces the tragic destiny of her family, stressing the responsibilities of each member but also the impossibility for them to escape their ineluctable fate. She includes these events within a broad narration, rooted in the myth, in which she describes an all-female constellation. Her aim is to hold Creon accountable, claiming that he left her with no alternative but to violate his edict and to lose her right to live in the city.

Many critical readings have highlighted Antigone's tragic isolation at the end of the play. Mark Griffith has remarked on Sophocles' repeated use of the first-person pronoun in the lamentation (893, 895, 900, 904, 913, and 928).[61] With similar arguments, Simon Goldhill and Davide Susanetti have retraced elements in this section that, according to their readings, clearly express Antigone's solitude and constant isolation within the political community.[62] The isolation of a radical claimer contesting the king's authority also emerges in Judith Butler's reading. Butler argues that, when Sophocles' protagonist acts out performing the funeral rituals (twice) and verbally repeats her transgression, "she becomes manly" and does not maintain her "position within gender".[63]

Although isolation is an inescapable element that Antigone herself remarks on in her self-portrait, she is not an entirely solitary figure at this point. It is necessary to take into account her vocal interactions, and particularly her attempt to communicate with the citizens of Thebes, to whom she addresses her self-narration. Firstly, she compares herself to Kore/Persephone, daughter of Demeter, the goddess of earth fertility and agriculture, imagining her own ideal marriage with Hades. Secondly, she refers to the myth of Niobe, punished by the gods after boasting about how many sons and

---

61 Griffith (1999) 276.
62 See in particular Goldhill (2012) 111f. and Susanetti (2012) 325.
63 Butler (2000) 10.

daughters she had given birth to. Moreover, she notes that she is Jocasta's and Oedipus' offspring in the first place, which makes her Polyneices' sister as well as Eteocles'. For her, these ties seem to be more important than the one with Haemon, which would make her a wife and a mother, as she declares in the disputed lines 905–7: "Never, if I had been a mother of children, or if a husband had been rotting after death, would I have taken that burden upon myself in violation of the citizens' will."[64]

While singing and talking to Antigone, the Chorus proves an active and agonistic engagement with her self-narration. They force her to clarify some aspects of her speech and give her the assistance to add details when, at the highest point of the *climax* of her lamentation, she mentions her father (858), the entire lineage of Labdacus' descendants (861), her mother's bed (862), and her brother's unhappy marriage (870). It is no coincidence that Antigone eventually presents herself as a μέτοικος in front of her fellow citizens. With these words, she responds to the Chorus' consolation speech that reminds her that she is one of the θνητογενεῖς ("mortal-born", 835), namely one of them. She complains that her own identity within the political community has been jeopardized, since Creon has made it impossible for anyone to recognize her as a legitimate member. Therefore, she does not seek recognition; rather, she refuses the terms by which recognition is accorded.

It is precisely for this reason that I have interpreted Antigone's lamentation as a gendered performance of vulnerability. Indeed, a close reading of lines 806–928 shows that Oedipus' daughter delivers her self-narration as a spectacular performance, with the aim of sending a message to the citizens of Thebes. In hindsight, in this passage Antigone does not spend any time expressing hatred or rage against Creon, although the king's accountability emerges clearly in her speech. She is communicating a message to her fellow citizens, and the agonistic exchange with the Chorus makes it evident that they are listening and interacting with her. I call it a performance, comparing the situation in which Antigone pronounces her lamentation to the model of the theatre and remarking on the publicness of the context in which she speaks. Antigone's register and expressiveness in the lines I have commented on are highly dramatic. She is aware that this is her last chance to speak to a "public" and she organises it as a fully theatrical interaction.

Its "spectacular" connotation is due to the fact that she chooses to communicate not only with words but also with images, by means of visual descriptions. Indeed,

---

[64] Commentators have been disputing the authenticity of the entire section 904–21 (which for this reason is very well-known) since the beginning of the nineteenth century. Griffith (1999) 277–9 explains that in this passage Sophocles has probably borrowed the argument of one episode from Herodotus (a dialogue between Dareius and Intaphernes' wife), which the poet has transposed into Antigone's speech: see Hdt. 3.119. Honig (2013) 132–40 reflects upon the possibility that, since the audience of the time probably had Herodotus' text in mind, perhaps Sophocles wanted to make Antigone's critique of Creon's despotism sound more effective by citing an episode in which another woman made a similar choice asking the sovereign to spare her brother's life.

she narrates the stories of three female characters – Kore/Persephone, Niobe, and her mother Jocasta – and describes their bodies, desires, losses, sorrows, and laments. She also involves her own body – in its physical appearance, with both its strengths and weaknesses – in this narration and compares her own lamentation with that of the goddesses she describes. The way in which she depicts herself evokes an active image of movement, rhythmically articulated by her mourning chant as a solemn procession. She does not pretend to be invincible when she leaves the scene; on the contrary, she displays her vulnerability, but she claims the right to choose how to be remembered. Eventually, she will take control over her own death by hanging herself in her tomb.

Several critical readings have insisted on Antigone's infertility, interpreting the Chorus' words as a way of reminding her that she has no chance either for rebirth (as Kore did) or for procreation (as Niobe did).[65] However, Antigone's body *is* indeed able to bear children and her lamentation proves that she does desire love and even motherhood. As Adriana Cavarero remarks, Demeter, the figure of the Great Mother, is a symbolical prefiguration of the crucial role played by natality for the individual and communal life of human beings.[66] The "maternal power", inscribed in Nature as a whole,[67] denotes a capacity – and a will – both to generate and to *refuse* to generate. According to the Italian feminist philosopher, Demeter's myth has been mistakenly read on the basis of its agricultural symbolism. This interpretation apparently reconciles a conflict between the two poles of life/generation and death/destruction but in fact obscures a process of gendering that has inscribed the "maternal power" within a patriarchal symbolical order.

Although Antigone chooses death (as a form of self-sacrifice) instead of generation (motherhood), she still aims to *generate* something new within the polis, that is, the possibility of new alliances and modes of cooperation that go beyond her own life. She does this by re-narrating her own story and that of her family and inscribing it within a genealogy that she creates by describing female bodies and desires – including those of her own mother, the outcome of which was incestuous intercourse. Her performance of vulnerability is therefore rooted in the narrative connection with this all-female mythology and characterized by gender attributions. The female and corporeal genealogy allows her to define her own identity *dialectically* by both comparing herself to the other female figures and marking her own *difference* as a woman who has chosen not to become a wife and a mother. This radical difference also emerges when she *autonomously* decides to violate the king's edict, to sing her own dirge, and, eventually, to die in the way she chooses.

---

65 For instance, Susanetti (2012) 317 writes that Antigone is the "anti-Demeter" characterized by "infertility" and "complete death".
66 Cavarero (1990) 60f.
67 Cavarero (1990) 61.

Bibliography

Texts and translations

Sophocles, *Antigone*, transl. by Richard C. Jebb, Cambridge 1966.
Sophocles, *Antigone*, ed. by Mark Griffith, Cambridge 1999.
Sofocle, *Antigone*, a cura di Davide Susanetti, Roma 2012.
Sophocles, *The Plays and Fragments, with critical notes, commentary, and translation in English prose. Part VI: The Electra*, transl. by Richard C. Jebb, Cambridge 1900.
Sophocles, *Electra*, ed. by Patrick Finglass, Cambridge 2007.
Sophocles, *Plays. Trachiniae*, transl. by Richard C. Jebb, London 2004.

Books and articles

Birmingham (2018): Peg Birmingham, "Superfluity and Precarity in Advance. Reading Arendt against Butler", *Philosophy Today* 62, 319–335.
Butler (2000): Judith Butler, *Antigone's Claim. Kinship between life and death*, New York.
Butler (2004): Judith Butler, *Precarious Life: The Power of Mourning and Violence*, London/New York.
Butler (2009): Judith Butler, *Frames of War. When is Life Grievable?*, London/New York.
Cantarella (2005): Eva Cantarella, "Gender, Sexuality, and Law", in: Michael Gagarin and David J. Cohen (eds.), *The Cambridge Companion to Ancient Greek Law*, Cambridge, 236–253.
Casadei (2018), "La vulnerabilità in prospettiva critica", in: Orsetta Giolo and Baldassare Pastore (eds.), *Vulnerabilità. Analisi multidisciplinare di un concetto*, Roma, 73–99.
Cavarero (1990): Adriana Cavarero, *Nonostante Platone. Figure femminili nella filosofia antica*, Roma.
Cavarero (2016): Adriana Cavarero, *Inclinations. A Critique of Rectitude*, Stanford.
Cavarero (forthcoming): Adriana Cavarero, "Niobe's hypermaternity", in: Andrew Benjamin and Mario Telo (eds.), *Niobes: Antiquity/Modernity/Critical Theory*, Columbus.
Ferrarese (2017): Estelle Ferrarese, *The Politics of Vulnerability*, New York.
Fineman and Grear (2013): Martha Albertson Fineman and Anna Grear (eds.), *Reflections on a New Ethical Foundation for Law and Politics*, Farnham.
Foley (2001): Helene P. Foley, *Female Acts in Greek Tragedy*, Princeton.
Futo Kennedy (2014): Rebecca Futo Kennedy, *Immigrant Women in Athens. Gender, Ethnicity, and Citizenship in the Classical City*, New York.
Gilson (2014): Erinn Gilson, *The Ethics of Vulnerability: A Feminist Analysis of Social Life and Practice*, New York.
Giolo (2018): Orsetta Giolo, "La vulnerabilità neoliberale. Agency, vittime e tipo di giustizia", in: Orsetta Giolo and Baldassare Pastore (eds.), *Vulnerabilità. Analisi multidisciplinare di un concetto*, Roma, 253–273.
Goldhill (2012): Simon Goldhill, *Sophocles and the Language of Tragedy*, New York.
Guaraldo (2012): Olivia Guaraldo, *Comunità e vulnerabilità. Per una critica politica della violenza*, Pisa.
Guaraldo (2018): Olivia Guaraldo, "La vulnerabilità come paradigma fondativo", in: Orsetta Giolo and Baldassare Pastore (eds.), *Vulnerabilità. Analisi multidisciplinare di un concetto*, Roma, 57–71.
Harris (2006): Edward M. Harris, *Democracy and the Rule of Law in Classical Athens. Essays on Law, Society, and Politics*, New York.

Henao Castro (2013): Andrés Fabiàn Henao Castro, "Antigone Claimed: 'I Am a Stranger!'. Political Theory and the Figure of the Stranger", *Hypatia: A Journal of Feminist Philosophy* 28, 307–322.
Honig (2013): Bonnie Honig, *Antigone, Interrupted*, Cambridge/New York.
Kasimis (2018): Demetra Kasimis, *The Perpetual Immigrant and the Limits of Athenian Democracy*, Cambridge/New York.
King (2002): Helen King, "Bound to Bleed: Artemis and Greek Women", in: Laura K. McClure (ed.), *Sexuality and Gender in the Classical World. Readings and Sources*, Oxford, 77–102.
Lape (2010): Susan Lape, *Race and Citizen Identity in the Classical Athenian Democracy*, Cambridge/New York.
Lewis (2015): Virginia M. Lewis, "Gendered Speech in Sophocles' *Electra*", *Phoenix* 69, 217–241.
Lévinas (1996): Emmanuel Lévinas, "Peace and Proximity", in: Robert Bernasconi, Simon Critchley and Adriaan T. Peperzak (eds.), *Emmanuel Lévinas: Basic Philosophical Writings*, Bloomington, IN, 161–169.
Lyons (2012): Deborah Lyons, *Dangerous Gifts. Gender and Exchange in Ancient Greece*, Austin.
Loraux (1990): Nicole Loraux, *Les Mères en deuil*, Paris.
Maragno (2018): Giorgia Maragno, "Alle origini (terminologiche) della vulnerabilità: *vulnerabilis, vulnus, vulnerare*", in: Orsetta Giolo and Baldassare Pastore (eds.), *Vulnerabilità. Analisi multidisciplinare di un concetto*, Roma, 13–35.
McClure (1999): Laura K. McClure, *Spoken like a Woman: Speech and Gender in Athenian Drama*, Princeton.
Mills (2018): Sophie Mills, "Images and Effects of Incest in *Antigone*", in: David Stuttard (ed.), *Looking at Antigone*, London, 47–61.
Moro (2021): Valentina Moro, "Sailing together. The agonistic construction of sisterhood in the language of Sophocles' Antigone", *Ramus* 50, 109–126.
Murnaghan (2009): Sheila Murnaghan, "Tragic Bystanders: Choruses and Other Survivors in The Plays of Sophocles", in: J. R. C. Cousland and James R. Hume (eds.), *The Play of Texts and Fragments. Essays in Honour of Martin Cropp*, Leiden/Boston, 321–333.
Nooter (2011), Sarah Nooter, "Language, Lamentation, and Power in Sophocles' Electra", *CW* 104, 399–417.
Ormand (1999): Kirk Ormand, *Exchange and the Maiden. Marriage in Sophoclean Tragedy*, Austin.
Pateman (1988): Carole Pateman, *The Sexual Contract*, Stanford.
Pulcini (2009a): Elena Pulcini, *La cura del mondo: paura e responsabilità nell'età globale*, Torino.
Pulcini (2009b): Elena Pulcini, "Paura, legame sociale, ordine politico in Thomas Hobbes", in: Giulio Maria Chiodi and Roberto Gatti (eds.), *La filosofia politica di Hobbes*, Milano, 65–79.
Rehm (1994): Rush Rehm, *Marriage to Death: the Conflation of Wedding and Funeral Rituals in Greek Tragedy*, Princeton.
Sebillotte Cuchet (2017): Violaine Sebillotte Cuchet, *Familles et société à Athènes à l'époque classique: un éclairage par les études de genre*, 2017: https://hal.archives-ouvertes.fr/hal-01618996 (03/05/2022).
Sissa (1987): Giulia Sissa, *Le corps virginal, La virginité féminine en Grèce Ancienne*, Paris.
Sourvinou-Inwood (1987): Christiane Sourvinou-Inwood, "A Series of Erotic Pursuits: Images and Meanings", *JHS* 107, 131–154.
Sutton (1997/8): Robert F. Sutton, "Nuptial Eros: The Visual Discourse of Marriage in Classical Athens", *The Journal of the Walters Art Gallery* 55/56, 27–48.
Todd (1993): Stephen C. Todd, *The Shape of Athenian Law*, Oxford.
Weiss (2017): Naomi Weiss, "Noise, Music, Speech: The Representation of Lament in Greek Tragedy", *AJPh* 138, 243–266.

Therese Fuhrer

A Female View of the Tragic Action: On the Function of Collective First-Person Statements in the Women's Choruses in the (ps.-)Senecan Tragedies *Troades* and *Hercules Oetaeus*

Abstract: By analysing the women's choruses in the (ps.-)Senecan tragedies *Troades* and *Hercules Oetaeus* I will try to show how Seneca and the anonymous author deploy and use the 'gender' aspect to give female voices greater scope – not only through the protagonists but also through the pronouncements of a group of women. This article will focus on the first-person statements of three women's choruses in the two tragedies. It also examines the extent to which, by subjectivising the voice of a female choral collective speaking in the first person, an additional external perspective relating to the social status of the protagonists can or should be made visible. It also looks at whether these utterances can or should be considered as specifically female or as a female staged confirmation, or provocation, of values with male connotations (power, war, status, wealth).

Keywords: choral I, identity of the tragic chorus, female discourse, social status, *Fallhöhe*

1 Introduction: the moulding of a 'choral I'

It is notoriously difficult to assign a clear-cut identity to the 'I' of classical choral lyric. As a rule this consists of a group of singing and dancing men, who, depending on the nature of the event – sacred, ritual, theatre performance – may be joined by or stand facing a chorus of young women.[1] The choruses in the tragedies and in classical comedy are composed of men, women or animals representing a collective that is relevant to the action of the drama. In archaic Greek choral lyric, the first-person statements of the singing choir are made, sometimes explicitly, in the name of the

---

[1] On the spectrum of possible functions of the choral person (festive, cultic, ritual, encomiastic, dramatic) and identities (public, the poet's, the chorus' own persona, just one more speaking persona) cf. Ford (2020) and the contribution of Emily Hauser in this present volume; on ancient discussions of the choral persona's identity cf. Schironi (2020).

poet.² Attempts have been made to detect the voice of the author in the choral passages of the drama, i.e. in the choral odes or in songs sung by the choir alternately with an actor or in the utterances recited in verse that can be attributed to the chorus or to the chorus leader.³

The identity of the chorus is relevant in the following because I propose to study the function of the first-person utterances in the choral passages of the (ps.-) Senecan tragedies *Troades* and *Hercules Oetaeus* in their immediate context. In both tragedies the choruses represent part of the female population of a particular town: Troy in *Troades* and Oechalia or Calydon in *Hercules Oetaeus*. They stand as a group⁴ of women by the side of one or more heroines who appear in the play and who come from the same place: Hecuba, Andromacha and – in a silent role – Polyxena in the *Troades*, Iole or Deianira in *Hercules Oetaeus*. This means that in both dramas the chorus has the theoretical possibility of stating its viewpoint either on the fate of its female compatriots or on its own situation.⁵

According to the tradition of Attic tragedy,⁶ such comments by the chorus take the form of a general reflection which slows down the action of the tragedy and gives the audience the possibility of a time-out or pause. Or they refer specifically to a particular utterance or action which immediately precedes or is announced just before the choral passage and is imminent, usually in the act following the choral song. In this second category too a distinction must be made as to whether the chorus makes utterances concerning itself or others: about its own mental and physical state, about the role it is playing or is about to play in the action, about the situation of the figures beside whom it appears and the consequences for the chorus itself as individuals or as a collective. Although the Senecan choral songs frequently and to a large extent take the form of general reflections, they are never entirely divorced from the dramatic action and in some cases are even deeply embedded in the action.⁷

---

2 Cf., again, Hauser in this volume.
3 See Fantham (1982) 85 and 263 and Fantham (2000) 263 on the second choral song of Seneca's *Troades*; cf. p. 186 below (with n. 29). See also Kirichenko (2013) 251 with n. 12; Gärtner (2003) 12.
4 The question of whether the chorus in the (ps.-)Senecan tragedies consists not of a group of singers or actors but appears as a "chorus of one" and that we have to assume a "radically different model of chorality", as Slaney (2013) puts it, is not relevant at this point. I am mainly interested here in passages where the chorus defines itself as a group and so wishes to be perceived as a (female) collective.
5 This function is also assigned to the chorus in the third choral song and in the fourth act of Seneca's *Agamemnon*, where together with Cassandra the chorus are captives and prizes of Agamemnon returning to Mycene and/or Argos. On the (traditional) tragic chorus of female prisoners supporting their mistress see Walde (1992) 26–33; Marcucci (1997) 111–16; Degiovanni (2017) 88f.
6 On the typology and function of choral songs in Attic tragedy cf. Hose (1990) 32–397; Gärtner (2003) 1f., 28 and *passim*; Slaney (2013) 100–102; Tarrant (2017) 93f. See also Valentina Moros's chapter on Antigone's exchange with the Chorus of Theban citizens in Sophocles' *Antigone* in this volume, esp. p. 154.
7 Bishop (1972) 331f. talks of the "odic line" of Senecan choral songs that have "the philosophy of the tragedy" as their subject. However, they could also reflect the "dramatic line" of the acts; cf. Kirichenko (2013) 251. Cf. also Mazzoli (2014) 567–74 on the "syntagmatic cohesion" and "mimetic

In the following I would like to analyse to what extent the moulding of a specifically female persona is relevant for the question of the function of the choral songs in the two tragedies.[8] I will attempt to underpin the theory that Seneca in the *Troades* and the anonymous poet in *Hercules Oetaeus* place female choruses next to the female protagonists to unmask their thinking and action as controlled by male values. In the following exploration, the general and reflective choral passages are also significant because they are to be understood as the performance of a group designated as female.

2 The Trojan women in Seneca's *Troades*

The title of the Senecan tragedy, modelled on the eponymous drama by Euripides, points to the central role of the female population in the city of Troy.[9] The appearance of Hecuba as the speaker of the prologue underlines that Troy is defeated, the city is destroyed and the Trojan women now face the fate that is typical for women in this situation: they are prisoners, they become the prizes of the victors and as such they are distributed among the men. All the characters in the title are Trojan women, the above-mentioned heroines Hecuba, Andromacha and Polyxena, the queen, her daughter-in-law and daughter as well as the women who appear as a group in the chorus.[10]

From its first appearance, the chorus is visually as well as acoustically identifiable in the first choral song. This means it is also identifiable for readers as a group

---

function" versus "detachment from the logical and chronological cogency of the *fabula*"; cf. Kugelmeier (2007) 151. Tarrant (2017) 93f. argues that the difference between the chorus in Attic and in Senecan tragedy consists in the level of information they possess: "I am suggesting that the ignorance of the chorus in Seneca is an essential aspect of its role and is itself a powerful component of the play's overall impact." The position taken by Slaney (2013) that the Senecan choral songs are "notoriously detached from the plays' dramatic action" is indebted to the argument of her thesis (cf. n. 4 above) that "as groups, Seneca's choruses have no positive identity, and minimal presence within the acts" (quotations p. 99). – For the variety of subjects covered in the choral songs of the Senecan tragedies see the compilations by Davis (1993) and Gärtner (2003).
8 I understand the term persona in drama analysis in its literal sense as a role, a *dramatis persona*, which in classical drama was also defined and depicted by a real mask. See also Fitch/McElduff (2008), who do not include the chorus. – On women's speech in Attic tragedy in general cf. Moro in this volume; Mossman (2001); and particularly with reference to "discours des personnages féminins" in Seneca's tragedies cf. Vandersmissen (2019), on the chorus cf. ibid. 81–3. On "feminine discourse" in Roman comedy see Dutsch (2008) 2f., considering the fact that the feminine characters were impersonated by male actors.
9 On the form see Georges s.v. "1. Tros . . . E) Troas, -ados": "trojanisch", "a) die Trojanerin", "b) die Landschaft Troas". On the title cf. Keulen (2001) 14–39 against Stroh (2008) 200 with n. 14 and Stroh (2014) 435.
10 The title therefore also includes the female protagonists, not only the chorus; cf. Keulen (2001) 14.

of mourning women.[11] They are part of the "crowd" (67, 81: *vulgus*, 87, 96, 409: *turba*), indicating that they have a lower social status than the above-mentioned protagonists. However, we learn nothing about their age, their social roles, about whether individual chorus members are wives or mothers. Nor do we find out whether they – like Hecuba, Andromacha and Polyxena – as survivors of the destruction of the city have lost or will lose their children, their grandchildren, their husbands or their virginity.

2.1 The first choral ode: the Trojan women as professional mourners – emotions on command

The chorus accompanies the performance of the mourning Hecuba and so it is present on the stage from the beginning of the play.[12] The members of the chorus hear the aged queen lamenting the sight of the once-proud city that is now in ruins and is being plundered by the victorious Greeks (1–27). As the mother of Paris, Hecuba feels responsible for the downfall of the royal family (28–40); she has had to witness the murder of king Priam (41–56); now the victors are drawing lots for her daughters-in-law, her daughters and herself as prizes (57–62). As Hecuba's words at the end of her prologue speech make clear, her companions do not remain silent but express their sorrow by the usual gestures of mourning and lamentation. When they cease,[13] she urges them for the first time to continue and thus to pay Troy its due homage (63–6). Hecuba addresses the chorus as "my crowd of captives" (63: *turba captivae mea*, cf. 96);[14] thus she confirms her solidarity with this group of women, already expressed in their joint performance as mourners.

The first choral song is a *kommos* in the form of an *amoibaion*, an antiphony between the chorus and Hecuba, in which the impression of solidarity is further

---

11 On the identity of the chorus as Trojans, cf. Kohn (2013) 112: this is said to be "unusually clear, just as remarkable as its level of participation in the play itself". A similar point is made by Davis (1993) 39f. and 46; Keulen (2001) 126. On the female identity of the ritual mourners cf. Foley (2001) 19–56, esp. 26–8.
12 This is also the view of Fantham (1982) 219f.; Keulen (2001) 65, 71 and 120, disagreeing with Boyle (1994) 142, who argues that the chorus comes onstage during Hecuba's prologue (v. 56) and with Heldmann (1974) 80 n. 220 who assumes that the chorus does not come onstage until the end of Hecuba's speech. Marshall (2000) 27 says that both of these variants are possible. On the question of whether the chorus is present during the entire play cf. Davis (1993) 20f. and 25–7.
13 In v. 63 Hecuba asks: *lamenta cessant?* ("is the wailing dying down?"). On the question of why the chorus has stopped wailing see the remarks by Shelton (2016) 189: "Perhaps Hecuba's mention of the lottery left them stunned and silent as they contemplated the loss of their old identity and the new miseries awaiting them."
14 The translations of the *Troades* here and in the following are by Dressler (2017).

reinforced.[15] The nature of the relationship between the queen and her companions is again underlined: the women address Hecuba directly, replying that her instruction to mourn (68: *lugere iubes*, "whom you ask to weep") does not fall on 'deaf ears'. They describe themselves as "not a crowd without experience, nor new with tears" (67: *non rude vulgus lacrimisque novum*; cf. 82).[16] After ten years of uninterrupted mourning, there is now "some new reason" for weeping after the fall of Troy (78). So they call on themselves to perform the ritual lamentation: "go to grieving" (79: *ite ad planctus*) for which the queen raises her hand as a sign, at which they will join her: "we will follow our mistress" (81: *dominam . . . sequemur*). With the repeated self-identification of the group as a "common crowd" (81: *vulgus . . . vile*) the women define their social status. They thus indicate a certain distance from Hecuba, whom they address as "queen" (80: *regina*) and refer to as "mistress" (81: *dominam*).

Hecuba assumes the role of the choral leader[17] and instructs her "faithful companions to my downfall" (83: *fidae casus nostri comites*) to loosen their hair and sprinkle it with Troy's ashes, to raise their arms, to pull their dresses up to their stomachs, to bare their breasts and to beat themselves again and again "with furious hands" (84–96). They are urged to excel themselves in their gestures of lamentation as together with Hecuba they "cry for Hector" (98: *Hectora flemus*). The women obey immediately and perform the mourning-ritual, the *planctus* ("lament", 93; cf. 108, 130, 132) as instructed by the queen, describing it in their own words as they do it. They bare their upper bodies, uttering loud lamentations and tell their hands to beat their breasts wildly, because: "We are crying for Hector" (116: *Hectora flemus*). As Hecuba says in the hymnic lamentation addressed to Hector, "the pillar of our country" (124: *columen patriae*),[18] her arms and shoulders bleed, she beats her head, tears her breasts, opening the scars that she inflicted on herself when Hector died, so that blood again flows from them (116–23). The mourning for Hector is staged as a bloody ritual[19] in which the women,

---

15 On the form of the *amoibaion* cf. Keulen (2001) 124–9; cf. also ibid. 120: "in no other Senecan tragedy do we find such a smooth transition from the prologue to the first choral ode as here"; similarly ibid. 126.
16 Marshall (2000) 28 translates *rude vulgus* as "no raw mob"; however, *rude* here means 'unexperienced' and is similar to *novum* (67).
17 See Davis (1993) 220f.; Kirichenko (2013) 253; Fabre-Serris (2015) 106f.
18 Hector is "the protector of the exhausted Trojans" (125: *praesidium Phrygibus fessis*), "our wall" (126: *murus*); cf. 126f.: "on your shoulders stood that city" (*umerisque tuis / stetit illa*). See the remarks by Bishop (1972) 330f. On the tradition of "Trauer-Laudationes" cf. Kudlien (1995) 180 and 183.
19 See Kohn (2013) 17: "As part of the mourning in the *Troades* (120ff.), the captive women beat and tear at their breasts, causing blood and scarring"; Shelton (2016): "Lamentation has a physically violent component"; Fabre-Serris (2015) 106: "This is a deliberately indecent state . . . there is no longer any possibility of decency for a captive who is destined for a forced union."

flouting all the rules of modesty (90f.), are called on to explicitly transgress the limits of normality.[20]

After Hecuba's exhortation to the chorus to turn to Priam in their mourning ritual, the women directly address the *rector Phrygiae* and ask him to accept their lament and their tears (133). But then they are immediately instructed by Hecuba to re-direct their tears and instead to praise Priam as happy (145: *'felix Priamus' dicite cunctae*) because death spares him from humiliation by the victors (144–55).[21] The chorus promptly replies: *'felix Priamus' dicimus omnes* (156) and concludes the *kommos* with the required macarism.

The chorus of the captive Trojan woman first has the task of mourning, but not for their own suffering.[22] At the behest of the queen, they start by lamenting Troy's defeat, then join in mourning the death of prince Hector, then the murder of king Priam. They place themselves entirely at the service of the rulers, both in their obedient response to Hecuba's instructions and in the hierarchisation of suffering, the hymnic lament for Hector and finally the paean to the king. In accordance with their social status as a "common crowd" (*vulgus, turba*), they fulfil their designated role in this situation as professional mourners, professional "lamentation artists", "sophisticated sufferers", who have mastered the 'art of lamentation'.[23] By carefully performing the gestures of lamentation according to the script prescribed by Hecuba, even to the extent of self-exposure and self-injury, sometimes repeating Hecuba's instructions word for word, they come across as a well-trained 'mourning team'.[24] They underline their skill as mourners by referring to their ten years of practice (69–77), describing themselves as *non rude vulgus* (67: "not a crowd without experience") and *non indociles* (82: "not unversed in weeping"). They adapt their mood and the volume

---

[20] Hecuba says in v. 98: *solitum flendi vincite morem* ("surpass your usual norms in weeping") and the chorus in v. 115: *non sum solito contenta sono* ("I am not satisfied with the usual sound"). On this cf. Boyle (1994) 148, who points to the legal restriction on exaggerated mourning gestures in Rome since the sixth century BCE, consolidated by the legislation of Twelve Tables. Cf. also Kudlien (1995) *passim*; Foley (2001) 22f.

[21] On this mourning motif cf. Shelton (2016) 192–4. This is not an exhortation "to the captive women . . . to lament their own fate too" as Kirichenko (2013) 253 argues.

[22] *Contra* Gärtner (2003) 29: "Der Chor . . . ist eben nicht nur ein kontemplativ-reflektierend beteiligter Beobachter aus der Stellung des ungefährdeten Mittelstands . . . Er ist vielmehr durch sein eigenes Geschick genauso von den Kriegsereignissen betroffen wie Hecuba und Andromache und kann sich dementsprechend nicht einer distanzierten Analyse der Handlung hingeben"; ibid. 30: "Der Chor ist . . . gewissermaßen in seinem eigenen Leid absorbiert." See also n. 38 below.

[23] The term "mourning artists" ("Klagekünstlerinnen") was coined by the Swiss classicist and ethnologist Karl Meuli; see Kudlien (1995) 178 on this. The term "sophisticated sufferers" is used by Marshall (2000) 28: "trained and regimented in their laments". – On the "lamentations as a gendered self-narration in Sophocles" cf. Moro in this volume.

[24] Fantham (1982) 226f. also refers to "elements . . . that are not reciprocal" and "a theme independent of her [i.e. Hecuba's] speech" ("calling on the response of shore and mountain" in 56f.). Cf. also Kohn (2013) 115.

of their singing to the requirements of the situation. They express their lamentation loudly. They are not satisfied with conventional lamentation (115: *non sum solito contenta sono*, "I am not satisfied with the usual sound").

By their submission, clearly indicated in the text, to the script that Hecuba demands, in which the women not only support the queen's ritual lament but also at her behest transgress conventional boundaries, the chorus acquires an effective stage presence both visually and acoustically.[25] The repeated we/I utterances give the impression that they have taken the emotions on board,[26] but because of the responsion the lament comes across as ritualised and stereotyped; it has the character of commissioned work that is performed in a highly professional, impact-oriented manner. The emotions staged and presented to us by the "mourning artists", including Hecuba in her function as chorus leader are not those of dejection, fear or hopelessness. Rather the emotions mentioned by the chorus are pain (107: *dolor*), rage (113: *saevite manus*, "be savage, hands"), tears (116: *flemus*; 133: *fletus*) and – when Hecuba addresses the chorus – incandescent fury (94: *furibunda manus*, "frenzied hands"), mourning (97: *luctus*) and finally joy at Priam's 'happy life' and imminent reunion with his son Hector in the afterlife (156–63).

The choral song sung by the aged queen and her companions and the exaggerated mourning ritual are certainly not to be read as symptoms of weakness but as anger at the defeat and the loss of the support provided by royal power. As such they contain potential for the emergence of new strength. In the speech led by Hecuba about the prince and the king, the women in the chorus represent the official perspective of the now dead and defeated male rulers. Like Hecuba, they adopt the male hierarchization of values. It becomes clear in the course of the play that the dead men will not permit the surviving women to abandon the claim to power and to revenge. Hecuba and Andromacha will do everything in their power to fight for the survival of Astyanax, the only surviving male member of the royal family, in order to gain revenge and to win back power for their family.[27]

---

25 On the visual aspect, or the possibilities of male actors in a male chorus staging nakedness and bleeding, cf. Kohn (2013) 115: "It is doubtful that the Chorus members are actually inflicting real wounds upon themselves. It is possible to use some kind of makeup or prosthetic effect. But I think it more likely, in a theater of convention, that the audience would simply believe that the women are physically scarred just because they say that they are."
26 V. 69: *hoc* (i.e. *lugere*) *continuis egimus annis*; 74: *Ide nostris nudata rogis*; 99: *solvimus omnes . . . crinem*; 115f.: *non sum solito contenta sono: / Hectora flemus*; 156: *'felix Priamus' dicimus omnes*; also in the self-exhortation v. 79: *ite ad planctus*. Cf. the list in Hill (2000) 582f.
27 See Fuhrer (2018); similarly McAuley (2015) 257–94; Fabre-Serris (2015) 108.

2.2 The second choral ode: Trojan women as philosophers?

In the second act, the messenger Talthybius reports the appearance of the dead Achilles, who like all the other Greeks wants to have a woman as his prize. He wishes the king's daughter Polyxena to be a human sacrifice at his grave. Achilles' son Pyrrhus defends this wish in an altercation with Agamemnon. Their dispute is settled by the seer Calchas, who announces that not only the sacrifice of Polyxena but also the death of the young prince Astyanax are commandments of the gods. Calchas warns that the Greeks will not be able to start their journey home unless the two royal children are killed.

The second choral song contains reflections on the nature of death, which is seen not as living on in the hereafter (371f.; 377) but as "nothingness" (397), as the end of earthly hopes (399) and of the body and soul (378–81; 401f.). The chorus does not speak in the first person. Most commentators attribute this section, following a note in the manuscript group A (*chorus grecorum*) to another chorus, consisting of Greeks whom we are to assume to be soldiers. They appear at the beginning of the second act together with Talthybius and they then address him briefly after his introductory words (166f.).[28] Others interpret the choral song as a voice "from outside the dramatic action", which can be understood as "the poet's own manifesto".[29] The chorus of Trojan women withdraws either at the end of the *kommos*[30] or after the first scene in the second act with the arrival of the messenger Talthybius[31] or else they retire to the back of the stage.[32] The Trojan women then return to the stage or come to the foreground together with Andromacha. Alternatively this is said to happen only after the performance of the third choral song (from v. 814).

The reason proposed for attributing the second choral song to a second chorus is that the overall tenor of the reflections with their Epicurean tone form a "philosophical antidote to archaic superstition".[33] It is argued that this jars with the

---

28 See Keulen (2001) 166 and 268–70; Stroh (2013) 437f.; Heil (2013) 130f. and 153–9. Dissenting views by: Fantham (2000) 17f.; Kugelmeier (2007) 95; Mazzoli (2014) 562 with n. 1.
29 According to Fantham (1982) 263 and 85; similarly Marshall (2000) 37, both with reference to the Aristotelian concept of *embolimon* ('interlude'). Fantham and Kugelmeier (2007) 153–6 thus draw the conclusion that Seneca was not writing for the stage.
30 Thus Keulen (2001) 165f.; Stroh (2014) 437.
31 Thus Davis (1993) 221; Boyle (1994) 156f. Marshall (2000) 36 and 39 sees the chorus as exiting via the wings and towards the "Troyward side" (so also Kohn 2013, 117) and also as entering and exiting "seawards".
32 According to Heil (2013) 127–32, esp. 131: "We must not imagine that the Trojan women actually go away – where are they supposed to go? . . . The Trojan women continue their lament offstage."
33 Thus Fantham (1982) 263; a dissenting view by Stroh (2014) 440 n. 18; cf. Boyle (1994) 172.

lament of the first choral song, which assumes that life continues in the hereafter.[34] The philosophical competence displayed in this ode, "one of the most fascinating pieces of ancient contemplative poetry", is a "tribute to the Greeks as the inventors of philosophy".[35]

However, the moulding of the Trojan women in the first choral song as professional "mourning artists" undoubtedly opens up the possibility that the same chorus would also be capable of producing general reflections on the nature of death, thereby reacting to the demand for the killing of two more members of the Trojan royal family: When the members of the chorus explicitly negate continued existence after death, the appearance of the prize-hungry dead Achilles is unmasked as a fiction of myth.[36] Such an idea expressed by Greek soldiers would be downright subversive. Likewise, the confirmation of the finitude of all human beings (390) and the idea of dissolution into nothingness can be just as consoling as the notion of the continued existence of the dead in the hereafter.[37] There is no need to argue that the chorus has changed its mind.[38] Rather the chorus represents a group of people who are capable of thinking and acting as the situation demands. This implies that they are able to react to the changing scenes and the stage action and can express themselves accordingly, though without subjectively coloured statements. The absence of first-person utterances clearly marks the choral song as a supra-individual reflection. It is quite reasonable to assume that a female collective possesses this reflective potential and the capacity to react to the given situation.[39] The profound reflections on the nature of mourning in the fourth choral song, which is undoubtedly sung by the Trojan women, confirm this.

This results in the following scenario: after Hecuba exits, the Trojan women either remain visibly in the background while the four male figures appear one after

---

[34] See Fantham (1982) 84; Boyle (1994) 172; Marshall (2000) 37; Keulen (2001) 269f.; Heil (2013) 153; this is also the view of Davis (1993) 46f., who attributes philosophical content to the first choral song (ibid. 221: "the doctrine of the immortality of the soul"); cf. Keulen (2001) 13.
[35] This is the view of Stroh (2014) 439f., who does not want to ascribe this high level of reflection to a Trojan chorus and would obviously prefer to assign it to a male chorus.
[36] Boyle (1994) 172: "'Death-as-nihilation' kills Ach. once and for all."
[37] See Fantham (1982) 85: "The tone is one of calm requiescence". On this gesture of the chorus, giving consolation through reflection, see Moro in this volume (p. 165): The members of the chorus in Sophocles' *Antigone* (consisting of elderly men, belonging to distinguished families in Thebes) "do not lament with Antigone. Nevertheless, they *engage with her* in her lamentation and even try to console her."
[38] Against Davis (1993) 48: "The chorus's change of mind then is a direct result of the events in Act 2". See also Lawall (1982) 249. A different opinion is held by Gärtner (2003) 29–35, esp. 31: "Die Lösung liegt einfach in der Fixierung dieses Chors auf die Bewältigung des eigenen Leidens"; ibid. 32: "das zweite Chorlied" hat "den Charakter einer psychologischen Selbstbeschwichtigung"; ibid. 34: "autistische Betrachtungsweise . . . völlige Fixierung auf das eigene Leiden und dessen Bewältigung"; but cf. n. 22 above.
[39] See also Davis (1993) 47f.; Boyle (1994) 172f.; Hill (2000) 580–84.

the other; or they exit the stage and reappear in the same configuration at the end of the second act when the stage is empty and then sing the second choral song. At the start of the third act, immediately after the second song, Andromacha plausibly and dramatically addresses the women as a "bleak crowd of Phrygia" (409: *maesta Phrygiae turba*) who tear out their hair, beat their breasts and weep.[40] The women maintain their mourning gesture. They did not have to dress up especially for their philosophical reflection.[41] On the contrary, the idea of blood and nakedness[42] evoked in the first choral song and now updated in Andromacha's address gives their reflection on the finitude and transience of human existence greater forcefulness and plasticity.

In the first verse of her opening speech, Andromacha identifies the women as 'Phrygians', i.e. as her own people, and describes their function as ritual mourners. However, she also now ascribes to them emotions which, according to Hecuba's instruction in the *kommos* were not permitted – sorrow and weeping for their own fate after the fall of Troy. Andromacha interprets the gestures and traces of the mourning-ritual that the chorus performed *lege artis* in the first song, understandably but wrongly, as an expression of personal grief. But this interpretation also contains a rebuke: She describes the subjective sorrow of the Trojan women as "light" (411: *levia*). In other words it is irrelevant compared with the grief that she has had to endure since Hector's, i.e. her royal husband's, death.[43] She is also burdened with responsibility for Astyanax, the potential heir to the throne (409–15). Andromacha downplays the personal grief of the Trojan women compared to her own and, ultimately just like Hecuba, denies them the right to genuine grief. This again underlines the male hierarchization of values that determine the thinking and the power interests of the women of the nobility.

---

40 Heil (2013) 131 and 154f. reads Andromacha's speech as an address to absent persons. Keulen's argument (2001) 166 that Andromacha's description of the chorus in vv. 409–11 would be "more appropriate, when the preceding intellectual choral ode has not been sung by the Trojan women" is not convincing.

41 Kirichenko (2013) 255 says that "in the second choral song . . . the choir simply drops the mask that it wore in the first" but adds that this "splitting of the choral voice . . . is perceptible only outside this fiction – by us." But the audience still has in mind the chorus in the form evoked at the beginning. The chorus always keeps its mask on (cf. my remarks on pp. 182–5 above). Nevertheless I find Kirichenko's idea of the "instructive illusion" (cf. ibid. 256) interesting as the chorus never expresses the specific emotions of the captive Trojan women as such but always reacts to the situation.

42 Cf. n. 19 above.

43 Hector's burial mound is visible on the stage set, which means that no 'real' change of scene is necessary, as Heil (2013) 131f. and 159 points out: the scene is always that of Troy in flames. In front of it the camp of the Trojan women captives, the camp of the Greeks and the *tumulus* are visible and to be understood as two different locations *in front of* the city. This is also the view of Marshall (2000), who speaks of a "fluid sense of space" (p. 28). Cf. also Kohn (2013) 112–16.

2.3 Choral odes 3 and 4: thoughts and emotions in the service of others

At the end of the third act, when Andromacha submits to Ulyxes' demand and has to deliver Astyanax to him, one of the two obstacles preventing the Greeks from setting off home is removed. As if anticipating this event, the chorus now presents a sung outline of Greek geography, listing as in a catalogue the places that are likely to be the future residences of the captive women (814: *quae vocat sedes habitanda captas?*).[44] However, the Greek place names are not assigned to specific Trojan women, with the exception of Hecuba, whom the chorus addresses at the end of the ode and who then (859f.) re-appears on the stage. As the *captae* and *miserae* (851) are referred to only in the third person, the chorus too seems strangely uninvolved (and largely for this reason this choral song has received little praise or attention).[45]

In the fourth act the chorus is forced to witness prince Astyanax and the king's daughter Polyxena being led off to the scene of the sacrifice. This is where the fourth choral song begins. Now finally the Trojan women have the chance to express their own emotions in the chorus. They express this in the form of a lyrical lament, always with reference to the suffering of all the Trojans, which is contrasted with the suffering of individuals. As a "throng of mourners" they are "sweet to someone who grieves" (1009: *dulce maerenti populus dolentum*), and "sweet are populations noisy with weeping" (1010: *dulce lamentis resonare gentes*). The grief is assuaged, when the sufferers see that the "crowd" (1012: *turba*) is shedding tears in a similar way.[46] It is "sweet" for those who stand "in unmeasured ruins" (1024: *in immensis posito ruinis*) to see that no one around them has "a happy face" (1025). The impression of unhappiness is put into perspective by the fact that in principle it arises only when it is compared with happiness (1023).[47]

Again the chorus puts itself wholeheartedly in the 'service' of the Trojan dynasty: the chorus of the Trojan women as the *populus dolentum* (1009) and *turba* is the 'resonating body' (1010: *resonare*) that reduces the grief of the royals (1012). As a group of women appearing together, they block any view of those who are happy or rejoicing. The chorus makes a first-person statement only in one place: the Greek "fleet will scatter these tears of ours" in all directions (1042f.: *lacrimasque nostras / sparget huc illuc agitata classis*).[48]

---

44 On the motif of the geographical catalogue, cf. Fantham (1982) 324–6; Keulen (2001) 415f.
45 See Keulen (2001) 416. An (unconvincing) 'rescue act' is attempted by Davis (1993) 48f.: "this ode underlines the women's fears about their uncertain future . . . it is in fact an entirely appropriate one to be sung by these women at this time"; a similar view is proposed in Boyle (1994) 202.
46 On the connection to and contrast with the proem of Lucr. 2 cf. Boyle (1994) 220.
47 See Lawall (1982) 249: "There is a high level of abstraction in examining the relativity of misery."
48 Hill (2000) 585f., who attributes this ode to a second chorus, changes the transmitted text and reads *vestras*; cf. Fabre-Serris (2015) 114.

In this way the women make clear, though only *en passant*, that they too are affected by the defeat and destruction of the city, by the extermination of the male members of the royal family and thus by the dissolution of the political and social order. Although they do not belong to the aristocracy and to those who once held power, as a female chorus, as a *turba* and *vulgus*, they represent the surviving part of the Trojan people, for whom the loss of their husbands, of their family structures and the consequences of captivity – abduction, enslavement, rape – also mean great suffering.[49] But here, too, the chorus puts its own pain below that of the *royal* Trojan women: as a gesture of support in *their* crisis caused by the loss of royal power and as a dark foil against which *their* – the royal family's – suffering can appear more bearable.

2.4 The Trojan women throughout the play

It has often been noted that the chorus in the *Troades* has a more dramatic role to play than the choruses in the other Senecan tragedies,[50] and this is one of the main reasons why from the outset it has a more clear-cut identity than most choruses in classical tragedy.[51] At the beginning of the play, the chorus of Trojan women adopts the conventional female role of ritual mourners. They appear as women of the people characterised by their role of mourners and sharing the grief of their rulers Hecuba and Andromacha. However, their self-presentation in the first choral song as professional wailing women or keeners whose task is to put their emotions entirely at the service of others also underlines their social distance from the royal family. Although they lament at the behest of, or in response to, queen Hecuba or the prince's wife Andromacha, they do not make the additional royal interests and negative emotions their own: anger at the recent or imminent deaths of the male members of the royal family and the concomitant loss of power. In the subsequent choral songs, a certain philosophical and emotional competence is attributed to the women, by means of which they reflect and accompany the action of the play on a general level. In this way, as in the first choral song, they become involved in the situation but as women – more clearly than a male chorus representing the male perspective – they keep a distance to the tragic heroes and heroines. The captive Trojan women can therefore be regarded not only as a contrast to the aristocrats Hecuba and Andromacha, but also to

---

49 See Boyle (1994) 219: "The main and final subject of the ode is social dissolution (1042ff.)". However, I cannot endorse his view that "the individualisation of *Tro.*'s chorus climaxes here" (ibid. 220).
50 See Davis (1993) 25; Gärtner (2003) 29; Marshall (2000) 27: "Choral presence must continually be read and re-read into scenes once they have begun."
51 On this, see p. 181f. with n. 11.

the male figures. The grief that they articulate in each of the choral songs thus displays a supra-individual perspective.

In their political and social position and in their physical condition, the women of the people in Troy are always dependent on other groups – the rulers or male-dominated families. So captivity and imminent enslavement would not make a fundamental difference to their social status and their prospects: in each situation they will not belong to the social elite. In these conditions these women are of course more flexible than the female members of the royal dynasty. They adapt to the changing circumstances not by submitting to them but by their ability to view them and to evaluate them from a different angle. The chorus of the Trojan women does not represent the type of the "uninformed informer",[52] but rather speaks in the role of loyal but distanced and resigned observers. The height from which they fall is less great and also less spectacular. The chorus of the *Troades* does, however, assign to the female "common crowd" a central function and a crucial voice: they will have to and can bear the loss of their home and their freedom. The last glimpse of Troy's smoking ruins as the captives look back from the Greek ships is not claimed as their own but is attributed to the *Troes*, the (male) Trojans, in general (1055: *Troes hoc signo patriam videbunt*, "the Trojans will recognize their homeland by this sign").

3 The choruses in *Hercules Oetaeus*: in the service of two royals

This tragedy by an unknown author[53] shows the two female protagonists, Iole – abducted by Hercules from Oechalia – and Hercules' legitimate wife Deianira, each accompanied by a female choir.

3.1 The community of Oechalian women: sharing the disaster

At the end of Hercules' appearance in the first act, in which he explains to Jupiter his right to a place in Olympus, he tells his follower Lichas to announce his triumph over Eurytus, the king of Oechalia.[54] Then a female chorus appears with Iole and in

---

52 According to Mazzoli (2014) 572: "the simultaneously blind and prophetic chorus". Cf. also the view of Tarrant (2017), quoted in n. 7.
53 On the authorship and dating see the overview in Littlewood (2014) 515; Degiovanni (2017) 3–11; Fitch, transl. (2018) 338. Rozelaar (1985) argues for the authorship of Seneca, as does Konstan, transl. (2017) 107.
54 Together with Braun (1997) and Konstan, transl. (2017) I assume that the scene at the beginning of the tragedy is Trachis. A different view is taken by Walde (1992) 81–4 and Degiovanni (2017) 71f.

an alternating song with their mistress they declare their identity as a group of captive Oechalians.

The women in this first chorus make a number of 'we' and 'I' statements describing themselves as the prize of Hercules and bemoaning their fate: they are emaciated and grieving (119f.: *nos turpis macies et lacrimae tenent / et crinis patrio pulvere sordidus*, "we waste away disgracefully, we weep, our hair is filthy with our country's soil").[55] True, they are still standing (123: *stamus*, "we abide") but their home country cannot produce any more harvests and will be ruined (123f.),[56] the temples will be used as homes and desecrated (124f.), in the centre of the town shepherds will graze their flocks (125–7); they will "sing our days in tearful strains" (130: *cantu nostra canet tempora flebili*); the town will be forgotten (131f.). When once they were happy as dwellers in "no barren hearths in the not infertile acres of Thessaly" (133f.: *felix incolui non steriles focos / nec ieiuna soli iugera Thessali*), i.e. wives with husbands and homes,[57] they are now being forced to go to Trachis (135: *ad Trachina vocor*). After vituperating Hercules' mother, the women enumerate the many victims of his destructive power, which now include the walls of Oechalia (162: *muros Oechaliae . . . propulit*). For them the high point of their misfortune is having seen the "angered Hercules" (172: *iratum miserae vidimus Herculem*). This remark is an effective conclusion to their lament, which here becomes a ritual vituperation.[58]

In her solo aria Iole first bewails the fact that she cannot lament the "shared wrong" (177: *commune malum*): the ruined holy places, the destruction of her home, the death of children and their fathers, the overthrow of the sacred order (173–7). Her fate tells her to mourn "other ruins" (179f.: *alias flere ruinas / mea fata iubent*). She had to witness her father and her brother being clubbed to death by Hercules in the "royal hall" (207–14). All that remains for her is the lament that she could not die with her parents (215f.). The fate awaiting her now is to spin and weave for her mistress (Hercules' wife Deianira, 218). For this she blames herself. Her beauty is the cause of her misfortune (219f.); her father did not want to let Hercules marry her because he feared him as a son-in-law (222f.). So now she is doomed to "approach my mistress's house" (224: *sed iam dominae tecta petantur*).

---

who argue that there is a change of scene between the first and the second act from Oechalia (located not on Euboea but on the Thessalian mainland) to Trachis, the move taking place during the first choral song.

55 The translations from *Hercules Oetaeus* here and in the following are by Konstan (2017).
56 Together with Averna (⁴2014) 149 and Konstan, transl. (2017) 119 I read here (123f.): *nec patriae messibus heu locus / sed silvis dabitur* ("no area will be granted for our nation's crops, only for the forests"). Zwierlein (1986) 347, Fitch, transl. (2018) 350–52 and Degiovanni (2017) 237 read *sed patriae . . . / et silvis . . .* ("but the place where our city stood will be given to crops and trees").
57 The term "chorus of Oechalian maidens" (in Konstan, transl. 2017, 115) is therefore not correct.
58 See Walde (1992) 114f.: "sarkastischer Selbsttrost", "ironische Pointe".

It is Iole herself, orphaned and isolated, who underlines the contrast between her situation and that of the chorus of the Oechalian women.[59] As the daughter of the king she was not part of the rural and urban population and the sacral community represented by the chorus and therefore she cannot join in their laments as a part of the group. She had neither a husband nor children, she was neither a wife nor a mother, and with her family she has lost the status of a royal. The ignominy of having to serve a mistress from now on is not only harder to endure but also completely new.

In the following address to the lamenting Iole, the chorus now assumes the role of a stoic advisor, urging her not to look back on her past affluence and on the kingdom of her father and her ancestors (225–7): Only those "who can suffer the state of slave and king alike" and "are able to adjust their look" can be happy (228–30: *felix quisquis novit famulum / regemque pati / vultusque suos variare potest*). Here the *kommos* ends.

The author assigns to the chorus the clearly traditional role of captive women who – in contrast to the choir of the *Troades* – first lament the loss of their family and possessions. As a result, the chorus acquires clear contours when the Oechalian women identify themselves as wives, mothers and housewives. Then, however, they put their own suffering aside and place themselves at the service of Iole, trying to distract their mistress from her far greater loss – given the height of her fall (*Fallhöhe*)[60] –, the loss of her status. They try to boost her morale with philosophical advice. In this subservient, resigned but self-assured role the ordinary women from the people seem to be superior to the lonely princess lamenting her beauty and her social humiliation.

3.2 The Calydonian women in Trachis: Deianira's 'old friends'

In the second act Deianira and her nurse appear, having been informed that Hercules will return in triumph to Trachis, with Iole as his prize, whom he wants to keep as a concubine (*paelex*) next to Deianira. Deianira proves to be a woman crazed with rage and thirsting for revenge, who at first wants to murder Hercules. She wants revenge for the humiliation that Hercules inflicts on her by bringing the *paelex* Iole as a captive to the house, threatening to oust her from the marriage bed and from her position as the wife of Hercules and daughter-in-law of Jupiter.[61] Deianira

---

59 Thus Iole and the chorus perform an *amoibaion* in the strict sense, *contra* Walde (1992) 117.
60 On the topic of *Fallhöhe* (fall from a height) as a reason for lamentation cf. Walde (1992) 106; Gärtner (2003) *passim*, and see below p. 195 with n. 65.
61 Vv. 287 and 291f.: *capta praeripiet toros? / . . . Herculis tantum fui / coniunx timentis*; 401f. and 405f.: *quem Iovi socerum parem, / altrix, habebo? / . . . toris caruisse regnantis leve est: / alte illa cecidit quae viro caret Hercule*. This aspect is stressed more forcefully here than in Sophocles' *Trachinian Women*. Cf. Walde (1992) 141f. and *passim*.

at first considers conventional male methods of murder until her nurse persuades her to use magic to win Hercules back. The two women devise a plan to follow the advice of the centaur Nessus, who was killed by Hercules. Before his death, Nessus had told Deianira to catch his blood and to keep it as a magic potion with which she could bind him to her again (527–30).

Deianira wants to return to the royal palace to soak with Nessus' blood a garment that she wove herself from wool spun by her servants,[62] intending to give it to Hercules when he returns home in triumph. Here the chorus comes towards her. She addresses them as her *comites* from Calydon, whom she brought to Trachis from their "fathers' hearths" (581f.: *quas paternis extuli comites focis, / Calydoniae*). With her instruction to the "women from Calydon" to lament the sorrowful change in their fortunes (582: *Calydoniae, lugete deflendam vicem*), she gives a 'text-internal stage direction' for the second choral song to begin.[63] The chorus follows the instruction.

In their address to Deianira as the "daughter of Oeneus" (583), the king of Calydon in Aetolia, the chorus confirms its identity as 'an old friend':[64] "your throng of friends in your first years" (584: *comitum primos turba per annos*) who are now willing to stand by her once again: "now too . . . take us as your fate's faithful friends" (600f.: *nunc quoque . . . / fidas comites accipe fatis*). The women "weep for" the fate of the king's daughter, as they are told to do (583: *flemus casus, Oenei, tuos*) and the wife of Hercules in Trachis as her marriage now seems to be threatened (585: *flemus dubios, miseranda, toros*, "we weep for your doubtful marriage bed"). With the anaphoric *flemus* (583 and 585) the chorus stresses the constancy of its sympathy as well as Deianira's doubly noble status as the daughter of the king of Aetolia and the wife of Hercules and hence the 'queen' of Trachis.

The ode begins with a reminiscence of the "first years" of their services for Deianira, a time when they were young women. The pronoun *nos* (586, 592, 504) is used three times to evoke memories of certain events when they were "constantly together" (586 and 595: *solitae*), as companions or followers in cultic rituals – including as a chorus of virgins (593) – at Deianira's side (586–99). The women were obviously still young girls when they left their families behind in Calydon to accompany Deianira to Trachis.

---

[62] Vv. 563f.: *prolata vis est quaeque Palladia colu / lassavit omnem texta famularem manum*; 571–4: *cape hos amictus, nostra quos nevit manus, / dum vagus in orbe fertur et victus mero / tenet feroci Lydiam gremio nurum, / dum poscit Iolen.*
[63] This differs from Sophocles' *Trachiniae*, in which the chorus following Deianeira consists of women from Trachis, whereas the female choruses in *Hercules Oetaeus* do not consist of native women. Cf. Walde (1992) 10f.; Marcucci (1997) 33f. On the constellation of 'mistress and chorus of companions' see n. 5 above.
[64] See Gärtner (2003) 36: "Eine solch praezise [sic] Identifikation findet sich in keiner echten Seneca-Tragödie, ebensowenig eine derartig enge Verbundenheit mit einer Hauptperson."

The women's view of the present (600: *nunc quoque*) and the allusion to their many years of loyalty (601) evokes a sequence of thoughts and *topoi* on male loyalty to those in power. Depending on the fate of the king, this loyalty is more or less stable, often going hand in hand with deception, cunning or envy (604f.), as the (male) followers of kings are seeking only glory and wealth (616–39). The contrast between the advantages of poverty compared to the dangers of wealth ends with the image of a wife at the side of a husband who is living a life of moderation (658: *coniunx modico nupta marito*, "a wife wed to a humble husband"). The wife also leads a simple life, spins wool and her marriage is not "doubtful" (659–72). This is followed by the conventional praise of the middle way (675–99) which the women's collective, speaking in the first person, claims as its own: Let others be hailed as "blessed and great", "but let no crowd hail me as mighty" (693: *me nulla vocet turba potentem*), "my small boat" should always hug the shore and not have to sail out on to the high seas (694–9). The women here define the great height from which the powerful can fall,[65] a height to which they never wish to be raised. This wish is directed against the possibility that a "crowd" can even raise members of a lower class into a position of power.[66]

The song itself concludes with the announcement of Deianira's appearance "like a maenad struck by Bacchus" (701).[67] It becomes clear in the third act that Deianira must already have suspected that Nessus had deceived her (716–21). In a conversation with her son Hyllus, who has just returned from the victory celebrations on Mount Oeta, she realises that Hercules, who during the sacrificial ritual had put on the cloak prepared by Deianira, is now being burnt by Nessus' poison.

Against this background the chorus's praise for the modest, wool-spinning and faithful wife and the wish to be spared from elevation into a position of power is retrospectively turned into a warning: Deianira and Hercules do not correspond to this ideal. They cannot possibly do so because they are not "humble people". Hercules is no *modicus maritus* (658) and Deianira makes her servants spin the wool from which she weaves the cloak (564). They are both members of the ruling class, subject to the dangers described by the chorus – the falseness, betrayal and resentment of their subordinates – and they have plunged each other into misfortune and ruin. The third act ends with Deianira's announcement that she intends to commit suicide; her son Hyllus follows her in a vain attempt (1465) to prevent her death, even though he thus becomes guilty in his father's eyes (1024–30).

---

65 The example of Icarus illustrates the downfall in its literal sense (674: *cecidisse*). Cf. Deianira in 406: *alte illa cecidit quae viro caret Hercule*.

66 The *turba* is the mob that helps tyrants to gain power, not the crowd from which people withdraw in order to lead a 'hidden Epicurean life', as Averna puts it (^{4}2014) 184.

67 On the question of whether the chorus remains onstage and in v. 715 asks Deianira about her panic (according to the stage direction in manuscript group A, followed by Zwierlein's OCT and Degiovanni 2017, 470) or whether the verse should again be attributed to the nurse, i.e. the chorus leaves the stage, cf. Averna (^{4}2014) 187.

With Deianira's death the chorus of the Aetolian women is now leaderless and does not return to the stage. Or it changes its identity.

3.3 The chorus turning male: the praise of male valour

The third song reflects themes from the story of Orpheus and his song in the underworld. Hercules' imminent death is sublimated by the thought of the inevitability and inescapability of death. In the absence of first-person utterances the chorus remains neutral. It is obvious that after the third choral song another chorus appears on the scene, marking the transition from the Deianira tragedy to the Hercules tragedy.[68]

In a number of lyrical interludes in the fourth act, the chorus observes and comments on Hercules' agonising death (1151–60; 1207–17; 1279–89),[69] before Hyllus and Alcmene announce the apotheosis of their father and son respectively. Then follows the fourth choral song, a hymn to the sun god Titan and to Hercules, who will join him, and to Hercules' father Jupiter (1518–1606). Here the chorus becomes identifiable as a male group (1587: *te, pater rerum, miseri precamur*). At the beginning of the fifth act the chorus asks Philoctetes, who gave Hercules the bow before his death, for an account of the hero's end, repeatedly insisting on hearing the details (1607f.; 1613; 1617; 1691f.).[70] A final choral song concludes the tragedy.

The stance adopted by the male chorus is to simply observe the events, although their comments also show awe and admiration for the "valour" (*virtus*) displayed by the hero (1207; 1285; 1564; 1834f.) in his struggle with death. The chorus praises Hercules' capacity to endure suffering and celebrates his imminent apotheosis. It clearly and uncritically adopts Hercules' judgement and values. It does not react to Hercules' repeated complaint that after years of struggle against Juno's machinations he has now been defeated by a mortal woman of all people (1177–91, 1318, 1352–8, 1455), i.e. by Deianira, the ruler of the singers of the second chorus. There are no reflections on the height from which the hero has fallen, nor are there

---

[68] See Rozelaar (1985) 1412f.; Averna (⁴2014) 203; more cautious Walde (1992) 11f. It is generally assumed that there are only two choruses (Zwierlein OCT, 336; Davis 1993, 264; Gärtner 2003, 36f.; Konstan, transl. 2017, 115). Fitch, transl. (2018) identifies it in the first and second choral song as a "Chorus of Oechalian women" and as a "Chorus of Aetolian women". From the third choral song onwards it is only called the "Chorus".

[69] Hercules has clearly (like Hyllus) returned to Trachis after the victory celebrations on Mount Oeta (on the "unity of place", cf. Braun 1997). According to Averna (⁴2014) 203, the choral parts in the fourth act are sung by Hercules' followers, which means a change of location would be presupposed and the "unity of place" within the drama would be given. However, Averna does not assume this but, like Rozelaar (1985) 1412–14, speaks of a "dramma originariamente indipendente".

[70] According to Zwierlein (1986) the consolation of Alcmene in vv. 1831–6 is also attributed to the chorus (according to the A-tradition to Philoctetes, according to E to Hyllus). Averna (⁴2014) 267; Konstan, transl. (2017) 174; Fitch, transl. (2018) 492f. all opt for Philoctetes.

any traces of criticism, for example of Hercules' behaviour towards Iole and her father when he conquers Oechalia, of the husband's infidelity to his wife, of the gesture of the triumphant hero, who proudly accepts and dons the cloak as the gift and product of the (deceived) wife. No criticism is made of his complaint that he is prevented from performing the final heroic deed, the *summus . . . Herculeus labor* (1455) – that of killing his wife.[71]

4 Conclusion

The function of questioning, to some degree at least, the values of the tragic heroes and heroines in the two (ps.-)Senecan tragedies is assigned to the female choruses. They play the conventional roles attributed to them and in their subjective utterances they comment on them critically or affirmatively. They adopt the traditional stance of a chorus as a body that observes, comments and steps outside the action in which it is itself involved to a greater or lesser degree. However, a meta-narrative of this kind, in which, as the drama unfolds, the chorus expresses its views directly or indirectly on questions of supra-individual relevance – issues of power, war, prestige, marriage and faithfulness, justice and retaliation –, acquires further dimensions by the fact that the choral persona can be identified as female.

As soon as a choral persona is defined as female, the spectrum of opportunities for the tragic chorus to reflect events becomes wider. In the context of tragic events, women are not merely followers of male and female rulers. They are also spoils of war, objects of the striving for possessions and power. They suffer a fate that differs from those of members of the ruling family and they have a role to play that changes according to the situation and the circumstances that they face. As subordinates at the side of the female protagonists, the women in the chorus are under an obligation to share their suffering and lamentation. Their essential competence is their ability to assist in the lamentations. There is little or no room in the choral song for reference to their situation, their emotions and their judgements.

The 'choral I' or 'choral we' in the two tragedies *Troades* and *Hercules Oetaeus* – apart from ethnic ascriptions and the qualities typical of female roles: their ability to lament, their place in the family and their virginity – remain rather pallid, not displaying any trace of individuality. Every subjectivisation of utterances, thoughts and emotions by the chorus persona is overshadowed by the women's role as

---

[71] See Fuhrer (2022). Littlewood (2013) 517 also points out the problematisation of "Herculean virtue" by the chorus, but he is referring only to the chorus of Oechalian women. In comparison with the female chorus, the male counterpart appears to be more devoted to his master. By praising Hercules' virtue the male chorus too indirectly conveys the *Fallhöhe* of the hero (my thanks to Maria Mertsching for this point).

companions and hence as subordinates of noble female protagonists. As the subjects of statements, they have to place themselves at the service of those who shape the events on the stage or who are destroyed by them.

Despite or perhaps because of the inferior status, the choral ode sung by the women provides an opportunity to reflect on the role of tragic heroes and heroines. Unlike the latter, the women cannot fall from a great height. This allows them to keep an agile mind and adopt different perspectives. For them the downfall of the tragic heroes and heroines does not represent a disaster but a chance to adapt to new circumstances, now in the entourage of other masters and mistresses, but still as subordinates. As such this role does not change.[72]

For the same reason, a voice that is clearly differentiated as female in the choruses of the *Troades* and in *Hercules Oetaeus* can certainly take on supra-individual characteristics. The voices attributed to a specific collective of women – Trojans, Oechalians, Calydonians – retain their female identity even when expressing themselves in general terms about subjects such as power, wealth, death and immortality.[73]

Bibliography

Texts and translations

L. Annaei Senecae *Tragoediae*, ed. Otto Zwierlein, Oxford ⁶2009.
Lucius Annaeus Seneca, *The Trojan Women*, transl. Alex Dressler, in: *The Complete Tragedies*, vol. 1, ed. Shadi Bartsch, Chicago/London 2017, 141–190.
Lucius Annaeus Seneca, *Hercules on Oeta*, transl. David Konstan, in: *The Complete Tragedies*, vol. 2, ed. Shadi Bartsch, Chicago/London 2017, 105–179.
Seneca, *Hercules on Oeta*, ed. and transl. John G. Fitch, in: *Seneca IX Tragedies*, vol. II, Cambridge Mass./London 2018, 329–505.

---

[72] This aspect is emphasized by Bishop (1972) who relates the "dissolution of a way of life" to the situation under the principate, in which people are forced to conform: "The tragedy comes in the total evil of the breakup and in the compelled joining to a new group which grants only a lessened role" (p. 337). Cf. also Slaney (2013) 116: "Seneca's imperial tragedies no longer have a role for collective authority. Instead, Senecan tragic lyric is mediated by the individual, and this individual is mute, animated by language directing him from without. This radical concentration of energy is entirely appropriate for a socio-political context in which the citizen group has no authority, but absolute imperial power is vested in one man." Cf. the title of the article by Gärtner (2003): "Besser, dem gemeinen Volk anzugehören" (the quotation marks seem to refer to a specific passage: *Ag.* 104 or *Thy.* 533f.?); yet according to Gärtner the chorus in the *Troades* does not support this view (cf. n. 22 above). – Slaney's (2013) thesis of a "Chorus of One" attributes a too strong individuality to the voice of the chorus which is clearly to be perceived as a collective.
[73] I would like to thank Paul Knight for translating this article from German.

Books and articles

Averna (⁴2014): Daniela Averna, *Lucio Anneo Seneca, Hercules Oetaeus. Testo critico, traduzione e commento*, Roma [¹2002].
Bishop (1972): J. David Bishop, "Seneca's *Troades*: Dissolution of a Way of Life", *RhM* 115, 329–337.
Boyle (1994): Anthony J. Boyle, *Seneca's Troades. Introduction, Text, Translation and Commentary*, Leeds.
Braun (1997): Ludwig Braun, "Die Einheit des Ortes im 'Hercules Oetaeus'", *Hermes* 125, 246–249.
Davis (1993): Peter J. Davis, *Shifting Song. The Chorus in Seneca's Tragedies*, Hildesheim et al.
Degiovanni (2017): Lucia Degiovanni, *L. Annaei Senecae, Hercules Oetaeus. Atti I–III (vv. 1–1030)*, Firenze.
Dutsch (2008): Dorota M. Dutsch, *Feminine Discourse in Roman Comedy: On Echoes and Voices*, Oxford.
Fabre-Serris (2015): Jacqueline Fabre-Serris, "Women after War in Seneca's *Troades*", in: Jacqueline Fabre-Serris and Alison Keith (eds.), *Women & War in Antiquity*, Baltimore, 100–118.
Fantham (1982): Elaine Fantham, *Seneca's Troades. A Literary Introduction with Text, Translation, and Commentary*, Princeton.
Fantham (2000): Elaine Fantham, "Production of Seneca's *Trojan Women*, ancient? and modern", in: George W. M. Harrison (ed.), *Seneca in Performance*, London, 13–26.
Fitch/McElduff (2008): John G. Fitch and Siobhan McElduff, "Construction of the Self in Senecan Drama", in: John G. Fitch (ed.), *Oxford Readings in Classical Studies: Seneca*, Oxford, 157–180, originally in: *Mnemosyne* 55 (2002) 18–40.
Foley (2001): Helene P. Foley, *Female Acts in Greek Tragedy*, Princeton.
Ford (2020): Andrew Ford, "Linus: The Rise and Fall of Lyric Genres", in: Margaret Foster, Leslie Kurke and Naomi Weiss (eds.), *Genre in Archaic and Classical Greek Poetry: Theories and Models*, Leiden et al., 57–81.
Fuhrer (2018): Therese Fuhrer, "Töten für den Frieden. Ambiguität in Senecas *Troades*", in: Christine Walde and Georg Wöhrle (eds.), *Gender und Krieg. Gender Studies in den Altertumswissenschaften*, Trier, 51–68.
Fuhrer (2022): Therese Fuhrer, "Das Kleid als tödliche Waffe. Senecas *Medea*, Ps.-Senecas *Deianira*", in: Henriette Harich-Schwarzbauer and Cédric Scheidegger Lämmle (eds.), *Women and Objects*, Trier, 109–127.
Gärtner (2003): Thomas Gärtner, "'Besser, dem gemeinen Volk anzugehören' – Zur Rolle des Chors in der senecanischen Tragödie", *Studia Humaniora Tartuensia* 4, 1–53.
Heil (2013): Andreas Heil, *Die dramatische Zeit in Senecas Tragödien*, Leiden et al.
Heldmann (1974): Konrad Heldmann, *Untersuchungen zu den Tragödien Senecas*, Wiesbaden.
Hill (2000): Donald E. Hill, "Seneca's Choruses", *Mnemosyne* 53, 561–587.
Hose (1990): Martin Hose, *Studien zum Chor bei Euripides*, Teil 1, Stuttgart.
Keulen (2001): Atze J. Keulen, *L. Annaeus Seneca, Troades. Introduction, Text & Commentary*, Leiden et al.
Kirichenko (2013): Alexander Kirichenko, *Lehrreiche Trugbilder. Senecas Tragödien und die Rhetorik des Sehens*, Heidelberg.
Kohn (2013): Thomas Kohn, *The Dramaturgy of Senecan Tragedy*, Ann Arbor.
Kudlien (1995): Fridolf Kudlien, "Berufsmäßige Klageweiber in der Kaiserzeit", *RhM* 138, 177–187.
Kugelmeier (2007): Christoph Kugelmeier, *Die innere Vergegenwärtigung des Bühnenspiels in Senecas Tragödien*, München.
Lawall (1982): Gilbert Lawall, "Death and Perspective in Seneca's *Troades*", *CJ* 77.3, 244–252.

Littlewood (2014): Cedric A. J. Littlewood, "Hercules Oetaeus", in: Gregor Damschen and Andreas Heil (eds.), *Brill's Companion to Seneca: Philosopher and Dramatist*, Leiden, 515–520.

Marcucci (1997): Silvia Marcucci, *Analisi e interpretazione dell'*Hercules Oetaeus, Pisa/Roma.

Marshall (2000): C. W. (Toph) Marshall, "Location! Location! Location! Choral Absence and Dramatic Space in Seneca's *Troades*", in: George W. M. Harrison (ed.), *Seneca in Performance*, London, 27–51.

Mazzoli (2014): Giancarlo Mazzoli, "The Chorus: Seneca as a Lyric Poet", in: Gregor Damschen and Andreas Heil (eds.), *Brill's Companion to Seneca: Philosopher and Dramatist*, Leiden, 561–574.

McAuley (2015): Mairéad McAuley, *Reproducing Rome: Motherhood in Virgil, Ovid, Seneca, and Statius*, Oxford.

Mossman (2001): Judith Mossman, "Women's Speech in Greek Tragedy: The Case of Electra and Clytemnestra in Euripides' *Electra*", *CQ* 51, 374–384.

Rozelaar (1985): Marc Rozelaar, "Neue Studien zur Tragödie 'Hercules Oetaeus'", *ANRW* II 32,2, 1349–1419.

Schironi (2020), Francesca Schironi, "The Speaking Persona: Ancient Commentators on Choral Performance", in: Margaret Foster, Leslie Kurke and Naomi Weiss (eds.), *Genre in Archaic and Classical Greek Poetry: Theories and Models*, Leiden et al., 109–132.

Shelton (2016): Jo-Ann Shelton, "The Fall of Troy in Seneca's *Troades*", in: Mary R. Bachvarova, Dorota Dutsch and Ann Suter (eds.), *The Fall of Cities in the Mediterranean. Commemorations in Literature, Folk-Song, and Liturgy*, Cambridge, 183–211.

Slaney (2013): Helen Slaney, "Seneca's Chorus of One", in: Joshua Billings, Felix Budelmann and Fiona Macintosh (eds.), *Choruses, Ancient and Modern*, Oxford, 99–116.

Stroh (2008): Wilfried Stroh, "Staging Seneca: The Production of *Troas* as a Philological Experiment", in: John G. Fitch (ed.), *Oxford Readings in Classical Studies: Seneca*, Oxford, 195–220, transl. of: "Inszenierung Senecas. Die Aufführung der 'Troas' als philologisches Experiment", in: Anton Bierl and Peter von Möllendorff (eds.), *Orchestra. Drama Mythos Bühne*, Stuttgart/Leipzig 1994, 248–263.

Stroh (2014): Wilfried Stroh, "Troas", in: Gregor Damschen and Andreas Heil (eds.), *Brill's Companion to Seneca: Philosopher and Dramatist*, Leiden, 435–447.

Tarrant (2017): Richard Tarrant, "*Custode rerum Caesare*: Horatian Civic Engagement and the Senecan Tragic Chorus", in: Martin Stöckinger and Kathrin Winter (eds.), *Horace and Seneca: Interactions, Intertexts, Interpretations*, Berlin/Boston, 93–112.

Vandersmissen (2019): Marc Vandersmissen, *Discours des personnages féminins chez Sénèque. Approches logométriques et contrastives d'un corpus théâtral*, Bruxelles.

Walde (1992): Christine Walde, *Herculeus Labor. Studien zum pseudosenecanischen Hercules Oetaeus*, Frankfurt et al.

Zwierlein (1986): Otto Zwierlein, *Kritischer Kommentar zu den Tragödien Senecas*, Stuttgart.

IV The Gender Parameter in Erotic First-Person Discourse

Giulia Sissa
Elle sait. Elle dit. Elle rit. L'éloge paradoxal d'éros par Diotime de Mantinée

Abstract: In Plato's *Symposium*, Diotima is credited with teaching Socrates that Ἔρως is a quest for immortality, through the generation of λόγοι. Diotima concludes her praise of Ἔρως with a famous metaphor: the steps that take a lover, from beautiful bodies to beautiful souls, to the form of Beauty. This ascent of desire from the embodied beauty of boys to its paradigmatic and unalloyed version, has attracted considerable scholarly attention. I argue that Ἔρως is not a mystical energy. It is an experience that occurs in a particular erotic culture, that of Athens and its sophisticated practice of παιδεραστεῖν. Athenian young men live in that culture and share that experience. They know about love, and how they live it through language. These amorously inclined youth, ἐρωτικοί, are the potential philosophers Socrates is interested in. For having grown used to that kind of Ἔρως – talkative and libertine, flattering and unfaithful – an Athenian ἐρωτικὸς is the best candidate for philosophical improvement. Socrates will take him from there. But it takes a woman to articulate this profoundly ironic understanding of Ἔρως: the more promiscuous, the more promising.

Keywords: Enounciation, love, desire, childbirth, laughter, incongruity

Y-a-t-il une énonciation genrée dans la situation dialogique Platonicienne ?[1] Cette question exige que nous acceptions, comme prémisse majeure, le montage théâtral de la situation philosophique, à savoir la mise en scène d'un échange dramatique entre des personnages qui ne cessent de se parler. Bavardage, questions, réponses, humour et, surtout, réfutation (ἔλεγχος) : les dialogues déploient un vaste répertoire de possibilités interlocutoires. Protagoniste de ces épisodes en série : Socrate, l'homme qui n'écrit pas, mais qui a déposé le modèle d'une façon de faire, l'εἰρωνεία. Εἰρωνεία n'est pas simplement une forme de dissimulation. Ce n'est pas non plus un accident de parcours dont l'un ou l'autre s'aviserait : c'est plutôt un jeu de rôles méthodique, un chassé-croisé inhérent à la rencontre avec Socrate. Comme l'affirme Thrasymaque dans la *République*, chez Socrate, l'εἰρωνεία est une habitude (1,337a). C'est en effet le scénario de parole qui rend possible le dialogue, tel que Socrate l'entend. Je te flatte (toi qui es tellement savant, dis-moi ce que tu penses !) ; je me minimise (quant à moi, le malheureux, je n'en sais rien !), mais uniquement afin de te faire causer. Et, comme par hasard, dès que tu ouvres la bouche, te

---

[1] Je me réjouis d'avoir présenté ces réflexions dans quelques occasions collectives. Je remercie Jacqueline Fabre-Serris, Sandra Boehringer, Irene Calà, Giulia Maria Chesi, Pierre Destrée, Arnaud Zucker et les Éditrices de ce volume pour leurs remarques et leurs conseils.

voilà tombé dans le panneau de la prétention, de la présomption, de l'illusion de savoir, bref : de la « doxosophie » (δοξοσοφία). Or, dans le *Philèbe*, Socrate théorise cet aveuglement sur soi-même, cet agrandissement de ses propres mérites, cette vanité et cette vantardise comme la cause du ridicule et le ressort de la comédie.[2]

Dans toute situation dialogique, dès que je joue le rôle de Socrate, je te pousse sournoisement à dire ce que tu penses et, une fois que tu t'es fait surprendre en flagrant délit d'ignorance ignorée, te voilà « doxosophiste ». Tu es marrant, mon pauvre ami ! Je pourrais sans doute me moquer ouvertement de toi, mais je vais plutôt te poser quelques petites questions supplémentaires sur ce que tu viens de dire. Tu veux-bien ? Et l'ἔλεγχος commence.

Toute situation dialogique est une situation ironique. Pourquoi donc le genre serait-il pertinent ? Le genre est pertinent parce que, tout d'abord, tous les personnages du théâtre platonicien sont des hommes. Ces hommes se parlent entre eux, à partir de, et au sujet de, leurs expériences intellectuelles, sportives, sociales et politiques partagées. C'est une vie qui leur est commune et qui les sépare des femmes. De surcroît, ils devisent de leur vie amoureuse, une entente d'homme à homme, qui soude leur amitié dans une complicité esthétique, érotique, sexuelle. Dans le petit clan platonicien, on s'aime entre soi. Même genre, littéralement. Ensuite, le genre pose question, parce que, dans cet univers homogène et homosensuel Platon fait parfois – et soudainement – résonner des voix de femmes. Enfin, Socrate métaphorise la situation

---

[2] Platon, *Philèbe* 48c–d : « L'ignorance est certainement un mal, tout comme ce que nous appelons une disposition stupide. Protarque : Sûrement. Socrate : Ensuite, considère la nature du ridicule. Protarque : S'il te plaît, continue ! Le ridicule est, principalement, une sorte de vice qui donne son nom à une condition ; et c'est cette partie du vice en général qui implique le contraire de la condition mentionnée dans l'inscription de Delphes. Protarque : Tu veux dire 'Connais-toi toi-même', Socrate ? Socrate : Oui ; et le contraire, dans la langue de l'inscription, serait évidemment de ne pas se connaître du tout » (ΣΩ. Κακὸν μὴν ἄγνοια καὶ ἣν δὴ λέγομεν ἀβελτέραν ἕξιν. ΠΡΩ. Τί μήν; ΣΩ. Ἐκ δὴ τούτων ἰδὲ τὸ γελοῖον ἥντινα φύσιν ἔχει. ΠΡΩ. Λέγε μόνον. ΣΩ. Ἔστι δὴ πονηρία μέν τις τὸ κεφάλαιον, ἕξεώς τινος ἐπίκλην λεγομένη· τῆς δ' αὖ πάσης πονηρίας ἐστὶ τοὐναντίον πάθος ἔχον ἢ τὸ λεγόμενον ὑπὸ τῶν ἐν Δελφοῖς γραμμάτων. ΠΡΩ. Τὸ "γνῶθι σαυτὸν" λέγεις, ὦ Σώκρατες; ΣΩ. Ἔγωγε. τοὐναντίον μὴν ἐκείνῳ δῆλον ὅτι τὸ μηδαμῇ γιγνώσκειν αὑτὸν λεγόμενον ὑπὸ τοῦ γράμματος ἂν εἴη). – *Philèbe*, 48e–49a: « Socrate : Mais de loin le plus grand nombre, je crois, se trompent dans le troisième domaine, les qualités de l'âme, en pensant qu'ils excellent dans la vertu alors que ce n'est pas le cas. Protarque : Oui, absolument. Socrate : Et de toutes les vertus, la sagesse n'est-elle pas celle à laquelle les gens en général prétendent, se remplissant ainsi de querelles et d'une fausse prétention de sagesse ? Protarque: Oui, bien sûr. Socrate: Et nous devrions sûrement avoir raison d'appeler tout cela une mauvaise condition. Protarque : Tout à fait » (ΣΩ. Πολὺ δὲ πλεῖστοί γε, οἶμαι, περὶ τὸ τρίτον εἶδος τὸ τῶν ἐν ταῖς ψυχαῖς διημαρτήκασιν, ἀρετὴν δοξάζοντες βελτίους ἑαυτούς, οὐκ ὄντες. ΠΡΩ. Σφόδρα μὲν οὖν. ΣΩ. Τῶν ἀρετῶν δ' ἆρ' οὐ σοφίας πέρι τὸ πλῆθος πάντως ἀντεχόμενον μεστὸν ἐρίδων καὶ δοξοσοφίας ἐστὶ ψευδοῦς; ΠΡΩ. Πῶς δ' οὔ; ΣΩ. Κακὸν μὲν δὴ πᾶν ἄν τις τὸ τοιοῦτον εἰπὼν ὀρθῶς ἂν εἴποι πάθος. ΠΡΩ. Σφόδρα γε).

Sauf précision contraire, c'est moi qui traduis.

dialogique/ironique elle-même, dans son intimité toute masculine, comme une expérience de grossesse et d'accouchement dont les hommes deviennent l'improbable sujet. Et voilà que ce petit monde se révèle être plus *queer* qu'il n'y paraît. Surtout dans le *Banquet*.

1 Chez Agathon

Agathon, jeune poète tragique, reçoit dans sa maison, pour célébrer la performance de sa première tragédie. Il y a son amant, Pausanias. Il y a quelques amis : Phèdre, Eryximaque, Aristophane. Plus tard dans la soirée, Alcibiade et d'autres se joindront à eux. Ils font la fête. Ils sont joyeux. Ils décident de faire une ronde de discours en l'honneur d'Éros. Lorsqu'il est temps qu'il prenne la parole, Agathon s'élance dans un véritable hymne à l'amour. Il glorifie le dieu dans une prose savamment rythmée qui se mue en vers et qui, par une profusion de parallélismes, tels que l'assonance, la consonance et l'allitération, produit de véritables effets de rime.[3] D'après Aristodème, le narrateur, son discours, est aussi beau que lui (198a). On aperçoit le poète lui-même dans ses mots et ses fioritures. Le discours à l'image du discoureur. Mais nous entrevoyons aussi Agathon tel qu'il apparaît dans les *Thesmophories* d'Aristophane, ou plutôt dans une nouvelle incarnation du même personnage.

Sur la scène comique, la plaque tourne, et l'intérieur de la maison du poète se révèle au public. Agathon est là, à l'œuvre. On le surprend en plein acte créatif, pendant qu'il compose une pièce chorale – pour un chœur de femmes. Sa voix. Son corps. Sa poétique. Tout se tient, car au parent d'Euripide, qui lui demande quel est son genre, au juste, Agathon répond que, lorsqu'il crée des personnages de femme, il sait comment faire pour devenir féminin (1–152). Or, Platon récrit le personnage d'Agathon d'après les *Thesmophories*, ai-je argumenté ailleurs, en le replaçant encore une fois chez lui, mais, cette fois-ci, son salon douillet se trouve à l'abri des regards du peuple athénien dont le Parent incarne la bêtise et la méchanceté.[4] Le poète n'est plus un caméléon indéchiffrable, en transition continue d'un genre à l'autre, ce qui provoque les insultes de l'homme du commun, velu, phallique et adepte de la logique binaire (130–145). La variante platonicienne d'Agathon est un artiste raffiné qui réconcilie les aspects sensuels de l'expérience érotique avec les vertus morales, dont ἀνδρεία, le courage/virilité (196d). Cet homme est admiré de ses amis. Nous sommes, chez Platon, dans l'ambiance de la pédérastie « aristocratique »,

---

[3] Wesling (1980) x–xi, 38–42.
[4] Sissa (2012). Skinner (2013) 248–251 a tort de voir Agathon comme le même cinède, à la fois dans les *Thesmophories* et dans le *Banquet*. Cela fausse la caractérisation du personnage et son rôle dans le dialogue.

ou, plus précisément, dans une réunion mondaine où des intellectuels publiques, Socrate et Aristophane, croisent un médecin, mais aussi un jeune homme de haute naissance comme Alcibiade. Cette atmosphère est favorable à un couple aussi stable que celui de Pausanias et d'Agathon, l'hôte qui reçoit ses amis. Les propos qui s'échangent célèbrent une relation symétrique et complice, au lieu de mettre face à face un macho tout fier de son agressivité sexuelle et un homme qui serait destiné soit à subir cette sexualité soit à s'y soumettre – et dont on se moquerait.

La perception de l'amour entre mâles est en effet profondément différente, dans des milieux sociaux différents. Quelle qu'ait pu être la réalité des pratiques sexuelles, les représentations ne sont pas du tout les mêmes.[5] Les discours adressés à un large public tournent en dérision ce que les échanges entre soi, au sein d'une société policée, mettent en valeur. Plus fondamentalement encore, le rapport sexuel fait l'objet de descriptions empiriques opposées. La culture populaire invente la distinction entre l'homme à l'anus dilaté et le satyre en érection, toujours prêt à violer l'autre par derrière.[6] L'environnement philosophique n'en a cure. Autant la pensée

---

[5] Cette différence est un fait textuel. On verra par exemple ce qu'Éphore et Strabon racontent des mœurs crétoises (10,4,21) : « Ils ont une coutume particulière en ce qui concerne les affaires d'amour, car ils gagnent les objets de leur amour, non par la persuasion, mais par l'enlèvement... Il est déshonorant pour les belles personnes ou les descendants d'ancêtres illustres de ne pas trouver d'amants, la présomption étant que leur caractère est responsable d'un tel sort. Mais les 'partenaires' reçoivent des honneurs (ἔχουσι δὲ τιμὰς οἱ παρασταθέντες) – car c'est ainsi qu'ils appellent ceux qui ont été enlevés. En effet, dans les danses et les courses, ils occupent les postes les plus honorifiques, et il leur est permis de s'habiller mieux que les autres, c'est-à-dire avec l'habit que leur a donné leur amant ; et non seulement cela, mais même après avoir atteint l'âge adulte, ils portent un vêtement spécial, destiné à faire connaître le fait que le jeune homme est devenu 'illustre' (κλεινός), car ils appellent l'être aimé κλεινός et l'amant φιλήτωρ ». Il faut remarquer l'emphase sur le mot « partenaire » (participe aoriste du verbe παρίστημι, « se trouver à côté »). – Différents aspects de la pertinence du milieu social one été reconnus depuis longtemps par Percy (1996), Hubbard (1998), Skinner (2013). *Contra* Shapiro (2015).

[6] Aristophane, *Thesmophories* 153–158, le Parent à Agathon : οὐκοῦν κελητίζεις, ὅταν Φαίδραν ποιῇς; ἀνδρεῖα δ' ἦν ποιῇ τις ἐν τῷ σώματι ἔνεσθ' ὑπάρχον τοῦθ'. ἃ δ' οὐ κεκτήμεθα, μίμησις ἤδη ταῦτα συνθηρεύεται. ὅταν σατύρους τοίνυν ποιῇς, καλεῖν ἐμέ, ἵνα συμποιῶ σοὔπισθεν ἑστυκὼς ἐγώ (« Donc quand tu crées une Phèdre, tu montes dessus ? Si l'on crée des sujets virils, ce morceau du corps est à portée de main. Mais les qualités que nous n'avons pas, c'est l'imitation qui les déniche. Eh bien, préviens-moi quand tu créeras des satyres, pour que je puisse t'aider, en me mettant derrière toi en pleine érection »). Sur Agathon, comme l'objet désigné de l'action du verbe transitif βινεῖν : 35 (βεβίνηκας) ; 50 (βινεῖσθαι) ; 206 (βινεῖσθαι) ; 1215 : l'Archer scythe se plaint qu'une vieille femme lui a volé son coffret à flute et qu'il a été « complètement baisé » (συβήνη 'στί· καταβήνησι γάρ). Sur la vision érotique de l'archer (pénétrer tout ce qui s'y prête, y compris une planche en bois trouée), voir 1118–1124. Pour une focalisation sur l'anus d'Agathon, voir 200 s. : le Parent, toujours lui, rebondit sur les propos du poète au sujet des « maux qu'il faut subir » (παθήμασιν), en attribuant à ce mot une signification sexuelle. « Toi, l'enculé, tu es grand-ouvert dans l'anus non pas aux discours, mais à ce qu'il faut subir » (καὶ μὴν σύ γ', ὦ κατάπυγον, εὐρύπρωκτος εἶ οὐ τοῖς λόγοισιν, ἀλλὰ τοῖς παθήμασιν).

comique provoque la raillerie aux dépens de l'homosexuel qui aime à se faire pénétrer, autant la pensée érotique amène à apprécier une connivence amoureuse. C'est l'Athénien ordinaire qui, sur la scène aristophanesque, réclame une différenciation bien nette entre les genres (130–145) et les rôles sexuels. Pourtant, contrairement à une idée reçue, cela le rend à son tour ridicule, d'une part parce qu'il a l'air d'un imbécile, d'autre part parce qu'il finit par tout confondre lui-même. Ainsi le Parent d'Euripide tout en menaçant de sodomiser Agathon (157 s.), dit ressentir « un chatouillement monter dans l'anus, rien qu'en écoutant » le chant du poète (ὥστ' ἐμοῦ γ' ἀκροωμένου ὑπὸ τὴν ἕδραν αὐτὴν ὑπῆλθε γάργαλος, 132 s.). C'est ce gros ballot, finalement, qui va subir une dépilation et emprunter les habits d'Agathon pour se faufiler incognito parmi les femmes qui célèbrent les rites de Déméter et de Perséphone. Le blâme sépare les partenaires ; l'éloge les réunit. Passivité *versus* activité, le soi-disant modèle de l'amour des garçons à Athènes, est une illusion comique.[7]

Dans le *Banquet*, nous sommes chez Agathon lui-même, entre gens de qualité qui, le temps de cette réception, s'imposent une contrainte conversationnelle et conviviale. Ici et maintenant, au début d'une fête, ces agréables conviennent de dire du bien d'Éros, dans une visée encomiastique et sur un régistre superlatif – ce qui promet un discours flatteur sur tous les aspects de l'amour. Tout commence par le regret qu'il n'y ait pas d'hymnes adressés à ce grand dieu. Vite ! Il faut combler cette lacune. Il faut tisser les louanges de l'amour. Le programme de cette soirée est, précisément, tout le contraire de ce qui se passe conventionnellement sur la scène comique ou dans les tribunaux, à savoir l'injure, la vilification, la dérision d'une sexualité anale, passive et efféminée. Chez Agathon, le seul amoureux « mauvais » est l'éraste libidineux que dépeint Pausanias, c'est-à-dire l'homme hyperactif qui poursuit un grand nombre de garçons de ses assiduités, uniquement pour leur jeunesse (183e–184a).

---

[7] Lorsque le discours sur le sexe entre hommes emprunte le registre du blâme et de la moquerie, les deux partenaires d'un couple homosexuel peuvent être distingués, tout en faisant, l'un et l'autre, l'objet d'un grand mépris. J'ai approfondi cette argumentation dans Sissa (2011), surtout au sujet du discours d'Eschine, *Contre Timarque*. Le discours Démosthène, *Contre Conon*, est encore plus intéressant à ce propos, puisque l'orateur met l'accent sur une réciprocité phallique entre des jeunes qui, tous se conduisent ignomignieusement: « Les fils de cet homme sont les bienvenus, en ce qui me concerne, pour être Ithyphalli et Autolecythi . . . ; car ils sont ceux qui s'initient les uns les autres aux rites d'Ithyphallus, et se livrent à des actes qui comportent une grande honte aussi à les mentionner, sans parler de les accomplir, pour des hommes mésurés » (οὗτοι γάρ εἰσιν οἱ τελοῦντες ἀλλήλους τῷ ἰθυφάλλῳ, καὶ τοιαῦτα ποιοῦντες ἃ πολλὴν αἰσχύνην ἔχει καὶ λέγειν, μή τί γε δὴ ποιεῖν ἀνθρώπους μετρίους, 16 s.). Ces hommes « lorsqu'ils se réunissent et sont seuls, ne s'abstiennent d'aucune forme de vice ou d'indécence » (ἐπειδὰν δὲ συλλεγῶσι καὶ μετ' ἀλλήλων γένωνται, κακῶν καὶ αἰσχρῶν οὐδὲν ἐλλείπουσι, 34 s.). Lorsque l'on fustige, et que l'on souhaite scandaliser son public, l'on met tous les partenaires sur le même plan. La distinction entre passif et actif n'a aucune importance. Vice versa, dès que l'on fait l'éloge de cette sexualité, l'on célèbre l'un et l'autre amant.

Quel est donc le rôle de ce poète tragique, qui est devenu un personnage comique et que, dans une sorte de palinodie, Platon ramène enfin dans le milieu qui est le sien ? Nous avons mis en évidence le premier aspect de sa caractérisation : Agathon n'a rien de l'efféminé de comédie. C'est un homme parmi des hommes. Deuxième aspect de sa réincarnation platonicienne : il est l'encomiaste par excellence. Son rôle consiste à pousser l'éloge au comble de l'hyperbole comme si ce poète incarnait l'esprit même de la parole épidictique jusqu'à son expression poétique. Souvenons-nous : c'est Phèdre qui déplore l'absence d'hymnes en l'honneur d'Eros, d'où la suite des discours, mais c'est Agathon lui-même qui porte Éros aux nues. Tandis que les autres symposiastes, tout en attribuant des qualités au dieu, appuient leurs propos sur des exemples (Phèdre), des récits (Aristophane), des mœurs (Pausanias), des principes (Eryximaque), Agathon se borne à aligner des adjectifs. Pure prédication amplifiée. Tel que ses amis l'entendent, se plaint en effet Socrate, l'éloge « est l'attribution de toutes les qualités les plus grandes et les plus belles à une chose, que ce soit le cas ou non – peu importe vraiment si elles sont fausses » (ἀλλὰ τὸ ὡς μέγιστα ἀνατιθέναι τῷ πράγματι καὶ ὡς κάλλιστα, ἐάν τε ᾖ οὕτως ἔχοντα ἐάν τε μή· εἰ δὲ ψευδῆ, οὐδὲν ἄρ᾽ ἦν πρᾶγμα, 198d-e). Agathon ne fait que cela : attribuer des superlatifs. Voilà la pensée/parole épidictique, dans sa plus simple expression.

Puisque le jeune poète s'énonce avec une telle facilité, étant tellement certain de toutes les qualités superlatives d'Éros, il est tout naturel que Socrate le choisisse, lui et lui seul, pour lui chercher noise à propos de ce que signifie le verbe ἐγκωμιάζειν, donc au sujet de ce que c'est, au juste, que d'énoncer des propos encomiastiques. Agathon s'y prend tellement bien, qu'il doit en savoir un bout. Tous ont merveilleusement célébré l'amour, remarque Socrate, mais c'est Agathon qui a prononcé le discours le plus admirable – bouleversant même. Ne serait-on pas mis hors de soi (ἐκπλήσσω), en écoutant la beauté des mots et des phrases (τὸ δὲ ἐπιτελευτῆς τοῦ κάλλους τῶν ὀνομάτων καὶ ῥημάτων τίς οὐκ ἂν ἐξεπλάγη ἀκούων, 198c). On en serait même médusé. Ce Gorgias est une Gorgone ! Sublime.

Lorsque Socrate flatte ainsi le beau parleur, nous ne sommes pas dupes. En se targuant de tout savoir sur l'Amour, Agathon excelle dans la δοξοσοφία. En déclamant son éloge sans la moindre hésitation et avec le dogmatisme du superlatif, Agathon s'est montré sûr de lui. En célébrant l'amour, d'ailleurs, il s'est célébré lui-même, l'amant de Pausanias. Son discours est aussi beau que lui (198a). Rien qu'en recevant ses amis à une soirée en son honneur, il baigne dès le début dans son propre succès. Socrate va donc lui infliger, à lui seul, une bonne dose d'εἰρωνεία. Dire de lui qu'il est une pure merveille : voilà son « ironie habituelle ». Εἰρωνεία est bel et bien une façon de moquerie. En conformité avec le *Philèbe*, Agathon apprête à rire. Et pourtant personne ne se gausse. Nous ne sommes pas sur la scène comique.

Le bel Agathon, le doxosophiste, est plutôt la victime désignée de l'ἔλεγχος qui va suivre. Socrate va lui faire avouer que son attribution (ἀνατιθέναι) de qualités superlatives à Éros est absurde. Pourquoi ? Parce que, si seulement Agathon s'écoutait parler, il ne pourrait s'empêcher de s'entendre dire que le mot Ἔρως appelle toujours un complément de spécification, un génitif objectif, un objet intentionnel. Éros est essentiellement Ἔρως *de* quelque chose. Éros, le dieu appelé Désir, ne fait que désirer (comme son nom l'indique). Son objet, pour être désiré, doit nécessairement ne pas être là. Or, on pourrait penser qu'il est question ici de l'objet du désir amoureux et de son manque. Mais l'ἔλεγχος va plus loin dans le métalangage. Il s'agit bien pour Socrate d'attirer l'attention sur la langue et sur l'attribution de qualités, puisque son questionnement s'engage dans la direction suivante : de même qu'une personne de haute taille ne saurait désirer cet attribut particulier, une haute taille, puisqu'elle le possède déjà, ainsi Éros ne désire que ce qu'il n'a pas. Ce qu'il désire, il ne saurait l'avoir. Dans la même logique, si Éros désire la beauté, comme Agathon a pu l'affirmer, c'est que la beauté lui fait défaut : éros ne saurait être beau (201b) :

> Ἐνδεὴς ἄρ' ἐστὶ καὶ οὐκ ἔχει ὁ Ἔρως κάλλος.
> Ἀνάγκη, φάναι.
> Τί δέ; τὸ ἐνδεὲς κάλλους καὶ μηδαμῇ κεκτημένον κάλλος ἆρα λέγεις σὺ καλὸν εἶναι;
> Οὐ δῆτα.
> Ἔτι οὖν ὁμολογεῖς Ἔρωτα καλὸν εἶναι, εἰ ταῦτα οὕτως ἔχει;
> Καὶ τὸν Ἀγάθωνα εἰπεῖν Κινδυνεύω, ὦ Σώκρατες, οὐδὲν εἰδέναι ὧν τότε εἶπον.

> « Et ce qui manque à l'Amour, n'est ce pas la beauté ? » – « Oui, nécessairement », dit-il. « Ce qui manque de beauté, et qui n'en possède pas, est-il beau ? » – « Sûrement pas. » – « Pouvez-vous encore permettre à l'Amour d'être beau, si c'est le cas ? » Sur quoi Agathon dit : « J'ai très peur, Socrate, que je ne savais rien de ce dont je parlais. »

Cette réfutation représente un point de non retour dans le déroulement de la soirée. Éros se retrouve dépouillé de tous ses attributs. À la lumière de cette déflation d'Éros, en effet, les propos de tous les convives se révèlent un bavardage de buveurs. On ne peut tout simplement pas dire du bien d'Éros, on ne peut tout simplement pas lui attribuer (ἀνατιθέναι) de propriétés qu'il ne saurait posséder, et a fortiori dans la forme intensifiée du superlatif – μέγιστα, κάλλιστα. Éros/Désir ne tolère pas qu'on en fasse un éloge. Quelle idée saugrenue ! Le bel Agathon devient le bouc émissaire d'une soirée insensée dont le thème (éros) et la contrainte (l'éloge) sont incompatibles. Si Socrate a raison, tout le monde a tort.

Socrate ridiculise Agathon. Il lui fait jouer le rôle du précieux ridicule. Dans une situation ironique qu'il a mise en place en s'excusant de sa propre prétention, Socrate oblige son « bienaimé Agathon » à admettre sa δοξοσοφία. « J'ai très peur, Socrate, que je ne savais rien de ce dont je parlais. » Et pourtant, Socrate ne s'esclaffe pas. Les autres symposiastes non plus. Arrêt sur image. Pourquoi ne pas rire du ridicule ? Parce que nous ne rions pas de nos amis. C'est Socrate qui l'affirme, encore une fois, dans le *Philèbe*. Précisément lorsque ceux-ci se rendent ridicules, l'amitié fait obstacle à la dérision, qui serait un mélange de plaisir et d'envie (φθόνος, 50a) :[8]

---

8 Pour un commentaire à ce texte, on verra Fussi (2017), qui met en avant la visée non-agressive du φθόνος entendu comme *Schadenfreude* dans le *Philèbe*, ce qui me paraît sous-estimer son aspect

> Γελῶντας ἄρα ἡμᾶς ἐπὶ τοῖς τῶν φίλων γελοίοις φησὶν ὁ λόγος, κεραννύντας ἡδονὴν αὖ φθόνῳ, λύπῃ τὴν ἡδονὴν ξυγκεραννύναι· τὸν γὰρ φθόνον ὡμολογῆσθαι λύπην τῆς ψυχῆς ἡμῖν πάλαι, τὸ δὲ γελᾶν ἡδονῆς, ἅμα γίγνεσθαι δὲ τούτω ἐν τούτοις τοῖς χρόνοις.

> Alors notre argument déclare que lorsque nous rions des qualités ridicules de nos amis, nous mélangeons le plaisir à la douleur, puisque nous le mélangeons à l'envie ; car nous sommes d'accord depuis le début que l'envie est une douleur de l'âme, et que le rire est un plaisir, et pourtant ces deux éléments sont présents en même temps dans de telles occasions.

Voilà qui explique le fait que Socrate ne raille jamais ouvertement ses interlocuteurs, quoi qu'ils disent. Pierre-Yves Testenoire a mis en évidence ce fait textuel : « Socrate est assez éloigné du personnage 'toujours riant, toujours beuvant d'autant à chacun, toujours se guabelant' décrit par Rabelais. Chez Xénophon comme chez Platon, Socrate rit en réalité très peu ».[9] Socrate, nous dit Pierre Destrée, rit sous cape afin de nous indiquer la place du Lecteur Modèle et de la Lectrice Modèle des dialogues platoniciens.[10] J'en conviens. Mais j'ajouterai que Socrate suspend son éclat de rire parce que le passage à l'acte hilare dans sa réalité corporelle, retentissante et ostensible, serait une « jouissance » (χαίρειν) « injuste » (ἄδικον) aux frais de ceux qui se rendent eux-mêmes ridicules – ce qui ne sied point à l'amitié. En l'occurrence, Agathon et les autres symposiastes ont tout fait pour offrir à rire. En ascrivant des qualités à un sujet qui ne saurait les recevoir, ils ont fait preuve d'ignorance et de prétention de savoir. Socrate pourrait s'amuser à leur sujet, en faire le but de ses plaisanteries. C'est comme s'il était sur le point d'éclater, mais s'en empêchait. Au lieu de cela, il se rabaisse lui-même dans une pirouette d'εἰρωνεία. Ah, que je suis bête ! Au lieu de cela, il procède à l'ἔλεγχος. La sienne est une moquerie sans éclat. Une façon différente de sévir.

La possibilité du rire est là. Agathon fait donc un discours virtuellement ridicule. Mais non pas comme un poète comique, qui s'efforcerait de faire rire les spectateurs des travers de ses personnages. Agathon, le poète tragique, compose, par mégarde, une comédie virtuelle – sur lui-même. Agathon prend l'amour trop au sérieux et se prend lui-même au sérieux. Un comédien malgré lui. On entend déjà sourdre la remarque qu'un même poète peut composer tragédie et comédie. Plus généralement, dans bien des dialogues, Socrate se tient à l'orée du rire. Pensons au *Protagoras*, ou au *Théétète*. En tant que lecteurs et lectrices, nous sommes invité/e/s à nous situer dans l'interstice entre ridicule et dérision, là où le rire est possible et, pourtant, retenu. Chaque fois qu'il se confronte à une situation de δοξοσοφία parfaitement comique – une situation que, le plus souvent, il a créée lui-même délibérément –, l'on

---

injuste et le fait qu'il faille s'en abstenir. La violence du rire moqueur et comique se trouve à l'arrière-plan de l'argument de Socrate, ce que Fussi reconnaît par ailleurs, lorsqu'elle évoque la vengeance que le rire pourrait susciter chez un puissant.

9 Comme le remarque Testenoire (2013) 9 s.
10 Destrée (2013).

pourrait s'attendre à ce que Socrate s'esclaffe, mais non : Socrate garde son sérieux. Le *Philèbe* nous ouvre une ligne d'interprétation.

D'abord, la civilité a une valeur morale. Le silène ne se moque pas de ces jeunes parce que son propos n'est pas de prendre du plaisir à leur dépens. Pensons à ses manières érotiques : il ne cesse de faire croire à l'éventualité d'une séduction, mais il se défile à la toute dernière minute, avant de (au lieu de) passer à l'acte sexuel. La relation érotique doit continuer sur le mode de l'excitation d'un désir, de la provocation à un contact, mais sans que le maître aille jusqu'à jouir du corps des élèves. De façon analogue, Socrate s'interdit l'éclat de rire. Son propos n'est pas se délecter des malheurs des autres. Ce genre d'amusement, accompagné de φθόνος serait forcément maligne. Il est l'apanage d'individus aussi insolents que le Parent d'Euripide, dans les *Femmes aux Thesmophories*. L'Agathon d'Aristophane se plaint de cela, précisément : en écoutant les moqueries de cet Athénien hirsute et agressif, le poète entend le blâme du φθόνος (146 s). Dans la situation dialogique, la δοξοσοφία doit être mise en lumière et mise à l'épreuve, certes, mais sans aboutir à la raillerie. Socrate n'est là ni pour jouir de ses interlocuteurs dans l'acte sexuel, ni pour s'en jouer dans l'acte comique. Il est là pour mobiliser leur désir de savoir, leur pulsion philosophique.

Ensuite, Socrate s'abstient de se moquer ouvertement de ces jeunes, parce qu'il souhaite les retrouver. La politesse est une stratégie de sociabilité. Ainsi qu'il le raconte dans l'*Apologie* et comme nous le comprenons dans l'allégorie de la caverne, Socrate n'a de cesse de revenir vers les gens qui sont passibles de bénéficier de son amitié. Il fait retour vers ses interlocuteurs. Agathon, par exemple, se retrouve parmi les hôtes de Callias, dans le *Protagoras*. Le fait même que Platon écrive de nombreux dialogues qui, tous, commencent par une rencontre, des amabilités, du badinage avant d'évoluer dans la réfutation ou dans l'argumentation, exige que Socrate soit cordial, aimable, enjoué. À chaque fois, il faut redémarrer dans une atmosphère favorable à la bonne entente. Ainsi, tout en cultivant l'εἰρωνεία dont il est célèbre, Socrate ne pourrait pas se permettre une fâcheuse réputation de moqueur. Il a tout intérêt à ne pas froisser ses amis, à ne pas les offenser de manière irréversible, à ne pas les faire fuir. Bien au contraire, dans sa bizarrerie, il les attire. Sa mission consiste à se joindre à leurs conversations et à attiser leur souhait de le fréquenter. La situation dialogique exige la courtoisie. C'est pourquoi, tout en se conduisant en grossier personnage, Socrate finit toujours par s'adapter à l'urbanité de ses fréquentations. Εἰρωνεία, c'est sa façon de négocier avec la politesse. En l'occurrence, dans la situation conversationnelle du symposium, l'amitié est cruciale. Cher Agathon, cher Phèdre, cher Alcibiade – le vocatif « ὦ φίλε » revient une dizaine de fois dans le *Banquet*. Nous sommes entre nous, entre amis. L'amitié crée une complicité sociale et intellectuelle, telle que, malgré les manœuvres socratiques, les positions peuvent s'échanger pendant que la dérision est retenue.

2 Chez Diotime

Nous nous en avisons par contraste avec la situation ironique qui va suivre. Tout de suite après la réfutation d'Agathon, le même travail de démystification de l'éloge continue, mais sur un tout autre régistre. Une femme savante, Diotime de Mantinée, fait son apparition en flash-back sur la scène toute masculine de cette soirée. Socrate s'en souvient. Dans un entretien datant d'il y a plusieurs années, Diotime avait déjà fait éclater en pleine lumière l'incongruité d'une attribution de qualités au dieu nommé Désir. Socrate raconte en effet que Diotime l'avait mis à la question. Elle s'était enquise de ce qu'il pensait au sujet d'Éros et avait écouté attentivement ses réponses, qu'elle avait jugées contradictoires. Socrate avait admis qu'Éros, tout en étant un dieu, n'était pas beau et bon, avant de reconnaître que tous les dieux, en tant que tels, sont beaux et bons. Du coup, Diotime avait éclaté de rire. « À ce propos, en riant elle avait dit : 'Mais comment est-ce possible, Socrate, que l'on s'accorde à dire qu'Éros est un grand dieu, chez ceux qui disent qu'il n'est pas dieu du tout ?' » (202c).[11] Ensuite, elle avait expliqué que ce soi-disant dieu n'en était pas un et que, par conséquent, il ne méritait surtout pas l'admiration qu'on lui témoignait. Nous allons revenir sur la nature démonique (et non pas divine) d'Éros, d'après Diotime. Arrêtons-nous un instant à ce rire.

Dans cet échange qui remonte à un temps révolu, Socrate tombe en contradiction avec lui-même, car, si les dieux sont beaux et bons, Éros aussi doit l'être. Affirmer le contraire, c'est se démentir. Or, cette faiblesse logique se révèle systématiquement dans la réfutation que Socrate inflige à ses interlocuteurs. Il leur fait admettre qu'ils disconviennent avec eux-mêmes. C'est précisément ce que reconnaît humblement Agathon. Il croyait savoir ce qu'il ne savait point. Or, devant la δοξοσοφία de Socrate, Diotime ne se retient pas : elle rit avec effusion, la gorge déployée.

Dès que Diotime fait son entrée dans l'horizon du dialogue, son rire résonne haut et fort. A la différence de Socrate, elle s'en donne à cœur joie ! Diotime éclate du rire que Socrate, lui, ne s'autorise pas. Elle est ce que Socrate serait s'il ne se gênait pas, comme s'il ne prenait pas garde de ménager ses amis, comme s'il leur faisait la leçon sur leurs erreurs, dogmatiquement et ouvertement. Diotime pratique l'ἔλεγχος, mais sans recourir au truchement d'εἰρωνεία. Ansi, tandis que lui, en homme malin et

---

[11] Testenoire (2013) 8 : « Aussi γελάω au participe présent ou aoriste est-il, de façon archétypale, apposé à un verbe d'énonciation conjugué. Le tour *[Nom du personnage] γελάσας, [propos au discours direct], ἔφη* (« en riant, un tel dit : . . . ») apparaît pas moins de huit fois chez Platon et la formule *[Nom du personnage] γελάσας εἶπε [propos au discours direct]* figure deux fois dans les dialogues socratiques de Xénophon. Le rire, dans ces formules, n'est qu'un simple circonstant de l'action principale de parler. Mais, fait remarquable chez ces deux auteurs, c'est toujours après un propos de Socrate et en s'adressant à lui – la fréquence de l'apostrophe ὦ Σώκρατες après cette formule, le prouve – que le rire vient moduler la prise de parole d'un personnage. » Voir la même construction : *Phédon* 64a ; 103b ; *Parménide* 136d ; *Charmide* 156a ; *Lysis* 208d ; *Euthydème* 298e ; *Protagoras* 310d ; *République* 451b.

sournois, il se protège du ridicule par l'εἰρωνεία, elle s'en protège d'abord en riant et, ainsi que nous le verrons, par sa verve comique. L'éloge ne sied pas à Éros, quelle idée extravagante ! Et ça, c'est à mourir de rire.

Diotime est marrante. – Rentrons dans le détail de sa stratégie argumentative, qui commence par un éclat de rire et continue sur le registre de l'incongruité.

Socrate raconte aux symposiastes que, avant de rencontrer Diotime, il ne savait pas non plus ce qu'il se piquait de savoir, puisque lui aussi, il avait tendance à magnifier la divinité de l'Amour. À l'époque, il pensait exactement comme Agathon, avoue-t-il. L'incohérence de ses propos avait révélé à Diotime l'incongruence de son illusion comique : se croire plus savant qu'il ne l'était. Δοξοσοφία, comme dans le *Philèbe*. Voilà donc que Socrate se met à la place du jeune homme dont il vient de démolir le discours. David Sedley a attiré l'attention sur Agathon comme un jeune Socrate, un « sous-Socrate ».[12] Ce qui nous importe ici, est qu'il n'y a pas que les places assises qui soient interchangeables, sur les banquettes et les coussins de cette maison. Aujourd'hui, Agathon répond à Socrate comme, il y a bien longtemps, Socrate lui-même a pu répondre à Diotime. L'un et l'autre doxosophiste partagent une expérience commune. Cela crée une connivence entre eux. Agathon se trompe sur Éros et sur lui-même, d'accord. Mais Socrate, maintenant plus âgé, est passé par là.

Platon soigne le montage de son récit. Premier plan sur Agathon. Longue séquence de sa réfutation. Flash-back sur Diotime. Très longue scène qui enchaîne la réfutation de Socrate, une nouvelle généalogie de l'amour et, pour finir, une redescription, paradoxalement normative, de l'expérience érotique athénienne. Si nous lisons en philosophes analytiques pressés d'en venir à ce que devait penser Platon en personne, nous allons sans doute aligner Diotime sur Socrate afin d'atteindre, par leur entremise, l'auteur du *Banquet* lui-même. Voilà donc, dans la bouche fictionnelle de la prêtresse de Mantinée, la théorie platonicienne d'éros ! Mais Platon, le narrateur « cinématographique » de cette soirée, crée une focalisation toute différente : Socrate tient à se placer au même niveau que son ami, Agathon. Tout contre lui, sur la même banquette. Tout près de lui, dans la même δοξοσοφία juvénile. C'est cette affinité, unique dans le corpus des dialogues, qui devrait nous faire réfléchir.

Cette proximité entre les deux hommes doit nous aider à apprécier la différence entre Socrate, l'Athénien festoyant chez Agathon, et Diotime, la femme étrangère. Il convient de placer Socrate *versus* Diotime. Dans sa lecture du *Banquet*, Christian Keime distingue leur façons respectives de subir la réfutation.[13] Attentif aux multiples stratégies de communication mises en œuvre dans les dialogues platoniciens, Keime se concentre sur la polyphonie et sur l'énonciation. Son travail novateur rejoint ainsi l'approche que je tâche de mener à bien dans mes propres réflexions sur la situation philosophique. En l'occurrence, j'argumente que le décalage entre Dio-

---

12 Sedley (2006). Voir aussi Wersinger (2012).
13 Keime (2014).

time et Socrate tient à la différence de genre et se manifeste, tout d'abord, dans son hilarité. Puisqu'il est impératif pour Socrate de retenir le rire malgré le ridicule de ses amis, Diotime, par le simple fait de s'esclaffer, dit toute son étrangeté. Tandis que Socrate dissimule la satisfaction maligne qu'il éprouve devant quelqu'un qui donne sujet qu'on se moque de lui, Diotime ne se gêne pas, mais vraiment pas du tout. Socrate ne saurait rire de ses amis que dans sa barbe, Diotime n'hésite pas à rire au nez de Socrate, et de tout cœur. Tandis que Socrate confond Agathon, mais sans le railler et, de surcroît, en se mettant dans sa peau par un geste de sympathie épistémique, on dirait que les femmes qui vous aident à énoncer vos discours sont sans pitié. Socrate donne une belle preuve d'amitié entre des hommes au banquet ; Diotime, une femme hors-norme, donne une bonne leçon. Une complicité ironique dans un réseau d'amis ; la leçon magistrale d'une étrangère. Pas de copinage, en somme, avec une sophiste de Mantinée !

Un éclat de rire est un acte sémiotique inarticulé, énoncé dans le langage du corps.[14] Mais il ne s'agit pas d'une « énonciation » ponctuelle. Le rire de Diotime met en route un long discours sur Éros, dont le contenu relève de l'incongruité depuis la récriture comique de la généalogie d'Éros, jusqu'à une théorie normative de la pédérastie qui est structurée par le paradoxe.

3 Une dissonance genrée

Pour commencer, il convient de reposer la question : pourquoi Diotime, pourquoi une femme ? On a pu affirmer, et moi-même j'ai argumenté en ce sens, qu'il fallait une femme, un « je » féminin, pour dire la natalité.[15] Dès que l'amour devient une affaire d'immortalité et de génération, et non pas de possession, il serait culturellement « naturel » que l'on fasse parler une femme – comme si l'énonciatrice colorait au féminin ses propres énoncés. À qui viendrait-il à l'esprit de mettre en branle une métaphore maternelle, sinon à une femme ? Mais j'aimerais cibler de manière plus exigeante la pertinence du genre de la locutrice par rapport au contenu sémantique de ses propos. Je souhaite me concentrer sur la situation dialogique.

Socrate, comme toujours, et encore davantage chez le bel Agathon, s'évertue à s'effacer, à se minimiser, à se mettre à l'écart. Ravi de son triomphe, le beau poète chante l'amour. Mais les autres aussi encensent Éros. Il se mettent en compétition à

---

14 Pour cette lecture du rire comme une « énonciation » non verbale, je prends appui sur le travail de Phillip Glenn (2003), une approche appelée « Conversation Analysis ». Cette linguistique du rire met en évidence l'interaction sociale et les effets du rire dans une conversation, notamment l'affiliation et le clivage (rire avec ; rire de). La séquentialité aussi devient un phénomène tout à fait important.
15 Sissa (2000) 69–106.

qui en fera l'éloge le plus élogieux. Ce qui montre leur aveuglement. Personne, aux yeux de Socrate, ne tâche de dire vrai. Personne ne voit la nature indigente du désir. Ainsi, à cette heure tardive, lorsque tant de parole encomiastique a coulé entre les buveurs, il faut que Socrate fasse un grand écart, pour ainsi dire. Car maintenant il lui faudrait réfuter chacun des symposiastes qui ont tissé les louanges d'Éros l'un après l'autre et qu'il a laissé parler, sans jamais intervenir, sinon sur le malheureux Agathon, le plus inconditionnel et le plus débridé des panégyristes. Au lieu de revenir à retardement sur les plaidoyers de chacun d'entre eux, Socrate ressuscite une conversation ancienne, qu'il a eue ailleurs, avec une femme savante. Retour en arrière : Socrate avec Diotime.

Socrate fait donc parler Diotime, laquelle désarçonne tous ces hommes en même temps. Si elle a raison, ils ont tous tort. Si l'amour est une affaire d'accouchement – et non pas de possession –, *tous* les discours de cette soirée ont raté leur cible. Engendrer, expulser de l'utérus, c'est le contraire de prendre, de posséder et de garder pour soi. La présence virtuelle de Diotime, un fantasme du passé, permet donc à Socrate de cacher son jeu : il n'a pas à chercher misère à chacun de ses amis ici et maintenant. L'étrangère s'en charge. La « délicate courtoisie » de cette invention a été vue depuis longtemps, notamment par un grand lecteur de Platon, Francis Cornford :[16]

> Socrates then opens with a conversational criticism of Agathon. By a masterstroke of delicate courtesy, he avoids making his host look foolish. He pretends that he himself had spoken of Eros in similar terms to Diotima, a wise priestess of Mantinea, and he represents the criticism as administered by Diotima to himself. This is a sufficient reason for the invention of Diotima. Socrates, moreover, can put forward the whole doctrine not as his own, but as hers, and so escape professing to know more about Eros than his fellow-guests.

Platon crée une mise en abîme. Après avoir réfuté Agathon, le champion de l'éloge irréfléchi, Socrate avoue avoir partagé le sort de celui-ci. Socrate raconte que, naguère, cette femme savante l'avait mis lui, Socrate, dans l'embarras, en le plaçant exactement dans la position d'Agathon. Ce récit rétrospectif, avons-nous dit, permet à Socrate de faire cause commune avec lui. Mais Diotime produit un effet dont l'ampleur dépasse la courtoisie. La prêtresse n'est pas une simple figure « extra », le masque d'un Socrate soucieux de ne pas froisser le maître de maison et ses invités. Car, en répercutant les propos de Diotime à son endroit, Socrate met en échec tous les symposiastes pour la simple raison qu'ils ont cru pouvoir louer l'amour. En citant Diotime, sans s'en démarquer, il énonce ses énoncés. Hier, il se trompait comme le jeune poète ; aujourd'hui, il a appris la leçon de la sophiste. Pire encore, Diotime place Socrate dans la situation de toutes les victimes de l'ἔλεγχος. Au-delà du discours sur l'amour, elle sait manier le redoutable traitement cathartique et maïeutique, que Socrate inflige à ses patients – la soi-disant « méthode socratique ». Diotime est le seul personnage platonicien qui sache battre Socrate à son propre

---

[16] Cornford (1950) 71.

jeu – démolir vos opinions contradictoires, sous prétexte de vous aider à les énoncer. Elle est un super-Socrate, en plus méchant. Platon construit donc un personnage aux virtualités inquiétantes, qui montre ce que Socrate pourrait faire s'il n'était pas profondément impliqué dans le monde de ses amis. Diotime est une figure deux fois étrangère – en tant que femme et en tant que non-Athénienne. Tandis qu'elle parle, le petit cercle se referme.

C'est déjà énorme, et nous pourrions en rester là. Mais nous devrions aller plus loin.

Socrate fait parler Diotime, mais, pour commencer, il la fait rire aux éclats. Cet acte de langage inarticulé, et pourtant significatif, enclenche le très long discours que l'étrangère va tenir au sujet d'Éros. Ce λόγος, je vais argumenter, renforce la perception d'une sociabilité érotique masculine qui rapproche Socrate de ses amis, tout en amplifiant la distance de la locutrice. La prêtresse, en effet, s'adresse à Socrate comme s'il était fasciné par les beaux garçons exactement comme les Athéniens qu'il fréquente (211d). Ils sont tous du même bord. L'énonciation par une voix féminine rieuse est donc solidaire du contenu « gynécologique » du discours, certes, mais aussi du ton, d'abord comique et ensuite paradoxal, d'un λόγος inouï. Puisqu'ils sont tous également attirés par les beaux corps, qu'il y aillent ! Que ce rire retentissant nous accompagne dans le vif d'un λόγος qui est genré et dissonant.

Voici la mise en place de la métaphore maternelle (208e–209a) :

Οἱ μὲν οὖν ἐγκύμονες, ἔφη, κατὰ σώματα ὄντες πρὸς τὰς γυναῖκας μᾶλλον τρέπονται καὶ ταύτῃ ἐρωτικοί εἰσι, διὰ παιδογονίας ἀθανασίαν καὶ μνήμην καὶ εὐδαιμονίαν, ὡς οἴονται, αὑτοῖς "εἰς τὸν ἔπειτα χρόνον πάντα ποριζόμενοι·" οἱ δὲ κατὰ τὴν ψυχήν – εἰσὶ γὰρ οὖν, ἔφη, οἳ ἐν ταῖς ψυχαῖς κυοῦσιν ἔτι μᾶλλον ἢ ἐν τοῖς σώμασιν, ἃ ψυχῇ προσήκει καὶ κυῆσαι καὶ τεκεῖν· τί οὖν προσήκει; φρόνησίν τε καὶ τὴν ἄλλην ἀρετήν· ὧν δή εἰσι καὶ οἱ ποιηταὶ πάντες γεννήτορες καὶ τῶν δημιουργῶν ὅσοι λέγονται εὑρετικοὶ εἶναι· πολὺ δὲ μεγίστη, ἔφη, καὶ καλλίστη τῆς φρονήσεως ἡ περὶ τὰς τῶν πόλεών τε καὶ οἰκήσεων διακοσμήσεις, ᾗ δὴ ὄνομά ἐστι σωφροσύνη τε καὶ δικαιοσύνη· τούτων αὖ ὅταν τις ἐκ νέου ἐγκύμων ᾖ τὴν ψυχὴν θεῖος ὤν, καὶ ἡκούσης τῆς ἡλικίας τίκτειν τε καὶ γεννᾶν ἤδη ἐπιθυμῇ, ζητεῖ δή, οἶμαι, καὶ οὗτος περιιὼν τὸ καλὸν ἐν ᾧ ἂν γεννήσειεν· ἐν τῷ γὰρ αἰσχρῷ οὐδέποτε γεννήσει. τά τε οὖν σώματα τὰ καλὰ μᾶλλον ἢ τὰ αἰσχρὰ ἀσπάζεται ἅτε κυῶν, καὶ ἐὰν ἐντύχῃ ψυχῇ καλῇ καὶ γενναίᾳ καὶ εὐφυεῖ, πάνυ δὴ ἀσπάζεται τὸ συναμφότερον, καὶ πρὸς τοῦτον τὸν ἄνθρωπον εὐθὺς εὐπορεῖ λόγων περὶ ἀρετῆς.

Or, ceux qui sont enceintes dans le corps se tournent plutôt vers les femmes, et sont amoureux de cette manière : en ayant des enfants, ils acquièrent immortalité, souvenir et bonheur, dont ils pensent que c'est « pour toujours ». Mais la grossesse de l'âme – car il y a des hommes, dit-elle, qui, dans leur âme plus encore que dans leur corps, conçoivent les choses qu'il est propre à l'âme de concevoir et de faire naître (et qu'est qui lui est propre ? La raison pratique, et la vertu en général) ; et les générateurs sont tous les poètes et les artisans que l'on appelle « inventeurs ». Or, la partie de loin la plus grande et la plus belle de la raison pratique est celle qui concerne l'ordonnance des cités et des maisons ; elle s'appelle modération et justice. Ainsi, lorsque l'âme d'un homme est si divine qu'elle en est enceinte dès sa jeunesse et que, lorsqu'il atteint l'âge approprié, il désire immédiatement donner naissance et engendrer, il va lui aussi, j'imagine, à la recherche du beau dans lequel il peut engendrer, car il n'engendrera jamais rien dans ce qui est laid. Ce sont donc les beaux corps, et non pas les laids, qu'il aime pendant sa grossesse, et s'il a aussi la chance de rencontrer une âme qui soit belle et noble et d'un bon naturel, il chérit volontiers les deux combinés ensemble ; et, en s'adressant à une telle personne, il parvient rapidement à prospérer dans les discours sur la vertu.

Si l'amour est une affaire d'accouchement – et non pas de possession –, *tous* les discours de cette soirée ont raté leur cible.[17] Ainsi que Miglena Nikolchina l'a montré dans le détail, Diotime décrit tous les aspects de l'expérience érotique et de la biographie d'Ἔρως dans l'idiome de la génération au féminin.[18] C'est sa mère, Penia, qui souhaite se faire faire un enfant par Poros ; c'est le désir d'immortalité qui cause la pulsion de mettre au monde des discours, pour des hommes qui sont déjà enceints dans l'âme ; c'est ce même désir qui pousse ces hommes à rechercher des partenaires qui soient beaux, puisqu'ils ne peuvent accoucher que dans la beauté ; Beauté agit comme une déesse accoucheuse ; la relation amoureuse produit une progéniture (poèmes, vertus, sagesse, lois etc.) que les « parents » nourrissent ensemble. Rien, dans ce discours, n'échappe à la métaphore maternelle. En changeant de langage, Diotime transforme radicalement la vision d'Éros. Elle remplace la « dichotomie » entre amant et bienaimé par la coopération d'un couple uni, en vue de la procréation. En conclusion, « Eros in Diotima's account is displaced by *tokos*. It is as *tokos* that Eros effects the transition from a discourse of desire to a discourse of knowledge ».[19]

J'ajouterai deux considérations. La première est que la métaphorisation de l'amour dans le langage de la naissance – « concevoir », « être enceint », « enfanter » – oriente l'activité amoureuse de l'intérieur du corps féminin dans une direction contraire par rapport à celle qu'exprime le vocabulaire de « prendre », « posséder » et de « garder pour soi ». Cette réorientation spatiale est solidaire de la perspective radicalement nouvelle qu'introduit Diotime : éros devient un instrument, indispensable à la création d'objets, tels que poèmes, pensées ou lois qui viennent enrichir l'univers moral, politique et culturel.[20] Éros est généreux, et non pas égoïste. Il est un moyen, et non pas une fin en soi. La projection d'une métaphore gynécologique sur l'amour entre mâles modifie l'érotique masculine dont il a été question dans les

---

17 Sur la distance entre Diotime et les symposiastes voir Pender (1992) ; Hawthorne (1994) 89.
18 Nikolchina (1993) 247 s. Voir aussi Halperin (1990) ; Hobbs (2006) ; DuBois (1994). Je partage l'approche de Wersinger (2012), qui montre la polyphonie du dispositif d'énonciation dans le *Banquet*, en dégageant la spécificité de la voix de Diotime. Wersinger ramène la métaphore maternelle au modèle du corps féminin, contre l'assimilation (par David Halperin) de l'accouchement et de l'éjaculation, ce qui est bienvenu (paragraphes 32 et 39), puisque la détresse et la souffrance d'une femme en couche n'a rien à voir avec la jouissance éjaculatoire. Je reviens sur ce point plus loin.
19 Nikolchina (1993) 248.
20 Neumann (1965) 47 souligne l'instrumentalité de l'amour : « Diotima's eros does not share the Aristophanic yearning for an ultimate union with its object, since that object is attractive solely as a medium in which the lover may give birth. Originally, as it were, there is a pregnancy within the lover and intercourse with the beloved is merely a means to give birth to child. Basically sophistical, this eros has little of the grandeur leading Aristophanes' love to sacrifice everything for a kind of mystical union with its beloved. »

discours précédents. L'amour n'est pas une passion entre deux amants qui se prennent dans les bras en rêvant de fusionner en un corps unique, au point d'en oublier tout le reste. L'amour n'est ni une motivation à l'excellence qui serait limitée aux couples, ni une gratification bien méritée, ni une force de liaison cosmique, ni le désir insatiable pour un objet qui manque. L'amour n'est pas non plus ce que Diotime admet tout au début de son discours, notamment « la possession du bien pour toujours » (206a). Non, tout à coup, l'amour cesse de se définir en termes d'intimité, d'exception, d'avoir, de recevoir, de posséder et de garder pour soi. Voici, tout à coup, un Éros inouï : l'amour est la quête d'un partenaire dont la beauté va agir en tant que sage-femme, afin de faire accoucher des hommes, en urgence, d' « enfants » discursifs. Ces enfants vont vivre dans la cité pour le bien de tous, tels les poèmes homériques ou les lois de Lycurgue. Beauté elle-même est la condition de possibilité pour la forme la plus haute de génération – celle de la véritable excellence.[21] Cette génération est possible. La grossesse signifie que nous pouvons faire un monde.

La seconde considération est une invitation à prendre la mesure de ce paradoxe. L'amour entre deux individus d'âge différent, mais qui partagent le même genre masculin, se trouve réécrit comme l'expérience d'un corps féminin et maternel, un corps qui a déjà été fécondé (on ne sait comment) et qui est désormais en mal d'enfants.[22] La grossesse et l'accouchement sont des phénomènes *gynécologiques*, irréductibles au modèle phallique de l'anatomophysiologie féminine.[23] Certes, le *Corpus Hippocratique* décrit l'appareil génital féminin par analogie avec l'appareil génital masculin, pour autant qu'il produit un fluide séminal dont l'émission dans le coït est fort agréable.[24] Mais la correspondance des parties anatomiques et de leur fonctions s'arrête là. La capacité d'accueillir la semence par la voie génitale, de contenir un embryon, de protéger la croissance d'un fœtus et d'enfanter est tout

---

[21] Cf. White (1989) ; White (2004) 372–374 ; White (2008).
[22] Pierce (1994) a problématisé la spécificité homosexuelle de l'éros qui conduit à la philosophie. À l'encontre du bannissement (devenu impératif dans les études sur la sexualité grecque et romaine) des mots « homosexualité » et « hétérosexualité », elle soutient que le fait de partager le même genre serait un facteur d'expérience tout à fait significatif, pour les amoureux dont parle Diotime, donc pour les effets épistémiques d'éros : « Homoeroticism provides the foundation for acquaintance with Beauty because the immediacy in homosexual encounters is akin to the way in which Beauty is known. Still, as Shapiro notes, it might be objected that the only genuine acquaintance or genuine knowledge is of the Forms, i.e., that knowledge of erotic properties is not really knowledge. We might then, she suggests, characterize homoeroticism as a kind of 'psychological preparation' for genuine knowledge by acquaintance that will make possible the recollection of Beauty. It is clear that Plato intends that sexuality be the starting point for the ascent, and heterosexuality cannot provide the appropriate preparation because heterosexual 'knowledge' of erotic properties must always be inferential » (p. 38). Je ne suis pas cette argumentation, mais je partage la ligne interprétative de Pierce, qui vise à rétablir le caractère physique de l'éros platonicien. Selon Hughes Dominik (2013) 560 l'aspect « genre » n'est pas pertinent.
[23] Contra Lear (2015), qui nie le modèle féminin de la maternité.
[24] Hippocrate, *Génération* 4 ; 7.

à fait spécifique aux femmes.²⁵ Davantage, le travail de l'enfantement est notoirement laborieux, pénible, interminable et même insupportable – et non pas voluptueux.²⁶ Or, c'est précisément l'aspect ardu et douloureux de la maternité que Socrate met en avant, lorsqu'il transpose l'enfantement – et non pas la filiation, tout court sur l'activité intellectuelle. Pour mettre son bébé au monde, une femme en couche souffre mille maux et, surtout, éprouve le besoin d'être aidée par autrui. Le ventre commence à se dilater, mais ne parvient pas tout seul à s'ouvrir comme il faut, d'où les douleurs lancinantes, la détresse, l'impuissance.²⁷ Il lui faut absolument l'assistance d'une sage-femme, humaine ou divine. L'indispensable secours d'une accou-

---

25 Contra Halperin (1990) 113–115, qui fait grand cas de l'analogie anatomo-physiologique entre femmes et hommes, ce qui créerait une contamination entre accouchement et éjaculation. Platon introduirait une femme, pour en effacer la présence. Pour une critique de la théorie des deux semences, dans le travail de Thomas Laqueur, je me permets de renvoyer à Sissa (1992) 80–86.
26 Hippocrate, *Nature de l'enfant* 7 : « Le début des douleurs de l'accouchement chez la femme est le suivant : le sang est remué dans la femme et fortement réchauffé par le mouvement violent du fœtus. Lorsqu'il est remué, le fœtus est d'abord expulsé et, avec lui, un liquide épais et sanguin qui lui sert de chemin comme l'eau sur une table. Puis après cela, la purification lochiale se produit sur l'ensemble » (c'est moi qui traduis). Dans le même chapitre, le médecin recommande d'aider la jeune mère à expulser les lochies immédiatement, ou elle risque de mourir. Sur la naissance, Demand (1994). Sur les difficultés et les aléas de l'accouchement, dans la tradition médicale tardive, Calà (2016). Sur l'expérience fondamentalement douloureuse de l'accouchement, et sur la métaphorisation de la douleur par cette expérience genrée, voir Loraux (1981) ; Holmes (2007).
27 J'ai argumenté en ce sens dans Sissa (1986) ; Sissa (1990) ; Sissa (2000). Wersinger (2012) compare aussi la métaphore maternelle entre le *Banquet* et le *Théétète*, mais en suivant une ligne interprétative différente. En s'appuyant sur l'expression « accoucher dans le beau » (ἐν τῷ καλῷ), dont elle soutient l'ambiguïté, puisque cela peut signifier soit « dans le beau » entendu au neutre, soit « dans le beau » pris au masculin, comme signifiant « le beau garçon » en position d'éromène, elle en vient à conclure que Diotime se place face à Socrate comme un éraste face à un éromène – un bienaimé qui, de surcroît, fait accoucher. Dans le *Théétète*, en revanche, « il convient de noter que Socrate n'y est plus un 'éromène-accoucheur' mais un *maieutikos*, expert en accouchements (149a4) ... Bien au contraire, dans le *Banquet*, la figure de l'accoucheur est essentiellement passive. Toute la part active se trouve dans celui qui est enceint : il retient ou non son fruit (*kuèma*, 206d7) ; de plus, il est capable de produire lui-même le diagnostic de son état, contrairement à ce qui se passe dans le *Théétète* où la faculté de diagnostiquer est entièrement médiatisée (148e6 s.). Comment interpréter de tels changements et substitutions de valeur ? » (paragraphe 51). La réponse est que, dans le dispositif d'énonciation du *Banquet*, Diotime viendrait jouer le rôle de l'énonciatrice de « beaux discours », ce qui expliquerait sa présence. Car en amont des récits emboîtés de la soirée, elle se charge de théoriser l'acte même de parler. Elle dirait en effet que la grossesse et le travail de l'enfantement seraient plus importants que le bébé (paragraphe 52). J'ai quelques objections. Socrate ne devient un « éromène » que pour Alcibiade. Diotime encourage les jeunes à aller vers des garçons. Il paraît difficile qu'elle les aiguille ainsi vers Socrate lui-même, son interlocuteur. C'est la beauté du garçon (Καλλονή), qui agit en sage-femme, dans le *Banquet*, et non pas le garçon lui-même. La qualité du produit (donc de l'énoncé), pour finir, me paraît revêtir une importance primordiale dans le discours de Diotime.

cheuse est le point de contact entre la corvée de faire naître un enfant et le tourment d'exprimer ses pensées.

4 Un logos genré : la sage-femme

Un dialogue tout entier, le *Théétète*, nous aide à comprendre le sens de la métaphore maternelle. Un jeune mathématicien se trouve mis à la question par un Socrate qui se présente comme étant une « sage-femme ». C'est Socrate lui-même qui opère sur le jeune homme, mais en tant que fils d'une accoucheuse, qui saurait faire accoucher la psyché de Théétète de ses opinions sur ἐπιστήμη. La tâche d'une sage-femme au masculin, explique-t-il, est tout d'abord d'« éveiller les douleurs » (ἐγείρειν τε τὰς ὠδῖνας) ou de les atténuer ; ensuite, de juger si un bébé est viable ou pas.[28] En l'occurrence, Socrate aide l'âme du jeune homme à mettre bas des opinions qui se révèlent être fausses et confuses. Ce sont des « œufs de vent », à jeter sur le champ. Tout cet effort, ce labeur, cette peine – pour rien du tout. La maïeutique, c'est l'ἔλεγχος le plus ironique qui soit.

Arrêtons-nous sur Socrate en sage-femme. Tout d'abord, la grossesse aboutit à un travail qui se prolonge dans le temps. Théétète expulse trois définitions de ἐπιστήμη, mais c'est seulement à la fin de sa longue réfutation que Socrate émet son verdict : ces bébés, ce sont des « œufs de vent » (ἀνεμιαῖα). Il faut les jeter (210b). La délivrance aura été interminable parce qu'elle demande un grand nombre de questions. Et cela, parce que le contenu de l'âme est prêt à sortir, mais n'y parvient pas tout seul. Théétète a beau ressentir l'inquiétude qui le tourmente, il est néanmoins incapable d'avancer. C'est justement cet état d'aporie que Socrate diagnostique comme étant une « grossesse » (148e–149a). Le corps de la femme, et l'âme masculine qui lui ressemble, résistent à s'ouvrir et à laisser passer l'enfant qui, pourtant, exerce une pression douloureuse sur les tissus. Le résultat de cette situation est le besoin

---

[28] Platon, *Théétète* 149c–d : « De plus, les sages-femmes, au moyen de médicaments et d'incantations, sont capables de réveiller les douleurs du travail et, si elles le souhaitent, de les rendre plus douces, et de faire naître ceux qui ont des difficultés à porter; et elles provoquent des fausses couches si elles les jugent souhaitables » (καὶ μὴν καὶ διδοῦσαί γε αἱ μαῖαι φαρμάκια καὶ ἐπάδουσαι δύνανται ἐγείρειν τε τὰς ὠδῖνας καὶ μαλθακωτέρας, ἂν βούλωνται, ποιεῖν, καὶ τίκτειν τε δὴ τὰς δυστοκούσας, καὶ ἐὰν νέον ὂν δόξῃ ἀμβλίσκειν, ἀμβλίσκουσιν;) ; 150b–d : « Tout ce qui est vrai de leur art de sage-femme l'est aussi du mien, mais le mien diffère du leur en ce qu'il fait accoucher des hommes, et non des femmes, et en ce qu'il surveille leur âme dans le travail, et non leur corps. Mais ce qu'il y a de plus important dans mon art, c'est qu'il peut tester de toutes les manières possibles si l'intelligence du jeune homme produit une simple image, une imposture, ou une progéniture viable et vraie » (τῇ δέ γ' ἐμῇ τέχνῃ τῆς μαιεύσεως τὰ μὲν ἄλλα ὑπάρχει ὅσα ἐκείναις, διαφέρει δὲ τῷ τε ἄνδρας ἀλλὰ μὴ γυναῖκας μαιεύεσθαι καὶ τῷ τὰς ψυχὰς αὐτῶν τικτούσας ἐπισκοπεῖν ἀλλὰ μὴ τὰ σώματα. μέγιστον δὲ τοῦτ' ἔνι τῇ ἡμετέρᾳ τέχνῃ, βασανίζειν δυνατὸν εἶναι παντὶ τρόπῳ, πότερον εἴδωλον καὶ ψεῦδος ἀποτίκτει τοῦ νέου ἡ διάνοια ἢ γόνιμόν τε καὶ ἀληθές).

d'assistance. Il est impératif qu'une auxiliaire médicale vienne prêter secours à la parturiente pour débloquer l'impasse, en suscitant et en maîtrisant les douleurs. Ensuite, la sage-femme des âmes « examine » (βασανίζειν) le nouveau-né et décide s'il est viable ou non, s'il mérite de vivre ou d'être mis au rebut (150a–c). Une sage-femme vous met à la torture et vous débarrasse de vos œufs clairs, sans pitié. Les bébés de Théétète, encore une fois, ne sont pas dignes de survivre.

Le discours de Diotime aussi se focalise sur l'urgence de trouver une obstétricienne. Les hommes enceints éprouvent le besoin de se faire aider par une accoucheuse. En l'occurrence, il s'agit de Beauté (Καλλονή), dans le rôle d'Ilithye (Εἰλείθυια), la déesse qui, depuis la poésie archaïque préside aux accouchements (206b–e). C'est pourquoi ils recherchent de beaux garçons :

> Μοῖρα οὖν καὶ Εἰλείθυια ἡ Καλλονή ἐστι τῇ γενέσει. διὰ ταῦτα ὅταν μὲν καλῷ προσπελάζῃ τὸ κυοῦν, ἵλεών τε γίγνεται καὶ εὐφραινόμενον διαχεῖται καὶ τίκτει τε καὶ γεννᾷ· ὅταν δὲ αἰσχρῷ, σκυθρωπόν τε καὶ λυπούμενον συσπειρᾶται καὶ ἀποτρέπεται καὶ ἀνείλλεται καὶ οὐ γεννᾷ, ἀλλὰ ἴσχον τὸ κύημα χαλεπῶς φέρει. ὅθεν δὴ τῷ κυοῦντί τε καὶ ἤδη σπαργῶντι πολλὴ ἡ πτοίησις γέγονε περὶ τὸ καλὸν διὰ τὸ μεγάλης ὠδῖνος ἀπολύειν τὸν ἔχοντα.

> C'est ainsi que Beauté préside à la naissance en tant que Destinée et Ilithye ; et c'est pourquoi, lorsque celui qui est enceint s'approche du beau, il devient non seulement gracieux mais exalté, il engendre et met au monde ; mais lorsqu'il rencontre la laideur, il se recroqueville dans une consternation maussade : retiré et réprimé, il ne met pas au monde, mais en gardant le fœtus se porte mal. C'est pourquoi, lorsqu'une personne est grosse et mûre à souhait, elle a envie de ce qui est beau, car celui qui possède la beauté peut la soulager de sa grande douleur.

Faute de trouver une sage-femme, l'homme enceint est destiné à aller mal (χαλεπῶς φέρει). Car il lui faut se débarrasser de son fardeau. Éros, c'est cela. « Car tu as tort, Socrate, de supposer que l'amour est amour du beau. Qu'est-ce que c'est alors ? Il s'agit d'engendrer et d'engendrer dans le beau. Ainsi soit-il !, dis-je » (ἔστι γάρ, ὦ Σώκρατες, ἔφη, οὐ τοῦ καλοῦ ὁ ἔρως, ὡς σὺ οἴει. Ἀλλὰ τί μήν; Τῆς γεννήσεως καὶ τοῦ τόκου ἐν τῷ καλῷ. Εἶεν, ἦν δ' ἐγώ, 207e). – Que les hommes soient en mal d'enfant, en somme, c'est une surprise.[29] Théétète croyait être un brillant mathématicien et un soldat valeureux, et voilà que son âme est une femme en couches. Il apprend son état avec stupeur. Diotime instruit Socrate sur l'amour des garçons, et voilà que la masculinité redoublée d'un couple d'hommes devient une gésine à traiter en toute urgence. La masculinité hétérosexuelle d'un père de famille, aussi. Rien ne saurait être plus ostensiblement non-masculin que le travail de la parturition. Rien ne saurait être plus hétéronormatif qu'une métaphorisation *obstétricale* de l'amour.

Depuis Homère, les Grecs connaissent bien les douleurs lancinantes de l'enfantement. Dans l'*Hymne à Apollon*, Léto est « percée » (πέπαρτο), neuf jours et neuf nuits, par des « douleurs désespérées » (ἀέλπτοις ὠδίνεσσι). Les plus grandes déesses,

---

29 Wersinger (2012) 45 et 52 reconnaît à juste titre l'aspect « choquant », « paradoxal » et « subversif » de ce discours qui suscite l'« étonnement » de Socrate.

Dioné, Rhéa, Ichnée, Thémis, Amphitrite l'accompagnent. Mais tant qu'Ilithye, « déesse des douleurs de l'accouchement » (μογοστόκος Εἰλείθυια), ne vient pas à son aide, le travail n'avance pas. « Dès qu'Ilithye, la déesse des douleurs de l'enfantement (μογοστόκος Εἰλείθυια), eut posé le pied sur Délos, l'enfantement la saisit (Léto), et elle eut une forte envie d'enfanter (δὴ τότε τὴν τόκος εἷλε, μενοίνησεν δὲ τεκέσθαι) ; elle jeta ses bras autour d'un palmier et s'agenouilla sur la douce prairie, tandis que la terre riait de joie sous elle. Puis l'enfant bondit (θρώσκω) vers la lumière, et toutes les déesses poussèrent un cri » (91–119). Dans l'*Iliade*, ces douleurs aiguës deviennent le paradigme de la souffrance d'Agamemnon blessé, et dont la blessure s'est refermée.[30]

Depuis le *Corpus Hippocratique*, l'on connaît bien l'urgence de pousser le bébé de toutes ses forces hors d'un ventre qui, tout en se contractant, mets des heures à se dilater. Surtout, il est impossible de parvenir à donner naissance, sans l'aide d'autrui. Il faut gérer les douleurs et ensuite s'inquiéter de faire s'écouler les lochies.[31] Il y a, par conséquent, une incongruité indélogeable dans le fait de transporter, pour ainsi dire, cette signification qui est « propre » au corps maternel à une toute autre signification, celle d'un désir d'immortalité, « qui ne lui convient qu'en vertu d'une comparaison qui est dans l'esprit ».[32] Dans l'esprit de Diotime, le « bébé » se fraie un chemin à la fois chez les hommes qui vont fonder une famille, en épousant des femmes qui, elles, se chargent d'enfanter ; et chez ceux qui préfèrent discuter avec des beaux garçons, ce qui les « transforme » en femmes en couches. Elle évoque ainsi une grossesse masculine, qui est deux fois absurde. Cette grossesse ne saurait être banalisée, sous prétexte que, dans la tradition poétique, Zeus aurait enfanté Athéna par sa tête et Dionysos par sa cuisse.[33] La cuisse ou la tête de Zeus sont des adaptations surnaturelles

---

30 11,127–172. Sur ce passage, voir Loraux (1981) ; Holmes (2007).
31 Hippocrate, *Nature de l'enfant*, 7. Sur la difficulté d'accoucher dans la médecine plus tardive, on verra Aétios d'Amida 16,12–15.
32 Je reprends ici le beau français de César Chesneau Du Marsais, *Œuvres*, 7 vol. in-8, Paris, 1797.
33 Hésiode, *Théogonie* 885–900 (Athéna) : « Zeus, roi des dieux, prit pour première épouse Metis, celle qui, parmi les dieux et les mortels, en sait le plus. Mais alors qu'elle allait donner naissance à la déesse Athéna, aux yeux brillants, il trompa son esprit par des ruses et par des paroles trompeuses et il la mit dans son ventre (ἐσκάτθετο νηδύν), par les conseils de la Terre et du Ciel étoilé: car c'est ainsi qu'ils lui avaient prophétisé, de peur qu'un autre des dieux éternellement vivants ne détienne l'honneur royal à la place de Zeus. Car il était prévu que des enfants extrêmement intelligents naissent d'elle : elle donnerait d'abord naissance à une jeune fille, Tritogéneia aux yeux brillants, possédant une force égale aux conseils et à la sagesse de son père, puis à un fils, roi des dieux et des hommes, possédant un cœur très violent. Mais avant que cela n'arrive, Zeus la mit dans son ventre (ἐσκάτθετο νηδύν), afin que la déesse le conseille sur le bien et le mal » ; ibid. 924 : « Lui-même, il engendra de la tête la déesse Athéna aux yeux bleu-vert » (αὐτὸς δ' ἐκ κεφαλῆς γλαυκῶπιδα γείνατ' Ἀθήνην). Euripide, *Bacchantes* 525–530 (Dionysos) : « Viens, Dithyrambe, dans mon ventre masculin. Je te ferai apparaître, Bacchus, aux Thébains pour qu'ils t'appellent ainsi ! » (Ἴθι, Διθύραμβ', ἐμὰν ἄρσενα τάνδε βᾶθι νηδύν: ἀναφαίνω σε τόδ', ὦ Βάκχιε, Θήβαις ὀνομάζειν). Le « ventre masculin » est la cuisse.

du corps masculin à la capacité de porter aisément un enfant. Diotime, au contraire, attribue la grossesse et, ce qui est plus étonnant, la parturition assistée aux hommes tels qu'ils sont. C'est comme s'il fallait imaginer qu'ils doivent relever le défi du *travail* de l'accouchement – grâce à cette sage-femme divine qu'est Beauté.

À première vue, j'aimerais insister encore davantage, ce langage métaphorique s'appuie sur une analogie : le corps est à l'âme, comme le féminin est au masculin. Mais cette mise en rapport vient oblitérer une profonde distance, culturellement codée. C'est, comme le dirait Paul Ricoeur, une « métaphore vive ».[34] Ensuite, si l'on suit le texte pas à pas, l'on s'avise que, d'une part, les mâles qui épousent les femmes pour faire des enfants en chair et en os sont *eux-mêmes* « enceints » (ἐγκύμονες) et, de surcroît, enceints « dans le corps » (κατὰ σώματα, 208e). Voilà une image qui trouble les genres et les préférences sexuelles : les pères de famille athéniens, dûment soucieux de progéniture, seraient enceints « dans le corps » et, en même temps, copuleraient avec des femmes. Par conséquent, ou bien, tout en étant féminisés par leur grossesse, ils/elles s'orienteraient néanmoins vers des femmes. Ou bien, tout en étant des hommes conventionnels, ils seraient néanmoins dans l'état d'une femme enceinte. Première incongruité. D'autre part, les mâles qui sont enceints (ἐγκύμονες) « dans l'âme » (κατὰ τὴν ψυχήν, 208e) cherchent des partenaires masculins attrayants, pour pouvoir mener à bien leur projet intellectuel, accoucher de discours « dans la beauté », une beauté qui est, cependant, incarnée et physique. Car tout en n'ayant aucun intérêt pour une descendance corporelle, ils poursuivent non pas des garçons quelconques, mais ceux qui sont beaux. Ils courent après une qualité sensible. Seconde incongruité. L'analogie brouille ce qu'elle a l'air de différencier. Nous sommes en pleine « métaphore conflictuelle ».[35]

Mis en examen, mis à la question et réfuté, Socrate s'est retrouvé naguère face à Diotime dans la position de Théétète face à Socrate – à un Socrate *queer*, fils de sa mère, qui pratique un métier de femme sur les âmes des hommes. Si nous lisons le *Banquet* avec le *Théétète*, il nous apparaît que Diotime ne se borne pas à parler un idiome de femme, notamment à métaphoriser l'amour en termes d'accouchement : elle a opéré sur Socrate, exactement comme une accoucheuse et comme Kallonè/Ilithye qui, dit-elle, doit toujours être là pour assister les hommes, dans leurs efforts de mettre bas des λόγοι. Beauté est une cause de désir ; c'est aussi une aide-soignante. Diotime a accompagné le « travail » de Socrate. Son genre, par conséquent, est doublement pertinent dans le *Banquet* : oui, elle voit l'amour en termes de natalité, mais, de surcroît, elle fait accoucher et, si le parturient le mérite, elle n'hésite pas à lui rire au nez – sans pitié. De nouveau : l'entente masculine se confirme. Socrate lui-même a pu être aussi bête qu'Agathon. Nous avons tous été, les amis, à un moment ou à un autre, pleins de vent. La sage-femme s'amuse.

---

[34] Ricoeur (1975).
[35] Sur l'incohérence conceptuelle de la métaphore Prandi (2002) ; Prandi (2016).

5 Le pauvre type

Diotime est la seule qui ait été toujours savante. Quel est son savoir, au juste ? Et nous voici, encore une fois, à réfléchir ensemble à son éloge d'Éros, qui n'en est pas un.

Tout d'abord, Éros n'est pas un dieu, dit-elle. Il est un δαίμων, fils d'une dénommée Penia et d'un certain Poros (203b–e). Sans blague ! Encore une fois, il nous faut prendre la mesure de cette audace.[36] Socrate vient à peine de faire émerger l'indigence d'Éros/Désir – le manque qui est le sien de son objet intentionnel et, aussi, l'absence des qualités qu'il ne saurait posséder. L'éloge en est impossible, nous avons compris. Maintenant, Diotime va carrément faire d'Éros l'enfant d'une mère dont le nom est Pauvreté. Diotime achève le travail de Socrate sur Agathon, à l'échelle collective. La filiation maternelle d'Éros renverse la perspective élogieuse de tout le dialogue. Diotime déstabilise les récits et les prouesses rhétoriques de tout le monde en même temps. Fini, l'amour comme source d'excellence selon Phèdre ; oubliées, les deux Aphrodites de Pausanias ; rien à voir avec la puissance cosmique du docteur Eryximaque ; terminée, l'attraction fusionnelle des moitiés d'une sphère primordiale, dans le récit d'Aristophane ; et que reste-t-il d'Éros, le dieu le plus beau, le plus jeune, le meilleur entre tous, la source de tout ce qui est beau et bon et vertueux dans le monde, d'après le panégyrique d'Agathon ? Que reste-t-il de cet amour-là ? Rien du tout. Diotime met un terme à l'adulation. Si elle a raison, de nouveau, ils ont tous tort. Éros, c'est un pauvre type.

Penia est un personnage connu dans la tradition poétique et historiographique.[37] Mais elle brille de tout son éclat sur la scène comique. Aristophane l'introduit dans *La Richesse*. Platon semble y puiser son portrait de la mère d'Éros. Cette provenance intertextuelle a été reconnue.[38] Je propose que nous lisions le discours de Diotime à la lumière de la comédie. Car tout commence par-là. Dans la pièce d'Aristophane, Richesse est aveugle, d'où la distribution injustifiée des biens matériels. Les riches sont souvent injustes. Il faudrait que Richesse recouvre la vue ! Chrémylos et Blepsidémos, deux Athéniens entreprenants, s'apprêtent à amener Richesse se faire soigner les yeux chez Asclépios, lorsqu'un personnage étrange fait irruption sur scène. « Qui es-tu ? Tu me sembles pâlichonne », demande Chrémylos (σὺ δ' εἶ τίς; ὠχρὰ μὲν γὰρ εἶναί μοι δοκεῖς). « Probablement, c'est une Erinye de tragédie ! Elle te regarde d'un air fou furieux et tragique », s'exclame Blepsidémos (ἴσως Ἐρινύς ἐστιν ἐκ τραγῳδίας· βλέπει γέ τοι μανικόν τι καὶ τραγῳδικόν, vv. 422–424).[39] Serait-elle une servante qui

---

[36] Ce qui n'a pas échappé à Hadot (1974) 47 : « C'est pourquoi la description d'Éros par Diotime a quelque chose de comique. »
[37] Avant la *Richesse*, Pauvreté apparaît chez Théognide (v. 351–354, 649–652), dans un fragment d'Alcée (fr. 364 V.) et chez Hérodote (VIII 111).
[38] Chevrolet (1989).
[39] Pour une synthèse des études sur les allusions à Eschyle, déjà commentées dans les scholies, on verra Caciagli *et al.* (2016) 78.

triche sur le vin ? Elle se présente. « Je suis Penia », dit-elle, « je suis Pauvreté » (v. 437). Les deux hommes annoncent leur intention de la chasser, mais Pauvreté argumente sur les avantages de sa présence parmi les hommes, car la pénurie, à ne pas confondre avec la misère totale des mendiants, est bénéfique.[40] Il faut qu'il existe des pauvres. Car c'est seulement lorsqu'ils ont besoin de ce qui leur manque que les hommes travaillent, produisent, font du commerce. Pauvreté est débrouillarde. Andrea Capra a bien montré les résonances entre Aristophane et Platon.[41]

La généalogie comique et, plus précisément Aristophanesque, d'Éros acquiert une signification stratégique dans le seul dialogue platonicien où Aristophane lui-même fait partie du casting. Platon fait une triple fleur au poète. D'abord, en le conviant au symposium. Ensuite en l'accueillant dans la maison même d'un de ses personnages, Agathon, qu'il avait représenté, dans les *Femmes aux Thesmophories*, dans une version parodique de ce même intérieur.[42] Enfin, en lui empruntant une autre créature fictionnelle, Penia. Du coup, on change de registre. On commence à s'amuser ouvertement, comme au théâtre – avec Aristophane et en écho de ses créations.[43] Diotime emboîte le pas à la comédie.

Pour conclure sur la naissance de l'amour, revue et corrigée dans cet éloge paradoxal : Éros, fils de sa mère, est un bâtard de la pire espèce. Voilà qu'il se débrouille avec les moyens du bord, exactement comme sa mère, cette laideronne au teint blafard, à la mine tragique, qui vous harcèle et vous donne l'irrésistible envie de déguerpir le plus vite possible, mais dont la présence, se vante-t-elle dans la *Richesse*, profite à tout le monde, et qui a elle-même profité, dans le *Banquet*, du sommeil de Poros pour se faire faire un enfant. Éros, fils de sa mère, est un fieffé coquin.

6 L'amour des garçons

Après cet exorde hilarant, Diotime semble changer de registre. Elle va enseigner un art d'aimer : non pas seulement « les choses de l'amour » (τὰ ἐρωτικὰ), mais, dans une visée pédantesque, « l'amour des garçons tel qu'il faut le pratiquer » (τὸ ὀρθῶς παιδεραστεῖν).[44] Cette leçon se veut normative et, puisqu'elle culmine avec la contempla-

---

[40] Sommerstein (1984).
[41] Dans Caciagli *et al.* (2016) 88 s.
[42] Sissa (2012).
[43] Diotime fait allusion aux idées qu'Aristophane injecte dans son éloge d'Éros. Pour prendre la mesure de l'enjeu de cette résonance, voir Fussi (2008).
[44] 211b–c : « Ainsi, lorsqu'un homme qui aime les garçons correctement s'élève de ces particularités et commence à contempler cette beauté, il est presque capable de toucher au but. Telle est l'approche droite aux choses de l'amour » (ὅταν δή τις ἀπὸ τῶνδε διὰ τὸ ὀρθῶς παιδεραστεῖν ἐπανιὼν ἐκεῖνο τὸ καλὸν ἄρχηται καθορᾶν, σχεδὸν ἄν τι ἅπτοιτο τοῦ τέλους. τοῦτο γὰρ δή ἐστι τὸ ὀρθῶς ἐπὶ τὰ ἐρωτικὰ ἰέναι).

tion de l'idée pure et simple de Beauté, elle a inspiré bien des lectures fort sérieuses.[45] Voilà l'amour platonicien et platonique. Je propose, tout au contraire, d'écouter Diotime dans la foulée de son éclat de rire et à la suite de sa mythologie farcesque. Encore une fois, je me trouve en accord avec Christian Keime, lorsqu'il argumente qu'il faudrait envisager

> l'ensemble du discours de Diotime comme un discours ironique ou parodique : il s'agit seulement de suggérer que les aspects sophistiques et religieux de ce discours, et le mode de transmission direct et autoritaire du savoir qu'ils induisent, expriment une conception de l'enseignement qui correspond davantage au point de vue du public de Socrate, qu'à celui de Socrate lui-même. Diotime *en tant que prêtresse et en tant que sophiste* peut être considérée comme le porte-parole, non de Socrate, mais de son auditoire. Diotime et son discours sont donc des objets littéraires et philosophiques ambivalents. On ne s'étonnera plus, dans ce cas, que le personnage de la prêtresse fasse l'objet d'interprétations aussi contradictoires ; il faut même considérer que c'est à raison que les interprétations se contredisent à son propos : la voix de Diotime est à la fois le chant et le contre-chant de la philosophie.[46]

Cette lecture parodique d'un discours circonstanciel, ciblé, ajusté à ses destinataires est compatible avec celle que je propose dans ce texte. L'éloge paradoxal d'Éros continue, ainsi va mon argument, dans une incongruité systématique. Rendre justice à Éros signifie se rendre à l'évidence que son pouvoir édifiant ne peut s'étayer que sur une sensibilité première au scintillement des surfaces, aux nuances d'une carnation, aux traits d'un visage – des riens qui changent tout. La perception sensorielle attire l'attention, frappe les sens, cause un désir, sans quoi l'on ne saurait aller nulle part. Au lieu de se ruer sur l'escalier qui mène vers l'océan de la Beauté pure, désincarnée, sans mélange, il vaudrait donc mieux apprécier le « tempo » de cette pensée.[47] La « frivolité mortelle » dont un jeune homme serait prêt à se détourner, si – et seulement si – il connaissait par avance l'existence de la Beauté, est néanmoins sa seule chance de se mettre en marche – précisément, et paradoxalement, dans la bonne direction. Ainsi, au lieu de s'empresser de jeter à la poubelle ces « déchets », ces « ordures », un jeune Athénien devrait savoir gré à ses yeux de l'éveiller aux couleurs et aux formes, comme il devrait être reconnaissant à Socrate lui-même pour ses piqûres et ses absurdités (211e).

Comment donc se déroule-t-il τὸ ὀρθῶς παιδεραστεῖν (211b) ? La façon correcte, droite, juste d'aimer les garçons doit commencer par aimer les beaux corps, et cela dès son plus jeune âge (210a–d) :

---

45 Keime (2014) offre une synthèse remarquable de ces diverses interprétations, tout en proposant une lecture tout à fait intéressante de la pensée de Diotime et, en même temps, de son énonciation dans la mise en abîme qu'opère le dialogue.
46 Keime (2014) paragraphes 21 s.
47 J'emprunte cette expression à Loraux (1993).

Δεῖ γάρ, ἔφη, τὸν ὀρθῶς ἰόντα ἐπὶ τοῦτο τὸ πρᾶγμα ἄρχεσθαι μὲν νέον ὄντα ἰέναι ἐπὶ τὰ καλὰ σώματα, καὶ πρῶτον μέν, ἐὰν ὀρθῶς ἡγῆται ὁ ἡγούμενος, ἑνὸς αὐτὸν σώματος ἐρᾶν καὶ ἐνταῦθα γεννᾶν λόγους καλούς, ἔπειτα δὲ αὐτὸν κατανοῆσαι, ὅτι τὸ κάλλος τὸ ἐπὶ ὁτῳοῦν σώματι τῷ ἐπὶ ἑτέρῳ σώματι ἀδελφόν ἐστι, καὶ εἰ δεῖ διώκειν τὸ ἐπ᾽ εἴδει καλόν, πολλὴ ἄνοια μὴ οὐχ ἕν τε καὶ ταὐτὸν ἡγεῖσθαι τὸ ἐπὶ πᾶσι τοῖς σώμασι κάλλος· τοῦτο δ᾽ ἐννοήσαντα καταστῆναι πάντων τῶν καλῶν σωμάτων ἐραστήν, ἑνὸς δὲ τὸ σφόδρα τοῦτο χαλάσαι καταφρονήσαντα καὶ σμικρὸν ἡγησάμενον· μετὰ δὲ ταῦτα τὸ ἐν ταῖς ψυχαῖς κάλλος τιμιώτερον ἡγήσασθαι τοῦ ἐν τῷ σώματι, ὥστε καὶ ἐὰν ἐπιεικὴς ὢν τὴν ψυχήν τις κἂν σμικρὸν ἄνθος ἔχῃ, ἐξαρκεῖν αὐτῷ καὶ ἐρᾶν καὶ κήδεσθαι καὶ τίκτειν λόγους τοιούτους καὶ ζητεῖν οἵτινες ποιήσουσι βελτίους τοὺς νέους, ἵνα ἀναγκασθῇ αὖ θεάσασθαι τὸ ἐν τοῖς ἐπιτηδεύμασι καὶ τοῖς νόμοις καλὸν καὶ τοῦτ᾽ ἰδεῖν ὅτι πᾶν αὐτὸ αὑτῷ συγγενές ἐστιν, ἵνα τὸ περὶ τὸ σῶμα καλὸν σμικρόν τι ἡγήσηται εἶναι·

Celui qui va procéder correctement dans cette affaire doit commencer dès sa jeunesse à rencontrer de beaux corps. En premier lieu, en effet, si son guide le conduit correctement, il doit aimer un corps particulier, et là il doit accoucher de beaux discours ; mais ensuite il doit remarquer comment la beauté attachée à tel ou tel corps est la sœur de celle qui est attachée à n'importe quel autre, et que s'il veut poursuivre une beauté dans la forme, c'est une grosse bêtise de ne pas considérer comme une seule et la même la beauté appartenant à tous. Ayant saisi cette vérité, il doit se faire l'amant de tous les beaux corps, et relâcher la force de son sentiment pour un seul en le méprisant et en le comptant pour une petite chose. Après cela, il lui faudra accorder une plus grande valeur à la beauté des âmes qu'à celle du corps, de sorte que, aussi peu que puisse s'épanouir la « fleur » dans une âme, il lui suffira d'aimer et de s'en soucier, et d'engendrer une conversation qui tendra à l'amélioration des jeunes ; et enfin il sera contraint de contempler le beau tel qu'il apparaît dans nos observances et nos lois, et de voir qu'il est dans une totale parenté avec lui-même – de manière à estimer ce qui se rapporte à un beau corps comme une petite affaire.

Dès l'abord, il « faut donc » (δεῖ γάρ) emprunter un parcours balisé. La « rectitude » de la pédérastie consiste à aller de l'avant (ἰέναι), vers des corps masculins qui sont beaux (ἐπὶ τὰ καλὰ σώματα).[48] Je souhaite souligner la relative jeunesse de l'amant

---

[48] Wedgwood (2009) argumente avec vigueur que Diotime présente une théorie de la motivation rationnelle, et que τὸ καλόν dénote tout ce qui a une valeur intrinsèque. Il ne s'agirait surtout pas de « sensuous or physical beauty », puisque Diotime applique cet adjectif à la sagesse, à la vertu et aux discours. C'est vrai, bien entendu. Mais ce discours est une narration normative, structurée par le temps. Il faut commencer quelque part, pour pouvoir mettre en train ces jeunes Athéniens qui, apparemment, ne trouvent pas tous seuls le chemin de la rationalité. Il faut donner le coup d'envoi. Ainsi, Socrate va les cueillir là où ils sont, dans leur monde (qui est aussi le sien), en les faisant réfléchir sur ce qu'ils font déjà. D'où l'importance de l'ordinaire. Ce commencement est décisif pour le déroulement de la suite. Dans une note, Wedgwood concède que Platon admet, peut-être, que l'appréciation de la beauté physique est facile, donc heuristique : « Indeed, Plato's view seems to be that the sensuous beauty of physical things is trivial (σμικρόν, 210c6) compared to the beauty that can be exemplified by souls, customs, and laws. Admittedly, he does not deny that physical beauty is a species of beauty; so a correct appreciation of beauty will presumably involve some appreciation of physical beauty as well as of the higher forms of beauty. Moreover, it may be that, given the nature of our embodied human souls, it is heuristically easier for us to start out with an appreciation of physical beauty and then ascend from there to an appreciation of the beauty of souls, customs, laws, and branches of knowledge (210a–c). The point remains, however, that the

qui prend l'initiative de ces approches (νέον ὄντα), envers des παῖδες.⁴⁹ En compagnie de ces corps – un, pour commencer ; ensuite, plusieurs – un jeune homme éprouve un désir urgent de parler, déborde de choses à dire, comme si toutes ses pensées se pressaient de sortir. Le déplacement de son désir d'un corps à l'autre se déroule tout seul puisqu'il remarque (κατανοῆσαι) l'air de famille entre la beauté de l'un et de l'autre garçon, mais encore faut-il qu'il puisse comprendre ce que cette transition signifie. Si c'est le beau qu'il recherche, alors il serait une « grosse bêtise » (πολλὴ ἄνοια) de ne pas considérer que tous ces beaux corps ont en commun une même qualité – la beauté. Un amant pas trop bête comprend, chemin faisant, ce qu'il est en train de percevoir. Puisque sa perception fait partie d'une expérience intentionnelle, le désir érotique, il comprend aussi ce qu'il est en train de « poursuivre ». Appréciation et attirance vont ensemble, ce qui provoque une induction. Aha, voilà donc la beauté de ces corps ! Aha, un adjectif se décline aussi au neutre !

Éros est une expérience esthétique, langagière et, bientôt, intellectuelle. Le jeune homme va vite apprendre sur le tas. Il réalise que le tout premier mouvement « vers les beaux corps » (ἰέναι ἐπὶ τὰ καλὰ σώματα) lui donne envie de parler. Cela n'exclut ni nécessairement ni explicitement une relation qui toucherait à ces corps, dont l'apparence lui plait tant. Au contraire, Diotime insistera plus loin sur ce moment d'immersion sensorielle : voilà une beauté « remplie des chairs et des couleurs qui sont humaines et de toute autre frivolité mortelle en abondance » (ἀνάπλεων σαρκῶν τε ἀνθρωπίνων καὶ χρωμάτων καὶ ἄλλης πολλῆς φλυαρίας θνητῆς, 211e). Elle mettra l'accent sur le désir que l'amant éprouve de s'en repaître les yeux (ὁρῶντες τὰ παιδικὰ ; θεᾶσθαι), en restant tout le temps en compagnie de de ces beaux garçons (συνεῖναι ; καὶ συνόντες ἀεὶ αὐτοῖς, 211d).

L'insistance de Diotime sur le regard est essentielle pour le développement de son discours. Car c'est justement la vision de ces chairs et de ces couleurs qui permet aux amoureux d'apprécier τὰ καλὰ σώματα. Le jeune homme va pouvoir prendre un virage cognitif, parce qu'il traverse cette première phase de l'expérience pédérastique. C'est grâce à l'impact esthétique de ces corps qu'il perçoit l'existence de la beauté. Car en présence de ces corps, il est saisi d'émerveillement, d'une impression forte sur les organes de la vue (ἐκπέπληξαι), ce qui l'enchante, mais l'amène aussi à cogiter (211d). Assurément, un jour, il lui faudra se détourner de tout

---

term 'καλόν' is not used here just for specifically sensuous beauty, but has a much more general application. » L'originalité du discours de Diotime réside précisément dans l'expérience de τὸ ὀρθῶς παιδεραστεῖν, depuis son démarrage sensuel et trivial, jusqu'à l'épiphanie de Beauté.

49 Cantarella (1990) explique la stratification des âges dans le contexte amoureux. Elle commente les textes qui montrent le souci de protéger les enfants des adultes et des jeunes plus âgés, dans les écoles et les gymnases. Les jeunes dont l'âge s'étale à cheval des vingt ans sont doublement dangereux, parce qu'ils peuvent déjà séduire les enfants et parce qu'ils peuvent continuer à se laisser pénétrer par des hommes mûrs. Je suis d'accord, à ceci près que les ἄνδρες ne semblent pas être plus bienvenus que les νεανίσκοι autours des παῖδες. Les sources ne prouvent guère l'existence d'une bonne pédérastie « institutionnelle », entre hommes faits et enfants.

cela, mais, pour l'instant, le jeune homme est affecté par les matières, les couleurs, les textures de ce spectacle – et il pense.

Pour finir, contrairement à la lecture et à la traduction que fait Martha Nussbaum de ce texte, ce tournant est épistémique, plutôt que décisionnel.[50] Certes, Nussbaum a raison d'insister sur l'homogénéité qualitative de la beauté. Le jeune homme découvre précisément que, sous des formes différentes, c'est la beauté qui ne cesse de se représenter à ses yeux. Cela devient encore plus clair dans un passage de la *République*.[51] Mais s'agit-il d'une « décision » ? S'agit-il d'un « devoir » ? Il semble plutôt que le même verbe impersonnel « il faut » (δεῖ) commande le processus tout entier, dès le tout premier mouvement vers le tout premier garçon. Un corps après l'autre, l'amoureux des garçons se rend à une évidence perceptuelle.

Il se trouve que le désir, y compris chez les intellectuels, s'accroche au corps et, plus précisément, à des corps dont l'attrait est éphémère. C'est là que, d'entrée de jeu, cela se passe. Les amoureux dont parle Diotime se conduisent déjà, d'eux-mêmes, en amateurs de garçons tels qu'ils sont à Athènes. Davantage, ils se conduisent comme certains des érastes dont nous parle Pausanias (183e–184a) :

> Πονηρὸς δ' ἐστὶν ἐκεῖνος ὁ ἐραστὴς ὁ πάνδημος, ὁ τοῦ σώματος μᾶλλον ἢ τῆς ψυχῆς ἐρῶν· καὶ γὰρ οὐδὲ μόνιμός ἐστιν, ἅτε οὐ μονίμου ἐρῶν πράγματος. ἅμα γὰρ τῷ τοῦ σώματος ἄνθει λήγοντι, οὗπερ ἤρα, "οἴχεται ἀποπτάμενος," πολλοὺς λόγους καὶ ὑποσχέσεις καταισχύνας· ὁ δὲ τοῦ ἤθους χρηστοῦ ὄντος ἐραστὴς διὰ βίου μένει, ἅτε μονίμῳ συντακείς. τούτους δὴ βούλεται ὁ ἡμέτερος νόμος εὖ καὶ καλῶς βασανίζειν, καὶ τοῖς μὲν χαρίσασθαι, τοὺς δὲ διαφεύγειν. διὰ ταῦτα οὖν τοῖς μὲν διώκειν παρακελεύεται, τοῖς δὲ φεύγειν, ἀγωνοθετῶν καὶ βασανίζων ποτέρων ποτέ ἐστιν ὁ ἐρῶν καὶ ποτέρων ὁ ἐρώμενος.

> Par « mauvais », nous entendons cet amant populaire, qui désire le corps plutôt que l'âme : comme il n'est pas amoureux de ce qui est stable, il n'est pas lui-même stable. Dès que la fleur du corps qu'il aimait commence à s'étioler, 'en s'envolant il disparaît', laissant tous ses discours et ses promesses déshonorés. En revanche, l'amoureux d'un caractère superlativement bon reste toute sa vie, comme étant fusionné avec l'autre dans la durée. Notre loi dispose maintenant d'un test sûr et excellent pour mettre à l'épreuve ces hommes, qui montre qui sont ceux qui doivent être gratifiés et ceux qu'il faut fuir. Dans un cas, il encourage donc la poursuite, mais la fuite dans l'autre, en appliquant des épreuves et des tests dans chaque cas, ce qui nous permet de classer l'amant et l'aimé de tel ou tel côté.

Les amoureux terriens qui aiment sous les auspices de l'Aphrodite pandémique passent d'un garçon à l'autre. Le rythme de leur désir dépend de l'objet qu'ils poursuivent. Car « la fleur du corps » ne s'incarne pas dans des traits anatomiques stables, comme la taille, un visage harmonieux ou des membres proportionnés. L'attrait, c'est

---

50 Nussbaum (1986) 179.
51 Platon, *République* 5,474c–475a.

la jeunesse.⁵² La beauté, c'est du temps. Or, si la désirabilité d'un corps tient à une saison de la vie qui passe très vite, l'inconstance est inévitable. Dans son discours d'éloge et de blâme, Pausanias reprouve ces manières érotiques parce qu'elles nuisent aux garçons, d'abord séduits et bientôt abandonnés. Il loue les bons amants, en revanche, parce qu'ils choisissent des garçons plus mûrs, étant prêts à s'attacher à leurs bienaimés pour toujours, dans une véritable « symbiose ».⁵³ L'opposition entre l'Aphrodite Toute Populaire et l'Aphrodite Céleste n'a rien à voir avec une dichotomie de la chair et de l'esprit, mais distingue deux régimes temporels : la volatilité d'une quête, aussi répétitive que discontinue, de la « fleur » et de la « saison » ; la constance d'une fixation durable sur un individu singulier.⁵⁴ Comme les couples dont Aristophane raconte qu'ils seraient ravis de se faire « fusionner et unifier en une même chose » (συντῆξαι καὶ συμφυσῆσαι εἰς τὸ αὐτό) par le dieu forgeron, Héphaïstos, les amants ouraniens « restent ensemble toute la vie et uni en symbiose » (τὸν βίον ἅπαντα συνεσόμενοι καὶ κοινῇ συμβιωσόμενοι).⁵⁵ Alcibiade participe à cette même expérience érotique.

---

52 Bien des études sur la sexualité antique examinent l'association entre la beauté et un âge de la vie, qui est le même pour les deux sexes : Konstan (2014) ; Gherchanoc (2012) ; Gherchanoc (2016) ; Loscalzo (2008) ; Vattuone (2004).

53 181d–e : « Ils n'aiment les garçons que lorsqu'ils commencent à acquérir un certain esprit – cela va avec le duvet sur le menton. Ceux qui commencent à aimer un garçon à cet âge, je pense, sont prêts à être toujours avec lui et à tout partager avec lui tant que durera la vie : ils ne se précipiteront pas en courant vers un autre, en décevant le garçon, en le prenant dans da sottise de petit jeune, et en se moquant de lui» (οὐ γὰρ ἐρῶσι παίδων, ἀλλ' ἐπειδὰν ἤδη ἄρχωνται νοῦν ἴσχειν· τοῦτο δὲ πλησιάζει τῷ γενειάσκειν. παρεσκευασμένοι γάρ, οἶμαι, εἰσὶν οἱ ἐντεῦθεν ἀρχόμενοι ἐρᾶν ὡς τὸν βίον ἅπαντα συνεσόμενοι καὶ κοινῇ συμβιωσόμενοι, ἀλλ' οὐκ ἐξαπατήσαντες, ἐν ἀφροσύνῃ λαβόντες ὡς νέον, καταγελάσαντες οἰχήσεσθαι ἐπ' ἄλλον ἀποτρέχοντες). Eryximaque se dit d'accord sur ce point, 186b–c (ἔστι δή, ὥσπερ ἄρτι Παυσανίας ἔλεγε τοῖς μὲν ἀγαθοῖς καλὸν χαρίζεσθαι τῶν ἀνθρώπων, τοῖς δὲ ἀκολάστοις αἰσχρόν).

54 Sur l'éloge de l'amour ouranien voir Renaut (2017), qui conteste une lecture de ce discours comme simple faire-valoir du discours de Diotime, pour en dégager la visée morale et éducative. Il insiste notamment sur la différence entre l'eros pandémien avec ses buts purement sexuels et l'éros céleste qui, étant concerné par le *caractère* du bienaimé, tient compte du garçon en entier. Le passage cité dans la note qui précède précise, en effet, que l'amant ouranien préfère un jeune dont l'esprit (νοῦς) s'accompagne « à la première barbe » (τῷ γενειάσκειν). Renaut ne se penche pas sur le potentiel cognitif de la promiscuité sexuelle que Diotime, paradoxalement, met à profit. Il atténue cependant le contraste entre le ciel et la terre, entre l'âme et le corps – ce qui contribue à nuancer l'avilissement du corps, qu'une lecture hâtive du texte pourrait suggérer. Sur la différence entre la complexité du discours de Pausanias et le simplisme de celui de Xénophon au sujet des deux Aphrodites, on verra Pentassuglio (2012).

55 Platon, *Banquet* 192a–e, Héphaïstos leur offre ses services : « Vous souhaitez être réunis dans l'union la plus étroite possible, afin de ne pas être divisés de jour comme de nuit ? Si tel est votre désir, je veux bien vous fusionner et vous souder en une seule pièce (ἐθέλω ὑμᾶς συντῆξαι καὶ συμφυσῆσαι εἰς τὸ αὐτό), afin que vous ne soyez plus que deux, que tant que vous vivrez, vous ne fassiez plus qu'un (ὥστε δύ' ὄντας ἕνα γεγονέναι καὶ ἕως τ' ἂν ζῆτε, ὡς ἕνα ὄντα, κοινῇ ἀμφοτέρους ζῆν). . . . Personne, en entendant cela, ne s'y opposerait ou ne souhaiterait autre chose: chacun considérerait sans réserve qu'on lui a offert ce qu'il désirait depuis toujours, à savoir être uni et fusionné (συντακεὶς) avec son bien-aimé de telle sorte que les deux ne fassent plus qu'un ». Les propos de Pausanias sur les amants ouraniens : 181d–e.

Pausanias fait reproche à l'amant pandémien, ὁ ἐραστὴς ὁ πάνδημος, de circuler trop vite d'un corps à l'autre. D'après Diotime, tout au contraire, la transférabilité du désir devient une bonne chose.

7 Éloge de l'ordinaire

J'insiste sur ce commencement qui relève de l'ordinaire, sinon d'une certaine vulgarité. Il peut paraître paradoxal que tout commence par une pulsion esthétique, charnelle, indifférente aux sentiments d'autrui, bref : une pulsion qui, pour l'instant, vise le beau « infecté » de matérialité, d'une frivolité empreinte de mortalité.[56] Tant que le jeune homme se tourne vers des corps, surtout des corps multiples, cette pulsion ne saurait être bonne. L'on pourrait écouter Diotime dans l'ombre de Pausanias, comme si elle stigmatisait le désir corporel, en tant que tel. Ainsi, bien des lectures savantes du *Symposium* prennent au sérieux le crescendo mystique du discours de Diotime. J'en présente un échantillon.

Luc Brisson voit dans son discours une « opposition between physical beauty, which is an object of consumption, and incorporeal beauty (intelligible Beauty and that of the soul), which presides over the birth of fine discourses and fine actions, thereby making this birth possible; the transition from the sensible to the intelligible is described in the terms of the Mysteries. »[57] Je ne saurais en convenir. Aux yeux de Diotime, la beauté des beaux garçons n'est pas un objet de consommation. Diotime n'a cure de la distinction chère à Pausanias, entre deux amours – dont l'un serait « mauvais ». D'une part, Diotime n'appelle jamais « mauvais » (πονηρὸς) « cet amant populaire » (ἐκεῖνος ὁ ἐραστὴς ὁ πάνδημος) qui poursuit les très jeunes garçons. Bien au contraire, l'amour des corps est un excellent début. Non seulement parce qu'il n'y en a pas d'autres, mais parce que cet amour, nécessairement transitoire, permet à un jeune homme de « relâcher la force de ce qu'il éprouve pour un seul » (ἑνὸς δὲ τὸ σφόδρα τοῦτο χαλάσαι, 210b). Le voilà libre de se déplacer, de circuler, de prendre le large. Cet amour ne vous cloue pas à un seul objet d'infatuation, ce qui serait une impasse.

D'autre part, Diotime ne s'évertue non plus à « reformer » l'amour pédérastique. Luc Brisson, encore une fois, nous propose une telle lecture.[58] Il faudrait résumer le

---

[56] Platon, *Banquet* 211e. Dillon (2003) prête une attention remarquable à la première phase de l'amour, que les amoureux transformeraient ensemble au fil du temps, au lieu de se séparer. L'argument de Dillon vise cependant à défendre Platon contre les accusations de Gregory Vlastos. Pour une lecture qui n'hésite pas à reconnaître l'intimité physique de ces premières rencontres, Pierce (1994) 29.
[57] Brisson (2007).
[58] Je suis d'accord avec Brisson (2007) sur la pertinence de la maïeutique et de l'anamnèse par rapport à la métaphore maternelle, comme j'ai pu l'écrire naguère, en tâchant de dégager le point crucial de cette métaphorisation, qui est la difficulté et d'accoucher et de penser/parler (Sissa 1986 ; Sissa 1990 ; Sissa 2000). Mais je vois mal sur quelle preuve textuelle l'on peut appuyer l'affirmation que le

dialogue sur le mode du « renversement » entre les scénarios qu'esquisse l'amant d'Agathon et le grand final platonicien qu'expose Diotime, en attribuant ainsi à cette dernière une critique radicale du παιδεραστεῖν athénien. Bien au contraire, elle préconise de le pratiquer tel quel, justement parce que le désir se promène. Comparé aux couples qu'Héphaïstos aurait fondu en seul bloc métallique (Aristophane), ou au couple « soudé » que doivent former les amants ouraniens (Pausanias), ou encore au couple qu'Alcibiade semble vouloir créer en collant à Socrate, le jeune homme qui suit la façon correcte d'aimer les garçons (τὸ ὀρθῶς παιδεραστεῖν) fait cela, purement et simplement – il aime les garçons.[59] Ce qui nous dérange. Diotime théorise une manière de pédophilie.

Dans une visée interprétative analogue, l'on pourrait être tenté de regarder ce début du parcours, du point de vue de sa fin. Au rebours du long discours de l'étrangère de Mantinée, l'on fera apparaître la cohérence d'une allégorie téléonomique – ascèse mystique, théorie (ratée) de l'amour, et autres versions d'un Platon moralisé et d'une Diotime dont on s'étonne qu'elle ne soit pas assez romantique.[60] Dans cette modélisation initiatique, c'est comme si les amants savaient déjà où ils vont, tels des individus qui se rendraient à Éleusis afin de se faire initier aux Mystè-

---

bienaimé subirait une forme d' « esclavage », alors que, dans la pédérastie ouranienne, que décrit Pausanias, ce sont d'abord et surtout les ἐρασταί qui se rabaissent en devenant des esclaves volontaires par rapport à leurs jeunes bienaimés, πρὸς τὰ παιδικά, 183a–c ; sur l'esclavage amoureux dans le *Banquet*, on verra désormais Regali (2020). Or, cette affirmation devient cruciale dans l'argument de Brisson, parce que Diotime, par la métaphore de la génération, « renverserait » cette relation de pouvoir. Que faut-il retenir de cette argumentation ? Oui, le paradigme de la conception / grossesse / parturition permet de redécrire l'expérience du désir (une fois que Socrate a fait dire à Agathon que ἔρως, c'est ἐπιθυμία) dans une perspective nouvelle, par rapport au début du dialogue. Oui, les amants sont repensés de manière tout à fait intéressante et, dirais-je, surprenante, comme étant enceints depuis longtemps. Oui, la beauté des jeunes qui les attirent agit non seulement comme cause de désir, mais aussi comme un « trigger » du travail de l'accouchement de discours, donc Beauté joue un rôle de sage-femme. Mais rien dans tout cela ne nous amène à conclure que le παιδεραστεῖν serait critiqué, au sens de blâmée comme une espèce d'amour vulgaire. Ça, c'est Pausanias qui le dit – l'homme qui a tout intérêt à distribuer éloge et blâme à des manières érotiques qui le concernent de près. Quant au pouvoir, il n'a rien à faire dans cette discussion. Candiotto (2017) montre bien comment Socrate « reforme » la relation pédérastique entre un maître et son élève, en l'occurrence entre lui-même et Alcibiade, en refusant de passer à l'acte sexuel. Elle a raison de mettre en évidence la façon dont Socrate se démarque de la mauvaise foi de ces amants qui offrent des bienfaits intellectuels, dans l'espoir d'obtenir une gratification érotique. C'est ainsi que se conduisent les amants ouraniens, d'après Pausanias ; c'est ainsi qu'Alcibiade se méprend sur les intentions de Socrate (p. 227).

59 Éromène et éraste et à la fois, prêt à coucher avec un homme plus âgé qui lui offre sagesse et savoir, Alcibiade est la caricature de l'amoureux Ouranien – qui, aux yeux de Socrates, n'a rien compris. Sur l'embarras, l'esclavage, les conflits d'Alcibiade, voir en dernier lieu Regali (2020).

60 Je fais allusion à l'article canonique de Vlastos (1973/1981) qui dénonce l'égoïsme de l'amant qui emprunte l'escalier vers la Beauté, aux dépens de son partenaire initial. Martha Nussbaum, Anthony Price et John Dillon (dans des textes cités) répondent à Vlastos, surtout dans le but de défendre Platon d'une telle accusation. Vlastos a vu juste.

res de Déméter.⁶¹ L'initiation se déroulerait progressivement, en vue d'un but bien précis, espéré d'avance. Mais une telle interprétation crée une distorsion de la temporalité que Diotime met en perspective. Car son discours fait émerger deux points de vue différents. Diotime elle-même se place à l'endroit précis où elle peut prévoir (et faire entrevoir à son auditeur) la conclusion de l'expérience érotique : la vision de la Beauté en soi. Les amoureux dont elle parle à Socrate (et que Socrate lui-même ne cesse de fréquenter), en revanche, vivent cette même expérience dans le présent le plus immédiat et le plus quotidien. Ils aiment ici et maintenant, dans l'espace/temps de la pédérastie athénienne, telle que Pausanias la décrit et qu'Alcibiade la pratique. Faire l'amour ou, du moins, flirter avec de multiples jeunes hommes : c'est cela le but, pour l'instant, rien d'autre.

Certes, cette façon de procéder dans l'amour des garçons – passer du singulier au pluriel – nous est présentée comme le départ vers une destination, comme un premier pas dans la montée de l'« escalier » métaphorique (ὥσπερ ἐπαναβαθμοῖς χρωμένου, 211c) qui conduit vers le ciel, océan de beauté. Mais sommes-nous sûrs que le sens du discours serait qu'il faille se presser d'arriver au but le plus vite possible, pour s'y installer à jamais ? J'en doute. Tout d'abord, il n'est pas possible ou même souhaitable de se fixer là-haut. Debra Nails insiste sur la distance entre le sommet de l'échelle mystique et le « worthless stuff » que devient l'expérience érotique aux yeux de l'initié, tout en soulignant que la contemplation de l'idée de Beauté ne correspond pas du tout à la pratique sociale et dialogique de Socrate, puisque celui-ci cultive un tout autre idéal d'existence : la vie examinée.⁶² Je suis entièrement d'accord. Je ne peux qu'abonder dans ce sens. Diotime décrit le point d'arrivée de l'ascension comme un pinacle, en regard duquel l'amour des garçons dans les rues et les gymnases d'Athènes apparaît – après-coup – comme faisant partie d'une vie quotidienne, vécue dans la multiplicité des corps et des rencontres. Mais cette vie-là continue, dialogue après dialogue. Car, malgré son « initiation » par Diotime, Socrate, le philosophe (à ne pas confondre avec le mystique d'un jour), reste pleinement engagé dans la parole ordinaire, dans l'attribution de beauté à des objets plus ou moins beaux, bref : dans la vie athénienne. Socrate ne couche *jamais* avec les beaux garçons, mais il ne cesse de revenir vers eux, de se mettre à leur niveau dans l'espoir que l'un ou l'autre puisse changer d'existence. Ensuite, Diotime elle-même donne une importance capitale au moment « pandémique » de la pédérastie puisque, sans cette première impulsion, rien ne peut commencer. C'est pourquoi je défends une lecture patiente de son discours à elle. J'insiste, autrement dit,

---

61 Pour une discussion des références à Éleusis, dans une interprétation qui en fait le support du discours de Diotime voir Evans (2006). Je ne rentre pas dans le détail, mais je nous met en garde contre l'aplatissement téléonomique de l'expérience pédérastique.
62 Nails (2007) examine les interprétations du discours de Diotime par Martha Nussbaum et Jonathan Lear, en présentant une critique tout à fait pertinente du paradigme mystique dans le dialogue. Socrate ne s'y conforme pas, affirme-t-elle, parce que la vie contemplative que la prêtresse prospecte est en fait très différente de celle que Socrate choisit de vivre, au milieu de ses amis.

sur la valeur de cette situation initiale que les interprètes téléonomiques ont tendance à voir comme une phase à dépasser le plus vite possible (« worthless stuff »), mais que Diotime présente, bien au contraire, comme tout à fait précieuse. Certes, pour ceux qui auront gravi les échelons, il y aura un dilemme entre pluriel et singulier. Mais, ici-bas, les beaux garçons restent beaux à leur manière, et il faut leur savoir gré de donner l'impulsion au mouvement du désir car, sans cette intentionnalité première, il ne se passerait rien du tout.[63]

Ou encore, il peut sembler évident que l'amour des garçons ne serait que le contexte dans lequel Socrate trouve un exemple efficace, la beauté, pour illustrer la quête des Formes. Nikolas Pappas nous conduit dans cette direction. En tant que qualité visible, désirable et transférable, la beauté serait la seule propriété que Platon utilise dans le *Phèdre* et dans le *Banquet*, pour décrire « the first movement into philosophizing ».[64] Dans ces deux dialogues, Platon ferait donc preuve d'« optimisme » sur la possibilité d'atteindre les Formes en prenant appui sur l'expérience érotique. Et Pappas d'ajouter : « Those optimistic moments are not easy to sustain. » En effet, si le but était de prendre son envol vers le ciel océanique où rayonne Κάλλος, il semble bien que l'injonction d'aller voir de beaux garçons serait étrangement contreproductive. Pourquoi faire perdre du temps aux jeunes Athéniens, au lieu de les encourager à s'arracher illico à leur frivolité ?

Ces lectures savantes sous-estiment la stratégie didactique de l'étrangère de Mantinée. C'est bien elle qui, au lieu de les en détourner, dirige ces jeunes vers « tous les beaux corps ». Aussi incongru que cela puisse nous paraître, il est certain qu'il faut en passer par là.

8 Vous, les ἐρωτικοί

Mais que dit Diotime, au juste ? Elle dit que, si l'on veut bien faire les choses dans l'amour des garçons, l'on doit débuter par tout ce qu'il y a de plus spontané : le désir

---

[63] Lear (2015) reconnaît la grande valeur que Platon attribue à la génération d'œuvres et de pensée, dans un environnement de beauté. Je ne saurais le suivre au sujet de la grossesse masculine comme étant un phénomène premier, et non pas une métaphore.

[64] Pappas (2008/2020) résume ainsi la manière dont Platon utilise la beauté comme exemple privilégié de l'accès à la conceptualisation. Il le dit d'une manière très claire et très pertinente, à ceci près que l'expérience de la beauté se fait d'abord dans l'attrait *sexuel*, et que cette expérience n'est pas seulement un exemple plus commode que d'autres, mais la vie même de ces hommes à qui Socrate est en train de parler. S'ils ont la chance de comprendre l'accès aux Formes, c'est qu'ils sont des ἐρωτικοί, donc qu'ils sont déjà sur la bonne voie vers l'intelligence du neutre. La beauté, en somme, n'est pas un exemple de Forme plus utile qu'un autre (parce que visible), mais la cause d'un désir vécu, partagé, unique – qui produit des effets spéciaux. C'est le désir physique et mouvant qui mène des hommes enclins à l'amour vers le « moment aha » où ils reconnaissent, tout simplement, que οἱ καλοί partagent τὸ καλόν.

pour les beaux corps. Ce désir advient. Il faut tout simplement « y aller ». Autrement dit, c'est là qu'il faut aller. « Il faut » (δεῖ γάρ) devenir « l'amant de tous les beaux corps » (πάντων τῶν καλῶν σωμάτων ἐραστήν), au pluriel. Puisqu'il ne s'agit pas de se rendre à une partouse, l'on commence par un premier beau garçon. Mais, encore une fois, c'est par là qu'« il faut » commencer, et le pluriel n'a pas l'air d'être difficile à cultiver. Bien au contraire, la sérialité est inscrite dans τὸ ὀρθῶς παιδεραστεῖν. Si, par définition, le beau corps qui excite le désir est celui d'un παῖς, c'est-à-dire d'un garçon dans la fleur de l'âge, l'inconstance est aussi prévisible que la progression de la puberté. Diotime prend donc acte de cette attirance, sans cesse renouvelée, pour des corps en devenir. Mais elle ajoute qu'il peut se passer quelque chose d'imprévu : il peut arriver que, chemin faisant, ces amoureux découvrent la vérité de leur désir. En poursuivant de multiples partenaires, ils s'aperçoivent – s'ils ne sont pas trop stupides – qu'ils désirent toujours la même chose. Au départ, ils se laissent charmer par des corps qui, l'un après l'autre, méritent le même adjectif, καλόν. Et, ensuite, l'attribut qu'ils répètent – et dont ils éprouvent l'attrait – se révèle une qualité commune à tous ces corps, toujours la même et transférable : τὸ καλόν, τὸ κάλλος, ce qui revient à dire la jeunesse.

Ainsi, par le simple fait de se focaliser non pas sur l'amour, mais sur l'amour des *garçons*, Diotime fait écho à Pausanias. La première épiphanie de τὸ κάλλος ne saurait être l'affaire d'une Aphrodite venue du ciel, mais plutôt d'une déesse qui circulerait ici-bas, les pieds sur terre. Car c'est l'éros vagabond qui part à la rencontre (ἰέναι ἐπὶ) de τὰ καλὰ σώματα, c'est l'éros qui nous fait aimer la conversation, pourvu que ce soit avec des gens ravissants, c'est l'éros sensuel, bavard et volage qui nous fait avancer et nous délie la langue. C'est cet éros-là, et non pas l'amour fusionnel, qui pave la voie à une quête qui a la chance de *devenir* philosophique – en cours de route. À force de distribuer des compliments à droite et à gauche, peut-être que l'on s'entend parler. Imaginez, en revanche, de faire comprendre que la beauté est une qualité transférable – donc qu'il existe une idée de beauté – à un jeune homme éperdument amoureux d'une seule et unique personne ! Hélas, pour apprendre à réfléchir, il faut faire l'expérience du pluriel, donc il faut se conduire comme les séducteurs cruels dont parle Pausanias.[65]

Sont-ils si méchants que ça, après tout ? Ne sont-ils pas tout simplement de jeunes Athéniens qu'il faut prendre au piège de leurs habitudes ? Peut-être que leur genre de vie présente un atout majeur car, grâce à la promiscuité, il peut leur arriver de se rendre à l'évidence. Peut-être que leur inconstance est une cohérence paradoxale, que leur frivolité est une quête – pour l'instant inconsciente. Il faudra en détourner la visée du corps – ce qui est encore un autre tournant – vers les âmes et,

---

[65] Le potentiel moralisateur du discours de Pausanias se trouve exploité dans le *Banquet* de Xénophon, où Socrate oppose les deux Aphrodites, Ourania et Pandemos, comme si l'une apportait l'amour des âmes et l'autre, l'amour des corps ; l'une, l'amitié et l'affection durables, surtout dans le couple hétérosexuel ; l'autre, la poursuite de l'amour physique des garçons. Sur ce contraste, on verra l'article éclairant de Pentassuglio (2012).

finalement, vers la qualité elle-même qui affecte tout ce qui est beau. Le bon pédagogue facilite ce détournement.

C'est une vignette dans la *République* qui nous aide à comprendre le scénario que théorise Diotime. Vous, les ἐρωτικοί, explique Socrate, vous savez bien que vous trouvez toujours les mots pour dire l'attrait des garçons les plus différents. Pourvu qu'ils soient dans la fleur de l'âge, votre désir s'accroche à l'un ou l'autre détail de leur aspect, détails que vous montez en épingle et que vous « accentuez », au fil d'analogies aussi flatteuses que contradictoires (5,474c–475a) :

> Ἀναμιμνῄσκειν οὖν σε, ἦν δ' ἐγώ, δεήσει, ἢ μέμνησαι ὅτι ὃν ἂν φῶμεν φιλεῖν τι, δεῖ φανῆναι αὐτόν, ἐὰν ὀρθῶς λέγηται, οὐ τὸ μὲν φιλοῦντα ἐκείνου, τὸ δὲ μή, ἀλλὰ πᾶν στέργοντα; "Ἀναμιμνῄσκειν, ἔφη, ὡς ἔοικεν, δεῖ· οὐ γὰρ πάνυ γε ἐννοῶ". Ἄλλῳ, εἶπον, ἔπρεπεν, ὦ Γλαύκων, λέγειν ἃ λέγεις· ἀνδρὶ δ' ἐρωτικῷ οὐ πρέπει ἀμνημονεῖν ὅτι πάντες οἱ ἐν ὥρᾳ τὸν φιλόπαιδα καὶ ἐρωτικὸν ἀμῇ γέ πῃ δάκνουσί τε καὶ κινοῦσι, δοκοῦντες ἄξιοι εἶναι ἐπιμελείας τε καὶ τοῦ ἀσπάζεσθαι. | ἢ οὐχ οὕτω ποιεῖτε πρὸς τοὺς καλούς; ὁ μέν, ὅτι σιμός, ἐπίχαρις κληθεὶς ἐπαινεθήσεται ὑφ' ὑμῶν, τοῦ δὲ τὸ γρυπὸν βασιλικόν φατε εἶναι, τὸν δὲ δὴ διὰ μέσου τούτων ἐμμετρώτατα ἔχειν, μέλανας δὲ ἀνδρικοὺς ἰδεῖν, λευκοὺς δὲ θεῶν παῖδας εἶναι· μελιχλώρους δὲ καὶ τοὔνομα οἴει τινὸς ἄλλου ποίημα εἶναι ἢ ἐραστοῦ ὑποκοριζομένου τε καὶ εὐχερῶς φέροντος τὴν ὠχρότητα, ἐὰν ἐπὶ ὥρᾳ ᾖ; καὶ ἑνὶ λόγῳ πάσας προφάσεις προφασίζεσθέ τε καὶ πάσας φωνὰς ἀφίετε, ὥστε μηδένα ἀποβάλλειν τῶν ἀνθούντων ἐν ὥρᾳ. "Εἰ βούλει, ἔφη, ἐπ' ἐμοῦ λέγειν περὶ τῶν ἐρωτικῶν ὅτι οὕτω ποιοῦσι, συγχωρῶ τοῦ λόγου χάριν".

« Avez-vous besoin qu'on vous rappelle, ai-je demandé, ou peut-être vous rappelez-vous que celui qui prétend être amoureux de quelque chose doit prouver, si la prétention est juste, non pas qu'il aime une partie, mais l'ensemble. » – « Il semble qu'il faudra me le rappeler », dit-il, « car je n'y pense pas du tout pour le moment. » – « Quelqu'un d'autre aurait dû dire ce que tu dis, Glaucon. Il n'est pas convenable pour un homme enclin à l'amour d'oublier que tous ceux qui sont dans la fleur de l'âge éprouvent et excitent l'amoureux des garçons quand ils lui paraissent dignes d'attention et d'étreintes amoureuses. Ou n'est-ce pas ainsi que vous réagissez aux beaux garçons ? Celui qui a le nez retroussé sera qualifié de 'charmant' et sera approuvé par vous, le nez aquilin d'un autre vous le dites 'royal', et un autre qui se situe entre les deux, il aura les proportions les plus harmonieuses ; les basanés sont 'virils', les beaux sont 'les fils de dieu'. » – « Pensez-vous que 'teint de miel' soit autre chose qu'un nom inventé de toutes pièces pour un amant qui passe outre et tolère un teint pâle, à condition qu'il appartienne à un garçon dans la fleur de l'âge ? En un mot, vous avancez toutes les excuses et faites tous les bruits nécessaires pour vous assurer de ne rejeter personne qui est dans la fleur de l'âge. » – « Si vous voulez parler de moi, au sujet de la façon dont les amoureux se comportent, » dit-il, « alors je suis d'accord pour le bien de notre argument. »

Dans leurs éloges à tout prix, les ἐρωτικοί sont marrants.[66] Mais l'argument est sérieux. Cela montre que, quand on aime une chose, on l'aime en entier, dans toutes

---

[66] Périllié (2015) paragraphe 8, comprend très bien le sens de ἐρωτικός : « . . . il apparaît que l'*erôtikos anèr* n'est pas simplement l'homme amoureux – à savoir l'homme qui se trouve momentanément sous l'emprise de l'amour – mais qualifie la nature d'un homme qui est porté à l'amour, ici en particulier l'amour de jeunes garçons qui sont, comme le dit le texte, 'dans l'éclat de leur jeunesse'. En d'autres termes, cette expression prise dans son contexte indique une constance, une

ses occurrences. Cela implique, aussi, que les façons de faire dans le domaine de τὰ ἐρωτικὰ peuvent devenir paradigmatiques, parce qu'elles sont spontanées, habituelles et tellement familières que l'on peut partir de là, pour en faire l'exemple d'autre chose. Éros, tel que vous-mêmes le pratiquez déjà, les enfants, vous révèle comment fonctionne la pensée et vous apprend à mieux penser. Suivez votre propre exemple !

La parole entre en jeu et, plus exactement, la rhétorique amoureuse. Les ἐρωτικοί font des compliments fallacieux, et c'est justement leur créativité épidictique *mensongère* qui les expose à la chance de comprendre une chose capitale : c'est la beauté/jeunesse qu'ils recherchent, qu'ils poursuivent, qu'ils affectionnent, et non pas tel ou tel jeune homme, Agathon ou Charmide. Ces amants-là, ce sont des êtres de fuite et, de surcroît, des flatteurs en série. Ils sont, par conséquent, des futurs philosophes. L'adulation répétée, c'est cela qui peut, éventuellement, vous alerter au fait que, lorsque vous aimez une qualité, vous l'aimez complètement, dans toutes ses variations et instanciations. Les ἐρωτικοί athéniens se conduisent comme cela – tels quels. Dans leur désir métonymique, indiscriminé et flagorneur, ils sont *déjà* en train de découvrir le neutre. Il leur faut seulement un « moment aha ». Et voilà que Socrate, le bon pédagogue, vient les cueillir là où ils sont, sur ce terrain-là, à ce moment-là – lorsqu'ils sont fin prêts à s'entendre parler. Il les aide à s'écouter parler d'éros. Cet instant est unique. Pourquoi ? Parce que dans l'expérience du sexe parlé, il y a une intelligence cognitive. Mais il y a un plus : cette intelligence est vécue comme une intention. Diotime met en avant l'envie de coucher avec un autre beau garçon, et encore un autre, autrement beau – à l'infini. Donc le souhait de jouir de leur beauté/jeunesse. C'est l'intention sexuelle qui insiste dans la répétition – le désir est insatiable. Et, d'après Diotime, – même si le terme ἀπληστία, qui d'habitude est connoté négativement, n'apparaît pas dans son discours – l'idée d'insatiabilité est une bonne chose.

9 Conclusion

Par toute une série de mises en échec Diotime, la femme, l'étrangère, la rieuse renverse allègrement la perspective épidictique de la soirée chez Agathon. Elle soumet Socrate à la réfutation. Elle n'hésite pas à se moquer de lui pour son attribution de qualité flatteuse à Éros. Elle raille ainsi ouvertement la présomption de savoir que cet éloge implique, alors que Socrate se garde bien de ricaner aux dépens d'Agathon, parce que les amis s'abstiennent de se moquer d'un ami. Elle réinvente un récit de la naissance honteuse d'Éros, aux échos aristophanesques. Elle remplace le

---

continuité, une qualité qui s'inscrivent dans la durée. Nous sommes autorisés en cela à parler d'une nature . . . » Garani (2014) rend justice à l'humour de ce catalogue. Price (2017) évoque ce passage, dans le contexte de sa réponse à Gregory Vlastos au sujet de l'amour égoïste. Voir aussi Price (1981).

langage de la possession par celui de la procréation, et surtout de l'accouchement dans la douleur. Elle transforme la Beauté en aide-soignante, en sage-femme. Elle féminise tout ce qu'il y a de plus masculin, la paternité et la philosophie, par l'attribution d'une grossesse généralisée à tous les mâles. L'éros le plus physique et la rhétorique la plus spécieuse deviennent le paradigme – improbable à souhait – de l'inférence. Bref : nous assistons, avec Diotime, à l'introduction jubilatoire d'une incongruité systématique. On dirait que la sophiste de Mantinée travaille à la pharmacie de Platon. Il n'y a rien de plus *queer*, que cet éros-là.

Encore une fois, une dernière fois : pour s'être habitué à ce genre d'éros – bavard et libertin, volage et flatteur – un ἐρωτικὸς athénien (et non pas Perse ou Béotien) est le meilleur candidat à une formation philosophique. Coïncidence inattendue des opposés. Diotime montre que les hommes, y compris Socrate, sont tous passibles de tomber dans la prétention de savoir. Pour commencer, ils se prennent pour des mâles, alors qu'ils sont tous des femmes (surtout les pères de famille). Ensuite, ils s'adonnent volontiers au plaisir de la parole encomiastique, ce piège à prétentieux. Et pourtant, ils ont la chance d'aboutir. L'éros qui fait du bien, dit-elle, est l'éros le plus vulgaire qui soit : cruel parce que fixé sur la jeunesse ; instable et insatiable, parce que glissant d'un objet partiel à l'autre, d'une cause de désir à l'autre. Cet éros ne sait pas encore qu'il se dirige vers l'Idée. Car il faut « justement » que cet ὀρθῶς παιδεραστεῖν – et c'est cela, sa « justesse » – soit un désir indiscriminé qui se déplace d'un corps à l'autre (pour que vous vous rendiez compte que vous cherchez un attribut) et un désir qui se traduise par des marivaudages insensés (pour que vous commenciez à articuler votre conscience de cet attribut). C'est cet éros pandémique, accroché aux petits bouts les plus risibles du corps – le profil d'un nez, une nuance de la peau – et flottant de l'un à l'autre par la parole ; c'est cet éros que d'autres pourraient blâmer ; c'est cet éros de comédie qui, paradoxalement, vous ouvre la voie de la pensée.

En créant cette incongruité suprême, Diotime fait tout son possible pour que nous riions – amicalement ou pas. En Lectrices et Lecteurs – Modèles du *Banquet*, au lieu de nous précipiter à gravir les marches de l'escalier mystique, nous devrions trouver tout cela exhilarant.

En osant s'esclaffer, Diotime actualise la possibilité du rire dont Socrate préfère s'abstenir. Les amoureux épidictiques, Socrate lui-même va les débusquer dans les rues, les salons et les gymnases d'Athènes. Mais s'il les tourne en ridicule, il n'en rit pas pour autant. L'on ne rit point du ridicule de ses amis. Socrate, ai-je répété, expose le potentiel comique d'Agathon, mais il ne s'en gausse pas. Ces égards font partie de sa palinodie du poète. Il faut une sophiste venue d'ailleurs – et qui n'appartient pas au petit cercle homosensuel – pour oser la comédie.

Bibliographie

Brisson (2007) : Luc Brisson, « Agathon, Pausanias and Diotima in Plato's *Symposium*: *Paiderastia* and *Philosophia* », *dans* : James Lesher, Debra Nails et Frisbee Sheffield (dir.), *Plato's Symposium: Issues in Interpretation and Reception*, Washington, DC, 229–251.

Caciagli *et al.* (2016) : Stefano Caciagli, Andrea Capra, Maddalena Giovannelli et Mario Regali, « Penia da Aristofane alla scena contemporanea. La forza drammatica di un personaggio anti-comico », *Lessico del Comico* 1, 78–97.

Calà (2016) : Irene Calà, « Terapie tra magia e religione. La gravidanza e il parto nei testi medici della tarda Antichità », *dans* : Martia Terese Santamaría Hernández (dir.), *Traducción y Transmisión doctrinal de la medicina grecolatina desde la Antigüedad hasta el mundo moderno: nuevas aportaciones sobre autores y textos*, Cuenca, 11–24.

Candiotto (2017) : Laura Candiotto, « On the Epistemic Value of *Eros*. The Relationship Between Socrates and Alcibiades », *PEITHO / EXAMINA ANTIQUA* 1 (8), 225–236.

Cantarella (1990) : Eva Cantarella, « *Neaniskoi*. Classi di età e passaggi di status nel diritto ateniese », *dans* : *Mélanges de l'École française de Rome. Antiquité* 102, 37–51.

Chevrolet (1989) : Teresa Chevrolet, « L'eros de Diotime comme mythe intertextuel : lectures néo-platoniciennes d'un passage du *Banquet* », *Bibliothèque D'Humanisme Et Renaissance* 51, 311–330.

Cornford (1950) : Francis Cornford, « The Doctrine of Eros in Plato's *Symposium* », *dans* : Id., *The Unwritten Philosophy and Other Essays*, Cambridge, 68–80.

Demand (1994) : Nancy Demand, *Birth, Death and Motherhood in Classical Greece*, Baltimore.

Destrée (2013) : Pierre Destrée, « Platon et l'ironie dramatique », *Revue de métaphysique et de morale* 80, 543–556.

Dillon (2003) : John Dillon, « The Platonic sage in love », *Studia Humaniora Tartuensia* 4 (En ligne).

DuBois (1994) : Page DuBois, « The Platonic Appropriation of Reproduction », *dans* : Nancy Tuana (dir.), *Feminist Interpretations of Plato*, University Park, Pa, 139–156.

Evans (2006) : Nancy Evans, « Diotima and Demeter as Mystagogues in Plato's *Symposium* », *Hypatia* 21, 1–27.

Fussi (2008) : Alessandra Fussi, « Tempo, desiderio, generazione. Diotima e Aristofane nel 'Simposio' di Platone », *Rivista di Storia della Filosofia* 63, 1–27.

Fussi (2017) : Alessandra Fussi, « *Schadenfreude*, envy and jealousy in Plato's *Philebus* and *Phaedrus* », *Philosophical Inquiries* 5, 73–90.

Garani (2014) : Myrto Garani, « *Rideamus igitur*! A Platonic palimpsest in Lucretius' treatise against love (*DRN* 4.1160-9) », *dans* : Πρακτικά του Θ΄ Πανελληνίου Συμποσίου Λατινικών Σπουδών Αθήνα, 19–22 Μαΐου 2011, Athens, 77–84.

Gherchanoc (2012) : Florence Gherchanoc, « Beauté, ordre et désordre vestimentaires féminins en Grèce ancienne », *Clio. Femmes, Genre, Histoire* 36, 19–42 (En ligne).

Gherchanoc (2016) : Florence Gherchanoc, *Concours de beauté et beautés du corps en Grèce ancienne. Discours et pratiques*, Bordeaux.

Glenn (2003) : Phillip Glenn, *Laughter in Interaction*, Cambridge.

Hadot (1974) : Pierre Hadot, *Éloge de Socrate*, Paris.

Halperin (1990) : David Halperin, « Why is Diotima a woman? », *dans* : Id. (dir.), *One Hundred years of homosexuality*, London, 113–151.

Hawthorne (1994) : Susan Hawthorne, « Diotima Speaks Through the Body », *dans* : Bat-Ami Bar On (dir.), *Engendering Origins, Critical Feminist Readings in Plato and Aristotle*, New York, 81–96.

Hobbs (2006) : Angela Hobbs, « Female Imagery in Plato », *dans* : James Lesher, Debra Nails et Frisbee Sheffield (dir.), *Plato's Symposium. Issues in Interpretation and Reception*, Washington, DC, 252–271.

Holmes (2007) : Brooke Holmes, « The *Iliad*'s Economy of Pain », *TAPhA* 137, 45-84.
Hubbard (1998) : Thomas K. Hubbard, « Popular Perceptions of Elite Homosexuality in Classical Athens », *Arion* 6, 48-78.
Hughes Dominik (2013) : Yamcy Hughes Dominik, « Images for the sake of the truth in Plato's 'Symposium' », *CQ* 63, 558-566.
Keime (2014) : Christian Keime, « La fonction de Diotime dans le *Banquet* de Platon (201d1-212c3) : le dialogue et son double », *Études platoniciennes* 11 (En ligne).
Konstan (2014) : David Konstan, *Beauty. The fortune of an ancient Greek idea*, Oxford.
Lear (2015) : Jonathan Lear, « Ironic eros. Notes on a fantastic pregnancy », *Journal of Philosophical Research* 40, 181-190.
Loraux (1981) : Nicole Loraux, « Le lit, la guerre », *L'Homme* 21, 37-67.
Loraux (1993) : Patrice Loraux, *Le Tempo de la pensée*, Paris.
Loscalzo (2008) : Donato Loscalzo, « Prima e dopo Socrate », dans : Gilberto Marconi (dir.), *Il fanciullo antico*, Alessandria, 65-83.
Nails (2006) : Debra Nails, « Tragedy off-stage », dans : James Lesher, Debra Nails et Frisbee Sheffield (dir.), *Plato's Symposium: Issues in Interpretation and Reception*, Washington, DC, 179-207.
Neumann (1965) : Harry Neumann, « Diotima's Concept of Love », *AJP* 86, 33-59.
Nikolchina (1993) : Miglena Nikolchina, « Feminine erotic and paternal legacy : revisiting Plato's 'Symposium' », *Paragraph* 16, 239-260.
Nussbaum (1986) : Martha Nussbaum, *The Fragility of Goodness: Luck and Ethics in Greek Tragedy and Philosophy*, Cambridge.
Pappas (2008/2020) : Nikolas Pappas, « Plato's Aesthetics », dans : *Stanford Encyclopedia of Philosophy* (En ligne).
Pender (1992) : Elizabeth E. Pender, « Spiritual Pregnancy in Plato's *Symposium* », *CQ* 42, 72-86.
Pentassuglio (2012) : Francesca Pentassuglio, « Duplice Afrodite, duplice Eros : un caso di intertestualità nei *Simposi* socratici », *Elenchos* 33, 335-356.
Percy (1996) : William A. Percy, *Pederasty and Pedagogy in Archaic Greece*, Urbana.
Périllié (2015) : Jean-Luc Périllié, « Socrate, 'homme érotique' (*erôtikos anèr*)? », *Kentron* 31 (En ligne).
Pierce (1994) : Christine Pierce, « Eros and Epistemology », dans : Bat-Ami Bar On (dir.), *Engendering Origins, Critical Feminist Readings in Plato and Aristotle*, New York, 25-39.
Prandi (2002) : Michele Prandi, « Métonymie et métaphore : parcours partagés dans l'espace de la communication », *Semen* 15 (En ligne).
Prandi (2016) : Michele Prandi, « Les métaphores conflictuelles dans la création de concepts et de termes », *Langue française* 189, 35-48.
Price (1981) : Anthony W. Price, « Loving Persons Platonically », *Phronesis* 26, 25-34.
Price (2017) : Anthony W. Price, « Generating Beauty for the Sake of Immortality. Personal Love and the Goals of the Lover », dans : Pierre Destrée et Zina Giannopoulou (dir.), *Plato's Symposium: A Critical Guide*, Cambridge, 176-193.
Regali (2020) : Mario Regali, « Alle origini di un topos : l'eros come δουλεία nel *Simposio* di Platone e il *servitium amoris* nell'elegia latina », dans : Giovanni Polara (dir.), *OMNE TULIT PUNCTUM QUI MISCUIT UTILE DULCI. Studi in onore di Arturo De Vivo*, Napoli, 819-838.
Renaut (2017) : Olivier Renaut, « La pédérastie selon Pausanias : un défi pour l'éducation platonicienne », dans : Luc Brisson et Olivier Renaut (dir.), *Érotique et politique chez Platon*, Baden-Baden, 219-230.
Ricoeur (1975) : Paul Ricoeur, *La Métaphore vive*, Paris.
Sedley (2006) : David Sedley, « The Speech of Agathon in Plato's *Symposium* », dans : Burkhard Reis (dir.), *The Virtuous Life in Greek Ethics*, Cambridge, 49-67.

Shapiro (2015) : Julia Shapiro, « Pederasty and the Popular Audience », dans : Ruby Blondell et Kirk Ormand (dir.), *Ancient Sex: New Essays*, Columbus, 177–207.
Sissa (1986) : Giulia Sissa, « L'aveu dans le dialogue », dans : *L'aveu. Antiquité et Moyen Âge. Actes de la table ronde de Rome (28–30 mars 1984)*, Rome, 53–67.
Sissa (1990) : Giulia Sissa, « Le sage/femme. Maïeutique et anamnèse », *Esquisses psychanalytiques* 13, 131–149.
Sissa (1992) : Giulia Sissa, « Membres à fantasmes. À propos d'un ouvrage récent de Thomas Laqueur (*Making Sex. Body and Gender from the Greeks to Freud*. Harvard, Harvard University Press, 1990) », *Terrain* 18, 80–86.
Sissa (2000) : Giulia Sissa, *L'Âme est un corps de femme*, Paris.
Sissa (2011) : Giulia Sissa, *Sexe et sensualité. La culture érotique des anciens*, Paris.
Sissa (2012) : Giulia Sissa, « Agathon and Agathon. Male Sensuality in Aristophanes' *Thesmophoriazusae* and Plato's *Symposium* », *Eugesta* 2, 25–70.
Skinner (2013) : Marilyn Skinner, *Sexuality in Greece and Rome*, Malden, MA, 2nd ed.
Sommerstein (1984) : Alan H. Sommerstein, « Aristophanes and the Demon Poverty », *CQ* 34, 314–333.
Testenoire (2013) : Pierre-Yves Testenoire, « Pragmatique du rire dans les écrits socratiques de Xénophon », *L'Information grammaticale* 136, 7–11.
Vattuone (2004) : Riccardo Vattuone, *Il Mostro e il sapiente: Studi sull'erotica greca*, Bologna.
Vlastos (1973/1981) : Gregory Vlastos, « The Individual as Object of Love in Plato », dans : Id., *Platonic Studies*, Princeton, 3–34.
Wedgwood (2009) : Ralph Wedgwood, « Diotima's Eudaemonism: Intrinsic Value and Rational Motivation in Plato's *Symposium* », *Phronesis* 54, 297–325.
Wersinger (2012) : Anne-Gabrièle Wersinger, « 'La voix d'une savante' : Diotime de Mantinée dans le *Banquet* de Platon (201d–212b) », *Cahiers « Mondes anciens »* 3 (En ligne).
Wesling (1980) : Donald Wesling, *The Chances of Rhyme: Devices of Modernity*, Berkeley/Los Angeles.
White (1989) : F.C. White, « Love and Beauty in Plato's Symposium », *JHS* 109, 149–157.
White (2004) : F.C. White, « Virtue in Plato's 'Symposium' », *CQ* 54, 366–378.
White (2008) : F.C. White, « Beauty of Soul and Speech in Plato's 'Symposium' », *CQ* 58, 69–81.

Christoph Mayr
Gender und Rollen in Horaz *carm*. 1,13

Abstract: Depending on text-type, content, intended effect, etc., the first-person speaker in Horace's *Odes* ascribes different roles to himself and to other figures. This makes it possible for both the figures within a text and the readers to set up opposing models of roles, and to deduce from them expectations about the manners of behaviour of the speaker and of other figures. In Hor. *carm*. 1.13, such role expectations are invited above all by the ascription of the parameter 'gender'. The present paper investigates the question of which role or roles are ascribed by the speaker in Hor. *carm*. 1.13 to himself and to other figures and what relation these have to the gender of the figures as presented in the text. I argue that the speaker is wooing the addressee Lydia with the aid of the role-parameter 'gender' and the expectations it invites at the level of the figures: by engaging with the gender of his rival Telephus and the role expectations this engagement invites, the speaker adapts the staging of his own gender status in such a way that at the end of the poem he is able to praise himself as a sensitive and faithful lover, and thus as an anti-model of his rival. Counterpointing this is the effect at the level of reception: the readers of the collection of *Odes* know on the basis of their intratextual reading experience of Books 1–3 that the speaker of this promise of faithfulness cannot keep it, and so the success of this wooing strategy at the level of the figures ultimately has to remain unknown.

Keywords: staging (male) gender, self-promotion, role-expectations, effeminate behaviour, ideals of beauty

1 Einleitung: Das Konzept der Rolle

Die folgende Interpretation von Horaz *carm*. 1,13 stützt sich auf das Konzept der Rolle, das ausgehend von der Theatersprache über die Sozialwissenschaften Einzug in die Literaturwissenschaft gefunden und sich dort etabliert hat, um soziale Interaktions- und Kommunikationsprozesse zu beschreiben und zu analysieren.[1] In Anlehnung an die sozialwissenschaftliche Verwendung des Begriffs verstehe ich unter Rolle ein Bündel von Erwartungen, das an einen sozialen Akteur als Inhaber einer sozialen Position

---

[1] Goffman (2017) 232 f. reflektiert die Übernahme von Konzepten und Begriffen der Theatersprache in die Soziologie, Platz-Waury (2007) 313 f. die Übernahme aus der Soziologie in die Literaturwissenschaft.

Danksagung: Ich danke den Herausgeberinnen für die Einladung zu der diesem Band zu Grunde liegenden Tagung in München sowie allen Teilnehmerinnen und Teilnehmern für hilfreiche Rückmeldung in der Diskussion.

bzw. eines sozialen Status gerichtet wird, d. h. ein Bündel von Erwartungen, die von außen an ein Individuum gestellt werden oder die ein Individuum an sich selbst stellt.[2] Entsprechende Erwartungen können ganz unterschiedliche Aspekte wie z. B. das äußere Erscheinungsbild, innere Einstellungen, Sprechweisen oder durch Gender beeinflusste Verhaltensweisen betreffen. Ein Individuum kann eine oder mehrere Rollen selbst übernehmen oder von anderen zugeschrieben bekommen, indem es sich anderen gegenüber mit bestimmten Rollenparametern präsentiert oder indem andere diese Rollenparameter in ihm wahrnehmen.[3] Die mit der Übernahme bzw. Zuschreibung von Rollen einhergehenden Erwartungen können absichtlich oder unabsichtlich erfüllt oder enttäuscht werden, so dass Übereinstimmungen oder Konflikte mit Rollen entstehen können, die in anderen Kontexten übernommen oder zugeschrieben werden.[4] Dabei hat jede Rollenübernahme bzw. -zuschreibung auch ein persuasives Ziel, das vor allem dazu dient, ein Gegenüber als Rezipientin oder als Rezipienten einer Rollenübernahme oder -zuschreibung zu einer bestimmten Handlung oder Einstellung zu bewegen.[5]

Bereits in der römischen Antike ist ein Denken in vorgeprägten Rollenmustern klar erkennbar. Jochen Martin bezeichnet die Gesellschaft des republikanischen Roms als eine „mask-to-mask-society" und betont, dass diese zum Ziele der sozialen Kontrolle „ausgeprägte Vorstellungen von Rollen entwickelt [hat], die das Handeln jedes Einzelnen in der Gesellschaft jederzeit erwartbar machen sollten."[6] Rollendenken ist in philosophisch-theoretischen Schriften fassbar[7] und war in Form der Übernahme der Perspektive und Sprecher-Haltung anderer bzw. des

---

[2] So die Definition bei Jordan (2015) 247.
[3] Mit Fuhrer (2012) verstehe ich unter Rollenparametern Merkmale, Eigenschaften und Verhaltensweisen, deren Vorhandensein oder Nicht-Vorhandensein eine Rolle modellieren. So lässt sich die Rolle ‚Vater' aus biologischer Sicht u. a. durch das Vorhandensein des Parameters ‚männliches Geschlecht' sowie durch das Nicht-Vorhandensein des Parameters ‚weibliches Geschlecht' definieren. Ein weiterer Parameter ist ein gewisses Alter (mindestens das Alter der Geschlechtsreife), der aber – verwendet man den Begriff z. B. im übertragenen Sinne von ‚Vaterfigur' – nicht unbedingt gegeben sein muss. Im hier verwendeten Beispiel können u. a. die Verhaltensweisen ‚ernähren', ‚erziehen', ‚loben' oder ‚strafen' die Rolle ‚Vater' bestimmen. In Abhängigkeit vom jeweiligen Kontext können Teilaspekte einer Rolle also durch das Hervorheben einzelner Parameter unterschiedlich stark gewichtet werden. S. zur persuasiven und performativen Funktion literarischer Rollenmodellierungen auch den Beitrag von Lisa Cordes im vorliegenden Band.
[4] Goffman (2017) 99–128 und Jordan (2015) 248 thematisieren Rollenkonflikte aus soziologischer Perspektive. Aus literaturwissenschaftlicher Sicht untersucht Fuhrer (2007) Rollenkonflikte in Catulls erotischer Dichtung.
[5] Ontrup/Schicha (1997) 7 zeigen, dass die Zuschreibung und Übernahme von Rollen „auf eine Effektdramaturgie hin konzipiert werden [und dass] ein kalkuliertes Auswählen, Organisieren und Strukturieren von Darstellungsmitteln [stattfindet], das in besonderer Weise strategisch auf Publikumswirkung berechnet ist". S. dazu auch Willems (2009) 78–81. Fuhrer (2012) überträgt diese soziologische Perspektive auf die Literaturwissenschaft.
[6] Martin (2002) 157 f. Ich danke Bianca Schröder für diesen Hinweis.
[7] Zu nennen ist insbesondere die auf Panaitios zurückgehende und bei Cic. *off.* 1,107–125 beschriebene stoische *persona*-Theorie. Es wird dort zwischen vier Rollen (*personae*) unterschieden, die

Hineinversetzens in andere Personen zentraler Bestandteil der rhetorischen Ausbildung und Praxis.[8]

Die folgende Analyse von Horaz *carm.* 1,13 geht von der Vorstellung aus, dass sowohl der Autor den im Text auftretenden Figuren als auch diese Figuren sich gegenseitig ein bestimmtes Rollenkonzept und das entsprechende Verhalten zuweisen.[9] Der Ich-Sprecher der *Oden* nimmt in Abhängigkeit von Textsorte, Inhalt, Wirkungsabsicht etc. unterschiedliche Rollen ein, wobei er als eine insgesamt konsistente Figur anzusehen ist, und schreibt zugleich anderen Figuren Rollen zu. Dies ermöglicht es der Leserschaft, verschiedene Rollenentwürfe gegenüberzustellen und aus ihnen Erwartungen an Verhaltensweisen sowohl des Sprechers als auch anderer Figuren abzuleiten. Vor diesem Hintergrund steht die folgende Interpretation von *carm.* 1,13. Die bisherige Forschung hat sich vor allem mit den intertextuellen Bezügen und der damit gegebenen Auseinandersetzung der Ode mit Sappho 31 und Catull 51 befasst.[10] Auch wurde des Öfteren auf den ‚feierlichen Ton' der letzten Strophe eingegangen,[11] in welcher von ewiger Treue geprägte Liebesverhältnisse gepriesen werden. Dieser Lobpreis wurde oftmals als ein zentraler Punkt der Ode erkannt, jedoch sehr unterschiedlich gedeutet, z. B. als „scheues Bekenntnis tiefer Liebesglut",[12] als „ernst gemeintes Ende", das satirisch auf die „Absurditäten des hellenistischen Epigramms" hinweise,[13] als eine idealisierte und illusorische Welt des „‚So müsste es sein.'",[14] oder als Gedenken der „glücklichen Tage", in denen der Ich-Sprecher „in einem unbelasteten Liebesverhältnis mit Lydia lebte".[15] Ohne diese exemplarisch genannten Forschungsmeinungen bestätigen oder widerlegen zu wollen, argumentiere ich im Folgenden dafür, dass in der Ode mit Rollenerwartungen gearbeitet wird, die vor allem durch die Zuschreibung des Parameters ‚Gender' geweckt werden. Mit Hilfe die-

---

jeder Mensch zu übernehmen hat, um seinen sozialen Pflichten in angemessener Weise gerecht werden zu können. S. dazu Fuhrmann (1979); Gill (1988); Bartsch (2006) 217–224.
8 Z. B. Bloomer (1997). S. zur Übernahme weiblicher Perspektiven durch Männer in den fiktiven Gerichtsprozessen in Sen. *Contr.* den Beitrag von Lisa Cordes im vorliegenden Band.
9 Dazu ausführlich Fuhrer/Zinsli (2003); Fuhrer (2007).
10 Diese Bezüge sind für die vorliegende Interpretation der Ode nur bedingt relevant, weshalb ich im Folgenden nicht näher darauf eingehe. Untersuchungen dazu finden sich bei Commager (1962) 153; Nisbet/Hubbard (1970) 169f.; Syndikus (2001) 154–159; Owens (1992) 241–244; Thome (1994) 26f.; Freis (2005); Sutherland (2005) 63–65; Johnson (2012) 195f.; Mayer (2012) 130–133.
11 In der Forschung finden sich zahlreiche Beschreibungen der letzten Strophe mit Bezeichnungen wie „solemnity", „almost sanctimonious calm", „sententious objectivity" (Segal 1973, 40); „solemn and philosophic calm", „solemn sentiment" (Owens 1992, 237f., 244); „tiefe Ernsthaftigkeit" (Heßen 2000, 248); „ruhige, glückliche, gleichmäßige Stimmung" (Syndikus 2001, 159); „solemn, romantic tone" (Mayer 2012, 133).
12 Kiessling/Heinze (1961) 68.
13 Nisbet/Hubbard (1970) 170: „Our poem should be regarded as a skit of the absurdities of Hellenistic epigram, set off against a more serious Roman attitude."
14 Maurach (1992) 514; ähnlich Eicks (2011) 145f. mit Anm. 372.
15 Heßen (2000) 248–250.

ses Parameters und der durch ihn geweckten Erwartungen kann der in der Ode auftretende Ich-Sprecher auf der Figurenebene um die Adressatin Lydia werben, indem er sich vor allem am Ende des Gedichts als gefühlvoller sowie treuer Liebhaber und dadurch als Gegenmodell zu seinem Rivalen Telephus anpreist. Zugleich weiß das Lesepublikum der Odensammlung auf Grund seiner intratextuellen Lektüreerfahrung der Bücher 1–3 jedoch, dass der Sprecher dieses Angebot der Treue nicht einhalten kann, so dass der Erfolg seiner Werbestrategie letzten Endes auch auf der Figurenebene offenbleiben muss.

2 Strophe 1

In der ersten Strophe werden die drei Figuren der vorliegenden Ode eingeführt und ihre Beziehung zueinander skizziert.[16]

> *Cum tu, Lydia, Telephi*
>   *cervicem roseam, cerea Telephi*
> *laudas bracchia, vae, meum*
>   *fervens difficili bile tumet iecur.*

Immer wenn Du, Lydia, den rosafarbenen Nacken des Telephus und die wachsweichen und weißen[17] Arme des Telephus lobst, wehe, dann schwillt meine wütende Leber von schwer zu kontrollierender[18] Galle.

Die Ausgangssituation des Gedichts ist folgende: Der Ich-Sprecher stellt in seiner Anrede an Lydia fest, dass diese wiederholt die physische Schönheit des Telephus lobe.[19] Er hat also – so die im Text evozierte Situation – von Lydia selbst erfahren,

---

16 Zwar finden sich auch in anderen Oden Figuren mit dem Namen Lydia (1,8; 1,25; 3,9) bzw. Telephus (3,19; 4,11), doch geht das Folgende auf eventuelle Bezüge dieser Oden untereinander nicht ein. Auch Maurach (1992) 502 Anm. 2 spricht sich dagegen aus, „alle horazischen Lydien miteinander zu identifizieren". Zum Verhältnis des Telephus aus dem Mythos und Drama zu gleichnamigen Figuren in Liebesdichtungen s. Nisbet/Hubbard (1970) 170 f.; Sutherland (2005) 61 f. mit Anm. 38.
17 Die Übersetzung von *cereus* mit „wachsweich und weiß" soll nicht nur die Farbe, sondern auch die Weichheit der Haut zum Ausdruck bringen. Kiessling/Heinze (1961) 68 beziehen *cereus* eher auf den „matten Glanz der Haut" als auf die Hautfarbe. Nisbet/Hubbard (1970) 171 f. deuten *cereus* als „white as refined wax", weisen aber darauf hin, dass das Adjektiv auch eine „firm and smooth texture" hervorhebt; so auch Maurach (1992) 502 Anm. 4; Mayer (2012) 130.
18 Nach Kiessling/Heinze (1961) 69 bedeutet der Ausdruck *difficilis bilis*, dass „sich [der Sprecher] vergebens gegen den aufsteigenden Groll" wehrt; ähnlich Maurach (1992) 502 f.; Freis (2005) 68. Nisbet/Hubbard (1970) 172 übersetzen *difficilis* mit „hard to swallow, indigestive".
19 Die Wiederholung des Namens *Telephus* legt nahe, dass Lydia immer wieder von ihm spricht (so Kiessling/Heinze 1968, 68; Nisbet/Hubbard 1970, 170 f.). Der *cum*-Satz ist demnach mit Maurach (1992) 502 iterativ aufzufassen. Ancona (1994) 122 deutet die Wiederholung als „obsession with an erotic rival he wishes to eliminate". Nach Mayer (2012) 130 erinnert die Stellung von *Lydia Telephi*

dass sie Telephus körperlich attraktiv findet. Dies ruft bei ihm Eifersucht und Zorn hervor, was sich in körperlichen Reaktionen manifestiert. Den drei Figuren werden dadurch folgende Rollen zugewiesen: Lydia ist an Telephus interessiert, von Intimitäten der beiden erfährt man jedoch erst in der dritten Strophe aus dem Munde des Ich-Sprechers. Dieser ist, wie seine Eifersucht zeigt, seinerseits an Lydia interessiert;[20] es bleibt offen, ob er ein intimes Verhältnis mit Lydia hatte oder hat.[21]

Zwei Aspekte in der ersten Strophe sind bemerkenswert: Zum einen kommt hier – wie auch in allen weiteren Strophen – nur der Sprecher selbst zu Wort: Er gibt Lydias Worte sowie ihre Sicht auf Telephus wieder, ihr Lob ist keine direkte Rede. Zum anderen wird die Aufmerksamkeit von Beginn an auf Körperliches gelenkt. So lobt Lydia ausschließlich physische Eigenschaften des Telephus und auch die Reaktionen des Sprechers werden auf diejenigen körperlichen Aspekte reduziert, in denen sich seine Emotionen manifestieren. Zudem fällt auf, dass Telephus und nicht die adressierte Lydia im Zentrum der Strophe steht. Zwar ist Lydias Lob Ausgangspunkt und Auslöser dafür, dass sich der Sprecher überhaupt mit Telephus auseinandersetzt, doch geht er abgesehen von der Anrede in V. 1 erst wieder in V. 13 auf sie ein. Vielmehr setzt er sich zunächst nur damit auseinander, was Lydia an Telephus preist, d. h. mit seinem „rosenfarbenen Nacken" (2: *cervix rosea*) sowie seinen „wachsweichen und weißen Armen" (2f.: *cerea bracchia*). Er weiß also, dass Lydia von einem Mann angezogen wird, an dessen Körper sie Eigenschaften hervorhebt, die in der literarischen Tradition als Ausdruck weiblicher Schönheitsideale verwendet werden.[22] Er sieht sich mit einem effeminierten Schönling als Rivalen konfrontiert. Vor diesem Hintergrund schildert er, wie als Reaktion auf diese Erkenntnis seine Leber von Galle anschwillt (3f.: *vae, meum / fervens difficili bile tumet iecur*). Durch dieses Bild präsentiert er sich in zweierlei Hinsicht als Kontrast zu seinem Rivalen: Zum einen evoziert das Anschwellen seiner Leber als Folge von Zorn und Eifersucht anders als die Beschreibung des schönen Telephus Hässlichkeit bzw. ein vor Zorn verzerrtes Ge-

---

an die römische Namensbezeichnung von Frauen und zeigt damit eine gewisse Zugehörigkeit der Lydia zu Telephus an.
20 Owens (1992) stellt die m. E. wenig überzeugende These auf, dass der Ich-Sprecher auch in Telephus verliebt und somit auch auf Lydia eifersüchtig sei; ähnlich Harrison (2018) 174f.
21 Ohne Anhaltspunkte im Text zu nennen, gehen von einer früheren und/oder aktuellen Liebesbeziehung zwischen Ich-Sprecher und Lydia aus: Ancona (1994) 122; Heßen (2000) 248f.; Johnson (2012) 192; Mayer (2012) 132.
22 Thome (1994) 26 weist darauf hin, dass eine *rosea cervix* „sonst Symbol von Frauenschönheit" ist (z. B. als Attribut der Venus in Verg. *Aen.* 1,402; 2,593 oder der Lavinia in 12,606). Sowohl weiße Hautfarbe als auch die Entfernung von Körperbehaarung und daraus resultierende weiche (= ‚wächserne') Haut sind weiblich konnotiert (Edwards 1993, 81). Catull verwendet das Farbadjektiv *roseus* für die Beschreibung weiblicher Brüste (55,12) und der Lippen eines *irrumator*

sicht.[23] Zum anderen lässt sich die Leber als Sitz erotischer Begierde und aggressiver Emotionen identifizieren.[24] Das Anschwellen steht demnach für männlich konnotierte Emotionen und Aggression. Dadurch werden folgende Erwartungen geweckt: dass der Ich-Sprecher im Folgenden als eifersüchtiger Liebender in einer Rolle auftreten werde, in der er sich aggressiv und/oder zumindest invektiv spottend gegenüber Lydia und Telephus verhalten werde;[25] dass Telephus als effeminierter Schönling dem nichts entgegenzuhalten habe.

3 Strophe 2

Doch diese Erwartungen werden nicht erfüllt. Denn im Folgenden handelt der Sprecher nicht aktiv und nimmt somit im Gegensatz zu V. 3f. keine Gegenposition zu Telephus zu ein, dem als Objekt der Begierde Lydias eine passive Rolle zugewiesen wird.

> *tum nec mens mihi nec color*
>   *certa sede manet, umor et in genas*
> *furtim labitur, arguens*
>   *quam lentis penitus macerer ignibus.*

> Daraufhin bleiben weder meine Gemütslage noch meine Gesichtsfarbe unverändert und das Nass [meiner Tränen] fließt unwillkürlich[26] auf meine Wangen und zeigt, wie sehr ich im Inneren von schwelenden Gluten verzehrt werde.

Anders als in V. 3f. angedeutet, tritt der Sprecher in Folge (5: *tum*) der in Strophe 1 skizzierten Ausgangssituation hier nicht aggressiv, ja nicht einmal aktiv handelnd auf. Vielmehr ist er seinen Emotionen machtlos ausgeliefert: Seine Gemütsstimmung und Gesichtsfarbe verändern sich, er kann seine Tränen als Folge seiner emotionalen Leiden nicht zurückhalten und wird von Liebesgluten verzehrt, die in seinem Inneren schwelen. Anders als in Strophe 1 drücken seine körperlichen Reaktionen hier keine aggressiven Emotionen aus. Vielmehr zeigt er sich in Strophe 2

(80,1), Martial zur Beschreibung von *pueri delicati* (7,80,9; 8,55,15); vgl. dazu Nisbet/Hubbard (1970) 171; Syndikus (³2001) 155 Anm. 4.
23 Vgl. Eicks (2011) 145f.
24 Vgl. Kiessling/Heinze (1961) 68f. mit Verweis auf Hor. *carm.* 1,25,15; Nisbet/Hubbard (1970) 172f. Sutherland (2005) 64 sieht die Leber als mögliches „substitute for sexual display" an.
25 Vgl. Johnson (2012) 194–196 mit Anm. 25, der darauf hinweist, dass an vier weiteren von insgesamt acht Belegstellen in Horaz' Werk die Verwendung von *bilis* in einer Invektive resultiert oder dieser vorausgeht (*sat.* 1,9,66; *sat.* 2,3,141; *epod.* 11,16; *epist.* 1,9,20).
26 Die Bedeutung von *furtim* ist in den Kommentaren nicht befriedigend erklärt. Nach Kiessling/Heinze (1961) 69 verweist *furtim* hier auf die Scham des Ich-Sprechers; bei Nisbet/Hubbard (1970) und Mayer (2012) finden sich keine Erläuterungen. Nach Freis (2005) 69 bedeutet es im vorliegenden Kontext „silent". Die überzeugendste Erklärung findet sich bei Sutherland (2005) 64f.: *furtim* bringe zum Ausdruck, dass die Tränen des Ich-Sprechers gegen seinen Willen fließen.

mit typischen Attributen eines Liebeskranken, wie er vor allem aus der römischen Liebeselegie, aber auch prominent aus den Vorlagen der Ode Sappho 31 und Catull 51 bekannt ist.[27] Dadurch weckt er entsprechende Erwartungen an sein künftiges Verhalten[28] und gesteht zudem mit Passivität, Kontrollverlust und mangelnder Selbstbeherrschung Eigenschaften ein, die in antiken Diskursen als weiblich angesehen wurden.[29] Er übernimmt somit, anders als Strophe 1 erwarten lässt, die Rolle des passiven, leidenden und somit als ‚unmännlich' konnotierten Liebenden, der seinen Gefühlen machtlos ausgeliefert ist und seinem Rivalen bzw. dessen in Strophe 1 gepriesener physischer Attraktivität nichts entgegenzusetzen hat.

4 Strophen 3 und 4

Diese Selbstdarstellung setzt sich in den Strophen 3 und 4 fort.

> *uror, seu tibi candidos*
> *turparunt umeros immodicae mero*
> *rixae sive puer furens*
> *impressit memorem dente labris notam.*
>
> *non, si me satis audias,*
> *speres perpetuum dulcia barbare*
> *laedentem oscula, quae Venus*
> *quinta parte sui nectaris imbuit.*

Ich brenne, egal, ob Dir von unvermischtem Wein zügellos gewordene Rangeleien die weißen Schultern entstellt haben oder ob der rasende Knabe mit seinen Zähnen ein vielsagendes Mal auf Deine Lippen gedrückt hat.

Du darfst, wenn Du recht auf mich hörst, nicht hoffen, dass Dir der ewig treu sein wird,[30] der barbarisch die lieblichen Lippen verletzt, die Venus mit dem fünften Teil ihres Nektars benetzt hat.

---

27 Zu Parallelen mit dem Motiv der Liebeskrankheit in der römischen Liebeselegie s. z. B. Ancona (1994) 123. Commager (1962) 152–155 sieht Strophe 2 als Parodie liebeselegischer Motive an.
28 Zu Erwartungen, die bei der Einnahme einer durch literarische Traditionen vorgeprägten Rolle geweckt werden, s. den einleitenden Abschnitt oben.
29 Föllinger (2003) zeigt an homerischen Helden, dass Weinen in der Antike nicht per se als unmännlich angesehen wurde. Unmännlich ist im vorliegenden Fall also nur der Mangel an Selbstkontrolle; zur Assoziation von Mangel an Selbstkontrolle mit Weiblichkeit s. Edwards (1993) 81–87, 91 f.
30 Nach Kiessling/Heinze (1961) 70 ist das Adjektiv *perpetuus* „singulär von *amor* auf den *amans* übertragen" und deutet auf Strophe 5 voraus. Ancona (1994) 124 mit Anm. 36 schlägt vor, *perpetuum* als Adverb mit der Bedeutung „repeatedly, continually" aufzufassen, und übersetzt: „you would not hope for him to continuously harm like a barbarian your sweet lips."; ähnlich Owens (1992) 238 f.

Strophe 3 beginnt mit einer Selbstaussage des Ich-Sprechers: *uror*. Angesichts seiner männlich-aggressiven Pose in Strophe 1 weckt dieses Verb erneut die Erwartung, dass er sich im Folgenden aggressiv gegenüber Lydia und/oder Telephus verhalten werde.[31] Doch wie schon in Strophe 2 werden diese Erwartungen auch hier nicht erfüllt. Vielmehr wird das mögliche Bedeutungsspektrum des Verbs *urere* reduziert und bezeichnet hier allein den emotionalen Leidenszustand des Ich-Sprechers. Denn im weiteren Verlauf der Ode ist keinerlei Rede mehr von seinem Zorn und seiner Wut, so dass das Verb *urere* – auch in Anknüpfung an den unmittelbar vorausgehenden Ausdruck *lentis penitus macerer ignibus* (8) – hier nur die für Liebeskontexte typische Bedeutung emotionalen Leidens trägt.[32] Der Ich-Sprecher tritt abgesehen von der Aussage in der passiven Verbform *uror* in der gesamten dritten Strophe nicht in Erscheinung, sondern lenkt die Aufmerksamkeit auf Lydias Körper sowie auf das Verhalten seines Rivalen in Bezug auf diesen Körper: Aus den darauf sichtbaren Liebesmalen schließt er auf ein sexuelles Verhältnis der beiden, in dem nun vielmehr Telephus, entgegen der in Strophe 1 geweckten Erwartung, eine männlich-dominante, ja sogar aggressive Rolle einnimmt. Anders als zu Beginn der Ode nimmt der Sprecher seinen Rivalen jetzt nicht mehr als weiblich und weichlich sowie als passives Objekt der Begierde Lydias wahr, sondern als ihren aktiv und dominant auftretenden Liebhaber. So bezeichnet er die von Telephus verursachten Liebesmale als ‚Entstellung' (10: *turparunt*), seine Küsse als „barbarische Verletzung" (14 f.: *barbare laedentem*)[33] Lydias und ihrer Schönheit. Zwar nimmt er Telephus ausschließlich aus Lydias Perspektive wahr, indem er von ihrem Lob berichtet (Strophe 1) und die Spuren seiner sexuellen Handlungen an ihrem Körper sehen kann – ob er seinen Rivalen jemals gesehen hat, bleibt offen. Doch ist Telephus in dieser Wahrnehmung nicht der effeminierte Schönling, als den Lydia ihn in Strophe 1 preist, sondern ein ‚barbarischer' *puer furens* (12).[34] Deshalb lenkt der Spre-

---

[31] Vgl. Johnson (2012) 196. Nach Freis (2005) 70 richtet sich der Zorn des Ich-Sprechers jetzt nur noch gegen Telephus, nach Johnson (2012) 196 gegen Lydia.

[32] Das Bedeutungsspektrum des Verbs *urere* umfasst sowohl ‚Brennen vor Liebe' als auch ‚Brennen vor Zorn oder Eifersucht', vgl. *OLD* s.v. *uro* 6 und 7: „(of love, an object of passion, etc.) To inflame with desire" bzw. „To cause to burn or smart with resentment, jealousy, grief, anxiety, etc." Sutherland (2005) 68 mit Anm. 65 betont, dass *urere* in der Liebeselegie i. d. R. nur emotionales Leiden ausdrückt.

[33] Quadlbauer (1975) zeigt, dass die Junktur *laedere oscula* (die er mit *pressu violare* umschreibt) im vorliegenden Kontext aus Sicht des Ich-Sprechers ein tatsächliches Verletzen der Lippen Lydias bezeichnet. Wenig überzeugend schlägt Owens (1992) 238 f. neben Quadlbauers Deutung eine weitere vor: „*laedo* on occasion could take a direct object of the thing which is struck down or pressed on something else." Das auf *oscula* bezogene Relativpronomen *quae* deute dann an, dass der Ich-Sprecher wisse, dass Telephus' Küsse *dulcia* seien, er ihn also selbst geküsst habe und deshalb auch in ihn verliebt sei.

[34] Nach Johnson (2012) 196 f. hat *furor* bei Horaz immer negative Bedeutung. Mayer (2012) 131 erklärt *furens* m. E. unzutreffend als „passionate" mit Verweis auf TLL VI 1,1627,28–42, dort jedoch: *amore, libidine quasi demens, vecors*.

cher bei der Beschreibung des Liebesaktes der beiden Figuren in den Strophen 3 und 4 die Aufmerksamkeit vor allem darauf, dass sein Rivale Gewalt auf den Körper Lydias ausgeübt habe. In der Forschung wird aus den als „von unvermischtem Wein zügellos gewordenen Rangeleien" genannten Intimitäten zwischen Telephus und Lydia (10 f.: *immodicae mero / rixae*) oftmals der Schluss gezogen, dass sich Telephus gegenüber Lydia gewalttätig verhalten habe und dass die Liebesmale an ihrem Körper tatsächliche, daraus resultierende Verletzungen seien.[35] Doch lässt sich der Text auch anders verstehen: Der Sex von Telephus und Lydia ist von körperbetonter und mithin physisch manifester Leidenschaft geprägt, die bei Lydia nicht auf Ablehnung stößt.[36] Hierfür spricht auch, dass die hier geschilderten Intimitäten zum typischen Repertoire der Liebesdichtung gehören.[37] Nur aus Sicht des eifersüchtigen, zornigen und vor Liebesqualen vergehenden Sprechers ist der „junge Knabe" Telephus „rasend" (V. 11: *puer furens*).[38]

Durch diese Beschreibung wird deutlich: Es ist der zunächst als effeminiert geschilderte *puer* Telephus, der in die *immodicae rixae* mit Lydia verwickelt ist und dabei eine aktive, dominante und somit männliche Position einnimmt. Telephus, nicht der Sprecher hinterlässt als Zeichen seiner sexuellen Dominanz und seiner Überlegenheit über den Rivalen Spuren an Lydias Körper. Der Sprecher ist seinem Rivalen in der Werbung um Lydia also nicht nur hinsichtlich physischer Attraktivität (Strophe 1), sondern auch in Bezug auf sexuelle Aktivität unterlegen (Strophe 3 und 4). Telephus vereint in sich die Qualitäten eines attraktiven und jugendlichen Körpers mit denen eines potenten und männlich auftretenden Liebhabers. Der Sprecher hat dem

---

35 Die *communis opinio* beruht vor allem auf Yardley (1976); vgl. auch Kiessling/Heinze (1961) 68, die die Strophe wie Maurach (1992) 508 mit der völlig anderen Situation in Ov. *am.* 1,7 gleichsetzen („trunkene Mißhandlungen und wilden Liebkosungen"); Nisbet/Hubbard (1970) 169 („violent habits"); Ancona (1994) 124 („barbarian harm"); Syndikus (³2001) 157 („wüste, wilde Leidenschaft"), 158 („barbarische Hemmungslosigkeit"); Freis (2005) 68 („violent passion"); Eicks (2011) 146 („ungestümer Grobian"; „brachiale Gewalt"); Johnson (2012) 196 („drunken brawls and rough sex", „[the rhythm] imitate[s] fists landing"). Dass Telephus als ‚Stellvertreter' des Ich-Sprechers „abusive actions" gegenüber Lydia ausübe, und sich der Ich-Sprecher voyeuristisch an dessen Gewalt gegen Lydias Körper erfreue, wie Sutherland (2005) meint, lässt sich m. E. am Text nicht belegen.
36 Gleicher Auffassung sind Sutherland (2005) 72 f. („Lydia in all likelihood enjoys the bodily marks that the lyricist frames as violence.") und Mayer (2012) 131 f. („erotic tussels"; Lydia is „besotted with him [Telephus], despite (or perhaps even because) of his rough treatment of her."). Maurach (1992) 505 stellt zumindest die Frage, ob Lydia den Schmerz „so ganz wider ihren Willen, ob mit der Lust der Hingabe an den so herrlich Aggressiven [erfuhr]".
37 Eine durch Beißen verursachtes Liebesmal (*nota*) erwähnen z. B. Prop. 4,3,25 f.; Tib. 1,8,37 f.; Ov. *am.* 1,7,41 f.; 3,14,33 f.; auch Plaut. *Pseud.* 67 und Catull 8,18 thematisieren einen „Beiß-Kuss" (so Bender unter dem Lemma ‚Kuss' im DNP). In Ov. *ars* 1,663–676 fordert der *praeceptor amoris* dazu auf, Frauen, die sich spielerisch ‚wehren', mit ‚Gewalt' zu küssen, da Frauen diese Form von ‚Gewalt' willkommen sei; in 3,307–310 beschreibt er genau das Verhalten, dass der Ich-Sprecher hier von Lydia und Telephus annimmt.
38 Ähnlich Quadlbauer (1975) 353.

nichts entgegenzusetzen und muss sich somit für die Werbung um Lydia in anderer Hinsicht attraktiv machen. Dazu präsentiert er sich als Gegenmodell zu Telephus, indem er sich in seiner Selbstdarstellung weder auf Schönheit noch auf Männlichkeit und damit verbundener sexueller Dominanz bezieht, sondern auf Eigenschaften, mit denen er sich gerade davon abgrenzen kann. Zunächst will er dazu mit der Schilderung seiner Leiden in Strophe 2 die Tiefe seiner Gefühle veranschaulichen[39] und nutzt dort die Zuschreibung unmännlich konnotierter Gendereigenschaften für die Werbung um Lydia.[40]

In der Du-Ansprache (9: *tibi*; 13: *audias*; 14: *speres*) wendet sich der Ich-Sprecher mit der Beschreibung bzw. mit seiner Imagination des Liebesaktes in den Strophen 3 und 4 nochmals explizit an Lydia. Die Strategie seiner Werbung umfasst in diesen Strophen zwei Aspekte. Zum einen erfolgt sie wenig überraschend über den Lobpreis ihrer Schönheit: Ihre Schultern sind weiß (9f.: *candidos . . . umeros*), ihre Lippen lieblich (14f.: *dulcia . . . oscula*) und von Venus' Nektar benetzt (15f.: *quae Venus / quinta parte sui nectaris imbuit*).[41] Zum anderen wirbt er um Lydia jedoch auch, indem er ihr mitteilt, welche Botschaften er aus ihrem Körper ‚herausliest':[42] Aus den Liebesmalen an ihrem Körper leitet er ab, dass Telephus sich nicht entsprechend Lydias in Strophe 1 artikulierten Erwartungen verhalten habe und somit nicht ihrem Ideal entspreche. Denn Lydias Liebesmale zeigen, dass Telephus gerade im direkten sexuellen Kontakt nicht effeminiert, sondern dominant, aggressiv und ‚männlich' auftritt.

5 Strophe 5

Diesem potenten und männlichen Auftreten seines Rivalen muss der Sprecher anderes entgegensetzen. Um Lydia umwerben zu können, lenkt er die Aufmerksamkeit im Folgenden deshalb mit der Eigenschaft der Treue auf einen Bereich, in dem er Telephus übertreffen kann. Bereits in Strophe 4 warnt er Lydia: Wer sich – wie es Telephus aus seiner Sicht tut – ihr gegenüber respektlos und aggressiv verhalte, von dem dürfe sie keine Treue erwarten: *non . . . / speres perpetuum dulcia barbare /*

---

39 Vgl. Ancona (1994) 123; Freis (2005) 70.
40 So auch Mayer (2012) 133; Hutchinson (2018) 202. Ähnlich Sutherland (2005) 65f.
41 Zum Preis von Lydias Schönheit s. Freis (2005) 70–72, der jedoch zu weit geht, indem er von der „near divinity" Lydias spricht (S. 71) und sie als „repository of divinity" (S. 72) bezeichnet. In Verbindung mit dem Nektar der Venus ist *dulcis* hier i. S. v. ‚honigsüß' o. ä. aufzufassen. Was mit dem Ausdruck *quinta parte sui nectaris* gemeint ist, bleibt unklar. Zwei Erklärungsversuche finden sich bei Nisbet/Hubbard (1970) 175–177: der Nektar der Venus symbolisiere die Liebe; Lydias Küsse seien so süß wie Nektar. Syndikus (^{3}2001) 158 Anm. 23 geht von einer nicht näher bestimmten, „uns nicht mehr erhaltene[n] Dichterstelle" als Vorbild für den Topos von mit Honig, Nektar oder Ambrosia benetzten Lippen aus.
42 Zum ‚Schreiben auf' und ‚Lesen von' Körpern s. Sutherland (2005).

laedentem oscula. In Strophe 5 fordert er implizit dazu auf, diese Eigenschaft bei ihm selbst anzunehmen.

> *felices ter et amplius*
>   *quos irrupta tenet copula nec malis*
> *divulsus querimoniis*
>   *suprema citius solvet amor die!*
>
> Dreimal und mehr glücklich sind die, die ein unzerreißbares Band zusammenhält und die ihre Liebe, die nicht durch böse Streitereien zerrüttet ist, nicht früher trennt als am letzten Tag![43]

Überschwänglich preist der Sprecher hier Menschen, deren Beziehung von fester Treue geprägt ist und ein ganzes Leben lang anhält. Dadurch ‚ersetzt' er die physische Attraktivität und das männliche Auftreten seines Rivalen – in beiden Aspekten kann er nicht mit Telephus konkurrieren – durch die Eigenschaft der Treue[44] und lenkt so die Aufmerksamkeit von den Qualitäten des Telephus weg, hin zu allgemein als positiv geltenden Qualitäten, über die er selbst zu verfügen behauptet. In seiner Werbung um Lydia betont er durch die Zuschreibung unmännlich konnotierter Gendereigenschaften, sie gerade nicht sexuell verführen oder dominieren zu wollen, sondern sie vor allem auf einer emotionalen Ebene als leidenschaftlich *und* treu Liebender zu begehren.[45] Auch wenn sich im Text selbst keinerlei Anzeichen dafür finden, dass Lydia überhaupt an einem von Treue geprägten Verhältnis mit Telephus interessiert ist – sie lobt in Strophe 1 ja ausschließlich dessen physische Attraktivität – kann der Ich-Sprecher durch die vom konkreten Bezug auf die Protagonisten der Ode abstrahierten Formulierungen und der damit verbundenen Erzeugung einer ‚feierlichen' Stimmung erreichen, dass Lydia sich von seiner Werbung angesprochen fühlt. Ob Lydia von dem Ideal, das ihr offeriert wird, angetan ist oder sich gar überzeugen lässt, bleibt freilich offen.

Diesem um Lydia werbenden Persuasionsversuch, der auf Figurenebene auf Rollenmodellierungen anhand von Gendereigenschaften basiert, steht die Wirkung auf der Rezeptionsebene entgegen. Auch hier arbeitet der Text mit Rollenerwartungen: Geht man davon aus, dass der Ich-Sprecher in Horaz' Odenbüchern 1–3 zwar unterschiedliche Rollen einnimmt, jedoch eine insgesamt relativ konsistente Figur darstellt, stellt das Lesepublikum bestimmte Erwartungen an ihn. Egal, ob die Lektüre

---

43 Die hier abgedruckte Übersetzung ist eine von mir adaptierte Version derjenigen von Holzberg (2018). Ich folge dabei Mayer (2001) 66 und beziehe die Negation *nec* sowohl auf *malis divulsus querimoniis* als auch auf *citius solvet*; anders Heßen (2000). Ancona (1994) bezieht *nec* nur auf *citius solvet* („Happy three times and more are those whom a bond that has suffered temporary ruptures holds and whom a love torn apart by serious complaints will not loosen sooner than the final day."); der Ich-Sprecher werbe somit um Lydia, indem er sich als kurzzeitigen und somit für ihre gefestigte Beziehung zu Telephus gefahrlosen Seitensprung anbiete.
44 Vgl. Freis (2005) 71 f.; Hutchinson (2018) 202.
45 Vgl. Sutherland (2005) 73 f.

der Oden linear oder nur in Auswahl erfolgt, wird – z. B. mit den vorausgehenden Oden 1,5 und 1,11 früh in der Sammlung – deutlich, dass der Sprecher Liebesverhältnisse mit verschiedenen Frauen eingegangen ist und eingeht. Das legt nahe, dass er das hier in Strophe 5 implizit gegebene Versprechen von Treue also kaum einhalten wird.[46] Dieser Eindruck und die damit verbundene Erwartungshaltung wird durch die Tatsache verstärkt, dass eine derart emphatische Betonung und damit implizierte Forderung von Treue wie hier in Strophe 5 in Horaz' *Carmina* einmalig ist. Denn in Oden mit erotischer Thematik stehen sonst fast ausschließlich sexuelle Beziehungen im Zentrum. Auch wird vom Sprecher der Oden nur hier Treue als Ideal in Liebesbeziehungen propagiert.[47] Die intratextuelle Lektüre der Bücher 1–3 stellt somit seinen in *carm.* 1,13 präsentierten Rollenentwurf in Frage, so dass auch der Erfolg seiner Werbestrategie auf der Figurenebene letztlich fraglich bleiben muss.

Literaturverzeichnis

Texte und Übersetzungen

Q. Horatius Flaccus, *Opera*, ed. David Roy Shackleton Bailey, Berlin [4]2008.
Q. Horatius Flaccus, *Sämtliche Werke*. Lateinisch-Deutsch, hrsg. und übers. von Niklas Holzberg, Berlin/Boston 2018.

Forschungsliteratur

Ancona (1994): Ronnie Ancona, *Time and the Erotic in Horace's Odes*, Durham/London.
Bartsch (2006): Shadi Bartsch, *The Mirror of the Self: Sexuality, Self-Knowledge, and the Gaze in Early Roman Empire*, Chicago.
Bloomer (1997): William Martin Bloomer, „Schooling in Persona: Imagination and Subordination in Roman Education", *ClAnt* 16, 57–78.
Commager (1962): Steele Commager, *The Odes of Horace. A Critical Study*, New Haven.
Edwards (1993): Catharine Edwards, *The Politics of Immorality in Ancient Rome*, Cambridge.
Eicks (2011): Mathias Eicks, *Liebe und Lyrik: Zur Funktion des erotischen Diskurses in Horazens erster Odensammlung*, Berlin/New York.
Föllinger (2003): Sabine Föllinger, „Männerbilder in der frühgriechischen Dichtung", in: Therese Fuhrer u. Samuel Zinsli (Hgg.), *Genderstudies in den Altertumswissenschaften. Rollenkonstrukte in antiken Texten*, Trier, 24–42.
Freis (2005): Richard Freis, „*Amor* and *Pietas*: The Catullan Revolution and the Horatian Counter-Revolution", in: William W. Batstone u. Garth Tissol (Hgg.), *Defining Genre and Gender in Latin*

---

[46] Vgl. z. B. Hutchinson (2018) 202: „The narrator's offer of permanence is at the least unverifiable, and Pyrrha (1.5) and Leuconoe (1.11) already make it seem implausible."
[47] Darauf weisen unter anderem hin: Kiessling/Heinze (1961) 68; Segal (1973) 40; Mayer (2012) 133; Hutchinson (2018) 202.

Literature: Essays Presented to William S. Anderson on His Seventy-Fifth Birthday, New York, 61–77.

Fuhrmann (1979): Manfred Fuhrmann, „Persona, ein römischer Rollenbegriff", in: Odo Marquard u. Karlheinz Stierle (Hgg.), Identität, München, 83–106.

Fuhrer u. Zinsli (2003): Therese Fuhrer u. Samuel Zinsli, „Einleitung", in: Therese Fuhrer u. Samuel Zinsli (Hgg.), Gender Studies in den Altertumswissenschaften: Rollenkonstrukte in antiken Texten, Trier, 7–13.

Fuhrer (2007): Therese Fuhrer, „Rollenerwartung und Rollenkonflikt in Catulls erotischer Dichtung", in: Elke Hartmann, Udo Hartmann u. Katrin Pietzner (Hgg.), Geschlechterdefinitionen und Geschlechtergrenzen in der Antike, Stuttgart, 55–64.

Fuhrer (2012): Therese Fuhrer, „Autor-Figurationen: Literatur als Ort der Inszenierung von Kompetenz", in: Therese Fuhrer u. Almut-Barbara Renger (Hgg.), Performanz von Wissen. Strategien der Wissensvermittlung in der Vormoderne, Heidelberg, 129–147.

Gill (1988): Christopher Gill, „Personhood and Personality. The Four-Persona Theory in Cicero, De officiis I", OSAPh 6, 169–199.

Goffman ([17]2017): Erving Goffman, Wir alle spielen Theater. Die Selbstdarstellung im Alltag. Aus dem Amerikanischen von Peter Weber-Schäfer, München.

Harrison (2018): Stephen Harrison, „Hidden Voices. Homoerotic Colour in Horace's Odes", in: Sebastian Matzner u. Stephen Harrison (Hgg.), Complex Inferiorities: The Poetics of the Weaker Voice in Latin Literature, Oxford, 169–184.

Heßen (2000): Bern Heßen, „Liebe bis zum Tod? Bemerkungen zur letzten Strophe von Horaz, carm. 1,13", in: Andreas Haltenhoff u. Fritz-Heiner Mutschler (Hgg.), Hortus litterarum antiquarum: Festschrift für Hans Armin Gärtner zum 70. Geburtstag, Heidelberg, 243–251.

Hutchinson (2018): Gregory Hutchinson, „On not Being Beautiful", in: Sebastian Matzner u. Stephen Harrison (Hgg.), Complex Inferiorities: The Poetics of the Weaker Voice in Latin Literature, Oxford, 169–204.

Johnson (2012): Timothy S. Johnson, Horace's Iambic Criticism: Casting Blame (Iambikē Poiēsis), Leiden.

Jordan (2015): Stefan Jordan, „Rolle", in: Sina Farzin u. Stefan Jordan (Hgg.), Lexikon Soziologie und Sozialtheorie, Stuttgart, 247–248.

Kiessling u. Heinze (1961): Adolf Kiessling u. Richard Heinze, Quintus Horatius Flaccus, Satiren, Berlin.

Martin (2002): Jochen Martin, „Formen sozialer Kontrolle im republikanischen Rom", in: David Cohen (Hg.), Demokratie, Recht und soziale Kontrolle im klassischen Athen, München, 155–172.

Maurach (1992): Gregor Maurach, „Hor. c. 1,13: einige Methodenprobleme", Gymnasium 99, 501–517.

Mayer (2001): Roland Mayer, „,Not' again?", Glotta 77, 65–74.

Mayer (2012): Roland Mayer, Horace. Odes. Book 1, Cambridge.

Nisbet u. Hubbard (1970): Robin G. M. Nisbet u. Margaret Hubbard, A Commentary on Horace: Odes, Book 1, Oxford.

Ontrup u. Schicha (1999): Rüdiger Ontrup u. Christian Schicha, „Die Transformation des Theatralischen – Eine Einführung", in: Rüdiger Ontrup u. Christian Schicha (Hgg.), Medieninszenierungen im Wandel. Interdisziplinäre Zugänge, Münster, 7–18.

Owens (1992): William M. Owens, „Double Jealousy: An Interpretation of Horace, Odes 1.13.VI", in: Carl Deroux (Hg.), Studies in Latin Literature and Roman History 6, Brüssel, 237–244.

Platz-Waury (2007): Elke Platz-Waury, „Rolle", in: Klaus Weimar et al. (Hgg.), Reallexikon der deutschen Literaturwissenschaft, Bd. 3, Berlin/New York, 313–315.

Quadlbauer (1975): Franz Quadlbauer, „laedentem oscula. Zu Hor. carm. 1,13,15", in: E. Lefèvre (Hg.), Studien zur augusteischen Zeit. Kieler Festschrift für Erich Burck zum 70. Geburtstag, Amsterdam, 347–358.

Segal (1973): Charles Segal, „*Felices ter et amplius*. Horace, *Odes*, I. 13", *Latomus* 32, 39–46.
Sutherland (2005): Elizabeth H. Sutherland, „Writing (on) Bodies: Lyric Discourse and the Production of Gender in Horace *Odes* 1.13", *CPh* 100, 52–82.
Syndikus (^{3}2001): Hans Peter Syndikus, *Die Lyrik des Horaz. Eine Interpretation der Oden*. Bd. 1: Erstes und Zweites Buch, Darmstadt.
Thome (1994): Gabriele Thome, „Die Funktion der Farben bei Horaz", *AClass* 37, 15–39.
Willems (2009): Herbert Willems, „Theatralität als (figurations-)soziologisches Konzept: Von Fischer-Lichte über Goffman zu Elias und Bourdieu", in: Herbert Willems (Hg.), *Theatralisierung der Gesellschaft*, Bd. 1: *Soziologische Theorie und Zeitdiagnose*, Wiesbaden, 75–112.
Yardley (1976): John C. Yardley, „Lover's Quarrels. Horace Odes 1, 13, 11 and Propertius 4, 5, 40", *Hermes* 104, 124–128.

Jacqueline Fabre-Serris
Enquête sur l'identité du « je » féminin de l'élégie 3.11 du *Corpus Tibullianum* : méthodes et conjectures

Abstract: Elegy 3.11 of the *Corpus Tibullianum* is written in the first person. Is the author a woman, or a man pretending to be a woman? Both hypotheses were supported. The first was put forward in 1755 by Heyne, who attributed elegies 3.9 and 3.11 to a Sulpicia living in the Augustan age. In 1838, Gruppe attributed poems 8–13 to an unknown poet and epigrams 14–18 to Sulpicia, Messalla's niece. This second assumption was accepted until the late twentieth century. Insofar as it was based on the ideas of his time about the kind of texts a woman was able to write, Gruppe did not have to strongly argue for his attribution, which was only contested in the following years about epigram 13. It is more surprising that this attribution continued to be accepted in the twentieth century and beyond, even after gender conceptions have changed significantly. This is particularly the case since, in 1994, Holt Parker argued that all eight poems in the first person were by Sulpicia by putting forward a whole series of arguments based on, among other ideas, the use of the first person (there is no example in Antiquity of a poet pretending to be someone else by using the 'I'). In this paper I will also support the assumption that the author of elegy 3.11 is Sulpicia by using two methods of modern text analysis: intertextuality and intratextuality, with the aim of showing how Sulpicia constructs herself as an elegiac author whose work is both original and 'feminine'.

Keywords: Sulpicia, Tibullus, Propertius, Gallus, reciprocity, frankness

L'élégie 3.11 du *Corpus Tibullianum* est un texte élégiaque sur les amours de Sulpicia et de Cerinthus, écrit à la première personne. Ce 'je' recouvre-t-il également un auteur féminin ? Ou est-il produit par un homme feignant d'être une femme ? Les deux hypothèses ont été soutenues. La première a été avancée en 1755 par Christian Gottlieb Heyne, qui attribua les élégies 3.9 et 3.11 à une Sulpicia vivant à l'époque augustéenne,[1] puis reprise par Holt Parker en 1994, par Judith Hallett en 2002 et par Peter Dronke en 2003, pour lesquels l'auteure de ces poèmes serait Sulpicia, fille ou petite-fille de Servius Sulpicius Rufus, et nièce de Valerius Messalla Corvinus.[2] J'ai ultérieurement tenté de conforter la même hypothèse dans différents articles.[3] La seconde

---
[1] Skoie (2002) 128.
[2] Parker (1994) ; Hallett (2002a), pour qui tous les poèmes du cycle ont été écrits par Sulpicia (c'est aussi la thèse qu'elle soutient dans sa contribution dans le présent volume) ; Dronke (2003).
[3] Fabre-Serris (2009), (2017), (2018a) et (2020a).

conjecture a fait florès depuis *Die Römische Elegie* d'Otto Gruppe parue en 1838. Le savant allemand attribua les poèmes 8–13, qu'ils soient à la première ou à la troisième personne, à un poète inconnu, désigné sous le nom d'*auctor de Sulpicia* ou d'*amicus Sulpiciae*. Sa répartition a été acceptée par la majorité des critiques, à une exception près : le poème 13 a été rajouté par August Rossbach en 1855 au groupe des épigrammes attribuées à Sulpicia.[4]

Dans la mesure où elle était basée sur une conviction issue des idées de son époque sur le genre de textes qu'une femme était en capacité d'écrire (de courts billets peu élaborés),[5] Otto Gruppe n'avait nul besoin d'argumenter réellement sa répartition. Une cinquantaine d'années plus tard, en 1891, c'est le même genre de préjugés qui explique le jugement de Georges Doncieux sur les épigrammes 13–18 : de « petits billets[6] amoureux, d'une versification gauche, d'un style dur et enchevêtré, mais d'une extraordinaire intensité de passion et qui, pour tout dire, 'respirent la femme à chaque ligne' ».[7] Il est assez singulier que cette répartition, jamais réellement argumentée, ait perduré au 20ième siècle et après, alors que les conceptions en matière de Gender ont considérablement évolué. Et ce, d'autant que Holt Parker avait développé une série d'arguments, basés à la fois sur l'usage de la première personne (on n'a aucun exemple dans l'Antiquité de poète se faisant passer pour un autre en utilisant le 'je') et sur la règle de composition des guirlandes poétiques (les auteurs sont alternés).[8]

Ce sont d'autres types d'arguments que j'utiliserai dans cet article pour défendre également l'identification du 'je' féminin de l'élégie 3.11 avec Sulpicia. Je recourrai à deux méthodes d'analyse moderne des textes : l'intertextualité et l'intratextualité. L'une et l'autre de ces techniques d'analyse visent à mettre en évidence l'ensemble des relations qu'un auteur a créées dans son texte, le plus souvent volontairement, avec d'autres textes écrits par d'autres auteurs ou par lui-même. Ce qui autorise l'emploi de ces deux méthodes modernes pour interpréter un texte poétique latin, est qu'elles rencontrent, en permettant de la déconstruire, la pratique d'écriture, tout à fait particulière, utilisée par les auteurs romains pour composer leurs poèmes. Cette

---

[4] Rossbach (1855) 6 et 55.

[5] Les raisons de son choix reposaient sur deux suppositions : l'une était tirée de la structure du recueil (les poèmes regroupés devaient être du même auteur), l'autre résultait d'un jugement stylistique, sous-tendu par ses convictions sur les capacités respectives des deux sexes : Gruppe attribua à Sulpicia les textes courts qu'il assimilait à des 'billets', à son avis, typiquement féminins, retraçant les événements réels d'une histoire d'amour, ce qui revenait à limiter leur intérêt à une valeur documentaire.

[6] Voir des jugements similaires par exemple chez Schanz-Hosius (1959) 190 ; Smith (1913) 79 s. ; Luck (1969) 108.

[7] Doncieux (1891) 77.

[8] Sur le fait que curieusement l'opinion (non fondée) de Gruppe ait continué de prévaloir malgré les « argomenti persuasivi » par lesquels Parker a appuyé la thèse que Sulpicia était l'auteure des élégies 9 et 11, voir Dronke (2003) 90.

pratique, analysée d'abord à travers le concept d'"écriture allusive',[9] consistait pour chaque poète à reprendre certains mots, expressions et motifs sélectionnés dans les textes d'autres auteurs et/ou dans les siens propres, et à les organiser dans une combinaison nouvelle de façon à produire des variations personnelles et se constituer en auteur original dans le cadre du genre poétique particulier qu'il avait choisi ou, plus largement, de la littérature de son temps. Ce qu'en écrivant ainsi, les poètes romains attendaient des lecteurs de l'époque, c'est à la fois qu'ils identifient comme telles les reprises verbales et thématiques effectuées et qu'ils comprennent, en confrontant les contextes (d'origine et d'arrivée) de leur utilisation, pourquoi l'auteur les avait choisies, comment et pour quels effets de sens il les avait modifiées. Cela n'implique pas toutefois que telle ait été, dans les faits, la pratique de leurs lecteurs, ni surtout qu'il en ait résulté une seule lecture possible des textes.[10] Aujourd'hui l'intertextualité et l'intratextualité peuvent permettre aux lecteurs modernes d'opérer le même genre de déconstruction d'un texte dans ses éléments constitutifs, stylistiques et thématiques, en identifiant l'origine des éléments repris à d'autres textes, en tant que préalable à l'analyse de la façon originale dont ce texte a été conçu.[11]

Que l'auteur de l'élégie 3.9 ait été un homme ou une femme,[12] en tant que poète élégiaque, je partirai du principe qu'elle ou il a cherché à s'intégrer, stylistiquement,

---

9 Voir Pasquali (1942), à qui se réfère Conte au début de *Memoria dei poeti e sistema letterario* (1974), un livre qui changea radicalement les méthodes d'analyse dans le domaine de la littérature latine. Sur l'influence de Conte sur les critiques anglo-saxons, voir Fowler (2000) 117. Pour une approche de l'intertextualité à travers l'étude des concepts d'auteur, texte et lecteur, et un rappel de leur théorisation par différents critiques, voir le livre fondamental d'Edmunds (2001). Pour le concept de l'intratextualité et son usage, voir Sharrock/Morales (2000).
10 La pratique de l'intertextualité, telle que je la conçois et la décris, suppose la croyance en une intentionnalité de l'auteur. Elle implique aussi la conviction qu'il n'y pas un seul sens du texte, mais des sens différents selon les lecteurs, qui peuvent identifier ou non tous les renvois insérés par l'auteur et de toute façon comprennent le texte non seulement en fonction de la façon dont ils font jouer entre eux ces renvois, mais aussi à partir d'autres paramètres, dont leur jugement personnel sur l'auteur, sa personnalité, son sexe, ses particularités stylistiques, ses choix thématiques, l'appréciation de l'impact du contexte politique et idéologique . . . sans compter les effets produits par leur propre sexe, éducation, convictions, croyance Comme le précise Barchiesi (1997) 211, « l'intenzione dell'autore è una componente in un gioco di forze che include anche la ricezione del testo 'prevista' dall'autore : entrambe sono sole strategie di letture non traguardi finali ».
11 Comme l'a souligné Barchiesi (1997) 217, il serait illusoire de penser qu'identifier des rapports intertextuels soit « soprattutto un modo di restringere e vincolare il significato di un testo. L'esperienza insegna che tracciare dei rapporti intertestuali arricchisce e complica, apre dialettiche e tensioni più che chiudere e semplificare l'atto dell'interpretazione. » Mon projet est d'utiliser l'intertextualité dans une autre perspective : je chercherai à lister les motifs et expressions repris à d'autres textes essentiellement dans le but d'appréhender la façon dont ils ont été agencés dans des combinaisons nouvelles.
12 Je me situe dans la ligne des études menées par les critiques féministes, qui considèrent Sulpicia comme engagée, à l'instar de ses alter-egos masculins, dans des rapports intertextuels avec ses contemporains. Voir, par exemple, Merriam (2006) et Hallett (2009). Le premier toutefois à avoir

thématiquement et métriquement, dans la tradition poétique, inaugurée par Gallus, l'inventeur de l'élégie érotique romaine, et poursuivie par ses successeurs, tout en proposant, ce qui en soi était d'une totale nouveauté, un point de vue féminin. Le fait de présenter ce point de vue féminin, en utilisant le pronom 'je', impliquait une inversion de genre dans les rôles attribués au poète et à l'être aimé, le 'je' étant dans l'élégie habituellement masculin et le 'tu', soit féminin, soit masculin. Il impliquait aussi, que cet auteur ait été ou pas Sulpicia, une conscience et une prise en compte du comportement moral attendu d'une femme et plus particulièrement d'une femme de l'élite sénatoriale, ce qui a priori était difficile à accorder avec le genre élégiaque, centré sur la célébration d'amours illicites. À cela s'ajoute le fait que la femme en question était la nièce du patron du cercle dans lequel le texte a été écrit et lu. C'est en ayant à l'esprit cette situation complexe que je vais vous proposer une double enquête intertextuelle et intratextuelle à propos de l'élégie 3.11.[13]

1 Les choix intertextuels du poète de l'élégie 3.11

Premier point : j'utiliserai le nom Sulpicia en mettant des guillemets simples quand je désigne l'auteur de l'élégie 3.11 qui, du fait de l'utilisation de la première personne, est censé être Sulpicia, que ce soit le cas ou non, et je parlerai de Sulpicia, la poétesse, pour désigner la nièce de Messalla. Tibulle est le poète élégiaque auquel 'Sulpicia' renvoie le plus, ce qui n'est pas surprenant puisqu'il s'agit du poète majeur du cercle de Messalla.

L'élégie 3.11 s'ouvre sur le rappel du premier jour de la liaison entre le 'je', non nommé, et un Cerinthus, placé en position d'objet d'amour et de destinataire privilégié (par l'emploi de la deuxième personne) :[14]

> *qui mihi te, Cerinthe, dies dedit, hic mihi sanctus*
> *atque inter festos semper habendus erit.*
> *te nascente* **nouum Parcae cecinere** *puellis*
> *seruitium et dederunt regna superba tibi.*

---

mis les textes de Sulpicia en relation avec ceux des poètes de son temps est Heyne, qui considère Sulpicia comme un poète élégiaque comme les autres : il met ses textes en relation principalement avec ceux de Properce, voir Skoie (2002) 145 et 149.

13 J'ai évidemment conscience de la part de subjectivité (genrée et personnelle, elle aussi) qui conditionne une lecture s'apparentant à une campagne visant à rendre justice à une auteure, trop longtemps 'maltraitée'. Pour une discussion sur l'impact du contexte personnel et historico-culturel sur les lectures produites par les critiques, impact qui est réel mais ne doit pas non plus être surestimé, voir Thomas (2001) xi–xii.

14 En fait ce ne sera pas le seul destinataire, ni surtout le plus important. Je me base dur l'édition de Ponchont (^{9}1989).

Le jour qui te donna à moi, Cerinthus, est pour moi sacré et devra toujours être mis au nombre des jours de fête. Quand tu es né, les Parques ont annoncé dans leur chant un nouvel esclavage pour les jeunes femmes et elles t'ont accordé (d'exercer) une fière souveraineté.

'Sulpicia' considère ce jour (évoqué préalablement dans l'épigramme 13, dont l'auteur est Sulpicia, la poétesse) comme sacré[15] et à célébrer chaque année parmi les jours de fête (1 s.). Dans les deux vers suivants (3 s.), *nouum*, *Parcae* et *cecinere* sont sans doute repris du début de l'élégie 1.7, dans laquelle Tibulle célèbre le jour où Messalla a triomphé des peuples d'Aquitaine (1–8) :[16]

> hunc **cecinere** diem **Parcae** fatalia nentes
>   stamina, non ulli dissoluenda deo,
> hunc fore Aquitanas posset qui fundere gentes,
>   quem tremeret forti milite uictus Atax.
> euenere : **nouos** pubes Romana triumphos
>   uidit et euinctos bracchia capta duces ;
> at te uictrices lauros, Messalla, gerentem
>   portabat nitidis currus eburnus equis.

C'est ce jour qu'ont annoncé les Parques, quand elles ourdissaient les fils du destin qu'aucun dieu ne doit dénouer, en chantant qu'il se produirait de telle façon qu'il pourrait mettre en déroute les peuples d'Aquitaine et faire trembler l'Aude, vaincue par un vaillant guerrier. C'est arrivé : le peuple romain a vu un nouveau triomphe et des chefs vaincus les bras enchaînés tandis que toi, arborant les lauriers de la victoire, tu étais porté par un char d'ivoire aux chevaux éclatants.

Le jour annoncé par les Parques à la naissance de Messalla correspond, au sens large, au moment de sa victoire définitive lors de de sa campagne militaire en Gaule, et, plus précisément, au jour de son triomphe, qui en fut est la consécration et le signe patent. C'est 'ce jour' que Tibulle célèbre 'le jour même de l'anniversaire de Messalla', ce qui a pu créer une confusion et faire croire à une concomitance : on a supposé que l'anniversaire de Messala serait tombé peu après son triomphe.[17]

---

15 Fulkerson (2017) 255 note que *sanctus* est employé aussi à propos d'un jour anniversaire par Horace (*Odes*, 4.11.16 s. : . . . *sanctiorque / paene natali proprio*, « . . . plus sacré presque que mon propre jour anniversaire »).
16 Sur le fait qu'avec les mots *cecinere* et *Parcae*, Tibulle renvoie lui-même au *carmen* 64 de Catulle, où les Parques célèbrent à la fois les amours de Pélée et le destin guerrier de son fils, Achille : *talia praefantes quondam felicia Pelei / carmina diuino* **cecinerunt** *pectore* **Parcae** (382 s.), voir Gaissler (1971) 223 ; Ball (1975) 730 ; Fabre-Serris (2009) 155 s.
17 Les avis des commentateurs divergent. Selon Smith (1913) 323, qui ne donne aucune justification, « Messalla had been sent into Gaul to quell a serious outbreak among the Aquitanians, returned successful, and was given a triumph Sept. 25, 27 BC. Soon after that date occurred the birthday for which the poem was written. » Pour Murgatroyd (1980) 213, il y aurait eu concomitance entre les deux jours, « A solemn and stately opening concerns a prophecy made on the day of Messalla's birth that his victory over the Aquitanians was destined to fall on this day's anniversary. » Selon

On a le même type d'associations entre deux 'jours' dans l'élégie 3.11. 'Sulpicia' commence proclamer que 'le jour qui inaugura sa liaison avec Cerinthus' est à mettre au nombre des jours de fêtes, autrement dit, à célébrer chaque année à sa date anniversaire, puis elle présente implicitement 'ce jour' comme la réalisation d'une annonce des Parques à la naissance de son amant, dont elle célèbre alors 'le jour anniversaire'.[18] À ce dernier fut promise une 'domination', non pas militaire et sur des peuples étrangers comme à Messalla, mais amoureuse et sur les jeunes femmes. Comme l'élégie 1.7, centrée sur 'le jour du triomphe' de Messalla, rappelé à l'occasion de 'son jour anniversaire', l'élégie 3.11 a pour circonstance la célébration du 'jour anniversaire' de Cerinthus, mais elle est centrée sur sa liaison amoureuse avec Sulpicia, dont l'amorce est présentée comme 'le jour de la réalisation de la promesse des Parques'.

Pourquoi qualifier l'esclavage annoncé à Cerinthus de « nouveau » ? Soit parce qu'il a consisté en une inversion de genre (l'amant-poète est, dans les autres textes élégiaques, un homme qui se déclare l'esclave de sa *puella*, qualifiée alors de *domina*), soit parce que la domination amoureuse promise à Cerinthus est exceptionnelle en ce qu'elle s'exerce sur 'toutes' les jeunes femmes.[19] Alors que l'adjectif *nouum* fait écho à *nouos triomphos* (1.7.5), *superba regna* est la reprise d'une métaphore militaire, utilisée par Tibulle, dans l'élégie 1.9, pour décrire la domination qu'exercera un jour sur lui un autre amant que l'infidèle Marathus : *tum flebis cum me uinctum puer alter habebit / et geret in regno regna superba tuo* (« alors tu pleureras quand un autre garçon me tiendra enchaîné à lui et exercera une fière souveraineté à la place de la tienne », 79 s.). Toutefois on n'a pas un parfait décalque des circonstances narratives de l'élégie 1.7. Si l'élégie 3.11 a pour circonstance la célébration du jour anniversaire de celui qui reçut une promesse de domination lors de sa naissance, contrairement à l'élégie 1.7, la réalisation de cette promesse ne semble pas correspondre exactement à l'annonce faite par les Parques. Il est question ici de deux dons et de deux bénéficiaires : les Parques ont 'donné' à Cerinthus une domination sur les jeunes femmes, mais lui-même a été 'donné' à Sulpicia. Comment ces dons s'articulent-ils ? La suite de l'élégie l'explique d'une façon qui amène à revoir la notion de *superba regna*.[20]

Outre l'ouverture, 'Sulpicia' a repris toute la construction narrative de l'élégie 1.7. Après avoir évoqué divers lieux en Gaule, qui peuvent témoigner des exploits

---

Lee (1990) 134, « we need not to suppose that either Messalla's victory or his Triumph fell on his birthday (though it may have done). »

18 C'est ce que met en evidence Fredericks (1976) 779 sans avoir perçu clairement la connexion entre les deux jours : « This (the first couplet) alone would lead one to think the day under consideration was that on which they met and fell in love, not, as it turns out, the day of Cerinthus' birth (*te nascente*). »

19 Une autre possibilité, proposée par Batstone (2018) 106, serait de prendre *nouus* au sens de « récent » : « The phrase could refer to the generic novelty (*nouus* = 'unheard of') of a male dominating a female in elegy, or to this latest re-instantiation (*nouus* = *recens*) of male domination. »

20 La répétition du verbe *dare* (*dedit*, 1 ; *dederunt*, 4) est relevée par Platnauer (1951) 53.

de Messalla, mais aussi d'autres pays (Cilicie, Syrie, Phénicie et Égypte) parcourus au cours de ses expéditions militaires,[21] Tibulle s'arrête longuement sur le Nil, qu'il loue en l'identifiant à Osiris et à Bacchus. Il demande à Bacchus de venir (*huc ades...*, 49) et de participer à la célébration du Génie de Messalla (**Genium** ... *concelebra*, 49 s.). Puis il demande au Génie de venir, lui aussi, « aujourd'hui » (*sic uenias hodierne*, 53) en ajoutant qu'il lui offrira de l'encens (*tibi dem **turis** honores*, 53). Enfin, après divers souhaits adressés à Messalla (*at tibi...*, 55), Tibulle invoque un Natalis, le jour anniversaire qu'il est en train de célébrer et dont il espère qu'il sera célébré longtemps, ou le dieu de ce jour : ***at tu Natalis** multos celebrande per annos / candidior semper candidiorque ueni* (« et toi, jour anniversaire, qui sera à célébrer durant plusieurs années, viens, plus éclatant et toujours plus éclatant encore », 63 s.).

'Sulpicia' a repris les trois invocations : à une divinité majeure, au Génie de son destinataire, à qui elle offre également de l'encens (9) :

> *mane*[22] ***Geni**, cape **tura** libens uotisque faueto.*
>
> Bon Génie, reçois l'encens de bon cœur et sois favorable à mes vœux.

et à Natalis en usant de la même expression que Tibulle (19) :

> ***at tu, Natalis**, quoniam deus omnia sentis...*
>
> Et toi, jour anniversaire, puisque, en tant que dieu, tu perçois tout...

Mais il s'agit clairement du dieu. Par ailleurs, 'Sulpicia' introduit deux modifications, sur lesquelles je reviendrai : elle substitue à Bacchus Vénus, qu'elle place en position centrale, et elle assortit chacune de ses adresses de prières qui ont trait à ses relations amoureuses avec Cerinthus.[23]

Si l'ensemble de l'élégie 3.11 est structurée sur le modèle de l'élégie 1.7, c'est à un autre texte de Tibulle que 'Sulpicia' emprunte son final : l'élégie 2.1. Elle reprend, en la modifiant, l'ingénieuse distinction faite par Tibulle entre deux catégories de vœux : ceux qui sont formulés « ouvertement » (*palam*) et ceux qui sont formulés « en secret » (*clam*, 83–86) :

---

[21] Sur les diverses interprétations données au développement du poème, qui part d'une description du triomphe de Messalla pour arriver à une évocation du Nil et d'Osiris (ce qui revient à faire allusion à la récente intégration de l'Égypte dans l'empire), avant de revenir à la célébration de l'anniversaire de Messalla, voir Gaisser (1971) ; Ball (1975) ; Konstan (1978) ; Lee-Stecum (1998) ; Fabre-Serris (2005) ; Lowell Bowditch (2012).
[22] Pour le choix de *magne* à la place de *mane*, voir Tränkle (1990) 285.
[23] Sulpicia opère un détournement du genre de poème composé pour célébrer un anniversaire (habituellement désigné sous le terme *genethliacon*). Ses trois requêtes consistent en demandes à propos de sa liaison, inaugurée le jour qui 'lui donna Cerinthus', alors que, le jour de l'anniversaire de la naissance de son ami, on s'attendrait à des vœux pour son bonheur à lui.

> *uos celebrem cantate deum pecorique uocate*
> *uoce ; **palam** pecori, **clam** sibi quisque uocet,*
> *aut etiam sibi quisque **palam** : nam turba iocosa*
> *obstrepit et Phrygio tibia curua sono.*

> Vous, chantez le dieu fêté par tous et invoquez-le à haute voix pour votre troupeau : que chacun l'invoque ouvertement pour son troupeau et en secret pour lui ; ou même que chacun l'invoque ouvertement pour lui : en effet la foule joyeuse et le son de la flûte phrygienne au bec recourbé feront obstacle.

Dans l'élégie 2.1, l'amoureux formulera ses vœux en secret (par pudeur ? par prudence ? aucune raison n'est donnée), ou il le fera ouvertement, mais c'est parce qu'il ne pourra pas être entendu. 'Sulpicia' affirme que son ami souhaite la même chose qu'elle, mais qu'il le fait « d'une façon plus dissimulée » parce qu'il « a honte » (la raison est ici donnée) d'exprimer ce souhait « ouvertement » (contrairement à elle donc), 'Sulpicia' prie *Natalis* d'agréer tout de même cette prière, même si elle est formulée « en secret » et non « ouvertement » (17–20):

> *optat idem iuuenis quod nos, sed **tectius** optat:*
> *nam pudet haec illum dicere uerba **palam**.*
> *at tu, Natalis, quoniam deus omnia sentis,*
> *adnue : quid refert, **clam**ne **palam**ne roget ?*

> Mon ami fait le même souhait que moi, mais il le fait d'une façon plus dissimulée : en effet il a honte de prononcer ces paroles ouvertement. Mais toi, jour anniversaire, puisqu'en tant que dieu, tu perçois tout, donne ton assentiment : qu'importe s'il adresse sa requête en secret ou ouvertement ?

Le début de l'élégie 3.11 semble annoncer un texte qui sera à la fois à la gloire de Cerinthus, comparé dans le domaine amoureux à Messalla dans le domaine militaire, et centré sur le motif gallien du *seruitium amoris*. 'Sulpicia' insère, dans son poème, des mots : *uror* (deux fois au vers 5), *uincla* (14) et *catena* (15), qui, probablement, renvoient à l'élégie 2.4. de Tibulle sur ce même motif du *seruitium amoris* (3–6) :

> *seruitium sed triste datur, teneorque **caten**is,*
> *et numquam misero **uincla** remittit Amor,*
> *et, seu quid merui seu quid peccauimus, **ur**it ;*
> ***uror**, io ! remoue, saeua puella, faces.*

> Mais un triste esclavage m'est imposé, je suis attaché par des chaînes, et jamais Amour ne relâche ses liens pour mon malheur, et soit que je l'ai mérité, soit que j'ai commis une faute, il me brûle, je suis brûlé, ah ! écarte tes torches, cruelle jeune femme !

Pour conclure, l'auteur(e) de l'élégie 3.11 se positionne comme un poète élégiaque du cercle de Messalla : elle/il rend hommage à Tibulle, le poète majeur de ce cercle quand elle/il traite des motifs (fréquents dans ce cercle) tels que la célébration du jour anniversaire, les prières à des divinités protectrices et le *seruitium amoris*, tout en introduisant des variations qui lui sont propres (et sur lesquelles je reviendrai dans ma deuxième partie). Comme je l'ai rappelé, c'est toujours le cas dans la poésie romaine, où les poètes situent leur propre pratique dans la continuité et/ou dans la rupture avec leurs prédécesseurs dans le même genre littéraire. À côté de ces renvois intertextuels, on peut lister une série d'éléments stylistiques et thématiques qui présentent des similitudes avec des choix textuels et des motifs que l'on trouve dans les épigrammes 13–18, attribuées à Sulpicia, la poétesse. Je défendrai l'idée qu'il s'agit là de traits intratextuels, autrement dit, d'éléments spécifiques à un poète, qui définissent son style, sa manière et sa modulation personnelle des motifs du genre qu'il a choisi de pratiquer.

2 Les traits intratextuels de l'élégie 3.11

2.1 Le choix du mot *iuuat*

Immédiatement après son rappel de la prédiction des Parques, annonçant un *seruitium* (*amoris*) pour les jeunes femmes, 'Sulpicia' précise qu'elle brûle plus que les autres, mais elle ajoute qu'il y a une condition à cet ardent désir (5 s.) :

> uror ego ante alias : iuuat hoc, Cerinthe, quod uror,
>   si tibi de nobis mutuus ignis adest.

> Je brûle plus que les autres, mais il me plaît de brûler, Cerinthus, à condition qu'il y ait pour toi, en ce qui me concerne, un feu réciproque/mutuel.

La formulation choisie peut sembler contournée, mais elle vise à exprimer, dans toute sa complexité, l'interaction entre les deux partenaires, souhaitée par 'Sulpicia'. Si l'on se réfère aux études stylistiques menées sur les épigrammes 13–18, cette formulation compliquée peut être vue comme un premier trait intratextuel.[24] À propos de ce vers, Parker remarque, à juste titre, « the use of *quod* at 3.11.5 s. . . . is very close to that of 3.16.1 s. (*gratum est, securus multum quod iam tibi de me / permittis, subito ne male inepta cadam*). »[25] J'ajouterai que *tibi de nobis* est également très proche de *tibi de me*.

'Sulpicia' a combiné, dans ces deux vers, plusieurs mots typiques du vocabulaire élégiaque : *iuuat, uror* et *mutuus*. Je vais passer rapidement sur *uror* et *mutuus*, qui

---

[24] Voir les études sur le style compliqué de Sulpicia, la poétesse, dans les épigrammes 13–18, en particulier Lowe (1988) et Tränkle (1990). Comme le souligne Parker (1994) 47 s., « Sulpicia's was a marker style . . . Lowe has identified a number of features characteristic of Sulpicia's style, though not hers exclusively, which can serve to unite 3.9 and 11 with 3.13–18, features not shared by the *auctor de Sulpicia* in 3.8, 10 and 12. »

[25] Parker (1994) 49.

étaient probablement présents dans les *Amores* de Gallus. Pour ce qui est d'*uror*, c'est ce que l'on peut supposer à partir de son emploi par Properce dans un contexte renvoyant ouvertement au fondateur du genre.[26] Quoi qu'il en soit, quand on confronte entre eux les élégiaques, on constate que les mots *uro, uror, exurere* (au sens figuré) ont été fréquemment utilisés dans le cercle de Messalla : 5 fois chez Tibulle en 1.5.5 (*ure ferum*, « brûle un homme fier »), en 1.8.7 (*deus crudelis urit*, « le dieu brûle plus cruellement »), en 2.4.5 s. ([*Amor*] . . . *urit* ; / *uror*, « [Amour] . . . brûle . . . je suis brûlé ») et en 2.6.5 (*ure, puer*, « brûle, enfant ») et 4 fois chez l'*amicus* en 3.8.5 (*cum uult exurere diuos*, « quand il veut enflammer les dieux »), en 11 s. (*urit . . . urit*, « elle enflamme . . . elle enflamme ») et en 3.12.17 (*uritur, ut celeres urunt altaria flammae*, « elle brûle comme les flammes brûlent rapidement l'autel »). L'adjectif *mutuus* est, dans l'élégie 3.11, utilisé une fois avec *ignis* au vers 6 et une fois avec *amor* dans le vers suivant. Que l'une ou les deux expressions étaient présentes dans les *Amores* peut être induit du fait qu'Horace a inclus *mutuus amor* dans son *Épode* 15, un poème où il parodie le genre élégiaque à une époque où le seul poète à avoir écrit des élégies était Gallus : *in uerba iurabas mea / . . . fore hunc amorem mutuum* (« tu jurais en répétant mes paroles . . . que cet amour entre nous serait réciproque », 4 et 10).[27]

---

26 Ce qui authentifie le verbe *uror* comme gallien est que Properce l'a employé, en 2.3.43 s., dans deux vers où il fait l'éloge de Cynthie en utilisant un jeu verbal célèbre de la poésie latine sur les deux noms de la planète de Vénus, selon qu'elle est vue le matin ou le soir : *siue illam* **Hesperiis**, *siue illam ostendet* **Eois**, / **uret** *et Eoos,* **uret** *et* **Hesperios** (« qu'il la montre à l'Occident, qu'il la montre à l'Orient, elle enflammera l'Orient, elle enflammera l'Occident »). Ce jeu verbal ne remonte pas à Gallus : à Rome on le trouve chez Catulle en 62.34 s. et chez Cinna (fr. 6 Courtney). Mais on peut inférer que le fondateur du genre élégiaque l'a repris dans un passage devenu, lui aussi, assez célèbre car Ovide l'utilise aussi, d'une part dans l'éloge conjoint qu'il fait de Gallus et de sa *puella* dans les *Amores* 1.15.29 s.: *Gallus et* **Hesperiis** *et Gallus* **notus Eois**, / *et sua cum Gallo* **nota** *Lycoris erit* (« Gallus sera connu des peuples de l'Occident, Gallus sera connu de ceux de l'Orient et avec Gallus sera connue sa Lycoris chérie »), d'autre part, de nouveau à propos de Lycoris, dans le passage de l'*Ars amatoria* 3 où il évoque les poètes romains dont la gloire durera toujours : **Vesper** *et* **Eoae nouere** *Lycoride terrae* (« l'étoile du soir et les terres de l'Orient connaissent Lycoris », 537). Il s'agit de deux passages où étant donné leur objet : l'éloge de Gallus, il y a probablement reprise de mots et motifs utilisés dans les *Amores*. Vu que le contexte est similaire (l'éloge de sa *puella*), on peut supposer que, comme l'écrit Cairns (2006), 98 : « Propertius writing of his Cynthia, but obviously recalling the same (lost) lines of Gallus to which Ovid refers . . . offers a more discreet variation. The whole world will fall in love with a portrait of Cynthia. » Sur le fait que *notus, nomen, nouere* sont des mots galliens, voir aussi Cairns (2006) 97–100. La répétition de *notus* dans le premier passage d'Ovide que j'ai cité équivaut à celle d'*uret* chez Properce, ce qui conforte la probabilité d'un usage similaire (de mots répétés) chez Gallus, ce qu'on retrouve d'ailleurs à la fois dans l'élégie 3.8.11 s. (*urit . . . urit*) et dans l'élégie 3.11.5 (*uror . . . uror*). Sur la particularité des formes de première personne qui se terminent en -r- dans les élégies de Sulpicia voir Hallett dans le présent volume, p. 17 avec la note 15.
27 Horace utilise aussi *mutuus* avec *amor* (. . . *bene mutuis / fidum pectus amoribus*, « . . . son cœur bien fidèle à des amours mutuelles », *Ode* 2.12.15 s.) pour caractériser l'amour réciproque unissant Mécène et Licymnia (en qui on s'accorde à reconnaître, désignée par un pseudonyme, l'é-

Le mot qui m'intéresse le plus est *iuuat*. C'est un verbe souvent utilisé dans la poésie latine, qui signifie soit « il plaît, il fait plaisir, il est agréable », soit « il est utile », en particulier dans l'expression *quid iuuat ?*, pris souvent comme un équivalent de *quid prodest ?*[28] Mais il est rarement employé dans un contexte érotique. Outre dans l'élégie 3.11, on le trouve au sens de « il plaît, il fait plaisir » dans le cercle de Messalla, chez Tibulle en 1.1.45 s. : *quam iuuat immites uentos audire cubantem / et dominam tenero continuisse sinu* (« quel plaisir d'entendre de mon lit les vents souffler sans douceur et de tenir tendrement ma maîtresse contre ma poitrine ! ») et chez Sulpicia, la poétesse, dans l'épigramme 13 : *peccasse iuuat* (« il me plaît d'avoir commis cette faute »), les deux fois à propos de l'union sexuelle. L'autre poète qui emploie *iuuat* avec le même sens dans un contexte érotique est Ovide : dans les *Amores* 1.13.5 (*nunc iuuat in teneris dominae iacuisse lacertis*, « c'est maintenant qu'il me plaît de rester étendu dans les bras tendres de ma maîtresse », une variation sur Tibulle 1.1.46, avec qui Ovide partage trois mots : *iuuat*, *tener* et *domina*) et dans sept passages à propos du plaisir sexuel (*Am.* 3.4.31 ; *Hér.* 15.134 ; 19.64 ; *Ars* 1.674 ; 2.308 ; *Rem.* 13 ; *Met.* 9.487).[29] Je propose de voir dans le *iuuat* des vers 5 s. de l'élégie 3.11, utilisé avec le même sens que dans l'épigramme 13, un

---

pouse de ce dernier). Tibulle emploie deux fois *mutuus amor* en 1.2.63 s. (*non ego totus abesset **amor** sed **mutuus** esset / orabam . . .*, « ce n'est pas la disparition totale de l'amour, mais la présence d'un amour mutuel que je demandais . . . ») et en 1.6.75 s. (*. . . sed mente fideli / **mutuus** absenti te mihi seruet **amor***, « . . . qu'avec ta fidélité un amour mutuel te conserve à moi en mon absence »). On trouve l'adjectif *mutuus* avec *cura* chez Lygdamus (*illa me referet si nostri **mutua cura** est / an minor, an toto pectore deciderim*, « elle me fera savoir s'il y a chez elle un amour pour moi qui répond au mien pour elle ou s'il est moindre, ou si j'ai totalement chuté de son cœur », 3.1.19 s.). Properce l'emploie une fois, et c'est en contexte gallien, dans l'élégie 1.5 adressée au fondateur du genre (*sed pariter miseri socio cogemur amore / alter in alterius **mutua** flere sinu*, « mais également malheureux dans un amour qui nous sera commun, nous serons contraints de pleurer des maux mutuels sur la poitrine l'un de l'autre », 29 s.). Ovide emploie *mutuus* avec *gaudia* dans les *Amours* 2.3.2 (*mutua nec Veneris gaudia nosse potes*, « et (parce que) tu ne peux pas jouir des plaisirs mutuels de l'amour »), et 3.6.87 s. (*. . . quid mutua differs / gaudia ?*, « . . . pourquoi diffères-tu des plaisirs mutuels ? ») et dans les *Métamorphoses* 7.800 (*mutua cura duos et amor socialis habebat*, « un souci mutuel et un amour commun (nous) possédait tous les deux »). Je reviendrai sur l'emploi de *mutuus* chez Catulle (45.20), page 270 et chez Lucrèce (4.1201, 1205, 1216 ; 5.854, 963), page 269.

28 Sur ces deux sens du mot et son emploi chez les élégiaques, voir Bréguet (1946) 225–227.
29 Ovide, *Am.* 3.4.31 : *indignere licet, iuuat inconcessa uoluptas* (« il est permis de s'indigner, mais une volupté interdite plaît ») ; *Hér.* 15.134 : *et iuuat, et siccae non licet esse mihi* (« et j'ai du plaisir et il ne m'est pas permis d'être sèche ») ; *Hér.* 19.63 s. : *multaque praeterea lingua reticenda modesta / quae fecisse iuuat, facta referre pudet* (« et beaucoup de choses en outre qui doivent être tues par une langue réservée, qu'il y a du plaisir à faire mais qu'on a honte de rapporter ») ; *Ars* 1.671 s. : *uim licet appelles, grata est uis ista puellis ; / quod iuuat, inuitae saepe dedisse uolunt* (« tu peux appeler cela de la violence, mais cette violence est agréable aux femmes ; ce qui procure du plaisir, souvent elles veulent l'avoir donné malgré elles ») ; *Ars* 2.307 s. : *ipsos concubitus, ipsum uenerere licebit / quod iuuat et quae clam gaudia noctis habet* (« vos étreintes elles-mêmes, cela même

autre trait intratextuel.[30] La prière que Sulpicia adresse ensuite à Vénus est basée sur une ingénieuse combinaison des deux motifs galliens précédemment convoqués, le *seruitium amoris* et le *mutuus amor*. Cette combinaison est rendue possible par l'utilisation d'une des étymologies de Vénus, supposée mettre en lumière un des pouvoirs spécifiques de la déesse: sa capacité à lier (*uincire*) deux amants. Il s'agit du passage le plus original sans doute de l'élégie 3.11, et sans surprise donc, celui où l'on peut reconnaître plusieurs 'marques' auctoriales, si on le compare aux épigrammes attribuées à la nièce de Messalla.

2.2 Le rôle de Vénus, l'étymologie *uincire* et le motif de la réciprocité

Dans son deuxième vœu, adressé à Vénus, placée en position centrale, donc, en position d'honneur,[31] 'Sulpicia' explicite la façon très particulière dont elle conçoit la notion de *seruitium amoris*, à laquelle elle renvoie par le verbe *seruiat* (13–16) :

> nec tu sis iniusta, Venus : uel seruiat aeque
>   **uinc**tus uterque tibi uel mea **uincla** leua ;
> sed potius ualida teneamur uterque **catena**,
>   **n**ulla queat posthac quam **sol**u**isse dies**.

> Et toi, ne sois pas injuste, Vénus : fais que chacun de nous soit (ton) esclave, lié de façon égale par toi, ou bien allège mes liens ou plutôt fais que nous soyons tenus, l'un et l'autre, par une chaîne solide qu'aucun jour ensuite ne puisse délier.

L'étymologie de Vénus, à laquelle 'Sulpicia' fait ici allusion à travers les mots *uinctus*, *uincla* et *catena*, a été largement exploitée par Lucrèce, puis reprise par Gallus

---

qui procure du plaisir, il te sera permis de le révérer et aussi les joies nocturnes qu'elle éprouve en secret ») ; *Rem.* 13 s. : *si quis amans, quod amare iuuat, feliciter ardet / gaudeat* (« si un amant, pour l'objet qu'il a plaisir à aimer, brûle en étant heureux, qu'il s'en réjouisse ! ») ; *Mét.* 9.485 : *ut meminisse iuuat ! quamuis breuis illa uoluptas* (« combien j'ai du plaisir à me souvenir, quelque brève qu'ait été cette volupté »).

30 C'est une mise en relation que fait aussi Dronke (2003) 95 : « L'espressione-chiave di quest'esametro è *iuuat*, che non può non ricordare il distico finale di *Tandem uenit amor : sed peccasse iuuat* . . . »

31 On trouve le même schéma narratif dans l'élégie 2.32 de Properce. Bien qu'il suspecte Cynthie d'avoir une autre liaison, Properce finalement minore l'importance de cette infidélité : « de petites accusations qui ne m'émeuvent pas » (*non me crimina parua mouent*, 30) en donnant trois exemples de femmes ayant eu des relations hors mariage sans que leur réputation en ait pâti, Hélène, Vénus et Œnone. La position de Vénus au centre de ce trio en fait la garante divine des deux autres : malgré son infidélité (*corrupta libidine Martis*, « corrompue par le désir de Mars ou par son désir pour Mars », 33) sa réputation dans le ciel n'en fut pas altérée : *nec minus in caelo semper honesta fuit* (« et elle n'en fut pas moins toujours considérée comme honorable dans le ciel », 34).

et utilisée par tous les élégiaques,[32] mais jamais de façon aussi importante que dans l'élégie 3.11. Lucrèce renvoie à cette étymologie, de façon implicite, dans la scène où il décrit Mars dans les bras de Vénus, qui l'enlace : *hunc tu, diua, tuo recubantem corpore sancto / circumfusa super ...* (« toi, ô divine, répandue au-dessus de lui et l'entourant de ton corps sacré, alors qu'il est étendu ... », 1.38 s.). Puis il l'utilise, au livre 4, pour nourrir une réflexion sur ce qu'est l'amour dans ses descriptions de l'union sexuelle, où il emploie aussi l'adjectif *mutuus*, en l'associant à *uoluptas* (*nonne uides etiam quos **mutua** saepe uoluptas / **uinxit**, ut in **uinclis** communibus excrucientur ?*, « ne vois-tu pas comment même ceux que souvent une volupté mutuelle a liés sont à la torture dans leurs liens communs ? », 1201 s.), à *gaudia* (*quod facerent numquam nisi **mutua** gaudia nossent, / quae iacere in fraudem possent **uinctos**que tenere*, « ils ne le feraient jamais <l'amour> s'ils ne connaissaient pas des joies réciproques telles qu'elles puissent les induire en erreur et les tenir enchaînés », 1205 s.) ou à *ardor* (1216).

Dans quels contextes les élégiaques ont-ils recouru à l'étymologie *uincire* à propos de Vénus ? Impossible de le savoir dans le cas de Gallus. Toutefois on trouve un emploi de l'étymologie *uincire* dans la description que fait Properce d'une nuit d'amour dans l'élégie 1.13, adressée à Gallus : *uidi ego te toto **uinctum** languescere collo* (« moi, je t'ai vu, le cou complètement enlacé, languir », 15). Si l'on le prend dans un sens métalittéraire,[33] comme on le fait pour *memini*, l'emploi de *uidi* engage à supposer un précédent dans les *Amores*, où l'amant se serait décrit dans la même position que Mars dans les bras de Vénus.[34] Chez Tibulle, l'emploi des mots de la famille de *uincire* est associé, non à une scène d'union sexuelle, mais au *seruitium amoris* : *me retinent **uinctum** formosae **uincla** puellae* (« je suis retenu enchaîné par les chaînes d'une belle jeune femme », 1.1.55) ; *uidi ego qui iuuenum miseros lusisset amores / post **Veneris uinclis** subdere colla senem* (« moi, j'ai vu qui s'était moqué des amours malheureuses de jeunes gens, tendre ensuite le cou aux chaînes de Vénus, une fois devenu vieux », 1.2.89 s.) ; *... detrecto non ego **uincla** pedum* (« ... je ne repousse pas les chaînes de mes pieds », 1.6.38) ; *non ego me **uinclis** uerberibusque nego* (« moi, je ne me refuse pas aux chaînes et aux coups », 2.3.80) ; *seruitium sed triste datur, teneorque **catenis**, / et numquam misero **uincla** remittit Amor* (« mais un triste esclavage m'est imposé, je suis attaché par des chaînes, et jamais l'amour ne relâche ses liens pour mon malheur », 2.4.3 s., que j'ai déjà cités parce que 'Sulpicia' emploie les mêmes mots). Chez Properce, *uinctus* et *uincla* sont utilisés, la plupart du temps, dans le contexte d'un *seruitium amoris* : *quid mirare ... / quod nequeam fracto rumpere **uincla** iugo* (« pourquoi s'étonner ... que je ne puisse pas, brisant mon joug, rompre

---

32 Voir Hinds (2006). Sur le rôle des étymologies romaines de Vénus dans la réception des théories d'Empédocle dans le *prooemium* de Lucrèce et leur utilisation par Gallus, voir Fabre-Serris (2014).
33 Sur l'emploi de *uidi* pour signaler un renvoi dans un sens métalittéraire, voir Cairns (2006) 117.
34 Properce, 1.13.19 s. : *non ego complexus potui diducere uestros : / tantus erat demens inter utrosque furor* (« moi, je n'ai pu séparer vos étreintes, si grand était entre vous deux le délire de la fureur »).

mes chaînes ? », 3.11.1, 4) ; . . . *nec femina post te / ulla dedit collo dulcia* **uincla** *meo* («. . . aucune femme après toi n'a imposé de douces chaînes à mon cou », 3.15.9 s.) ; **uinctus** *eram uersas in mea terga manus* (« j'étais enchaîné, les mains tournées dans mon dos », 3.24.14). Toutefois, comme Lucrèce, Properce utilise aussi *uincire* et *uincla* deux fois (outre l'élégie 1.13) dans le contexte d'une union sexuelle : *atque utinam haerentis sic nos* **uincire** *catena / uelles, ut numquam solueret ulla dies* (« puisses-tu vouloir nous lier ainsi attachés par une chaîne de sorte qu'aucun jour jamais ne la délie », 2.15.25 s.) ; *namque ubi non certo* **uincitur** *foedere lectus . . . / et quibus imposuit,* **soluit** *mox* **uincla** *libido* (« en effet quand un lit n'a pas été lié par un pacte assuré . . . bientôt le désir sexuel a délié les liens pour ceux à qui il les a imposés », 3.20.21, 23). Un autre texte est peut-être aussi à l'arrière-plan de l'élégie 3.11 : le *carmen* 45 de Catulle,[35] où l'on trouve une scène érotique (avec l'expression *in gremio* comme chez Lucrèce, mais ici c'est le garçon qui tient la fille dans ses bras) et une réflexion sur l'amour, qui met l'accent sur l'idée d'esclavage partagé (les deux amants 'servent l'amour'), et souligne, avec l'emploi de l'adjectif *mutuus*, la réciprocité des sentiments éprouvés (1 s., 10, 14, 20) :

> Acmen Septimius suos amores
> tenens in gremio "mea" inquit "Acme . . ."
> at Acme leuiter caput reflectens . . .
> huic uni domino usque **seruiamus** . . .
> **mutuis** animis amant amantur.

> Septimius tenant Acmé, ses amours, dans ses bras, dit « Mon Acmé . . . » De son côté Acmé tournant légèrement la tête en arrière . . . continuons de servir ce seul maître . . . avec des sentiments réciproques ils aiment et sont aimés.

L'idée qu'aimer c'est être au service et, au sens fort, être l'esclave de l'amour a été reprise par Tibulle dans l'élégie 2.3. Après avoir longuement décrit le *seruitium amoris* d'Apollon, devenu le bouvier d'Admète, il définit l'amour comme 'un esclavage' qui soumet l'amant au pouvoir de Vénus : *felices olim, Veneri, cum fertur aperte / seruire aeternos non puduisse deos* (« heureux les hommes d'autrefois, quand les dieux éternels, dit-on, ne rougissaient pas de servir ouvertement Vénus », 29 s.).

Pour conclure, en combinant dans sa prière à Vénus les mots *seruiat*,[36] *uinctus*, *uincla* et *catena*, 'Sulpicia' inscrit sa réflexion sur ce qu'est l'amour dans un arrière-plan complexe, où l'on trouve tous les poètes romains qui, avant elle, ont cherché à

---

35 Sur ce texte, voir Cairns (2012), qui considère, ce que je ne crois pas (cf. la note 35), qu'il n'y a pas d'ironie dans ce passage.

36 Dans un contexte amoureux, on trouve *seruire* seulement chez Tibulle 1.2.97 s. : *At mihi parce, Venus : semper tibi dedita seruit / mens mea . . .* (« mais épargne-moi, Vénus : mon esprit, qui t'a toujours été dévoué, est ton esclave . . . ») ; Properce 1.7.7 s. : *nec tantum ingenio quantum seruire dolori / cogor . . .* (« je suis forcé de servir non pas tant mon talent que ma douleur . . . ») ; 2.26b.21 s. : *Nunc admirentur quod tam mihi pulchra puella / seruiat . . .* (« maintenant que l'on

décrire et analyser le sentiment amoureux : Catulle,[37] Lucrèce, Gallus et Tibulle.[38] Il faut rajouter à ce panorama poétique Properce : l'idée qu'aucun jour ne déliera les chaînes entre deux amants est un élément commun entre l'élégie 3.11 et l'élégie 2.15 (un passage que j'ai déjà cité, dont le contexte est une nuit d'amour) : *atque utinam haerentis sic nos* **uincire catena** / *uelles, ut numquam* **solueret ulla dies** ! (« puisses-tu vouloir nous lier ainsi attachés par une chaîne de sorte qu'aucun jour jamais ne la délie !», 25 s.).

Comparée à ses prédécesseurs, 'Sulpicia' propose une version du *seruitium amoris*, revu et corrigé, pour lequel elle sollicite l'usage par Vénus du pouvoir qui lui est spécifique : lier, et qu'elle exerce dans l'acte amoureux. Au lieu que l'un des amants soit l'esclave de l'autre, tous deux doivent l'être de la déesse, solidement tenus par des 'liens partagés' comme c'est le cas dans l'acte amoureux. Cette égalité et réciprocité entre partenaires amoureux (déjà suggérée par les expressions *mutuus ignis* et *mutuus amor*) constitue, me semble-t-il, un autre trait intratextuel. C'est ce qui fait en effet la double particularité de la notion la plus importante que Sulpicia, la poétesse met en avant pour justifier sa liaison dans l'épigramme 3.13, celle de *dignitas* 'mutuelle' : *sed peccasse iuuat, uultus componere famae / taedet : cum digno digna fuisse ferar* (« mais il me plaît d'avoir commis cette faute; composer mon visage pour ma réputation me dégoûte ! J'ai été avec quelqu'un qui était digne de moi et dont j'étais digne, que ce soit cela que l'on dise ! », 9 s.).

Une autre particularité de la prière adressée à Vénus est qu'elle suggère un lien personnel entre 'Sulpicia' et la déesse : c'est à elle qu'elle demande une aide majeure en matière d'amour, et elle le fait dans des termes laissant supposer une intimité particulière : *nec tu sis iniusta, Venus* (« et toi, Vénus, ne sois pas injuste » 13). Je crois qu'on peut y voir un autre trait spécifique, soutenu par l'intratextualité. Dans l'épigramme 3.13, Sulpicia la poétesse, fait, elle aussi allusion à l'aide décisive qu'elle a reçue de Vénus : *exorata meis illum Cytherea Camenis / attulit in nostrum*

---

admire qu'une si belle femme soit mon esclave . . . ») ; 3.25.3 : *quinque tibi potui seruire fideliter annos* (« pendant cinq ans j'ai pu être ton fidèle esclave ») ; Ovide, *Am*. 1.3.5 : *accipe, per longos tibi qui deseruiat annos* (« accepte quelqu'un qui soit totalement ton esclave pendant de longues années ») ; *Am*. 2.17.1 : *siquis erit qui turpe putet seruire puellae* (« si quelqu'un pense honteux d'être l'esclave d'une jeune femme ») ; *Hér*. 20.92 : *tam bene qui seruit, seruiat iste mihi* ! (« qui sert si bien, que cet homme-là me serve »). Je laisse de côté les vers 9 s. de l'élégie 3.12 du *Corpus Tibullianum*, qui sont à prendre comme une 'reprise avec variation » répondant à l'élégie 3.11.

37 Sur les rapports entre Catulle et Sulpicia, voir Hallett (2002b) 147, qui met en rapport les emplois de l'adjectif *mutuus* dans l'élégie 3.11 avec le vers 26 du *carmen* 45. Il est à noter que, dans le *carmen* 45, l'idéal incarné par les deux amants qui jurent d'être pour toujours les esclaves du même maître, l'amour, est présenté avec humour par Catulle, ce qui n'est pas le cas chez 'Sulpicia'. Mais on ne trouve pas non plus chez elle la tonalité 'tragique' qu'a la peinture de l'amour chez Lucrèce.

38 Je laisse de côté Ovide, la question des rapports de priorité entre Sulpicia et Ovide ayant donné lieu à des opinions divergentes qu'il serait trop long de rappeler et de discuter. Voir Hinds (1987) ; Parker (1994) ; Fabre-Serris (2018b) et (2020a).

deposuitque sinum (« fléchie par mes Camènes, Cythérée l'a amené et déposé dans mes bras », 3 s.). C'est un passage qui a été rapproché de l'*Ode à Aphrodite*,[39] où Sappho met en scène son lien personnel avec la déesse : « et toi, Bienheureuse, ayant souri de ton visage immortel, tu me demandas ce qui m'était advenu, et quelle faveur j'implorais et ce que je désirais le plus dans mon âme insensée[40] » (13–18). La déesse promet à Sappho que sa bien-aimée, qui maintenant la méprise, viendra rapidement la rejoindre : καὶ γὰρ αἰ φεύγει, ταχέως διώξει, « et en effet celle qui fuit loin de toi, rapidement te poursuivra » (21). Toutefois, la situation décrite par 'Sulpicia' ne correspond pas à la promesse d'Aphrodite. Elle renvoie en fait au proème du *De rerum natura*, où Lucrèce dit de Mars qu'il « vient souvent se jeter dans les bras de Vénus » (*in gremium qui saepe tuum / se reicit . . .*, 33 s.), en substituant à *gremium* le mot gallien, *sinum*.[41] Or l'allusion faite ici aux amours de Mars et de Vénus, on la retrouve aussi dans l'élégie 3.11, ainsi que dans l'autre élégie à la première personne, l'élégie 3.9 : c'est donc, je crois, un autre trait intratextuel.[42]

2.3 Un exemple récurrent évoqué toujours allusivement dans les différents textes de Sulpicia : les amours de Mars et de Vénus

Aux vers 7 s. de l'élégie 3.11, 'Sulpicia' adresse une prière à Cerinthus :

> *mutuus adsit amor, per te dulcissima furta*
> *perque tuos oculos per Genium rogo.*

> Puisse-t-il y avoir, entre nous, un amour réciproque, je t'en supplie au nom de nos si doux larcins/si douces amours secrètes, au nom de tes yeux et au nom de ton Génie !

---

39 Sur Sulpicia et Sappho, voir, par exemple, Piastri (1998) 139 s. ; Merriam (2006) 12 ; Fabre-Serris (2009) 150 s.
40 La traduction est celle de Renée Vivien (1903).
41 Sur le fait que *sinum* est probablement un mot gallien, voir Fabre-Serris (2017) 120 s. Sur les possibles renvois de Lucrèce à Sappho dans le *prooemium* du *De rerum natura*, voir Fulkerson (2017). Elle pointe en particulier l'instabilité dans les attachements amoureux, qui lui semble un point commun entre le discours d'Aphrodite dans Sappho qui « emphasizes the natural reversals in love rather than offering any form of permanent stability » et la vision, influencée par Empédocle, que Lucrèce propose de la déesse (« seen through the eyes of Lucretius, Aphrodite becomes rather like Empedocles' impersonal Love, a force that brings things together », 67).
42 Ce qui va dans le même sens est que l'*amicus Sulpiciae* dans l'élégie 3.8, composée en réponse à l'épigramme 13, propose, lui aussi un scénario remanié des amours de Mars et de Vénus qui inclut Sulpicia. Voir Fabre-Serris (2017) 121 s.

Dulcissima furta est une expression rare. On n'en trouve au 1ier siècle av. J.-C. que trois autres occurrences, sous la forme *dulcia furta*, l'une dans les *Géorgiques* 4, où Virgile résume ainsi le contenu du chant de Clyméné (345–347) :

> *inter quas curam Clymene narrabat inanem*
> *Volcani Martisque dolos et dulcia furta*
> *aque Chao densos diuom numerabat amores.*

> Parmi elles, Clyméné racontait le vain souci amoureux de Vulcain, les ruses de Mars et ses doux larcins/douce liaison secrète et elle énumérait depuis le chaos les amours abondantes des dieux.

La seconde se trouve chez Properce en 2.30.27 s. :

> *illic aspicies scopulis haerere Sorores*
>   *et canere antiqui dulcia furta Iouis.*

> Là tu apercevras les <neuf> Sœurs immobiles sur leurs rochers en train de chanter les doux larcins du Jupiter des anciens temps.

et la troisième chez Ovide à propos des amours interdites entre Byblis et son frère (*Mét.* 9.558) :[43]

> *dulcia fraterno sub nomine furta tegemus.*

> Nous couvrirons nos doux larcins en nous servant du nom de frère et sœur.

Je laisserai de côté l'emploi de l'expression chez Ovide pour les raisons données dans la note 38. On peut supposer que Properce, lui, renvoie aux *Géorgiques* 4, étant donné la similitude des situations : deux chants de femmes, et d'objet : des amours divines d'autrefois. Dans les *Géorgiques*, ces deux vers figurent dans un passage préliminaire au récit des amours d'Orphée et d'Eurydice, dont Gian Biagio Conte a montré que Virgile l'avait conçu comme une critique de la conception élégiaque du *furor* amoureux.[44] Dans la mesure où *cura*[45] et *dolos* appartiennent au glossaire élégiaque, il en est, sans doute, de même pour *dulcia furta,* et, si l'on tient compte du contexte narratif (Orphée, le protagoniste de l'épisode suivant, aurait

---

43 Voir Fabre-Serris (2020b).
44 Voir Conte (1984) et (1998).
45 Sur l'origine gallienne de *cura* au sens élégiaque de 'beloved', voir Cairns (2006) 115 s. Que *cura* ait eu ce sens chez Gallus n'est pas un obstacle à une utilisation du mot par Virgile avec un sens légèrement différent : « (vain) souci/soin amoureux ». Cf. l'usage relevé par Cairns, p. 116, du mot *cura* par Properce en 1.8.1 au sens de 'my love for you' qu'il considère comme une allusion à l'usage du mot chez Gallus.

été, de l'avis d'une partie des critiques, évoqué par Gallus[46]), il s'agit probablement d'une expression gallienne. L'épisode homérique des amours de Mars et de Vénus auquel il est fait allusion dans ces deux vers de Virgile a été lu allégoriquement par les Anciens comme une mise en scène de la victoire du principe empédocléen de l'Amour. C'est cette même lecture qui a été faite par David Sedley[47] pour la scène des amours de Mars et de Vénus dans le proème du *De rerum natura*, où Lucrèce évoque la déesse en insérant plusieurs renvois aux étymologies romaines sur le nom de Vénus (*uenire, uis, uincire, uincere*). Il y a de bonnes raisons pour supposer que l'analyse lucrétienne du pouvoir de Vénus à la lumière d'Empédocle ait joué un rôle générateur dans la conception de l'amour amorcée par Gallus et développée par ses successeurs.[48] J'en reviens à l'élégie 3.11 *dulcissima furta* me semble à prendre non seulement comme la reprise ou adaptation d'une *iunctura* gallienne, mais aussi, et surtout, comme un renvoi au passage des *Géorgiques* 4, où Virgile utilise une expression similaire dans le contexte narratif des amours de Mars et de Vénus en faisant de ces amours le modèle de toutes les amours divines ultérieures.

Dans l'élégie 3.11, ce renvoi aux *dulcia furta* expérimentés par tous les amants élégiaques précède en effet une prière à Vénus, où Sulpicia fait appel au pouvoir qu'a la déesse de 'lier' 'également' les amoureux. Ce pouvoir, à l'origine du couple qu'elle forme avec Mars, est aussi à l'origine de tous les couples d'amants mortels, enchaînés par le désir comme leur modèle divin. L'allusion voilée aux amours de Mars et de Vénus que le lecteur peut inférer d'une part de l'emploi de *per . . . dulcissima furta*, d'autre part de l'appel adressé à la déesse pour qu'elle use de son pouvoir de lier les amants me semble pouvoir être rapprochée de l'allusion aux amours de Mars et de Vénus faite, elle aussi, de façon voilée dans l'épigramme 3.13, où l'image du dieu enlacé par Vénus est à l'origine de celle de Cerinthus apporté par la déesse dans les bras de Sulpicia. On trouve le même genre d'allusion indirecte aux amours de Mars et de Vénus dans l'élégie 3.9, écrite également à la première personne. Comme l'a noté Stephen Hinds,[49] la situation décrite dans les vers 15 s. : *tunc mihi, tunc placeant siluae, si, lux mea,*[50] *tecum / arguar ante ipsas concubuisse plagas* (« c'est alors, alors que les forêts me plairaient si, lumière de ma vie, j'étais

---

46 Sur la probabilité que Gallus ait évoqué Orphée, voir Ross (1975) 23–38 ; Kennedy (1987) 53 s. ; Cairns (2006) 113 et 121, Fabre-Serris (2008) 67 n. 38. Sur le contexte gallien de ce passage des *Géorgiques*, voir Fabre-Serris (2014) par. 13–15.
47 Voir, par exemple, Sedley (2007), pour qui tout le début du *De rerum natura* est calqué sur le Περὶ Φυσέως d'Empédocle.
48 Sur l'hypothèse que Gallus aurait mentionné, décrit ou raconté les amours de Mars et de Vénus en usant des mêmes étymologies que Lucrèce, pour développer des motifs comme la victoire d'Amor (*uicit Amor*) ou l'étreinte étroite des amants quand ils font l'amour (*uincire*), qui deviendront typiques du genre qu'il a inventé, voir Fabre-Serris (2014) par. 19–44.
49 Hinds (1987) 35.
50 Comme le note Parker (1994) 47, *lux mea* est utilisé en 3.9.15 et en 3.18.1, et nulle part ailleurs dans le *Corpus Tibullianum*.

convaincue d'avoir fait l'amour ou si on révélait que j'avais fait l'amour avec toi devant les filets mêmes ») : « a copulating couple, nets and exposure », semble (en effet) faire allusion, de la même façon voilée, à l'épisode où les deux amants divins furent pris sur le fait. Cette convergence entre les deux élégies à la première personne va dans le sens d'une identification de l'auteur avec un seul et même auteur, le même que celui de l'epigramme 3.13, Sulpicia.

2.4 Le refus de souffrir, une variation sur un motif majeur de l'élégie

Une autre particularité de l'élégie 3.11 est le refus de souffrir, qui ressort du glissement de l'annonce d'un *seruitium amoris* général pour les jeunes femmes à la requête d'un *mutuus amor* entre Cerinthus et Sulpicia.[51] Dans le *seruitium amoris* les poètes font l'expérience de la souffrance amoureuse, tout en appelant de leurs vœux, un *mutuus amor*. Les prières adressées au Génie de Cerinthus et à Natalis, que j'ai laissées de côté jusqu'ici, mettent en évidence la volonté qu'a 'Sulpicia' de supprimer toute occasion de souffrir. Ces prières sont toutes destinées à garantir la constance et la fidélité de Cerinthus. La faveur de son Génie est conditionnée à la bouffée d'ardeur dont le jeune homme doit être saisi quand il pense à Sulpicia (9–12) :

> *mane Geni, cape tura libens uotisque faueto.*
> *si modo, cum de me cogitat, ille calet.*
> *quodsi forte alios iam nunc suspiret amores,*
> *tunc precor infidos, sancte, relinque focos.*

> Bon Génie, reçois l'encens de bon cœur et sois favorable à mes vœux, si seulement, lorsqu'il pense à moi, il brûle. Mais si par hasard il soupire dès maintenant après d'autres amours,[52] alors je t'en prie, dieu vénérable, abandonne ce foyer devenu infidèle !

Cerinthus espère, affirme 'Sulpicia' après sa prière à Vénus, la même chose qu'elle (autrement dit, les liens éternels demandés à la déesse) : *optat idem iuuenis quod nos* (« le jeune homme <que j'aime> souhaite la même chose que moi », 17). Que Natalis donne son assentiment à ce vœu ! (*at tu, Natalis . . . / adnue*, 19 s.).

Ces prières pour éliminer toute infidélité future de Cerinthus peuvent être aussi mises au nombre des traits intratextuels de l'élégie 3.11, le souci d'échapper aux souffrances amoureuses étant en effet constant dans les épigrammes 3.13–18. Dans le genre élégiaque, les principales occasions des souffrances amoureuses sont la séparation,

---

[51] C'est l'observation que fait aussi Fulkerson (2017) 259, quand elle commente les vers 13 s. : « S, at least as she is described here, is not interested in elegiac suffering ».
[52] *Alios . . . suspiret amores* est la reprise d'une expression au vers 35 de l'élégie 1.6 de Tibulle : *te tenet, absentes alios suspirat amores* (« elle te tient dans ses bras, mais soupire après d'autres amours absents »). À cette élégie renvoie aussi l'expression *mutuus amor* également présente en 3.11.7 et 1.6.76.

l'infidélité et le *seruitium amoris*. Que ce soit dans l'élégie 3.11, dans les épigrammes 3.13–18 ou dans l'élégie 3.9, aucun de ces motifs ne donne lieu aux souffrances qui leur sont traditionnellement associées dans le genre élégiaque. Sulpicia, la poétesse, appréhende une séparation dans l'épigramme 3.14, mais c'est seulement une possibilité, qui est aussitôt annulée dans l'épigramme 3.15. L'infidélité de Cerinthus n'est évoquée que comme une éventualité dans l'élégie 3.11, que 'Sulpicia' cherche à éliminer avec l'aide du Génie du jeune homme. Dans l'épigramme 3.16, où il semble que Cerinthus ait préféré à Sulpicia une prostituée, celle-ci paraît envisager, si c'est le cas, de lui rendre la pareille,[53] mais ces deux situations sont évoquées dans des termes qui ne permettent pas de savoir si elles sont autre chose que des suspicions ou des éventualités. Quant au *seruitium amoris*, ce n'est pas un hasard si non seulement l'élégie 3.11, mais l'élégie 3.9 en proposent un traitement nouveau, où sont éliminées les souffrances dont il s'accompagne dans les textes des autres élégiaques. Dans l'élégie 3.11, on l'a vu, 'Sulpicia' substitue au *seruitium amoris* des requêtes de *mutuus amor*. Dans l'élégie 3.9, le maniement des filets et les ronces des buissons qu'on s'attendrait à voir associés au *seruitium amoris* accompli par 'Sulpicia' font souffrir, non l'amante devenue chasseresse sur le modèle de Milanion, mais le jeune chasseur lui-même, ce que 'Sulpicia' déplore parce que sa beauté en est altérée. 'Sulpicia' imagine ensuite que, si elle se faisait sa compagne de chasse, elle et lui y mettraient fin en faisant l'amour en plein air. Finalement elle demande à Cerinthus de rester chaste en son absence et de revenir vite se jeter dans ses bras.

2.5 Le choix provocant de parler ouvertement de ses amours

À la fin de l'élégie 3.11 'Sulpicia' reprend une opposition faite précédemment par Tibulle entre deux prières, l'une faite ouvertement, l'autre en secret parce que la seconde a trait à des vœux amoureux. J'ai déjà cité ce passage. Je rappelle que, chez Tibulle, les deux prières sont attribuées aux mêmes personnes. Ici l'une des prières est celle que 'Sulpicia' vient d'adresser à Vénus pour que la déesse assure à sa 'liaison' avec Cerinthus une durée sans fin. Elle attribue l'autre à Cerinthus en précisant que son contenu est le même, mais que son ami formule ses vœux d'une façon plus dissimulée (17 s.).

> *optat idem iuuenis quod nos, sed tectius optat :*
> *nam pudet haec illum dicere uerba palam.*
>
> Le jeune homme <que j'aime> souhaite la même chose que moi, mais il formule ce souhait d'une façon plus dissimulée, car lui, il a honte de dire ces paroles ouvertement.

---

[53] C'est le poème le plus difficile à interpréter, en raison en particulier des expressions *ne male inepta cadam* et *ne cedam ignoto . . . toro*, dont le sens a donné lieu à plusieurs hypothèses.

Or c'est aussi un trait propre à la manière d'écrire de Sulpicia, la poétesse, que le choix de 'parler ouvertement' de ses amours.[54] On a donc ici aussi un trait intratextuel, confirmé d'ailleurs par des reprises textuelles. Les mots *tectius* et *pudet* trouvent des échos dans les mots *texisse* et *pudori* utilisés au début de l'épigramme 3.13 pour soutenir le choix de parler ouvertement de sa liaison que Sulpicia non seulement fait, mais proclame qu'elle fait, en écrivant son poème : *tandem uenit amor qualem* **texisse pudori** */ quam nudasse alicui sit mihi fama magis* (« enfin l'amour est venu tel que la réputation de l'avoir caché serait davantage pour moi une source de honte que celle de l'avoir dévoilé à quelqu'un », 1 s.). Le choix du mot *nudasse* versus *texisse* correspond à celui de *palam* versus *tectius* dans l'élégie 3.11, avec un zeste de provocation en plus, si considère que l'absence ou la présence de vêtements couvrant le corps est directement en relation avec le respect ou non de la pudeur attendue des femmes.[55]

J'ai déjà signalé le caractère provocateur du vers 3.11.5 (. . . *iuuat hoc, Cerinthe, quod uror*), par lequel 'Sulpicia' proclame ouvertement le plaisir qu'elle a à éprouver une ardeur amoureuse (illicite) en précisant que cet emploi pouvait être rapproché du *peccasse iuuat* de l'épigramme 3.13, où Sulpicia, la poétesse, revendique, d'une façon provocatrice, une liaison érotique, potentiellement problématique pour une femme ayant son statut social. Que *dicere uerba palam* soit à prendre comme un trait intratextuel est confirmé par la dernière épigramme du cycle sulpicien. Si Sulpicia y proclame son regret d'avoir quitté Cerinthus durant la nuit « par désir de lui dissimuler son ardeur » (*ardorem cupiens dissimulare meum*, 3.18.6), elle le fait en présentant ce regret comme la chose dont elle 'avoue' (*fatear*) se repentir le plus. Ce qui a pour effet de donner plus de force encore à l'aveu a posteriori de cette ardeur.

3 Conclusion

En conclusion, si l'on admet que : l'emploi de *iuuat* au sens de « il me plaît » dans un contexte érotique provocateur (la revendication du désir ou de la faute) ; l'affirmation ou l'exigence d'une réciprocité en amour ou entre amants ; la mise en évidence d'un lien personnel avec Vénus qui se traduit par une aide majeure de la déesse, demandée ou obtenue ; des allusions voilées aux amours de Mars et de Vénus liés par le désir ; le refus de souffrir et le choix de parler ouvertement de ses amours sont des

---

[54] Ce choix de parler ouvertement de ses amours était déjà souligné par Heyne : voir Skoie (2003) 145 s.
[55] Comme on l'a noté Milnor (2002) 260, Sulpicia utilise le verbe *texisse* ('couvrir en tissant'), ce qui est la tâche recommandée et louée pour les femmes) versus *nudasse* ('mettre à nu'), ce qu'elle a fait de son corps durant cette première nuit d'amour.

traits propres aux épigrammes 3.13–18, également présents dans l'élégie 3.11, l'auteur de ce poème est Sulpicia elle-même, qui, par ces traits stylistiques et thématiques, marque de sa *persona* poétique ce poème dans lequel, en même temps, avec ingéniosité et virtuosité, elle rend hommage à Tibulle.

J'ajoute que tous ces éléments me semblent cohérents avec le fait que Sulpicia est une patricienne. Dans l'élégie 3.11, comme dans les épigrammes 3.13–18, elle se comporte, quand il s'agit de morale ou de sexe, 'au moins en paroles', avec une assurance, un orgueil et sans doute un sentiment d'impunité, qui aura peut-être été altéré par les Lois Juliennes,[56] mais qui est typique de son origine familiale. On peut en trouver indirectement une confirmation dans le comportement qui sera plus tard celui de la fille d'Auguste, Julia.[57] Inversement aucun poète masculin du cercle n'aurait pu écrire des choses aussi hardies en les attribuant à la nièce de Messalla, ce que confirme l'élégie 3.12, qui reprend en les modulant différemment certains des motifs de l'élégie 3.11.[58] Je n'en donnerai qu'un exemple : comme Tibulle, l'*amicus* oppose deux types de vœux prononcés par une seule personne : l'une ouvertement, l'autre en secret. Cette même personne est Sulpicia, à qui sa mère, qualifiée de « dévouée », recommande (de souhaiter) « ce qu'elle-même souhaite » pour sa fille (*praecipit et natae mater studiosa quod optat*, 15), tandis que cette dernière formule « mentalement » et « silencieusement » (*tacita . . . sua mente*, 16) un autre vœu inspiré par son amour.

Ce double effet de la position sociale de Sulpicia n'avait pas échappé à Georges Doncieux. Dans l'article que j'ai cité plus haut, intitulé « De qui sont les élégies 2–6 du livre IV de Tibulle ? », le critique français attribue à Sulpicia les élégies 3.9 et 3.11, parce qu'il y retrouve la personnalité de l'auteure de l'épigramme 3.13. Voici ce qu'il écrit à propos de l'élégie 3.9 et du vers *arguar ante ipsas concubuisse plagas* (16): « Cela est d'une amoureuse violente, et *née grande dame*,[59] bref je ne sais *qu'une personne au monde capable de parler en ces termes de Sulpicia, c'est Sulpicia elle-même* ; c'est celle qui disait une autre fois : *sed peccasse iuuat ; uultus componere famae / taedet* »,[60] et à propos de l'élégie 3.11 et du vers 5: « Parallèlement, dans l'élégie 5, mais ceci est affaire d'impression plutôt que de raisonnement, ce beau vers tout de feu : *Vror ego ante alias : iuuat hoc, Cerinthe, quod uror* me semble inspiré par elle ». « Inspiré » : parce que Georges Doncieux conclut tout de même que ces textes ne peuvent pas être de Sulpicia toute seule ; elle a dû se faire aider . . . par

---

[56] Sur l'hypothèse qu'elle ait écrit avant la publication des Lois Juliennes, voir Hallett (2009) 141 et (2011) 83–85.
[57] Voir les anecdotes rassemblées par Macrobe et la très intéressante analyse qu'en a faite Richlin (2014) 81–109.
[58] C'est ce que j'ai essayé de montrer dans une étude en cours qui fait partie du livre que je suis en train d'écrire sur Sulpicia.
[59] Les italiques sont de moi.
[60] Doncieux (1891) 80.

Tibulle (« Quoi de plus *naturel* que cette 'docte fille' le prie d'arranger un peu et d'embellir ses vers ? »[61]). Autre temps, autres conceptions du genre !

Bibliographie

Édition

Tibulle et les auteurs du Corpus Tibullianum, texte établi et traduit par Max Ponchont, Paris ^{9}1989.

Articles et ouvrages de critique

Ball (1975) : Robert J. Ball, « The structure of Tibullus 1.7 », dans : *Latomus* 34, 729–744.
Barchiesi (1997) : Alessandro Barchiesi, « Otto punti su una mappa dei naufragi », *MD* 39, 209–226.
Batstone (2018) : William W. Batstone, « Sulpicia and the Speech of Men », dans : Stavros Frangoulidis et Stephen Harrison (dir.), *Life, Love and Death in Latin Poetry*, Berlin, 83–109.
Cairns (2012) : Francis Cairns, « Poem 45. The wooing of Acme and Septimius », dans : Ian M. Le M. Du Quesnay et Tony Woodman (dir.), *Catullus. Poems, Books, Readers*, Cambridge, 112–129.
Conte (1974) : Gian Biagio Conte, *Memoria dei poeti e Sistema letterario*, Torino.
Conte (1984) : Gian Biagio Conte, « Aristeo, Orfeo e le *Georgiche*. Struttura narrativa e funzione didascalica di un mito », dans : *Virgilio. Il genere e i suoi confini*, Milano, 13–42.
Conte (1998) : Gian Biagio Conte, « Aristeo, Orfeo e le *Georgiche*. Una seconda volta », *SCO*, 103–128.
Currie (1983) : Harry MacL. Currie, « The poems of Sulpicia », dans : *ANRW* II 30.3, 1751–1764.
Doncieux (1891) : Georges Doncieux, « De qui sont les élégies 2–6 du livre 4 de Tibulle? », *Revue de Philologie, de littérature et d'histoire anciennes* 15, 76–81.
Dronke (2003) : Peter Dronke, « Alcune osservazioni sulle poesie di Sulpicia: c. a. 25 a. C. », dans : Ferruccio Bertini (dir.), *Giornate filologiche "Francesco Della Corte"* III, 81–99.
Edmunds (2001) : Lowell Edmunds, *Intertextuality and the Reading of Roman Poetry*, Baltimore.
Fabre-Serris (2005) : Jacqueline Fabre-Serris, « L'élégie et les images romaines des origines : les choix de Tibulle », dans : Jürgen P. Schwindt (dir.), *La représentation du temps dans la poésie augustéenne, Zur Poetik der Zeit in augusteischer Dichtung*, Heidelberg, 141–157.
Fabre-Serris (2008) : Jacqueline Fabre-Serris, *Rome, l'Arcadie et la mer des Argonautes. Essai sur la naissance d'une mythologie des origines en Occident*, Lille.
Fabre-Serris (2009) : Jacqueline Fabre-Serris, « Sulpicia: An/other Female Voice in Ovid's *Heroides*. A New Reading of *Heroides* 4 and 15 », *Helios* 36,2, 149–172.
Fabre-Serris (2014) : Jacqueline Fabre-Serris, « La réception d'Empédocle dans la poésie latine : Virgile (*Buc.* 6), Lucrèce, Gallus et les poètes élégiaques », *Dictynna* 11.
Fabre-Serris (2017) : Jacqueline Fabre-Serris, « Sulpicia, Gallus et les élégiaques. Propositions de lecture de l'épigramme 13 », *Eugesta* 7, 115–139.

---

[61] Doncieux (1891) 81.

Fabre-Serris (2018a): Jacqueline Fabre-Serris, « Intratextuality and Extratextuality in the *Corpus Tibullianu*m 3.8–18 », dans : Stephen Harrison, Stavros Frangoulidis et Theodore Papanghelis (dir.), *Intratextuality and Latin literature*, Berlin, 67–79.

Fabre-Serris (2018b) : Jacqueline Fabre-Serris, « Love and Death in Propertius 1.10, 1.13 and 2.15: Poetic and Polemical Games with Lucretius, Gallus and Virgil », dans : Stavros Frangoulidis and Stephen Harrison (dir.), *Life, Love and Death in Latin Poetry*, Berlin, 37–50.

Fabre-Serris (2020a) : Jacqueline Fabre-Serris, « The authorship of Tibullus 3.9: methods and criteria », dans : Tristan E. Franklinos et Laurel Fulkerson (dir.), *Constructing Authors and Readers in the Appendices Vergiliana, Tibulliana, and Ovidiana*, Oxford, 170–185.

Fabre-Serris (2020b) : Jacqueline Fabre-Serris, « Ovide lecteur de Sulpicia? Déclaration amoureuse et stratégies d'énonciation dans le *Corpus Tibullianum* 3.11, 3.13 et l'*Héroïde* 4 », *Dictynna* 17.

Fowler (2000) : Don Fowler, « On the Shoulders of Giants! Intertextuality and Classical Studies », dans : Id. (dir.), *Roman Constructions. Readings in Postmodern Latin*, Oxford, 115–137. Première publication dans le numéro spécial de *MD* 39, 1997, *Memoria, arte allusiva, intertestualità / Memory, Allusion, Intertextuality*, 13–34.

Fredericks (1976) : Sigmund C. Fredericks, « A Poetic Experiment in the Garland of Sulpicia (*Corpus Tibullianum* 3.10) », *Latomus* 35, 761–782.

Fulkerson (2017) : Laurel Fulkerson, *A literary commentary on the elegies of the « Appendix Tibulliana »*, Oxford.

Gaisser (1971) : Julia Gaisser, « Tibullus 1.7: a tribute to Messalla », *CP* 66, 221–229.

Gruppe (1838) : Otto Gruppe, *Die römische Elegie*, Leipzig.

Hallett (2002a) : Judith P. Hallett, « The eleven elegies of the Augustan poet Sulpicia », dans : Laurie J. Churchill, Phyllis R. Brown et Jane E. Jeffrey (dir.), *Women writing Latin from Roman Antiquity to early modern Europe*, vol 1: *Women writing Latin in Roman Antiquity, Late Antiquity and the Early Christian Era*, New York/ London, 45–65.

Hallett (2002b) : Judith P. Hallett, « Sulpicia and the Valerii. Family Ties and Politic Unity », dans : Bettina Amden (dir.), *Noctes Atticae: 34 articles on Graeco-Roman Antiquity and its Nachleben, studies presented to Jørgen Mejer on his sixtieth birthday, March 18, 2002*, Copenhagen, 141–149.

Hallett (2009) : Judith P. Hallett, « Sulpicia and her resistant intertextuality », dans : Danielle van Mal-Maeder, Alexandre Burnier et Loreto Núñez (dir.), *Jeux de voix. Enonciation, intertextualité et intentionnalité dans la littérature antique*, Bern, 141–155.

Hallett, J. (2011) : Judith P. Hallett, « Scenarios of Sulpiciae: Moral Discourses and Immoral Verses », *Eugesta* 1, 79–97.

Hinds (1987) : Stephen Hinds, « The poetess and the reader. Further steps towards Sulpicia », *Hermathena* 143, 29–46.

Hinds (2006) : Stephen Hinds, « Venus, Varro and the *vates*: towards the limits of etymologizing interpretation », *Dictynna* 3.

Kennedy (1982) : Duncan Kennedy, « Gallus and the *Culex* », *CQ* 32, 371–389.

Konstan (1978) : David Konstan, « The Politics of Tibullus' 1.7 », *RSC* 26, 173–185.

Lee (1990) : Guy Lee, *Tibullus: Elegies*, Wiltshire.

Lee-Stecum (1998) : Parshia Lee-Stecum, *Powerplay in Tibullus: Reading Elegies Book One*, Oxford.

Lowe (1988) : Nicholas J. Lowe, « Sulpicia's Syntax », *CQ* 38, 193–205.

Lowell Bowditch (2011) : Phebe Lowell Bowditch, « Tibullus and Egypt. A post-colonial reading of elegy 1.7 », *Arethusa* 44,1, 89–122.

Luck (1969) : Georg Luck, *The Latin Love Elegy*, London.

Luck (1976) : Georg Luck, « An Interpretation of Horace's Eleventh *Epode* », *ICS*, 122–126.

Merriam (2006) : Carol Merriam, « Sulpicia, just another poet », *CW* 100, 11–15.

Murgatroyd (1980) : Paul Murgatroyd, *Tibullus 1. A Commentary on the First Book of the Elegies of Albius Tibullus*, Pietermaritzburg.
Parker (1994) : Holt Parker, « Sulpicia, the Auctor de Sulpicia, and the Authorship of 3.9 and 3.11 of the *Corpus Tibullianum* », *Helios* 21, 39–62.
Pasquali (1942) : Giorgio Pasquali, « Arte allusiva », dans · Id., *Pagine stravaganti*, Firenze, 2, 275–282.
Piastri (1998) : Roberta Piastri, « I carmi di Sulpicia e il repertorio topico dell'elegia », *Quaderni del Dipartimento di Filologia, Linguistica e Tradizione classica* 11, 137–170.
Platnauer (1951): Maurice Platnauer, *Latin Elegiac Verse. A study of the metrical usages of Tibullus, Propertius and Ovid*, Cambridge.
Richlin (2014) : Amy Richlin, *Arguments with Silence*, Ann Arbor.
Ross (1975) : David O. Ross, *Backgrounds to Augustan Poetry. Gallus, Elegy and Rome*, Cambridge.
Rossbach (1855) : August Rossbach, *Albii Tibulli libri quattuor*, Leipzig.
Schanz-Hosius (1959) : Martin Schanz et Carl Hosius, *Geschichte der römischen Literatur*, Leiden.
Sedley (2007) : David Sedley, « The Empedoclean Opening », dans : Monica Gale (dir.), *Oxford Readings in Classical Studies: Lucretius*, Oxford, 48–87.
Sharrock/Morales (2000) : Alison Sharrock et Helen Morales, *Intratextuality. Greek and Roman Textual Relations*, Oxford.
Smith (1913) : Kirby F. Smith, *The Elegies of Albius Tibullus*, New York.
Thomas (2001) : Richard Thomas, *Virgil and the Augustan Reception*, Cambridge.
Tränkle (1990) : Hermann Tränkle, *Appendix Tibulliana*, Berlin.
Vivien (1903) : Renée Vivien, *Sapho. Traduction nouvelle avec le texte grec*, Paris.

V The Gender Parameter in Ovid's First-Person Discourse

Alison Sharrock

Living to Tell the Tale: Male and Female First-Person Narrators of Metamorphosis

Abstract: Ovid's *Metamorphoses* is well supplied with variant narrators, many of whom are female. Among the few characters who live to tell the tale of their own metamorphosis, there are some interesting gendered effects: I shall concentrate on Cornix, Ocyroe, and Hippolytus. Of these three, Hippolytus-Virbius maintains the greatest control over his post-metamorphic existence. Ocyroe does not, strictly speaking, live to tell the tale, in that her account of her metamorphosis into a horse is prophetic. Cornix, the first female storyteller of the poem, retains the ability to speak in crow-form, but remains caught in a web of storytelling delay. After suggesting negatively-charged gendered implications arising from these first-person narrators, I shall address a problem in contemporary feminist theory, in which attempts to expose female suffering and to pay attention to female voices risk re-enacting the very oppression they seek to expose. If access to the Symbolic is more available to Hippolytus than to Ocyroe, is that because my act of reading has made it so?

Keywords: Ovid, *Metamorphoses*, Symbolic, storytelling, author-poet, narrators

1 Introduction

Most of the stories of transformation that feature in Ovid's great epic of change, *Metamorphoses*, are told by third parties, be that extradiegetically by the primary narrator, whom we can call Ovid himself, extradiegetically by one of the many storytellers internal to the poem but external to the stories they tell, or sometimes in tales in which the speaker him- or herself is involved as witness or even agent of metamorphosis.[1] Indeed, the first true metamorphosis of a human, that of Lycaon into a wolf, is narrated by its agent Jupiter, although hardly with the sympathy which more often characterises the relationship between narrator and metamorphic subject of narration. Any narrating character partakes to some extent in the action of the primary narrator, who partakes to some extent in the action of the author. The work of an author is a paradigm case of what in feminist theory has been characterised as the

---

1 See especially Wheeler (1999) 188, on variant narrators in the *Metamorphoses*.

Acknowledgments: I am grateful to Therese Fuhrer and Lisa Cordes for their kind invitation to contribute and their patience with me in the process. I would also like to thank my assistant, Julene Abad Del Vecchio, for numerous forms of help in the production of this paper.

Symbolic, that is, the world order controlled by men, including education, politics, literature, the professions, and so on.[2] While no character within a work of fiction can ever attain full control of the Symbolic, being also controlled by an external author, I would like to suggest that the distinction between characters and author is not absolute, on either side. On the one hand, the 'author' is himself constructed by the poem, while on the other hand it is a commonplace of reading to see at least some of the internal narrators of the poem as 'ciphers' for the poet.

Many of the tales include extended and empathetically drawn-out descriptions of metamorphosis, the majority of which, I argue elsewhere, are of female victims, especially when the metamorphosis itself is described at length.[3] In most cases, empathetic narration gives voice to characters who cannot speak for themselves: speech, or rather the lack of it, constitutes an important element in the enactment of metamorphosis.[4] A natural concomitant of this situation is that very few characters in the poem narrate their own transformation, for the simple reasons of narrative time and the fact that metamorphosis generally involves the loss of voice. There are, however, a few cases where narrative tricks are employed to circumvent the logical constraints on first-person narration of metamorphosis. This paper explores the situation of three such characters: the crow, who (with help from Callimachean intertextuality) partakes in the fable-like world of the talking animal and so is able to tell her own tale; the prophetic Ocyroe, who foretells the future up to the point when future and present meet; and the divinised Hippolytus, whose metamorphosis is subsumed in apotheosis. I shall explore how these first-person narrators tell their own stories, how they interact with the primary narrator – as all internal storytellers must do, whether they are telling their own or someone else's story – and how differences of gender play themselves out in storytelling and in criticism.

---

2 Moi (2002) 12 characterises "liberal feminism" as women "demand equal access to the Symbolic order".
3 I discuss the gendered nature of metamorphosis in Sharrock (2020a).
4 Explicit reference to loss of speech is an especially marked element in Ovidian metamorphosis, especially, although not exclusively, of female characters, including Byblis, Callisto, Chione, Cyane, Dryope, Echo, Galanthis, Hecuba, Heliades, Harmonia, Io, Minyeides, Myrrha, Niobe, Ocyroe, Philomela, Pierides. On this, see above all Natoli (2017), who notes (34) that "Ovid mentions speech loss in roughly 40 of the 250 stories [*referring to his Appendix A*]. In each of these episodes, Ovid routinely follows a schematic model and associates speech loss with the nonhuman, the emotional, and the curtailment of community. When a character is transformed from a human into a nonhuman (e.g., an animal, an inanimate object, a plant), like Kafka, Ovid focuses his attention on the character's inability to speak in his or her transformed state. Likewise, often when a character is transformed into a speechless animal, Ovid indicates that the character also experiences an increase in emotion. As a result of the transformed character's speech loss and heightened emotion, the character is also removed from community, as she or he is no longer able to communicate with it."

2 Ocyroe: A woman following in her father's footsteps

I begin with an early figure in the poem, whose status as prophet of the future allows her to tell her own story before it happens. Ocyroe, daughter of the prophetic centaur Chiron, enters the poem when her father is granted tutelage of the baby Aesculapius, son of Apollo and Coronis, who is saved from the womb and funeral pyre of his mother after she has been killed by Apollo in a fit of vengeance for her affair with a human youth (2.542–7, 598f.). Chiron is happy in his role as guardian and teacher of epic and semidivine heroes. He is accompanied in this task by his daughter, who has had a remarkably Symbolic-friendly upbringing and education in her father's profession (2.635–9).[5]

> ecce uenit rutilis umeros protecta capillis
> filia Centauri, quam quondam nympha Chariclo
> fluminis in rapidi ripis enixa uocauit
> Ocyroen. non haec artes contenta paternas
> edidicisse fuit; fatorum arcana canebat.

> Look, here comes the daughter of the Centaur, her shoulders covered in red-gold hair, she whom the nymph Chariclo once bore on the banks of a fast-flowing river and called Ocyroe. She was not content to have learnt her father's arts; she kept prophesying the secrets of the fates.

Ocyroe foretells the future of the baby Aesculapius, who will first die then become a god, and also that of her centaur father, who will turn from immortal to mortal in order to escape suffering. The problem is that her Symbolic ambition to know and to speak is deemed a threat to world order, and the extent of her exposure of the future is not acceptable. *Vates* are supposed to speak divine prophecy as a vehicle of Apollo, not to take the initiative into their own hands as Ocyroe does in telling the secrets of the fates. Ocyroe will have her capacity to speak taken from her, but not before she offers the most immediate, contemporaneous, intradiegetic account of metamorphosis in the whole poem.[6] Here we see not only a clever narrative trick to enable someone to speak about losing the capacity to speak, but also the merged consciousness of human and metamorphosed creature (in this case, horse) from the point of view of the individual (2.655–64).

> restabat fatis aliquid; suspirat ab imis   655
> pectoribus, lacrimaeque genis labuntur obortae,
> atque ita 'praeuertunt' inquit 'me fata uetorque

---

[5] All quotations from Ovid's *Metamorphoses* are from the edition of Tarrant (2004). Translations are my own.
[6] See Merli (2004) 459 apropos *restabat fatis aliquid* (*Met.* 1.655): "Il testo stesso tematizza così la propria incompletezza, invitando e autorizzando il lettore a integrare la storia".

> *plura loqui **uocisque meae praecluditur usus.***
> *non fuerant artes tanti, quae numinis iram*
> *contraxere mihi; mallem nescisse futura.* 660
> *iam mihi subduci facies humana uidetur,*
> *iam cibus herba placet, iam latis currere campis*
> *impetus est; in equam cognataque corpora uertor.*
> *tota tamen quare? pater est mihi nempe biformis.'*

There remained something from the fates; she sighed from the depths of her breast and the rising tears fell over her cheeks, and thus she spoke: 'The fates are preventing me and I am forbidden to speak more, and **the use of my voice is shut off in advance.** The arts which drew the anger of the godhead against me were not worth it; I would have preferred not to have known the future. Now human appearance seems to be drawn away from me, now grass is pleasing as food, now there is the desire to run over the broad fields; I am being turned into a filly, a cognate body. But why totally? To be sure my father is of twofold nature.'

In her very last moments of speech, Ocyroe's final act is to apply logic to her case, in her question of why she should be totally horse, rather than at least half-humanoid centaur. In doing so, she holds onto the Symbolic to the end. It is not irrelevant, in this battle for narratological control, that just before Ocyroe began her final prophetic speech, the narrator interrupted with an external account of her grief (2.655f.). Once Ocyroe's ability to express her logic is suppressed, the poet wholly snatches back the storyline, and it is he who narrates the process of change in real-time and in intense detail, playing on the complex relationship between metamorphosis, simile, appearance, and reality, and observing the transformation in minute detail. Note how the first lines in the passage quoted below draw out the loss of the communicative, the intelligible, the Symbolic, as the first stages in the transformation from human to equine sounds. Ocyroe's words are characterised as a *querela*, a complaint in which the details of logical argument are undermined (2.665–75).[7]

> *talia dicenti pars est extrema querelae* 665
> *intellecta parum, confusaque uerba fuerunt;*
> *mox ne uerba quidem nec equae sonus ille uidetur,*
> *sed simulantis equam, paruoque in tempore certos*
> *edidit hinnitus et bracchia mouit in herbas.*
> *tum digiti coeunt et quinos alligat ungues* 670
> *perpetuo cornu leuis ungula, crescit et oris*
> *et colli spatium, longae pars maxima pallae*

---

[7] In this regard, the account of Ocyroe's loss of speech has affinities with the suppressive characterisation of Euryalus' mother's speech as *ululatus*, as I argued in Sharrock (2011). See Merli (2004) 462, on the *Fasti* passage, on *querimonia* with its correlates as a key-word for the elegiac genre, although *querela* in the *Met.* passage is not noted. Its presence here might detract from Merli's Heinze-inspired generic reading, although the fact that Ocyroe's *querela* is suppressed by the action of Apollo could perhaps be interpreted from a generic point of view.

cauda fit, utque uagi crines per colla iacebant,
in dextras abiere iubas, pariterque nouata est
et uox et facies; nomen quoque monstra dedere. 675

As she spoke thus, the final part of her complaint was barely intelligible and the words were confused; soon the sound didn't seem to be either words or that of a horse, but rather of someone imitating a horse, but in a short time she gave forth definite whinnies and moved her arms to the grass. Then her toes came together and a light hoof tied together her five toenails in a single horn, the length of both her face and her neck increased, and the largest part of her long cloak became a tail, and as her dishevelled hair lay on her neck, it turned into a mane on the right-hand side, and equally her voice and face were made new; the prodigy also gave her a name.

The final line of the narrator's account forcefully enacts narratorial control over intellectual poetry, with its oblique reference to the alternative name Hippe (or Hippo or Melanippe).[8]

It might seem that Ocyroe has lost her battle for self-expression, for a career as *uates*, and even for personhood. Her role as narrator does, however, have greater force in the macroscopic structure of the *Metamorphoses*, in that her prophecy of Aesculapius' destiny will be reprised by the poem in Book 15. Her 'thou, child' moment (2.642–8) tells how Aesculapius will bring health to the world, even bringing people back to life, attracting the anger of the gods in much the same way as Ocyroe's own prophesying does. She tells how he will twice move between divine and human status. For those of us observing from the outside, we might note that the male Aesculapius will end up as a god, whereas the female Ocyroe will end up as an animal.[9] The story of Aesculapius plays an important role in the poem's crescendo towards apotheosis.[10] We might, furthermore, see a reprise of Ocyroe's battle with the fates not only in the account of the healing god in Book 15 but also in the poem's visit, through Jupiter, to the Record Office of Fate (15.808–15). As Hardie argues, the poem constitutes a kind of a "stand-off between *Fama* and *Fatum*, [in which] *Fama* will finally have the upper hand", in the epilogue where poetic fame overcomes mortal, political, and even divine fate.[11]

How far does Ocyroe get to share in the Symbolic as embodied by the poet, the poem, and poetic fame? We might want to say that the fact that her story reaches out beyond itself into the deeper structures of the poem enables her to share in the vatic and Symbolic status of Ovid as poet. She herself, however, does not seem to be aware of the poetic, rather than purely prophetic, aspects of her foreknowledge. Whether or not this vatic status raises her to the Symbolic is something which, perhaps, can only be decided by the reader. I shall return to this issue at the end of this paper.

---

8 See Keith (1992) 66 on the *lusus etymologicus* here; Heath (1994).
9 In Sharrock (2020b), I discuss the gendered patterns of metamorphic destination.
10 Hardie (1997); Barchiesi (1997).
11 Hardie (2012) 166f.

3 Cornix: A story of herself

My next example of a self-told narrative of metamorphosis comes just before Aesculapius and the centaur family. As the Raven was rushing to tell Apollo about Coronis' infidelity, he was stopped by a Crow, who told her own story to dissuade him from interference. These two characters, the only speaking animals in the *Metamorphoses*, resist the poem's usual suppression of speech along with the loss of human form. They are enabled to do so by plugging into the general tradition of animal fables and, as is well known, by the more specific literary authority of Callimachus.[12] Cornix as narrator is remarkable within the totality of the poem in a number of ways: she is the first of many female storytellers of the poem, the first of fewer to recount her own experience of attempted rape, and the first of very few to recount her own experience of metamorphosis. Indeed, the only other female self-narrator of metamorphosis is Ocyroe, discussed above. The account of Cornix thus constitutes an important meditation on the female voice and metamorphosis. She is the only female character who retains the ability to speak in animal form. Many characters can feel and do attempt to communicate – Callisto and Io, who can even write her name, are nearby examples – but no one else has the fabular gift of articulate speech. The only male character who speaks in animal form is her interlocutor the Raven, almost all of whose speech is reported by the primary narrator rather than represented directly in the poem. The only exception is his brief rejection of Cornix's warning (2.596f.).

Considering the significance of her role as female narrator of her own story, it is perhaps surprising (or perhaps not) that the Crow bustles her way into the poem without any justification in the narrative macrostructure or any elevated status. That the talking Crow has her intertextual origin in Callimachus' *Hecale* is well known, but there she is probably talking directly to some other bird, not to the Raven, whose transformation from white to black she prophesies in the third person.[13] Ovid has brought them face-to-face, by having Cornix interrupt his (Ovid's) larger narrative rather untidily and with stereotypical female inquisitiveness.[14] Another way of looking at it would be that Cornix is cawing to be heard (2.547–52):

---

12 Barchiesi (2005) 279; Keith (1992), esp. 19; Zissos/Gildenhard (2004); Hollis (²2009) 33; Fermi (2011), suggesting that the Homeric episode where Helenus listens in on Apollo and Athena metamorphosed into vultures sitting on an oak tree (*Il.* 7.17–60) could be an intertext for Callimachus here, which would add an interestingly darker element to the Ovidian-Callimachean fable. For the construction of gender regarding a speaking animal in Martial (10.63 and 11.69), see Baumann in this volume. On the wider theme of the Raven and the Crow in antiquity, see Schmidt (2002).
13 Hollis (²2009) 12, 224 ("an old crow . . . is speaking to another bird").
14 See Tissol (1997) 159f. on the playful and confusing narrative line in this section.

> quem garrula motis
> consequitur pennis, scitetur ut omnia, cornix
> auditaque uiae causa 'non utile carpis'
> inquit 'iter; ne sperne meae praesagia linguae. 550
> quid fuerim quid simque uide meritumque require:
> inuenies nocuisse fidem.

The talkative Crow followed him [the Raven] with flapping wings, in order to know everything, and hearing the cause of his journey said, 'the path you undertake is not useful; do not scorn the prognostications of my tongue. Look at what I was and what I am and ask how I earned it: you will find that I damaged trust.

She is perhaps herself not a very good listener, as the cause of his journey is only alluded to very briefly. Instead, she is keen to tell her own story of *delatio* and the (un)gratefulness of divine recipients of bad news (2.552–64). She tries to warn the Raven that it will not be a good idea to tell Apollo about Coronis' infidelity, taking the example of what happened when she herself observed (or rather, spied on) the daughters of Cecrops as they peeked into the basket containing a snake and a baby – who Cornix has just told us is Ericthonius, born without a mother (2.553).[15] The Crow told Minerva, who promptly punished her by expelling her – and thus crows – from service in the Acropolis.[16] Seeking additional self-justification in front of the Raven, Cornix launches further back in her own history. She is determined to be heard and to present herself to anyone who will listen, even for a moment (2.569–72).

> nam me Phocaica clarus tellure Coroneus
> (nota loquor) genuit fueramque ego regia uirgo 570
> diuitibusque procis (ne me contemne) petebar;
> forma mihi nocuit.[17]

For renowned Coroneus fathered me in the land of Phocis (I say things well known) and I had been a royal maiden wooed by rich suitors (do not despise me); my shape/beauty harmed me.

Her self-presentation begins in epic style. Royal parentage, geographical identity, and the attentions of many suitors give Cornix status in the aristocratic human world of epic. Although she claims that her status is well known, the implication

---

15 The detail which the Crow omits to mention in her self-serving account to the Raven is an additional reason why her mistress might be especially sensitive about discussion of the event: the child born without a mother is the result of the attempted rape of Minerva by Vulcan. See Barchiesi (2005) 283.
16 For the aetion, see Hollis (²2009) 7, 31 (in connection with the reference to this phenomenon at Lucr. 6.749–85); Myers (1994) 149 n. 71.
17 Julene Abad Del Vecchio draws my attention to the echo between *forma . . . nocuit* here and *nocuisse fidem* at 552. Like Daphne, Cornix seems all too ready to internalise the blame associated with the beauty of rape victims.

being that (surely) she hardly needs to mention it, her second parenthesis ('do not despise me') betrays her anxiety regarding her status and ability to hold her audience by speech. Before the Raven can reply, the Crow launches into her tale with one of the iconic words of the poem, *forma*, both beauty and shape, that of which Ovid undertook to speak in the opening line of the epic, and which Daphne prayed to lose in her attempt to escape Apollo. Cornix encountered the same problem with Neptune. Unlike Daphne, however, who, after her metamorphosis into a tree, could only ambiguously nod, Cornix speaks with the voice of the survivor (2.572–80).

>   nam cum per litora lentis
> passibus, ut soleo, summa spatiarer harena,
> uidit et incaluit pelagi deus, utque precando
> tempora cum blandis absumpsit inania uerbis,   575
> uim parat et sequitur. fugio densumque relinquo
> litus et in molli nequiquam lassor harena.
> inde deos hominesque uoco, nec contigit ullum
> uox mea mortalem; mota est pro uirgine uirgo
> auxiliumque tulit.   580

For when I was walking along the shore with slow footsteps, as is my custom, on the top of the sand, the god of the sea saw me and blazed, and, after he has wasted time in prayers with flattering words, he prepares violence and comes after me. I flee and I leave the dense shore and in vain I am wearied in the soft sand. Then I call on gods and men, but my voice reached no mortal; the virgin was moved on behalf of a virgin and brought me aid.

Cornix's voice was no use then in enlisting male help (*ullum . . . mortalem*), but a divine female did hear and answer. The Crow now has another attempt at making her voice reach male ears, as she gives an account of her metamorphosis from her own point of view (2.580–88).

>   tendebam bracchia caelo: 580
> bracchia coeperunt leuibus nigrescere pennis;
> reicere ex umeris uestem molibar: at illa
> pluma erat inque cutem radices egerat imas;
> plangere nuda meis conabar pectora palmis:
> sed neque iam palmas nec pectora nuda gerebam;   585
> currebam, nec ut ante pedes retinebat harena,
> sed summa tollebar humo; mox alta per auras
> euehor et data sum comes inculpata Mineruae.

I was stretching out my arms to heaven: my arms began to grow black with light feathers; I strove to cast the cloak from my shoulders: but it was plumage and had driven deep roots into my skin; I tried to beat my naked breast with my hands: but now neither hands nor naked breast did I bear; I ran, but the sand did not as previously hold back my feet, but I was raised up from the top of the earth; soon I am borne on high through the breezes and given as a blameless companion to Minerva.

There is an interesting twist to the story here. Cornix becomes the first character, and perhaps the only one, openly to question the meaning of metamorphosis. Others will debate the justice of metamorphosis, such as in the response to Diana's punishment of Actaeon by turning him into a stag who is torn to pieces by his own dogs. One could say, however, that in that case the discussion is over the justice of him being punished by being torn apart, rather than the meaning of the metamorphosis that functions as a tool along the way. By contrast, Cornix notices that while she has become a bird-companion of Minerva as rescue and (implied by *inculpata*) reward, it seems as though the owl Nyctimene has gained the same metamorphic status as punishment (2.589–95).[18]

> *quid tamen hoc prodest, si diro facta uolucris*
> *crimine Nyctimene nostro successit honori?*   590
> *an quae per totam res est notissima Lesbon*
> *non audita tibi est, patrium temerasse cubile*
> *Nyctimenen? auis illa quidem, sed conscia culpae*
> *conspectum lucemque fugit tenebrisque pudorem*
> *celat et a cunctis expellitur aethere toto.'*   595

But what use is it, if Nyctimene, turned into a bird by a dread crime, has succeeded to my honour? Have you not heard the story which is very well known throughout all of Lesbos, how Nyctimene violated her father's bed? She indeed is a bird, but conscious of her fault she avoids sight and light and hides her shame in the shadows and is rejected by all in the whole sky.'

It seems as though Cornix is reflecting on the instability in the meaning of metamorphosis with which so many readers have grappled over the centuries. In asking this question of meaning, of logic, and of justice, at the end of her story, she foreshadows the case of Ocyroe, railing against her metamorphosis on the grounds that her parentage should mean that she ought at least only to have to go halfway from human to horse. Both females, because of their own stories of attempted rape and metamorphosis, therefore, respond with a logical question – which remains unanswered by the poem.

The only answer Cornix receives is a total block. The Raven finds his voice only to reject her story and, undeterred, carries on with his journey (2.597f.).

> *talia dicenti 'tibi' ait 'reuocamina' coruus*
> *'sint precor ista malo; nos uanum spernimus omen.'*

As she was saying this, the Raven said 'I pray that this story of delay may be a source of evil to you; I spurn the empty omen.'

---

[18] Barchiesi (2005) 285 suggests that Cornix is not being entirely fair on the owl here, in that in versions of the story in Hyginus *Fab.* 204 and Servius on Virgil *Georg.* 1.403 Nyctimene was raped by her father and became an owl, a night bird, out of shame. It seems to me that those stories add to the question of the meaning of metamorphosis at work here – at work, but never resolved.

The Raven's story continues and goes somewhere – it contributes to the story of Apollo and Coronis that has been interrupted by Cornix, and thus to the longer story arc of Aesculapius. But Cornix's story just stops.[19]

4 Hippolytus: A hero's death – as told by himself

To contrast with Ocyroe's and Cornix's accounts of their own metamorphosis, I offer one more case of a character who narrates his own transformation, who is able to do so because there is a form of metamorphosis open to him, as male character, which is almost entirely closed to females – deification.[20] Hippolytus/Virbius may not be the most impressive of deified humans, living out his life as a minor god in secret under the protection of Diana, but he does have a very loud voice.[21] The story occurs in Book 15, as the minor deities of Latium are attempting to console the nymph Egeria in her grief at the death of her husband Numa. In an extraordinary piece of insensitive consolation, the *Theseius heros* ('hero-son of Theseus', 15.492) kept on telling her to stop crying, because he had it much worse.[22] He then launches into a 50-line account of his life, death, resurrection, and deification, in which he is the hero. I shall suggest that there are some interesting similarities and differences between this passage and the story of Cornix.

Hippolytus/Virbius begins, as Cornix did, in epic mode, implying that his story is already well known to the audience, even if they do not realise that this is the same person (15.497–500).

fando aliquem Hippolytum uestras si contigit aures
credulitate patris, sceleratae fraude nouercae
occubuisse neci, mirabere uixque probabo,
sed tamen ille ego sum . . .

---

19 One might consider that it has some degree of continuation in the brief backwards reference which explains Minerva's unfriendly attitude towards Aglauros in the story of Mercury and Herse (at 2.749), to the Cecropides' (or, rather, now only Aglauros') transgression. This seems to me, however, more like a case of Ovid the narrator seizing the initiative from Cornix.
20 It is true that there are some examples of women who become goddesses in the poem, including Io, Ino, and Hersilia, the wife of Romulus, but their share in the big structural and political theme of apotheosis in the poem is, to put it mildly, limited.
21 In this discussion, I am mainly concerned with Hippolytus as a narrator, and the gendered narrator at that. As a result, I perhaps downplay his heroic role, compared with what might be perceived if the passage is viewed in the wider context of the poem's progression towards Rome, deification, and ultimately Augustus. See Hardie (2015) 560 for Hippolytus' role in this movement. On Hippolytus' story in the context of resurrection, see Waldner (2017).
22 While Roman literature of consolation often feels insensitive and ineffective to modern ears, I think it is unlikely that we are meant to read Hippolytus/Virbius' attempts positively.

> If by any chance you have heard how Hippolytus succumbed to death by the credulity of his father and the fraud of his wicked stepmother, you will be amazed and hardly will I prove it, but nonetheless I am he . . .

However well-known this story of Greek myth/Euripidean tragedy might or might not be to Egeria and the other Latin nymphs, to the external audience it is certainly famous. The speaker takes no chances with the moral interpretation of the tale, however, in his opening with the credulity of his father Theseus and the fraud of the stereotypical wicked stepmother, Phaedra. The story is set up to exculpate the male and condemn the female. Where Cornix told the much-repeated story of *forma nocuit* and running away from a divine would-be rapist, Hippolytus/Virbius is able to present his experience of unwanted erotic attention with greater narrative complexity and specificity, while making it clear where the blame lies (15.500–505).

> me Pasiphaeia quondam 500
> temptatum frustra patrium temerare cubile,
> quod uoluit, finxit uoluisse et crimine uerso
> (indiciine metu magis offensane repulsae?)
> damnauit, meritumque nihil pater eicit urbe
> hostilique caput prece detestatur euntis. 505

> Once upon a time, the daughter of Pasiphae fabricated the story that I had rashly made an attempt in vain on my father's bed, and what she wanted she pretended I had wanted and by turning the charge back on me (was it more through fear of betrayal or offence at the repulse?) she damned me, and my father cast me out, deserving nothing of it, from the city, and as I went cursed my head with hostile prayer.

That was how a hero deals with a sexual advance. Next, he grandly relates how, in his view, a true hero responds to a threat from the sea (15.506–23).

> Pittheam profugo curru Troezena petebam
> iamque Corinthiaci carpebam litora ponti,
> cum mare surrexit cumulusque inmanis aquarum
> in montis speciem curuari et crescere uisus
> et dare mugitus summoque cacumine findi. 510
> corniger hinc taurus ruptis expellitur undis
> pectoribusque tenus molles erectus in auras
> naribus et patulo partem maris euomit ore.
> corda pauent comitum, mihi mens interrita mansit
> exiliis contenta suis, cum colla feroces 515
> ad freta conuertunt arrectisque auribus horrent
> quadripedes monstrique metu turbantur et altis
> praecipitant currum scopulis. ego ducere uana
> frena manu spumis albentibus oblita luctor
> et retro lentas tendo resupinus habenas. 520
> nec uires tamen has rabies superasset equorum,
> ni rota, perpetuum qua circumuertitur axem,
> stipitis occursu fracta ac disiecta fuisset.

> I was making for Pittheus' Troezen on exiled chariot and was already skirting the shore of the Corinthian Sea when the waves rose up and a huge pile of waters seemed to curve into the shape of a mountain and to grow and rumble and split in its highest peak. From here a horned bull charged out from the breakers and reared up its breast into the soft airs and vomited forth part of the sea from its nostrils and its wide-open mouth. The hearts of my companions were afraid, but my mind remained unterrified, content in its exile, when the ferocious horses turn their necks to the waters and bristle with their ears pricked up and are disturbed by fear of the monster and throw the chariot headlong over the high rocks. I struggle in vain to pull the bits smeared with white foam and leaning back as far as possible I pull on the pliant reins. Yet the madness of the horses would not have overcome my powers had not the wheel, where it continually turns the axle, been broken and torn apart when it hit a stump.

We should note here not only the epic account, but also the fact that he is not alone (unlike Cornix), nor has he lost his regal and epic status. Like Cornix, he tells us about his own feelings, or at least the version that he would like to relate: while his companions are terrified, his mind is stoically composed (514f.). He almost had the chariot and horses under control, when a wheel fell off and he was thrown. It was, therefore, the chariot's fault. Now comes the even more narratively privileged account, as Hippolytus/Virbius tells the story of his own death, wallowing proudly in the extremity of his bodily destruction (15.524–34).

> *excutior curru, lorisque tenentibus artus*
> *uiscera uiua trahi, neruos in stipe teneri*   525
> *membra rapi partim, partim reprensa relinqui,*
> *ossa grauem dare fracta sonum fessamque uideres*
> *exhalari animam nullasque in corpore partes*
> *noscere quas posses, unumque erat omnia uulnus.*
> *num potes aut audes cladi conponere nostrae,*   530
> *nympha, tuam? uidi quoque luce carentia regna*
> *et lacerum foui Phlegethontide corpus in unda,*
> *nec nisi Apollineae ualido medicamine prolis*
> *reddita uita foret;*

> I am thrown from the chariot, and as the reins hold onto my limbs, you could see my living entrails dragged, my nerves stuck on the stump, my limbs in part snatched away, in part held fast, my broken bones giving a heavy sound and my exhausted spirit being breathed out. There would be no parts in my body which you could recognise, for everything was a single wound. Surely you cannot and dare not compare your trouble to my disaster, nymph? I also saw the lightless realms and I bathed my lacerated body in the river of Phlegethon, and life was only returned to me by the strong medicine of the child of Apollo [Aesculapius] . . .

Somehow, although the details of this narrative, with its open wounds and voyeuristic counting of innards, have affinities with the flaying of Marsyas, the first-person narrative here seems to me to lack the emotive qualities of the third-person narrative in that story, perhaps because the narrator himself is speaking from a point of view of comfortable detachment and pride in his own magnificent experiences. Hippolytus/Virbius is in the unusual position of being able to recount not only his deeds but also his own death, in a kind of katabasis which has the unusual feature of occurring through literal death. On his return to the upper world, Hippolytus (as told by Hippolytus/Virbius) continues his heroic role under the protection of Diana, like Odysseus with Athene and Aeneas with Venus, when he is hidden in a protective divine cloud (15.537), after which comes the formal metamorphosis (15.534–40):

> quam postquam fortibus herbis
> atque ope Paeonia Dite indignante recepi,   535
> tum mihi, ne praesens augerem muneris huius
> inuidiam, densas obiecit Cynthia nubes,
> utque forem tutus possemque inpune uideri,
> addidit aetatem nec cognoscenda reliquit
> ora mihi.

After I received my life back through strong herbs and with the aid of Paeon, though Dis objected, then Diana cast dense clouds around me, lest I should by my presence increase the envy of this gift, and so that I should be safe and could be seen with impunity, she made me older and unrecognisable.

Here, instead of a great revelation, as in the heroic precedents, Diana decides that she has to protect Hippolytus from the enmity that might arise out of his resurrection, by keeping his identity hidden. Like Aeneas, Hippolytus is brought to Latium, but the latent hidden agenda of that place is actualised in his case. He is, moreover, made to look older and unrecognisable than he had been previously – again, a similarity with both Odysseus and Aeneas, but one that does not quite perhaps give Hippolytus/Virbius the heroic status he wishes to portray. Odysseus is made to look older and unrecognisable in order to help him in his vengeance over the suitors. Both he and Aeneas, when revealed to the right people, are made to look *younger* and more heroic. Indeed, when Odysseus is finally recognised by Telemachus, at *Od.* 16.202–12, Odysseus remarks on the fact that Athene has made him look both old and young at different times.[23] By contrast, Hippolytus is simply disguised in order to lie hidden forever.

A further metamorphosis comes in nomenclature, swapping one speaking name (loosened by horses) for another (twice man, or man-life).[24] Finally, he is instituted as a minor local deity. The goddess considers Crete (the place of Odyssean liars) and Delos (centre of the world), before finally choosing Latium – a hidden place, although of course quietly part of the great transfer of culture from Greece to Rome (15.540–46):

---

23 See Nagy (2010) 159–64. On Aeneas' variously doctored appearance, see Griffith (1985).
24 See Hardie (2015) 560 for the etymologies.

> *Cretenque diu dubitauit habendam* 540
> *traderet an Delon; Delo Creteque relictis*
> *hic posuit nomenque simul, quod possit equorum*
> *admonuisse, iubet deponere, 'qui' que 'fuisti*
> *Hippolytus' dixit, 'nunc idem Virbius esto.'*
> *hoc nemus inde colo de disque minoribus unus* 545
> *numine sub dominae lateo atque accenseor illi.*

> For a long time she wondered whether to hand me over to Crete or to Delos. Having rejected Delos and Crete, she placed me here and ordered me to put aside my name, which might remind me of the horses, and said "you who were Hippolytus, now be Virbius." From then on I inhabit this grove and as one among the lesser gods I lie hidden beneath the godhead of my mistress and I am accounted to her.

Hippolytus/Virbius has narrated his adventures, death, immortalisation, and treble metamorphosis (deification, change of appearance, change of name), but throughout his extended self-narrative it seems to me that we are also enabled to read between the lines, and perceive him as a somewhat unreliable narrator. For all his posturing, he has not managed to tell us very much about what it is like to die, or to be metamorphosed. And perhaps his final position, hiding in Latium under the protection of Diana, with a name sensitively chosen to avoid upsetting him, is not quite so impressively heroic as he would have us believe.

5 Cornix and Hippolytus

As I have suggested above, there are a number of interesting similarities and differences between Cornix and Hippolytus/Virbius. Both have virginal divine patrons, Minerva and Diana, although Hippolytus' experience with Diana is much more consistently positive, while Cornix is rejected by Minerva after the initial rescue. Both tell their stories, presenting their account, 'this is me', in ways that betray anxiety about the speaker's identity, as both seek to establish their aristocratic and epic status. Both suffer catastrophe which arises from sexual victimisation and is directly or indirectly brought about by Neptune. Perhaps most interestingly, both are very unsuccessful in reaching their audience. Cornix is ignored by the Raven, who goes on to repeat her mistake; Egeria is not comforted by Hippolytus/Virbius, instead continuing to grieve and inverting his upward metamorphosis by her own transformation into water.[25]

---

[25] It is perhaps worth noting that the author of Egeria's metamorphosis, like that of Hippolytus, is Diana (15.550). Regarding further links between the stories of Book 2 and that of Hippolytus, it may be worth noting that the narrative of Hippolytus in *Fasti* 6 features the matronymic Coronides (*Fast.* 6.746) and links to Ocyroe's story. See Keith (1992) 69f. On the linked stories of Aesculapius and Chiron in *Metamorphoses* and *Fasti*, see Merli (2004).

As for the differences, I note a number of points with regard to which the two characters are related but opposite. The first is, as mentioned above, the way in which Cornix is rejected by her tutelary goddess whereas Hippolytus is deified by his. Second, metamorphosis for Cornix is downward (human to animal), whereas for Hippolytus it is upward (human to god). Cornix is unusual in her metamorphosis being not the telos of her story but only the punctuation mark of its first chapter. For Hippolytus, by closely-connected contrast, death is the punctuation mark for his first chapter, with metamorphosis functioning more conventionally as its climax. The relationship between death and metamorphosis is always complex in the poem, but for both these two characters it is sublimated, although in different ways. Cornix's ongoing ability to speak after transformation grants the possibility of post-metamorphic continuation to her story to an extent that is rare for metamorphic subjects, while for Hippolytus undergoes a more cleanly literal death followed by a series of metamorphoses that either undo death (immortalisation) or have nothing to do with it (the change of appearance and name). In many of the poem's stories, the metamorphosis functions as a quasi-death, although rarely is it clearly a true death.[26]

But the most interesting difference between our two intradiegetic narrators is in the narrative concentration. For Cornix, this consists of predominantly internal self-perception, whereas for Hippolytus/Virbius it is driven by concern for an external picture of heroism. Both characters are keen to present themselves as righteous victims, and more than once: Cornix is the righteous victim of Neptune's attempted rape, but also of Minerva's unjust punishment; Hippolytus is the righteous victim of Phaedra's sexual approach and deceit, but also of his father's misguided curse – and again of equipment when the wheel fell off his chariot. For all that neither of them is consistently the most attractive or likeable character, for all that both seek to present an overly positive version of themselves, it is, I suggest, significant that it is the female speaker who concentrates on her feelings and internalised experience, while the male concentrates on how he looks to the outside world. Readers will perhaps not be surprised by the gendered nature of this difference, but the existence of such a difference would seem to tell against the claim that there is no difference in the voices of the various storytellers of the poem.[27] Two episodes is

---

[26] Cases where metamorphosis causes unambiguous death are collateral to the actual transformation. There is, for example, Actaeon torn to pieces by his dogs because they do not recognise him in stag-form, and there is Periclymenus, the shape-changer who takes the form of an eagle while in battle with Hercules and is shot, not of itself fatally but with the result that he falls out of the air and is killed. I consider different aspects of the relationship between death and metamorphosis in Sharrock (2018) and Sharrock (forthcoming a).

[27] According to Barchiesi (1989), the *Metamorphoses* cannot be regarded as polyphonic, because there is no significant difference between the different narrating voices. There is an important discussion of narrating voices and vatic status in Wheeler (1999) throughout, but especially 185–93.

perhaps not enough to certify a pattern, but it does tally with gendered features of the poem that I have identified elsewhere, including the significant (not universal) connection between female gender and the process of transformation within the *Metamorphoses*.[28]

6 A problem in theory

How far can these first-person narrators gain access to the Symbolic? To what extent can they move from storyteller to author? For these purposes, an author, as opposed to a flesh-and-blood writer, is a metaphorical composite drawn out of both text and reading.[29] The author is the embodiment of access to the Symbolic and the controller of that access within the text. While for modern and contemporary authors, including women and other traditionally suppressed voices, access to the Symbolic through writing is a matter of ongoing struggle, as the writer negotiates a path to establish herself as an author through the publishing business, literary hierarchies such as major prizes, advertising and visibility through both social and mainstream media, for a text such as the *Metamorphoses* all that contestation is in the past. Sulpicia may still be involved in an ongoing struggle for access, being a paradigm case for the tendency of literary history and practice to relegate women to the role of object rather than subject,[30] and Ovid himself might claim to have struggled to make his voice heard from exile, but the fact is that he won. His access to the Symbolic is a matter of much more than just being read. It consists in being a 'classic', as the patron of a recurring *aetas Ovidiana*, as a regular set text in schools, colleges, and universities.

Indeed, this article, like many others, contributes to enabling Ovid's access to the Symbolic. While it is a regular feature of Ovidian criticism to regard the various storytellers of the poem as in some way sharing in the action of the poet, the extent to which they do so, and the ease with which it can be perceived, has considerable variation. The character who most clearly presents himself as a self-aware poet of metamorphosis, and hence having closest association with the author, is Pythagoras, whose extended discourse in Book 15 is explicitly concerned with change for change's sake. Most other storytellers, even when they gather together many different metamorphic tales, do not show explicit awareness of the fact that they are

---

28 I argue this in particular in Sharrock (2020a).
29 The best and most accessible account I know of the relationship between flesh-and-blood authors, internal authors, and authors in the tradition of reading is Bennett (2005). I explore this matter with regard to classical literary criticism in Sharrock (forthcoming b).
30 On the discussion of female literary agency see the contributions of Hauser and Hafner in this volume; on Sulpicia see Fabre-Serris and Hallett in this volume.

narrators of metamorphosis in a poem called *Metamorphoses*. The daughters of Minyas would be a good case in point – their stories all happen to involve some transformation, but they do not display any explicit awareness of the fact.[31]

Great figures, both male and female, do indeed succeed in sharing in Ovid's work, via the work of professional readers. Arachne's tapestry is regularly interpreted as a particularly Ovidian (playful, chaotic, 'Hellenistic') epic challenge to the monolithic, 'Virgilian' work of her combatant Minerva.[32] Orpheus, who dominates the poem for more than a whole book with his metapoetically charged performances, is easily seen as a version of Ovid, complete with self-deprecating intertextual playfulness.[33] It is difficult not to see a gendered difference between the ongoing opportunities of each character: Arachne, the spider, is condemned to produce work that is indeed beautiful and delicate, but without any Symbolic content, while Orpheus escapes metamorphosis and instead is happily reunited with Eurydice in the underworld.[34] To return to our narrators of their own stories, I would find it easy to say that Hippolytus, whose tale has much more in common with epic narrative than does that of Cornix, and who would, moreover, have a good case for claiming to be the last alternative narrator of the poem, has greater affinity with the poet and therefore better access to the Symbolic. If that is the case, if that access is more available to Hippolytus than to Ocyroe or Cornix, to what extent is that greater access enabled by the feminist criticism that exposes it? That is, to what extent do I reinforce, or even create, the oppression that I seek hereby to expose? In order to attempt to redress the balance, I would like, finally, to explore a way of gifting the Symbolic to Cornix, not as an interpretation of what 'Ovid intended' but as an act of

---

[31] On the tales of the Minyeides at *Met.* 4.1–415, see Keith in this volume.
[32] See Harries (1990), and the seminal von Albrecht (1979). Hardie (2002) 176 points out that both tapestries can "in their different ways, reflect the themes and structures of the *Metamorphoses* as a whole". For a recent full discussion, see Lobe (2021).
[33] Campbell (2019) offers a good recent example of the metapoetic force of the Orpheus passage and character in interaction with literary tradition. Her primary purpose is to explore the underworld connotations of the shade(s) cast by the trees who are drawn by Orpheus' song, but this is constructed in interaction with pastoral shade, the epic catalogue of trees, lyric and erotic elegy, such that "Orpheus' grove represents a transformation across both levels of narrative, as Ovid transforms the topos of the epic tree catalogue and Orpheus transforms the Thracian landscape into his personal version of the Underworld" (14). See also Pavlock (2009), esp. 169.
[34] I have suggested elsewhere, however, that the silence of Orpheus on his second, as opposed to first, entry into the underworld in the poem is an archly ironic comment, which could even be seen as a rejection of Orpheus' poetic status. See Sharrock (2018) 131: "Orpheus in this underworld has ceased to be a poet, has stopped constructing Eurydice as his artistic work, stopped destroying her by his consuming unidirectional vision, and has achieved a degree of mutuality which was previously impossible. Ovid replaces Virgil's underworld with one that has room for women and for love."

reading in the contemporary world.[35] I suggest that we could do so by drawing attention to her flight, and its potential for being poetic flight.

Cornix interrupts Ovid's tale of Coronis with a story about the daughters of Cecrops and Ericthonius, followed by the account of her own victimisation by Neptune and rescue by Minerva. Ovid will seize back the narrative line later in the same book, when he returns to the daughters of Cecrops for the metamorphosis of Aglauros. Ocyroe's story of Aesculapius is crucial to the macrostructure of the *Metamorphoses*, but Cornix's *infans* (Ericthonius, 2.553) goes nowhere, despite his aetiological importance for Athens. On the other hand, something special about the Crow is that, among all the metamorphosed human-birds in the poem, she is the only character to speak in the first person about how it feels to take flight. In general, flight is a well-known poetic metaphor. To what extent, then, might the flight of Cornix be poetological? Let us return to her aviotransformation (2.580–88).

> *tendebam bracchia caelo:* 580
> *bracchia coeperunt leuibus nigrescere pennis;*
> *reicere ex umeris uestem molibar: at illa*
> *pluma erat inque cutem radices egerat imas;*
> *plangere nuda meis conabar pectora palmis:*
> *sed neque iam palmas nec pectora nuda gerebam;* 585
> *currebam, nec ut ante pedes retinebat harena,*
> *sed summa tollebar humo; mox alta per auras*
> *euehor . . .*

I was stretching out my arms to heaven: my arms began to grow black with light feathers; I strove to cast the cloak from my shoulders: but it was plumage and had driven deep roots into my skin; I tried to beat my naked breast with my hands: but now neither hands nor naked breast did I bear; I ran, but the sand did not as previously hold back my feet, but I was raised up from the top of the earth; soon I am borne on high through the breezes. . .

Two interconnected links, one intertextual and the other intratextual, suggest the possibility of a metapoetic reading.

Cornix's account of her metamorphosis into a bird resonates with that of another first-person narrator of his own aviotransformation, Horace (*Carm.* 2.20.9–12):

> *iam iam residunt cruribus asperae*
> *pelles, et album mutor in alitem*
>   *superne, nascunturque leves*
>   *per digitos umerosque plumae.*

---

35 In making this explicit attempt to 'release' the voice of Cornix by an act of interpretation, this reading would come into the category of optimistic interpretations of classical female speakers, usually but not always fictional, which became popular in the early part of this millennium. In brief, it seems to me that there is a significant, although certainly not absolute, distinction between an earlier feminist exposure of female subjugation, with which I would generally associate myself, and a more recent desire to hear (and create) stronger women out of our classical texts.

> Now, now the rough skin sits back on my legs, and I am being changed into a white bird on high, and smooth feathers are being born over my fingers and shoulders.

Horace's transformation into a poetic bird is striking, if not bizarre, but is explicitly metapoetic. It is mediated to the reader also via Ennius, and the association he makes (or made for him) between poetic flight and poetic fame which transcends death, in the epitaph attributed to him by Cicero (Enn. *Var.* 17f. Vahlen):

> nemo me lacrimis decoret nec funera fletu
>   faxit. cur? uolito uiuos per ora uirum.

> Let no one honour me with tears or perform my funeral with weeping. Why? I fly living over the lips of men.

This nexus of allusions, from Ennius to Virgil[36] to Horace to Ovid, is well known. Francesca Martelli eloquently describes the Ennius epitaph as "writ[ing] the script of literary immortality for all Latin poets (of the Augustan era, at least)".[37] She points out that the image in Ennius itself draws on a "distinguished literary predecessor", Theognis, where the image appears in an amatory context as the poet "proclaims his power to confer immortality by giving his beloved wings".[38] She also points out that the allusion here "to one of Greece's best-known *elegists* is a highly self-conscious choice" (her emphasis), in that "it is with distichs like this one that Ennius is credited with having introduced elegiacs to Latin verse". I am not proposing a specifically generic aspect to Cornix's metamorphosis into a bird, at least not simply – although it might be possible to see some sort of elegiac trace in her bodily experience of transformation, in contrast with the climactic epic force of Ovid's own employment of the motif in Book 15. My point, rather, is that Cornix's account of her metamorphosis makes a claim for Symbolic status both by replaying, in more appropriate context (a literal shape-change, in a poem overtly about transformation), the metaphorical metamorphosis of Horace into the (Pindaric) swan, and also by linking that metamorphic passage with Ovid's own claims to poetic immortality via the tradition of intertextuality and canon formation, i.e., precisely the Symbolic order for authors.[39]

---

[36] *Temptanda uia est, qua me quoque possim / tollere humo uictorque uirum uolitare per ora* ('A way must be sought, by which I may rise up from the ground and as victor fly over the lips of men', *Georg.* 3.8f.).
[37] Martelli (2018) 71.
[38] *Ibid.*
[39] Martelli (2018) 72 n. 12: "As symbolic father of this tradition, Ennius might be said to instantiate this principle of substitution for other reasons too: in Lacanian thought, the paternal function or *nom-du-père* authorises the subject's entry into the Symbolic, and, above all, provides him/her with access to the processes of substitution, or metaphoric functioning, which mobilise the play of signifiers within the Symbolic."

Here is Ovid's version of the topos, in the final lines of the poem (15.875f. and 878f.).

parte tamen meliore mei super alta perennis
astra ferar, nomenque erit indelebile nostrum;
. . .
ore legar populi, perque omnia saecula fama
(si quid habent ueri uatum praesagia) uiuam.

In the better part of myself I shall be borne perennial above the high stars and my name will be indelible . . . I shall be spoken on the lips of people, and in fame through all the ages (if the prophecies of bards have any truth) I shall live.

Cornix shares with Horace the details of avian corporeal physicality; with Virgil her elevation from the ground (Cornix *tollebar humo*, Virgil can *tollere humo*); with Horace and Ovid the first-person passive (Cornix *tollebar, euehor*; Horace *mutor*; Ovid *ferar, legar*).

While the opportunity to tell her own story of becoming a bird may well enable Cornix to partake in this grand tradition of poetic immortality, the problem is that whereas the male poets are lifted up from the ground and fly on the lips of men in eternal fame, Cornix, by contrast, bumps back down to earth. Her metamorphosis and institution as a companion of Minerva is quickly undermined. She tells, or at least half tells, another bird story, that of Nyctimene (2.589f.), with its Ovidian incestuous aetiology for the owl's liking for darkness, but she does not get to be a poet. We must acknowledge that the text does not grant her self-awareness of the poetological possibilities of her flight. And then narrative leaves her with the Raven's rejection of her warning, and she is forgotten.[40]

---

[40] Julene Abad Del Vecchio suggests to me that we might usefully think about Medea's flight as a metapoetic alternative to that of both Cornix and Ovid. Women, in the end, must perhaps simply resort to fleeing the Symbolic (world), in order to exist in their own right, perhaps no longer bound by the stories that the male poets tell about them. It is then up to the reader how to interpret the flight, whether as a more pessimistic move that denotes a halt to textual existence, or something conducive to a different reality, perhaps even a new creative process to which we are not privy within the world shaped by Ovid. While writing this paper, I am also teaching a graduate class on 'Reimagining Virgil', in which Ursula Le Guin's *Lavinia* (2008) offers an example of this new creative process outside the control of the poet. The narrator Lavinia has kept up a metapoetic conversation with 'the poet' (Virgil) throughout the novel, becoming the author of her own story when the tale moves beyond that narrated or foreshadowed in the *Aeneid*. At the end, she cannot die, as Aeneas and Dido and Creusa died, because, she says, the poet did not give her enough life to be able to die. Instead, she narrates the process of her metamorphosis into an owl (or, perhaps, the owl). This is not stated explicitly, but the reader of Ovid and Virgil has little difficulty in perceiving it. While we might say that no first-person narrator, however metapoetically self-conscious, can ever spread her wings and fly away from authorial control entirely (Le Guin's, even if she has escaped Virgil's), the final pages of that novel seemed to come as close as might be possible to setting free the voice of epic's suppressed female characters.

But if we expose the struggles of female characters to gain access to the Symbolic, are we in fact (also) enacting that failure? That seems to me to be a double bind that feminist criticism can never escape. It is related to an even wider issue in feminist criticism: how far should feminist reading seek to create equality of opportunity on a level playing field (minimising distinctions between male and female speakers) or tease out the specificity of the gendered, especially female, voice (thus maximising such distinctions)? I think all we can hope to do is knowingly to hold both in balance.

Bibliography

Text

P. Ovidi Nasonis *Metamorphoses*, ed. Richard J. Tarrant, Oxford 2004.

Books and articles

Barchiesi (1989): Alessandro Barchiesi, "Voci e istanze narrative nelle *Metamorfosi* di Ovidio", *MD* 23, 55–97.
Barchiesi (1997): Alessandro Barchiesi, "Endgames: Ovid's *Metamorphoses* 15 and *Fasti* 6", in: Deborah H. Roberts, Francis M. Dunn and Don Fowler (eds.), *Classical Closure: Reading the End in Greek and Latin Literature*, Princeton, 181–208.
Barchiesi (2005): Alessandro Barchiesi, *Ovidio, Metamorfosi, Volume I: Libri I–II*, Milan.
Bennett (2005): Andrew Bennett, *The Author, The New Critical Idiom*, Abingdon.
Campbell (2019): Celia Campbell, "The Shade of Orpheus: Ambiguity and the Poetics of *Vmbra* in *Metamorphoses* 10", *Dictynna* 16.
Fermi (2011): Damiano Fermi, "Gli avvoltoi di Omero e le cornacchie di Callimaco: uccelli a colloquio nell'epica", *Eikasmos: Quaderni Bolognesi di Filologia Classica* 22, 151–170.
Griffith (1985): Mark Griffith, "What does Aeneas look like?", *Classical Philology* 4, 309–319.
Hardie (1997): Philip R. Hardie, "Questions of Authority: The Invention of Tradition in Ovid's *Metamorphoses* 15", in: Thomas Habinek and Alessandro Schiesaro (eds.), *The Roman Cultural Revolution*, Cambridge, 182–198.
Hardie (2002): Philip R. Hardie, *Ovid's Poetics of Illusion*, Cambridge.
Hardie (2012): Philip R. Hardie, *Rumour and Renown: Representations of Fama in Western Literature*, Cambridge.
Hardie (2015): Philip R. Hardie, *Ovidio, Metamorfosi. Volume VI: Libri XIII–XV*, Fondazione Valla, Milan.
Harries (1990): Byron Harries, "The Spinner and the Poet: Arachne in Ovid's 'Metamorphoses'", *Proceedings of the Cambridge Philological Society* 36, 64–82.
Heath (1994): John Heath, "Prophetic Horses, Bridled Nymphs: Ovid's Metamorphosis of Ocyroe", *Latomus* 53, 340–353.
Hollis (^{2}2009): Adrian S. Hollis, *Callimachus Hecale: Introduction, Text, Translation and Enlarged Commentary*, Oxford.
Keith (1992): Alison M. Keith, *The Play of Fictions: Studies in Ovid's Metamorphoses Book 2*, Ann Arbor.

Le Guin (2008): Ursula Le Guin, *Lavinia*, London.

Lobe (2021): Michael Lobe, "Augusteische Arachnophobie. Verschiedene Lesarten der Bildteppiche in Ovids *Metamorphosen* 6,70–128", in: Bernhard Zimmermann (ed.), *29. Salemer Sommerakademie: Frauen und Frauenbild in der Antike*, Baden-Baden, 37–56.

Martelli (2018): Francesca Martelli, "Ennius' *imago* between tomb and text", in: Nora Goldschmidt and Barbara Graziosi (eds.), *Tombs of the Ancient Poets: Between Literary Reception and Material Culture*, Oxford, 69–82.

Merli (2004): Elena Merli, "Esculapio e Chirone in 'Fasti e Metamorfosi': tradizione mitologica e definizione del genere letterario", *Hermes* 132, 459–471.

Moi (2002): Toril Moi, *Sexual-textual Politics: Feminist Literary Theory* (1st ed. 1985), London/Methuen.

Myers (1994): Karen S. Myers, *Ovid's Causes, Cosmogony and Aetiology in the Metamorphoses*, Ann Arbor.

Nagy (2010): Gregory Nagy, "The Meaning of homoios (ὁμοῖος) in *Theogony* 27 and Elsewhere", in: Phillip Mitsis and Christos Tsagalis (eds.), *Allusion, Authority, and Truth. Critical Perspectives on Greek Poetic and Rhetorical Praxis*, Berlin/Boston, 153–168.

Natoli (2017): Bartolo A. Natoli, *Silenced Voices: The Poetics of Speech in Ovid*, Madison, Wisconsin.

Pavlock (2009): Barbara Pavlock, *The Image of the Poet in Ovid's Metamorphoses*, Madison, Wisconsin.

Schmidt (2002): Gudrun Schmidt, *Rabe und Krähe in der Antike: Studien zur archäologischen und literarischen Überlieferung*, Wiesbaden.

Sharrock (2011): Alison R. Sharrock, "Womanly wailing? The mother of Euryalus and gendered reading", *Eugesta* 1.

Sharrock (2018): Alison R. Sharrock, "Till Death do us Part . . . or Join: Love beyond Death in Ovid's *Metamorphoses*", in: Stavros Frangoulidis and Stephen Harrison (eds.), *Life, Love and Death in Latin Poetry: Studies in Honor of Theodore D. Papanghelis*, Berlin, 125–136.

Sharrock (2020a): Alison R. Sharrock, "Gender and Transformation: Reading, Women, and Gender in Ovid's *Metamorphoses*", in: Alison R. Sharrock, Mats Malms and Daniel Möller (eds.), *Metamorphic Readings: Transformation, Language, and Gender in the Interpretation of Ovid's Metamorphoses*, Oxford, 33–53.

Sharrock (2020b): Alison R. Sharrock, "*noua . . . corpora*: New Bodies and Gendered Patterns in the *Metamorphoses*", *Dictynna* 17.

Sharrock (forthcoming a): Alison R. Sharrock, "*ambobus pellite regnis*: Between Life and Death in Ovid's *Metamorphoses*", in: Joe Farrell, John Miller, Damien Nelis and Alessandro Schiesaro (eds.), *Ovid, Death, and Transfiguration*.

Sharrock (forthcoming b): Alison R. Sharrock, "Authors, Texts, Readings", in: Roy Gibson and Christopher Whitton (eds.), *The Cambridge Critical Guide to Latin Literature*, Cambridge.

Tissol (1997): Garth Tissol, *The Face of Nature: Wit, Narrative, and Cosmic Origins in Ovid's Metamorphoses*, Princeton.

von Albrecht (1979): Michael von Albrecht, "L'épisode d'Arachné dans les Métamorphoses d'Ovide", *Revue des Études Latines* LVII, 266–277.

Waldner (2017): Katharina Waldner, "Hippolytus and Virbius: Narratives of 'Coming Back to Life' and Religious Discourses in Greco-Roman Literature", in: Frederick S. Tappenden and Carly Daniel-Hughes (eds.), *Coming Back to Life: The Permeability of Past and Present, Mortality and Immortality, Death and Life in the Ancient Mediterranean*, Montreal, 345–374.

Wheeler (1999): Stephen M. Wheeler, *A Discourse of Wonders: Audience and Performance in Ovid's Metamorphoses*, Philadelphia.

Zissos/Gildenhard (2004): Andrew Zissos and Ingo Gildenhard, "Ovid's *Hecale*: Deconstructing Athens in the *Metamorphoses*", *JRS* 94, 47–72.

Federica Bessone
Autofiction al femminile. Arte di raccontare ed effetti di genere in Ovidio

Abstract: Ovid experiments with feminine writing in the *Epistulae heroidum*. This experiment with 'gender effects' within the conventions of a poetic genre continues in the female *Ich-Erzählungen* in the *Metamorphoses*. Here, too, the author's narrative complicity with his feminine characters is combined with irony at their expense, which insinuates a male perspective between the lines. The erotic pursuit, a recurrent pattern in this 'epic of desire', undergoes interesting variations when the narrating voice is that of a victim, or a fugitive. This can be seen in Arethusa's autobiographical tale to Ceres. Arethusa's version of Alpheus' love for her defies expectations, as it stops before the well-known end of the story. Here, the 'nymph-hunting' scheme, established by the Apollo and Daphne paradigm, frames the figure usually characterised as a victim of rape as a winner. This nymph shapes her 'autofiction' self-consciously; nevertheless, Ovid's irony is felt between the lines. The nymph's tale challenges the hero's tale in the *Aeneid*: Arethusa corrects Aeneas in her story, and strives to create a heroic profile for herself. This female re-interpretation of a typical Ovidian narrative scheme fosters further gender effects: the nymph's nonchalant description of her beauty is a 'sporting' version of Ovid's voyeuristic descriptions of the female body; her self-definition as *rustica* seems to align with the male point of view expressed throughout Ovid's erotic elegy; and metanarrative features comment on her estranged appropriation of stereotyped Ovidian similes for the female victim's fear.

Keywords: *Heroides*, *Metamorphoses*, Irony, relativism, Arethusa, rape, metanarrative

> *Come riesce, lei che è un uomo, a creare figure femminili?*
> Nessuno se ne accorge, ma in effetti tutti i personaggi femminili nei miei romanzi sono variazioni di tre persone soltanto:
> Mia moglie.
> La donna immaginaria che è il negativo di mia moglie e con cui ho dovuto rinunciare a vivere nel momento in cui ho deciso di sposarmi.
> La donna che sono io.
> Per quanto sia imbarazzante ammetterlo, quella che mi attrae di più è la terza.
>
> Eshkol Nevo, *L'ultima intervista*, tr. it. 2019

1 Voce femminile, ironia d'autore, complicità narrativa

Mettersi nei panni dei personaggi più diversi è il mestiere di chi scrive storie, e impersonare l'altro sesso è uno strumento del mestiere, da sempre. La letteratura antica esercita il potere *trans-gender* della scrittura di finzione a senso unico, ma, in questa unidimensionalità, offre un campo di studio più che stimolante. Tra gli autori, quasi invariabilmente maschi, che meglio rappresentano il mondo femminile 'dall'interno', assumendo la voce di una donna che dice 'Io', il più ricco di sperimentazioni, dopo Euripide, è Ovidio.[1]

A partire dalle *Eroidi*. L'elegia al femminile non è un'invenzione ovidiana: già Properzio fa lamentare Cinzia gelosa e fa scrivere una lettera di lamento da Aretusa a Licota. Ma è Ovidio che, dopo aver dato la parola a una *lena* negli *Amores* (1,8) e aver messo in scena Medea nella tragedia perduta, nelle *Epistulae heroidum* inventa una scrittura femminile in serie e crea un genere nuovo (*ignotum hoc aliis ille novavit opus*, "questo genere, ignoto ad altri, lui l'ha reso nuovo", *Ars* 3,346).[2] Esperimento nell'esperimento, le tre coppie di epistole doppie (*Ep.* 16–21) oppongono una prospettiva maschile a una femminile: in questi confronti diretti Ovidio dà forma a una scrittura elegiaca diversificata (in certa misura) secondo il genere del mittente,

---

[1] L'assunzione della voce femminile tocca un vertice di sperimentalismo con la ricreazione di una voce *poetica* femminile, quella di Saffo, nell'*Ep.* 15, che ritengo ovidiana: Bessone (2003a). Sull'ampliamento di prospettiva costituito dalla rappresentazione del femminile in Ovidio cf. Rosati (2018) 313sq., che richiama analoghe considerazioni sul teatro attico di Zeitlin (1996) 363. Nel caso di Aretusa, che esaminerò qui, la riflessione teorico-letteraria sulla *Ich-Erzählung* al femminile coinvolge il tema politicamente sensibile della violenza erotica. Su voce e linguaggio femminile in rapporto con la violenza sessuale nelle *Metamorfosi*, e sulle diverse valutazioni 'politiche' della rappresentazione ovidiana, Enterline (2000) cap. 1, con bibliografia in n. 5, pp. 227sq. Per la discussione su violenza erotica, visione maschile della sessualità e rischi di spettacolo voyeuristico per il lettore si vedano soprattutto Curran (1978), Richlin (1992) e, di recente, Newlands (2018) 141, con opportune riflessioni sulla pluralità di prospettive e di risposte suggerite dal testo, sulla critica dello sguardo maschile implicita nella stessa rappresentazione ovidiana, e sulla possibilità di resistere al compiacimento voyeuristico con una lettura eticamente responsabile; cf. anche Scourfield (2018), spec. 322sq. Morales (2020) 65–82; sull'aggressione erotica al femminile nell'episodio di Salmacide si veda Fabre-Serris (2018). Per l'applicazione alle *Metamorfosi* di una prospettiva di lettura femminile (con la donna nel ruolo di *resisting reader*, per cui cf. Fetterley 1978) si veda Liveley (1999), che, alle pp. 197–200, discute le diverse posizioni di Cahoon (1996), Richlin (1992) e Sharrock (1991); nuova, stimolante discussione teorica ora in Sharrock (2020) 33–37.
[2] Rosati (1992); sulle dinamiche di genere nell'elegia latina, da Properzio a Ovidio, e sulla loro ricezione nella critica femminista, discussione in Wyke (2002) 155–191 (*Gender and Scholarship on Love Elegy*).

ma omogenea nelle forme e nel linguaggio, e ugualmente esposta all'ironia d'autore, allo sguardo superiore del lettore e alla prefigurazione ironica del futuro.[3]

Tocchiamo così una prima questione teorico-critica che la scrittura al femminile di Ovidio solleva. Per un verso, la finzione autoriale di voci di donne ignare del proprio destino, che è invece ben noto al pubblico, pone le eroine ovidiane in una condizione di inferiorità: un'inferiorità conoscitiva, che si aggiunge alla debolezza, fisica e sociale, lamentata da molte *Heroides* in formule stereotipate.[4] Il *cliché* della debolezza femminile accomuna, in superficie, le mittenti epistolari, ma corrisponde solo in parte al loro profilo mitico: possiamo credere a Fillide, ma non dobbiamo credere a Medea, quando tutte e due usano per sé il termine *femina* come sinonimo di 'debolezza femminile'.[5] Analogamente, l'inferiorità conoscitiva delle eroine, rispetto alla competenza intertestuale di autore e lettori, non esclude che una parte di queste donne sia artefice, più che vittima, del proprio destino. Ovidio lo ricorda al lettore anche quando, nello spazio virtuale dell'epistola, gioca a travestire ognuna di loro sotto le forme convenzionali del lamento e della persuasione elegiaca.[6] Per lettera, Penelope *inganna* l'astuto Ulisse descrivendosi come una donna indifesa, che tesse la tela come una matrona qualunque, e ha bisogno del sostegno del marito; Didone, se non sarà ascoltata, è pronta a realizzare il suicidio, minacciato fin dall'*incipit*, come una maledizione per Enea e una macchia sulla sua reputazione;[7] Fedra – ci viene suggerito a ogni verso – scriverà presto una lettera ancor più micidiale per Ippolito; e Medea sta per uccidere i figli per lo stesso motivo per cui fa credere a Giasone che, al vederli, si commuove: "sono *troppo* simili a te"; una somiglianza letteralmente *eccessiva*, che chiede vendetta – la scrittura epistolare può avere una potenza pari alla *Trugrede* tragica.[8]

---

3 Con "ironia d'autore" intendo la distanza dal personaggio-mittente epistolare che l'autore fa avvertire per via allusiva: Ovidio rimanda ai modelli letterari che fissano la versione 'oggettiva' del mito, segnala le forzature soggettive e strumentali di chi scrive, e sottolinea la propria superiorità conoscitiva, condivisa col lettore; entro questo quadro, il meccanismo della "prefigurazione ironica del futuro" è analogo all'ironia drammatica, ma funziona grazie all'allusione a testi precedenti, in cui il futuro mitico è già scritto (per questi principi fondanti della poetica delle *Eroidi* cf. Bessone 1997, *Introduzione*, con bibliografia ed esempi). Non è questa la sede per tracciare relazioni tra i molteplici aspetti dell'ironia ovidiana e le diverse funzioni dell'ironia socratica, romantica o postmoderna. Qui mi interessa la funzione dell'ironia nelle dinamiche di genere innescate dall'assunzione della voce femminile da parte di un autore maschio: un autore che riflette sulla propria operazione e la commenta, rivolgendosi al lettore. Per una discussione teorica sulla dimensione 'politica' dell'ironia, come pratica e strategia discorsiva che implica relazioni di potere nella comunicazione, si veda Hutcheon (1994).
4 Per l'epistola elegiaca come lamento femminile, Rosati (1989) 30–46.
5 Ov. *Ep.* 2,65; 12,118 con Bessone (1997) 177sq. ad loc.
6 Questa doppia leggibilità delle *Eroidi* non impedisce letture, per così dire, unidimensionali, che valorizzano la superficie del lamento femminile, la posa elegiaca e l'autorappresentazione indifesa delle eroine: Farrell (1998) (cf. 326: "guileless female writing").
7 Barchiesi (1992) 24sq. e nn. a 9sq.; Bessone (2018) 199sq.; Bessone (2022).
8 Bessone (1997) a 183–206 e 187–190.

Dunque, la scarsa preveggenza delle eroine (talora non così scarsa) non è il segno che l'autore si faccia beffe di loro, né che certifichi la loro inferiorità in quanto donne: la scrittura elegiaca può anche essere un'arma potente, o un'abile mascheratura, o l'espressione di una debolezza momentanea, in mano a figure femminili che il destino mitico non favorisce, ma che il testo di Ovidio esalta nelle loro capacità, espressive e operative.

C'è un altro elemento che parte della critica vede come espressione di superiorità e quasi di sopraffazione maschile da parte dell'autore, ma che si rivela un argomento a doppio taglio. Nel riscrivere la loro storia, le eroine esercitano sui modelli letterari in cui sono 'vissute', e che garantiscono una versione 'oggettiva' dei fatti, forzature soggettive e strumentali: la loro *autofiction* in chiave elegiaca, e con intenti conativi, distorce il passato mitico, mentre lascia immutato un futuro già scritto.[9] È questo un modo di leggere le *Eroidi* che si è affermato dagli anni '80 del Novecento, in particolare nella scuola italiana.[10] Anche per reazione a queste letture intertestuali, la critica femminista anglosassone si è sentita in dovere di riscattare le eroine: vittime presunte di un'intesa tra autore e lettore che screditerebbe la loro voce femminile *in quanto tale*, alludendo a modelli letterari scritti da autori maschi.[11]

Ora, è senz'altro vero che l'autore gioca su tendenziosità, contraddizioni e velleità delle sue eroine, così come sui loro limiti conoscitivi. Ma, innanzi tutto, l'atteggiamento di Ovidio non è diverso nei confronti degli eroi maschi, quando sono loro a prendere l'iniziativa epistolare: nelle *Eroidi* doppie, la superiorità conoscitiva di autore e lettore si esercita anche a spese del genere maschile, lo stesso cui appartengono l'autore e i suoi modelli poetici. Su questo punto, il confronto tra eroi ed eroine è alla pari.[12]

---

9 Prendo a prestito il termine *autofiction*, coniato nel 1977 da Serge Doubrovsky per il suo romanzo *Fils* (e opposto al "patto autobiografico" definito da Philippe Lejeune), che la critica contemporanea applica a diverse forme di compromesso tra autobiografia e finzione romanzesca (cf. ad es. Donnarumma 2014, cap. III 8; Jordan 2013), e su cui vi è un'ampia discussione teorica (per una panoramica si veda http://autofiction.org/). Usando il termine, in accezione metaforica, per i 'racconti' autobiografici delle eroine ovidiane, intendo sottolineare il carattere tendenzioso di quei racconti rispetto alla 'verità' biografica, ovvero alla storia mitica dei personaggi fissata nei modelli poetici. All'interno della finzione letteraria di Ovidio, l'"autofinzionalità" delle mittenti epistolari, o delle narratrici interne all'epos, distorce dati ben noti, verificabili dal lettore sui testi-modello, e crea un ibrido tra 'verità' e inganno: una formazione provvisoria e come sospesa, fatta di illusione e ambiguità.

10 Questa linea critica ha preso le mosse da Rosati (1985) e Barchiesi (1986).

11 Spentzou (2003); parte da premesse simili (l'insoddisfazione per la critica intertestuale), ma segue un'impostazione teorica diversa, anche Lindheim (2003), su cui si veda la discussione di Casali (2006). In questo volume, Alison Sharrock si chiede come i narratori in prima persona possano avere accesso al Simbolico, l'ordine del mondo controllato dagli uomini, che include l'autore, e quale ruolo abbia il lettore (moderno) nel concedere questo accesso.

12 Basterebbe a mostrarlo una rassegna degli effetti paralleli di prefigurazione ironica prodotti dalla scrittura di Paride e di Elena: cf. Kenney (1996) alle *Ep.* 16 e 17, *passim*; Bessone (2003b).

C'è di più. La tecnica allusiva che segnala gli scostamenti di chi scrive rispetto al testo dei modelli, e smaschera le forzature delle mittenti epistolari, rivela le eroine come manipolatrici potenti, e proprio in quanto donne: 'autrici' fittizie di finzioni letterariamente efficaci; e, in più, lettrici controcorrente, capaci di reinterpretare testi di autori (maschi) secondo linee non autorizzate, o di immaginare alternative virtuali a storie già (autorevolmente) scritte. Nelle *Eroidi* la marginalità femminile, da elemento di debolezza, diventa un potente strumento di critica 'alternativa', una prospettiva antagonista da cui guardare le celebrazioni ufficiali degli eroi. Come ho cercato di mostrare altrove, queste lettere d'amore a destinatari mitici sono anche 'lettere aperte' sulla storia letteraria di quei miti: le eroine ovidiane condividono la competenza critica e storico-letteraria del loro autore. Penelope, Fillide, Briseide, Didone, Arianna si impegnano a contestare, screditare o ridimensionare la reputazione degli eroi e a rivendicare la propria: così, promuovendo interpretazioni poco compiacenti, ridisegnano il profilo dei protagonisti della grande letteratura antica (senza, per questo, risparmiare se stesse). La scrittura al femminile delle *Eroidi* è spesso un esercizio di 'critica militante' – che, tra le righe, diventa anche un'involontaria autocritica.[13]

C'è un altro punto che a me pare cruciale. Nelle *Epistulae heroidum*, la voce unica delle eroine è continuamente esposta all'ironia d'autore. Eppure, nelle opere ovidiane successive la parola dell'eroina diventa spesso parola d'autore: le voci delle *Eroidi* diventano la voce del precettore d'amore, e poi del narratore epico o elegiaco. La prospettiva femminile – anticonvenzionale, demistificante, spesso tagliente – si rivela un punto di vista letterariamente efficace per guardare alle cose del mito. Non è solo il punto di vista che il maestro d'amore assume quando si rivolge alle donne, in *Ars amatoria* 3, e interpreta gli *exempla* mitici dalla loro parte. È anche il taglio scelto dal narratore epico delle *Metamorfosi*, un poema eccentrico rispetto alla tradizione, in cui gli eroi più grandi sono messi di fronte alle loro *défaillances* e a versioni 'non autorizzate' e politicamente scorrette delle loro storie. Attraverso la voce delle loro donne, gli eroi nazionali di Atene e Roma, Teseo ed Enea, o gli eroi protagonisti dei poemi omerici, Achille e Ulisse, appaiono già nelle *Eroidi* come appariranno nelle *Metamorfosi*: non all'altezza della loro fama migliore. L'elegia al femminile è un laboratorio poetico per il relativismo dell'epos ovidiano.

Torniamo dunque alla questione teorica sollevata all'inizio. Nelle *Eroidi*, come si usa dire, Ovidio gioca alle spalle dell'eroina che scrive. Ma, in questo gioco intertestuale, l'eroina e l'autore possono essere i migliori alleati l'uno dell'altra. Per voce di Didone, nella settima *Eroide*, Ovidio rilegge l'*Eneide* anticipando la Scuola

---

[13] Bessone (2018). Uso l'espressione "tra le righe", qui e in seguito, per indicare gli effetti di ironia come presa di distanza autoriale da ciò che è detto esplicitamente nel testo, in particolare dalla voce di un personaggio: una presa di distanza rivelata indirettamente, soprattutto attraverso segnali intertestuali e autoriflessivi, che attivano nel lettore la memoria dei modelli e il confronto implicito con versioni diverse della storia, smascherando così la tendenziosità di chi parla. Per questa dimensione, spiccatamente intertestuale, dell'ironia ovidiana si veda Casali (2009); cf. *supra*, n. 3.

di Harvard; una lettura che riproporrà per tutta la sua carriera, dall'*Ars* in poi, e soprattutto nelle *Metamorfosi*: là le 'altre voci' dell'*Eneide*, filtrate attraverso l'*Eroide*, diventeranno la voce stessa del narratore epico.[14]

Nonostante le migliori intenzioni della critica femminista, non esiste un'autrice antica di nome Didone.[15] Esiste però un autore maschio che, impersonando la protagonista di un epos e dandole voce in elegia, reagisce al potenziale maschilista del poema nazionale e, mentre ne esaspera le tensioni, ne mette in discussione l'eroe – ovvero, il *vir*. Che l'epistola di Didone non abbia effetto su Enea può apparire una ri-affermazione di maschilismo; di fatto, tuttavia, è con le parole della protagonista femminile che Ovidio afferma per la prima volta una lettura 'femminista' dell'*Eneide* – quella che sarà poi, per sempre, la sua lettura di Virgilio.

È questo il punto su cui vorrei riflettere in questo contributo. Esiste una convergenza di interessi letterari, e una complicità narrativa, tra la persona poetica ovidiana e la voce femminile che dice 'Io'. Questa solidarietà di intenti è spesso una scelta di opportunismo, al servizio di una poetica anticonvenzionale e anticonformista: l'alleanza tra persona autoriale e personaggio femminile può essere funzionale a sovvertire, criticare o relativizzare narrazioni *mainstream* e discorsi culturali dominanti. Allo stesso tempo, c'è un'analisi acuta del mondo femminile che emerge da questo sforzo di rappresentazione dall'interno, e quasi di immedesimazione con l'altro genere, come è proprio della grande letteratura.

E tuttavia questa quasi-identificazione non esclude l'ironia. Questo, a mio parere, è un elemento decisivo. Dare potere letterario alle donne, facendole parlare – o 'scrivere' – in prima persona, mette in crisi la gerarchia (sociale e letteraria) tra i generi, ma non mette le donne al riparo dallo sguardo ironico che Ovidio riserva a tutti i suoi personaggi, e alla sua stessa persona autoriale. Il relativismo della poesia ovidiana è un relativismo *assoluto*. L'ironia 'involontaria' dell'eroina che parla o scrive – un'autoironia talvolta dissacrante – è l'ironia di un autore che sistematicamente smonta le pretese di chiunque prenda la parola nelle sue opere, compreso se stesso: un gesto autocosciente, che scopre contraddizioni, denuncia contraffazioni, mette a nudo debolezze, o semplicemente coglie idiosincrasie, sempre con superiore distacco – e magari con una punta di malizia maschile, quando l'autore impersona l'altro sesso.

Un tale groviglio di fili poetici può apparire quasi inestricabile. Ma, nello spazio che mi resta, vorrei fare almeno il tentativo di sbrogliarne un esempio.

---

14 Casali (1995); Casali (2004/2005); Piazzi (2007).
15 Per le eroidi come autrici cf. Fulkerson (2005).

2 La 'caccia alla ninfa' secondo Aretusa

Il discorso in prima persona, modellato secondo parametri di genere, conosce sviluppi nuovi nelle prove di *Ich-Erzählung* delle *Metamorfosi*: i racconti interni per voce delle protagoniste declinano al femminile l'arte ovidiana del narrare. Qui vorrei osservare quali variazioni esibisca uno schema tipico dell'"epica del desiderio",[16] quello dell'inseguimento erotico, quando a raccontare non è la voce maschile del narratore primario (o secondario), ma la voce della vittima, o della fuggitiva.[17]

Il caso di studio è il racconto di sé che Aretusa fa a Cerere, inserito nel canto di Calliope di fronte alle Ninfe giudici (nella gara tra le Muse e le Pieridi), a sua volta riferito da una Musa anonima a Minerva. Al centro di un complesso di racconti di donne ad altre donne, contenuti l'uno nell'altro, troviamo una versione inedita del convenzionale racconto ovidiano di 'caccia alla ninfa', costruito questa volta in chiave di *autofiction*. Nella struttura diegetica più complessa del poema, la tradizione degli "amori di Alfeo e Aretusa" è trasformata – su questo punto presuppongo le conclusioni di un mio studio recente.[18] *Fluminis Elei veteres narravit amores* ("narrò gli antichi amori del fiume di Elide", *Met.* 5,576) è la didascalia che introduce il racconto.[19] In questa sezione di narrativa al femminile, sul tema della violenza sessuale, Ovidio ci presenta, non 'la verità su Aretusa', ma 'la versione di Aretusa': una versione del mito tagliata su misura per il contesto, che si arresta prima della conclusione della vicenda e fa apparire vincitrice la ninfa in fuga, omettendo la celebre unione erotica (e coniugale) realizzata infine col 'mescolare le acque'. Tra tutte le versioni a noi note del mito, questa è l'unica in cui Alfeo rimane frustrato: in apparenza, il dio-fiume non raggiunge Aretusa e non si unisce con lei in Sicilia, dopo che la ninfa, rincorsa dall'Arcadia fino in Elide e qui mutata in fonte da Diana (che apre la terra davanti a lei), fluisce sotto il mare e riemerge a Ortigia.

---

16 La definizione è di Rosati (2008).
17 Prove preliminari alla narrazione di Aretusa, nel poema, sono il breve racconto della cornacchia sul suo passato di fanciulla, sfuggita alla violenza di Nettuno con la metamorfosi, in *Met.* 2,569–588 (una replica in miniatura dello 'schema di Dafne', con inseguimento, fuga, preghiera a una dea vergine, metamorfosi; cf. 572–580) e, nello stesso episodio di Minerva presso le Muse che contiene il resoconto del canto di Calliope su Proserpina rapita, il preambolo della Musa anonima alla dea vergine sulla violenza di Pireneo, a cui le Muse tutte sono sfuggite "prendendo le ali" (*Met.* 5,273–293: vedi *infra*; le narrazioni femminili di tema erotico sono schematizzate in tabelle da Nikolopoulos (2004) 141–160, che classifica impropriamente il caso di Aretusa come "successful rape", pp. 147sq.). Il racconto intessuto da Filomela della violenza subita da Tereo è al centro del dibattito sulla rappresentazione della violenza sessuale nelle *Metamorfosi*: cf. Segal (1994), Salzmann-Mitchell (2005) e la bibliografia citata *supra*, n. 1. Un'aggressione erotica da parte di Apollo è raccontata per lettera dalla ninfa Enone a Paride in *Ep.* 5,139–148.
18 Bessone (2020).
19 Le traduzioni delle *Metamorfosi* sono in parte mie, in parte (dove indicato) di Paduano; le *Eroidi* sono citate secondo la traduzione di Rosati, l'*Eneide* secondo quella di Fo.

Hac Arethusa tenus (*Met.* 5,642), "fin qui", e solo fin qui, arriva il racconto della protagonista. Questa versione, apparentemente inedita, è piuttosto una versione incompleta, accelerata e bruscamente interrotta nel finale, che viene fatta propria, per interesse, da due narratrici interne e dal narratore esterno. Il discorso diretto di Aretusa a Cerere è recitato da Calliope davanti alle Ninfe, è riferito da una Musa a Minerva ed è raccontato dal narratore primario al suo pubblico. Nessun commento o correttivo lo accompagna, e il discorso appare riportato integralmente: l'impressione creata da Ovidio è quella di una 'presa diretta'. Poco prima, al contrario, il canto irriverente della Pieride sulla Gigantomachia è stato riassunto dalla Musa anonima a Minerva con giudizi sprezzanti e con una drastica selezione in discorso diretto, mirata a screditare l'avversaria di Calliope: anche questo contrasto produce l'impressione di un'adesione piena di tutte le Muse alla 'versione di Aretusa'.

Il racconto di Aretusa, la ninfa-Musa, appare dunque 'autorizzato', con complicità professionale, da due Muse, dal narratore primario e, sembrerebbe, dal poeta stesso. Come è evidente, è impossibile, qui, districare fra loro le tre voci femminili sovrapposte, ed è un'operazione particolarmente delicata distinguerne inflessione e intento da quelli della voce autoriale. Il discorso diretto si colloca al quarto livello diegetico; in una struttura così complessa, non si può decidere se una scelta narrativa appartenga all'uno o all'altro livello della narrazione.[20]

Quello che è certo è che c'è *solidarietà* fra tutti e tre i livelli intra-diegetici, e tra questi e il piano extra-diegetico. Tutte le voci in questo coro, compresa quella del narratore primario – che le 'finge' tutte quante –, hanno interesse a costruire un racconto in cui, per una volta, un tentativo di violenza va a vuoto (come già nel caso di Pireneo e delle Muse); e tutte queste voci hanno interesse a far ascoltare un tale racconto a un uditorio simpatetico: la dea madre Cerere, che ha subìto il ratto di Proserpina; le Ninfe giudici della gara poetica, vittime abituali di violenza;[21] la dea vergine Minerva, scampata a uno stupro e 'refrattaria al sesso';[22] infine, il lettore delle *Metamorfosi*, curioso di variazioni narrative su uno schema ricorrente. La Musa compiace Minerva, come Calliope compiace le Ninfe, come Aretusa compiace Cerere: la ninfa protagonista evita di irritare la dea contro la Sicilia, evitando di ricordare che nell'isola è giunto anche il suo 'rapitore', e intanto attribuisce a se stessa tutta la gloria delle "acque di Elide" a Ortigia. La fluidità, motivo chiave del racconto, è anche una chiave per interpretarlo; come lettori delle *Metamorfosi*, restiamo incerti se Alfeo

---

20 Le avvertenze metodologiche di Wheeler (1999) 187–189 si fanno qui particolarmente problematiche: "These character-narrators may share stylistic traits with and be implicitly manipulated by the primary narrator, but their point of view is distinct . . . The external narrator addresses a generalized audience, but internal narrators orient themselves toward definite audiences and consequently may adopt different rhetorical strategies . . . we should not confuse Calliope's voice with Arethusa's, nor should their voices be confused with the primary narrator's".
21 Zissos (1999); Rosati (2009a) a *Met.* 5,577–641, p. 231.
22 Rosati (2009a) a *Met.* 5,271–274.

abbia infine mescolato le sue acque con quelle dell'amata, ma possiamo ammirare l'abilità di chi narra nel 'confondere le acque': l'abilità di Aretusa, e di tutte le voci che si sovrappongono alla sua.

Dunque, la finzione ovidiana del discorso di Aretusa risulta efficace e credibile a ognuno di questi livelli narrativi. E tuttavia, quando si percepiscono coloriture ironiche – se questa non è l'illusione di un'ovidianista –, sembra quasi di distinguere la voce dell'autore, rivolto al suo lettore. Come la scrittura per voce sola delle *Eroidi*, i pezzi per voce femminile delle *Metamorfosi*, quando non sono commentati da interventi del narratore primario o di narratori interni, e neppure relativizzati da reazioni polemiche dei personaggi del racconto, trovano però un implicito controcanto nell'ironia autoriale. La voce nascosta dell'autore può farsi sentire per via allusiva, attraverso la sottolineatura di mosse inattese, scarti di stile e sorprese linguistiche, o segnalando automatismi narrativi inappropriati, che risultano in pose improbabili e poco adatte al personaggio che narra di sé: attraverso più voci, distinte e concordi, l'autore disegna il carattere di una narratrice autobiografica con le sue ambizioni e velleità, esaltando idiosincrasie e tratti marcati, indicando contraddizioni o incongruenze, e rimandando a versioni alternative del mito fissate nei modelli poetici. Ovidio commenta tra le righe l'espressione della prospettiva femminile da lui stesso creata, mettendola in rapporto di senso con le convenzioni del poema e con la tradizione letteraria.

3 Storie di donne

Andiamo per ordine. Il primo degli effetti di genere ricercati da Ovidio nel racconto di Aretusa è anche il più ovvio: la scelta di un tema e di un taglio narrativo congeniali al discorso femminile. Esiste, secondo Ovidio, un compiacimento delle donne, e delle vergini (o presunte tali), nel raccontare ad altre donne, e ad altre vergini, non solo di amori (come mostra Virgilio col canto di Climene in *Georgiche* 4),[23] ma di innamorati respinti o di assalti erotici sventati. In questo episodio sono le stesse Muse, 'sorelle vergini' per definizione,[24] a istituire un paradigma autorevole: accogliendo Minerva sull'Elicona, la Musa anonima racconta alla dea ospite, come in un

---

23 Verg. *Ge.* 4,345–347 *inter quas curam Clymene narrabat inanem / Volcani Martisque dolos et dulcia furta, / aque Chao densos divum numerabat amores*, "Tra di loro Climene narrava la sorveglianza di Vulcano – inutile! – e gli inganni di Marte e i dolci furti; contava, a partire dal Caos, i fitti amori degli dei" [tr. Barchiesi]. Aretusa è nell'uditorio: cf. v. 344 *et tandem positis velox Arethusa sagittis*, "e la veloce Aretusa, spogliata infine delle sue trecce". Sulle narrazioni femminili nelle *Metamorfosi* si veda anche il contributo di Alison Keith in questo volume, incentrato sui racconti delle Minieidi.
24 Come del resto – ad esempio – Orfeo è per definizione figlio di una Musa: cf. Reed (2013) a *Met.* 10,148. Per la coesistenza tra il dato tradizionale della verginità delle Muse e le tradizioni mitiche sui figli delle Muse cf. Rosati (2009a) a *Met.* 5,271–274.

prologo, il recente assalto di Pireneo, che ha finito con lo sfracellarsi al suolo. Questa predilezione narrativa femminile per gli amori rifiutati è confermata anche più avanti nel poema: il narratore primario segnala l'abitudine di Scilla di raccontare di sé alle ninfe marine gli *elusos iuvenum amores* ("gli amori dei giovani a cui era sfuggita", *Met.* 13,737); e Galatea invidia alla *virgo* la capacità di sottrarsi ai pretendenti, mentre le racconta, a sua volta, le conseguenze tragiche del proprio rifiuto al Ciclope (*Met.* 13,735–745).[25]

Le molestie respinte, dunque, sono una predilezione narrativa femminile. Ma Aretusa non è solo una donna, e non è una narratrice qualsiasi: è una ninfa-Musa, fonte di ispirazione della poesia bucolica, invocata nell'*incipit* della decima *Egloga*. È una narratrice professionale, degna di prendere la parola nelle parole delle Muse. Ovidio ne fa una voce tra le più consapevoli delle *Metamorfosi* e le presta riflessioni metanarrative. Nel suo primo discorso a Cerere, rivelando la sorte di Proserpina, Aretusa rimanda il racconto autobiografico a quando la dea sarà *curaque levata et vultus melioris* (*Met.* 5,499–501 *veniet narratibus hora / tempestiva meis, cum tu curaque levata / et vultus melioris eris*, "verrà un momento opportuno per il mio racconto, quando sarai sollevata dall'ansia e avrai un'espressione più distesa"): una notazione competente sul momento opportuno per narrare e sull'opportunità della buona disposizione di chi ascolta. Addirittura, interrompendo il corso del suo racconto per farlo riemergere più avanti, la ninfa acquatica mima nella forma del testo il contenuto della storia, la traversata sottomarina che la fa riemergere in un punto distante della terra.[26]

4 Il racconto dell'eroe, il racconto della ninfa: Aretusa come Enea

L'Aretusa di Ovidio è una narratrice ambiziosa: e si misura niente meno che col racconto di *Enea* in Virgilio – il più celebre racconto inserito dell'epica latina.[27] La 'cornice di silenzio' del discorso cita l'*incipit* del secondo libro dell'*Eneide*. *Conticuere*

---

25 *Met.* 13,735–737 *hanc multi petiere proci; quibus illa repulsis / ad pelagi nymphas, pelagi gratissima nymphis, / ibat et elusos iuvenum narrabat amores*, "La chiedevano molti pretendenti, ma lei li respinse: andava dalle Ninfe del mare (carissima era alle Ninfe del mare), e raccontava come era sfuggita agli amori dei giovani" [tr. Paduano]. Cf. Rosati (2009a) 231 a 5,577–641.
26 Rosati (2002) 283sq.; (2009b) 240–245; cf. Barchiesi (2002) 20.
27 Ov. *Met.* 5,572–579 *exigit alma Ceres, nata secura recepta, / quae tibi causa fugae, cur sis, Arethusa, sacer fons. / conticuere undae, quarum dea sustulit alto / fonte caput viridesque manu siccata capillos / fluminis Elei veteres narravit amores. / 'Pars ego nympharum quae sunt in Achaide' dixit / 'una fui, nec me studiosius altera saltus / legit nec posuit studiosius altera casses'*, "L'alma Cerere, serena una volta riavuta la figlia, chiede quale sia la causa della tua fuga, perché tu, Aretusa, sia una fonte sacra. Tacquero le onde, dalla profonda sorgente la dea levò il capo e, asciugati con le mani i verdi capelli, narrò gli antichi amori del fiume di Elide. 'Io ero una parte delle ninfe che

undae (*Met.* 5,574) fa eco a *conticuere omnes* (Verg. *A.* 2,1) – e induce a chiedersi se in quelle "onde", così animate di presenze, qualcuno sia in ascolto. L'esordio della ninfa fa il verso all'esordio dell'eroe:[28] il racconto sui *veteres amores* del "fiume di Elide" gareggia con gli *apologoi* sulla caduta di Troia e le peregrinazioni dell'esule. Anche in chiusa la ninfa rilegge l'*Eneide*: riusa il verbo *renarro*, l'*hapax* con cui Virgilio chiudeva il racconto di Enea alla fine del terzo libro.[29]

Così, Aretusa in persona sembra correggere l'eroe virgiliano. Enea, verso la fine del suo racconto, accennava a Didone la storia di Alfeo, giunto – come lui – dall'Oriente in Sicilia, per confondere le acque con l'amata (Verg. *A.* 3,692–696):

Sicanio praetenta sinu iacet insula contra
Plemyrium undosum: nomen dixere priores
Ortygiam. Alpheum fama est huc Elidis amnem
occultas egisse vias subter mare, qui nunc
ore, Arethusa, tuo Siculis confunditur undis

Giace adagiata davanti a un golfo sicanio, di fronte
all'ondoso Plemurio, un'isola; il nome di Ortigia
gli avi le diedero. È fama che qui Alfeo, fiume dell'Elide,
venne per vie nascoste al di sotto del mare, e ora unito
alla tua bocca, Aretusa, si mischi alle sicule onde.

L'Aretusa di Ovidio, occultando Alfeo e la sua traversata, ruba la scena al *partner* e si mette lei stessa in parallelo con l'eroe nazionale. Un parallelismo anticipato nel primo discorso a Cerere, dove la ninfa si è presentata come *hospita* (*Met.* 5,493), *peregrina* che ha trovato in Italia i suoi *Penates* (vv. 495sq.) e transfuga *tanti . . . per aequoris undas* (5,498sq. *mota loco cur sim tantique per aequoris undas / advehar Ortygiam*, "Perché io abbia cambiato sede e, attraverso una così vasta distesa di mare, sia giunta a Ortigia").[30]

Mentre la ninfa promuove se stessa a 'doppio' di Enea, il testo fa ironia sulle differenze di genere, e di rango. Aretusa è come Enea, o quasi: la ninfa non "prende a parlare dall'alto divano" (*toro . . . ab alto*), come l'eroe ospite alla reggia, ma

---

sono in Acaia', disse, 'e nessun'altra percorreva con più passione le valli, e nessun'altra posava con più passione le reti'".

28 Verg. *A.* 2,1–6 *conticuere omnes intentique ora tenebant. / inde toro pater Aeneas sic orsus ab alto: / 'Infandum, regina, iubes renovare dolorem, / Troianas ut opes et lamentabile regnum / eruerint Danai, quaeque ipsa miserrima vidi / et quorum pars magna fui*', "Tacqero tutti, e tenevano intenti su lui i loro sguardi. / Quindi dall'alto giaciglio così incominciò il padre Enea: / 'Chiedi, regina, che io ripercorra un dolore indicibile: / come il regno potente di Troia, ora degno di lacrime, / abbiano i Danai divelto, e le tristi sventure che vidi / io, coi miei occhi, e di cui fui gran parte.'"
29 Verg. *A.* 3,716–718 *sic pater Aeneas intentis omnibus unus / fata renarrabat divum cursusque docebat. / conticuit tandem factoque hic fine quievit*, "Il padre Enea in questo modo a tutti, intenti, lui solo / ridescriveva i fati divini e narrava i suoi viaggi. / Tacque infine e, fermandosi qui, ritornava in silenzio".
30 Cf. Rosati (2009a) al v. 574; Ntanou (2020) 89.

"leva il capo dal profondo gorgo" delle onde (*alto / fonte*); e ricorda, non di avere avuto una "grande parte" in eventi luttuosi e letterariamente sublimi (*et quorum pars magna fui*), ma di essere stata "una parte" delle ninfe d'Acaia (*pars ego nympharum . . . una fui*): una fra le tante, ma abile nella caccia come nessuna; la più brava a percorrere i boschi e a tendere le reti.[31] C'è un divertimento nel trovare accostata l'autobiografia della ninfa a quella dell'eroe, e si creano effetti di genere nella forma del discorso in prima persona, che qui ci interessa analizzare.

L'eroe epico, da Omero in poi, si presenta dichiarando la propria patria, famiglia, virtù e fama.[32] La ninfa si appropria del modulo, ma deve fare i conti con la differenza di genere (*Met.* 5,580sq.):

> *sed quamvis formae numquam mihi fama petita est,*
> *quamvis **fortis** eram, formosae nomen habebam*
>
> Ma, benché non abbia mai cercato la fama di bella e benché fossi forte, avevo fama di bella.

Aretusa si qualifica come *fortis*, ma si rammarica di aver ottenuto, benché *fortis*, la *fama* di *formosa*.[33] Questa ex-ninfa-cacciatrice, a quanto pare estranea all'eros, che sta per rievocare la sua resistenza eroica a un assalto maschile, rivendica per sé una qualità propriamente virile, distintiva dell'eroe epico: e così dà l'impressione di modellarsi ancora su Enea, di cui Didone ricorda, in Virgilio, '*quam **forti** pectore et armis . . . quae bella exhausta canebat*', "Che forza nel petto e nelle armi! . . . Che guerre affrontate cantava!" (*A.* 4,11–14 [tr. Fo, modificata]). Se l'Aretusa di Ovidio vuol fare apparire diversa una storia che forse è rimasta la stessa, con questo suo racconto, mostrandosi vittoriosa su Alfeo, prende la sua rivincita sulla *fama*.

---

[31] *Met.* 5,577–579, cf. *supra*, n. 27.

[32] Hom. *Od.* 9,19–21 "Ulisse io sono, figlio di Laerte, che per ogni sorta di inganni / sono ben noto tra gli uomini e la mia fama va su fino al cielo. / La mia patria è Itaca, è facile scorgerla" [tr. Di Benedetto e Fabrini]; Verg. *A.* 1,378sq. *sum pius Aeneas, raptos qui ex hoste penates / classe veho mecum, fama super aethera notus*, "Sono il pio Enea, che, strappati al nemico i Penàti, li porto / su di una flotta con me, conosciuto per fama oltre l'ètere"; cf. Mastronarde (1994) a Eur. *Phoen.* 288–290.

[33] La qualifica di *fortis* per la cacciatrice Aretusa la accosta alla sua dea tutelare, Diana: *Am.* 3,2,31sq. *talia pinguntur succinctae crura Dianae / cum sequitur fortes, fortior ipsa, feras*, "tali sono nei dipinti le gambe di Diana dalla veste succinta, quando insegue forti fiere, più forte lei stessa"; cf. McKeown/Littlewood (c.d.s.) ad loc. In *Ars* 3,712 l'aggettivo qualifica Procri quando entra nel bosco, suggerendo il ruolo di cacciatrice a lei stessa attribuito in *Met.* 7,746: cf. Gibson (2003) ad loc. Una donna *fortis* è un'eccezione: in *Am.* 3,1,42 Elegia nega la qualifica per sé, affermando di non essere "più forte" della sua *materia*; in *Met.* 7,76 *fortis* è Medea, nel momento in cui sembra aver vinto e messo in fuga l'amore (cf. 7,73). Aretusa esprime più avanti la coscienza della sua inferiorità fisica femminile: *Met.* 5,610 *ego viribus impar*, "io, inferiore di forze".

Non è facile, per una ninfa, aspirare al ruolo letterario di un eroe. Spesso, nelle sue opere, Ovidio fa ironia sulla notorietà delle ninfe, una notorietà ristretta al loro piccolo mondo, perlopiù autoproclamata, o palesemente inventata da lui stesso.[34] Qui l'ironia sgonfia le ambizioni epico-eroiche di Aretusa, e misura la distanza irriducibile tra un eroe 'bello di fama' e una ninfa che ha 'fama di bella'.

5 Lo spettacolo della bellezza

La bellezza è il punto chiave del passo. L'elemento che Aretusa rifiuta è proprio quello su cui insiste e intorno a cui costruisce il racconto (*Met.* 5,582–584):[35]

> *nec mea me facies nimium laudata iuvabat,*
> *quaque aliae gaudere solent, ego rustica dote*
> *corporis erubui crimenque placere putavi*
>
> Ma la mia bellezza troppo lodata non mi era gradita, e mentre altre sono solite gioirne, io, rustica, arrossivo per le doti del corpo, e ritenevo una colpa piacere.

La lode eccessiva dell'aspetto fisico (*facies nimium laudata*, 5,582) non è per la protagonista narratrice – nelle sue parole – motivo di compiacimento, bensì di vergogna, e la consapevolezza di piacere equivale per lei addirittura alla coscienza di una colpa.[36]

Eppure, questa è proprio la premessa a una descrizione sapiente – fatta attendere, suggerita, interrotta e ripresa – del corpo nudo della ninfa in movimento, nella trasparenza delle acque, prima ancora che in fuga sulla riva: uno 'spettacolo della bellezza' offerto agli occhi e alla mente del lettore, come in tanti brani del poema gestiti dal narratore primario, spesso mediante focalizzatori interni (quasi sempre) maschili. Se le *Metamorfosi* sono 'poesia per gli occhi', e se è ad Ovidio che si deve "l'invenzione del corpo femminile", la narratrice interna prediletta dal poeta collabora con lui in una modalità peculiare, più suggestiva che dettagliata – più 'sportiva' che morbosa –, e ci regala un pezzo tra i più riusciti del suo repertorio. Un pezzo che

---

34 Cf. Ov. *Ep.* 5,3 *Pedasis Oenone, Phrygiis celeberrima silvis*, "Enone di Pedaso, celeberrima tra le ninfe di Frigia"; *Met.* 1,690sq. *inter Hamadryadas celeberrima Nonacrinas / Naias una fuit; nymphae Syringa vocabant*, "tra le Amadriadi di Nonacri c'era una naiade / che era la più famosa; le ninfe la chiamavano Siringa"; *Met.* 5,412 *inter Sicelidas Cyane celeberrima nymphas*, "Ciane, la più famosa tra le ninfe di Sicilia"; 5,539sq. *Orphne, / inter Avernales haud ignotissima nymphas*, "Orfne – non la meno famosa tra le ninfe d'Averno –" [tr. Paduano].
35 Il rammarico per i danni attirati su di sé dalla propria bellezza è anche in *Met.* 1,547 (Dafne) *qua nimium placui, mutando perde figuram*, "distruggi, trasformandola, questa mia figura che è troppo piaciuta" [tr. Paduano]; cf. *Met.* 2,572 (la cornacchia racconta il suo passato di fanciulla) *forma mihi nocuit*, "mi danneggiò la bellezza" [tr. Paduano].
36 Aretusa esaspera la posizione difensiva di Elena in *Ep.* 17,23: vedi *infra*.

inizia, del resto, citando l'*incipit* di *Amores* 1,5, "l'elegia più erotica della raccolta ovidiana" (*aestus erat*, "c'era caldo", *Met.* 5,586).[37]

Il discorso in prima persona della ninfa non esclude del tutto dallo sguardo i dettagli fisici della preda erotica: vediamo "la punta del piede", la gamba immersa "fino al polpaccio", "le braccia tese" nel nuoto (*pedis vestigia, poplite . . . tenus, excussa . . . bracchia*); tuttavia, la *Ich-Erzählung* fa a meno, qui, di similitudini descrittive (come quella impiegata per Ermafrodito in contesto identico)[38] e insiste piuttosto, semplicemente, sulla 'nudità' della ninfa (595 *nudaque mergor aquis*, "e mi immergo nuda nell'acqua", 601 *sicut eram . . . sine vestibus*, "così com'ero, fuggo senza vesti", 603 *nuda fui*, "ero nuda").

In questo non mancano effetti di *humour*, per lo sforzo della narratrice, da un lato di giustificare se stessa (per essere rimasta svestita), dall'altro di interpretare la reazione istantanea di Alfeo, immedesimandosi nella psiche maschile. Parentesi, nessi causali, uso di *videor* sono gli strumenti con cui Aretusa commenta, analizza, giudica la dinamica di un assalto erotico mosso da un maschio (5,601–603):[39]

> *sicut eram, fugio sine vestibus* **(altera vestes**
> **ripa meas habuit)**; *tanto magis instat et ardet,*
> *et* **quia** *nuda fui,* **sum visa** *paratior illi*

> così com'ero, fuggo senza vesti (le mie vesti le aveva l'altra riva); tanto più mi incalza e arde, e poiché ero nuda, gli sembravo più pronta.

Il testo guadagna così in ironia intellettualistica quello che perde in immediatezza, come mostra il confronto con la descrizione dell'infiammarsi di Salmacide al vedere la nudità di Ermafrodito (*Met.* 4,345–347 *mollia de tenero velamina corpore ponit. / tum vero placuit, nudaeque cupidine formae / Salmacis exarsit*, "depone le morbide vesti dal tenero corpo. Allora le piacque, e Salmacide arse di desiderio per la bellezza nuda").

---

37 Rosati (2009a) ad loc.; cf. Rosati (2018).
38 Cf. *Met.* 4,352–355 (Ermafrodito) *ille cavis velox applauso corpore palmis / desilit in latices alternaque* **bracchia** *ducens / in liquidis translucet aquis, ut eburnea siquis / signa tegat claro vel candida lilia vitro*, "Lui, colpendo il corpo col cavo delle mani, salta agilmente nell'acqua e, muovendo le braccia con moto alterno, traspare nelle acque limpide, come chi copre con lucido vetro una statua d'avorio o gigli candidi" [tr. Paduano].
39 Notevole anche l'effetto di genere nell'uso al femminile del part.-agg. *paratus*, che in contesti simili può indicare, con eufemismo sessuale, l'eccitazione erotica maschile, mentre qui connota la 'disponibilità' della donna, come preda, agli occhi del maschio: cf. la discussione in Bömer (1976) ad loc., Green (2004) a *Fast.* 1,437 e, per l'accostamento con *praeda*, ad es. *Ep.* 8,82 *ecce, Neoptolemo praeda parata fui* ("ecco che anch'io fui destinata in preda a Neottolemo"), con Pestelli (2007) ad loc.

6 *Forma* e *rusticitas*

Dunque, il rifiuto della propria bellezza dichiarato da Aretusa è un mezzo per introdurre nella *Ich-Erzählung* l'ingrediente essenziale di una storia di aggressione erotica – la bellezza, appunto –, e, allo stesso tempo, è una premessa necessaria a caratterizzare la ninfa, che con questo atteggiamento scagiona preventivamente se stessa dai sospetti di civetteria e di provocazione. Questa cacciatrice scontrosa costruisce se stessa come l'esatto contrario di Salmacide, la ninfa dedita all'*otium* e alla cura di sé, che il lettore ha conosciuto nel libro precedente, e che ha un ruolo opposto in una storia parallela (*Met.* 4,302–319):

> *nympha colit, sed nec venatibus apta nec arcus*
> *flectere quae soleat nec quae contendere cursu,*
> *solaque Naiadum celeri non nota Dianae.*
> . . .
> *nec iaculum sumit nec pictas ille pharetras,* 308
> *nec sua cum duris venatibus otia miscet,*
> *sed modo fonte suo **formosos** perluit artus,*
> *saepe Cytoriaco deducit pectine crines*
> *et quid se deceat spectatas consulit undas;*
> . . .
> *nec tamen ante adiit, etsi properabat adire,* 317
> *quam se composuit, quam circumspexit amictus*
> *et finxit vultum et meruit **formosa** videri*

> Vi abita una ninfa che non si dedica alla caccia, non piega l'arco e non fa gare di corsa; è la sola non nota alla rapida Diana. . . . Ma lei non prende giavellotti o faretre dipinte, non alterna i suoi ozi con la caccia faticosa; ma ora bagna nella sua fonte le belle membra, ora si liscia i capelli col pettine di legno del Citoro, e chiede all'acqua, specchiandosi, cosa le dona; . . . ma non gli si avvicinò, per quanto fosse ansiosa, prima di essersi tutta acconciata e avere aggiustato il velo, costruita un'espressione e guadagnato di sembrare bella [tr. Paduano].

Nelle parole di Aretusa, l'osservazione *quaque aliae gaudere solent* [sc. *dote corporis*] (*Met.* 5,583) è anche un rimando interno alle *Metamorfosi* e a un episodio che va letto in parallelo: i contatti esibiti tra i due brani – la descrizione delle acque trasparenti, l'aggettivo *perspicuus* usato solo in questi due passi, la scena del nuoto di Ermafrodito – esaltano il contrasto tra le due protagoniste, in ruoli rovesciati.[40]

---

[40] Cf. *Met.* 4,297–301 (v. 300 *perspicuus*) con 5,587sq. *aquas . . . perspicuas ad humum* ("acque . . . trasparenti fino al fondo"); 4,340–347 *at ille, / ut puer et vacuis ut inobservatus in herbis, / huc it et hinc illuc et in adludentibus undis / summa* pedum *taloque* tenus *vestigia tingit; / nec mora, temperie blandarum captus aquarum /* mollia *de tenero* velamina *corpore* ponit. */ tum vero placuit,* nudaeque *cupidine formae / Salmacis exarsit* . . . ("Ma il ragazzo, pensando di essere inosservato nel bosco vuoto, gira di qua e di là, e bagna la punta dei piedi e poi fino al tallone nelle onde che lo lambiscono; e senza indugio, attirato dalla temperatura dell'acqua carezzevole, depone dal tenero corpo le vesti. Allora sì che le piacque, e Salmacide arse dal desiderio della nuda bellezza" [tr. Pa-

Tuttavia, a dispetto delle dichiarazioni di Aretusa, possiamo chiederci se non emerga anche qui, fra le righe, un sospetto di vanità femminile. Mentre la ninfa proclama l'insofferenza per la propria bellezza, una serie di segnali ironici nel testo orienta il lettore in senso contrario. Il primo indizio è il gesto di strizzarsi le chiome emergendo dall'acqua, *viridesque manu siccata capillos*, "asciugàti con le mani i verdi capelli" (v. 575):[41] secondo Rosati, "quasi un segnale del racconto erotico che la ninfa sta introducendo" (cf. *veteres . . . amores*, v. 576). Qui la seguace di Diana assume una posa tipica di Venere – la celebre Venere *anadyomene* – e sembra tradire una sensibilità diversa da quella che dichiara.

Dall'iconografia dei gesti all'ideologia delle parole. Parlando di sé al passato, Aretusa si definisce **rustica** (*ego rustica*, v. 583 cit.), un termine che in Ovidio è un manifesto. *Rustica* non solo denota la ninfa dei boschi, ma la connota come 'rozza', 'inurbana', 'inesperta' delle arti d'amore.[42] L'Aretusa narratrice, qui, sembra prendere le distanze da se stessa: mentre sta per sedurre i lettori con un racconto erotico, giudica quasi dall'alto la ninfa che era un tempo, refrattaria alla seduzione. Gesti e termini rivelatori suggeriscono forse quello che Aretusa non dice: che anche questa ninfa non è del tutto estranea alla sfera dell'eros – o non lo è più.

Qualunque sia la nostra idea sulla versione del mito presupposta qui, *ego rustica* suona come un giudizio: il giudizio retrospettivo di una ninfa che (forse) ha conosciuto l'amore, o il giudizio maschile fatto proprio da una donna (come nelle parole di Penelope a Ulisse in *Ep.* 1,77sq. *forsitan et narres quam sit tibi rustica coniunx. . .*, "Forse le racconti anche com'è grossolana tua moglie"). Oppure – quel che ci interessa di più qui – un giudizio *insinuato nel testo* da una prospettiva maschile: se non la prospettiva del *partner* Alfeo segretamente in ascolto, certo quella del narratore esterno delle *Metamorfosi*, e di un autore che, nell'*Ars amatoria*, ha fatto della *rusticitas* l'antitesi della propria ideologia erotica.

L'effetto creato qui, attraverso le parole della protagonista narratrice, equivale a quello creato dal narratore esterno con il suo intervento nell'episodio di Dafne. Là, un'apostrofe alla protagonista le ricorda che – in base a una legge dell'eros – la sua bellezza non si concilia col suo voto di verginità: *sed te decor iste quod optas / esse vetat, votoque tuo tua forma repugnat*, "ma è quella tua bellezza che ti impedisce di essere ciò che vuoi, e il tuo aspetto avvenente contraddice il tuo voto" (*Met.* 1,488sq. [tr. Paduano, modificata]). Come osserva Barchiesi: "L'uso dell'apostrofe . . . è potenziato dal deittico *iste*: l'effetto coinvolge chi legge nel punto di vista ma-

---

duano]) con 5,585–603 (592sq. *primumque pedis vestigia tinxi, / poplite deinde tenus*, "bagnai dapprima la punta del piede, poi fino al polpaccio"; 594 *molliaque impono salici velamina curvae*, "appendo i morbidi veli al ramo pendente di un salice"; 595 *nudaque*); 4,352–355 cit. (353 *alternaque bracchia ducens*) con 5,595sq. cit. (. . . *excussaque bracchia iacto*).

41 Variazione sul v. 488 *rorantesque comas a fronte removit ad aures*, "scostò dalla fronte i capelli umidi sulle orecchie" [tr. Paduano].

42 Cf. Murgatroyd (2012) 179.

schile e suggerisce una reificazione di Dafne, da soggetto attivo a donna-oggetto, anche qui con richiamo alla mentalità elegiaca".[43]

Dall'interno del discorso di Aretusa, l'assunzione di una prospettiva maschile crea un gioco polifonico sul termine *rustica*, simile a quello costruito nelle *Eroidi* 16 e 17.[44] Paride, il *non rusticus hospes* dell'*Ars amatoria* (*Ars* 2,369), verso la fine della sua epistola accusa Elena di comportarsi da *rustica*: *a nimium simplex Helene, ne rustica dicam!* ("Oh troppo semplice – per non dire ingenua – Elena"); la sua *facies* – ammonisce l'eroe – la predispone ai *furta*, non si concilia con la *pudicitia* o con l'essere *dura*, e non può rimanere esente da *culpa*, perché *lis est cum forma magna pudicitiae*, "bellezza e pudicizia sono grandi nemiche" (*Ep.* 16,290).[45] Nell'ottica maschile, dall'essere bella al farsi rapire il passo è breve.

Scandalizzata, Elena controbatte l'accusa di essere *rustica* difendendo la *rusticitas* come alleata del *pudor*[46] (proprio l'accoppiata di valori che l'*Ars amatoria* bandisce, o smaschera come ingenua e ipocrita).[47] Ma la stessa Elena, verso la fine dell'epistola, si spoglia da sé della sua pretesa *rusticitas*, quando invita Paride a rapirla, scuotendo via la *rusticitas* con la *vis* (*Ep.* 17,185–188).[48] La prospettiva maschile, rifiutata nell'*incipit*, è fatta propria dall'eroina nella chiusa.

Torniamo alle *Metamorfosi*. Aretusa, in passato più integralista di Elena (che nel suo esordio definisce un *crimen* il *deleniri*, "lasciarsi sedurre"),[49] un tempo considerava

---

43 Barchiesi (2005) a *Met.* 1,488sq.
44 Cf. Bessone (2003b).
45 Ov. *Ep.* 16,287–290 *a nimium simplex Helene, ne rustica dicam! / hanc faciem culpa posse carere putas? / aut faciem mutes aut sis non dura necesse est: / lis est cum forma magna pudicitiae* ("Oh troppo semplice – per non dire ingenua – Elena, pensi che una bellezza come la tua possa evitare la colpa? O cambi la tua bellezza o bisogna che tu non sia inflessibile: bellezza e pudicizia sono grandi nemiche"). Con Elena, Aretusa condivide il *nomen*, la *fama*, la lode della bellezza/di bella: cf. 5,581 cit. *formosae nomen habebam* con *Ep.* 16,143sq. *nec. . . / inter formosas altera nomen habet*, "né un'altra ha, fra le belle, un nome pari al tuo"; 5,582 cit. *facies . . . laudata* con *Ep.* 16,133 *laudatam formam*; 141–146.
46 *Ep.* 17,11–14 *nec dubito quin haec, cum sit tam iusta, vocetur / rustica iudicio nostra querela tuo. / rustica sim sane, dum non oblita pudoris / dumque tenor vitae sit sine labe meae*, "E non ho dubbi che con questo mio lamento, per giusto che sia, apparirò scontrosa di fronte ai tuoi occhi. E va bene, sarò pure scontrosa, lo accetto, purché io non dimentichi il pudore, e purché sia senza macchia la mia condotta di vita".
47 *Ars* 1,607sq. *fuge rustice longe / hinc Pudor*, "via, lontano di qui, rozzo Pudore"; 1,672 *ei mihi, rusticitas, non pudor ille fuit*, "Ahimè! quello non fu pudore, ma soltanto rozzezza".
48 *Ep.* 17,185–188 *quod male persuades, utinam bene cogere posses! / vi mea rusticitas excutienda fuit. / utilis interdum est ipsis iniuria passis: / sic certe felix esse coacta forem*, "Oh, se quello di cui fai male a persuadermi, tu potessi costringermi a farlo senza colpa! con la forza bisognava strapparmi la mia goffa ritrosia. Talvolta la violenza è vantaggiosa perfino per chi la subisce; così certo sarei stata costretta a essere felice".
49 Ov. *Ep.* 17,23sq. *crimen erat nostrum si delenita fuissem; / cum sim rapta, meum quid nisi nolle fuit?*, "Sarebbe mia la colpa se fossi stata sedotta; ma essendo stata rapita, che avrei dovuto fare più che rifiutarmi?".

un *crimen* addirittura il *placere*, e per questo ora si giudica da sé: *ego rustica* (v. 583). Tacciando se stessa di *rusticitas*, la narratrice delle *Metamorfosi* fa propria l'ottica maschile: un po' come Elena, nel replicare alle parole di Paride, si vede *rustica* con gli occhi di lui (*nec dubito quin haec, cum sit tam iusta, vocetur / rustica iudicio nostra querela tuo*, "E non ho dubbi che con questo mio lamento, per giusto che sia, apparirò scontrosa di fronte ai tuoi occhi", *Ep.* 17,11sq.).

Dalle *Eroidi* alle *Metamorfosi*, l'eroina che dice 'Io' è complice di un autore che sa prendere le parti delle donne, ma che non rinuncia all'ironia, non rinnega la sua esperienza dell'eros, e non dimentica la sua appartenenza di genere. Nelle narrazioni femminili del poema, l'interferenza ironica tra le due prospettive crea 'effetti di genere' intriganti – come nel terzo libro dell'*Ars*, dove il maestro dà armi alle donne, ma qualche volta si ricorda che sta dall'altra parte del campo di battaglia, insieme ai suoi lettori maschi.[50]

La pretesa *rusticitas* di Aretusa non si sottrae alla legge universale della vanità – più specificamente, della vanità femminile – enunciata dal *praeceptor* nel primo libro dell'*Ars*: anche le vergini e caste si compiacciono della propria bellezza e sono sensibili alle sue lodi.[51] Così, la ninfa che rifiutava la sua *nimium laudata . . . forma* collude ora con l'autore epico, offrendo lo spettacolo del corpo femminile, e declinando in versione 'sportiva' il voyeurismo tipico di scene come questa. Aretusa ci appare desiderabile mentre scivola nell'acqua nelle "mille pose" del nuoto[52] (*Met.* 5,595sq. *nudaque mergor aquis. quas dum ferioque trahoque / mille modis labens excussaque bracchia iacto . . .*, "e mi immersi nuda nell'acqua. Mentre la batto e me la tiro dietro guizzando in mille modi, muovendo le braccia" [tr. Paduano]): quasi un preludio erotico; e il lettore è incerto se attribuire la malizia all'autore, o alla narratrice.

7 Una narrazione autoriflessiva

Concludo. Nelle *Metamorfosi* il racconto di un inseguimento erotico per voce della preda femminile è un'occasione per variare modalità narrative di uno schema ricorrente, con una riflessione sulle dinamiche di genere, e con tratti autoriflessivi che commentano i meccanismi consueti della rappresentazione ovidiana. Aretusa si appropria delle strutture e del linguaggio formulare delle scene di ratto con consapevolezza metanarrativa. Quando riusa un modulo della storia-archetipo di Apollo e Dafni, la similitudine animale per la paura della 'preda' ('come l'agnella coi lupi, o la lepre coi cani'),[53]

---

50 Miller (1993); Gibson (2003) 35sq. e n. ai vv. 7–28.
51 *Ars* 1,613–630; cf. Bessone (2005).
52 Murgatroyd (2012).
53 Cf. Rosati (2009a) a 5,626sq. e a 6,527–530 (Filomela); Barchiesi (2005) a 1,533–539 (Dafne).

la ninfa lo introduce con un'interrogativa retorica che chiama in causa il lettore (*Met.* 5,626–629):

> quid **mihi** tunc animi miserae fuit? **anne** quod agnae est,
> si qua lupos audit circum stabula alta frementes,
> aut lepori, qui vepre latens hostilia cernit
> ora canum nullosque audet dare corpore motus?

> Qual era allora il mio animo, povera me? Di un'agnella che sente i lupi ringhiare attorno alle alte stalle, o di una lepre che, nascosta tra i rovi, scorge i musi ostili dei cani e non osa muoversi? [tr. Paduano, modificata]

La movenza patetica[54] è anche un commento a un'operazione letteraria straniante. La vittima si sostituisce al narratore epico, si appropria della sua maniera narrativa e, così facendo, ne certifica l'efficacia, o – piuttosto – la mette alla prova: segnala uno stereotipo, mentre lo rinnova dall'interno; rappresenta se stessa nel ruolo di preda, ma una preda capace, poco dopo, di una reazione (in apparenza) vincente. Le narratrici create da Ovidio collaborano con lui alla costruzione di un poema polifonico – e Aretusa è tra le sue preferite.

Spero di aver mostrato che, tra Ovidio e le sue donne, esiste una complicità narrativa, che non esclude l'ironia; e che, tra *resisting reading* e *releasing reading*,[55] esiste forse una terza via. Nello spazio letterario classico, dominato da un genere solo, la voce femminile ha trovato una delle sue massime espressioni in un autore che, con il suo relativismo, ha saputo mettersi dall'una e dall'altra parte dei confini di genere.

Bibliografia

Testi e traduzioni

Omero, *Odissea*, a cura di Vincenzo Di Benedetto, traduzione di Vincenzo Di Benedetto e Pierangelo Fabrini, Milano 2010.
Ovidio, *Lettere di eroine*, a cura di Gianpiero Rosati, Milano 1989.
Ovidio, *Opere, II, Le metamorfosi*, traduzione di Guido Paduano, introduzione di Alessandro Perutelli, commento di Luigi Galasso, Torino 2000.
P. Ovidi Nasonis *Metamorphoses*, recognovit brevique adnotatione critica instruxit Richard J. Tarrant, Oxonii 2004.

---

[54] Per la formula '*quid mihi tunc animi* . . . ?' cf. *Met.* 14,177, con Hardie (2015) ad loc., e *Met.* 7,582sq. '*quid mihi tunc animi fuit? an quod debuit esse, / ut vitam odissem et cuperem pars esse meorum?*', "Cosa provai io allora? Non forse, com'è giusto, d'odiare la vita, bramando aver parte alla sorte dei miei?" [tr. Chiarini], con Kenney (2011) 283: "l'attenzione si sposta ora sulle emozioni del narratore, che osserva la peste con gli occhi di un governante di fronte a una calamità pubblica in cui le istituzioni sociali e religiose, nonché le norme del vivere civile, si dissolvono nel caos".
[55] Per questa alternativa si veda ora Sharrock (2020).

Publio Virgilio Marone, *Eneide*, traduzione a cura di Alessandro Fo, note di Filomena Giannotti, Torino 2012.

Publius Vergilius Maro, *Aeneis*, recensuit atque apparatu critico instruxit Gian Biagio Conte, editio altera, Berlin/Boston 2019.

Libri e articoli

Barchiesi (1986): Alessandro Barchiesi, "Problemi d'interpretazione in Ovidio: continuità delle storie, continuazione dei testi", *MD* 16, 77–107.

Barchiesi (1992): Alessandro Barchiesi (ed.), *P. Ovidii Nasonis Epistulae Heroidum 1–3*, Firenze.

Barchiesi (2002): Alessandro Barchiesi, "Narrative Technique and Narratology in the *Metamorphoses*", in: Philip Hardie (ed.), *The Cambridge Companion to Ovid*, Cambridge, 180–199.

Barchiesi (2005): Alessandro Barchiesi (ed.), *Ovidio, Metamorfosi, Volume I, Libri I–II*, Milano.

Bessone (1997): Federica Bessone (ed.), *P. Ovidii Nasonis Heroidum Epistula XII. Medea Iasoni*, Firenze.

Bessone (2003a): Federica Bessone, "*Saffo, la lirica, l'elegia. Su Ovidio, 'Heroides' 15*", *MD* 51, 209–243.

Bessone (2003b): Federica Bessone, "Discussione del mito e polifonia narrativa nelle *Heroides*. Enone, Paride ed Elena (Ov. *Her*. 5 e 16–17)", in: Marcella Guglielmo e Edoardo Bona (eds.), *Forme di comunicazione nel mondo antico e metamorfosi del mito: dal teatro al romanzo*, Alessandria, 149–185.

Bessone (2005): Federica Bessone, "Stile didascalico e verità del mito in un 'exemplum' ovidiano: *Ars Amatoria* 1, 623–6", *Dictynna* 2.

Bessone (2018): Federica Bessone, "Storie di eroi, scrittura di eroine. Storia e critica letteraria nelle *Heroides*", in: Paolo Fedeli e Gianpiero Rosati (eds.), *Ovidio 2017. Prospettive per il terzo millennio. Atti del Convegno internazionale (Sulmona, 3–6 aprile 2017)*, Teramo, 181–213.

Bessone (2020): Federica Bessone, "L'illusione del lettore. Aretusa e i suoi racconti in Ovidio, *Metamorfosi* 5", *Dictynna* 17.

Bessone (2022): Federica Bessone, "Oggetti di un discorso amoroso. La retorica delle cose nell'elegia al femminile delle *Heroides*", in: Henriette Harich-Schwarzbauer (ed.), *Women and Objects in Antiquity*, Trier, 81–108.

Bömer (1976): Franz Bömer (ed.), *P. Ovidius Naso, Metamorphosen, Vol. II, Buch 4–5*, Heidelberg.

Cahoon (1996): Leslie Cahoon, "Calliope's Song: Shifting Narrators in Ovid, *Metamorphoses* 5", *Helios* 23, 43–66.

Casali (1995): Sergio Casali, "Altre voci nell'Eneide' di Ovidio", *MD* 35, 59–76.

Casali (2004/2005): Sergio Casali, "Further Voices in Ovid 'Heroides' 7", *Hermathena* 177/178, 147–164.

Casali (2006): Sergio Casali, recensione a Lindheim (2003), *International Journal of the Classical Tradition* 13.1, 130–133.

Casali (2009): Sergio Casali, *Ovidian Intertextuality*, in: Peter Knox (ed.), *A Companion to Ovid*, Malden, MA et al., 341–354.

Curran (1978): Leo C. Curran, "Rape and Rape Victims in the *Metamorphoses*", *G&R* 24, 170–184.

Donnarumma (2014): Raffaele Donnarumma, *Ipermodernità. Dove va la narrativa contemporanea*, Bologna.

Enterline (2000): Lynn Enterline, *The Rhetoric of the Body from Ovid to Shakespeare*, Cambridge.

Fabre-Serris (2018): Jacqueline Fabre-Serris, "Desire and Rape in the Feminine: The Tales of Echo and Salmacis: An Ovidian Answer to Propertius 1.20?", *Helios* 45.2, 127–144.

Farrell (1998): Joseph Farrell, "Reading and Writing the *Heroides*", *Harvard Studies in Classical Philology* 98, 307–338.

Fetterley (1978): Judith Fetterley, *The Resisting Reader: A Feminist Approach to American Fiction*, Bloomington/London.

Fulkerson (2005): Laurel Fulkerson, *The Ovidian Heroine as Author. Reading, Writing, and Community in the Heroides*, Cambridge.

Gibson (2003): Roy K. Gibson (ed.), *Ovid, Ars amatoria, Book 3*, Cambridge.

Green (2004): Steven J. Green (ed.), *Ovid, Fasti 1: A Commentary*, Leiden/Boston.

Hardie (2015): Philip Hardie (ed.), *Ovidio, Metamorfosi, Volume VI, Libri XIII–XV*, trad. di G. Chiarini, Milano.

Hutcheon (1994): Linda Hutcheon, *Irony's Edge. The Theory and Politics of Irony*, London.

Jordan (2013): Shirley Jordan, "Autofiction in the Feminine", *French Studies* 67.1, 76–84, https://doi.org/10.1093/fs/kns235 (03/05/2022).

Kenney (1996): Edward J. Kenney (ed.), *Ovid, Heroides XVI–XXI*, Cambridge.

Kenney (2011): Edward J. Kenney (ed.), *Ovidio, Metamorfosi, Volume IV, Libri VII–IX*, trad. di G. Chiarini, Milano.

Lindheim (2003): Sara H. Lindheim, *Mail and Female: Epistolary Narrative and Desire in Ovid's Heroides*, Madison.

Liveley (1999): Genevieve Liveley, "Reading Resistance in Ovid's *Metamorphoses*", in: Philip Hardie, Alessandro Barchiesi e Stephen Hinds (eds.), *Ovidian Transformations: Essays on Ovid's Metamorphoses and its Reception*, Cambridge, 97–213.

Mastronarde (1994): Donald J. Mastronarde (ed.), *Euripides, Phoenissae*, Cambridge.

McKeown/Littlewood (c.d.s.): Jim C. McKeown e R. Joy Littlewood (eds.), *Ovid: Amores. Volume IV, A Commentary on Book Three*, Leeds.

Miller (1993): John F. Miller, "Apostrophe, Aside and the Didactic Addressee: Poetic Strategies in Ars amatoria III", *MD* 31, 231–241.

Morales (2020): Helen Morales, *Antigone Rising. The Subversive Power of Ancient Myths*, London.

Murgatroyd (2012): Paul Murgatroyd, "Entertaining Arethusa", *MH* 69, 177–189.

Newlands (2018): Carole E. Newlands, "Violence and Resistance in Ovid's *Metamorphoses*", in: Monica R. Gale e J. H. D. Scourfield (eds.), *Texts and Violence in the Roman World*, Cambridge, 140–178.

Nikolopoulos (2004): Anastasios D. Nikolopoulos, *Ovidius polytropos. Metanarrative in Ovid's Metamorphoses*, Hildesheim.

Ntanou (2020): Eleni Ntanou, "*HAC Arethusa TENUS* (Met. 5.642). Geography and Poetics in Ovid's Arethusa", in: Alison Sharrock, Daniel Möller e Mats Malm (eds.), *Metamorphic Readings. Transformation, Language, and Gender in the Interpretation of Ovid's Metamorphoses*, Oxford, 84–103.

Pestelli (2007): Angela Pestelli (ed.), *P. Ovidii Nasonis Heroidum Epistula VIII. Hermione Oresti*, Firenze.

Piazzi (2007): Lisa Piazzi (ed.), *P. Ovidii Nasonis Heroidum Epistula VII. Dido Aeneae*, Firenze.

Reed (2013): Joseph D. Reed (ed.), *Ovidio, Metamorfosi, Vol. V, Libri X–XII*, trad. di G. Chiarini, Milano.

Richlin (1992): Amy Richlin, "Reading Ovid's Rapes", in: Amy Richlin (ed.), *Pornography and Representation In Greece and Rome*, Oxford/New York, 158–179.

Rosati (1985): Gianpiero Rosati, *Forma elegiaca di un simbolo letterario: la Fedra di Ovidio*, in: Renato Uglione (ed.), *Atti delle giornate di studio su Fedra* (Torino, 7-8-9 maggio 1984), Torino, 113–131.

Rosati (1989): Gianpiero Rosati, *Epistola elegiaca e lamento femminile*, in: Id., *Ovidio, Lettere di eroine*, Milano, 5–46.

Rosati (1992): Gianpiero Rosati, "L'elegia al femminile: le *Heroides* di Ovidio (e altre *heroides*)", *MD* 29, 71–94.

Rosati (2002): Gianpiero Rosati, "*Narrative Techniques and Narrative Structures in the Metamorphoses*", in: Barbara Weiden Boyd (ed.), *Brill's Companion to Ovid*, Leiden, 271–304.

Rosati (2008): Gianpiero Rosati, "Le *Metamorfosi* di Ovidio, un'epica del desiderio", in: Renato Uglione (ed.), *Atti del convegno nazionale di studi "Arma virumque cano . . . ". L'epica dei Greci e dei Romani, Torino 23–24 aprile 2007*, Torino, 139–157.

Rosati (2009a): Gianpiero Rosati (ed.), *Ovidio, Metamorfosi, Volume III, Libri V–VI*, trad. di G. Chiarini, Milano.

Rosati (2009b): Gianpiero Rosati, "Tempo del desiderio e fuga delle forme: la donna-acqua Aretusa e un testo che corre", in: Hélène Casanova-Robin (ed.), *Ovide, figures de l'hybride. Illustrations littéraires et figurées de l'esthétique ovidienne à travers les âges*, Paris, 235–245.

Rosati (2018): Gianpiero Rosati, "Ovidio e l'invenzione del corpo femminile", in: Paolo Fedeli e Gianpiero Rosati (eds.), *Ovidio 2017. Prospettive per il terzo millennio*, Teramo, 313–331.

Salzmann-Mitchell (2005): Patricia B. Salzmann-Mitchell, *A Web of Fantasies: Gaze, Image and Gender in Ovid's Metamorphoses*, Columbus.

Scourfield (2018): J. H. David Scourfield, "Violence and the Christian Heroine: Two Narratives of Desire", in: Monica R. Gale e J. H. D. Scourfield (eds.), *Texts and Violence in the Roman World*, Cambridge, 309–337.

Segal (1994): Charles Segal, "Philomela's Web and the Pleasures of the Text: Reader and Violence in the *Metamorphoses* of Ovid", in: Irene J. F. de Jong e John Patrick Sullivan (eds.), *Modern Critical Theory and Classical Literature*, Leiden et al., 257–280.

Sharrock (1991): Alison Sharrock, "The Love of Creation", *Ramus* 20, 169–182.

Sharrock (2020): Alison Sharrock, "Gender and Transformation. Reading, Women, and Gender in Ovid's Metamorphoses", in: Alison Sharrock, Daniel Möller e Mats Malm (eds.), *Metamorphic Readings: Transformation, Language, and Gender in the Interpretation of Ovid's Metamorphoses*, Oxford, 33–53.

Spentzou (2003): Efrossini Spentzou, *Readers and Writers in Ovid's Heroides. Transgressions of Genre and Gender*, Oxford.

Wheeler (1999): Stephen M. Wheeler, *Audience and Performance in Ovid's Metamorphoses*, Philadelphia.

Wyke (2002): Maria Wyke, *The Roman Mistress*, Oxford.

Zeitlin (1996): Froma Zeitlin, *Playing the Other: Gender and Society in Classical Greek Literature*, Princeton.

Zissos (1999): Andrew Zissos, "The Rape of Proserpina in Ovid *Met.* 5.341–661: Internal Audience and Narrative Distortion", *Phoenix* 53, 97–113.

Alison Keith
Gender and Genre in First-Person Discourse: Three Case Studies in Ovid's *Metamorphoses*

Abstract: In the first half of *Metamorphoses* 4, the daughters of Minyas beguile their spinning and weaving by telling a series of mythological love stories (4.1–415). These tales have received a great deal of critical analysis in the last thirty-five years or so. Building on this impressive body of scholarship and on recent narratological studies of the relationship between narrators and their narratives in the *Metamorphoses*, this study argues that Ovid shaped the Minyads' tales in such a way as to offer reflection on stereotypically feminine narrative subjects, themes and settings that complement the exclusively feminine setting of wool-working in which the sisters tell their tales. In their tales of failed romance and elegiac trysts, the sisters overtly reject Bacchus' rites and the sexual immorality associated with them, while adapting the elegiac theme of illicit love in a manner calculated to appeal to a female audience. Female characters take the lead in all three of the Minyads' narratives: bold Thisbe, vindictive Venus and Clytië, and seductive Salmacis. Like their characters, moreover, who pursue love at all costs, the Minyads are motivated by the pleasure of (hearing) love (stories). In this, they, like their characters, lend credence to the popular view of women's interest in the amatory fictions of romance and, especially, in the first-person discourse of elegiac poetry.

Keywords: aetiology, elegy, epic, romance, storytelling, weaving

We know very little about the circumstances of Ovid's composition of his hexameter *Metamorphoses*, though we can surmise something of its compositional context – enough, at any rate, to articulate the importance of the text precisely as a document of 'scripted orality'. In all likelihood, Ovid's poem, or parts of it, also originally circulated orally. We have extensive evidence of authors trying out their work on a small group of friends in this period and, contemporary with Ovid's own poetic career, there developed the institution of the *recitatio*, the semi-public reading of an author to an audience of invited friends and acquaintances.[1] Seneca Rhetor explains

---

1 Dalzell (1955).

Acknowledgments: I am grateful to Therese Fuhrer and Lisa Cordes for their generous invitation to participate in the November 2019 EuGeStA conference on the gender parameter in the shaping of first-person discourse in classical literature, and for their hospitality in Munich; my thanks as well to the conference interlocutors for their helpful feedback on an earlier version of this paper. I am solely responsible for any remaining errors and infelicities.

https://doi.org/10.1515/9783110795257-016

that "Asinius Pollio never let a crowd in when he declaimed; but he was not without public ambition – indeed he was the first of all the Romans to recite what he had written before an invited audience" (*Contr.* 4 *praef.* 2, *Pollio Asinius numquam admissa multitudine declamauit, nec illi ambitio in studiis defuit; primus enim omnium Romanorum aduocatis hominibus scripta sua recitauit*).[2] Seneca also offers evidence for the oral reception of Ovid's poetry in the rhetorical culture of the early principate, for example in his picture of one speaker capping another with *bons mots* drawn from the *Ars* and *Metamorphoses* in the heat of declamation (*Contr.* 3.7, quoting Ov. *Met.* 8.877f.):

> EXTRA. *Alfius Flauus hanc sententiam dixit: 'ipse sui et alimentum erat et damnum.' hunc Cestius quasi corrupte dixisset obiurgans: 'apparet, inquit, te poetas studiose legere: iste sensus eius est qui hoc saeculum amatoriis non artibus tantum sed sententiis impleuit. Ouidius enim in libris metamorphoseon dicit: ipse suos artus lacero diuellere morsu / coepit et infelix minuendo corpus alebat.'*

> BY THE WAY: Alfius Flavus spoke this epigram: "He was his own nourishment – and his own damage." Cestius reproved him for something in such bad taste, and said: "It is obvious you are a careful reader of poetry. That idea came from a man who filled this generation with erotic handbooks – and erotic epigrams." For it is Ovid who says in the *Metamorphoses*: "He began to tear his own limbs, biting and rending; / Wretched man, he nourished his body – by taking from it."

Ovid's verse thus furnishes material for the elder Seneca's report of a game of wits amongst Roman declaimers, writers and politicians competing for cultural prestige in a rhetorical forum that consolidated elite social privilege. Critical discussion of his vignette has focused on its declamatory setting and rhetorical context, as an important framework for Ovid's poetic practice, rather than on the centrality of gender to literary expression in ancient Rome.[3]

Yet such male-voiced scripted orality, the norm in classical literature, can be fully appreciated only by paying the closest attention to the gender of the speaker(s) and the deep interconnection of gender with generic paradigms. The ancient evidence points to multiple and overlapping interconnections between oral discourse and literary texts in Latin rhetorical culture, such that any exploration of the gendered voicing of Latin literary texts must proceed with the fullest attention to the possibility, indeed probability, of multiple and variegated oral contexts informing this literature. It is this gendered void in studies of scripted orality that my chapter

---

[2] I cite the text and translation of Seneca Rhetor from the Loeb Classical Library edition of Winterbottom (2014).
[3] For the similar use of an anecdote about Ovid preserved by Seneca Rhetor, see Keith (2016). On the construction of masculinity through declamatory competition and rhetorical display, see Gleason (1995); Gunderson (2003). See also the chapter by Lisa Cordes in this volume.

seeks to address, specifically in connection with Ovid's *Metamorphoses*,⁴ where both song and storytelling are conceived in oral rather than in literary terms.⁵

An extended instance of scripted orality, with differently gendered and generic voicing of the embedded narratives, appears in the fourth book of Ovid's *Metamorphoses*, when the daughters of Minyas beguile their spinning and weaving with a series of mythological love stories (4.1–415). These tales have received a great deal of critical analysis: scholars have investigated the Minyads' artistic standards and the relationship of their narrative artistry to the poetic project of the *Metamorphoses* as a whole;⁶ the themes and imagery of the sisters' tales;⁷ and the application of psychoanalytic theories of subjectivity both to the sisters and to the female characters in their stories.⁸ Building on this impressive body of scholarship and on narratological studies of the relationship between narrators and their narratives in the *Metamorphoses*,⁹ I want to suggest that Ovid shaped the Minyads' tales in such a way as to offer reflection on stereotypically feminine first-person discourse in the sisters' choice of narrative subjects, themes, characters and conventional settings.

At the conclusion of *Metamorphoses* 3, the Theban women, warned by the ghastly demise of Pentheus, assiduously worship the new god Bacchus (3.732f.). Only the daughters of Minyas foolishly persist in denying to Bacchus both his descent from Jove and his divinity (4.1–4; cf. 4.272f.). Spurning his rites, the Minyads and their slave women remain inside to spin and weave, celebrating the rites of Minerva instead of Bacchus (4.32–5):¹⁰

> solae Minyeides intus
> intempestiua turbantes festa Minerua
> aut ducunt lanas aut stamina pollice uersant
> aut haerent telae famulasque laboribus urgent.

---

4 For narratological discussion of Ovid's *Metamorphoses*, see Nagle (1988a), (1988b), and (1988c); Keith (1992); Barchiesi (2001); Rosati (2002); Papaioannou (2005) and (2007).
5 Fully argued in Wheeler (1999).
6 Due (1974); Leach (1974); Lateiner (1984); Holzberg (1988); Henderson (1990); Rosati (1999) and (2007); Keith (2010).
7 On the first Minyad's 'Pyramus and Thisbe', see Duke (1971); Due (1974); Rhorer (1980); Knox (1986) 35–7; Newlands (1986); Janan (1994); Keith (2010). On the second sister Leuconoë's 'Amours of the Sun', see Janan (1994); Keith (2010). On the third sister Alcithoë's 'Salmacis and Hermaphroditus', see Nugent (1990); Keith (1999) and (2010); Robinson (1999); Pietropaolo (2014).
8 Nugent (1990); Janan (1994).
9 Ahl (1985); Keith (1992); Myers (1994a); Nagle (1988a), (1988b), and (1988c). See also the chapter by Alison Sharrock in this volume who is interested in the question whether the female narrators in the *Metamorphoses* are also controlled by the external (male) author.
10 I cite Ovid's *Metamorphoses* from Tarrant (2004); translations are either my own or adapted from Miller (³1977).

> Only the Minyads within, marring the festival with Minerva's untimely tasks, either spin wool or thumb the turning threads, keeping close to the loom and oppressing their slave women with work.

Wool working constituted women's labour *par excellence* in antiquity, and in ancient Rome a woman's worth was long defined by her performance of this household duty, as we can see in the story of Lucretia, famously reported in Augustan literature by both Livy (1.57.8–10) and Ovid (*Fasti* 2.741–60). Indeed, wool working enjoyed particular prestige in Ovid's day, when the *princeps* boasted that his sister, wife, daughter and granddaughters wove his clothing (Suet. *Aug.* 64.2, 73).[11]

The praise accorded Roman women for spinning and weaving within the domestic sphere stands in sharp contrast to the denunciation of women involved in Bacchic rites by contemporary Augustan authors such as Livy (39.8–18) and Vergil (*Aen.* 7.385–405). Thus, the Minyads implicitly assert their exemplary feminine virtue when they contrast the Theban women's misguided worship of the false god Bacchus with their own service in the rites of Minerva (4.37–41):

> 'dum cessant aliae commentaque sacra frequentant,
> nos quoque, quas Pallas, melior dea, detinet' inquit,
> 'utile opus manuum uario sermone leuemus
> perque uices aliquid, quod tempora longa uideri   40
> non sinat, in medium uacuas referamus ad aures!'

> "While the other women are deserting their tasks and thronging this so-called festival, let us also", she said, "who keep to Pallas, a better goddess, lighten with various tales the serviceable work of our hands, and to beguile the tedious hours, let us take turns in telling stories, while all the others listen."

Despite the sisters' disavowal of Bacchus (the embodiment of unruly emotionalism) and their concomitant endorsement of Minerva (the embodiment of disciplined domesticity), the suggestion that they might beguile their wool work by exchanging stories hints at the holiday spirit of Bacchus' festival. Ovid thus multiply overdetermines the gendered context in which the sisters tell their tales.

1 Pyramus and Thisbe: Romance and Elegy

The Minyads enthusiastically "endorse their sister's words and ask her to go first" (4.42, *dicta probant primamque iubent narrare sorores*). Ovid shows the first sister carefully weighing her options among a repertoire of four tales of metamorphosis (43–51): Dercetis of Babylon, transformed into a fish (in order to escape the attack

---

[11] Cf. Columella 12. *praef.* 9, for pervasive upper class Roman resentment of this platform.

of the Giants during the Gigantomachy, cf. 5.321–6.331); her daughter Semiramis, transformed into a dove, reputed like her mother to have had consuming passions for young lovers, whom they put to death when they grew tired of them; a Naiad, also transformed into a fish after she has so transformed many youths, apparently her lovers; or the transformation of the mulberry tree's fruit from white to black (4.51–4):

> ... an, quae poma alba ferebat,
> ut nunc nigra ferat contactu sanguinis arbor.
> hoc placet; hanc, quoniam uulgaris fabula non est,
> talibus orsa modis lana sua fila sequente.

> ... or how the mulberry-tree, which once had borne white fruit, now has fruit dark red, from the blood stain. This last pleases her. This tale, not commonly known as yet, she tells, spinning her wool the while.

Much has been made of the first sister's quasi-Callimachean fastidiousness in her rejection of three little-known myths by preference for a fourth still more obscure tale (*quoniam uulgaris fabula non est*, 53).[12] Yet we might also note the criterion of pleasure (*placet*, 53) that motivates both her selection of an obscure tale and her original suggestion to enliven the tedium of wool working (39–41, quoted above).

If the first sister's decision to narrate the story of the mulberry's transformation appears to constitute a move away from stories in which the central character is a woman or goddess and the central theme is female erotic passion (with its attendant dangers for the male), her subsequent treatment of the myth reveals an unabated gyno- and erotocentrism. She prefaces her story with the introduction of the two protagonists (4.55–8):

> 'Pyramus et Thisbe, iuuenum pulcherrimus alter,
> altera, quas Oriens habuit, praelata puellis,
> contiguas tenuere domos, ubi dicitur altam
> coctilibus muris cinxisse Semiramis urbem.'

> "Pyramus and Thisbe – he the most beautiful youth, and she, loveliest maiden of all the East – dwelt in houses side by side, in the city which Semiramis is said to have surrounded with walls of brick."

The juxtaposition of the teenagers' names at the outset looks like the title of an ancient romance,[13] and the tale is often discussed in relation to the generic conventions of the

---

12 Rosati (1999) and (2007) 254.
13 Cf., e.g., *Chaereas and Callirhoe*, *Parthenope and Metiochus*, *Daphnis and Chloe*, *Leucippe and Clitophon*; and the Ninos-romance, also called *Ninus and Semiramis*, which has been dated to between 100 BCE and 100 CE. On the titling conventions of the genre, see Whitmarsh (2005).

Greek novel.[14] In addition to the opening conjunction of the young lovers' names, romance conventions in the episode include the youngsters' superlative beauty;[15] the fabulous Eastern setting;[16] the reference to Semiramis, legendary queen of Babylon and heroine of the so-called Ninos-romance, *Ninus and Semiramis*;[17] the innocence of the love-struck teenagers; the obstacles to their love; their determination to marry one another; their departure from home and inadvertent separation; the encounter with a wild beast; and the apparent death of the heroine. The intensity of the Minyad's engagement with the genre of romance in 'Pyramus and Thisbe' emerges clearly when we recall the conventional plot-points of the Greek novel: "love, travel, wild beasts, and acts of violence."[18] Both her interest in sensational romance and her apparent assumption that this narrative will engage her female audience, moreover, align closely with a scholarly tradition that has viewed women as the primary readership for ancient Greek fiction.[19] Whether or not this traditional consensus is correct, it is at least consistent with the evidence of Apuleius' *Metamorphoses*, which introduces 'Cupid and Psyche', the longest embedded narrative in the novel, as "a charming narrative and old wives' tale" (*narrationibus lepidis anilibusque fabulis*, Apul. Met. 4.27), told by an old woman to the captive maiden Charite.[20]

As the narrative of the teenagers' love proceeds, the Minyad deploys rhetorical effects of parallelism, repetition, echo and balance to bravura effect (4.59–64):

notitiam primosque gradus uicinia fecit;
tempore creuit amor. taedae quoque iure coissent,   60
sed uetuere patres; quod non potuere uetare,
ex aequo captis ardebant mentibus ambo.
conscius omnis abest; nutu signisque loquuntur,
quoque magis tegitur, tectus magis aestuat ignis.

Proximity brought them together and engendered first steps; in time grew love. Marriage torches would duly have come too, but their fathers forbade it; what they couldn't forbid was that both began to burn equally, their minds captivated. Every witness was absent; with a nod and signs they converse, and the more it's concealed, the more their concealed fire blazes.

---

14 See Due (1974) 123–7; Newlands (1986); Holzberg (1988).
15 Cf. Chariton, *Chaereas and Callirhoe* 1.1; Ach. Tat. *Leucippe* 1.4; Long. *Daphnis and Chloe* 1.7; Hel. *Aeth*. 1.2; etc.
16 Cf. the Ninos-romance; the Sesonchosis-romance; Xenophon's *Ephesiaca*; Ach. Tat. *Leucippe* 1.1; Iamblichus' *Babyloniaca*; Heliodorus' *Aethiopica*; Lollianus' *Phoinikika*. For the question of setting and its relation to romance titles, see Whitmarsh (2005).
17 On the Ninos-romance, see Perry (1967) 153–66; Hägg (1983) 17–19; G.N. Sandy in Reardon (1989) 803–8, with further bibliography.
18 Renner (1981) 100, quoted in Sandy (1994) 133.
19 Hägg (1983) 90 and 95; Lefkowitz (1991); Pervo (1991); Montague (1992); Egger (1999); *contra* Sandy (1994) 133f.; Haynes (2003) 1–10.
20 Cf. Aristoph. *Lys*. and *Eccl*.; Enn. *Ann*. 34–44 Sk.

The rhetorical devices of *amplificatio*, epanalepsis, and pleonasm (59f., 63), chiasmus, alliteration, assonance, *adnominatio* and polyptoton (61, 64; cf. 71, 89), and balanced word arrangement (62), along with the tight focus on the youthful pair (62f.), vividly suggest the reciprocity of the teenagers' mutual love – the "symmetry", in David Konstan's words, of the lovers' amatory experience in Greek romance.[21] In Roman literature, however, these rhetorical figures are closely associated with contemporary Latin love elegy and its characteristic metre, the elegiac distich, and above all with Ovid's stylization of the genre and its metrical form.[22]

The importance of the genre of elegy for the Minyad's narrative emerges especially clearly in the young lovers' formulation of a plan "to try to elude their guardians' watchful eyes and steal out of doors, when all had become still that night" (84f., *ut nocte silenti / fallere custodes foribusque excedere temptent*). The Minyad here draws on the lexicon and conventional themes of Latin erotic elegy, and she underlines the elegiac stylization of her plot as she proceeds (93–6):

> *callida per tenebras uersato cardine Thisbe*
> *egreditur fallitque suos adopertaque uultum*
> *peruenit ad tumulum dictaque sub arbore sedit.*   95
> *audacem faciebat **amor**...*

> Now Thisbe, carefully opening the door, steals out through the darkness, seen of none, and arrives duly at the tomb with her face well veiled and sits down under the trysting-tree. Love made her bold...

Thisbe displays the boldness and initiative characteristic of the elegiac mistress in her escape from the walls of her house and city. The adjective *callida* (93) belongs, like the phrases *per tenebras* (93) and *uersato cardine* (93), to the contemporary elegiac *sermo amatorius*.[23] With her reference to *amor* as the controlling passion of the plot (96), moreover, the Minyad implicitly invokes the genre of Latin love elegy, collections of which were often titled *Amores*.[24] The fineness (*tenues amictus*, 104) of

---

21 Konstan (1994).
22 On Ovid's treatment of the elegiac distich, see esp. McKeown (1987) 1.108–28; cf. Platnauer (1951). On Ovid's elegiac style more broadly, see further Knox (1986) 9–47; McKeown (1987) vol. 1.11–107.
23 For the elegiac mistress as *callida*, cf. Tib. 1.6.5f.; for the elegiac poet-lover as *callidus*, cf. Ov. Am. 1.2.6, 1.10.3f., 2.19.10, Ars 1.490. For *per tenebras* of the dark of night in which illicit affairs could be prosecuted, cf. Tib. 1.2.25, 1.5.16, 1.6.6, 1.10.50; Ov. Am. 1.6.9f., Her. 18.55f. For *uersato cardine*, cf. Tib. 1.2.10, 1.6.12, 1.8.60; Ov. Am. 1.6.4. See further Pichon (1902) s.vv., for this vocabulary; and Knox (1986) 35–7, and Rosati (2007) 263 ad Met. 4.93–6, for Ovid's deployment of the lexicon of elegy in this passage.
24 Cf., e.g., Gallus (*apud* Serv. ad Verg. Buc. 10.1); Prop. 2.1.1f. (*quaeritis unde mihi totiens scribantur **amores**, / unde meus ueniat mollis in ora liber*); Ov. Am. 1.1.26, 3.15.1. For Ovid's use of *amor* as a generic cue elsewhere in the *Metamorphoses*, see 1.452 with Nicoll (1980); cf. *ardor* at 14.682f. with Myers (1994b).

the cloak (*uelamina*, 101) Thisbe wears to the rendezvous also aligns her with the *puellae* of elegy, who wear similarly elegant clothing to trysts with their lovers.[25] Indeed, *Elegia* herself, "Mistress Elegy", wears just this kind of transparent dress (*uestis tenuissima, Am.* 3.1.11) in a cameo appearance in Ovid's *Amores*, where she delivers a lengthy speech (35–60) and recalls teaching the poet-lover's mistress Corinna to accomplish the same kind of daring night escape from her guardians as Thisbe successfully undertakes (*Am.* 3.1.49–52):[26]

> *per me decepto didicit custode Corinna*
>   *liminis astricti sollicitare fidem*
> *delabique toro tunica uelata soluta*
>   *atque impercussos nocte mouere pedes.*

> Through me, Corinna has learnt to deceive her guardian and disrupt the faith of a narrow threshold, to slip from her bed concealed in a loose tunic and move through the night without noise.

Thus, although the Minyad speaks in the dactylic hexameters of Ovid's *Metamorphoses*, the romance narrative she recounts draws closely on the generic conventions of Latin love elegy, with its focus on the resourceful mistress.[27]

Like romance, moreover, the genre of elegy was closely associated with women, and accordingly presumed to enjoy a female readership. The genre was deemed quintessentially "soft" (*mollis*), effeminate in both form and content, by contrast to the "harsh" (*durus*) genre of hexameter epic, which conventionally memorialized the glorious deeds of men (κλέα ἀνδρῶν) whether in warfare, cosmogony, or instruction. Although the elegiac mistress is not normally termed *mulier*, "woman", Roman etymological theory derived the noun from the adjective *mollis*,[28] a programmatically-

---

25 Cf., e.g., Corinna's *tunica rara* on her epiphany to Ovid early in the collection (*Am.* 1.5.13).
26 The object of the elegiac affair is to cheat the guard set on the mistress, though Ovid plays with the conceit in *Amores* 2.19, to suggest that the mistress' deception keeps his amatory interest alive (*Am.* 2.19.7f.): *quo mihi fortunam, quae numquam fallere curet? / nil ego quod nullo tempore laedat amo* ("Why would I want Fortune never to bother to deceive me? I don't at all love what never gives me pain", or more strongly, "that she never deceives me"). On the paradoxes of that passage, see Booth (1991) 190f. ad loc.; McKeown (1998) vol. 3.411f. ad loc.
27 On the elegiac mistress, see Sharrock (1991); Wyke (2002); James (2003); Keith (2012a); Miller (2013).
28 Lactantius (*Opif.* 12.17) reports that "Varro derived *mulier* from *mollities*, with one letter changed and withdrawn, as though *mollier*" (*mulier, ut Varro interpretatur, a mollitie est dicta, inmutata et detracta littera uelut mollier*). The same etymology is reported by Caes. Arel. *Serm.* 43.1; Isid. *Diff.* 2.82, *Orig.* 11.2.18. Cf. Isid. *Orig.* 10.179: *mollis, quod uigorem sexus eneruiati corpore dedecoret, et quasi mulier emolliatur.* ("'Soft', inasmuch as it is unbecoming for the strength of the sex weakened in the body, and is softened as if a 'woman'"). See Maltby (1991), s. vv. *mollis* and *mulier*; Edwards (1993) 63–97.

charged descriptor of Latin elegy,[29] and the elegists positively embrace the resulting feminization of the genre in their self-characterization as unmanly and effete. They repeatedly acknowledge the significance of their female readership (Tib. 2.4.19; Prop. 3.2.10, 3.9.45; Ov. *Ars* 3.57, 333f.), and Ovid himself specifically addresses two books of didactic elegy to women (*Ars* 3, *Medicamina*).[30]

The double generic templates of romance and elegy inform the Minyad's narrative throughout, and are intertwined in its climactic denouement. When Thisbe encounters a lioness slaking her thirst at the spring beside Ninus' tomb, she displays a romance heroine's presence of mind in her retreat to a nearby cave (4.99f.). Despite this unnerving encounter, with its overtones of a romance plot, Thisbe sets aside her fears and returns to the appointed meeting place (128f.): *ecce metu nondum posito, ne fallat **amantem**, / illa redit* ("And now comes Thisbe from her hiding-place, still trembling, but fearful also that her lover will miss her"). The Minyad attributes her motivation to a desire not to fail her lover, in another evocation of the genre of elegy. In her gynocentric tale, the first sister thus endows Thisbe with the assertiveness of both a romance heroine and an elegiac *puella*.

The Minyad's double allegiance to the feminine genres of elegy and romance has the concomitant effect of implicitly unmanning the teenage hero Pyramus (105–8):

serius egressus uestigia uidit in alto
puluere certa ferae totoque expalluit ore
Pyramus; ut uero uestem quoque sanguine tinctam
*repperit, '**una duos**' inquit '**nox perdet amantes**'.*

Pyramus, coming out a little later, sees the lion's tracks plain in the deep dust and pales at the sight. But when he saw the cloak too, smeared with blood, he cried: "One night shall bring two lovers to death."

Like the young heroes of Greek romance, Pyramus arrives late (105), misreads the evidence of Thisbe's absence and her bloodied cloak (105–7),[31] laments his inadequacy in failing to protect her (108–14), and determines to fall upon his sword (118f.): so far so novelistic. At this point, however, the Minyad breaks dramatically

---

29 Propertius characterizes his composition of elegiac verse as ***mollem** componere uersum* (1.7.19), while his mistress walks in elegiac metre, ***molliter** ire pedes* (2.12.24). See Wyke (2002) 46–77.
30 For women as the implied audience of Latin elegy, cf. Prop. 1.7.11, 2.11.6, 2.13.7–14; Ov. *Am.* 2.1.7, 2.4.17, *Ars* 2.281; and see further James (2003). The very openness of elegy to female expressions of desire has been proposed to explain, in part, both the existence and the survival of the *elegidia* of Sulpicia ([Tib.] 3.9, 11, 13–18): see Keith (2012b) 392.
31 Cf., e.g., the apparent death of Leucippe no fewer than three times in Achilles Tatius' novel *Leucippe and Clitophon* (3.15, 5.7), including her 'decapitation' in front of her lover (5.7); and the apparent deaths of the hero Habrocomes and heroine Anthia of the Ephesian Xenophon's novel, who survive crucifixion (4.2) and live burial (4.5.1–5.1.1) respectively.

with the conventions of the romance plot by describing Pyramus' real, and very bloody, death (119–24).[32] Returning from the cave to meet her lover (131f.), Thisbe finds him gasping out his life beneath a tree whose berries have been stained purple from his blood (133f.). It is therefore she who dominates the conclusion of the tale, as the Minyad records her reaction to Pyramus' death in first-person discourse (142f., 148–61).

Thisbe determines to join her lover in death (148–50) and concludes a moving soliloquy over his prostrate form with an avowal of eternal love that evokes Latin elegy (151–3):

> *persequar* **extinctum letique miserrima** *dicar*
> ***causa comesque*** *tui, quique a me morte reuelli*
> *heu sola poteras, poteris nec morte reuelli.*

> I shall follow you in death and be called the most pitiable cause and comrade of your demise, and you who could have been parted from me by death alone, will not be parted from me by death.

The pervasive lexical doublets and rhetorical devices in these lines signal the generic provenance of Thisbe's speech in elegy. Indeed, in enunciating her commitment to her dead lover, she rephrases in the first person the very words with which Ovid describes Laodamia's eternal love for her dead husband (*Am.* 2.18.38): *et comes extincto Laodamia uiro.*[33] Her language is particularly evocative of Ovid's heroines, who speak for themselves in his *Heroides*. Ventriloquizing the heroines' letters, Thisbe plays Phyllis to Pyramus' Demophoon (*Her.* 2.147f., *ille* **necis causam** *praebuit, ipsa manum*), Dido to his Aeneas (*Her.* 7.195, *praebuit Aeneas et* **causam mortis** *et ensem*).[34] In applying the pathetic superlative *miserrima* to herself, moreover, she fashions herself as the complete elegiac lover, whose first-person discourse Latin erotic elegy records.[35] If the Minyad herself eschews the use of the first person in her narrative, she endows her leading protagonist with the voice of an elegiac heroine at the breaking point.

In her final words, Thisbe prays that their parents may relent and permit them to be joined together in death as they could not be in life (154–7), and that the mulberry tree's fruit (literally its "offspring", 161, the only children of the failed coupling of Pyramus and Thisbe) may remain dark as a fitting memorial of their deaths (158–61):

---

32 On the thematic implications of Pyramus' death and the simile that describes it, see Newlands (1986).
33 For the same conceit, cf. Ov. *Tr.* 1.6.20, *Pont.* 3.1.109f., both of Laodamia.
34 Other Ovidian elegiac comparanda at, e.g., *Ars* 3.39f., *F.* 3.549, *Ib.* 123.
35 Cf. Prop. 1.1.1; Ov. *Am.* 1.1.25, 1.14.51, etc., both looking back to Cat. 8.1.

> *at tu, quae ramis arbor miserabile corpus*
> *nunc tegis unius, mox es tectura duorum,*
> *signa tene caedis pullosque et luctibus aptos* 160
> *semper habe fetus, gemini monimenta cruoris.*

And you, tree who now shade with your branches the pitiable body of one, but will soon shade two, keep the marks of our death and always bear dark fruit, meet for mourning, memorial of our double death.

The fruit (*mora*, 127) of the mulberry tree (*morus*, 90), transformed from white to black (125–7), anagrammatically memorializes the teenagers' "love" (*amor*) and "death" (*mors*).[36] Thisbe's epitaphic lexicon is equally at home in the elegiac distichs of sepulchral epigram and engages closely with the genre's funerary associations.[37] The Minyad confirms the elegiac contours of the tale in her final lines, which deploy the elegiac rhetoric of parallelism, repetition, echo and balance to articulate the elegiac trope of the lovers' tragic union in death (164–6):[38]

> *uota tamen tetigere deos, tetigere parentes;*
> *nam color in pomo est, ubi permaturuit, ater,*
> *quodque rogis superest una requiescit in urna.*

Her prayers touched the gods and touched their parents; for the colour of the mulberry fruit is dark red when it is ripe, and all that remained from both funeral pyres rests in a common urn.

Resting in a single urn, the lovers achieve the amatory union Canace prays for in *Heroides* 11 (122–4) and the epitaphic tribute Ovid offers Tibullus in *Amores* 3.9 (67). The cadences of the Minyad's final line are especially reminiscent of the elegiac pentameter and its association with funerary epitaph.[39]

---

36 On the etymological play, see Newlands (1986) 149; Keith (2001).
37 Cf. Ov. *Am.* 3.9.3f.: *flebilis indignos, Elegia, solue capillos: / a, nimis ex uero nunc tibi nomen erit!* ("Loose your unworthy tresses, mournful Mistress Elegy; alas, your [mournful] name will now be too true!"). For the funereal associations of dark clothing, characterized by the colour-term *pullus*, cf. Ov. *Am.* 2.4.41, *Ars* 3.189f., *F.* 4.620. On the elegiac association of love and death, see Papanghelis (1987); Ramsby (2007); Keith (2011).
38 Cf. the elegiac tonality of Pyramus' impassioned response to his discovery of Thisbe's bloodied cloak (4.108, quoted above) and his acceptance of culpability (4.110, *ego te, miseranda, peremi*).
39 Cf., e.g., *AP* 7.666.5; Prop. 2.8.23, 4.7.94; Ov. *Ars* 3.21; *Epiced. Drusi* 163. The motif pervades sepulchral epigram: cf., e.g., *AP* 7.330.3f., 378.3f., 15.8.1f., and see further Bömer (1976) 66f. ad loc., for Latin inscriptional parallels. The motif is also at home in the genre of romance, Greek and Latin: cf. Ach. Tat. 3.5.4, κοινῇ ταφῶμεν; Apul. *Met.* 8.14.3.

2 The Loves of the Sun: Elegy and Aetiology

In her elaboration of the teenagers' love story, the first Minyad offers, in the lexicon of Latin erotic elegy a (failed) romance narrative of the kind generally assumed to be of special interest to women in antiquity (despite the fact that almost all our evidence concerning both these narratives and women's predilection for them is derived from male-authored texts).[40] In her tale, *amor* is not only an omniscient deity (68, *quid non sentit amor?*), but also the source of her pre-eminent plot points, themes, and characters. This central focus on *amor* recurs in the tale of the second sister, Leuconoë, who undertakes to narrate the "loves of the Sun" (169f.):

> *hunc quoque, siderea qui temperat omnia luce,*
> *cepit **amor** Solem; Solis referemus **amores**.*

> This god too, who governs all things with his starry light, the Sun was struck by love; I shall relate the amours of the Sun.

If the first Minyad's opening formulation announces a romance plot (*Pyramus et Thisbe*, 55), her sister's initial words cue an explicitly elegiac tale in the genre's programmatic lexicon (*amor . . . amores*, 170) and conventional rhetoric (polyptoton, chiasmus, 170). Even the metre of her second line has an elegiac quality, with a penthemimeral caesura that falls between the polyptotonic repetition *Solem – Solis*.

Leuconoë begins her tale with a Homeric preface, based on Demodokos' song in *Odyssey* 8.266–369. Recalling how the Sun informed Vulcan of his wife Venus' adultery with Mars (*Met.* 4.171f.) and the aggrieved husband avenged his wife's infidelity (173–89), she spins her tale from Venus' plot to avenge her humiliation (190–92). Homeric in origin, Leuconoë's Venus is especially reminiscent of the wrathful Juno of Vergil's *Aeneid* 1.4 (*saeuae **memorem** Iunonis ob iram*) in her determination to exact revenge on the Sun (Ov. *Met.* 4.190–2):

> *exigit indicii **memorem** Cythereia poenam*
> *inque uices illum, tectos qui laesit **amores**,*
> *laedit **amore** pari.*

> Cythereia exacted a penalty reminiscent of his evidence, and in turn harmed him with an equal love as he had harmed hers.

An astute reader of the *Aeneid*, the Ovidian Leuconoë transforms Aeneas' epic persecution by Juno into the Sun's erotic persecution by Venus, in an elegiacizing tale of love and betrayal. Leuconoë announces her tale's generic allegiance in emphatic repetition of the conventional elegiac lexicon (*amores, amori*, 191f.), characters (*Cythereia*, 190), and rhetorical figures (parallelism, amplification, polyptoton, 191f.). Venus

---

40 Janan (1994).

herself, while hardly unknown to epic audiences (especially in the wake of the *Aeneid*), was most familiar to audiences in Ovid's day as the presiding deity of the elegiac genre, especially of Ovid's.[41] Indeed, though drawn from the epic repertoire of Homer, Leuconoë's prefatory tale (171–89) was also familiar to contemporary Roman readers from Ovid's generic relocation of the myth to his own amatory elegy: in *Amores* 1.9.40, he refers to the tale as "more well known in heaven than any other story" (*notior in caelo fabula nulla fuit*), and in the *Ars amatoria* (2.561–88), he rehearses it at length, introducing it as "the best known story in all heaven" (*fabula narratur toto notissima caelo*, 561). Thus for all its epic pedigree, Leuconoë's preface resonates with the contemporary cadences of Latin erotic elegy, as the Minyad adapts Ovid's elegiac material to her own erotic narrative.[42]

Leuconoë's title (*Solis amores*, *Met.* 4.170) implies the Sun god's extensive experience in erotic affairs, enumerated later in her narrative (204–8), and heralds his discovery of Venus' adultery, *adulterium* (171), a word naturalized in Latin elegy.[43] Indeed, throughout the narrative, Leuconoë draws her lexicon and rhetoric from contemporary elegy (*furta tori furtique locum*, 174; *torum coniunx et adulter in unum*, 182; *in mediis ambo deprensi amplexibus haerent*, 184).[44] Also elegiac in resonance is the programmatically charged vocabulary she employs to describe the divine smith's elegant craftsmanship (176–81, 183f.):

> . . . *extemplo* **graciles** *ex aere catenas*
> *retiaque et laqueos, quae lumina fallere possent,*
> **elimat** *(non illud* **opus tenuissima** *uincant*
> *stamina, non summo quae pendet aranea tigno),*
> *utque* **leues** *tactus momentaque* **parua** *sequantur*   180
> *efficit*
> . . .
> **arte** *uiri uinclisque* **noua** *ratione paratis*
> *in mediis ambo deprensi* **amplexibus** *haerent.*

> . . . At once he perfected graceful chains of bronze and nets and halters such as could deceive the eyes – not the finest threads that a spider hangs from the highest beam could conquer his artistry – and he made them in such a way that they would follow a slight touch and small motions . . . The pair cling together, caught in the midst of their embraces by her husband's craft and the chains prepared by his novel plan.

Leuconoë's Callimachean lexicon (highlighted in bold) confirms both Vulcan's and her own adherence, like her sister's before her, to the Alexandrian poet's exacting

---

41 Cf. e.g., *Am.* 3.15.1, 15; *Ars* 1.7, 30, 33; *F.* 4.1–8.
42 On Ovid's adaptation of *Ars* 2 in *Met.* 4, see Bömer (1976) 67–75; Rosati (2007) 270–74.
43 See, e.g., Prop. 2.29.38; Ov. *Ars* 2.367, 484.
44 On the elegiac overtones of *furta* and *furtiuus*, see *TLL* 6.1644.42–97; Pichon (1902) 158.

standard of artistic polish, which the Roman elegists espoused in their verse.[45] Moreover, her description of Vulcan's sophisticated workmanship suggestively recalls the Minyads' own arts of spinning and weaving, which they ply as they tell their tales. The first sister proposes their story-exchange while "spinning thread with her slender thumb" (*leui deducens pollice filum*, 36), in self-conscious instantiation of Callimachean stylistic ideals,[46] and she proceeds to narrate the story of Pyramus and Thisbe "spinning her wool the while." Leuconoë too spins as she speaks (167f., *et orsa est / dicere Leuconoe; uocem tenuere sorores*, "And taking up the thread, Leuconoë began to speak; her sisters checked their voices"),[47] and the same domestic setting of women weaving in their quarters, surrounded by their slave women, reappears in *mise-en-abîme* structure as her narrative proceeds (see below).

Leuconoë describes Sol burning like a callow elegiac lover for Leucothoë (194–8, 202f.):

> *nempe tuis omnes qui terras* **ignibus uris**
> **ureris igne** *nouo, quique omnia cernere* **debes**   195
> *Leucothoen spectas et uirgine figis in una*
> *quos mundo* **debes** *oculos.* **modo** *surgis Eoo*
> *temperius caelo,* **modo** *serius incidis undis*
> . . .
> *nec tibi quod lunae terris propioris imago*
> *obstiterit* **palles***; facit hunc* **amor** *iste* **colorem***.*

> Indeed you who enflame all lands with your fires are yourself enflamed by a strange new fire, and you who ought to look on all things focus on Leucothoë and fix your eyes, which you owe the world, on one maiden. Now you rise earlier in the eastern sky and sink later in the waves . . . Nor are you pale because the image of the moon, nearer the earth, obstructs you; your love makes this your complexion.

The flame of love (194f.) is conventional in the elegiac lexicon, and Leuconoë implies the elegiac provenance of the Sun's behaviour by identifying *amor* (203) as its cause. She deploys the same rhetorical figures of repetition and parallelism (highlighted in bold), characteristic of the elegiac genre, that her sister employs in 'Pyramus and Thisbe'. She also draws on elegiac conventions in her comic description of the god's unwonted paleness, for pallor marks the languishing lover of contemporary Latin amatory elegy. As Ovid instructs his male pupils in the *Ars amatoria* (1.729):[48]

---

[45] On Leuconoë's Callimacheanism, see Rosati (2007) 272f. ad 176f. On the elegists' espousal of Callimachean artistry, see Wimmel (1960); Heslin (2018).
[46] Rosati (2007) 252f., ad 4.36.
[47] Ovid plays here on the basic sense of *ordior* – "begin a web", "lay a warp" (i.e., begin to weave) – which was early extended to the absolute sense of "begin, undertake".
[48] Cited by Rosati (2007) 276 ad loc.

palleat omnis amans, hic est color aptus amanti ("Let every lover be pale; this is the complexion suitable for a lover").

Like her sister, moreover, Leuconoë focuses in her tale on the feelings and activities of her female characters, from Venus to the Sun's mistresses Clytië and Leucothoë. Thus, in her catalogue of Sol's former girlfriends (204–8), now superseded (*Leucothoe mutarum obliuia fecit*, 208), Leuconoë lingers over the continuing love felt by his spurned mistress Clytië, whose jealousy – the elegiac emotion *par excellence*[49] – motivates her finale. She also supplies a genealogy for his latest love that focuses at greater length on her mother Eurynome's beauty (209–11) than on her father Orchamus' lineage (212f.). The emphasis on Leucothoë's maternal lineage has a narrative point, moreover, since Sol gains access to her chamber by assuming the form of her mother (218–21):

> . . . *thalamos deus intrat amatos*
> *uersus in Eurynomes faciem genetricis et inter*
> *bix sex Leucothoen famulas ad lumina cernit*   220
> *leuia uersato ducentem stamina fuso.*

> . . . The god entered his beloved's chambers in the guise of her mother Eurynome, and saw Leucothoe amidst her twelve slave women at the lamplight, turning her spindle and spinning light threads.

Leucothoë's domestic setting precisely mirrors that of the narrator Leuconoë, spinning in the company of her sisters and slave women (32–5).[50] But the context also sounds a contemporary elegiac note, in its reminiscence of the setting of Lucretia's rape in Ovid's aetiological calendar poem *Fasti* (2.741–6):

> *inde cito passu petitur Lucretia. nebat:*
>   *ante **torum** calathi lanaque **mollis** erant.*
> *lumen ad **exiguum** famulae data pensa trahebant;*
>   *inter quas **tenui** sic ait ipsa sono:*
> *'mittenda est domino (nunc, nunc properate, puellae)*   745
>   *quamprimum nostra facta lacerna manu.'*

> From there they proceeded swiftly to look for Lucretia. She was spinning: baskets of soft wool stood before her couch. By the fading light, her slave women were drawing out their allotments of wool; and among them she herself, in a faint voice, spoke thus: "it must be sent to the master (now, now hurry girls), as soon as his mantle has been finished by my own hand."

Like both Leucothoë and Leuconoë, Lucretia spins in the midst of her slave women and, like Leucothoë, she spins by lamplight. Ovid draws attention to the elegiac *color* of Lucretia's rape by the application of a conventional elegiac lexicon (highlighted in

---

[49] Caston (2012).
[50] Rosati (1999).

bold) to her setting and character: Lucretia spins soft wool (*lanaque mollis, F.* 2.742) in front of her couch (*torum*, 2.742) – presumably in her chamber like Leucothoë – by weak lamplight (*lumen ad exiguum*, 2.743) and speaking in a faint voice (*tenui sono*, 2.744). The domestic, urban setting is precisely the context for the erotic trysts of contemporary elegiac poetry.

Leuconoë relates how, in just such a highly charged feminine and elegiacizing context, the Sun trades on a mother's intimacy with her daughter to dismiss Leucothoë's attendants (*Met.* 4.223–5). The god thereby gains unimpeded access to Leucothoë and overcomes her resistance (230–33), despite her fear (228–30): *pauet illa metuque / et colus et fusus digitis cecidere remissis; / ipse timor decuit.* ("She trembles with fear, and in terror dropped distaff and spindle from her limp fingers; fear itself became her"). The terror with which Leucothoë reacts to the Sun's passion, recalls that of Lucretia when confronted by Tarquin's ardor (*F.* 2.79f., *sed tremit, ut quondam stabulis deprensa relictis, / parua sub infesto cum iacet agna lupo*, "but she trembles as when a small lamb, once caught in an empty manger, lies beneath the hated wolf"). Leucothoë drops her wool working tools just as the mythical Hero does when fatigue overwhelms her, waiting for Leander (*Her.* 19.197, *stamina de digitis cecidere sopore remissis*, "and the threads fell from my fingers, limp from sleep"). Leuconoë's emphasis on Leucothoë's beauty in her fear also strikes a very elegiac note: elsewhere in his amatory poetry, Ovid describes fear enhancing the Sabine women's beauty in the eyes of their rapists (*Ars* 1.126, *et potuit multas ipse decere timor*) and Europa's in the eyes of Jove (*F.* 5.608, *et timor ipse noui causa decoris erat*).[51]

Clytië's jealousy initiates the denouement of Leuconoë's tale (4.234–7):

> **inuidit** Clytie (neque enim moderatus in illa
> Solis **amor** fuerat) stimulataque paelicis ira   235
> uulgat **adulterium** diffamatamque parenti
> indicat . . .

> Clytië was jealous, for love of the Sun still burned uncontrolled in her. Burning now with wrath at the sight of her rival, she divulged the adultery and told the girl's father of her widely known shame . . .

Leuconoë employs the conventional lexicon of Latin erotic elegy to describe Clytië acting on the twin emotions of love and envy to denounce her rival's amatory triumph as "adultery". Her 'tale-telling' is quintessentially elegiac in subject and motivation (if anti-Callimachean in expression: *uulgat . . . diffamatamque*, 236).[52] The injured parent reacts with emphatically epic anger, burying his daughter (237–40) so deeply beneath the earth that Sol is unable to revive her bloodless corpse (*corpusque*

---

51 Both cited by Rosati (2007) 278f. ad loc.
52 On the passage, see Kenney (1959) 251–3.

exsangue iacebas, 244).⁵³ But Leuconoë draws on the elegiac register again in recounting the god's extravagant mourning for his dead beloved (251, *multaque praequestus*, "lamenting much"; cf. *dolentius*, 246). Propertius characterizes his elegiac verse as *querelae*,⁵⁴ and the elegists conventionally "lament" (*queror*) their haughty mistress' cruelty.⁵⁵ Leucothoë's metamorphosis into a frankincense plant suitably memorializes the dead girl in an aetiology for one of the costly perfumes of the fabled orient (250, 252f.).⁵⁶

> *nectare odorato sparsit corpusque locumque,*
> . . .
> *protinus imbutum caelesti nectare corpus*
> *delicuit terramque suo madefecit odore.*
>
> He sprinkled her body and the ground with fragrant nectar . . . Straightway the body, soaked with the celestial nectar, melted away and filled the earth around with its sweet fragrance.

An expensive eastern import, frankincense like other oils and unguents commonly features in contemporary erotic poetry as one of the luxurious accoutrements of the love-poets' demanding mistresses.⁵⁷

In an elegiacizing coda Leuconoë reports Clytië's unhappy fate (256–9):

> *at Clytien, quamuis **amor** excusare **dolorem***
> *indiciumque **dolor** poterat, non amplius auctor*
> *lucis adit **Veneri**sque modum sibi fecit in illa.*
> ***tabuit** ex illo **dementer amoribus** usa.*
>
> But Clytie, though love could excuse her grief, and grief her tattling, was sought no more by the Sun, and he made an end of his love for her. Thereafter, her love turned to madness and she pined away.

The Minyad's amatory lexicon assimilates Clytië to an elegiac lover driven mad by grief and passion.⁵⁸ Leuconoë literalizes the elegiac trope of wasting away from passion to make Clytië the very incarnation of elegiac love *in extremis*. Elegiac madness thus underwrites her metamorphosis into a heliotrope (4.266–70):

---

53 The phrase *corpus exsangue* looks like a bathetic play on the elegiac lover's characteristic pallor.
54 Saylor (1967).
55 Cf., e.g., Tib. 2.3.9; Ov. Am. 2.17.9f.
56 On this aetiology, see Myers (1994a) 80 n. 2; for the importance of aetiological narrative in the *Metamorphoses*, and its relationship to those in the *Fasti*, see further Myers (1994a) 61–94.
57 Cf., e.g., Cat. 13; Hor. C. 1.13.15f., with Nisbet/Hubbard (1970) 176f. ad loc.
58 Rosati (2007) 282 ad 259–63, comparing Prop. 2.15.30. For the motif of the elegiac lover's madness, cf. Gallus' *Amores*, with Tränkle (1960) 22; Ross (1975) 66–8; Cairns (2006) 111–13.

> *membra ferunt haesisse solo; partemque coloris*
> *luridus **exsangues pallor** conuertit in herbas,*
> *est in parte **rubor uiolae**que simillimus ora*
> *flos tegit. illa suum, quamuis radice tenetur,*
> *uertitur ad Solem mutataque seruat **amorem**.*

> They say that her limbs grew fast to the soil and her deathly pallor changed in part to a bloodless plant; but in part it was red, and a flower, much like a violet came where her face had been. Still, though roots hold her fast, she turns ever towards the sun and, though changed herself, preserves her love unchanged.

Clytië instantiates both the pallor (*luridus pallor*, 267) and the ardor of an elegiac lover in her transformation into a "bloodless" plant (*exsangues . . . in herbas*, 267) with the heliotrope's deep purple flower (*rubor uiolaeque simillimus ora / flos tegit*, 268f.). In this way, her transformation truly "memorializes her elegiac love" (*seruat amorem*, 270). Leuconoë's word choice annotates the generic register from which she has drawn her tale (*amorem*, 270) and in which she delights her audience (*factum mirabile ceperat auris*, 271).[59] Like her sister's 'Pyramus and Thisbe', her 'Amours of the Sun' exhibit the gendered features conventionally associated with the genre of elegy, an amatory discourse frequently represented as the subject of women's narratives in the (mostly male-authored) texts of antiquity.[60] Her tales of divine lust find a particularly suggestive parallel in the succession of love stories recounted by the nymph Clymene to her sisters in Vergil's *Georgics* (4.345–7):

> ***inter quas curam** Clymene narrabat inanem*
> *Vulcani, Martisque dolos et dulcia **furta**,*
> *aque Chao densos diuum numerabat **amores**.*

> Amongst them her sister Nereids, Clymene was telling the tale of Vulcan's unrequited love, Mars' treachery and the sweet thefts of love; she was recounting the gods' frequent love affairs from Chaos on.

3 Salmacis and Hermaphroditus: Elegy and Epic

The third sister, Alcithoë, takes up the narrative thread in a final bravura performance that mirrors the first Minyad's interest in obscure myths (275–9, 284):

---

59 On the undertone of paradoxography here, cf. Myers (1994a) 147–59, on ancient literary collections of 'marvels' in relation to Ovid's Pythagoras in *Met.* 15.
60 See n. 30, above.

> *quae* **radio stantis percurrens stamina telae**
> *'uulgatos taceo' dixit 'pastoris amores*
> *Daphnidis Idaei, quem nymphe paelicis ira*
> *contulit in saxum:* **tantus dolor urit amantes**;
> *nec* **loquor**, *ut quondam*
> . . .
> *praetereo dulcique animos nouitate* **tenebo**.'

> Running her shuttle swiftly through the threads of her loom, she said: "I will pass by the well-known love of Daphnis, the shepherd-boy of Ida, whom a nymph, in anger at her rival, changed to stone: so great is the pain that burns jealous lovers. Nor will I tell how once . . . All these stories I will pass by and will charm your minds with a tale that is pleasing because new."

Ovid reiterates the wool-working context of the sisters' narratives, while Alcithoë (named at 4.274) emphasizes her twin motivations of Callimachean discrimination (276, 278f., 284) and sheer pleasure (284) in the selection of a story to share with her sisters. Her disinclination to tell the myth of Daphnis (276–8) highlights the misalignment of pastoral with the feminine domestic context in which the Minyads exchange their amatory tales, as she frames the moral of the rejected tale in the elegiac lexicon of the burning passions of love and grief (*dolor urit amantes*, 277).

Like her sisters, Alcithoë pursues an elegiac course in her narrative (285–7): *unde sit infamis, quare male fortibus undis / Salmacis eneruet tactosque remolliat artus, / discite.* ("Learn whence arose Salmacis' ill-repute and how her spring enervates with enfeebling waters and softens the limbs it touches"). She sounds another moralizing note in the imperative *discite* (287), reminiscent of Latin didactic,[61] but the verbs *eneruet* and *remolliat* (286), whose programmatic undertones evoke the genre of elegy, suggest Ovid's elegiac innovations in erotic instruction rather than the hexameter tradition of didactic. As in her sisters' tales, moreover, the presiding deity of amatory elegy makes an appearance in her introduction of Herm**aphrodit**us, "a youth born from Mercury and the goddess of Cythera" (*Mercurio puerum* **diua Cythereide** *natum*, 288). But it is Salmacis herself, the nymph of her eponymous spring, who most fully embodies elegiac convention in Alcithoë's narrative (309–14):

> *nec sua cum duris uenatibus* **otia** *miscet,*
> *sed modo fonte suo* **formosos perluit artus**,   310
> *saepe* **Cytoriaco deducit pectine crines**
> *et quid* **se deceat** *spectatas* **consulit** *undas;*
> *nunc* **perlucenti circumdata corpus amictu**
> **mollibus** *aut foliis aut* **mollibus incubat** *herbis;*

---

[61] For the didactic tone of *discite* (287), cf. Ov. *Med.* 1; *Ars* 1.50, 459; 3.298, 315, 327, 455; *Rem.* 43, and see further Gibson (2003) 218 ad 298, on Ovid's prominent use of the verb *discere* in his elegiac didactic. For the aetiological undertones in the rest of the line (*discite.* **causa** *latet, uis est notissima fontis*), see Myers (1994a) 79f.

Nor does she vary her ease with the hardships of the hunt; but at times she bathes her shapely limbs in her own pool; often combs her hair with a boxwood comb, often looks in the mirror-like waters to see what best becomes her. Now, wrapped in a transparent robe, she lies down to rest on the soft grass or the soft leaves.

Salmacis' preference for the elegiac mistress' expensive accoutrements (hair-combs and see-through clothing) and leisured pursuits (bathing and beauty culture) distinguish her from the traditional nymphs of classical myth, whose passion for the hunt she emphatically rejects (302–9). Her sensual dress recalls that of both Thisbe in the first Minyad's tale (*tenues amictus*, 104) and *Elegia* herself in *Amores* 3.1 (*uestis tenuissima*, *Am.* 3.1.11),[62] while her pleasure in reclining on programmatically "soft" surfaces (*mollibus . . . mollibus incubat, Met.* 4.314) hints at an interest in erotic dalliance that will be realized the instant she catches sight of Hermaphroditus (316): *cum puerum uidit uisumque optauit habere* ("when she saw the boy, and longed to possess what she saw"). Like a seasoned elegiac courtesan,[63] moreover, she arranges her appearance for maximum sex appeal before presenting herself to the youth (317–19):

> *nec tamen **ante** adiit, etsi properabat adire,*
> ***quam se composuit**, quam circumspexit amictus*
> *et finxit uultum et meruit formosa uideri.*

> Not yet, however, did she approach him, though she was eager to do so, before she had pulled herself together, arranging her robes, composing her countenance, and taking every pain to appear beautiful.

The care with which she completes her toilette recalls that of Corinna, the mistress who holds sway over Ovid's earliest elegiac poetry (*Am.* 2.17.9f.): *scilicet a speculi sumuntur imagine fastus, / nec nisi **compositam se prius illa uidet*** ("Indeed her arrogance arises from her image in the mirror, nor does she view herself before she's composed herself"). Indeed, in this regard, Salmacis follows an elegiac script: in the *Ars amatoria*, Ovid counsels both men (1.513–22) and women (3.129f.) to look their best when meeting a lover.

Like her first sister, who endows Thisbe with first-person discourse (148–61), Alcithoë gives Salmacis a lengthy speech (320–28), which she introduces with the same phrase as that with which Ovid introduces her sister Leuconoë's narrative (320): *tum sic orsa loqui* ("then she began to speak"; cf. 167f., quoted above). In her words, Salmacis gives full voice to importunate elegiac desire (320–28). In her admiration of Hermaphroditus' beauty and address to him as a god (320f.), she employs longstanding

---

[62] The related adjective, *perlucida*, appears only in Latin elegy, at [Tib.] 3.12.13 *purpureaque ueni perlucida palla*, "and come, shining in your fine purple cloak." For the implication that Salmacis' dress is see-through, cf. Hor. *Serm.* 1.2.101f.; Mart. 8.68.7; Sen. *Ben.* 7.9.5.

[63] Cf. the precepts of the bawds Dipsas (Ov. *Am.* 1.8) and Acanthis (Prop. 4.5), with Myers (1996).

techniques of elegiac seduction.⁶⁴ Moreover, she brazenly adapts the Homeric Odysseus' delicate flattery of Nausikaa (*Od.* 6.149–59) to blatantly erotic purpose (*Met.* 4.325–8):

> *sed longe cunctis longeque beatior illis,*
> *si qua tibi sponsa est, si quam dignabere taeda.*
> *haec tibi siue aliqua est, mea sit **furtiua uoluptas**,*
> *seu nulla est, ego sim, **thalamum**que ineamus **eundem**.*

> But far, oh far happier than all, is she if any be your promised bride, if you deem any worthy to be your wife. If there be such, let mine be stolen pleasure; if not, let me be your bride, and may we be joined in wedlock.

Her suggestion that Hermaphroditus indulge in "clandestine" pleasure with her, lays bare her interest in an illicit (i.e., elegiac) affair.⁶⁵ Even her proposal of marriage (*seu nulla est, ego sim*, 328; cf. *sponsa, taeda*, 326) looks more like a sexual proposition, as her recommendation that they "enter the same bedchamber" (328) closely recalls an Ovidian distich describing how "beautiful Semiramis and the courtesan Lais are said to have entered bedchambers" (*Am.* 1.5.11f., *qualiter **in thalamos** formosa Semiramis **isse** / dicitur et multis Lais amata uiris*). Hermaphroditus, "not recognizing elegiac love" (*nescit enim quid **amor***, 330), rejects her advances, but Salmacis persists in her demand "at least for sisterly kisses" (*poscenti nymphae sine fine sororia saltem / oscula*, 334f.).⁶⁶

Alcithoë portrays the youth succumbing to elegiac temptation in her description of him stripping to bathe in Salmacis' pool (344f.): *nec mora, temperie **blandarum** captus aquarum / **mollia** de **tenero** uelamina corpore ponit* ("Without delay, captivated by the warmth of her seductive waters, he removed his soft cloak from his tender body"). The elegiac resonances of the adjectives *blandus, mollis,* and *tener* combine to characterize Hermaphroditus as the kind of "desirable youth" (*puer delicatus*) who, alongside the "harsh mistress" (*dura puella*), constitutes the object of the elegiac poet-lover's amatory advances, in Ovid's definition of the genre's characteristic subject (*Am.* 1.1.19f.):⁶⁷
... materia est numeris leuioribus apta, / aut puer aut longas compta puella comas ("material fit for elegiac measures, either a youth or a girl adorned with long tresses").

---

64 Cf. Ov. *Am.* 3.2.60, cited by Rosati (2007) 289 ad 320–28.
65 On the sexual valence of *uoluptas*, see Adams (1982) 197f.; cf. the sexual metaphor of *furtum*, "theft", on which see Adams (1982) 167f. and, for its elegiac provenance, 224f.
66 Knox (1986) 20, notes Ovid's play elsewhere in the *Metamorphoses* on "the amatory associations of *nosco* and *cognosco*"; cf. *ibid.* 25 n. 53. He also discusses (*ibid.* 41) the elegiac background, in Ovid's use of *denegat* in this passage, of his portrait of Hermaphroditus as "a reluctant lover".
67 Cf., e.g., Marathus in Tib. 1.4, 8, 9 vs. Delia in Tib. 1.1, 2, 5, 6. The gendered pair are already visible in Catullan lyric and elegy under the names Juventius (*c.* 24, 48, 81, 99) and Lesbia (*c.* 5, 7, 43, 51, 58, 72, 75, 79, 83, 86, 87, 92, 107).

The sight further inflames Salmacis' lust, until she can scarcely contain her desire (346f., 350f.):

> tum uero **placuit**, nudaeque **cupidine** formae
> Salmacis **exarsit**; **flagrant** quoque lumina nymphae
> . . .
> uixque moram patitur, uix iam sua **gaudia** differt,　　　350
> iam cupit **amplecti**, iam se male continet **amens**.

> Then indeed he pleased her, and Salmacis burned with desire for his naked body; the nymph's eyes blazed too . . . She can hardly bear the delay, now she can hardly postpone her joys, now she wants to embrace him, now she barely contains herself, mad with desire.

The nymph displays the conventional symptoms of elegiac love – lust (346, 351), impatience (350), and erotic madness (351) – described by Alcithoë in the familiar lexicon of the genre's figures and tropes (burning, madness).[68] Of particular interest is the Minyad's emphasis on Salmacis' "pleasure" (*placuit*, 346) at seeing Hermaphroditus naked, which recalls the pleasure both Alcithoë and her sister aim to give their audience (*dulcique animos nouitate tenebo*, 234; *hoc placuit*, 54). While the pleasures of storytelling ostensibly motivate the Minyads, the erotic themes of their tales hint at their own stereotypically feminine interest in illicit desire.

Alcithoë's tale unfolds in elegiac language and erotic imagery to a conclusion that overturns generic conventions. Salmacis dives into her pool after Hermaphroditus to embrace him but struggles to kiss him, in a parody of elegiac lovemaking (358): *pugnantemque tenet luctantiaque oscula carpit* ("she holds him as he struggles and snatches kisses from him"). The verbs *luctor*, "struggle" (Prop. 2.1.13, 2.15.5), and *pugno*, "fight" (Tib. 1.1.75f., 1.4.53f.; Ov. *Am.* 1.5.13f., *Ars* 1.665), belong to the elegiac lexicon of *militia amoris* (*Am.* 1.9.1) and conventionally describe the consummation of the elegiac affair, which may begin with snatched kisses (cf. Ov. *Am.* 2.4.26). But Salmacis' elegiac script is frustrated when "Hermaphroditus persists in denying the nymph the erotic satisfaction she hopes for" (*Met.* 4.368f., *perstat Atlantiades sperataque* **gaudia** *nymphae / denegat*). As J. N. Adams delicately puts it, "*gaudium* . . . commonly [has] a sexual implication",[69] and Salmacis seems to achieve her desire, "when their limbs come together in a clinging embrace" (377, *ubi* **complexu coierunt** *membra tenaci*). The clinging embrace is an elegiac ideal, travestied earlier in Leuconoë's account of Vulcan's entrapment of Mars and Venus (184).

But Alcithoë thoroughly perverts elegiac principle in her description of the pair's transformation into "a double form, such that can be called neither woman nor youth, and seems neither and both" (378f., *forma duplex, nec femina dici / nec*

---

68 For the Gallan provenance of *exarsit* (4.347), see Cairns (2006) 101f. On love's figures and tropes, see Kennedy (1993) 46–63.
69 Adams (1982) 197f., citing Ov. *Am.* 3.7.63.

puer ut possit, neutrumque et utrumque uidentur). Hermaphroditus' concluding wish, that "any man who enters the spring leave it emasculated, suddenly made soft by her waters' touch" (385f., *quisquis in hos fontes uir uenerit, exeat inde / **semi-uir** et tactis subito **mollescat** in undis*), provides an aetiology for the spring's enervating effect that literalizes the elegiac lexicon Alcithoë employs throughout her tale. Her final words confirm the tale's generic alignment with elegy (388): *et incesto fontem medicamine tinxit* ("And his parents touched the spring with an unclean drug"). The drug with which the gods infect Salmacis' pool is no "remedy" for love, but rather a substance that promotes the unchaste sexual relations celebrated in contemporary elegiac verse. In this regard, it mimics the genre of elegy itself, which conventionally canvases various "cures for love" (*remedia/medicina amoris*)[70] but attracts an audience eager to learn about illicit love affairs (*amores*, Prop. 2.1.1f.; *turpis liber*, 2.3.3f.; *nequitia*, Ov. Am. 2.1.1f.).

The stories the sisters exchange as they weave exhibit manifold points of contact in their subtle adaptations of one another's elegiac themes, settings, symbolism, and imagery, which produce an intricate web of connections between the inset tales and their gendered frame. In their tales of failed romance and elegiac trysts, the sisters overtly reject Bacchus' rites and the sexual immorality associated with them, while adapting the elegiac theme of illicit love in a manner calculated to appeal to a female audience. Female characters take the lead in all three of the Minyads' narratives: bold Thisbe, vindictive Venus and Clytië, and seductive Salmacis. Like their characters, moreover, who pursue love at all costs, the Minyads are motivated by the pleasure of (hearing) love (stories). In this, they, like their characters, lend credence to the popular view of women's interest in the amatory fictions of romance and, especially, in the first-person discourse of elegiac poetry.

Bibliography

Texts and translations

Ovid, *Amores II*, ed. Joan Booth, Warminster UK 1991.
Ovid, *Amores*, 3 vols., ed. J. C. McKeown, Leeds 1987–1998.
Ovid, *Ars amatoria* Book 3, ed. Roy K. Gibson, Cambridge 2003.
P. Ovidi Nasonis *Metamorphoses*, ed. Richard J. Tarrant, Oxford 2004.
Ovid, *Metamorphosen*, Buch IV–V, ed. Franz Bömer, Heidelberg 1976.
Ovid, *Metamorfosi*, Volume II, Libri III–IV, ed. Gianpiero Rosati, Rome/Milan 2007.

---

70 On *medicina furoris* as a Gallan complex, see Tränkle (1960) 22f.; Ross (1975) 67f., 91; Cairns (2006) 100f., 111–13, 134, 140f., 144, 160, 162; cf. Knox (1986) 15–17, on Ovid's use of the complex in the *Metamorphoses*.

Ovid, *Metamorphoses* Books 1–8, with an English translation by Frank J. Miller, revised by G.P. Goold, Cambridge, MA/London ³1977.
Seneca the Elder, *Declamations*, 2 vols., with an English translation by M. Winterbottom, Cambridge, MA/London 2014.

Books and articles

Adams (1982): James N. Adams, *The Latin Sexual Vocabulary*, Baltimore.
Ahl (1985): Frederick M. Ahl, *Metaformations*, Ithaca/London.
Barchiesi (2001): Alessandro Barchiesi, *Speaking Volumes: Narrative and Intertext in Ovid and Other Latin Poets*, London.
Cairns (2006): Francis Cairns, *Sextus Propertius, the Augustan Elegist*, Cambridge.
Caston (2012): Ruth Rothaus Caston, *The Elegiac Passion: Jealousy in Roman Love Elegy*, Oxford.
Dalzell (1955): Alexander Dalzell, "C. Asinius Pollio and the Early History of Public Recitation at Rome", *Hermathena* 86, 20–28.
Due (1974): Otto Steen Due, *Changing Forms*, Copenhagen.
Duke (1971): T.T. Duke, "Ovid's Pyramus and Thisbe", *CJ* 66, 320–327.
Edwards (1993): Catharine Edwards, *The Politics of Immorality in Ancient Rome*, Cambridge.
Egger (1999): Brigitte Egger, "The Role of Women in the Greek Novel", in: Simon Swain (ed.), *Oxford Readings in the Greek Novel*, Oxford, 108–137.
Gleason (1995): Maud W. Gleason, *Making Men: Sophists and Self-Presentation in Ancient Rome*, Princeton, NJ.
Gunderson (2003): Erik Gunderson, *Declamation, Paternity, and Roman Identity: Authority and the Rhetorical Self*, Cambridge.
Hägg (1983): Tomas Hägg, *The Novel in Antiquity*, Oxford.
Haynes (2003): Katharine Haynes, *Fashioning the Feminine in the Greek Novel*, London.
Henderson (1990): John Henderson, "A Turn-up for the Books: Yes, it's . . . Ovid's *Metamorphoses*", *Omnibus* 19, 15–20.
Heslin (2018): Peter J. Heslin, *Propertius, Greek Myth, and Virgil: Rivalry, Allegory, and Polemic*, Oxford.
Holzberg (1988): Niklas Holzberg, "Ovids Babyloniaka", *WS* 101, 265–277.
James (2003): Sharon L. James, *Learned Girls and Male Persuasion: Gender and Reading in Roman Love Elegy*, Berkeley.
Janan (1994): Micaela W. Janan, "'There Beneath the Roman Ruin Where the Purple Flowers Grow': Ovid's Minyeides and the Feminine Imagination", *AJP* 115, 427–448.
Keith (1992): Alison M. Keith, *The Play of Fictions*, Ann Arbor, MI.
Keith (1999): Alison M. Keith, "Versions of Epic Masculinity in Ovid's *Metamorphoses*", in: Philip Hardie, Alessandro Barchiesi and Stephen Hinds (eds.), *Ovid's Transformations. Essays on the Metamorphoses and its Reception*, Cambridge, 214–239.
Keith (2001): Alison M. Keith, "Etymological Wordplay in Ovid's 'Pyramus and Thisbe' (*Met.* 4.55–166)", *CQ* 51, 309–312.
Keith (2010): Alison M. Keith, "Tragic Themes and Allusions in Ovid, *Metamorphoses* 4", in: Ingo Gildenhard and Martin Revermann (eds.), *Beyond the Fifth Century: Interactions with Greek Tragedy from the Fourth Century BCE to the Middle Ages*, Berlin, 181–211.
Keith (2011): Alison M. Keith (ed.), *Latin Elegy and Hellenistic Epigram*, Newcastle.
Keith (2012a): Alison M. Keith, "The *Domina* in Roman Elegy", in: Barbara K. Gold (ed.), *A Companion to Roman Love Elegy*, Malden, MA, 285–302.

Keith (2012b): Alison M. Keith, "Women in Augustan Literature", in: Sharon L. James and Sheila Dillon (eds.), *A Companion to Women in the Ancient World*, Malden, MA, 385–399.

Keith (2016): Alison M. Keith, "Ovidian Itineraries in Flavian Epic", in: Laurel Fulkerson and Tim Stover (eds.), *Repeat Performances: Ovidian Repetition and the Metamorphoses*, Madison, WI, 196–224.

Kennedy (1993): Duncan F. Kennedy, *The Arts of Love*, Cambridge.

Kenney (1959): Edward J. Kenney, "Notes on Ovid: II", *CQ* 9, 240–260.

Knox (1986): Peter E. Knox, *Ovid's Metamorphoses and the Traditions of Augustan Poetry*, Cambridge.

Konstan (1994): David Konstan, *Sexual Symmetry*, Princeton.

Lateiner (1984): Donald Lateiner, "Mythic and Non-Mythic Artists in Ovid's Metamorphoses", *Ramus* 13, 1–30.

Leach (1974): Eleanor W. Leach, "Ekphrasis and the Theme of Artistic Failure in Ovid's Metamorphoses", *Ramus* 3, 102–141.

Lefkowitz (1991): Mary R. Lefkowitz, "Did Ancient Women Write Novels?", in: Amy-Jill Levine (ed.), *'Women Like This': new perspectives on Jewish women in the Greco-Roman world*, Atlanta, GA, 199–219.

Maltby (1991): Robert Maltby, *A Lexicon of Ancient Latin Etymologies*, Leeds.

Miller (2013): Paul Allen Miller, "The *puella*: accept no substitutions!", in: Thea S. Thorsen (ed.), *The Cambridge Companion to Latin Love Elegy*, Cambridge, 166–179.

Montague (1992): Holly Montague, "Sweet and Pleasant Passion: Female and Male Fantasy in Ancient Romance Novels", in: Amy Richlin (ed.), *Pornography and Representation in Greece and Rome*, Oxford, 231–249.

Myers (1994a): K. Sara Myers, *Ovid's Causes*, Ann Arbor, MI.

Myers (1994b): K. Sara Myers, "*Ultimus Ardor*: Pomona and Vertumnus in Ovid's *Met.* 14.623–771", *CJ* 89, 225–250.

Myers (1996): K. Sara Myers, "The Poet and the Procuress: The *Lena* in Latin Love Elegy", *JRS* 86, 1–21.

Nagle (1988a): Betty R. Nagle, "A Trio of Love-triangles in Ovid's Metamorphoses", *Arethusa* 25, 11–31.

Nagle (1988b): Betty R. Nagle, "Erotic Pursuit and Narrative Seduction in Ovid's Metamorphoses", *Ramus* 17, 32–51.

Nagle (1988c): Betty R. Nagle, "Ovid's Metamorphoses: A Narratological Catalogue", *Syllecta Classica* 1, 97–125.

Newlands (1986): Carole Newlands, "The Simile of the Fractured Pipe in Ovid's Metamorphoses 4", *Ramus* 15.2, 143–153.

Nicoll (1980): W.S.M. Nicoll, "Cupid, Apollo, and Daphne (Ovid, *Met.* 1.452ff.)", *CQ* 30, 174–182.

Nisbet/Hubbard (1970): R. G. M. Nisbet and M. Hubbard, *A Commentary on Horace Odes, Book I*, Oxford.

Nugent (1990): S. Georgia Nugent, "This Sex Which Is Not One: De-Constructing Ovid's Hermaphrodite", *differences* 2.1, 160–185.

Papaioannou (2005): Sophia Papaioannou, *Epic Succession and Dissension: Ovid, Metamorphoses 13.623–14.582, and the Reinvention of the Aeneid*, Berlin.

Papaioannou (2007): Sophia Papaioannou, *Redesigning Achilles: "Recycling" the Epic Cycle in the "Little Iliad" (Ovid, Metamorphoses 12.1–13.622)*, Berlin.

Papanghelis (1987): Theodore D. Papanghelis, *Propertius: A Hellenistic Poet on Love and Death*, Cambridge.

Perry (1967): Ben Edwin Perry, *The Ancient Romances: A Literary Historical Account of their Origins*, Berkeley.

Pervo (1991): Richard I. Pervo, "Aseneth and her Sisters: Women in Jewish Narrative and in the Greek Novels", in: Amy-Jill Levine (ed.), *'Women Like This': new perspectives on Jewish women in the Greco-Roman world*, Atlanta, GA, 145–160.

Pichon (1902): René Pichon, *Index uerborum amatoriorum de sermone amatorio apud Latinos elegiarum scriptores*, Paris.

Pietropaolo (2014): Mariapia Pietropaolo, "Metamorphic Composition in Ovid's Treatment of Salmacis and Hermaphroditus", *Mouseion* 11, 279–294.

Platnauer (1951): Maurice Platnauer, *Latin Elegiac Verse: A Study of the Metrical Usages of Tibullus, Propertius & Ovid*, Cambridge.

Ramsby (2007): Teresa R. Ramsby, *Textual Permanence: Roman Elegists and the Epigraphic Tradition*, London.

Reardon (1989): Bryan P. Reardon, *Collected Ancient Greek Novels*, Berkeley.

Renner (1981): Timothy Renner, "A Composition Concerning Pamphilus and Eurydice", in: Roger S. Bagnall (ed.), *Proceedings of the XVI Congress of Papyrology*, Chico, CA, 93–101.

Rhorer (1980): Catherine Campbell Rhorer, "Red and White in Ovid's *Metamorphoses*: the Mulberry Tree in the Tale of Pyramus and Thisbe", *Ramus* 9, 79–88.

Robinson (1999): M. Robinson, "Salmacis and Hermaphroditus: when two become one (Ovid, *Met.* 4.285–388)", *CQ* 49, 212–223.

Rosati (1999): Gianpiero Rosati, "Form in Motion: Weaving the Text in the *Metamorphoses*", in: Philip Hardie, Alessandro Barchiesi and Stephen Hinds (eds.), *Ovid's Transformations. Essays on the Metamorphoses and its Reception*, Cambridge, 240–253.

Rosati (2002): Gianpiero Rosati, "Narrative Techniques and Narrative Structures in the *Metamorphoses*", in: Barbara Weiden Boyd (ed.), *Brill's Companion to Ovid*, Leiden, 271–304.

Ross (1975): David O. Ross, Jr., *Backgrounds to Augustan Poetry: Gallus, Elegy, and Rome*, Cambridge.

Sandy (1994): Gerald Sandy, "New Pages of Greek Fiction", in: John R. Morgan and Richard Stoneman (eds.), *Greek Fiction*, London, 130–145.

Saylor (1967): Charles Saylor, "*Querelae*: Propertius' Distinctive Technical Name for his Elegy", *ΑΓΩΝ*, 142–147.

Sharrock (1991): Alison R. Sharrock, "Womanufacture", *JRS* 81, 36–49.

Tränkle (1960): Hermann Tränkle, *Die Sprachkunst des Properz und die Tradition der Lateinischen Dichtersprache*, Wiesbaden.

Wheeler (1999): Stephen Michael Wheeler, *A Discourse of Wonders*, Philadelphia.

Whitmarsh (2005): Tim Whitmarsh, "The Greek Novel: Titles and Genre", *AJP* 126, 587–611.

Wimmel (1960): Walter Wimmel, *Kallimachos in Rom. Die Nachfolge seines apologetischen Dichtens in der Augusteerzeit*, Wiesbaden.

Wyke (2002): Maria Wyke, *The Roman Mistress. Ancient and Modern Representations*, Oxford.

VI The Gendered 'I' in the Poetry of Late Antiquity

Henriette Harich-Schwarzbauer

In den Wind gesprochen – Die Ich-Reden der Ceres in Claudians *De raptu Proserpinae*

Abstract: Claudian is famous for the considerable number of I-speeches of the *personae* in his panegyrics; most of these speeches are delivered either by male speakers or female personifications. Interestingly, in Claudian's mythological epic *De raptu Proserpinae*, Ceres holds the record with six speeches. The proliferation of I-speeches by the female deity seems to be a clue for gendering these speeches, especially when compared to the Ovidian pretexts on the rape of Proserpine in the *Metamorphoses* and *Fasti*. The more her "I" is stressed, the more Ceres seems to lose her authority and to preach to the winds. A close reading of Ceres' speeches, compared to those of Iupiter, the nurse Electra and the complaints of Proserpina, will bring to the fore the fundamental chance in the character of Ceres, who gradually loses authority and undergoes a metamorphosis becoming a 'Rabenmutter'.

Keywords: Claudian, rape of Proserpine, Ceres, female 'i', loss of authority

1 Einleitung

In Claudians vermeintlich unvollendetem Poem *De raptu Proserpinae*[1] sticht die Gestalt der Ceres hervor. Sie ist die eigentlich tragische Figur des Gedichts. Sie ignoriert, dass ihre Tochter ins heiratsfähige Alter gelangt und nicht ihr uneingeschränkter 'Besitz' ist. Mit ihren Reden trägt Ceres den daraus resultierenden Konflikt mit Jupiter und den Olympiern, mit der Tochter und damit zugleich auch mit der kosmischen Ordnung aus. Ceres nimmt mit insgesamt sechs Reden die erste Stelle unter den Redenden ein. Proserpina hingegen spricht bloß zweimal. Weitere Protagonisten des Gedichts, beginnend bei Jupiter, über Pluto, Venus, Pallas Athena, die Parze Lachesis, Natura sowie den personifizierten Aetna,[2] bleiben hinsichtlich ihres Umgangs und der Gesamtzahl ihrer Reden deutlich hinter Ceres zurück. Auffällig wortreich ist indes nur noch der Redebeitrag der Amme Electra. Die dicht gesetzten Reden in *DRP* stellen eine der wesentlichen Modifikationen zu den Ceres-Erzählungen bei Ovid dar.[3] Sie

---

[1] Nachfolgend abgekürzt *DRP*. Der Frage der Unabgeschlossenheit des Kleinepos – dazu bereits Wheeler (1995) 113, mit neuen Argumenten Schirner (2017) 16 und Klebs (2019) 179 – wird hier nicht weiter nachgegangen.
[2] Analysen der Reden nach Genderkriterien fehlen für *DRP* weitgehend. Zur Rede des Aetna s. Lämmle und Scheidegger Lämmle (2017) 25 f.
[3] Zu Proserpina (Kore) als „mythological imaginery" in der weiblichen Rede (Antigone) s. Moro in diesem Band.

steuern die Mythentransformation, allen voran zu nennen sind die Reden der Ceres. In den *Metamorphosen* spricht Ceres bloß einmal,[4] während Proserpina gänzlich stumm bleibt. In den *Fasti* beschränkt sich der Redeanteil der Ceres auf Interjektionen und kurze klagende Fragen, Proserpina bleibt erneut stumm.[5]

Claudian geht es, wie gezeigt werden soll, um spezifische Ausdifferenzierungen des Mythos, welche durch die zahlreichen Ich-Reden der Ceres in einem überaus bekannten und in verschiedenen literarischen Genera von Ovid erzählten Mythos getroffen werden.[6] Mit dem Blick auf diese Ausdifferenzierungen werde ich mich im Rahmen von grundlegenden Annahmen der Narratologie bewegen. Ausgehend von Prämissen der Erzähltheorie, wie sie von Gérard Genette entwickelt wurde,[7] soll es darum gehen zu sichten, welche Tendenz und welche Dynamik das Epyllion im Vergleich mit den ovidianischen Prätexten nimmt, sobald nicht eine außenstehende Erzählinstanz über Ceres, sondern Ceres selbst mit ihrem Ich spricht. Es handelt sich also, um mit Genette zu sprechen, darum zu analysieren, was die „Erzählung von Worten" zu leisten imstande ist. Wirkt sich das Umschalten auf den dramatischen Modus genderspezifisch aus, wie wird die Unmittelbarkeit der Ich-Reden gesteuert, stellt die Erzähldistanz mit den Ich-Reden Distanz zur Erzählfigur her? Spezifisch für *DRP* ist schließlich – Genette ergänzend – zu fragen, welche Konsequenzen sich für die Erzählung aus dem fortgesetzten Wechsel der „Erzählung von Worten" und dem nahezu Innehalten, also der extremen Verlangsamung des Erzähltempos durch die Ceres-Reden, und das Formen einer weiblichen Rede ergeben?[8]

In meinem Beitrag werde ich also die Formung der Ich-Reden der Göttin in den Mittelpunkt stellen. Ausgehen möchte ich von der Überlegung, dass diese Reden in

---

4 Ov. *met.* 5,514–522, an die Adresse Jupiters. Dessen Replik folgt dort unmittelbar (5,523–532).
5 Ov. *fast.* 4,448 f.: Hilferufe der Proserpina an ihre Mutter; 456 und 483: Rufe der Ceres. Zur Relevanz von generischen Normen wie auch deren Inkonsistenz in Ovids Proserpina-Raubversionen s. Hinds (1987) 117–127, für den die generische Form (elegisches Distichon) mit der *querimonia* korrespondiert. In *DRP* spricht Ceres hingegen nicht nur als klagende Mutter. Ihre Reden reichen von epischer Höhe ‚hinunter' zur elegischen Klage.
6 Zum Proserpina-Mythos bei Ovid s. Hinds (1987); zur literarischen Rezeption des Proserpina-Mythos, die vom Hymnus auf Demeter ausgehend über Ovid und Claudian bis zu Elfriede Jelinek führt, Klebs (2019).
7 Genettes Beitrag zur Erzähltheorie (Genette 2010), die er in mehreren Etappen (mit Präzisierungen, Korrekturen und Ergänzungen) anhand der großen Erzählformen Roman und Epos – wobei er auf die Antike ausgreifend vor allem Homer berücksichtigte – entwickelte, ist offen genug, um auf Claudians Epyllion angewendet zu werden.
8 Ich beziehe mich für meine Beobachtungen auf Genette (2010) Kap. II (Neuer Diskurs der Erzählung), insb. 199–201, in dem sich der Verf. mit kritischen Stimmen zu seiner Erzähltheorie auseinandersetzt und diese produktiv verarbeitet. Insbesondere geht es mir dabei um die modale Kategorie „Distanz", mit deren Hilfe die quantitative Modulation (wieviel narrative Information?) und mit ihr die qualitative Modulation (über welchen Kanal?) unter dem Begriff der Perspektive reflektiert werden.

DRP ihrer Funktion entsprechend (z. B. Klage, Überredung) je anders akzentuiert werden. Zu beobachten wird sein, ob und wie das Ich in den Reden der Ceres konstruiert wird, wie häufig dieses Ich sich zeigt, und vor allem, worin sich, wenn dem so ist, ein spezifisch weibliches Ich in den Reden der Ceres manifestiert. Das mythologische Kleinepos bietet sich für eine Analyse vorzüglich an, da die Reden in *DRP* in einem relativ engen Rahmen auf verschiedene Personen in unterschiedlichen hierarchischen Positionen verteilt sind. Somit ist zum einen der Vergleich der Reden der Ceres an unterschiedliche Adressaten instruktiv, darunter ihre Rede an die sozial unterstellte Amme, aber auch die Rede an den allmächtigen Göttervater Jupiter, der zugleich der Vater der Proserpina ist. Zum andern gibt es mehrere weibliche Sprecherinnen, es sind Göttinnen, dann Proserpina wie auch die bereits erwähnte Amme Electra. Betrachtet man Claudians Œuvre in seiner Gesamtheit, so ist festzuhalten, dass die weibliche Rede in seiner Panegyrik und seinen historischen Epen weitgehend auf personifizierte Mächte beschränkt[9] und insgesamt unterrepräsentiert ist. Die Reden der Ceres können also darüber Aufschluss geben, ob der Dichter in *DRP* eine spezifische Sensibilität für die weibliche Rede erkennen lässt.[10]

2 Die Ich-Reden der Ceres

Ceres ergreift in *DRP* insgesamt sechsmal das Wort:[11]

> Abschiedsworte an Sizilien (1,194–200)
> Fragen an Proserpina (3,92–96)
> Abschiedsworte an Cybele (3,114–133)
> Scheltrede an Electra (3,179–192)
> Anklage der Olympier (3,270–291; 295–329)
> Selbstanklage gegenüber Proserpina (3,407–437)

Ihre Reden beleuchten die Situation der Göttin, die ihre Macht über die Tochter und zugleich die Tochter durch deren Vermählung mit Pluto verliert.[12] An Ceres' Situation werden Geschlechterverhältnisse thematisiert, wobei gleich mehrere Facetten der

---

9 So z. B. die Rede der *Roma* (28–127) und der *Africa* (139–200) im Epos *In Gildonem*. Zu den Gender-Markern dieser Personifikationen vgl. Harich-Schwarzbauer (2021) 256 f. Weibliche Personen der Historie (allen voran Serena) treten bei Claudian nicht mit Ich-Reden hervor.
10 In den Paratexten von *DRP* (Praefationes und Prooemium) spricht ein lyrisches Ich, welches in meinem Beitrag aber nicht berücksichtigt werden soll. Dazu, wie zu den Paratexten der Panegyrik Claudians, vgl. Felgentreu (1999).
11 Kellner (1997) 139–192 legt eine Übersicht und Interpretation aller Ceres Reden vor. Er betrachtet vor allem die rhetorische Durchführung und die argumentative Schlüssigkeit der Reden.
12 Klebs (2019) 179 bringt es auf den Punkt: „Sie wird zu einer von Trauer und Zorn überwältigten, sich zur Furie wandelnden Figur", die „gegenüber dem patrilinear fundierten Bündnis zwischen Ober- und Unterwelt machtlos bleibt."

Mutter-Rolle infrage gestellt werden.[13] Der Redeanteil der Ceres ist in *DRP*, wie oben erwähnt, der höchste. Der Umfang von Proserpinas Reden fällt vergleichsweise deutlich geringer aus. Nach ihren kurzen Hilferufen an Minerva und Diana (1,204 f.) ergreift sie nur zweimal das Wort. Nach ihrer Klage beim Raub, die sie an Jupiter und Ceres richtet (1,250–272), antwortet sie knapp auf die Klagen der Mutter in dem Traumgesicht, das Ceres erscheint (3,97–108). Dort tadelt sie die Unbekümmertheit der Mutter, die den Raub überhaupt erst ermöglicht habe. Ihre Hochzeit begleitet sie später nur noch wortlos mit Gesang (2,367–372), so wie sie mit Gesang ins Epyllion eingeführt wurde (1,246). Claudian entwickelt in der Erzählung ein Motiv, das in früheren Mythenvarianten fehlte: das von Jupiter oktroyierte Schweigegebot um das Verschwinden der Proserpina, das mit Bestrafung sanktioniert werden soll (3,55–65). Dieser Zwang zum Schweigen betrifft alle Personen, die über den Verbleib der Cerestochter wissen. Angesichts dieses bedrohlichen Schweigens kommt den Reden der Ceres überproportional Gewicht zu.

2.1 Ceres' Abschiedsworte an Sizilien (1,194–200)

Ceres spricht ein hymnisches Lob Siziliens, bevor sie nach Phrygien aufbricht. Doch schon da quälen sie Vorahnungen. Dennoch agiert sie als Göttin, die kraft ihrer (vermeintlich intakten) göttlichen Machtfülle der Insel verspricht, ihr ewigen Frühling zu schenken, wenn Sizilien ihre Tochter vor Übergriffen schützt. Ihrem Status entsprechend und um ihre Dignität zu demonstrieren, greift Ceres, so sie über sich dank ihrer Autorität als Göttin spricht, überwiegend zum majestätischen Plural „wir". Eine geschlechtsspezifische Differenzierung dieses „wir" ist nicht ablesbar. Indes scheint der Wechsel zum „ich" (*commendo*)[14] ein Indiz dafür zu sein, dass ein Gender-Moment hinzutritt, sobald die Göttin auf ihre Funktion als Gebärerin verweist (1,194–196):[15]

> *salve, gratissima tellus,*
> *quam nos praetulimus caelo: tibi gaudia nostri*
> *sanguinis et caros uteri commendo labores.*[16]

Leb' wohl, liebste Erde, die ich dem Himmel vorgezogen habe. Dir vertraue ich die Freuden meines Blutes an, dir die mir lieben Mühen meines Leibes.[17]

---

13 Zu den Facetten der Mutter-Rolle der Ceres aus genderspezifischer Perspektive s. Klebs (2019). Auf die Reden geht Klebs nicht eigens ein.
14 Die Begründung *metri causa* für den Wechsel zwischen Singular und Plural ist bei Beobachtungen zu den Ich-Reden der Ceres nie gänzlich auszuschließen. Sie soll jedoch bei meinen Überlegungen nicht vorrangig die Argumentation lenken.
15 Nicht so in Ov. *met.* 5,517, als sich Ceres an Jupiter wendet: *quod nostro est edita partu*.
16 Text: Hall (1985) mit vereinzelten Modifikationen bei der Interpunktion.
17 Übersetzungen: Harich-Schwarzbauer.

2.2 Ceres' Fragen an Proserpina (3,92–96)

Nachdem ihr die Tochter in einem schrecklichen Traumgesicht begegnet war, in Ketten gelegt, schmutzig und abgemagert, richtet Ceres, tief erschüttert, das Wort an Proserpina (3,92–96):

> . . 'cuius tui poenae criminis?', inquit:
> 'unde haec informis macies? cui tanta potestas
> in me saevitiae? rigidi cur vincula ferri
> vix aptanda feris molles meruere lacerti ?
> tu mea, tu proles? an fallimur umbra ?'

„Für welches Verbrechen eine solch große Strafe?" sprach sie, „Woher diese entstellende Ausgezehrtheit? Wer besitzt solche Macht zu Grausamkeit gegen mich? Weshalb verdienten zarte Arme die Fesseln harten Eisens, die man kaum wilden Tieren umlegen könnte? Bist du es, bist du es mein Kind? Oder täuscht mich ein Traum?"

Die Situation hat sich mit dem dritten Gesang merklich gewandelt. Ceres tritt plötzlich nicht mehr als selbstbewusste Göttin auf, die auf ihre göttliche Macht rekurrieren würde, Fruchtbarkeit zu gewähren. Im zweiten Gesang war Ceres – ihrer Absenz bei Cybele in Phrygien geschuldet – gänzlich abwesend. Die Erzählinstanz fokussierte ausschließlich auf das Verhältnis von Proserpina und Pluto, auf die Ängste der jungen Frau vor der Hochzeit, auf Plutos keimendes Begehren – es wird als *amor* bezeichnet –, womit sich die lastende Atmosphäre nach dem Raub plötzlich ins Positive zu wenden beginnt. In Konsequenz zu diesem Stimmungswandel zelebriert die Unterwelt die Hochzeit freudig und ausgelassen. Demgegenüber schlägt Ceres nun durch ein Traumgesicht der Tochter erschreckt dunkle und furchterregende Töne an. Es ist übrigens das einzige Mal, dass Ceres das Gespräch mit Proserpina aufnimmt, und dies zudem noch vermittelt, da sie ihr nicht physisch von Angesicht zu Angesicht gegenübersteht. Angst beherrscht die Göttin, ihre Unsicherheit ob des Realitätsgehalts des Traumes lässt sie zweifelnd fragen.[18] Ihre Ich-Position kehrt Ceres nun stärker hervor. Ihr *me* in prominenter Versposition (3,95), welches zudem mithilfe eines Hyperbatons hervorgehoben wird, legt nahe, dass ihr die entsetzliche Traumbotschaft ihre problematische Position als Mutter plötzlich drastisch vor Augen führt. Unterschwellig drängt sich ihr der Gedanke auf, dass sie mit Jupiter als dem Kindesvater, nunmehr ihrem Gegner, konfrontiert ist. Dieser Ahnung gibt sie Nahrung, wenn sie ihren ‚Besitz' infrage stellt: *tu mea, tu proles?* Das Ich der Ceres wird durch das doppelte *tu* ein-

---

18 3,132: *ah vereor, ne quid protendant omina veri*. Der Status des Traums zwischen Realität, Prophetie und Lüge wurde in der Spätantike eifrig diskutiert. Dazu allgemein Cox-Miller (1994), die jedoch die Träume in der spätantiken Dichtung allgemein, so auch den Ceres-Traum in DRP, in ihre Studie nicht einbezieht. Ein Reflex auf das Vermögen von Träumen ist an dieser Stelle nicht auszuschließen. Die Feststellung, dass Claudian auf epische Prätexte anspielt, steht dem nicht entgegen. Zu epischen Prätexten z. B. Charlet (1991) 167 f. ad loc.; Gruzelier (1993) ad loc.

gerahmt und betont wie kein zweites Mal. Offener hingegen nimmt sich das unmittelbar folgende „wir" (*fallimur*) aus, mit dem ein allgemeineres Problem, der Wahrheitsgehalt von Träumen, angesprochen wird.

2.3 Ceres' Abschiedsworte an Cybele (3,114–133)

Erst die Anschuldigungen der Tochter lassen Ceres die Tragweite der Ereignisse und ihr Versäumnis erkennen. Wenngleich sie den Wahrheitsgehalt der Traumerscheinung leugnet, kündigt sie Cybele ihren Abschied unvermittelt an. Aus ihren Worten spricht das Ich einer Göttin, die affektgeleitet (3,112: *amens prosilit*) auf Vorwürfe ihrer Tochter reagiert.[19] Mit ihrer Rede beginnt sie das Geschehene allmählich zu realisieren und endet damit, sich folgenträchtige Fehler einzugestehen (3,114–123; 130–133):

'*iam non ulterius Phrygia tellure morabor,*
sancta parens; revocat tandem custodia cari 115
pignoris et cunctis obiecti fraudibus anni.
nec mihi, Cyclopum quamvis exstructa caminis,
culmina fida satis. timeo ne fama latebras
prodiderit leviusque meum Trinacria celet
depositum. terret nimium vulgata locorum 120
nobilitas. aliis sedes obscurior oris
exquirenda mihi. gemitu flammisque propinquis
Enceladi nequeunt umbracula nostra taceri.
. . .
si buxus inflare velim, ferale gemiscunt, 130
tympana si quatiam, planctus mihi tympana reddunt.
ah vereor, ne quid portendant omina veri!
ah longae nocuere morae!'

„Nicht länger werde ich auf phrygischem Boden verbleiben, verehrte Mutter. Es ruft mich nun doch die Bewachung meiner lieben Tochter zurück, die all den Täuschungen ihrer Jugend ausgesetzt ist. Nicht sind mir die Dachfirste verlässlich genug, selbst wenn sie in von den Feuerstellen der Kyklopen stammen. Ich fürchte, dass ein Gerücht das Versteck preisgegeben hat und die Insel Trinacria zu leichtfertig mit dem Schutz des dort Verwahrten umgeht. Zu sehr bedroht die Veröffentlichung des berühmten Ortes. Ich muss eine Wohnstatt in einem weniger offenkundigen Landstrich suchen, durch das Seufzen des Enceladus und die nahen Flammen kann mein Versteck nicht ausreichend geheim bleiben . . . Sobald ich auf der Buchsbaumflöte blasen will, seufzt sie, einen Tod anzeigend. Wenn ich die Pauken schlagen will, geben die Pauken ein Wehklagen als Antwort. Ach, ich fürchte, dass diese Zeichen mir Wahres künden! Oh weh, das lange Verweilen hat geschadet!"

---

19 Kellner (1997) 144, 150 u. ö. hebt die überaus emotionsgeladenen Reden der Ceres hervor. Eine – gemäß rhetorischen Prinzipien respektive nach Kriterien der (z. B. stoischen) Affektenlehre – vertiefte Analyse beabsichtigt er allerdings nicht.

Mit dieser Ich-Rede wächst die Einsicht der Göttin, die Lage falsch eingeschätzt zu haben: Indem sie Sizilien, das Versteck der Tochter, zu sicher wähnte, ermöglichte sie den Raub. Verdichtete, darunter durch Possessivpronomina betonte Ich-Bezeugungen (114: *morabor . . .* , 117: *mihi*, 118: *timeo*, 119: *meum*, 122: *mihi*, 123: *nostra*, 130: *velim*, 131: *quatiam . . . mihi*, 132: *vereor*) und damit eine deutlich markierte Selbstanklage setzen ein. Das lange Verweilen in Phrygien und die Teilnahme an Riten der Cybele verdächtigt sie, fatale Entscheidungen getroffen zu haben. Die zweimalige Interjektion (132 f.: *ah . . . ah . . .*) hebt diese Selbstanschuldigungen effektvoll hervor. Dieses Bewusstwerden jedoch ist nicht gefestigt. Denn nach wie vor kann sie nicht anerkennen, dass ihre Lage aussichtslos ist, wenngleich selbst aus dem Kultbereich der Cybele untrügliche Hinweise auf Todbringendes kommen. In dieser Ich-Rede der Ceres spiegelt sich die beginnende Entmächtigung als Göttin. Cybeles Antwort mag verstörend wirken, als leichthin gesagte Beschwichtigung. Situativ aber ist sie trefflich gewählt, da Cybele auf Deeskalation setzt. Denn sie führt die Obsorge Jupiters zugunsten von Proserpina ins Treffen: *procul irrita venti / dicta ferant* (133 f.). Und dennoch: Transportieren diese Worte nicht eine doppelte Botschaft? Sind sie nicht auch ein Indiz dafür, dass Cybele vom Kreis der Wissensträger ausgeschlossen ist, die von Jupiter zur Ausgrenzung der Ceres aus dem Wissen um seine Entscheidungen verpflichtet wurden?

2.4 Ceres' Scheltrede an Electra (3,180–192)

In größter Eile kehrt Ceres zurück nach Sizilien. Das Haus findet sie verwaist vor. Ihre Vorahnungen haben sich bestätigt. Ihre Stimme versagt angesichts der Leere. Ceres verdoppelt damit die unheimliche Stille im Palast (3,148: *tacitae . . . aulae*), nicht einmal ihr Atem ist nunmehr vernehmbar. Eine die Dramatik steigernde Ich-Rede gibt es in dieser Situation nicht. Reden wird durch Trauergesten substituiert. Die wiederum tragen Züge einer Selbstanklage und eines Eingeständnisses ihres Versagens, wenn Ceres nicht nur ihr Gewand zerreißt und sich die Haare rauft, sondern diese sogar zusammen mit abgebrochenen Ähren ausreißt. Das Verstummen der Göttin dauert an. Anstatt zu klagen spricht sie gleichsam wortlos. Sie küsst das zurückgelassene Gewebe der Tochter, mehr noch, ihr lautloses Klagen bricht sie durch das Berühren des Stoffes abrupt ab (159 f.: *nec deflet plangitve malum: tantum oscula telae / figit et abrumpit mutas in fila querellas*).[20] Emotional gesteuert drückt sie die Spielsachen Proserpinas an sich und „liest" nochmals genau die Situation (165: *perlegit*) und beginnt zu begreifen. Sie ruft Erinnerungen an die Tochter in deren Gemach wach. Ihre Reaktion ist – aus der Perspektive traditionellen weiblichen Verhaltens betrachtet – stimmig, also 'regelkonform'. Sie korreliert mit der Be-

---

[20] Klebs (2019) 185 spricht vom „Ersticken" der Klage im Gewebe.

schreibung erster Reaktionen angesichts von extremem Schmerz beim Tod von Angehörigen.[21] Auffällig daran ist freilich der Transfer von Sprachverlust aufgrund von Schmerz in das Gewebe. Denn so sehr Realitätssinn dieser Geste innewohnt, so sehr kann er als Indiz dafür gelesen werden, dass die Klage der Göttin zugleich die Klage einer Frau ist, die sich selbst die Zunge auszureißen scheint.[22] Ceres findet danach allmählich zurück zum Wort. Electra, die alte Amme, nahezu eine Mutter für Proserpina, ist ihr Gegenüber, an dem sie ihren heftigen Schmerz, nun mit Worten, ausagiert (3,180–182; 189–192):

> . . . *'quod cernimus' inquit*   180
> *'excidium? cui praeda feror? regnatne maritus*
> *an caelum Titanes habent?*
> . . .
> *heu, ubi nunc est nata mihi? quo mille ministrae?*
> *quo Cyane? volucres quae vis Sirenas abegit?*   190
> *haecine vestra fides? sic fas aliena tueri*
> *pignora?'*

> „Welches Ende sehen wir", sagte sie. „Wem werde ich zur Beute gereicht? Herrscht mein Ehemann oder haben die Titanen den Himmel als Besitz? . . . Wehe, wo ist meine Tochter? Wohin sind die tausend Dienerinnen, wohin ist Cyane? Welche Macht hat die Sirenen vertrieben? Ist dies eure Treue? Ist es auf diese Weise schicksalshaft geregelt, ein fremdes Pfand zu beschützen?"

Diese Ich-Rede artikuliert die extreme emotionale Last der Ceres. Nicht sind es lange Jeremiaden, vielmehr kurze Fragen, die ihre Lage, mehr noch ihre Demontage, stichwortartig zum Ausdruck bringen. Zerstörung und Beute (181: *excidium*, *praeda*) sind die auf Gewalt verweisenden Zuschreibungen, die sie für ihre Lage mit ihren ersten Worten findet. Ein Machtverlust Jupiters gegenüber den Titanen wird von ihr erwogen. Dann nennt sie nicht ohne Bitterkeit Jupiter plötzlich ihren Ehemann. Erst nach diesen quälenden Fragen, mit denen sie ihre Konsternation sprachlich bekundet und ihre Position als Mutter nochmals betont, spricht sie die Leere des Palastes an, aus dem alle Dienerinnen, die Nymphen, zudem auch Cyane und die Sirenen, verschwunden sind. Die Ich-Rede kreist um den Vorwurf von totaler

---

21 Zur ersten Reaktion beim Tod eines Angehörigen in der römischen Tradition (darunter die letzte Berührung des Mundes des Sterbenden) vgl. Harich-Schwarzbauer (2011) 171–173. Zur *querela* (der Ocyroe, Ovid *met.* 2,665–675), die vom Erzähler explizit als Verlust logischen Argumentierens gekennzeichnet wird, s. Sharrock in diesem Band. Anders die Klage der Ceres, deren Fragen die Machtverhältnisse treffend analysieren, womit sie ihr vorgängiges affektgeladenes Sprechen (3,112) hinter sich lässt.

22 Es handelt sich gleichsam um eine Form der Selbstverstümmelung und eine Zuspitzung des Motivs des Transfers von weiblichem Sprechen auf Textilien, wenn Frauen, z. B. Philomela (Ov. *met.* 6,624–674), Gewalt erfahren und ihrer Zunge beraubt werden. Zur genderspezifischen Inszenierung von Klage in der griechischen und römischen Tragödie s. die Beiträge von Moro und Fuhrer in diesem Band.

Auslöschung. Das Verschwinden des gesamten Gesindes, hyperbolisch mit *mille ministrae* betont, unterstreicht das Schweigen, das Ceres nun umgibt.

Die Forschung fokussiert für diesen Textabschnitt auf die sich steigernde Pathetisierung des Geschehens, die durch die ruhige Reaktion der Amme konterkariert wird.[23] Electra schildert die Ereignisse aus der Perspektive einer wehrlosen alten Frau am unteren Ende der sozialen Hierarchie, die am Verschwinden Proserpinas auf ihre Art leidet. Die Fragen der Ceres werden von der Amme beantwortet. Damit schlüpft Electra in die Rolle einer intradiegetischen Erzählerin, womit sie die außenstehende Erzählinstanz ergänzt und eine persönliche Perspektive einbringt. So berichtet sie über Ereignisse, die aus dem Raub Proserpinas resultieren, darunter zum Verbleib der Dienerinnen, und gibt insbesondere über das Schicksal der Cyane und der Sirenen Auskunft (3,245–258). Ihre Rede charakterisiert und kontrastiert die Rede der Ceres. Sie ist die Frau, die die Ereignisse ruhig und besonnen zu deuten sowie die Gesamtsituation treffend einzuschätzen vermag. Zu diesem Zweck rekurriert sie sogar auf Sinnsprüche.[24] Auch Electra spricht mit ihrem Ich,[25] doch äußerst sparsam: Sie signalisiert mit der Geminatio von *mecum* pointiert und an prominenter Versstelle ihren engen Bezug zu Proserpina (3,205 f.: *sermonum gratia mecum / mecum somnus erat*), den sie mit dem betonten *ego* noch weiter untermauert (229 f.: *quos ego nequiquam planctus, quas inrita fudi / ore preces*).[26] Die innige Verbindung mit der Geraubten, nicht Rechtfertigung auf die Anwürfe der Ceres sprechen aus ihrer Rede.

2.5 Ceres' Anklage der Olympier (3,270–291; 295–329)

Ihre Wut, denn nicht länger hat der Schmerz die Oberhand, lässt Ceres zum Olymp aufbrechen. Sie klagt die Olympier pauschal an, entrüstet darüber, dass ihre Abstammung von Saturn und Cybele ignoriert würde – um dann drei Göttinnen reihum, nämlich Venus, Minerva und Diana, anzuklagen. Anschuldigungen geben den Takt an, wobei jede der drei Göttinnen in einem der ihr angestammten Bereiche infrage gestellt wird. Vor allem die Jungfräulichkeit von Minerva und Diana wird als Heuche-

---

[23] Zum gesteigerten Pathos s. Charlet (1991) ad loc. (mit Anm. 2, S. 170).
[24] 3,197: *levius communia tangunt*; 3,227: *teneris heu lubrica moribus aetas*.
[25] Mit dem Possessivpronomen *nostra* in Vers 215 spricht Electra präzise die geteilte Verantwortung für das unerfahrene Mädchen an. Weitere Ich-Bezeugungen Electras resultieren aus ihrer Rolle als Augenzeugin des Raubs.
[26] Electra übernimmt eine Funktion, die in der Tragödie dem Frauenchor zukommt. Aus kritischer Distanz reflektiert sie die Rolle der leiblichen Mutter. Eine „Fallhöhe", wie sie sich in den Klagereden der Ceres abzeichnet, bleibt ihr aufgrund ihres sozialen Status erspart; zur Denkfigur der „Fallhöhe" vgl. Fuhrer in diesem Band.

lei desavouiert. Neid auf ihre ‚Schwester' Proserpina wird den Göttinnen unterstellt (3,270–274; 282–288; 312–320):

> 'reddite' vociferans: 'non me vagus edidit amnis,   270
> non Dryadum de plebe sumus. turrita Cybebe
> me quoque Saturno genuit. quo iura deorum,
> quo leges cecidere poli? quid vivere recte
> proderit?
> . . .
> o templis Scythiae atque hominem sitientibus aris
> utraque digna coli! tanti quae causa furoris?
> quam mea vel tenui dicto Proserpina laesit?
> scilicet aut caris pepulit te, Delia, silvis,   285
> aut tibi commissas rapuit, Tritonia, pugnas !
> an gravis eloquio? vestros an forte petebat
> importuna choros?
> . . .
> quid tantum dignum fleri dignumque taceri?
> 'ei mihi, discedunt omnes. quid vana moraris
> ulterius? non bella palam caelestia sentis?
> quin potius natam pelago terrisque requiris?   315
> accingar lustrare diem, per devia rerum
> indefessa ferar. nulla cessabitur hora;
> non requies, non somnus erit, dum pignus ademptum
> inveniam, gremio quamvis mergatur Hiberae
> Tethyos et rubro iaceat vallata profundo'.

„Gebt sie zurück", rief sie laut, „mich hat nicht ein weithin strömender Fluss geboren; nicht gehöre ich zum niederen Volk der Dryaden. Die turmgekrönte Cybele hat mich dem Saturn geboren. Wohin sind die Rechte der Götter, wohin sind die Gesetze des Himmels? Was wird es nützen, rechtschaffen zu leben? . . . Ach, ihr beide verdient es, in den Tempeln Skythiens und an Altären, die nach Menschenblut dürsten, verehrt zu werden. Was ist der Grund für ein so großes Rasen? Wen hat meine Proserpina mit ihrer sanften Rede verletzt? Mag es sein, dass sie dich, Göttin aus Delos, aus den dir lieben Wäldern vertrieben hat, oder dir aufgetragene Schlachten geraubt, Tritonia, oder war sie hart mit ihren Worten? Oder wollte sie sich unverschämt in eure Reigen hineindrängen? . . . Was ist so würdig, dass man es beweint, was, dass man es verschweigt? Wehe mir, alle verschwinden. Was bleibst du ohne Erfolg noch länger? Spürst du nicht ganz offen die Kriege der Himmlischen? Warum suchst du nicht eher die Tochter zu Land und zu Wasser? Ich werde mich vorbereiten, die Welt, die dem Tag gehört, zu erkunden. Über alle Hürden hinweg werde ich unermüdlich gehen. Keine Stunde werde ich vergehen lassen. Keine Ruhe, keinen Schlaf wird es geben, bis ich mein Pfand, mein Kind, finde, mag sie auch im westlichen Meer ertrunken sein und tief unten im Roten Meer festgehalten liegen."

Diese Ich-Rede der Ceres ist als Wendepunkt in ihrem Verhalten anzusehen. Die Peripetie, in die ihr Rasen mündet, endet in einem Zusammenbruch. Aus der wütenden Göttin wird eine gedemütigte, verunsicherte, ja eine Orientierung suchende Frau. Kellner spricht im Anschluss an Potz generell von einer Vermenschlichung, welche die Götter in *DRP* durchmachen.[27] Doch geht es hier um eine Vermenschlichung, die sich in Ceres vollzieht? Werden Affekte der Götter im Epos nicht immer nach menschlichem Maß gestaltet? Produktiver dürfte es sein zu beobachten, was durch die Rede bewirkt wird, vor allem, wie die Transformation der Ceres vonstatten geht, als sie ihrer Macht beraubt wird.[28] Gerade mithilfe der Ich-Reden wird die Herabminderung der Ceres in Szene gesetzt. Damit im Gleichschritt verdichten sich ihre Anschuldigungen und ihre heftigen Attacken. Ein Gleichnis, das dem Rasen der Göttin vorausgeht, präludiert den Umschlag: Wie eine Tigerin wütend voranstürmt, bis sie ihr Rasen im Glas gespiegelt sieht und innehält (3,263–268), so hält Ceres in ihrem Furor plötzlich inne und wird sich der Ineffizienz ihrer Strategie, das meint ihres aggressiven Verhaltens, bewusst. In ihrer Rede vollzieht sich dieser ‚Bruch'. Die Zäsur zeigt sich in einem signifikanten Wechsel, indem sich Ceres einmal mit „du" anspricht (3,313–315: *quid vana moraris / ulterius? . . . sentis? / . . . requiris?*). Allerdings ist dieser Wechsel zum „du", aus narratologischer Sicht betrachtet, nicht so eindeutig Ceres zuzuordnen. Denn das „du" könnte ebenso als Apostrophe der außenstehenden Erzählinstanz an ihre Erzählfigur gelesen werden.[29] Dass damit auch eine Irritation, ein Innehalten einer intendierten Leserschaft beabsichtigt sein könnte, ist nicht von der Hand zu weisen. An diesem Punkt drängt sich noch stärker als für die übrigen Ceres-Reden die Frage auf, wie anders die außenstehende Erzählinstanz den Wandel der Ceres erzähltechnisch hätte anlegen oder welches Gleichnis diese Transformation auch nur annähernd effektvoll hätte vor Augen führen können. Hätte die Erzählinstanz vermeiden wollen/können, das Verhalten der Göttin zu beurteilen? Mit diesem Kunstgriff geht sie zumindest auf Distanz zur Erzählfigur. Nach der letzten Rede der Ceres scheint festzustehen: Die Göttin der Fruchtbarkeit hat jegliche Autorität eingebüßt. Resignierend droht sie nicht, die Ordnung der Natur auszuhebeln. Im Übrigen ist diese Frage in *DRP* andernorts und ohne Ceres schon geklärt. Denn es ist Jupiter, der, durch Klagen der Natura veranlasst, über Ceres' Abwahl als Stifterin des Getreidebaus bestimmt (3,19–54).[30] Schon hat die personifizierte Natura die Rolle der Obsorge über die Fruchtbarkeit übernommen (3,33).

---

[27] Kellner (1997) 216, 280 u. ö. Bereits Potz (1984) 23–26 u. ö. hatte die „Vermenschlichung" der Göttergestalten in *DRP* zu einem Leitthema erhoben.
[28] Taisne (2001) geht auf die Reden der Ceres als einheitsstiftendes Moment in *DRP* nicht ein; sie betont das Motiv der Mutterliebe, das Claudian anhand von Prätexten aus Statius entfaltet.
[29] Eine Ambivalenz wird von Gruzelier (1993) nur für Vers 311 behauptet: Die Worte *largis nunc imbribus ora madescunt* weist sie der Rede der Ceres zu. Kellner (1997) 171 mit Anm. 744 geht demgegenüber im Gefolge von Charlet (1991) 171 ad loc. für Vers 311 von einem auktorialen Einschub aus.
[30] Vgl. Kellner (1997) 85–89; Klebs (2019) 187.

2.6 Ceres' Selbstanklage gegenüber Proserpina (3,407–437)

Allein das sichere Wissen um den Ort des Verbleibs der Tochter erbittet Ceres in ihrer Verzweiflung. Sie akzeptiert vorerst das *fait accompli*. Ihre Worte an die verschwundene Tochter sind ein Einbekennen von Fehlern, sie bekräftigen den Mutterstolz und enden mit der Hoffnung auf ein Wiedersehen. Die Ich-Rede deckt die großen Probleme der Göttin auf: dass sie ihre Fehler nicht eingestehen wollte (ihre Weigerung, die Tochter in die Ehe freizugeben), dass sie im eifernden Besitzerstolz mit anderen Göttinnen konkurrierte, dass sie eigennützig agierte, indem sie zu Cybele nach Phrygien aufbrach. Mit der geschwächten Position der nun gedemütigten Göttin geht eine sichtliche Zunahme ihrer Ich-Bezeugungen einher. Auf 31 Verse kommen 23 Ich-Bezeugungen (408: *sperabam . . . mihi*, 411: *cingebar . . . mihi*, 412: *sublimis eram*, 415: *mihi . . . ferebar*, 417: *gessi*, 418: *fui*, 420: *ego . . . ademi*, 421: *deserui*, 422: *exposui . . . fruebar*, 424: *iungebam*, 425: *merui*, 428: *quaeram*, 429: *me*, 431: *deprendam*, 432: *ibo, ibo*, 436: *videbo*, 437: *vidi*).[31] Daher soll diese Rede in ihrer Gesamtheit vorgelegt werden (3,407–437):

> 'non tales gestare tibi, Proserpina, taedas
> sperabam, sed vota mihi communia matrum,
> et thalami festaeque faces caeloque canendus
> ante oculos hymenaeus erat. sic numina fatis   410
> volvimur et nullo Lachesis discrimine saevit!
> quam nuper sublimis eram quantisque procorum
> cingebar studiis! quae non mihi pignus ob unum
> cedebat numerosa parens? tu prima voluptas,
> tu postrema mihi! per te fecunda ferebar.   415
> o decus, o requies, o grata superbia matris,
> qua gessi florente deam, qua sospite nusquam
> inferior Iunone fui, nunc squalida, vilis!
> hoc placitum patri. cur autem adscribimus illum
> his lacrimis? ego te, fateor, crudelis ademi,   420
> quae te deserui solamque instantibus ultro
> hostibus exposui. raucis secura fruebar
> nimirum thiasis et laeta sonantibus armis
> iungebam Phrygios, cum tu raperere, leones.
> accipe, quas merui poenas. en ora fatiscunt   425
> vulneribus grandesque rubent in pectore sulci!
> immemor en uterus crebro contunditur ictu.
> qua te parte poli, quo te sub cardine quaeram?
> quis monstrator erit? quae me vestigia ducent?
> quis currus? ferus ille quis est? terraene marisne 430

---

31 Das zweimalige ‚wir' in dieser Rede wird präzise vom 'ich' abgesetzt: *sic numina fatis / volvimur* (410f.) ist sentenzenhaft (vgl. 3,96): Mit *adscribimus* (419) bezieht Ceres die Tochter in ihr Fragen mit ein.

incola? quae volucrum deprendam signa rotarum?
ibo, ibo quocumque pedes, quocumque iubebit
casus. sic Venerem quaerat deserta Dione.
proficietne labor? rursus te, nata, licebit
amplecti? manet ille decor? manet ille genarum   435
fulgor? an infelix talem fortasse videbo,
qualis nocte venis, qualem per somnia vidi?'

„Nicht solche Hochzeitsfackeln für dich, Proserpina, zu tragen, hoffte ich, sondern Gelübde, die mir mit den Müttern gemeinsam sind und die festlichen Fackeln des Brautgemachs und eine Hochzeit, die der Himmel besingen sollte, stand mir vor Augen. So werden wir Gottheiten durch das Schicksal überwältigt und Lachesis wütet ohne Unterschied! Wie herrlich war ich vor kurzem noch, von wie großen Bemühungen von Freiern war ich umgeben. Welche Mutter zahlreicher Kinder stand mir nicht nach aufgrund meines einzigen Kindes. Du bist die erste und auch die letzte Leidenschaft für mich! Durch dich nannte man mich fruchtbar. Oh, du meine Zierde, meine Seelenruhe, du mir lieber Stolz einer Mutter; als du erblühtest, war ich stolze Göttin, als du unversehrt warst, war ich Juno nie unterlegen, nun bin ich elend, armselig! Gefällt dies deinem Vater, warum schreiben wir den Grund dieser Tränen ihm zu! Ich habe dich, ich bekenne, ich Grausame habe dich vernichtet, da ich dich verlassen und dich, als Feinde drohten, überdies alleine dargeboten habe. Allzu sicher erfreute ich mich an den schrillen Umzügen, und freudig schloss ich mich mit klingenden Waffen den phrygischen Löwen an, während du entführt wurdest. Vernimm die Strafe, die ich verdient habe, mein Antlitz wird schlaff von den Wunden und rot zeichnen sich tiefe Furchen in meiner Brust ab. Mein Leib, bar jeder Erinnerung, wird von heftigen Schlägen heimgesucht. Auf welcher Seite des Pols, in welcher Weltgegend soll ich Dich suchen? Wer wird es mir anzeigen? Welche Spuren werden mich leiten? Welcher Wagen? Wer ist jener Wilde? Ein Bewohner der Erde oder des Himmels? Welche Zeichen soll ich von den hurtigen Rädern ablesen? Ich werde gehen, werde gehen, wohin mich die Füße zu gehen heissen, wohin es das Schicksal befiehlt. So möge die verlassene Dione Venus suchen. Wird diese Mühe erfolgreich sein? Werde ich dich, mein Kind, wieder umarmen dürfen? Wird ihre Zierde bleiben? Wird der Glanz ihrer Wangen Bestand haben? Oder werde ich Unglückliche dich vielleicht so sehen, wie du in der Nacht kommst, wie ich dich im Traum sah?"

Spät erst richtet Ceres Worte an die abwesende Tochter. Die Ich-Rede kann in drei inhaltliche Abschnitte geteilt werden, die bislang Erzähltes in ein neues Licht stellen: 1) die ‚Palinodie' ihrer Weigerung, die Tochter zu verheiraten, diese gepaart mit dem Mutterstolz (407–418), 2) die Selbstanklage und damit verbunden die Entlastung Jupiters (419–427) sowie 3) die Entscheidung, die Tochter zu Lande und zu Wasser zu suchen (428–435). Dabei tritt zutage, dass Ceres der Erzählinstanz mehrfach widerspricht oder zumindest eine partielle Korrektur vornimmt. Denn die Erzählinstanz hatte eingangs erkennen lassen, dass Ceres einer Verheiratung der Tochter entgegenstand (1,130–142), immerhin hatte sie neben einer stattlichen Zahl an Freiern selbst göttliche Werber wie Mars und Apollo abgewiesen. Dieser Widerspruch zum Bericht der außenstehenden Erzählinstanz beleuchtet die folgenträchtige Entscheidungsschwäche der Göttin, die ihre Fehleinschätzung nun selbst demaskiert. Das Welken des Gesichts, die Furchen, die der Schmerz in ihr Herz zeichnet, das Schlagen auf den Uterus, den Sitz der (so erschöpften wie vernachlässigten) Mutterschaft, schreiben das schuldbezeugende Ich zuletzt auch in den Körper ein.

3 Die Ceres-Reden und Jupiters Schweigegebot

Die Reden der Ceres ergeben in Summe das Bild einer Frau, der die Mitgestaltung am Schicksal ihrer Tochter abrupt genommen wird. Zu Beginn des Epyllions wirft die Erzählinstanz kein gutes Licht auf die Göttin, soweit es um ihre Verantwortung für Proserpina geht.[32] Zumal Ceres gesellschaftliche Konventionen zu ignorieren gewillt ist, vor allem, da sie ein indirekt sich abzeichnendes, freilich noch nicht näher definiertes erotisches Sehnen der nun erwachsenen Tochter nicht zur Kenntnis nimmt.[33]

Ceres, die im zweiten Buch von *DRP* keine Rolle spielt, steht dafür im dritten Gesang im Mittelpunkt, welchen sie mit gleich fünf ihrer insgesamt sechs Reden dominiert. Diese Ungleichgewichtung könnte als konzeptionelle Schwäche oder gar als Zeichen für die Unabgeschlossenheit des Epyllions gewertet werden. Der Ceres dicht gesetzte Reden, so könnte man folgern, lassen für weitere Redner keinen Raum. Doch wer hat angesichts der Umstände des Verschwindens der Proserpina überhaupt noch ein Rederecht? Electra legt Ceres ihre persönliche Sicht des Raubs dar. Sie allein ist vom Schweigegebot, das Jupiter unter massiven Drohungen ausgesprochen hat, nicht betroffen. Sie gehört nicht zum Kreis der Göttergestalten, die für seine Kundmachung zum Verschwinden der Proserpina in den Olymp geladen worden waren.[34] Sie verfügt nicht über das von Jupiter dort veröffentlichte (und mit Schweigegebot belegte) Wissen um die Identität des Räubers. Der Ausschluss von potentiellen Rednerinnen lässt sich auf der Folie der Cereserzählung in Ovids *Metamorphosen* erklären. Vorab: Die Amme Electra firmiert bei Ovid nicht.[35] Sie gehört daher nicht zu den Gestalten, die in Ovids Mythenbearbeitung Wissensträgerinnen des Raubes sind und Gegenstand einer Verwandlungserzählung werden. Arethusa ist, anders als bei Ovid, bei Claudian nur noch eine Quelle in Sizilien, nicht mehr die Personifikation der Quelle, sie scheidet als Rednerin somit aus.[36] Über den Verlust des Gefolges der Proserpina, das Auskunft geben könnte, äußert sich Electra. Als Berichterstatterin der Ereignisse rund um den Raub legt sie den Finger auf die Differenz zwischen Ovid – den sie zu diesem Zwecke kennen musste – und Claudian: Cyane habe sich in ihrem Schmerz über den Raub bereits in Wasser aufgelöst. Die Sirenen wiederum seien geflohen, eine Antwort sei von ihnen nicht mehr zu erwarten. Ihre Gesänge würden nur noch Verderben bringen (3,245–258). Wer also bliebe, um Ceres

---

[32] Vgl. Klebs (2019) 179 f.
[33] Anders als bei Ovid (*met.* 5,376 f.) ist nicht die Rede davon, dass sich Proserpina mit dem Gedanken trägt, jungfräulich zu leben.
[34] Zum Ausschluss der Ceres aus der Götterversammlung (Umkehr des Motivs des *Hymnus an Demeter*) siehe Klebs (2019) 186.
[35] Im homerischen *Hymnus auf Demeter* (418) ist die Okeanide Elektra eine Begleiterin Proserpinas. Vgl. Gruzelier (1993) 259 f.
[36] *DRP* 2,60: Quellnymphen begleiten Proserpina beim Blumenpflücken. Anders als bei Ovid (*met.* 5,487–508) ist Arethusa nicht mehr Nymphe, sie kann also zum Auffinden der Proserpina nicht beitragen. Vgl. Gruzelier (1993) 173.

Antwort zu geben? Aus der Sicht der Ceres sollte es – zum ‚Buchende', dann allerdings ohne Referenz auf Electra und mit Bezug auf Ovids *Fasti* (4,500) – Scylla sein. Doch auch sie scheint bereits ohne Redevermögen zu sein, da einer Verwandlung unterzogen.[37] Einige von Scyllas Hunden, und damit endet das Epos in der uns überlieferten Form, schweigen verblüfft. Andere bellen, noch nicht eingeschüchtert, als Ceres eintrifft (3,448 f.): *antra procul Scyllaea petit, cunlbusque reductis / pars stupefacta silet, pars nondum exterrita latrat.* Nicht mit Worten wird Ceres empfangen, sondern mit Schweigen respektive mit Tierlauten.[38] So als ob die Drohungen Jupiters bis in die Tierwelt Wirkung zeigten.

4 *procul irrita venti dicta ferant* – ein Fazit

Mit ihrer Antwort auf den Albtraum der Ceres hatte Cybele versucht, ihre Tochter zu beruhigen. Doch Cybele sollte sich irren. Denn sie gehörte nicht zu den Personen, die von Jupiter in die Götterversammlung eingeladen waren (3,133–136):

> '. . . *procul irrita venti*
> *dicta ferant*', subicit Cybele: 'nec tanta Tonanti
> segnities ut pro pignore fulmina mittat.
> i tamen et nullo turbata revertere casu.'

> „Weit weg mögen die Winde deine nutzlosen Worte tragen", warf Cybele ein. „Eine so große Nachlässigkeit ist nicht die Art des Donnergottes, sodass er für sein Kind sehr wohl Blitze sendet. Geh' dennoch und kehre zurück, ohne von einem Unglück irritiert zu sein."

Und dennoch: Cybeles Worte sollten sich auch bewahrheiten, allerdings nicht in dem von Ceres verstandenen Sinn. Denn Jupiter stimmte mit seinen Blitzen für die Ehe mit Pluto und damit für den Raub (2,228–230). Vergegenwärtigt man sich die Vergeblichkeit der Ceres-Reden, die auf sich und auf ihr Ich zurückgeworfen wird, dann spricht Ceres ihre Klagen in den Wind. Das Gewicht ihrer sich verdichtenden Ich-Bezeugungen steht diametral zu ihrem Gewicht als Göttin. Ihre Worte finden keine Resonanz, je mehr sie auf ihr Ich setzt, desto schwächer erscheint sie.[39] Ihre

---

[37] Zur Verwandlung der Scylla vgl. Ov. *met.* 14,51–67. Zu weiteren Prätexten zu Scylla und zu Scyllas Hunden vgl. Gruzelier (1993) 301 ad loc.
[38] Schirner (2017) 14 deutet diese Situation als „Ausnahmezustand" im Sinne ihrer Deutung von *DRP* als „Epik des Exzeptionellen". Ihre Interpretation schließt Überlegungen zum Reden und zum Redeverbot nicht ein. Ähnlich auch Onorato (2008), der etwas schematisch an einer Parallelisierung zwischen Pluto und Ceres festhält.
[39] Klebs (2019) 179 spricht in diesem Zusammenhang wohl zu Recht vom Ausschluss der Ceres aus dem Olymp. Dies gilt auch für Cybele, die per se nicht zu den Olympiern gerechnet wurde. Bei beiden geht es auch um den Ausschluss der Matrilinearität aus der Gesellschaftsordnung.

potenzierten Ich-Bezeugungen sind Manifestationen ihrer emotionalen Befindlichkeit, die zwischen Empörung, Zorn und tief empfundenem Schmerz um den Verlust ihrer Tochter oszillieren. Die direkten Reden der Göttin – Ceres ist in *DRP* nie Gegenstand einer berichteten, indirekten Rede – kreisen um den Verlust weiblicher Macht und um Trauer angesichts des Verlusts der Tochter. Bemerkenswert daran ist in *DRP* ein Punkt: Auf Ceres' gesteigertes Insistieren auf ihr Ich gibt es eine Antwort: Schweigen. Sie ist konfrontiert mit einem umfassenden Schweigegebot, das einem Redeverbot gleichkommt. Jede Reaktion auf ihre Worte muss kraft eines Götterspruchs unterbleiben. Das Ich der Ceres, so präsent es im Epyllion auch erscheinen mag, ist ohnmächtig. Dass sich Ceres selbst als ausgegrenzt wahrnimmt, zeigt sich aufgrund ihrer (alternativlosen) Entscheidung, Scylla aufzusuchen, um wenigstens von ihr eine Antwort zu erhalten. Aus den Ich-Reden spricht die Mutter, der bei all der inhärenten Problematik – indem sie das Heiratsalter der Tochter nicht wahrhaben will – jeglicher Dialog in dieser extremen und für sie schmerzhaften Situation verwehrt wird. Das Fazit von Julia Klebs, dass es „angesichts der in *DRP* angelegten Machtkonzentration in den Händen der männlichen Figuren kein Leichtes wäre, Ceres wieder ins Spiel zu bringen, zumal auch das Ausbleiben der Vegetation transformiert wird", ist wohl zutreffend.[40] Ergänzend dazu sei anhand der Analyse der Ich-Reden der Ceres festgehalten, dass die (zu späte) Einsicht der Göttin im dritten Buch plausibilisiert wird. Die außenstehende Erzählinstanz erkennt diese Leistung an. Doch aus der Position einer ‚Rabenmutter' entlässt sie Ceres, soweit uns das Epyllion vorliegt, nicht. Dem Konflikt einer Mutter angesichts des ‚Verlusts' einer heiratsfähigen Tochter, der in *DRP* mithilfe der gehäuften Ich-Reden vordergründig wird, wohnt eine zusätzliche Brisanz inne, so man ihn im Kontext von Claudians Epithalamium *c.* 10 liest. Dann entpuppen sich die Ceres-Reden in *DRP* gleichsam als ‚Gegenerzählung' zum harmonischen Übereinstimmen der Brauteltern im Epithalamium auf Honorius und Maria (*c.* 10), in dem die Brautmutter Serena – deren erst ‚heranreifende' Tochter Maria unvorbereitet verheiratet wird – nie das Wort ergreift, während die (panegyrische) Erzählinstanz das Heer die Vorfreude auf eine (männliche) Nachkommenschaft des Brautpaares sowie auf die Fruchtbarkeit des Herrscherhauses insgesamt verlauten lässt, nachdem die Soldaten zuvor umfänglich und in höchsten Tönen das Lob des Brautvaters (und Heermeisters) Stilicho verkündet hatten.[41]

---

40 Ibid.
41 Zur Rolle der Mutter in der römischen Hochzeitspoesie s. Harich-Schwarzbauer (2020) 129–139. Vgl. auch den Beitrag von Alison Sharrock im vorliegenden Band, die das Verstummen weiblicher Stimmen vor dem Hintergrund der feministischen Theorie zur männlich kontrollierten sozialen und symbolischen Ordnung erklärt. Zum Modus des ‚Verstummen-Lassens' weiblicher Stimmen vgl. auch die Ausführungen von Markus Hafner zur Delphischen Pythia oben S. 74–78.

Literaturverzeichnis

Texte und Übersetzungen

Claudii Claudiani *carmina*, ed. John B. Hall, Leipzig 1985.
Claudien, *Le rapt de Proserpine*, texte établi et traduit par Jean-Louis Charlet, Paris 1991.
Claudian, *Der Raub der Proserpina*, lat. und dt., eingeleitet und kommentiert von Anne Friedrich, übersetzt von Anne Friedrich und Anna Katharina Frings, Darmstadt 2009.
Claudio Claudiano, *De raptu Proserpinae*, a cura di Marco Onorato, Napoli 2008.

Forschungsliteratur

Cox-Miller (1994): Patricia Cox Miller, *Dreams in Late Antiquity. Studies in the imagination of a culture*, Princeton.
Felgentreu (1999): Fritz Felgentreu, *Claudians praefationes: Bedingungen, Beschreibungen und Wirkungen einer poetischen Kleinform*, Stuttgart.
Genette (2010): Gérard Genette, *Die Erzählung*, übers. von Andreas Knop, 3. durchgesehene und korrigierte Auflage, München.
Gruzelier (1993): Claire Gruzelier, *Claudian, De raptu Proserpinae*, edited with introduction, translation and commentary, Oxford.
Harich-Schwarzbauer (2011): Henriette Harich-Schwarzbauer, „Tod und Bestattung in der römischen Literatur", in: *ThesCRA* VI, 172–182.
Harich-Schwarzbauer (2020): Henriette Harich-Schwarzbauer, "Motherhood in Roman Epithalamia", in: Alison Sharrock and Alison Keith (Hgg.), *Maternal Conceptions in Classical Literature and Philosophy*, Toronto 2020, 129–139.
Harich-Schwarzbauer (2021): Henriette Harich-Schwarzbauer, „*Africa, famula Romae*. Constructions of Ethnic Identity in Claudian's Panegyrics", in: Jacqueline Fabre-Serris, Alison Keith and Florence Klein (Hgg.), *Identities, Ethnicities and Gender in Antiquity*, Berlin, 251–263.
Hinds (1987): Stephen Hinds, *The Metamorphosis of Proserpina. Ovid and the self-conscious muse*, Cambridge.
Kellner (1997): Thomas Kellner, *Die Göttergestalten in Claudians De raptu Proserpinae. Polarität und Koinzidenz als anthropologische Dialektik mythologisch formulierter Weltvergewisserung*, Stuttgart/Leipzig.
Klebs (2019): Julia Klebs, *Der Raub der Proserpina. Kultur- und Geschlechtergeschichte einer mythischen Figur*, Berlin.
Lämmle und Scheidegger Lämmle (2017): Rebecca Lämmle und Cédric Scheidegger Lämmle, „Der Raub der Persephone – Eine Blütenlese", in: Renate Möhrmann (Hg.), *„Da ist denn auch das Blümchen weg". Die Entjungferung – Fiktionen der Defloration*, Stuttgart, 3–31.
Potz (1984): Erich Potz, *Claudian: Kommentar zu De raptu Proserpinae, Buch 1*, Graz.
Schirner (2017): Rebecca Schirner, „Eine Epik des Exzeptionellen. Claudians Epos *De raptu Proserpinae*", *WJA* N.F. 41, 5–51.
Taisne (2001): Anne-Marie Taisne, „La Cérès de Claudien au miroir de Stace", *Bulletin de l'Association Guillaume Budé* 3, 298–316.
Wheeler (1995): Stephen Wheeler, „The Underworld Opening of Claudian's *De Raptu Proserpinae*", *TAPhA* 15, 113–134.

Ann-Kathrin Stähle
Medea *virago* in Dracontius' *Romulea*

Abstract: This paper aims to address Medea's speeches in Dracontius. An investigation of these speeches is worthwhile for several reasons. For one, Dracontius provides us with a highly inconsistent portrait of Medea: She is a priestess and is described as a *virgo* (*virago*); yet she's also characterised as a mother. In contrast to these thoroughly human aspects, however, she, when appearing as a fury-like sorceress, seems to possess a superhuman nature. Besides this, her speeches are interesting from a gender perspective: I maintain that the author does not assign any kind of feminine role to his Medea and thereby invalidates all gender attributions. In pursuing this thesis, I wish to explore how the male author lays out the speeches of Medea: What does she say and how does she say it? What gender-specific role manifests itself for Medea, or how does the parameter of 'gender' influence her speech? Alongside all of this, I want to clarify how the author moulds Medea's speeches in comparison to Iason's: How is the relationship between husband and wife presented? Finally, I want to highlight how Dracontius has altered the character of Medea, and her speeches, in comparison to his literary antecedents.

Keywords: priestess, mother, wife, male author, feminine figure

1 Einleitung

Die Medea des Dracontius, der um 500 n. Chr. im vandalischen Karthago lebt und ihre ‚Geschichte' in einem hexametrischen Epyllion (*Romulea* 10) erzählt,[1] ist eine interessante, weil zwiespältige Figur: Einerseits tritt sie als Mutter auf (*mater*, *parens* und *genitrix*), andererseits zeigt der Dichter sie als Priesterin (*sacerdos*) und charakterisiert sie als *virgo* oder *virago*. Auch letzteres ist widersprüchlich, insofern *virgo* das jungfräuliche Mädchen, *virago* die männergleiche Frau bezeichnet.[2] Im Gegensatz zu diesen menschlichen Aspekten zeigt sie eine übermenschliche Natur, wenn sie als furienartige Zauberin erscheint (1–16), Glaukes Brautkrone verzaubert (484–493) oder am Schluss in den Himmel aufsteigt (564–569). Selbst in dieser ihrer übermenschlichen Seite ist sie nicht eindeutig, wenn sie auf die Hilfe der Götter angewiesen ist,

---

[1] Eine Zusammenfassung von *Romulea* 10 bzw. einen Überblick über die Handlung bieten z. B. Schubert (1998) 83–89 und Kaufmann (2006a) 53 f.
[2] Zur Bedeutung(sdifferenz) sowie Verwendung der Begriffe *virgo* und *virago* s. Kaufmann (2006a) 109 und 115 f. Anm. 75 und 76. Zur ambivalenten Gender-Zuschreibung einer Priesterin als *virgo*/*virago* s. auch Cordes in diesem Band. Zur hündischen *venatrix* und *virago* Lydia in Mart. 11.69 s. Baumann in diesem Band.

Cupidos Pfeilen unterliegt (219–224, 240–243), an Dianas Vergebung (416), die Hilfe der Unterwelt (446–452) und Sols Eingreifen bei der Entzündung der Krone (505–508) appelliert.

Diese Widersprüchlichkeit zeigt, dass Medeas Macht, wie bei allen Gottheiten, nicht absolut, sondern relativ ist; sie vermag nur so viel, wie der Erzähler ihr zutraut. Da Medea nicht kultisch verehrt wird, untersteht ihr Handeln allein der Einschätzung des Dichters.[3]

Zu Beginn des Gedichts kündigt der Autor an, dass er ihre Reden formt bzw. nur selektiv wiedergibt: Ihre Zauberworte zu kennen und zu verbreiten, zieme sich nicht für ihn (*quae carmina linguis / murmuret aut urens species quae nomina dicat, / haec vatem nescire decet; quae nosse profanum est, / quod fuerit vulgasse nefas!*, 13–16). In meinem Beitrag möchte ich daher untersuchen, wie der männliche Autor Medeas Ich-Rede modelliert, zu welcher Gelegenheit er sie sprechen lässt und welche Rolle er der zwiespältigen Figur verleiht.

Im Folgenden geht es mir darum zu zeigen, dass der Autor seine Medea nicht mit einer rein weiblichen Rolle ausstattet, dass er mit der Figur der Medea vielmehr Gender-Zuschreibungen außer Kraft setzt. Ich werde also den Parameter ‚Gender' anhand ihrer Ich-Rede untersuchen: Welche geschlechterspezifischen Elemente werden einer Figur zugeschrieben, die in einer weder als rein männlich noch rein weiblich definierten Rolle spricht? Dabei scheint mir auch Medeas Beziehung zu Jason aufschlussreich; in welchem Verhältnis stehen die Reden von Mann und Frau?

Eine diachrone Betrachtung der Figur soll schließlich deutlich machen, wie sich Medea(s Rede) bei Dracontius zu seinen literarischen Vorgängern verändert hat.

2 Medeas Ich

In Dracontius' Gedicht erscheint Medeas Ich im Vergleich zu den anderen handelnden Personen am häufigsten: Nebst Medeas direkten Reden findet sich eine Rede der Göttin Juno an Venus, um Medeas Hochzeit zu planen, sowie Dianas Fluch. Ferner gibt es kurze Gesprächssequenzen zwischen Venus und Cupido sowie zwischen Medea, der Amme und Jason. Medeas Ich-Reden, die überwiegend im letzten Drittel des Textes auftreten, richten sich an Diana, die Unterweltsgötter und Sol.

---

3 Zum Prinzip der relativen Macht der Götter bei Dracontius s. Kaufmann (2006a) 55–58.

Das erste Gebet adressiert sie an Diana, deren Priesterin sie ist;[4] nach einer langen Anrede, einer ausführlichen Apostrophe und Lobpreisung der Göttin, kommt sie schließlich zu ihrer Bitte (416–430):[5]

> *da veniam, Medea precor: cum clade suorum*
> *non decet ira deos. mereor pro crimine poenam,*
> *te feriente tamen, non ut mendicus Iason*
> *sit vindex, regina, tuus, qui criminis auctor*
> *ipse fuit: miseram solus non puniat, oro,*   420
> *qui me cum feriendus erat; cuicumque iubebis,*
> *colla paro feriat: tantum ne virgo Creontis*
> *discidium pariat nautam ductura maritum.*
> *exaudi famulam: dolor est, non zelus Iason.*
> *quinque dabo inferias (sat erunt pro crimine nostro)*   425
> *illustres animas: niveam cum Iasone Glaucen,*
> *mortibus amborum regem superaddo Creonta*
> *et natos miseranda duos, mea pignora, supplex*
> *offero, sacrilegos nostro de corpore fructus,*
> *ne prosit peccasse mihi.*   430

Gewähre Verzeihung, ich, Medea, bitte dich. Zorn, der zugleich Verderben für die eigenen Leute bedeutet, ziemt sich nicht für die Götter. Für mein Vergehen verdiene ich Bestrafung, allerdings nur, wenn du mich bestrafst, so dass nicht der hergelaufene Jason dein Rächer ist, Herrin, der (420) selbst der Anlass meines Vergehens war: Mich Elende möge nur er, ich bitte dich, nicht bestrafen, der mit mir hätte bestraft werden müssen; wem auch immer du befehlen wirst, zuzuschlagen, halte ich den Hals hin, wenn nur Kreons heiratsfähige Tochter nicht unsere Scheidung zustande bringt, um den Seemann zu heiraten. Erhöre deine Dienerin: Schmerz, nicht eifernde Liebe bedeutet Jason für mich. (425) Fünf angesehene Seelen werde ich als Totengabe darbringen (das wird für unser Vergehen genug sein): mit Jason die schneeweiße Glauke, zu den Leichen der beiden füge ich noch den König Kreon hinzu, und demütig bringe ich beklagenswerte meine Söhne dar, die Beweisstücke meiner Ehe, die aus Frevel entstandenen Früchte meines Körpers, (430) damit mir mein vergangenes Vergehen keinen Nutzen bringt.

Zu Beginn ihrer Rede nennt Medea prägnant ihren Eigennamen (*Medea precor*, 416) und bringt sich so in Position für ihre Forderung, ihr den Fehltritt zu verzeihen, sich mit Jason verheiratet und damit gegen ihren Dienst als Diana-Priesterin verstoßen zu haben. Indem sich Medea selbst beim Namen nennt, macht sie ihre Rolle als Sprecherin des Gebets deutlich; darin zeigt sich ihr Selbstbewusstsein, das sie auch als Schuldige nicht verloren hat. Darüber hinaus verleiht sie ihrer

---

4 In Anlehnung an Dionysios Skytobrachion charakterisiert Dracontius Medea als eine der Iphigenie ähnliche Priesterin, die der Göttin Diana die Ankömmlinge opfern muss; vgl. Kaufmann (2006a) 48. Als Priesterin der Hekate steht ihr Zauberwissen im Vordergrund; indem Dracontius sie zu einer Priesterin der Diana macht, ermöglicht er die Charakterisierung ihrer Figur als *virago*.
5 Die Übersetzungen übernehme ich jeweils von Kaufmann (2006a).

Bitte mehr Gewicht, indem ihr Name an ihre Beziehung zur Göttin und ihre übernatürlichen Kräfte erinnert.[6]

Die Anmerkung, dass es Göttern nicht zukomme, zornig zu sein (416f.), wirkt in dieser Situation des Schuldbekenntnisses und der Reue unpassend. Sie bekennt dann zwar, dass sie Bestrafung verdient (417), sieht aber nicht sich selbst, sondern Jason als *auctor* ihres Vergehens (419f.). Die Entschuldigung wird hier gleichsam zur Verleumdung, wenn man bedenkt, dass nicht Jason sie verführte, sondern sie ihm, durch Amor zur Liebe bewegt, einen Heiratsantrag macht. An ihre Bestrafung stellt sie Bedingungen und Ansprüche, indem sie erklärt, wie bzw. durch wen sie bestraft werden möchte (418–424). Schließlich legt sie selbst Art und Größe ihrer Opfergabe fest (425–430).

Auch wenn man im Verhältnis von Göttin und Priesterin das *do-ut-des*-Prinzip geltend machen kann, zeigt sich Medea gegenüber ihrer Göttin, als deren Dienerin sie sich bezeichnet (*famulam*, 424), kaum reumütig, zurückhaltend und untertänig, sondern selbstbewusst, dominant und bestimmend: Zorn über das Vergehen gesteht sie ihrer Göttin nicht zu, die Schuld für ihren Fehltritt sieht sie bei Jason, über den Umfang ihres Opfers bestimmt sie selbst. Dass sich Medea gegenüber den Göttern besonders herrisch verhält, bemerkt der Dichter eigens im Prooemium: Die Götter sind ihre Gefangenen (*virginis atrae captivos deos*, 2), die sie nötigt, ihr zu gehorchen, während sie selbst ungestraft bleibt (*et superos impune premit prece nixa virago / invitos parere sibi*, 12f.). Daraus lässt sich ferner erkennen, dass die Opferung für sie keine Strafe bedeuten kann, sondern sie dadurch nur selbst bestraft.

Verschiedene Antithesen im Text machen diese Diskrepanz zwischen ihrer Rolle als Dienerin und ihrem dominanten Auftreten deutlich: Begriffe, die ihre Bitten zum Ausdruck bringen (*precor*, 416; *oro*, 420; *famulam*, 424; *supplex*, 428), kontrastieren mit Aufforderungen (*da veniam*, 416; *exaudi*, 424), die aber auch Ausdruck ihrer Untertänigkeit sind. Sie stellt sich als Dianas Opfer dar (422) und opfert dann selbst. In Vers 423 stehen sich zu Versbeginn und Versende Scheidung und Hochzeit (*discidium – maritum*) sowie gleichsam parallel dazu im folgenden Vers *dolor* und *zelus* gegenüber. Sie möchte einerseits ihr Vergehen gegenüber Diana sühnen, zeigt aber andererseits keine Reue für ihre Ehe mit Jason, wenn sie eifersüchtig befürchtet, dass Glauke diese zerstören wird (422f.). Auch dass der *fructus* (429, ihre Kinder) nicht nützen soll (*ne prosit,* 430), erscheint paradox. Einerseits bezeichnet sie sich wie schon in Vers 420 als *miseranda*, wobei nicht klar ist, ob sich darin ihre Gewissensbisse gegenüber ihren Kindern zeigen oder ob sie sich doch eher selbst als bemitleidenswert darstellt;[7] andererseits erscheint sie auch ganz gefühlskalt, wenn sie ihre

---

[6] Zu ihrer Namensnennung in anderen Mythenversionen (Euripides, Apollonios Rhodios, Ovid, Seneca) s. Kaufmann (2006a) 366.

[7] Nicht sicher ist auch, ob *mea pignora* ihre Muttergefühle oder eher ihr schlechtes Gewissen zum Ausdruck bringen, da sie nicht nur Beweise für ihre Ehe, sondern auch für ihre Verfehlung gegenüber der Göttin sind; vgl. Kaufmann (2006a) 371.

Kinder mit dem Adjektiv *sacrilegus* (429) versieht. Die Kinder sind deshalb *sacrilegi*, weil Medea *sacerdos* mit ihnen zur Frevlerin wurde. Das Adjektiv verweist so auch auf ihren Zwiespalt, zum einen Mutter, zum anderen Priesterin zu sein.[8]

Widersprüchlich wirkt auch ihre im Anschluss an die Furien gerichtete Aufforderung, die Hochzeit zwischen Glauke und Jason zu verhindern (453–458):

> cur mora? nam nihil est quod non me exaudiat umquam.
> virginitas si casta placet, retinere pudorem
> si libet et numquam contagia blanda mariti   455
> quaeritis, innuptae nuptam exhorrete sorores.
> si Furias saevire precor nec sponte nocetis,
> non estis Furiae.

> Weshalb die Weile? Es gibt nämlich nichts, was mich je nicht erhört. Wenn euch reine Jungfräulichkeit gefällt, wenn es beliebt, züchtigen Anstand (455) zu wahren und ihr nie die verführerischen und befleckenden Berührungen eines Ehemannes sucht, ekelt euch, unverheiratete Schwestern, vor der bald verheirateten Frau. Wenn ich die Furien bitten muss zu wüten und ihr nicht von selbst Schaden anrichtet, seid ihr keine Furien.

Zunächst wundert sie sich, warum ihr die Furien nicht sofort gehorchen, und streicht ihre mächtige Stellung heraus. Sie stellt sich in einer Litotes wie eine Befehlende dar, deren Befehle immer ausgeführt werden (*nihil est quod non me exaudiat umquam*, 453).

Durch folgende Argumente will sie die Furien überzeugen, sich für ihren Fall einzusetzen und Jason und Glauke für ihre Heirat zu bestrafen:
1. *si virginitas casta placet*
2. *si pudorem retinere libet*
3. *si numquam contagia blanda mariti quaeritis*

Sie beziehen sich auf das Konzept der Jungfräulichkeit und Reinheit, das den jungfräulichen, unverheirateten Furien geläufig sein muss. Dass die Bitte, Verunreinigung zu ahnden, nun gerade von einer *virgo* und Priesterin ausgeht, die sich durch Heirat selbst einer solchen schuldig gemacht hat, wirkt wiederum eigenartig und widersprüchlich.

Auf das Ahnden zielt dann die folgende Invektive gegen die Furien ab:
1. *si Furias saevire precor*
2. *si sponte non nocetis, (ergo) non estis Furiae*

Die Furien sollen (gewissermaßen wie ein Staatsanwalt) von Amtes wegen gegen Vergehen wie gegen einen Vertragsbruch vorgehen. Wenn sie aber gebeten werden müssen und nicht aus eigenem Antrieb schaden, können sie keine Furien sein. Es

---

8 Antithetische Wirkung entfalten jene beiden Wörter auch in den Versen 136 f. (*Medea sacerdos, / sacrilega quae voce solet compellere caelum*), wo Venus Medea beschreibt, die ihr Sohn Cupido auf Wunsch Junos mit seinem Pfeil treffen soll.

entsteht der Eindruck, als würde Medea die Furien für eine falsche oder minderwertige Racheinstanz halten, sich selbst dagegen für fähiger, deren Aufgabe zu übernehmen. Anstatt sich unterwürfig zu zeigen, wenn sie sie um Hilfe bittet, bringt sie sich in Opposition zu den Furien. Dies wird auch durch die Häufung der sich gegenüberstehenden Pronomina (*meis*, *vestros*, *vos*, *nostras*, *me*) ersichtlich.

Die kämpferische Haltung Medeas wird durch eine weitere Antithese unterstützt: Die jungfräulichen, ehelosen Furien werden der bald verheirateten Glauke gegenübergestellt (*innuptae nuptam*, 456). Auch das erscheint paradox, ist doch Medea selbst verheiratet,[9] wenngleich sie sich hier mit den unverheirateten Furien verbündet,[10] da sie sich offenbar immer noch als Diana-Priesterin sieht, für die Jungfräulichkeit eine Bedingung ist; kurz zuvor hatte sie zu Diana gebetet und ihre Kinder, die sie reumütig als *sacrilegos fructus* bezeichnet, als Opfergabe angeboten (396–430). Passend dazu charakterisiert sie die Ehe negativ als *contagia blanda mariti* (455).

Die Ambivalenz in Medeas Rede setzt sich, kurz bevor sie den Mord an den Kindern begeht bzw. das Opfer vollzieht, fort (543–546):

> *satis est punisse nocentes*
> *insontesque simul. miseros hoc ense necabo,*
> *quo genitor feriendus erat; nihil ipsa dolebo,*   545
> *si ingrata maneat nullus de gente superstes.*

> Es genügt, Schuldige und Unschuldige zusammen bestraft zu haben. Ich werde die Elenden mit dem Schwert töten, (545) mit dem ihr Erzeuger hätte getötet werden müssen: Mich meinerseits wird es überhaupt nicht schmerzen, wenn niemand aus der undankbaren Familie am Leben bleibt.

Die Schuldigen (Jason, Glauke und Kreon) werden den unschuldigen Kindern gegenübergestellt; mit dem Adjektiv *miseros* wird einerseits verdeutlicht, dass sie ihre Kinder als bemitleidenswert betrachtet, andererseits betont das Verspaar 545 f. mit der Litotes, dass sie nichts dagegen einzuwenden hat, Jasons Geschlecht vollständig und endgültig zu zerstören.[11]

In Medeas Ich-Reden treten die scheinbar konträren Eigenschaften ihrer Figur, Priesterin sowie Ehefrau und Mutter zu sein, zeitgleich auf und verschmelzen miteinander: Als Verheiratete schlüpft sie zurück in ihre Rolle als Priesterin, die sich nicht untertänig und gehorsam zeigt, sondern fordernd und furchteinflößend auftritt. Als Priesterin betet sie zu den Göttinnen, um ihr Vergehen zu sühnen, geriert

---

9 Sie bezeichnet Jason auch in dieser Rede noch als ihren Ehemann, den Glauke nun heiraten wird (*Glauce veniet nuptura marito*, 447).
10 So wird sie auch mit den Wörtern *furens* (181, 389), *furit* (230), *furor* (63, 536) oder *furibunda* (62, 531, 537) versehen; vgl. Kaufmann (2006a) 109, 125, 385.
11 Zum Aspekt des Mitleids gegenüber ihren Kindern s. genauer Kaufmann (2006a) 432.

sich dabei aber zugleich als betrogene Ehefrau. Aus Rachsucht mordet sie, opfert aber für Diana.

Dass Medea verschiedene Seiten in sich vereinigt, kündigt der Dichter ganz zu Beginn des Gedichts an, wo zugleich auch das Thema benannt wird (1–13):

> *fert animus vulgare nefas et virginis atrae*
> *captivos monstrare deos, elementa clientes,*
> *naturam servire reae, servire puellae,*
> *astra poli et Phoebi cursus et sidera caeli*
> *arbitrio mulieris agi, pendere Tonantem,*   5
> *quod iubeat Medea nefas, ubi mittere flammas*
> *imperet aethereas. penetrat vox illa per auras,*
> *cum vitas mortesque facit, cum fata retorquet*
> *ad cursus quoscumque velit. licet hospite caeso*
> *serviat et Scythiae currat per templa Dianae,*   10
> *possidet astrigerum funesto pectore caelum*
> *et superos impune premit prece nixa virago*
> *invitos parere sibi.*

Mein Sinn führt mich dazu, den Frevel allgemein bekannt zu machen und zu zeigen, dass die Götter die Gefangenen einer düsteren jungen Frau sind, die Elemente ihr untertan, dass die Natur einer Verbrecherin, einem Mädchen dient, dass die Sterne des Himmelsgewölbes, die Bahnen des Phoebus und die Gestirne des Himmels (5) durch das Walten einer Frau angetrieben werden, dass der Donnerer angespannt harrt, welche Untat Medea anordnet, wohin sie die himmlischen Flammen schicken heißt. Ihre Stimme dringt durch die Lüfte, sooft sie Leben und Tod bewirkt, sooft sie die Geschicke umlenkt auf die Bahnen ihrer Wahl. Mag sie auch durch die Tötung von fremden Gästen (10) ihren Dienst leisten und sich im Tempel der skythischen Diana verausgaben, sie hat dennoch den Sterne tragenden Himmel als Besitz in ihrer todbringenden Brust und sie, die herrische junge Frau, nötigt die Götter kraft ihrer Beschwörung, ihr sogar gegen den eigenen Willen zu gehorchen, ohne dass sie bestraft wird.

Medea wird hier als übermenschliche und allmächtige Hexe[12] beschrieben, der sich alles um sie herum unterordnet. Ihre Macht wird jedoch zugleich kontrastiert durch das in Vers 3 wiederholte *servire*. In demselben Vers stehen sich *rea* und *puella* gegenüber, insofern sie nicht als Mädchen zur Verbrecherin wird.

Ihre Bezeichnungen als *virgo* (1), *puella* (3), *mulier* (5) und *virago* (12) verdeutlichen, dass Medea in allen Lebensphasen über die Welt herrscht, können aber auch eine Entwicklung anzeigen, zumal *virgo* durch *virago* gesteigert wird.[13] Der Anfang *fert animus*, der Ovids *Metamorphosen* aufruft, macht auf eine Verwandlung Medeas

---

[12] Der Versanfang *fert animus* verweist auch (s.u.) auf Lucan, wodurch die Parallelen von Medea und der thessalischen Hexe Erictho, die im *Bellum civile* die Toten beschwört, betont werden; vgl. Kaufmann (2006a) 107 f.

[13] *Virago* bezeichnet Heldinnen oder Göttinnen, wie etwa Minerva oder Diana, die sowohl jungfräulich und weiblich als auch kriegerisch und männlich sind; vgl. Kaufmann (2006a) 115.

aufmerksam:[14] Sie wird durch Amor von der rasenden männergleichen *virago* zur schwachen Liebenden (*virgo*, 62–64), um dann in Theben spätestens wieder zur gebietenden *virago* zu werden. In den *Metamorphosen* wird die jedem Wesen innenwohnende *substantia* in der Verwandlung beibehalten. Es ist die Priesterin, die Medea männergleich (*virago*) ist und jungfräulich (*virgo*) weiterhin bleibt.

Dass der Dichter Medea Männlichkeit zuschreibt, wird auch am Wort *penetrat* (7) deutlich, was zugleich die für sie charakteristische Rhetorik beschreibt.[15] Dass es sich dabei um eine Verkehrung von Genderzuschreibungen handelt, wird in diese Passage ebenfalls ersichtlich, wenn sich eine Sterbliche, ein Mädchen, über die Götter erhebt (1–7), mit ihrer Magie den Lauf der Gestirne zu ändern vermag, Macht über alle Elemente der Natur ausübt (2–7, 11–13) und über Leben und Tod bestimmt (8 f.).[16]

3 Medea und Jason

Wenn Medea derart männliche Züge übernimmt, ergibt sich sogleich die Frage, ob und wie sich diese Männlichkeit auch gegenüber ihrem Ehemann Jason offenbart bzw. wie sich Medea ihm gegenüber verhält. In folgender Textstelle macht Medea *sacerdos* Jason äußerst unvermittelt einen Heiratsantrag (247–260):

```
                     conversa sacerdos
ad iuvenem: ‚dic, nauta fugax, pirata nefande:
est consors matrona decens an caelibe vita
degis adhuc nullum que domi < tibi > pignus habetur?'      250
‚solus' ait captivus, ego, mihi pignora nulla
coniugis aut subolis.' dictis gavisa virago
blanda refert: ‚vis ergo meus nunc esse maritus?'
‚servus' Jason ait, ‚tantum ne vita negetur
te precor et dominam fateor.' sic fatus. at illa            255
rumpi vincla umeris, virgo suspendit ab aris,
ut facinus purget; proprium vocat ipsa maritum
vestibus indutum Tyriis, quas sericus ambit
mollis et in medio fulvum distinxerat aurum,
blattea puniceo radiabant stamina filo.                     260
```

---

14 In den *Metamorphosen* findet eine Verwandlung Medeas vom liebenden Mädchen zur grausamen Hexe (7.1–158) statt; s. Schubert (1998) 67–75.
15 So verweist auch das Schwert (*mucro*), mit dem Medea in Raserei hantiert (*Medea nocens urgetque ministros / nudato mucrone furens*, 180 f.), insbesondere in Verbindung mit dem Adjektiv „nackt" (*nudus*), auf das männliche Glied; vgl. Adams (1990) 19 f.
16 Ebenso beschreibt die Göttin Venus Medea, wenn sie Cupido anweist, Medea in Jason verliebt zu machen (136–140).

Die Priesterin wandte sich zum Jüngling: „Sag, unstet flüchtiger Seefahrer, abscheulicher Seeräuber: Hast du eine ehrbare Frau zur Gattin oder lebst du noch ein eheloses (250) Leben und hast zu Hause kein Unterpfand deiner Liebe?" „Allein", sagte der Gefangene, „bin ich, ich habe keine Unterpfänder, weder eine Gattin noch Nachwuchs." Über die Worte freute sich die herrische junge Frau und erwiderte verführerisch: „Willst du also nun mein Ehemann sein?" „Auch dein Sklave", sagte Jason, „nur dass du mir das Leben nicht verweigerst, (255) bitte ich dich und als Herrin anerkenne ich dich." So sprach er. Aber sie löste die Fesseln von den Schultern, die junge Frau, und hängt sie am Altar auf, um ihre Missetat zu sühnen. Ihren eigenen Ehemann nannte sie ihn, der bekleidet war mit durch tyrischen Purpur gefärbten Gewändern, deren Rand weiche Seide umfasste und in deren Mitte sich dunkelgelbes Goldgewebe abhob: (260) Das purpurne Gewebe strahlte durch den leuchtend roten Faden.

Der Heiratsantrag ist nicht nur für eine Priesterin seltsam, auch für eine Frau entspricht er nicht den Konventionen: Medea *virago* (252) wirkt so äußerst männlich. Jason nimmt ihren Heiratsantrag an und gibt sich seiner *domina* (255) als *servus* (254) hin. Nachdem ihr Wille in Erfüllung gegangen ist, ist Medea besänftigt und wird zur *virgo* (256).[17] Dass es sich indes nicht um Liebe und echte Zuneigung handelt, wird auch an Medeas Anrede an Jason deutlich (*dic, nauta fugax, pirata nefande*, 248), in der eher Verachtung als Verliebtheit zu erkennen ist. Auch dass Jason ihrem Antrag zustimmt, erfolgt eher aus einer Notsituation denn aus Liebe heraus, liegt er doch gefesselt vor ihr auf dem Altar. Sie nennt ihn *proprium maritum* (257) und erachtet ihn so als ihr Eigentum, über das sie verfügen kann.[18] Die Rollenzuteilung von Mann und Frau werden hier deutlich sichtbar vertauscht.

Am Schluss dieser Passage wird ausführlich die Kleidung und das Aussehen Jasons beschrieben (258–260). Es steht in deutlichem Kontrast zu Medeas Erscheinung: Während Jasons Gewand rot-golden strahlt (*radiabant*, 260), ist Medea schwarz (*atra*, 1)[19] und blutrünstig (*cruenta*, 22, 152, 195, 549).[20] Jasons Schönheit wird immer wieder hervorgehoben: So wird er eigens mit dem Attribut *pulcher* versehen (56, 179); seine Schönheit scheint auch der Grund zu sein, weswegen sich Medea (179, 210) und Glauke (371–373) in ihn verlieben. Dadurch wird Jason gleichsam zum Objekt dieser Frauen, denen er sich hingibt.[21] Da jedoch gemeinhin die Frau das Objekt männlicher Begierde ist, wird auch durch diese Hervorhebung der Schönheit Jasons deutlich, wie

---

17 Zur Konnotation von *virgo* als gefährlich und bösartig s. Kaufmann (2006a) 109.
18 Mit einem *servitium amoris* der römischen Liebeselegie, auf das die Bezeichnungen *servus* und *domina* hier anspielen, hat diese Szene eher wenig gemein. Dass sich Jason im Sinne der Liebeselegie als elegischer Liebhaber stilisiert, würde voraussetzen, dass er sich tatsächlich in Medea verliebt hat. Dies erscheint angesichts der Tatsache, dass er sich auf einem Opferaltar befindet, absurd. Er begibt sich nicht aus Liebe in die Rolle des Sklaven, sondern weil er sein Leben retten will. Zu den Bezügen bzw. Nicht-Bezügen auf die Topoi der römischen Liebeselegie s. Kaufmann (2006b) 107–109.
19 Glauke wird dagegen als ihre Rivalin mit dem Adjektiv „weiß" versehen (*niveam Glaucen*, 426).
20 Medea ist einmal *fulgens*, allerdings in dem Moment, wo sie sich mit ihrem Gatten Jason vereinigt (*iungitur Aesonidi fulgens Medea marito*, 289).
21 Vgl. Simons (2005) 197.

die Zuschreibung von Männlichkeit und Weiblichkeit verkehrt wird. Während Medea den männlich aktiven Part einnimmt, erscheint Jason passiv und weiblich. Aktiv zeigt er sich nur, wenn er vor Kolchis von seinem Schiff springt und an Land schwimmt (41–44) und als er zu Cupido betet (201–208, 217–219). Sonst fügt er sich dem Willen und den Aufforderungen anderer: Aus Angst willigt er ein, Medea zu heiraten (254f.); als sich Glauke in ihn verliebt, stimmt er der Heirat gleichsam passiv zu: Er wurde ausgewählt, wofür er sich bedankt (*grates electus agit*, 380).[22] In der Beziehung zu Medea ist Jason klar unterlegen. Jason bleibt Medeas Opfer, auch nachdem er in der Opferszene verschont blieb. Die Verse 30f. (*cur hospes amatur / qui mactandus erat, vel cur mactatur amatus*), die das Prooemium abschließen und auf die beiden Teile des Epyllions, die Heirat in Kolchis und die Ermordung in Theben, vorausweisen, machen explizit auf Jasons durchgängige Opferrolle aufmerksam.

Auch ist er nicht der Held, den man aus dem Kontext der Argonautenfahrt kennt.[23] Die Seefahrt verbindet Dracontius vielmehr negativ mit Raub und Piraterie.[24] Dies schlägt sich in der Bezeichnung Jasons als *pirata* (210, 235, 248) bzw. *praedo* (368) nieder. Der Raub wird dabei anders als in den Argonautenepen nicht bewundert;[25] als *pirata* ist Jason vielmehr ein Feigling, der in Situationen der Bedrohung nur zittern oder um Rettung flehen kann.[26] Dass Jason derart charakterisiert ist, wird in folgenden Versen noch unterstrichen (330–333):

> *sic meruit veniam generum confessus Achilles,*
> *sic pater ignovit Lycomedes pectore natae*
> *et Pyrrhum suscepit avus gremioque nepotem*
> *fovit et ad Troiam post crimina misit Achillem.*

So wurde Achill Verzeihung zuteil, nachdem er sich als Schwiegersohn bekannt hatte, so verzieh der Vater Lykomedes im Herzen seiner Tochter, hob als Großvater Pyrrhus auf, herzte den Enkel auf seinem Schoß und schickte Achill später trotz des Vergehens nach Troja.

---

22 Vgl. Bright (1987) 71.
23 Jason wird zwar als *callidus heros* (41) bezeichnet, doch hat das Attribut *callidus* bei Dracontius die Bedeutung 'listig', 'verschlagen', wodurch sein Heroentum in Zweifel gezogen wird; vgl. Simons (2005) 196; Bright (1987) 49.
24 Zur negativen Konnotation des Begriffs *nauta* vgl. Kaufmann (2006a) 121; Simons (2005) 196.
25 Die Verse 367f. (*miratur rex ipse Creon, laudatur Iason, / quod freta, quod terras sic felix praedo vagetur*) zeigen Kreons Bewunderung und Lob für Jason. Kreon bewundert allerdings nicht ihn, sondern vielmehr das Vlies; auch lobt er Jason nicht für die Beute, die er selbst gar nicht erbeutet hat (vgl. 363f.), sondern er lobt lediglich, dass er als *pirata* umherreist; vgl. Kaufmann (2006a) 345.
26 Bei seiner Gefangennahme auf Kolchis wird Jason als ängstlich beschrieben (*paventem*, 48); in der Opferszene bittet er die Gottheit ängstlich um Hilfe (*precatur murmure sollicito*, 200f.). Cupido fragt ihn, was er fürchtet (*quid metuis*, 211); Jason ruft dann laut um Hilfe (*exclamat: 'Sucurre . . .'*, 218); er sieht sich als Opfer, fürchtet sich vor dem Tod und fühlt sich bedroht (*victima sum, pereo: iugulis male mucro minatur*, 239); Medea beschreibt ihn dann als unwürdiges Opfer, das zittert, den Schmerz fürchtet und blutlos vor ihr liegt (243–246); vgl. Simons (2005) 196–198.

Nachdem Medeas Vater Aietes über ihre Hochzeit mit Jason zunächst erzürnt, dann aber durch Bacchus von ihrer Nützlichkeit überzeugt wurde, zeigt er sich besänftigt und stellt hier einen Vergleich zwischen sich und Lykomedes bzw. zwischen Jason und Achill her. Lykomedes konnte Achill verzeihen, dass er mit seiner Tochter Deidameia Pyrrhus (Neoptolemus) gezeugt hatte. Das Gleichnis – anaphorisch durch *sic* (330, 331) und epiphorisch durch *Achilles . . . Achillem* (330, 333) betont – ist nun im Hinblick auf die Rolle des Jason deshalb bemerkenswert, weil sich der Held Achill im Hause des Lykomedes als Mädchen verkleidet hatte, um sich so einer Teilnahme am trojanischen Krieg zu entziehen; auch wird Achills unerlaubtes Verhältnis mit Deidameia als *crimina* bezeichnet. So zeigt auch dieser Vergleich, dass Jason als weiblicher und verbrecherischer Antiheld wahrgenommen wird.

Medea und Jason werden also jeweils wie folgt gegenübergestellt:

Medea	Jason
bestimmend, fordernd (*domina*)	willfahrend, unterwürfig (*servus*)
dunkel	strahlend
selbstbewusst, einschüchternd	ängstlich, feige
aktiv	passiv
männlich	*weiblich*

Darin, dass Medea ihre Liebe zu Jason als *crimen* (417, 419) bzw. als *sacrilegus amor* (293) und ihre Kinder als *sacrilegos fructus* (429) betrachtet, sieht die Forschung eine frühchristliche Sexualfeindlichkeit[27] oder generell misogyne Haltung des Autors: Medea sei nach dem Muster des Sündenfalls zugleich Ursache der Leidenschaft und Ursprung des Bösen.[28] Da jedoch Medea derart männlich gezeichnet wird und die Ursache der Leidenschaft gerade nicht die Frau, sondern der *pulcher Jason* ist, erweist sich diese Interpretation als keineswegs stichhaltig.[29]

Medeas Heiratsantrag ist auch deshalb so erstaunlich, weil er vor Dracontius nicht Bestandteil der Medea-Darstellungen war und mithin eine Neuerung des Dracontius darstellt. Damit komme ich zur diachronen Betrachtung der Medea Figur und zur Transformation, die sie bei Dracontius in der Spätantike erfährt.

---

27 S. Mallinger (1971) 187 f.; ebenso Glaser (2001) 73–75.
28 Ebenso Bright (1987) 83; dagegen aber Klein (2001) 237 f.
29 Simons (2005) 206 f. weist zudem darauf hin, dass die Hochzeit in Kolchis positiv bewertet wird, da sie generisch wie ein Epithalamium gestaltet und insofern legitimiert ist. Zu Dracontius' Gestaltung der Hochzeit als Epithalamium s. Selent (2011) 149–164.

4 Medea vor und bei Dracontius

In Kolchis ist Dracontius' Medea nicht die brave Königstochter, sondern eine grausame und emanzipierte Diana-Priesterin; im zweiten Teil, den Dracontius nicht in Korinth, sondern in Theben situiert,[30] ist Medea nicht damit beschäftigt, Jasons Treuebruch, sondern ihr Vergehen gegenüber der Göttin Diana zu sühnen.[31] Dracontius zeigt Medea nicht als naives junges Mädchen, das sich vom Helden Jason beeindrucken lässt und sich in ihn verliebt. Sie muss die Liebe stattdessen erst lernen (*discat amare*, 63). Amor wird von Venus eigens darauf hingewiesen, dass es Medea ist, die er mit seinem Pfeil durchbohren muss (*Medeam fixurus eris*, 144); er soll folglich sorgfältig und bedacht vorgehen (*sollicitus tamen ista para catusque memento*, 143).[32] Medea ist kein leichtes Opfer, sie ist nicht schwach, sie plagt sich nicht mit Gewissensbissen. Sie behält vielmehr auch hier die Oberhand: Jason wird als Gefangener geliebt (*captus amatur*, 18) und als Geliebter schließlich geopfert (*mactatur amatus*, 31). In der Szene, wo sich Medea selbst als Liebende bezeichnet, stellt sie klar, dass sie sich nicht etwa blind vor Liebe täuschen lässt (*non fallis amantem*, 344). Auch zeigt sich Medea nicht naiv, sondern kritisch und vorsichtig, wenn sie ihren Mann nach Kindern oder einer Ehe fragt (248–250).

Dadurch, dass Dracontius beide Motive, die Heirat mit Jason in Kolchis und den Kindermord in Theben, miteinander vereint, muss er sich in besonderem Maße mit einer liebenden und zugleich grausamen Frau auseinandersetzen. Dracontius zeigt die Ambiguität seiner Medea nicht dadurch, dass er sie im ersten Teil untertänig und liebend darstellt und im zweiten Teil böse und rächend, sondern dadurch, dass er sie durchgehend zwiespältig charakterisiert. Dadurch schafft Dracontius einen einheitlichen Charakter: Medea ist wie in Theben so auch in Kolchis dominant, dunkel und bedrohlich.[33]

Dass in der Medea des Dracontius besonders ihre Männlichkeit aufscheint, soll im Vergleich mit einer Passage Ovids, wo sie sich explizit als Frau bezeichnet, veranschaulicht werden. Eingangs wurde Medeas Schuldbekenntnis und Bitte an die Göttin Diana betrachtet (*Romul.* 10,416–430); zum Vergleich hier nun eine Textstelle aus Ovids *Heroides* (12,116–120):

---

[30] Zur Frage, warum Dracontius Medeas Kindermord nach Theben verlegt, s. Schetter (1980) und Kaufmann (2006a) 343.
[31] Auf folgende Vorgängertexte nimmt Dracontius Bezug: Eur. *Med.*, Apoll. Rhod. *Arg.*, Dion. Skyth. *Arg.*, Ov. *Met.* 7.1–424, Ov. *Her.* 12, Sen. *Med.*, Val. Fl. *Arg.*, Hos. Geta *Med.*; zu Dracontius' Neuerungen s. Kaufmann (2006a) 52f.
[32] Medea muss auch zweimal von Amors Pfeil getroffen werden, ehe sie der Liebe nachgibt; vgl. Simons (2005) 164f.
[33] Vgl. Simons (2005) 161.

> *sic ego, sed tecum, dilaceranda fui.*
> *nec tamen extimui – quid enim post illa timerem? –*
> *credere me pelago, femina iamque nocens.*
> *numen ubi est? ubi di? meritas subeamus in alto,*
> *tu fraudis poenas, credulitatis ego!* 120

So hätte ich zerfleischt werden müssen, aber zusammen mit dir! Und trotzdem habe ich keine Angst davor gehabt – was hätte ich denn danach noch fürchten sollen? – mich dem Meer anzuvertrauen, eine Frau und dazu noch schuldig. Wo ist der göttliche Wille? Wo sind die Götter? Wir sollten eigentlich auf dem hohen Meer die verdiente Strafe erleiden, (120) du für deinen Betrug, ich für meine Leichtgläubigkeit.

Hier spricht die liebende Medea: Sie möchte *zusammen* (*sed tecum*, 116) mit ihrem Geliebten bestraft werden. Die Liebe und der daraus resultierende Wille, Jason zu begleiten, macht Ovids Medea furchtlos und risikobereit (*nec tamen extimui*, 117). Diese Furchtlosigkeit ist jedoch, wie sie einräumt, insofern bemerkenswert, als sie eine Frau (daher schwach) und schuldig (daher der göttlichen Bestrafung ausgesetzt) ist. Sich als schwache und hilflose Frau zu charakterisieren und gleichzeitig schuldig zu sein, da sie ihren Bruder ermordet hat, erscheint paradox, doch ist (*femina*) *nocens* (118) in *Her.* 12 auch eine feste Bezeichnung für Medea (106) und weist als Schlüsselwort auf die tragische Tat voraus (124, 129).[34] Für Jasons Betrug und ihre Leichtgläubigkeit erwartet sie dann die Strafe der Götter, mit der sie sich schließlich an ihm rächen möchte. Chiastisch werden sein und ihr jeweiliges Vergehen gegenübergestellt, wobei mit den beiden Pronomina *tu* und *ego* künftig auch der jeweils andere gemeint sein kann. Die *credulitas* (120) ist für Liebende typisch; für Medea ist indes auch das darin mitklingende Wort *crudelitas* passend.[35]

Auch wenn der Begriff *femina* hier ironisch erscheint, insofern sie als *femina nocens* männliche Eigenschaften des weiblichen Geschlechts verkörpert, und auch wenn er an die Trugrede der euripideischen Medea erinnert und hier deutlich Medeas ambivalentes Schwanken zwischen schwacher Liebe und grausamer Rache zum Ausdruck kommt, betont die ovidianische Medea ihre Weiblichkeit und ihre Schwäche. Die dracontische Medea ist anders: Sie ist eine *virago*, die ihre Männlichkeit und Stärke hervorhebt. Entsprechend klagt sie nicht, sie fordert. Während die ovidianische Medea beinahe unterwürfig nach den strafenden Göttern fragt, fordert die dracontische Medea die Götter zur Strafe auf und knüpft Bedingungen daran. Bei Ovid rächt sich die Betrogene aus verletzter Liebe. Schmerz und Eifersucht treiben auch Dracontius' Medea an, doch mordet sie nicht deshalb, sondern sie opfert ihrer Göttin.

---

34 S. Bessone (1997) ad loc.
35 Vgl. Bessone (1997) 175–179.

5 Fazit

Zum einen ging es mir darum zu zeigen, wie der männliche Autor Medeas Ich-Reden modelliert, zu welcher Gelegenheit er sie sprechen lässt und welche Rolle die Ich-Sprecherin übernimmt. Darüber hinaus sollte der Beitrag darlegen, welche Gender-Parameter der Autor auf ihre Ich-Aussagen anwendet.

Medeas Ich-Reden sind überwiegend Gebete, die sie in ihrer Rolle als *sacerdos* an die Götter, Diana und die Furien richtet. Als solche spricht sie selbstbewusst und dominant; sie benimmt sich als Sterbliche nicht demütig und unterwürfig, was ihrer Situation eigentlich zukäme, sondern stellt Forderungen und zeigt sich als bestimmende und herrische *virago*.

Das dominante Auftreten wirkt mithin seltsam und unpassend, was durch verschiedene Antithesen im Text unterstützt wird. Als Priesterin hat sie sich durch ihre Heirat zu Jason sowie die damit verbundene Geburt ihrer Kinder schuldig gemacht; dennoch wendet sie sich an die Furien und fordert sie als betrogene Ehefrau auf, ihre Nebenbuhlerin Glauke zu bestrafen.

Dominant und bestimmend verhält sich Medea auch gegenüber Jason, der sich ihr im Gegenzug als sklavisches Opfer hingibt. Auch zu ihm spricht sie in dieser Opferszene als *sacerdos*. Dass sie ihm als Priesterin und als Frau einen Heiratsantrag macht, wirkt ebenfalls kurios und unpassend. Da sie typisch männlich agiert, entsteht der Eindruck einer Emanzipierten. Medea *virago* tritt Jason, der als weich und ängstlich modelliert wird, mächtig, willensstark und rigoros entgegen. Während er negativ bewertet wird, wird Medea nicht explizit verurteilt.

Diese Charakterisierung resultiert nun daraus, dass Dracontius seine Medea – und das ist das Spezifikum seiner Dichtung – als Priesterin anlegt und ihr Priestertum in den Vordergrund stellt. Als Priesterin ist sie ein Wesen ‚in-between'; sie vermittelt nicht nur zwischen Mensch und Gott, Dracontius formt sie auch als Wesen zwischen den Geschlechtern.[36] Sie zeigt sich nicht weiblich, wird daher nicht schwach und klagt auch nicht. Als dominante *virago* setzt sie sich über ihr Konfliktpotential hinweg und bleibt auch in ihrem Wandel von *virago* und *virgo* in ihrer Rolle als Diana-Priesterin bestehen. Indem der Dichter Medea als Priesterin konzipiert, verleiht er ihr trotz der Kombination des Kolchis- und des Kindermord-Stoffes einen einheitlichen Charakter.

---

[36] Zu dieser Gender-Hybridisierung der Stimme einer Priesterin s. auch Cordes und Hafner in diesem Band.

Literaturverzeichnis

Adams (1990): James Noel Adams, *The Latin Sexual Vocabulary*, Baltimore.
Bessone (1997): Federica Bessone, *Heroidum Epistula XII (Medea Iasoni), testi con commento*, Florenz.
Bright (1987): David F. Bright, *The Miniature Epic in Vandal Africa*, Norman.
Glaser (2001): Horst Albert Glaser, *Medea oder Frauenehre, Kindsmord oder Emanzipation: Zur Geschichte eines Mythos*, Frankfurt am Main.
Kaufmann (2006a): Helen Kaufmann, *Dracontius Romul. 10 (Medea), Einleitung, Text, Übersetzung und Kommentar*, Heidelberg.
Kaufmann (2006b): Helen Kaufmann, „Intertextualität in Dracontius' Medea (*Romul.* 10)", *MH* 63, 104–114.
Klein (2001): Richard Klein, „Medea am Ausgang der Antike. Bemerkungen zum Epyllion «Medea» des christlichen Dichters Dracontius", *WJA* NF 25, 229–238.
Mallinger (1971): Léon Mallinger, *Médée. Étude de littérature comparée*, Genf.
Schetter (1980): Willy Schetter, „Medea in Theben", *WJA* NF 6a, 209–221.
Schubert (1998): Werner Schubert, „Medea in der lateinischen Literatur der Antike", in: Annette Kämmerer, Margret Schuchard und Agnes Speck (Hgg.), *Medeas Wandlungen. Studien zu einem Mythos in Kunst und Wissenschaft*, Heidelberg, 55–91.
Selent (2001): Doreen Selent, *Allegorische Mythenerklärung in der Spätantike. Wege zum Werk des Dracontius*, Rahden.
Simons (2005): Roswitha Simons, *Dracontius und der Mythos. Christliche Weltsicht und pagane Kultur in der ausgehenden Spätantike*, München.

Notes on Contributors

Luca Basso got his Doctorate Degree from the University of Turin. He has studied in Heidelberg and Munich as a DAAD scholarship holder. He has published articles on Ovid's *Fasti* and a commentary on the first part of *Fasti* 5 (Alessandria 2022).

Helge Baumann is postdoctoral research assistant at the JLU Gießen, Germany. He has published on the reception of epics, literary role construction, and intertextuality in Martial's *Epigrams* and Statius' *Silvae*. Currently, his research is centered on the representation of acoustic phenomena and auditory perception in Latin literature, especially in Roman tragedy.

Federica Bessone is Professor of Latin at the University of Turin; she studied at the SNS, Pisa. She is the author of *P. Ovidii Nasonis Heroidum Epistula XII. Medea Iasoni* (1997) and *La 'Tebaide' di Stazio. Epica e potere* (2011); she co-edited *The Literary Genres in the Flavian Age. Canons, Transformations, Reception* (2017) and *Lettori latini e italiani di Ovidio* (2019). She is a member of the editorial board of *Eugesta*, *MD*, *RCCM*, and the *Oxford Commentaries on Flavian Poetry*.

Lisa Cordes is a Feodor Lynen Research Fellow at the University of Cambridge and a Juniorprofessor of Latin Philology at the Humboldt University of Berlin. She has held positions at the Freie University of Berlin and at the Ludwig Maximilians University of Munich. Her research focuses on ancient concepts of fiction, persona and authorship in Latin literature, on panegyric rhetoric, praise and critique of rulers in Antiquity, and on gender studies in Antiquity. She is a member of the editorial board of *Eugesta*.

Jacqueline Fabre-Serris is Professor of Latin Literature at the University of Lille. She is co-editor of *Dictynna* and *Eugesta*. Her research focuses on Latin literature, on mythology, on mythography, and on gender studies. Monographs include *Mythe et poésie dans les Métamorphoses d'Ovide* (1995), *Rome, l'Arcadie et la mer des origines* (2008). She is co-editor of *Women and War in Antiquity* (2015), and *Identities, Ethnicities and Gender in Antiquity* (2021). She is currently writing a book on Ovid and Sulpicia.

Therese Fuhrer has held Chairs of Latin at the Universities of Trier, Zurich, Freiburg, the Freie University of Berlin, and since 2013 at the LMU Munich. She has published on topics ranging from Hellenistic Greek through republican and Augustan poetry and prose to Augustine. She is currently engaged in a number of research projects in the field of ancient philosophy and rhetoric, on Roman historiography, on the authorial voice, and Late Antiquity.

Markus Hafner is Assistant Professor of Greek at the University of Graz. He has held positions at the Universities of Munich, Heidelberg, the Humboldt University of Berlin, and has been a Humboldt Research Fellow at the University of North Carolina at Chapel Hill. His focus ranges from Imperial Literature (especially Lucian) through conceptions of authorship and literary collaboration in Archaic and Classical Greek to the History of Classics in the twentieth century.

Judith Peller Hallett is Professor of Classics and Distinguished Scholar-Teacher Emerita at the University of Maryland, College Park. She has published widely in the areas of Latin language and literature; women, sexuality and the family in ancient Greek and Roman society; and the study and reception of classics in the Anglophone world, focusing on pioneering female classicists and Jewish scholars who fled Nazi-occupied Europe. A 2013 collection of essays from Routledge – *Domina Illustris: Latin Literature, Gender and Reception* – celebrates her academic career.

Henriette Harich-Schwarzbauer is professor of Latin Philology at the University of Basel since 2002. Her publications range from the History of Women Philosophers to Latin poetry in Late Antiquity as well as to Neo-Latin authors and to the History of Classical Scholarship. Currently she prepares an edition with commentary and translation on the 'minor poems' of Claudius Claudianus and is the main investigator of a research project on poetic 'books' in Late Antiquity and the Renaissance.

Emily Hauser is Lecturer in Classics and Ancient History at the University of Exeter. She has written articles on gender in Homer, women poets in antiquity and their reception in contemporary women's writing, and is the author of a trilogy of novels reworking the women of Greek myth, including *For the Most Beautiful* (2016, Penguin Random House). Her current book, *How Women Became Poets: A Gender History of Greek Literature*, looks at the gendering of authorship in Greek poetry and is forthcoming with Princeton University Press.

Alison Keith is Professor of Classics and Director of the Jackman Humanities Institute at the University of Toronto. She has published widely on the intersections of gender and genre in Latin literature and Roman society. Her current research projects include a biography of Sulpicia and the study of Roman Epicureanism in Latin literature.

Florence Klein is Associate Professor of Latin Literature at the University of Lille. She is co-editor of *Dictynna* and member of the editorial board of *Eugesta*. Her publications focus on Hellenistic and Roman poetry, literary theory and intertextuality, *enargeia*, and gender studies. Her current research projects include a lexicon of metapoetic imagery in Greek and Roman literature and several works on the reception of several Hellenistic poets in Augustan poetry.

Christoph Mayr is a research and teaching assistant at the LMU Munich. He is currently working on his doctoral thesis on the fallibility and failures of the author's persona in Horace, Ovid, and Seneca.

Valentina Moro is a postdoctoral researcher in Political philosophy at the University of Verona, where she collaborates with the "Hannah Arendt" Center for Political Studies. Her research combines Political philosophy, Feminist theories, and Classical studies (with a special focus on the Attic Tragedy). She has held postdoctoral positions at the Istituto italiano per gli studi filosofici (Italy) and at the Center for Advanced Studies of Southeastern Europe (Croatia). She co-edited the book *Polis, Erōs, Parrēsia. Letture etico-politiche contemporanee della tragedia greca* (Padova, 2018).

Alison Sharrock is Hulme Professor of Latin at the University of Manchester. She has published extensively on Latin poetry, and is author of *Seduction and Repetition in Ovid's* Ars Amatoria *2*, *Reading Roman Comedy: Poetics and Playfulness in Plautus and Terence* (2009), and co-author with Rhiannon Ash of *Fifty Key Classical Authors* (2002). She is the co-editor of numerous books, including *The Art of Love: bimillennial essays on Ovid's* Ars Amatoria *and* Remedia Amoris (2006) with Roy Gibson and Steven Green, *Metamorphic Readings: Transformation, Language, and Gender in the Interpretation of Ovid's* Metamorphoses (2020) with Mats Malm and Daniel Moller, and *Maternal Conceptions in Classical Literature and Philosophy* (2020) with Alison Keith.

Giulia Sissa is Professor of Political Science and Classical Studies at the University of California, Los Angeles (UCLA). She holds a PhD in Classical Studies from the École des Hautes Études en Sciences Sociales (EHESS) in Paris. Her research focuses on aspects of classical antiquity that are closely linked to important contemporary debates, including feminism, sexuality and the body, political emotions, addictions and utopian thought.

Ann-Kathrin Stähle studied Latin and Ancient Greek at the University of Basel and Geneva. She is engaged in the SNF project "Muse – Musse – Musseraum" doing her PhD on œuvre concepts and poetics of myth in Sidonius Apollinaris. She is a member of the PhD program at the Department of Classics at the University of Basel.

General Index

Achilles 186f., 261 n. 16, 311, 384f.
active / passive 48, 60–62, 73, 77, 112, 133–135, 137 n. 34, 151, 159, 174f., 207, 219 n. 27, 248–251, 323, 384f.
Aelius Theon 1f.
Aeneas 15f., 77 n. 20, 297, 304 n. 40, 307, 309, 311f., 316–318, 338, 340
Aesculapius (s. also apotheosis, Ocyroe) 287, 289, 290, 294, 296, 298, 302
aesthetic(s) 43, 45–47, 57, 60 n. 53, 65, 77, 88, 204, 228, 231
aetiology / aetiological 118, 302, 304, 329, 340, 343, 345, 347 n. 61, 351
Agathon of Athens (poet) 205–215, 224f., 232f., 237f.
age 1, 113, 116, 120, 165f., 182, 206 n. 5, 213, 218, 226, 228 n. 49, 230, 235f., 244 n. 3, 357
agency 4, 7, 71, 74, 76f., 79f., 83f., 87f., 118, 133, 300 n. 30
aggression 109, 248, 250, 252, 308 n. 1, 313 n. 17, 321, 367
Aglaurus 294 n. 19, 302
Alcibiades 205f., 211, 219 n. 27, 230, 232f.
Alcithoë 331 n. 7, 346–351
Alcmene 196
Alphaeus 307, 313f., 317f., 320, 322
ambiguity / ambivalence 4, 25, 31f., 36, 40, 43, 47–51, 54f., 72f., 75, 81 n. 37, 86f., 105, 154, 160, 219 n. 27, 226, 292, 299 n. 26, 310 n. 9, 367 n. 29, 375 n. 2, 380, 386f.
amoibaion 182f., 193 n. 59
amor s. love
amphitheatre 115, 117, 119, 122 n. 76
Andromacha 180–190
animal
 – attributed with human gender 106, 115f., 118f., 121–123
 – boar 115, 117, 119–121
 – dog 105, 107, 115–121
 – speaking 4, 106, 115f., 121f.
anniversary (s. also birthday) 261–264, 275
anthropomorphism 105f., 116f., 123
Antigone 6, 151–177, 187 n. 37, 375 n. 3
Aphrodite (s. also Venus) 30, 86 n. 60, 135–138, 224, 229f., 235, 272

Apollo (s. also vates) 17, 71–92, 138, 153, 162, 270, 287f., 290–292, 294, 296, 307, 313 n. 17, 324, 369
apotheosis (s. also Aesculapius, Hippolytus / Virbius, metamorphosis) 196, 286, 289, 294
appropriation / depossession 26 n. 3, 29f., 35–39, 106, 112, 135, 137 n. 36, 139, 145, 307
Arachne 301
Arethusa 99f., 307f., 313–325, 370
Arge 118
Argos 120, 180 n. 5
Aristonike 80, 84 n. 51
assonance 335
Atalante 118
Athena (s. also Minerva) 120, 222, 290 n. 12, 297, 332, 357
Athens 78 n. 25, 80, 82 n. 44, 134 n. 22, 159, 170, 203, 207, 229, 233, 238, 302, 311
attic drama / tragedy 152, 154, 156 n. 23, 180f.
authorship 3f., 7, 22, 71f., 74 n. 8, 77 n. 19, 79–85, 87, 129, 131f., 137, 140, 145, 191 n. 53, 257–281, 300–305
authority 3, 6, 11, 54, 73 n. 6, 75, 77, 79, 80, 87 n. 64, 113 n. 37, 130, 137 n. 36, 172f., 198 n. 72, 290, 357, 360, 367
autofiction 307–328
autonomy / autonomous 56, 72–74, 79f. n. 30, 87 n. 64, 100, 157, 162, 175

Bacchus 195, 222 n. 33, 263, 329, 331f., 351, 385
bard 4, 71, 73, 76 n. 15, 82 n. 42, 87f., 129, 131f., 135–137, 139, 304
beauty / *forma* 25 n. 2, 62 n. 58, 99f., 121, 192f., 203, 208f., 217–238, 243–252, 291f., 307, 318–324, 334, 343f., 348, 383
Bee Maidens 86f.
birthday / *natalis* (s. also anniversary) 261–264, 275
body 54, 111f., 119 n. 64, 145, 155f., 159, 161–164, 168–171, 175, 186, 189, 197, 247–252, 307, 318–321, 324f., 330, 336 n. 28, 339, 345, 349f., 369
boundaries s. transgression

burial 114 n. 43, 116 n. 48, 156, 162, 188 n. 43, 337 n. 31
Butler, Judith 155, 173

Caesar, Julius 11–13, 18, 20, 22
Calidorus 13–16
Callisto 118, 286 n. 4, 290
Callimachus / Callimachean 25f., 30–40, 286, 290, 333, 341f., 344, 347
Camilla 117f.
captive 180–193
Cassandra 48 n. 22, 77 n. 23, 180 n. 5
Cavarero, Adriana 155, 164 n. 44, 175
Cecropides 294
Cephalus 115, 119f.
Ceres (s. also Demeter) 6, 158 n. 29, 307, 313–317, 357–372
Cerinthus 17, 257–265, 272–277
Charite 334
chastity / *castitas* / *pudicitia* 48, 50f., 54, 56f., 61f., 107–109, 111f., 323
childbirth 5, 109, 114, 158, 174, 203, 206, 216f., 219, 221f., 225, 237, 388
children 12, 78 n. 26, 109, 114, 153, 159, 162, 174f., 182, 186, 192f., 309, 315 n. 24, 338, 378–380, 385f., 388
Chiron (s. also Ocyroe, *vates*) 75 n. 11, 287, 298 n. 25
Chloe 333f.
chorus 129–146, 151–175, 179–198, 205, 365 n. 26
Clodia 11–13, 19–22
Clodius Pulcher 19
Clytaemestra 48 n. 22
Clytië 329, 343–346, 351
collaboration 71–92, 319, 325
comedy 12–14, 43, 46 n. 12, 48, 60, 65, 179, 181 n. 8, 204, 208, 210, 224f., 238
communication 15, 22, 43, 45 n. 7, 47 n. 18, 57f., 79 n. 29, 83 n. 48, 88 n. 68, 105f., 123, 154, 213
Corinna 336, 348
Cornix (s. also metamorphosis) 6, 285, 290–304
Coronis (s. also Aesculapius, Apollo) 287, 290f., 294, 302
cosmogony 336
Creon 156f., 163f., 166f., 169–174
Croesus 74–76

Cupid and Psyche 334
Cyane 286 n. 4, 364f., 370
Cybele 359, 361–368, 371

Daphne (s. also Cornix) 72, 291f., 307
Daphnis 333f., 347
death 16, 33, 107–123, 153, 157–175, 184–198, 294–299, 303, 333f., 337–339, 364, 382
declaimer / declamation 4–6, 43–68, 330
dedicatee 106, 117, 133
Deianira 180, 191–196
deification s. apotheosis
Delphi 71, 73, 75f., 78, 82f., 85–87, 134–136, 138
Demeter (s. also Ceres) 151, 158f., 168, 173, 175, 207, 233
Demodocus 88, 340
Dercetis 332
desire (s. also pleasure) 5, 25 n. 2, 28, 30, 35–37, 96, 99, 154, 159f., 163f., 168, 171, 175, 203, 209, 217, 229, 250 n. 32, 302 n. 35, 307, 313, 320, 337, 348, 350
dialogue 1, 73, 96, 98, 101, 103, 152f., 157, 174 n. 64, 203, 205, 210–213, 220, 224–226, 232–234, 372
Diana (s. also Hippolytus / Virbius) 48 n. 22, 118f., 293f., 297f., 300, 313, 318 n. 33, 321f., 360, 365, 376–378, 380f., 386, 388
didactic 46, 337, 347
Dido 12–16, 19, 304 n. 40, 309, 311f., 317f., 338
dignitas 271
Diotima of Mantineia 203–241
dirge 157, 161, 175
dispersion (of the 'I') 37–39
divine speaker 4
domestic 117, 168, 332, 342–344, 347
dominance 57
doxosophia 204, 208, 213
dream 62, 360–362, 371

education 1 n. 3, 44, 78 n. 26, 117, 119 n. 63, 259 n. 10, 286f.
effeminate s. *mollis*
Egeria 294f., 298
Electra 152f., 162 n. 39, 164f.
elenchus 203f., 208–212, 215, 220, 229
Eleusis 232f.
Elis 313–317

General Index

emotions 2, 12, 15f., 20–22, 46, 53, 117, 122, 182, 185, 188–190, 197, 247f., 250, 253, 286 n. 4, 332, 343f., 362–364, 372
encomium 107 n. 8, 121, 179 n. 1, 207f., 215, 238
epideictic rhetoric 46
epigram 57, 105–126, 245, 257–281, 330, 339
epistolary conventions 6, 11–15
epitaph 105–123, 303, 339
epithalamium 34, 40 n. 37, 372, 385 n. 29
Ericthonius 291, 302
Erigone 115, 119
Eros 5, 86 n. 60, 203–238
erotic 5f., 15, 25, 78 n. 25, 100, 110 n. 23, 112, 117, 160, 204–207, 211, 213, 216f., 228, 230, 232–234, 246 n. 19, 295, 301 n. 33, 307f., 313, 315, 320–322, 324, 330–350

Fallhöhe 179, 193, 197 n. 71, 365 n. 26
fame / *fama* 16, 131, 134 n. 22, 141, 143, 145, 164 n. 45, 289, 303f., 311, 317–319, 323
family 153f., 157, 159f., 162, 166–175, 182, 185, 187, 190, 193, 197, 290
female
– becoming male / hybrid 4, 25–42, 48, 74, 83f., 87f., 133–139, 375–388
– collective 4, 154 n. 8, 179–198
– inspiration s. Muses, priestess, Pythia
– readership / audience 113 n. 37, 329, 334, 336f., 351
– view 179–200
feminist (theory) 5–7, 74 n. 8, 151, 155f., 175, 259 n. 12, 285, 300–305
– limits 302, 305
– *s. also* symbolic
feminization 25–41, 152, 337
fertility 151, 160, 162, 164, 168, 173, 175, 361, 367, 372
fiction / fictivity (*s. also* autofiction) 3 n. 14, 6, 14, 18f., 29, 43–65, 113, 122, 130 n. 5, 187f., 213, 225, 286, 302 n. 35, 329, 334, 351
fidelity / infidelity 62, 108, 165, 197, 245f., 252–254, 290f., 340, 386
Flora 93f., 98–103
foreigner / stranger 37–39, 76 n. 14, 153, 164, 170, 172f., 213–216, 232, 234, 237
forma s. beauty
funeral ritual 152, 160f., 166, 169f., 173

Gallus 257–274, 335 n. 24, 345 n. 58
genealogy 85, 103, 132, 158–168, 171, 175, 213f., 225, 343
genre 2, 6, 46, 65, 79 n. 30, 105–107, 111 n. 29, 130 n. 5, 132, 152, 259f., 266, 275f., 288 n. 7, 307, 329–351
gigantomachy 314, 333
Graces 4, 88 n. 66, 134–139, 145
Grossman, Igor 11–13
gynecology 216–218
gynocentric 333, 337

Hades 151, 158f., 161, 173
Harpalyce 118 n. 60
Hector 133, 183–185, 188
Hecuba 180–190, 286 n. 4
Helen of Troy 133–135, 146, 268 n. 31, 323
Heliotrope 345f.
Hercules 120, 179–181, 191–198, 299 n. 26
Hermaphroditus 320f., 331 n. 7, 346–351
Hermes 85, 89
Hero and Leander 14f., 344
hero / heroine / heroism 5, 15, 19, 48f., 54f., 61–63, 118, 120–122, 129, 140, 143–145, 157, 164, 169, 180f., 190, 196–198, 287, 294–299, 307, 309–311, 334, 337f., 384
Hippolytus / Virbius 6, 14, 285f., 294–301
homeridae 132, 137, 144
homosexuality 36, 207, 218 n. 22
Honorius 372
honey 85f., 252 n. 41
humiliation / humility 11, 13, 50f., 53, 55, 59, 184, 193, 340
humour 57 n. 42, 95, 116 n. 50, 203, 236 n. 66, 271 n. 37, 320
hunting 105–107, 116–123, 160, 307, 313, 318, 321, 324
husband 14, 62, 65, 96, 101, 108f., 112, 159, 162, 165, 174, 182, 188, 190, 192f., 195, 197, 294, 309, 338, 340, 364, 375, 380 n. 9, 382f.
Hyllus 195f.
hymn 21, 144, 160f., 183f., 196, 205–208
hypermaternity 164

Ida 118
identity 27, 75, 93–103, 122, 129, 131, 138, 146, 160, 166 n. 47, 171f., 174f., 179–198, 257–279, 291, 297f., 370

illaism / illeism 11–13, 15, 18f., 22
illusion 188 n. 41, 204, 207, 213, 310 n. 9, 315
impersonation 45f., 50, 58, 181 n. 8
incest 153f., 168, 175, 304
individuality 197f.
infertility 162, 175
inspiration 33, 73, 77f., 81 n. 38, 86–88, 129, 135 n. 26, 137–139, 146, 316
intertextuality 40, 46, 106, 115 n. 46, 120, 123, 224, 245, 258–265, 286, 290, 301–303
intratextuality 33–35, 45 n. 7, 246, 254, 258–260, 265–277, 302
Iole 180, 191–194, 197
irony 5, 50, 57 n. 42, 81, 97, 116 n. 48, 136 n. 29, 146, 164, 192 n. 58, 204f., 208f., 212, 214, 220, 226, 270 n. 35, 301 n. 34, 307–325, 387
Ismene 167 n. 49, 170

Jelinek, Elfriede 358 n. 6
Jocasta 151, 168, 170, 174f.
Juno 17, 94–96, 101, 103, 196, 340, 376, 379 n. 8
Jupiter 191, 193, 196, 285, 289, 331, 344, 357–371

kommos 152, 156f., 182, 184, 186, 188, 193
Kore / Persephone / Proserpina 6, 151, 158–164, 168, 170, 173, 175, 313f., 316, 357–372

Lachesis 357, 368f.
Lailaps 115, 119, 123
lamentation 151–175, 182–185, 187, 193, 197, 358–367
Lamprias 73, 76
Laodamia 14, 338
law / lawsuit / juridical 43–65, 79 n. 30, 155, 157, 159, 166f., 169–173
Lesbia / Lesbius 19–22
Leuconoë 254 n. 46, 331, 340–350
Leucothoë 342–345
Lévinas, Emmanuel 154f.
loss 3, 6, 38, 118, 135 n. 26, 152, 161, 165, 175, 182 n. 13, 185, 190f., 193, 249, 286, 288, 290, 357, 364, 370, 372
love / *amor* 16f., 30, 53, 61f., 86 n. 60, 98, 164, 175, 203–238, 245–254, 257–278, 307, 329–351, 361, 378, 382–387
Loxias 84f.

Lucretia 332, 343f.
Lycoris 266 n. 26
Lygdamus 267 n. 27

madness 78, 86f., 251, 345, 350, 366f., 382
Maira 115, 119, 123
Maria, daughter of Stilicho and Serena 372
man-fashioning 105, 142
mantic *s.* prophesy / prophet
marriage 16, 21, 95, 100, 108f., 112, 151, 159–174, 194f., 197, 278, 349, 360f., 369, 376, 378f., 385
Mars 16f., 96–98, 268f., 272–274, 277, 315 n. 23, 340, 346, 350, 369
mask / unmask 181, 187f., 215, 244, 311, 323, 369
matrilinearity 343, 371 n. 39
matron / *matrona* 5, 48, 95–98, 101, 103, 105–123, 309
Medea 6, 48 n. 22, 304 n. 40, 308f., 318 n. 33, 375–389
Meleager 120
memoir, personal 18, 21
mentula 107, 109–114
Messalla 257, 260–268, 278
metamorphosis 4, 162f., 268, 285–305, 329–351, 357
metapoetics *s.* poetics / poetry
metoikia / *metoikos* 151, 153, 164, 167, 170–172, 174
midwife 218–223, 232
Minerva 48 n. 22, 100 n. 14, 291–304, 313–315, 331f., 360, 365, 381 n. 13
Minyads, daughters of Minyas 5, 286 n. 4, 301, 329–351
mollis / soft 246f., 250, 321f., 336f., 348f., 388
mother 96, 98–100, 108, 118, 151, 159, 162–165, 168, 172, 174f., 182, 192f., 217, 219, 223–225, 229, 287f., 291, 314, 333, 343f., 357–372, 375, 379f.
mother-in-law 181f., 192
mourning 25f., 31, 35, 151–153, 157, 162, 169, 175, 182–188, 345
– mourning artists 182, 184f., 187
– ritual mourners 182, 188, 190
mouthpiece 71, 73, 77, 81, 85 n. 57
mulberry 333, 338f.
Muses 4, 16, 30 n. 9, 33 n. 23, 86–88, 129, 134–139, 143, 146, 313–316

narrator / narration / narrative 3–7, 18, 22, 48, 51, 57, 61, 63f., 76f., 84, 88, 93, 96, 98–101, 103, 105, 118, 205, 213, 227 n. 48, 254 n. 46, 262, 268 n. 31, 273f., 285–305, 307–325, 329–351, 357–372, 376
– embedded narrative 88 n. 66, 307f., 313, 316, 331, 334
– extradiegetic 285, 314
– heterodiegetic 3, 365
– homodiegetic 3, 99, 103
– intradiegetic 100, 287, 299, 314, 365
– meta-narrative 197, 307–325
– narrative complicity with female narrator 307, 325
– self-narration 151–175, 290–298
– s. also storytelling
narratology, historical 3
natality 175, 214, 223
Nausikaa 349
Neptune 292, 298f., 302
Niobe 151, 153, 162–165, 168, 172f., 175, 268 n. 4
norms / normative 4f., 46, 48, 55, 110, 118 n. 61, 123, 131, 143, 145, 153, 159, 213f., 221, 225, 227 n. 48, 325 n. 54, 330, 358 n. 5
novel (s. also romance, Ninos romance) 1, 22, 43–48, 60–65, 304 n. 40, 334, 337
Nussbaum, Martha 229, 232f.
Nyctimene 293, 304
nymphs 99–101, 118 n. 58, 287, 294–296, 307, 313–325, 346–350, 364, 370 n. 36

obscenity 22, 109–114
Ocyroe / Hippe (s. also metamorphosis) 285–302
Odysseus 88 n. 69, 120f., 297, 349
Oedipus 151f., 160, 165, 168f., 171, 174
Oeta 195f.
offspring 19, 151, 153, 162, 165, 171, 174, 338, 372
omniscience 75, 88, 340
onymity 71, 74, 79–81
oracle 71–89, 138
orality 43, 47, 57–59, 71, 74, 76 n. 15, 81–83, 132, 329–331
Orpheus (s. also vates) 196, 301, 315 n. 24
Ortygia 313f., 317

Pallas s. Athena
Paris 182
Parnassus 85, 89
passive s. active / passive
pederasty 5, 205, 214, 227f., 231–223
Penelope 13–15, 309, 311, 322
performance 7, 19, 56–58, 79 n. 29, 82f., 85, 87f., 113 n. 36, 129–136, 138, 144, 146, 151–154, 166, 169, 171, 174f., 179, 181f., 186, 205, 301, 332, 346
– s. also chorus
Perialla 79, 81, 84 n. 51
Pericles 170
persona 2f., 5f., 25, 46, 105, 110 n. 24, 113f., 129–131, 136f., 139, 141, 145f., 179 n. 1, 181, 197, 244 n. 7, 278, 312, 357
perspective(-taking) 1–6, 11, 13, 36, 46, 57, 60, 65, 86, 93, 101, 103, 130, 154–157, 167 n. 48, 179, 185, 189–191, 198, 217, 224, 232f., 237, 244f., 250, 259 n. 11, 307f., 311, 315, 322f., 358 n. 8, 360 n. 13, 363, 365, 375
Phaedra 13–15, 295, 299, 309
Phemius 87
Phemonoe 72, 77
Philomela 286 n. 4, 313 n. 17, 324 n. 53, 364 n. 22
Phoenicium 11–16, 19
Phrygia 164, 184, 188, 360–363, 368f.
pleasure (s. also desire) 88, 106, 112, 123, 209–211, 238, 267f., 277, 329, 333, 347–351
Pluto 357, 359, 361, 371
poet
– as craftsman 139–145
– etymology 131–133
– male-gendering of 129–146
– *poeta amator* 53, 262, 264, 335f., 345, 349
– poetic lineage 132
poetics / poetry
– metapoetics 6, 25–41, 97 n. 10, 102, 105, 110 n. 26, 111 n. 28, 112, 122, 133, 137, 301–304
– craft metaphors for 130–132, 139–145
political community (*polis*) 80 n. 35, 160, 162–166, 169–175, 190
Polyneices 151, 153, 156, 162, 166, 169, 172, 174

polyphony 58 n. 47, 71–92, 213, 217 n. 18, 299 n. 27, 323, 325
Polyxena 48 n. 22, 180–182, 186, 189
power 21, 48f., 51, 53, 59, 64f., 77 n. 22, 79, 132, 135, 137, 139, 141 n. 56, 152, 163f., 167, 169, 175, 179, 185, 188, 190, 192, 195, 197f., 226, 232 n. 58, 268, 270f., 274, 296, 303, 308f., 312, 359–361, 367, 372, 376, 379, 381f., 388
pregnancy 205, 216–223, 232, 234, 238
Priam 94, 182, 184f.
Priapus 111
priestess / priesthood 4, 6, 43, 45, 47–60, 64f., 71–80, 84–86, 213, 215f., 226, 233 n. 62, 375, 377–380, 382f., 386, 388
progeny 217, 220, 223
prophesy / prophet (s. also vates) 22, 71–89, 129, 133–139, 191 n. 52, 261 n. 17, 285–290, 304, 361 n. 18
– mantic 74 n. 10, 78, 85–88, 139
prosopopoeia 1f., 44 n. 4
prostitute 43, 45, 47f., 50f., 60f.
psychoanalysis 331
pudicitia s. chastity
purity / puritas 48, 159
Pygmalion 53
Pyramus 331–334, 337–342, 346
Pythagoras 72, 300, 346 n. 59
Pythia 4, 48 n. 25, 71–89, 134 n. 22, 138f.

queer 205, 223, 238

Rabelais, François 210
rape (s. also victim) 6, 34f., 40, 48–51, 53, 61, 64, 190, 290f., 293, 299, 307, 313 n. 17, 343, 357f., 360f., 363–365, 370f.
raven 290–294, 298, 304
reciprocity 34, 41, 207 n. 7, 257, 265f., 268–272, 277, 335
Rederecht 370
relativism 307, 311f., 325
Ricoeur, Paul 223
Robson, David 11–13
role (social, gender etc.) 1–5, 18, 30, 44–49, 54–65, 105–126, 138, 141, 153, 159, 161, 168, 171, 175, 180–184, 190f., 193, 197f., 203f., 207, 209, 221, 232 n. 58, 243–254, 274, 289f., 300, 360, 365, 372 n. 41, 375–388

romance (s. also novel) 5, 329, 332–340, 351
rusticus, rustica / rusticitas 307, 319–324

Salmacis 308 n. 1, 320f., 329, 331 n. 7, 346–351
Scylla 371f.
self-assertion 6f.
self-consciousness 43, 47, 53, 83, 94, 103, 303, 304 n. 40, 307, 309, 311, 316, 319, 322, 324, 342
self-fashioning / self-presentation 4–7, 12, 45, 55, 63–65, 94–97, 99, 103, 105f., 109, 113, 117, 137, 184, 190, 291, 298–300, 307, 309 n. 6, 325, 338
self-injury 184
Semiramis 333f., 349
Serena 359 n. 9, 372
sermocinatio 5, 43–68
servitium amoris 264f., 268–271, 275f., 308, 383 n. 18
sexual assault s. rape
sexuality 110, 112f., 159, 206f., 218 n. 22, 230 n. 52
Sicily 313–319, 359f., 363, 370
silence 22, 30, 37f., 51, 71, 74, 145, 301 n. 34, 360, 365, 370–372
slaves, slavery 11–13, 48, 61f., 170, 190f., 193, 331f., 342f., 383
social status 1, 3, 5, 65, 101, 108, 112f., 122, 166, 179, 182–184, 191, 244, 277, 359, 365
Socrates 5, 11, 73 n. 5, 72, 78, 86f., 203–238
Sol, sun 196, 331 n. 7, 340–346, 376
song (s. also chorus) 81, 83, 88, 111, 129–146, 152, 160, 180–197, 301 n. 33, 331, 340
stereotype 3–5, 46, 51, 60, 107f., 112, 185, 290, 295, 307, 309, 325, 329, 331, 350
Stilicho 372
stone 108, 116, 153, 162–164, 168
storytelling (s. also narrator / narration / narrative) 285f., 329, 331, 350
subjectivisation 3, 197
subordination 195, 197f.
suffering 162, 164, 166, 170, 184, 189f., 193, 196f., 275–277, 285, 287, 298
Sulpicia 1, 4, 11–22, 112 n. 32, 257–281, 300, 337 n. 30
symbolic (s. also feminist theory) 5f., 74 n. 8, 285–305
symposium 143, 203, 211, 225, 231

textuality / textual 35 n. 31, 47 n. 18, 57–60, 65, 83, 113f., 304 n. 40
theatre / theatricality 151, 154, 174, 179, 185 n. 25, 203f., 225, 308 n. 1
Thebes 156f., 165–174, 187 n. 37, 331f., 382, 384, 386
Themistocleia 72
Theon 73, 81
Theseus 294f.
third person 4, 6, 11–21, 54, 56, 62, 84, 105, 108, 189, 290, 296
Thisbe 329–351
Tiresias 72
tissue / Gewebe 363f., 383
Trachis 191–196
transformation 4, 25 n. 1, 33–35, 38, 56, 159, 163, 168, 285–303, 313, 319 n. 35, 333, 346, 350, 367, 385
transgression / crossing of (gender) boundaries 4, 48–51, 55, 57, 62, 64, 118 n. 61, 129, 131, 157, 173, 294 n. 19
translation 4, 6, 25–42
triumph 101, 191, 193f., 197, 261–264, 344
Troy 133, 180–184, 188, 191, 317

vates (*s. also* Apollo, Chiron, Ocyroe, Orpheus, prophet, Pythia) 287, 289
Venus (*s. also* Aphrodite) 61, 93f., 96–98, 101–103, 118, 247 n. 22, 252, 263, 266–272, 274–277, 297, 329, 340f., 343, 350f., 357, 365, 376, 379 n. 8, 382 n. 16, 386

Vesta / Vestal Virgins 43–65
victim (of violence, *s. also* metamorphosis, rape) 35 n. 31, 44, 99f., 103, 164, 192, 208, 215, 286, 291 n. 17, 298f., 302, 307, 309, 313, 325, 384 n. 26, 386, 388
virago 6, 43–65, 105, 117f., 122, 375–388
virgo / virgin / virginity 43–65, 72 n. 3, 117, 159 n. 30, 161, 182, 194, 197, 298, 313–316, 322, 324, 365, 370 n. 33, 375, 379–383, 388
virility 25 n. 2, 39, 48, 55f., 93, 96–98, 101, 103, 205f., 236, 252, 318, 382, 384, 386f.
voice 2, 4f., 12 n. 2, 25–27, 47f., 56–58, 71, 74f., 81–87, 105, 108, 110 n. 24, 112–117, 123, 130, 134–139, 145f., 151–157, 179f., 186, 188 n. 41, 191, 198, 285–294, 299f., 302 n. 35, 304f., 307–316, 324f., 338, 342–344, 348, 363, 372 n. 41, 388 n. 36
– collective 152, 154, 157
voyeurism 251 n. 35, 296, 307f., 324
Vulcan 291 n. 15, 340–342, 346, 350
vulnerability 6f., 151–177

weakness 6, 43, 49, 50, 55, 59, 175, 185, 309–312, 368, 371, 382, 386–388
weaving 73 n. 7, 133, 143, 192, 195, 329, 331f., 342, 351
wife 95, 100, 108–110, 112, 119 n. 66, 151, 159, 161, 164f., 172, 174f., 190–195, 197, 294 n. 20, 307, 322, 332, 340, 375, 380f., 388
womanufacture 43, 53

Index locorum

Achilles Tatius
Leuc.
passim — 333 n. 13
1.1 — 334 n. 16
1.4 — 334 n. 15
3.5.4 — 339 n. 39
3.15 — 337 n. 31
5.7 — 337 n. 31
6.21.3 — 62 n. 60
6.22.1–4 — 62f.

Aelianus
NA 12.32 — 80

Aeschines
In Tim. — 207 n. 7

Aeschylus
Ag. — 77 n. 23
Eu. — 72 n. 2f., 85, 87, 138 n. 41
Oed. Col. — 171
Pers. (Arg. 1) — 80 n. 33
Supp. — 170 n. 54
Th. — 170 n. 54

Aesop
121 — 122 n. 77

Aetius of Amida
16.12–15 — 222 n. 31

Alcaeus
fr. 364 V. — 224 n. 37

Alcman
fr. 3 PMG — 136 n. 32

Anthologia Graeca
7.189–216 — 115 n. 47, 116 n. 49
7.330–666 — 339 n. 39
15.8 — 339 n. 39

Apollodorus
1.9.4 — 120 n. 68
3.14.7 — 119 n. 65

Apollonius Rhodius
Arg. — 386 n. 31

Apuleius
met.
4.27 — 334
8.14 — 339 n. 39

Archilochus
passim — 80 n. 31
fr. 1 West — 88 n. 67

Aristophanes
passim — 121, 205–208, 211, 217, 224f., 230, 232, 237
Ach. — 136 n. 32
Av. — 82 n. 44, 121 n. 75
Eccl. — 334 n. 20
Lys. — 136 n. 32, 334 n. 20
Pl. — 224f.
Ran. — 121 n. 75
Th. — 79 n. 28, 205f., 211, 225

Aristotle
passim — 186 n. 29
fr. 399 Rose — 80

Athenaeus
10.425f. — 142 n. 63

Bacchylides
passim — 136, 140f.
5.3–6 — 141 n. 60
9.3 — 137 n. 38
10.11 — 141 n. 60

Caesar
b.G./civ. — 11–13, 18, 20, 22

Caesarius of Arles
serm. 43.1 — 336 n. 28

Callimachus
passim — 290, 333, 341f., 344, 347
Aet. fr. 110 Pf. (*Coma Berenices*) — 26, 30–36, 39f.

Carmina Priapea
passim — 110, 112

Catullus
passim — 110, 121f., 261, 266f., 270f., 349 n. 67
8 — 12, 21f., 25 n. 2, 251 n. 37, 338 n. 35
11 — 12, 20–22
13 — 345 n. 57
16 — 115 n. 45
45 — 267 n. 27, 270, 271 n. 37

50	114 n. 44	**Demosthenes**	
51	22 n. 21, 26–30, 39, 134 n. 24, 245, 249	21 (*Against Meidias*)	83 n. 47
55	247 n. 22	54 (*Against Conon*)	207 n. 7
56	12, 19f.	**Diodorus Siculus**	
58	12, 20	4.66.6	72
61	34	16.26.6	72 n. 3
62	34, 266 n. 26	**Diogenes Laertius**	
63	25 n. 1	8.1–50	72
64	33–35, 261 n. 16	**Dionysius Scythobrachion**	
65	29 n. 6, 33–35, 39, 40 n. 37	*Arg.*	386 n. 31
66	26f., 30–36, 39f.	**Dracontius**	
68	25 n. 2	*Romul.* 10 ('*Medea*')	375–389
72	25 n. 2		
76	25 n. 2	**Ennius**	
79	12, 19f.	*ann.* 34–44	
80	247f. n. 22	Skutsch	334 n. 20
Chariton		*fr. var.* 17f.	
Chaer.		Vahlen = 46	
passim	61 n. 57, 333 n. 13	Courtney	303
1.1	334 n. 15	**Epicedion Drusi**	
Cicero		339 n. 39	
div.		**Eratosthenes**	
1.38	73 n. 6	*Cat.* 1.33.1–10	119f. n. 67
fam.		*Erig.*	119 n. 65
9.22.3	109 n. 17	**Euripides**	
off.		*passim*	205, 207, 211, 222, 308
1.107–125	244 n. 7		
Verr.		*Ba.*	222 n. 33
2.5.36	98 n. 12	*Hipp.*	102 n. 19, 120 n. 68, 295
Cinna			
fr. 6 Courtney	266 n. 26	*Ion*	72 n. 2, 85 n. 56
Claudian		*Med.*	386 n. 31, 387
epithal. dict.		*Phoen.*	318 n. 32
Honorio (c. 10)	372	*Tr.*	77 n. 23, 136 n. 32, 181
in Gildonem (c. 15)	359 n. 9		
rapt. Pros.	158 n. 29, 357–373	**Eustathius**	
Clement of Alexandria		*Comm. in Il.*	
Strom. 5.14	80 n. 32	(ed. van der Valk) 8.97	
Columella		(p. 701)	80 n. 33
12 *praef.* 9	332 n. 11		
Corpus Hippocraticum		**Gallus**	
Genit.	218 n. 24	*am.*	257–274, 335 n. 24, 345 n. 58
Nat. Puer.	219 n. 26, 222 n. 31		
Corpus Tibullianum *s.* Tibullus			

Heliodorus
  Aeth.
  passim   334 n. 16
  1.2   334 n. 15
Heraclitus
  fr. 22 DK   80 n. 31
Herodotus
  1.13   74 n. 10, 84
  1.47–93   74–77, 81 n. 36/40,
                            82–84
  1.167–174   81 n. 40, 84
  3.57f.   84
  3.119   174 n. 64
  4.150–157   84, 170 n. 54
  5.63–92   81 n. 36/40, 84
  6.66–86   72 n. 2, 79, 81 n. 36/
                            40, 84 n. 51
  7.6   81 n. 36, 82 n. 44
  7.111   72 n. 2
  7.140–148   80, 82 n. 44/46, 84
  8.20   81 n. 36
  8.37   76
  8.77   81 n. 36
  8.96   81 n. 36, 82 n. 44
  8.111   224 n. 37
  8.141   81 n. 36
  9.43   81 n. 36, 82 n. 44
  9.95   81 n. 36
Hesiod
  Op.
  25f.   131 n. 10, 140
  Th.
  27f.   86
  31f.   88 n. 67
  64   134
  95–99   131 n. 10
  885–900   222 n. 33
  912–914   158 n. 29
  924   222 n. 33
Historia Apollonii Regis Tyri
  63
Homer
  passim   27, 72, 76 n. 15,
                            80 n. 31, 82 n. 42, 83,
                            129–146, 218
  Il.
  1.1   136 n. 32
  2.484–600   88 n. 66/69
  4.110   140 n. 51
  4.179   164 n. 45
  5.3   164 n. 45
  5.59   140 n. 51
  6.315   140 n. 51/54
  6.357f.   133
  7.17–60   290 n. 12
  7.91   164 n. 45
  8.192   164 n. 45
  9.539   121 n. 73
  11.127–172   222
  13.390   140 n. 51
  15.411   140 n. 51
  16.483   140 n. 51/54
  23.712   140 n. 51
  23.865   84 n. 49
  24.602–617   162 n. 40
  24.720   131 n. 10
  Od.
  1.1   129, 144
  3.267–270   131 n. 10
  4.17   131 n. 10
  6.149–159   349
  8.47   164 n. 45
  8.63f.   88
  8.87   131 n. 10
  8.266–369   88, 340
  8.491   88 n. 69
  9.19–21   164 n. 45, 318 n. 32
  9.126   140 n. 51/54
  10.212–219   120 n. 72
  14.29–36   120 n. 72
  16.4f./162f.   120 n. 72
  16.202–212   297
  17.291–327   120
  17.340–384   140 n. 51
  17.383–385   131 n. 10, 140
  19.56   140 n. 51
  19.449–451   121 n. 74
  21.43   140 n. 51
  22.347f.   87
Homeric Hymns
  2 (Demeter)   34 n. 27, 370 n. 35
  3 (Apollo)   85 n. 57, 134, 221f.
  4 (Hermes)   83, 85–89
  27 (Artemis)   134 n. 23
Horace
  carm.
  1.5   254
  1.8   246 n. 16

1.11	254	**Livy**	
1.13	243–256, 345 n. 57	1.57	332
1.25	246 n. 16, 248 n. 24	39.8–18	332
2.12	266 n. 27	**Lollianus**	
2.20	302f., 304	*Phoen.*	334 n. 16
3.9	246 n. 16	**[Longinus]**	
3.19	246 n. 16	*Subl.*	
3.30	114 n. 42	10.3	37f.
4.11	246 n. 16, 261 n. 15	13.2	87 n. 61
epist.		**Longus**	
1.9	248 n. 25	*Daphn.*	
epod.		*passim*	333 n. 13
11	248 n. 25	1.7	334 n. 15
15	266	**Lucan**	
sat.		5.96–211	77
1.2	348 n. 62	**Lucian**	
1.9	248 n. 25	*JTr.* 20	80 n. 33
2.3	248 n. 25	**Lucretius**	
Hosidius Geta		1.33–39	269, 272, 274 n. 48
Med.	386 n. 31	2.1–19	189 n. 46
Hyginus		4.1201–1216	267 n. 27, 269
astr.		5.739	98 n. 12
2.4	119 n. 65, 120 n. 67	5.854–963	267 n. 27
2.35	119f. n. 67	6.749–785	291 n. 16
fab.		**Lycophron**	
130	119 n. 65, 120 n. 67	*Alex.* 1416–1420	80 n. 33
193	118 n. 60		
204	293 n. 18	**Martial**	
205	118 n. 58	1–12 *passim*	105–126
		1.34f.	110–113
Iamblichus Philosophus		1.109	121f.
Myst. 3.11	78 n. 24	3.86	113
Iamblichus Scriptor Eroticus		7.80	248 n. 22
Bab.	334 n. 16	8.55	248 n. 22
Isidore of Seville		8.68	348 n. 62
diff.		10.63	107–116, 122f., 290 n. 12
2.82	336 n. 28	11.69	115–121, 123, 290 n. 12, 375 n. 2
orig.			
10.179	336 n. 28	13–14	121
11.2.18	336 n. 28	*epigr. (spectac.)*	121, 123
		Maximus of Tyre	
John Chrysostom		13.1	80 n. 33
hom. in I Cor		**Metiochus and Parthenope**	
29.12.1	78 n. 24		333 n. 13
Juvenal			
13.80	118 n. 58	**Ninos-romance**	
			333 n. 13, 334 n. 16f.
Lactantius			
opif. 12.17	336 n. 28		

Origen
   Cels. 7.3f.   78 n. 24
Ovid
   am.
   1.1   335 n. 24, 338 n. 35, 349
   1.2   335 n. 23
   1.3   271 n. 36
   1.5   320, 336 n. 25, 349f.
   1.6   335 n. 23
   1.7   251 n. 37
   1.8   308, 348 n. 63
   1.9   341, 350
   1.10   335 n. 23
   1.13   267
   1.14   338 n. 35
   1.15   266 n. 26
   2.1   337 n. 30, 351
   2.3   267 n. 27
   2.4   337 n. 30, 339 n. 37, 350
   2.17   271 n. 36, 345 n. 55, 348
   2.18   338
   2.19   335 n. 23, 336 n. 26
   3.1   318 n. 33, 336, 348
   3.2   318 n. 33, 349 n. 64
   3.4   267
   3.6   267 n. 27
   3.7   350 n. 69
   3.9   339
   3.10   102 n. 18
   3.14   251 n. 37
   3.15   335 n. 24, 341 n. 41
   ars
   1.7–33   341 n. 41
   1.50   347 n. 61
   1.126   344
   1.459   347 n. 61
   1.490   335 n. 23
   1.513–522   348
   1.607–630   323 n. 47, 324
   1.663–676   251 n. 37, 267, 350
   2.281   337 n. 30
   2.304–308   267
   2.367–369   323, 341 n. 43
   2.561–288   341
   3.21   339 n. 39
   3.39f.   338 n. 34
   3.57   337
   3.129f.   348
   3.189f.   339 n. 37
   3.298–315   347 n. 61, 251 n. 37
   3.307–310   251 n. 37
   3.333f.   337
   3.346   308
   3.455   347 n. 61
   3.537   266 n. 26
   3.712   318 n. 33
   fast.
   1.437   320 n. 39
   1.671   98 n. 12
   2.79f.   344
   2.304   98 n. 11
   2.741–760   332, 343f.
   3.1–260   97f., 338 n. 34
   3.549   338 n. 34
   4.1–16   96f., 341 n. 41
   4.448f.   358
   4.500   371
   4.620   339 n. 37
   5.183–378   98–102
   5.608   344
   6.15–64   94–96
   6.746   298 n. 25
   her.
   1   12, 14, 309, 311, 322
   2   309, 311, 338
   3   311
   4   12, 14
   5   313 n. 17, 319 n. 34
   6   309
   7   309, 311f., 338
   8   320 n. 39
   10   311
   11   339
   12   309, 386f.
   13   12, 14
   14   12, 14
   15   267, 308 n. 1
   16   308, 310 n. 12, 323
   17   308, 310 n. 12, 319 n. 36, 323f.
   18   14f., 308, 335 n. 23
   19   267, 308, 344
   20   271 n. 36, 308

21	308
Ib.	
123	338 n. 34
medic.	
passim	337
1	347 n. 61
met.	
1.110	102 n. 18
1.452	335 n. 24
1.488–691	319 n. 34f.
2.492	118 n. 58
2.542–675	287–294, 302, 304, 313 n. 17, 319 n. 35, 364 n. 21
3.265f.	95 n. 5
3.732f.	331
4.1–415	301 n. 31, 320f., 331–351
5.271–641	99, 100 n. 15, 313–325, 333, 358, 360 n. 15, 370 n. 33/36
6.118	98 n. 12
6.146–312	162 n. 40
6.624–674	364 n. 22
7.1–424	318 n. 33, 382 n. 14, 386 n. 31
7.582f.	325 n. 54
7.746	318 n. 33
7.759–793	120 n. 67, 267 n. 27
8.362–402	121 n. 74
8.877f.	330
9.485–487	267f.
9.558	273
10.148	315 n. 24
10.710–716	121 n. 74
13.735–745	316
14.51–67	371 n. 37
14.177	325 n. 54
14.682f.	335 n. 24
15.492–546	294–298
15.808–815	289
15.875–879	304
Pont.	
3.1.109f.	338 n. 33
rem.	
13f.	267f.

43	347 n. 61
trist.	
1.6.20	338 n. 33
Papyri	
P. Berol. 11517	81 n. 37
Pausanias	
1.18.2	80 n. 33
10.5.7	72
Phaedrus	
fab.	121, 122 n. 77
app.	8 77 n. 22
Philochorus	
FGrHist 328 F 116	80
Photius	
Bibl. 190	72 n. 4
Pindar	
fr.	
70 (= *Pae.* 21)	133 n. 16
76	134 n. 22
94	139 n. 45
150	138f.
Isthm.	
1.34	143
2.34	143
4.70	143
6.1	143
6.67	140 n. 52
8.1	143
9	139 n. 44
Nem.	
1.9	143
2.1–3	132, 137, 143, 144, 146
3	130, 133–143
5.1–15	141f., 144f.
5.49f.	140 n. 50, 145
6.1–5	114 n. 42, 144
7.62f.	143
8	141, 142 n. 64
9.50–54	130, 137 n. 37
Ol.	
1	130, 143
2.2	129f., 143
6	143f.
7.7–15	143, 144 n. 69
7.32	82 n. 46
9.13	143

14	134f., 137, 139, 145	1.5	267 n. 27
Pae.		1.7	270 n. 36, 337 n. 29f.
6	134–139, 143, 145f.	1.8	273 n. 45
21 (= fr. 70)	133 n. 16	1.13	269f.
Pyth.		2.1	335 n. 24, 350f.
1	133, 137, 143, 143 n. 68	2.3	266 n. 26, 351
		2.8	339 n. 39
2.52–56	80 n. 31	2.11	337 n. 30
3	140f.	2.12	337 n. 29
4.1	143f.	2.13	337 n. 30
4.60	74 n. 9, 86 n. 59	2.15	270f., 345 n. 58, 350
5.22	138 n. 44, 143	2.26	270 n. 36
5.36	140 n. 50	2.29	341 n. 43
5.107	143 n. 68	2.30	273
8.59	134 n. 22	2.32	268 n. 31
9.4	143	3.2	337
9.46–49	75 n. 11	3.9	337
10.6	138 n. 44, 143	3.11	269f.
10.22	143	3.15	270
Plato		3.20	270
Ap.	87 n. 62, 211	3.24	270
Chrm.	212 n. 11	3.25	271 n. 36
Euthd.	212 n. 11	4.3	251 n. 37, 308
Ion	87 n. 62	4.5	348 n. 63
Ly.	212 n. 11	4.7	339 n. 39
Men.	87 n. 62		
Phd.	212 n. 11	**Quintilian**	
Phdr.	78, 85 n. 56, 86f., 234	inst. 9.2	45 n. 6
		Ps.-Quintilian	
Phlb.	204, 208–211, 213	decl. mai.	44, 60 n. 54
Prm.	212 n. 11		
Prt.	210f., 212 n. 11	**Sappho**	
R.	203, 212 n. 11, 229f., 236f.	fr. 1 V.	272
		fr. 31 V.	26–30, 35–41, 134 n. 24, 245, 249
Symp.	203–238		
Tht.	210, 219 n. 27, 220–223	fr. 94 V.	40
		fr. 103 V.	134
Plautus		fr. 105A V.	39f. n. 37
passim	48, 60 n. 54	fr. 128 V.	134
Bacch.	14	**Seneca Rhetor**	
Curc.	14, 61	contr.	
Pseud.	11–15, 19, 251 n. 37	1 praef. 24.4	57 n. 47
Rud.	61f.	1.2	43–68, 245 n. 8
Plutarch		1.3	58 n. 50
De Def. Or.	73f., 76f.	1.5	59 n. 52
De E	73 n. 5	2.2	58 n. 49, 59 n. 52
De Pyth. Or.	73, 76, 81–83	2.5	58 n. 49, 59 n. 52, 62
Propertius		2.7	58 n. 49, 59 n. 52
1.1	338 n. 35	3.7	58 n. 49, 330

4 praef. 1f.	330, 57 n. 47	**Suetonius**	
4.4	59 n. 52	*Aug.*	332
4.6	58 n. 49, 59 n. 52	**Suidas Lexicon**	
5.3	58 n. 49	α 2371	80 n. 32f.
6.4	58 n. 49	**Sulpicia** s. Tibullus 3 and General Index s.v.	
6.6	58 n. 49, 59 n. 52	Sulpicia	
6.8	46 n. 13, 57 n. 42, 58 n. 50	**Theognis**	
7.2	59 n. 52	15	134
7.4	58 n. 49, 59 n. 52	19–23	83
7.8	49 n. 30, 58 n. 49, 59 n. 52	351–354	224 n. 37
		649–652	224 n. 37
8.1	59 n. 52	805–810	82f.
9.2	59 n. 52	**Theopompus of Chios**	
9.4	59 n. 52	*FGrHist* 115 F 336	83
9.6	59 n. 52	**Thucydides**	
10.4f.	59 n. 52	*passim*	13, 18
suas.		2.13	170 n. 54
passim	43f. n. 1	2.54.2f.	82 n. 41
1.13	44 n. 5	**Tibullus (*Corpus Tibullianum*)**	
Seneca the Younger		1.1	267, 269, 349 n. 67, 350
Ag.	180 n. 5		
benef. 7.9.5	348 n. 62	1.2	267 n. 27, 269, 270 n. 36, 335 n. 23
Med.	378 n. 6, 386 n. 31		
Tro.	154 n. 8, 166 n. 47, 180–191, 197f.		
		1.4	349 n. 67, 350
		1.5	266, 335 n. 23
(Ps.-)Seneca		1.6	267 n. 27, 269, 335 n. 23
Herc. O.	154 n. 8, 166 n. 47, 180f., 191–198		
		1.7	261–264
Servius		1.8	251 n. 37, 266, 335 n. 23
buc. 10.1	335 n. 24		
georg. 1.403	293 n. 18	1.9	262
Sesonchosis-romance		1.10	335 n. 23
334 n. 16		2.1	263f.
Sophocles		2.3	266 n. 26, 269f., 345 n. 55
Ant.	151–177, 180 n. 6, 184 n. 23, 187 n. 37		
		2.4	264, 266, 269, 337
El.	152f., 164f.	2.6	266
Tr.	152, 165f., 193 n. 61, 194 n. 63	3.1	267 n. 27
		3.8	12f., 16f., 258, 266, 272 n. 42
Statius			
silv.		3.9	13, 16, 17 n. 15, 257–260, 272, 274, 276, 278, 337 n. 30
2.3	114 n. 41/43		
2.4	116 n. 48		
Theb.			
9.616	118 n. 58	3.10	12f., 16f., 258
Strabo		3.11	13, 17 n. 15, 77 n. 19, 257–281
9.3.5	73f., 76		
10.4.21	206 n. 5		

3.12	13, 16f., 258, 266, 271 n. 36, 278, 348 n. 62	3.692–718	317
3.13	13, 16, 17 n. 15, 258, 261, 265, 267, 271f., 274–278	3.716–718	317 n. 29
		4 *passim*	11f., 15f., 19
		4.307–370	12, 15f., 19
		6.45–101	77 n. 20
3.14	13, 17 n. 15, 258, 265, 275f., 278	7.385–405	332
		9.178	118 n. 58
3.15	13, 258, 265, 275f, 278	11.539–781	117f.
		12.606	247 n. 22
3.16	13, 258, 265, 275f., 278	*ecl.*	
		10	316, 335 n. 24
3.17	13, 258, 265, 275f., 278	*georg.*	
		1.403	293 n. 18
3.18	13, 258, 265, 274 n. 50, 275f., 278	3.8f.	303 n. 36
		4.344–347	273f., 315, 346
Tzetzes			
H. 9.812	80 n. 32	**Xenophanes**	
		fr. 21 DK	80 n. 31
Valerius Flaccus		**Xenophon**	
Arg.		*passim*	13, 210, 212 n. 11, 230 n. 54, 235
passim	386 n. 31		
3.335	118 n. 58	*Anab.*	18
Vergil		*Kyn.* 10.1–3	121 n. 74
Aen.		*Smp.*	235 n. 65
1.4	340	**Xenophon of Ephesus**	
1.46f.	95 n. 5	*Ephes.*	
1.314–320	118 n. 58/60	*passim*	334 n. 16
1.378f.	318 n. 32	4.2	337 n. 31
1.402–405	102 n. 19, 247 n. 22	4.5–5.1	61, 337 n. 31
2.1–6	316f.	5.7f.	61f.
2.593	247 n. 22	6.22	62f.

www.ingramcontent.com/pod-product-compliance
Lightning Source LLC
Chambersburg PA
CBHW080406230426
43662CB00016B/2331